ZOMNIBUS

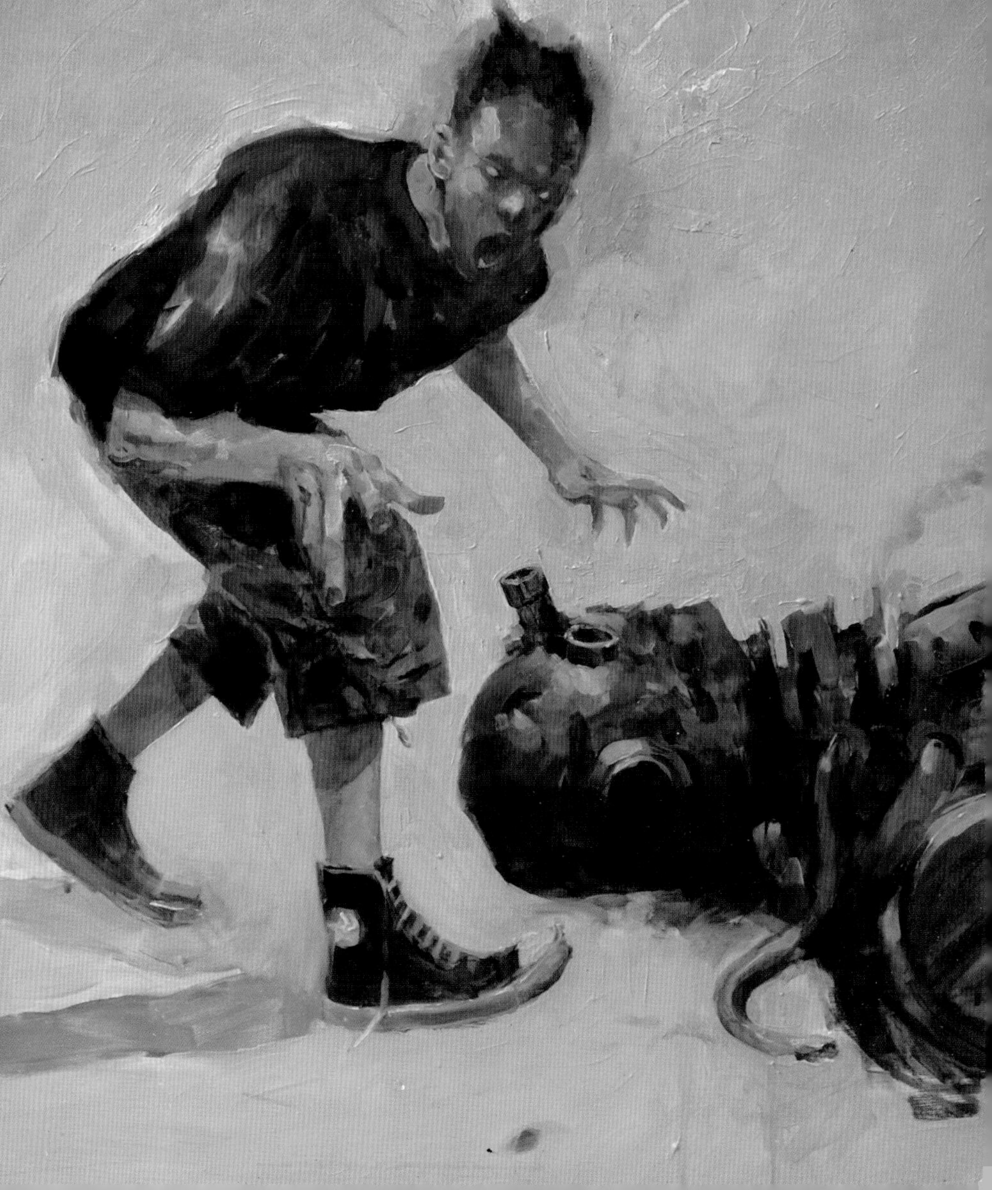

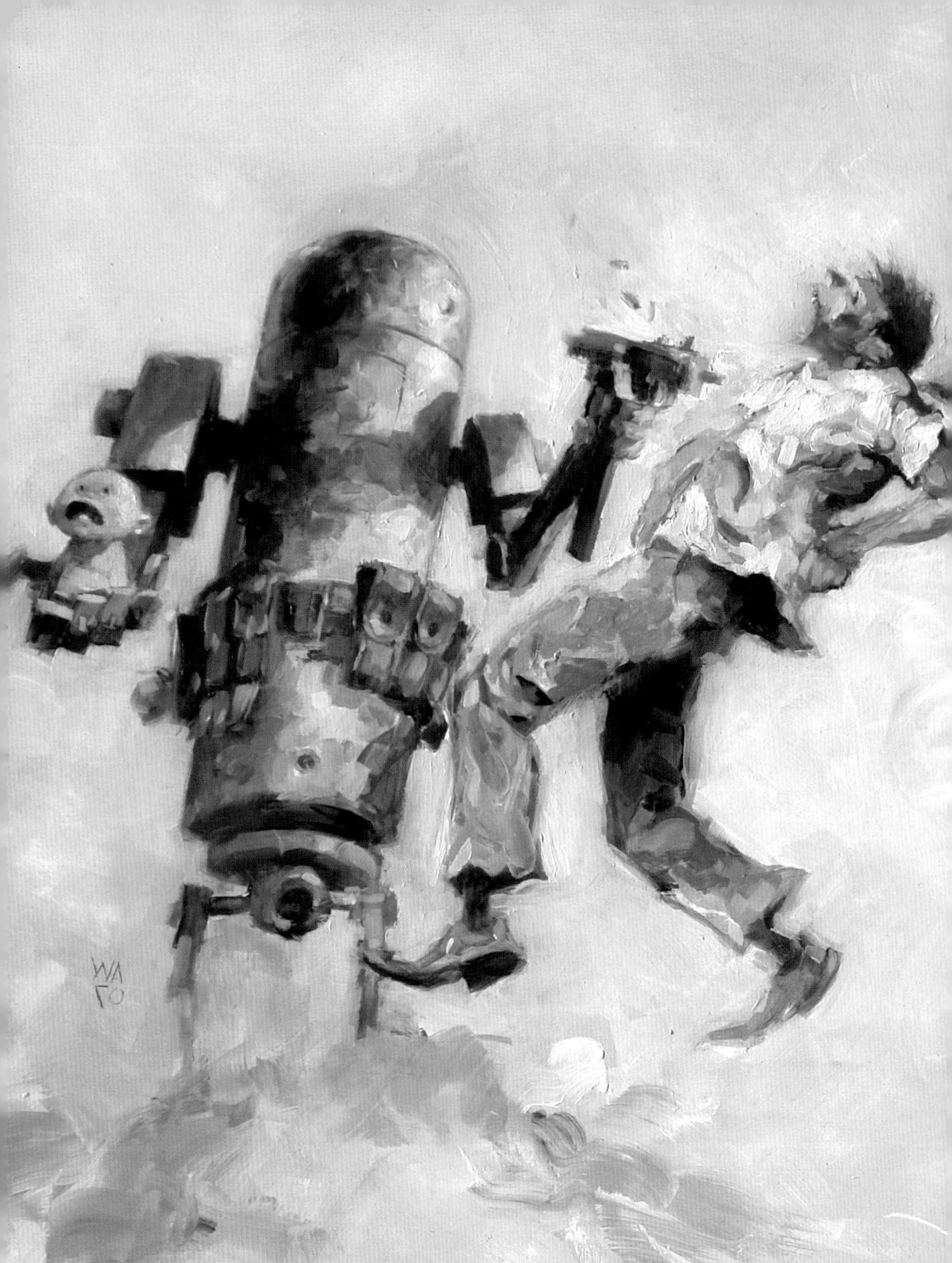

Collection Cover by Ashley Wood • Original Series Edits by Chris Ryall • Collection Edits by Justin Eisinger • Collection Design by Bill Tortolini

www.IDWPUBLISHING.com ISBN: 978-1-60010-527-2 13 12 11 10 2 3 4 5

IDW

Operations: Ted Adams, Chief Executive Officer • Greg Goldstein, Chief Operating Officer • Matthew Ruzicka, CPA, Chief Financial Officer • Alan Payne, VP of Sales • Lorelei Bunjes, Dir. of Digital Services • AnnaMaria White, Marketing & PR Manager • Marci Hubbard, Executive Assistant • Alonzo Simon, Shipping Manager • Angela Loggins, Staff Accountant • Cherrie Go, Assistant Web Designer • Editorial: Chris Ryall, Publisher/Editor-in-Chief • Scott Dunbier, Editor, Special Projects • Andy Schmidt, Senior Editor • Bob Schreck, Senior Editor • Justin Eisinger, Editor • Kris Oprisko, Editor/Foreign Lic. • Denton J. Tipton, Editor • Tom Waltz, Editor • Mariah Huehner, Associate Editor • Carlos Guzman, Editorial Assistant • Design: Robbie Robbins, EVP/Sr. Graphic Artist • Neil Uyetake, Art Director • Chris Mowry, Graphic Artist • Amauri Osorio, Graphic Artist • Gilberto Lazcano, Production Assistant • Shawn Lee, Production Assistant

Originally published as ZOMBIES!: FEAST Issues #1–5, ZOMBIES!: ECLIPSE OF THE UNDEAD Issues #1–4,and ZOMBIES VS. ROBOTS Issues #1–2, D'AIRAIN AVENTURE Issues #1–2, and ZOMBIES VS. ROBOTS VS. AMAZONS Issues #1–3.

ZOMNIBUS

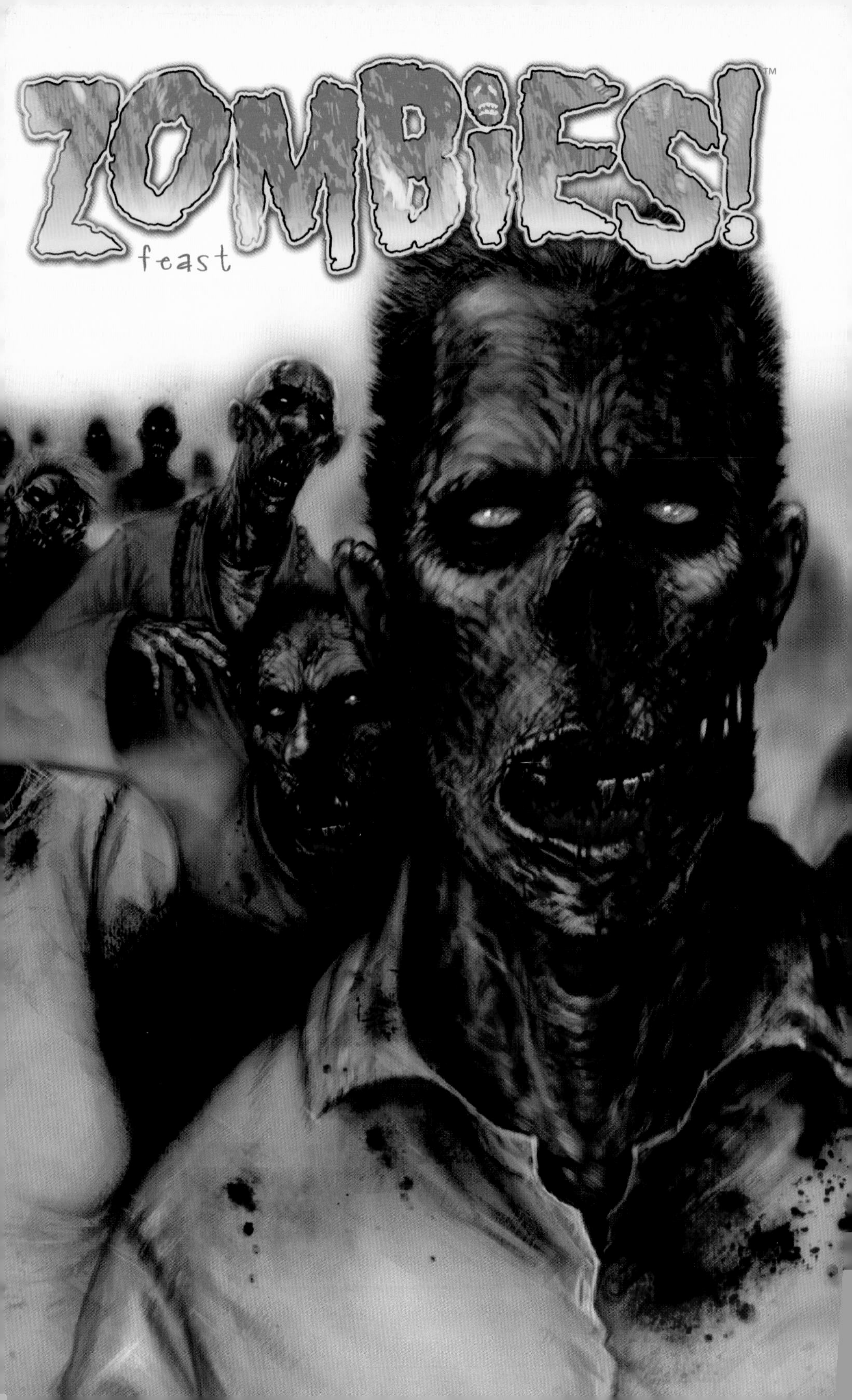
ZOMBIES!™
feast

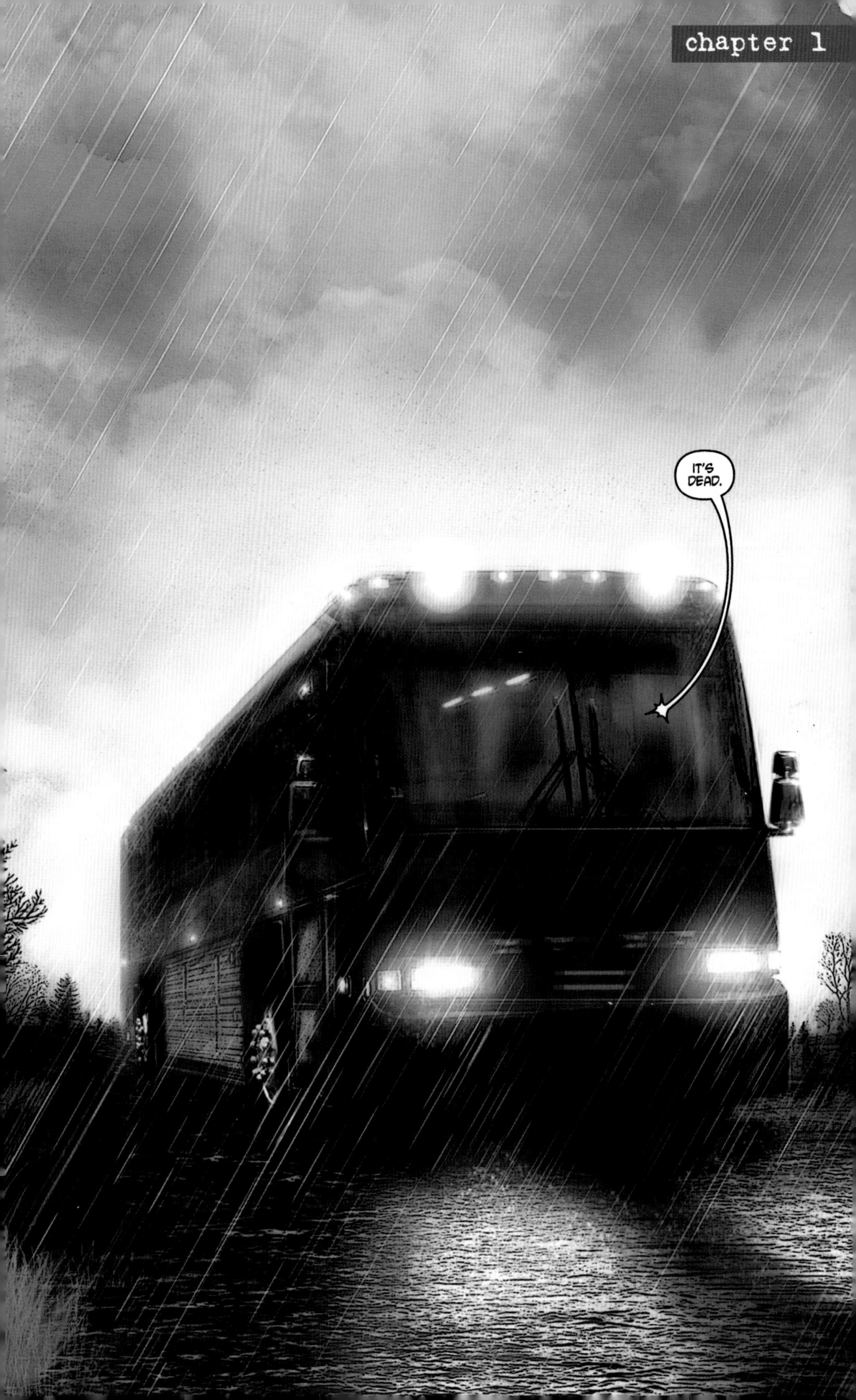
IT'S DEAD.

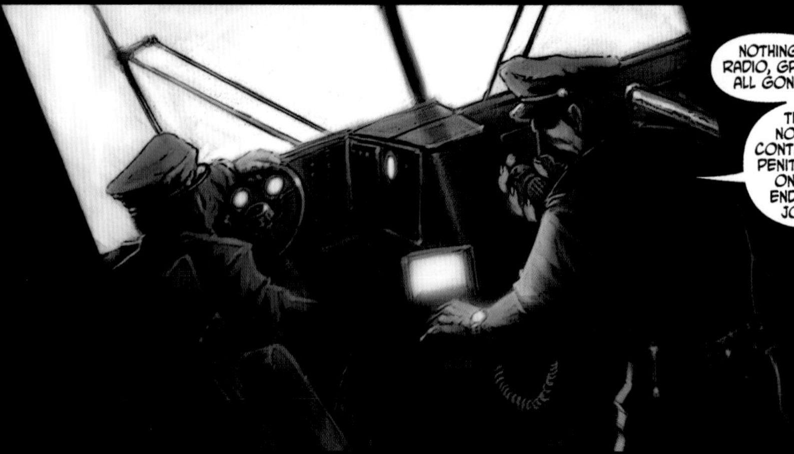
NOTHING. RADIO, GPS... ALL GONE.
THERE'S NO WAY OF CONTACTING THE PENITENTIARIES, ON EITHER END OF OUR JOURNEY.

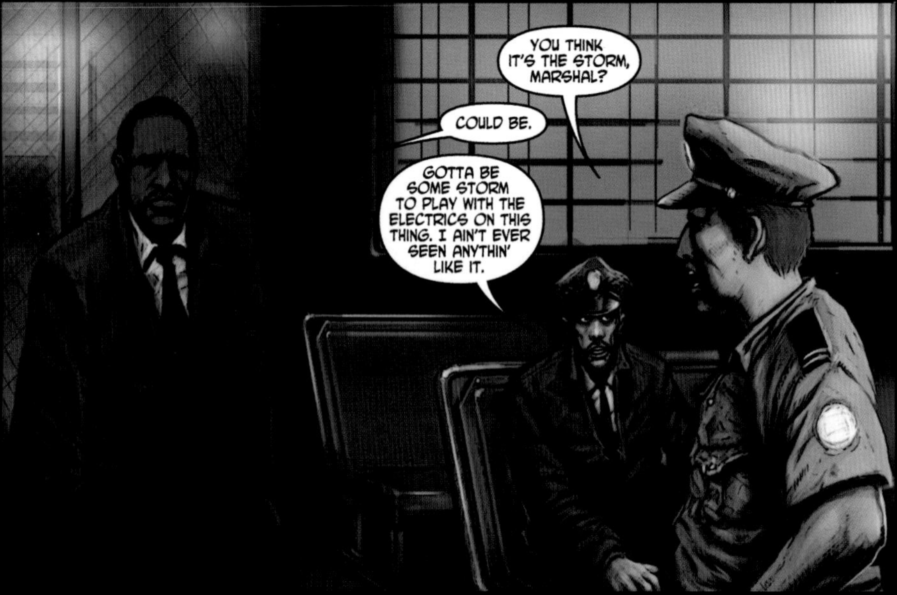
YOU THINK IT'S THE STORM, MARSHAL?
COULD BE.
GOTTA BE SOME STORM TO PLAY WITH THE ELECTRICS ON THIS THING. I AIN'T EVER SEEN ANYTHIN' LIKE IT.

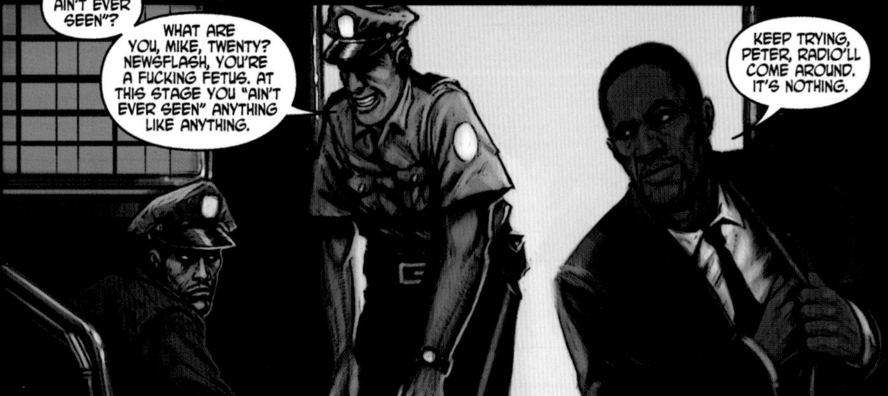
"YOU AIN'T EVER SEEN"?
WHAT ARE YOU, MIKE, TWENTY? NEWSFLASH, YOU'RE A FUCKING FETUS. AT THIS STAGE YOU "AIN'T EVER SEEN" ANYTHING LIKE ANYTHING.
KEEP TRYING, PETER, RADIO'LL COME AROUND. IT'S NOTHING.

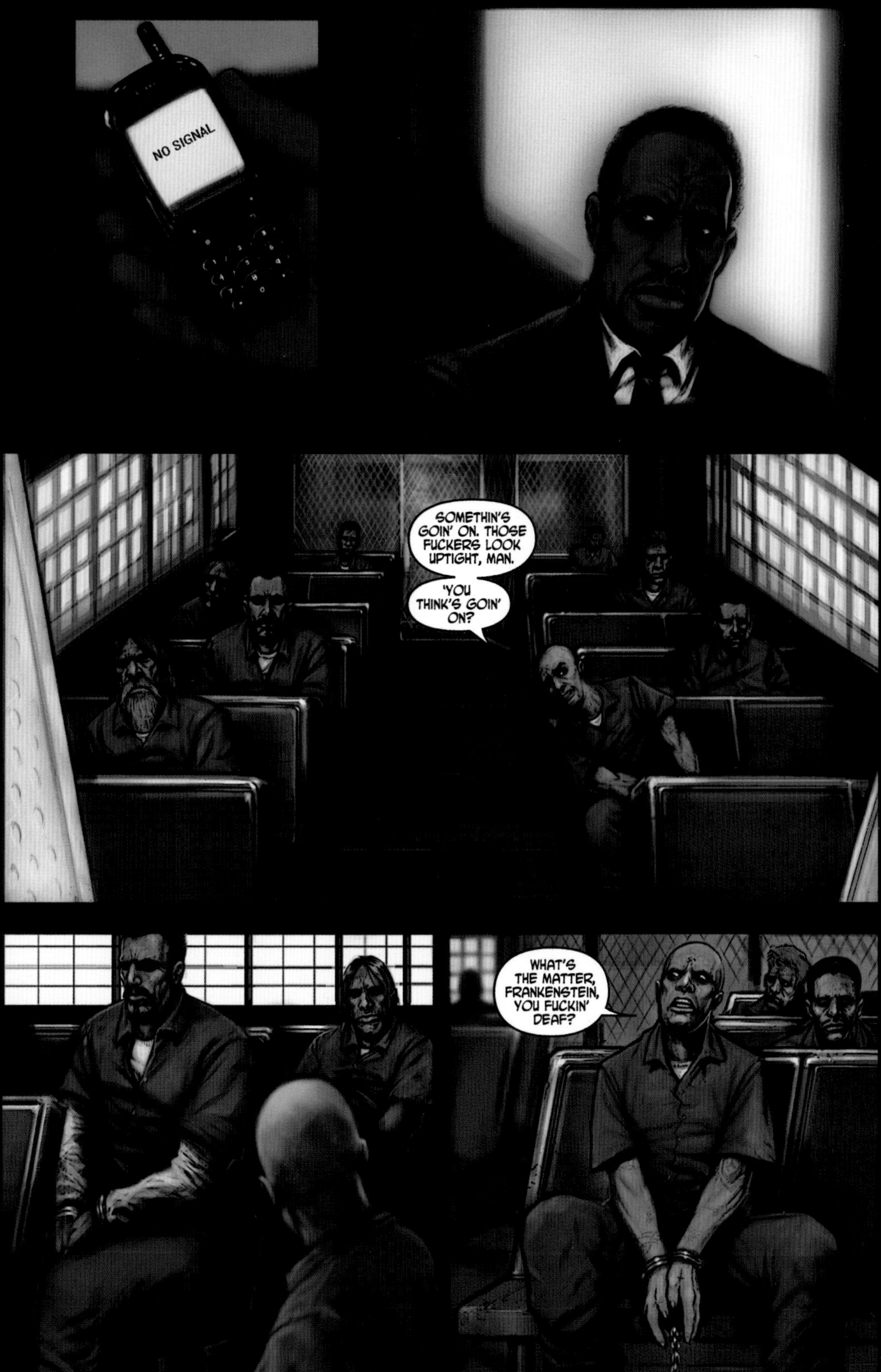
NO SIGNAL
SOMETHIN'S GOIN' ON. THOSE FUCKERS LOOK UPTIGHT, MAN.
'YOU THINK'S GOIN' ON?
WHAT'S THE MATTER, FRANKENSTEIN, YOU FUCKIN' DEAF?

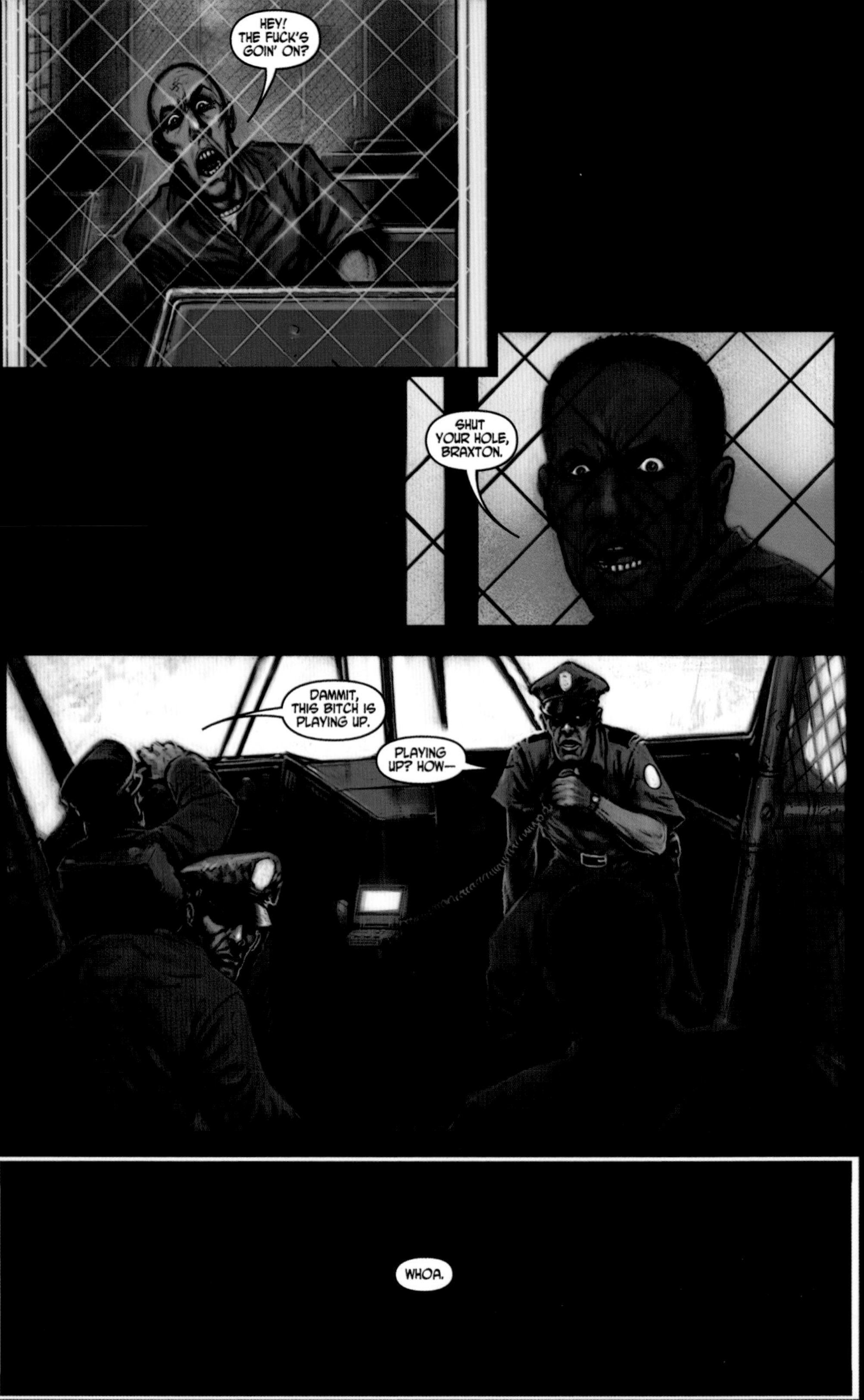
HEY! THE FUCK'S GOIN' ON?
SHUT YOUR HOLE, BRAXTON.
DAMMIT, THIS BITCH IS PLAYING UP.
PLAYING UP? HOW--
WHOA.

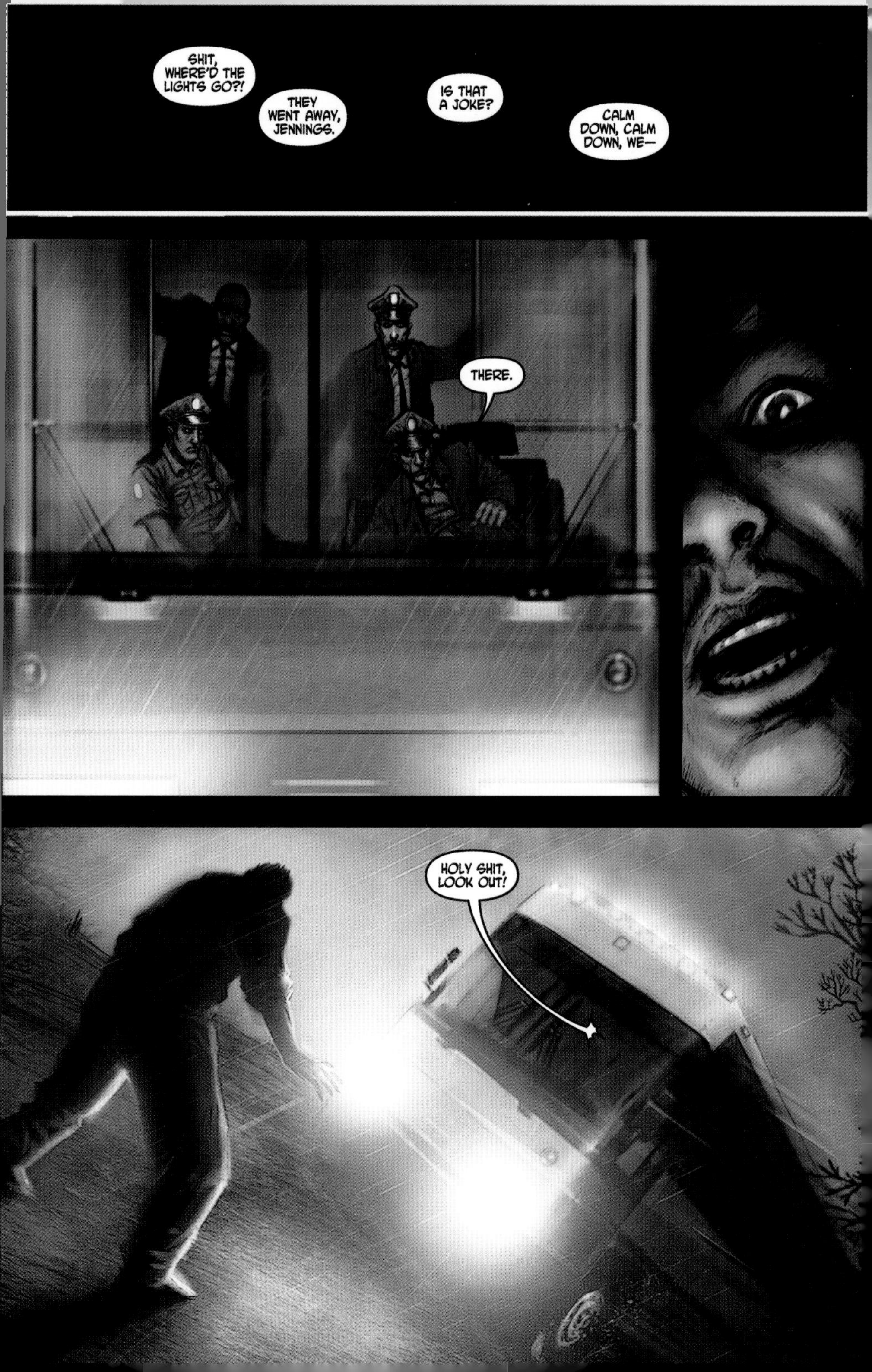
SHIT, WHERE'D THE LIGHTS GO?!
THEY WENT AWAY, JENNINGS.
IS THAT A JOKE?
CALM DOWN, CALM DOWN, WE—
THERE.
HOLY SHIT, LOOK OUT!

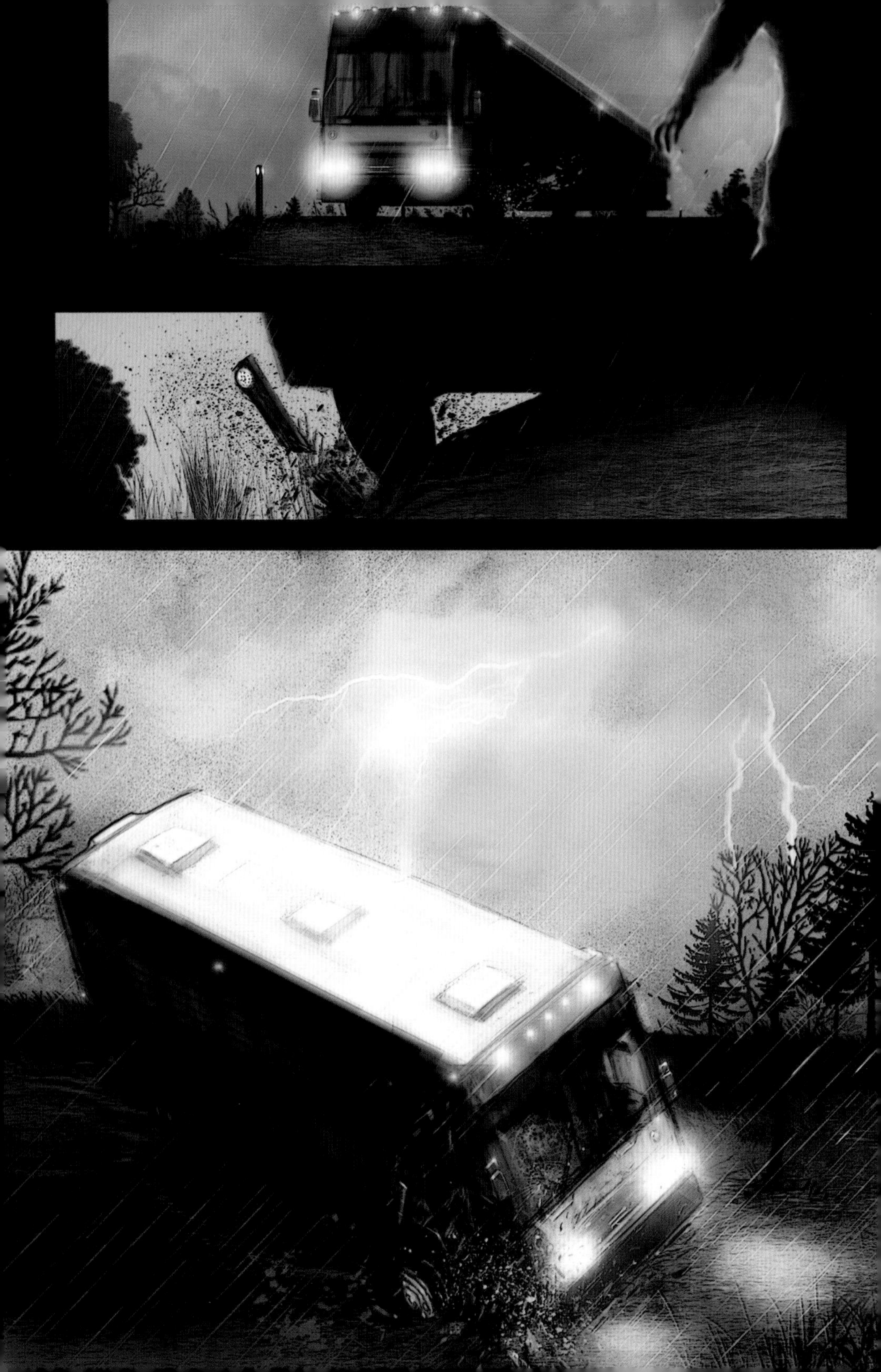

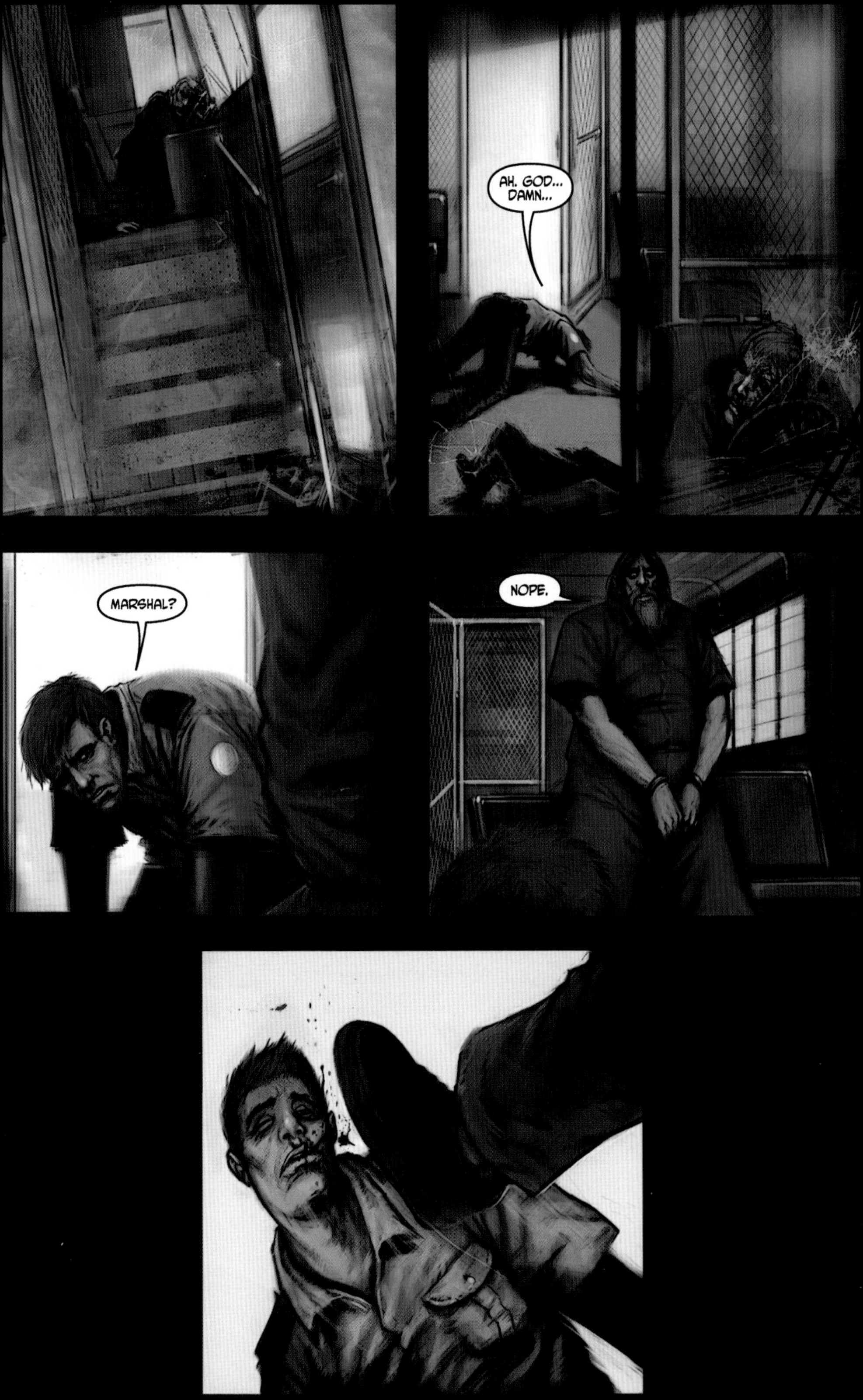
AH. GOD...
DAMN...
MARSHAL?
NOPE.

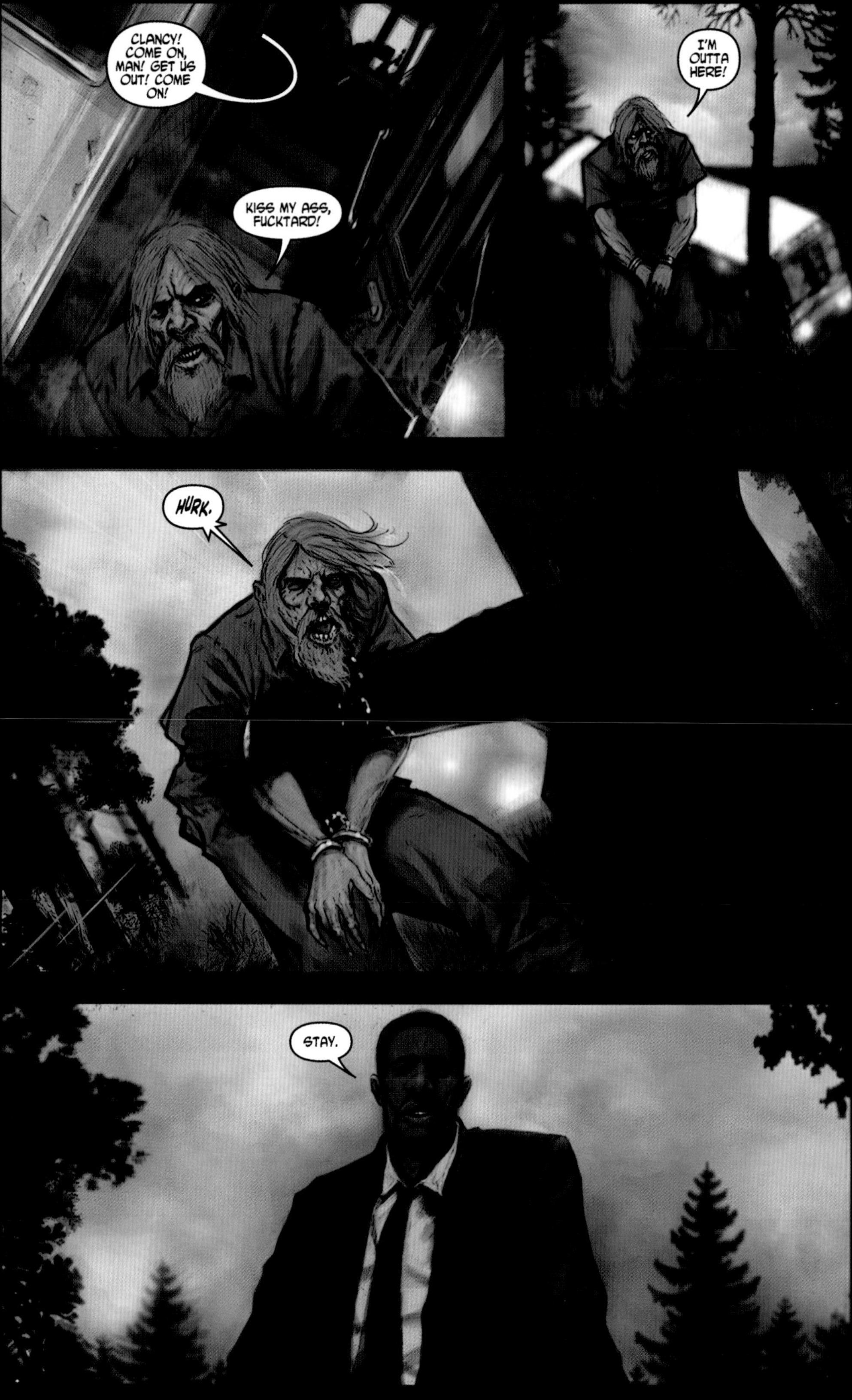
CLANCY! COME ON, MAN! GET US OUT! COME ON!
KISS MY ASS, FUCKTARD!
I'M OUTTA HERE!
HURK.
STAY.

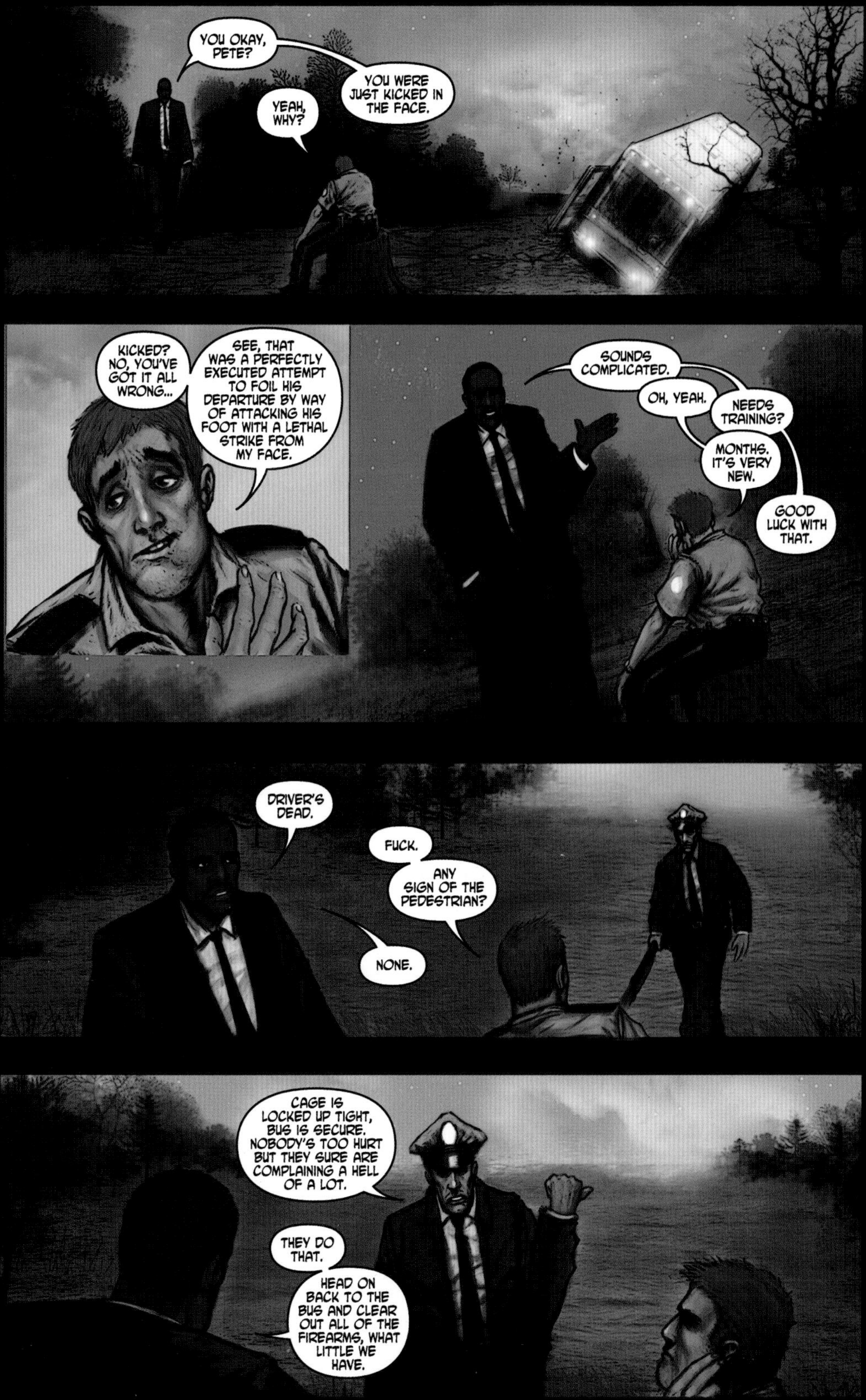
YOU OKAY, PETE?
YEAH, WHY?
YOU WERE JUST KICKED IN THE FACE.
KICKED? NO, YOU'VE GOT IT ALL WRONG...
SEE, THAT WAS A PERFECTLY EXECUTED ATTEMPT TO FOIL HIS DEPARTURE BY WAY OF ATTACKING HIS FOOT WITH A LETHAL STRIKE FROM MY FACE.
SOUNDS COMPLICATED.
OH, YEAH.
NEEDS TRAINING?
MONTHS. IT'S VERY NEW.
GOOD LUCK WITH THAT.
DRIVER'S DEAD.
FUCK.
ANY SIGN OF THE PEDESTRIAN?
NONE.
CAGE IS LOCKED UP TIGHT, BUS IS SECURE. NOBODY'S TOO HURT BUT THEY SURE ARE COMPLAINING A HELL OF A LOT.
THEY DO THAT.
HEAD ON BACK TO THE BUS AND CLEAR OUT ALL OF THE FIREARMS, WHAT LITTLE WE HAVE.

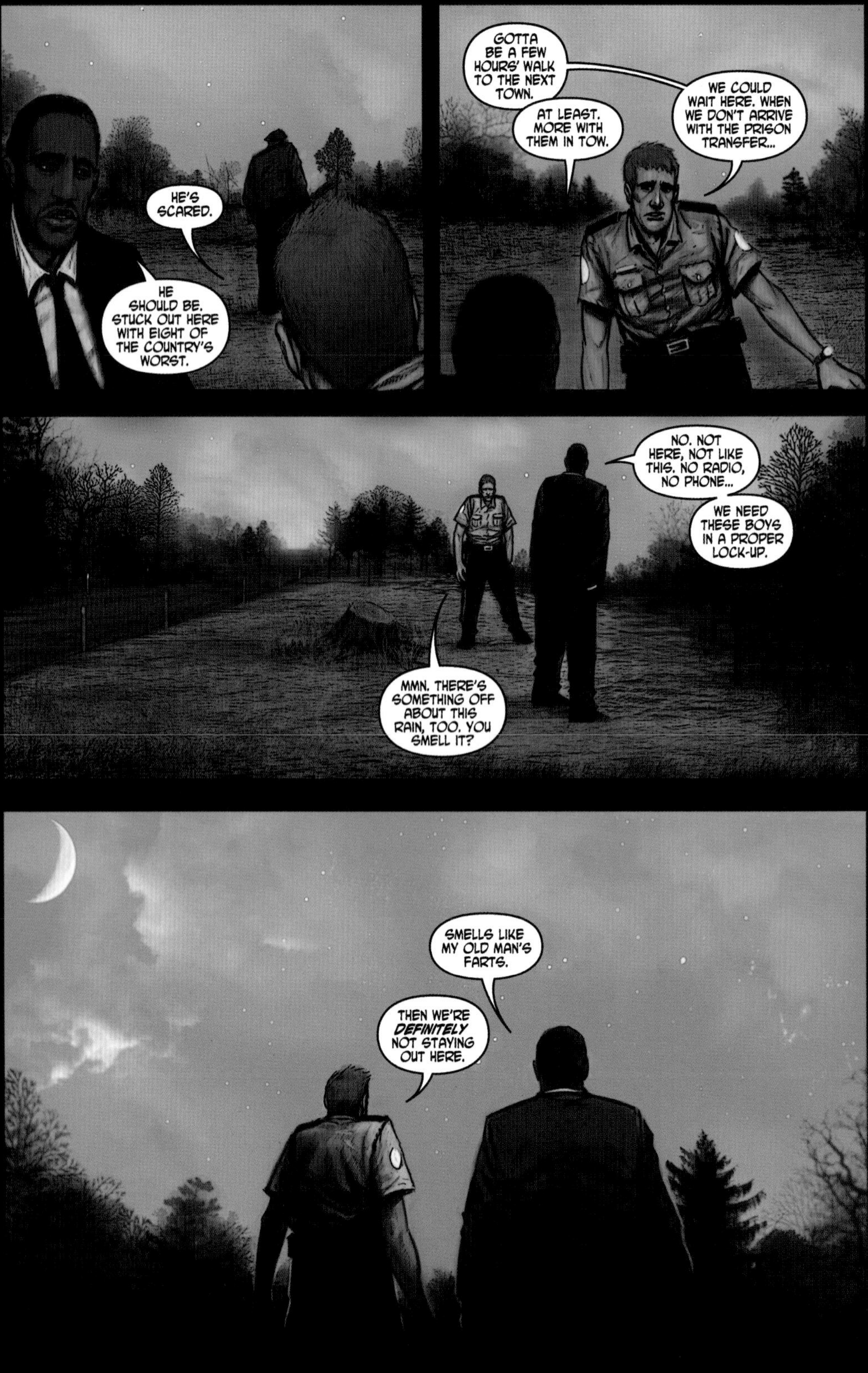
HE'S SCARED.
HE SHOULD BE. STUCK OUT HERE WITH EIGHT OF THE COUNTRY'S WORST.
GOTTA BE A FEW HOURS' WALK TO THE NEXT TOWN.
AT LEAST. MORE WITH THEM IN TOW.
WE COULD WAIT HERE. WHEN WE DON'T ARRIVE WITH THE PRISON TRANSFER...
NO. NOT HERE, NOT LIKE THIS. NO RADIO, NO PHONE...
WE NEED THESE BOYS IN A PROPER LOCK-UP.
MMN. THERE'S SOMETHING OFF ABOUT THIS RAIN, TOO. YOU SMELL IT?
SMELLS LIKE MY OLD MAN'S FARTS.
THEN WE'RE *DEFINITELY* NOT STAYING OUT HERE.

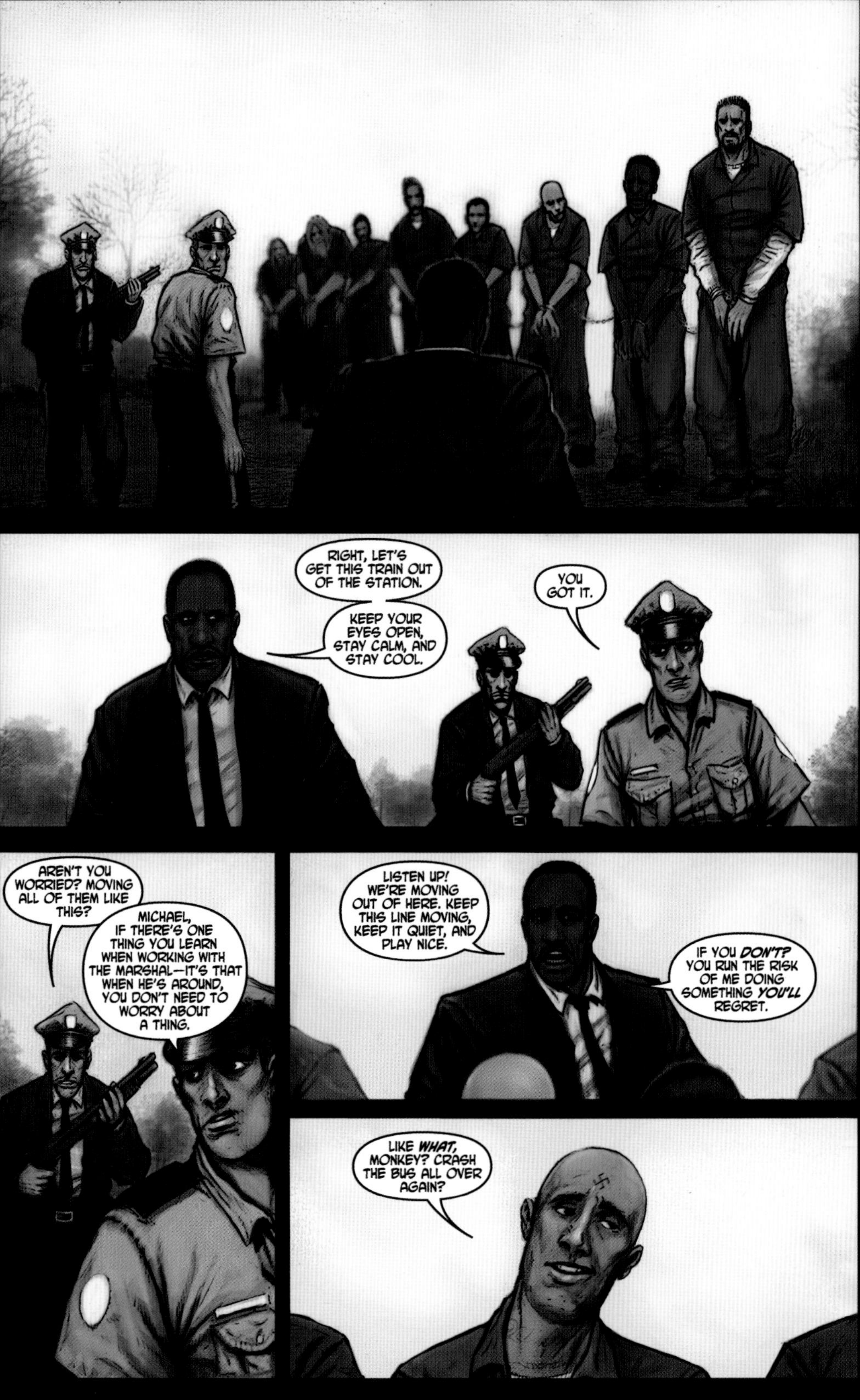

RIGHT, LET'S GET THIS TRAIN OUT OF THE STATION.
KEEP YOUR EYES OPEN, STAY CALM, AND STAY COOL.
YOU GOT IT.
AREN'T YOU WORRIED? MOVING ALL OF THEM LIKE THIS?
MICHAEL, IF THERE'S ONE THING YOU LEARN WHEN WORKING WITH THE MARSHAL—IT'S THAT WHEN HE'S AROUND, YOU DON'T NEED TO WORRY ABOUT A THING.
LISTEN UP! WE'RE MOVING OUT OF HERE. KEEP THIS LINE MOVING, KEEP IT QUIET, AND PLAY NICE.
IF YOU *DON'T?* YOU RUN THE RISK OF ME DOING SOMETHING *YOU'LL* REGRET.
LIKE *WHAT,* MONKEY? CRASH THE BUS ALL OVER AGAIN?

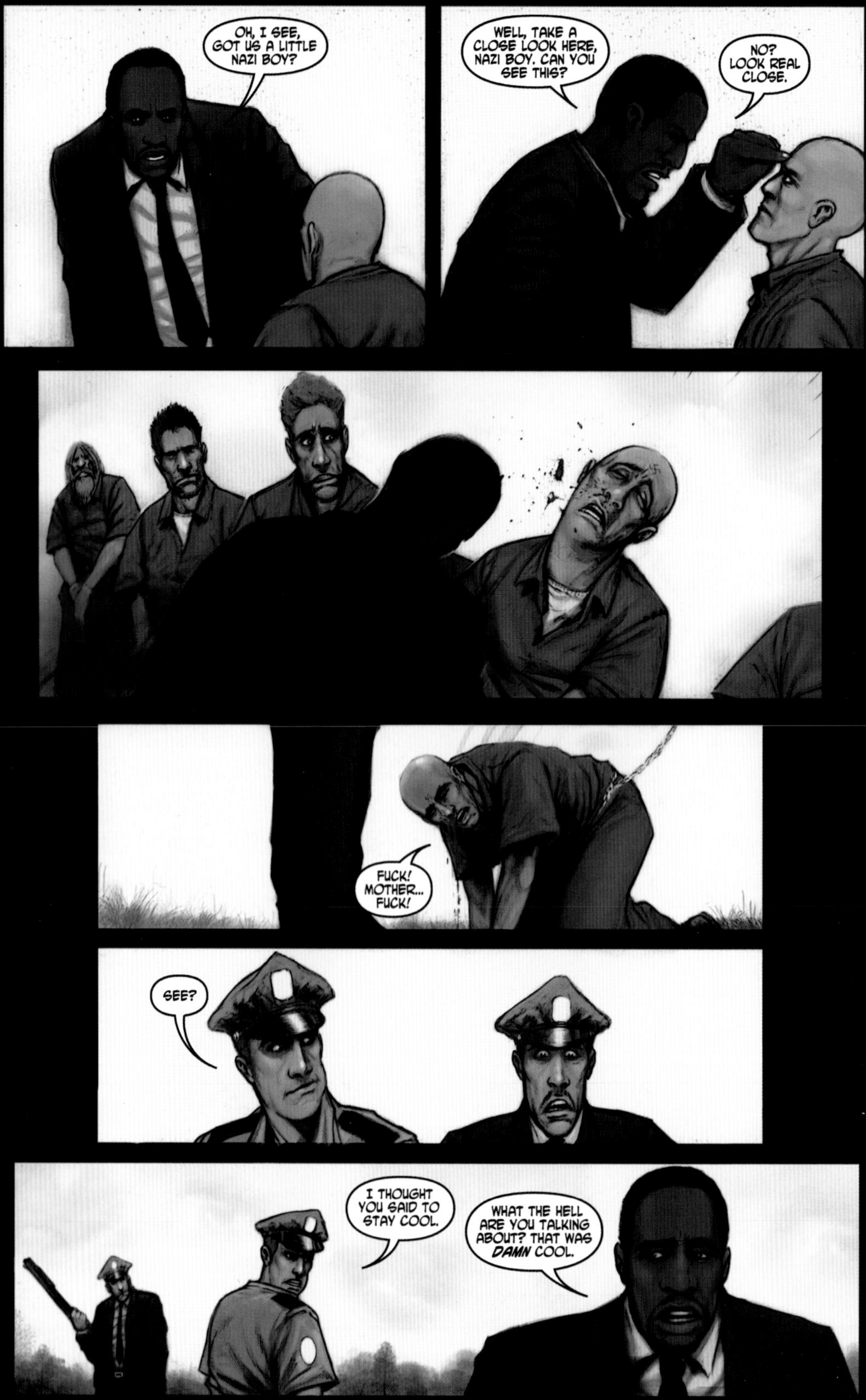
OH, I SEE, GOT US A LITTLE NAZI BOY?
WELL, TAKE A CLOSE LOOK HERE, NAZI BOY. CAN YOU SEE THIS?
NO? LOOK REAL CLOSE.
FUCK! MOTHER... FUCK!
SEE?
I THOUGHT YOU SAID TO STAY COOL.
WHAT THE HELL ARE YOU TALKING ABOUT? THAT WAS *DAMN* COOL.

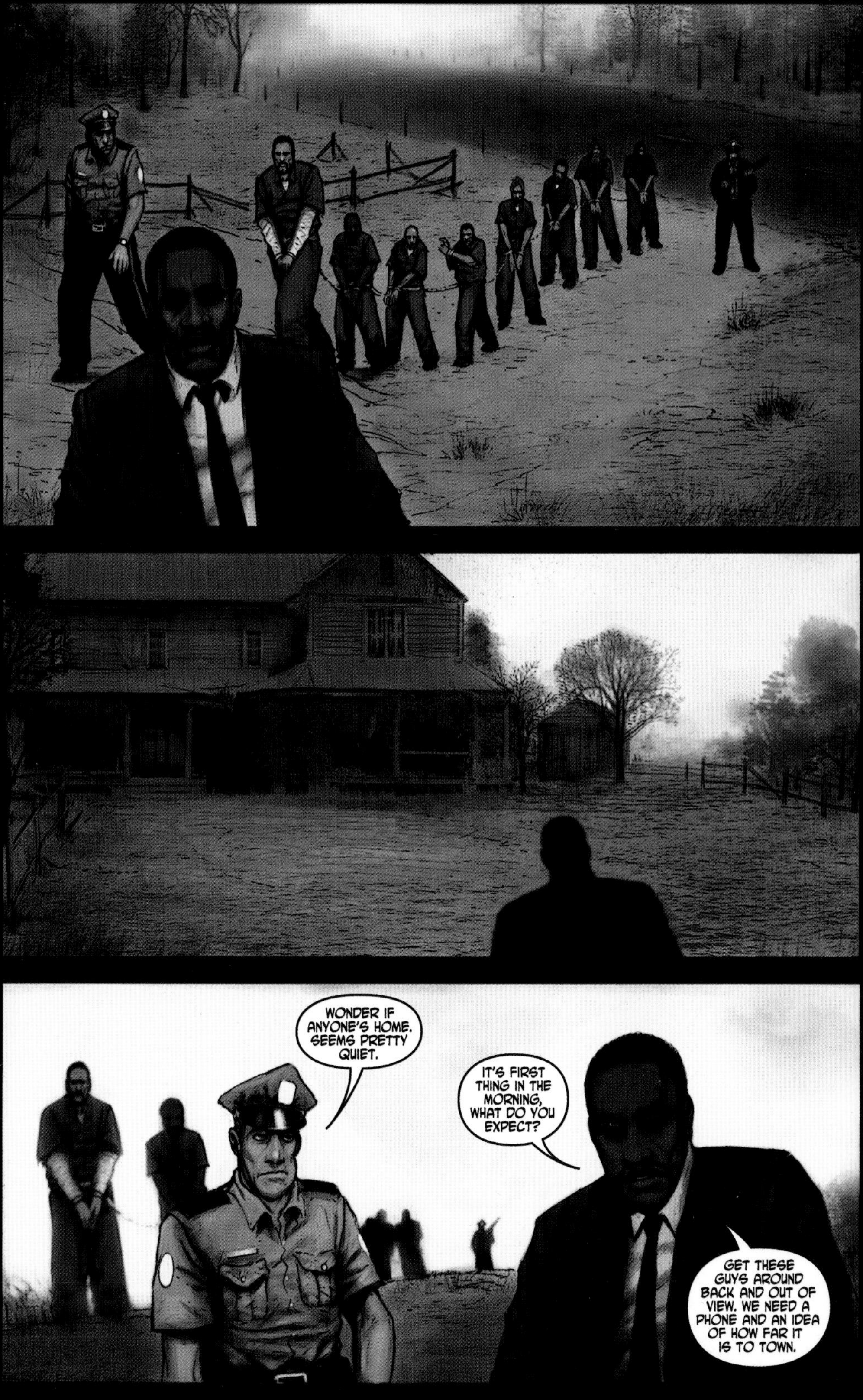
WONDER IF ANYONE'S HOME. SEEMS PRETTY QUIET.
IT'S FIRST THING IN THE MORNING, WHAT DO YOU EXPECT?
GET THESE GUYS AROUND BACK AND OUT OF VIEW. WE NEED A PHONE AND AN IDEA OF HOW FAR IT IS TO TOWN.

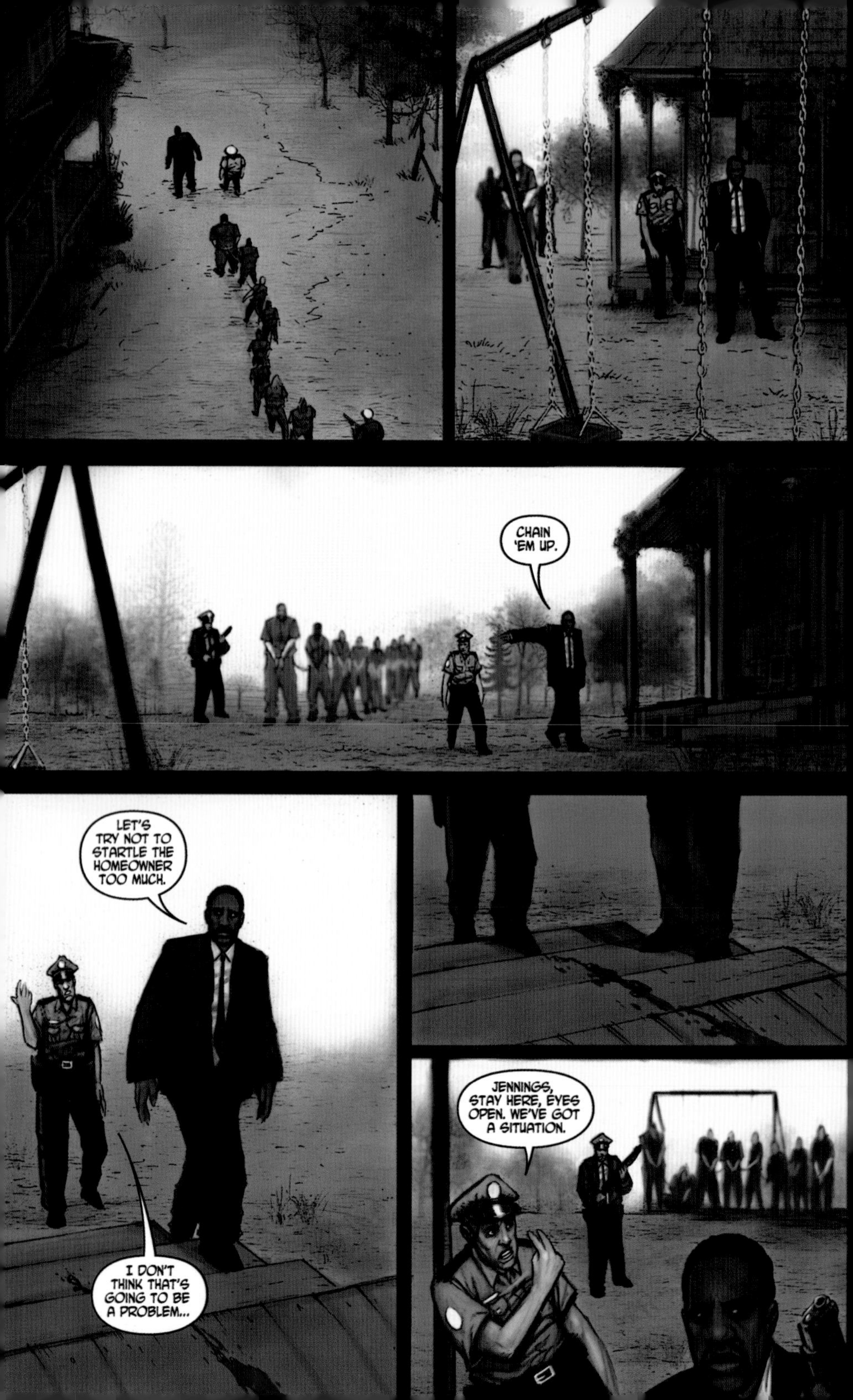
CHAIN 'EM UP.
LET'S TRY NOT TO STARTLE THE HOMEOWNER TOO MUCH.
I DON'T THINK THAT'S GOING TO BE A PROBLEM...
JENNINGS, STAY HERE, EYES OPEN. WE'VE GOT A SITUATION.

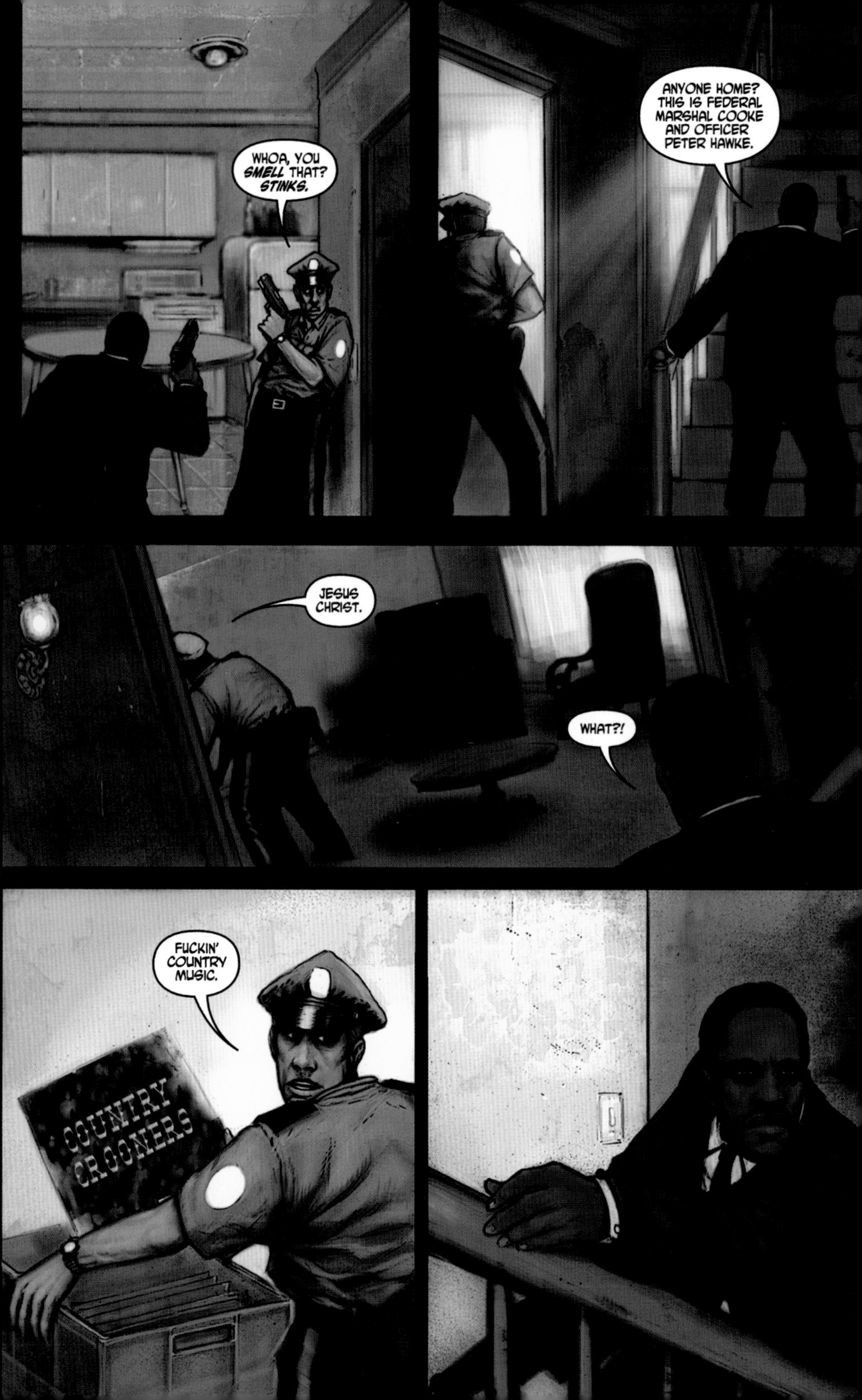
WHOA, YOU *SMELL* THAT? *STINKS.*
ANYONE HOME? THIS IS FEDERAL MARSHAL COOKE AND OFFICER PETER HAWKE.
JESUS CHRIST.
WHAT?!
FUCKIN' COUNTRY MUSIC.
COUNTRY CROONERS

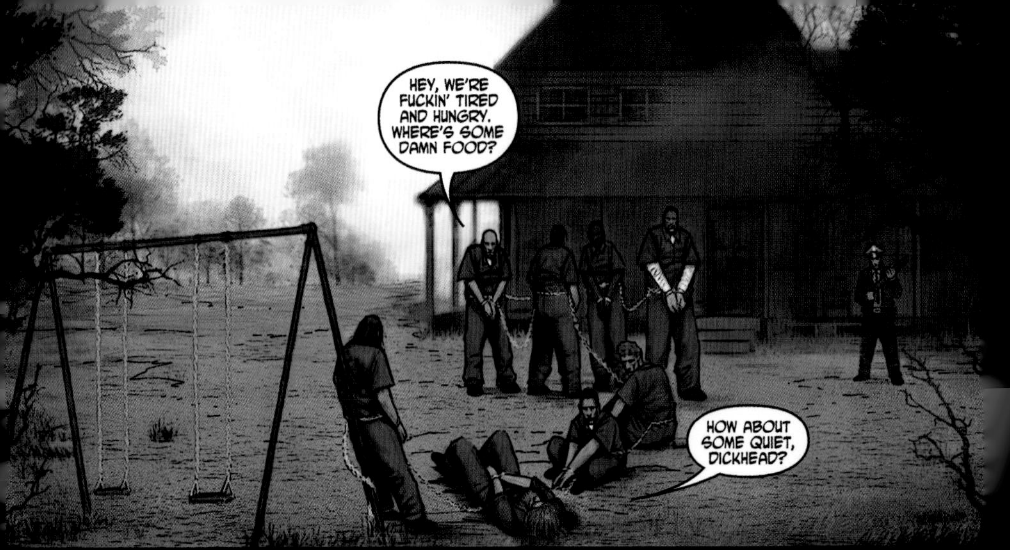
HEY, WE'RE FUCKIN' TIRED AND HUNGRY. WHERE'S SOME DAMN FOOD?
HOW ABOUT SOME QUIET, DICKHEAD?

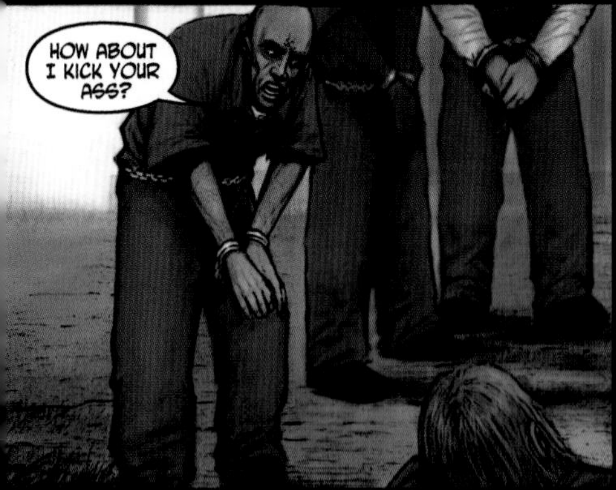
HOW ABOUT I KICK YOUR ASS?

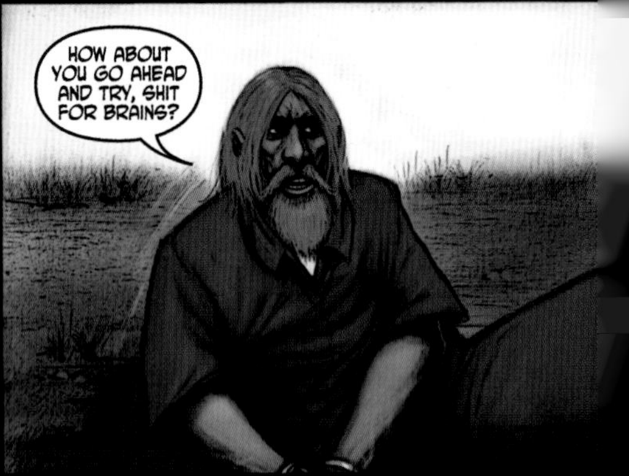
HOW ABOUT YOU GO AHEAD AND TRY, SHIT FOR BRAINS?

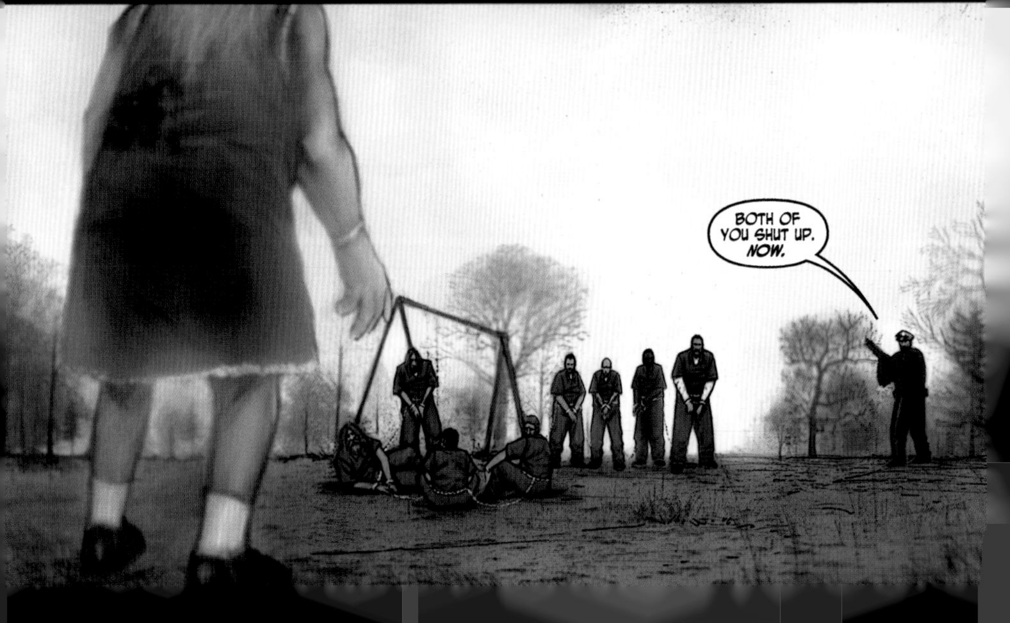
BOTH OF YOU SHUT UP. *NOW.*

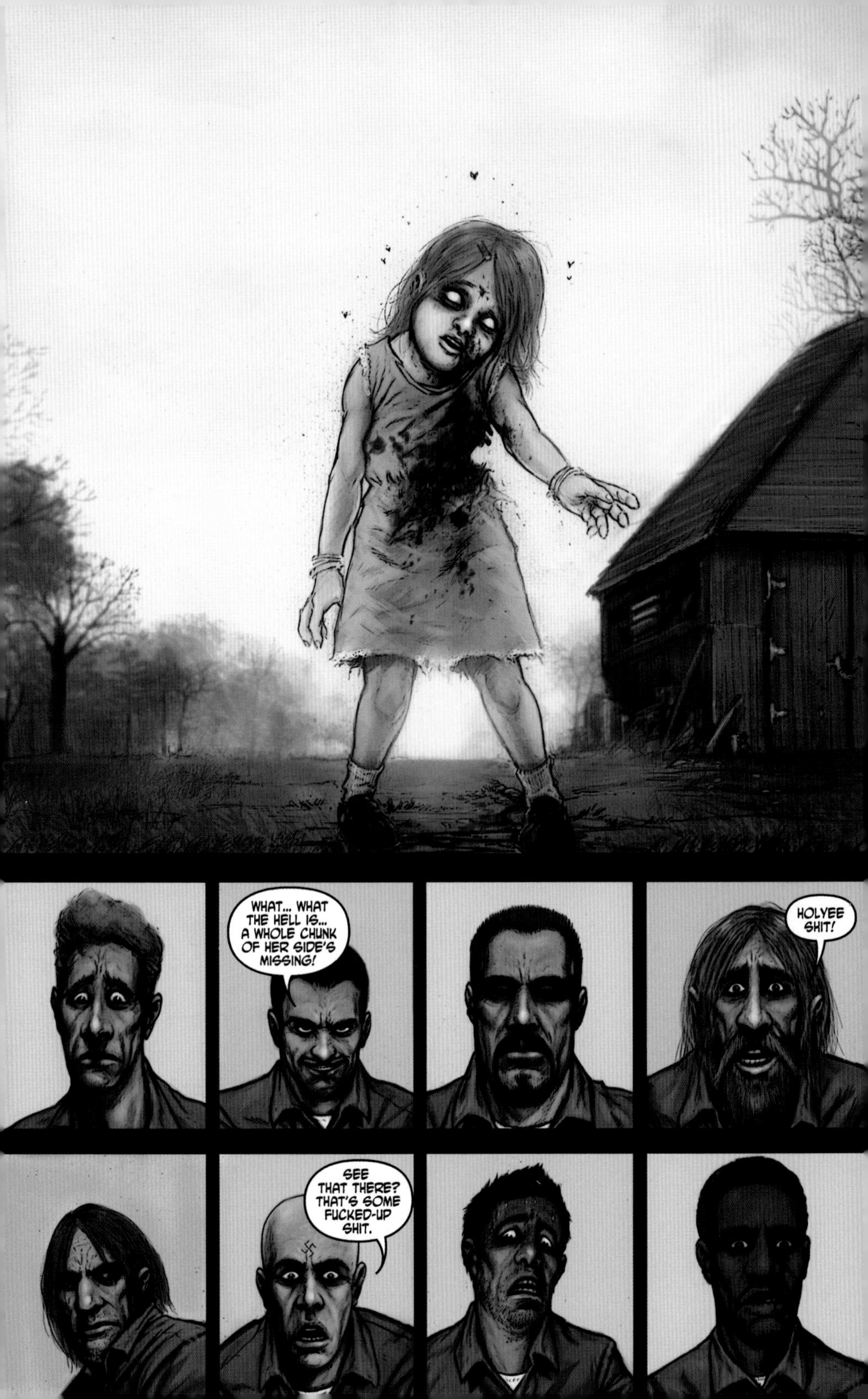
WHAT... WHAT THE HELL IS... A WHOLE CHUNK OF HER SIDE'S MISSING!
HOLYEE SHIT!
SEE THAT THERE? THAT'S SOME FUCKED-UP SHIT.

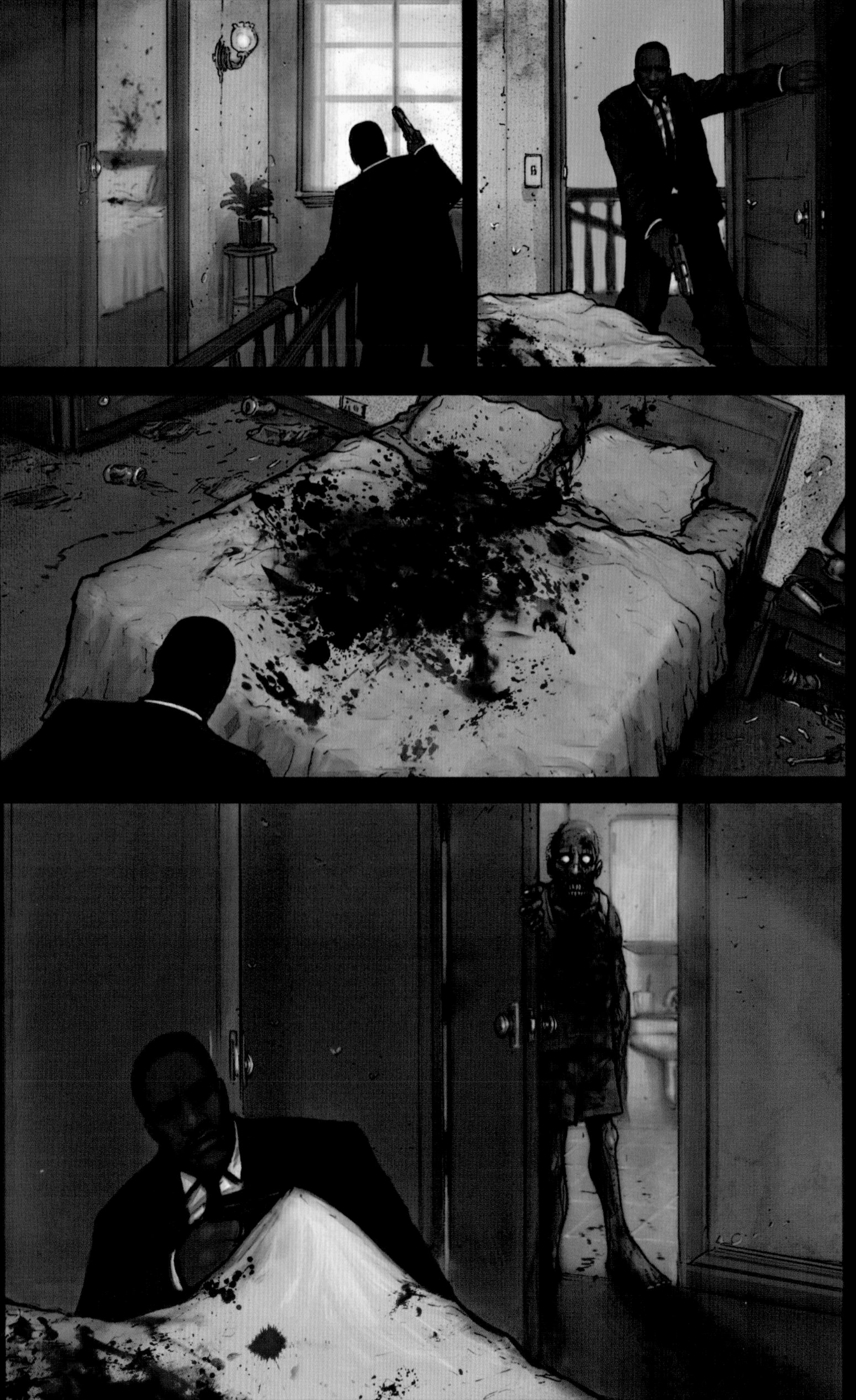

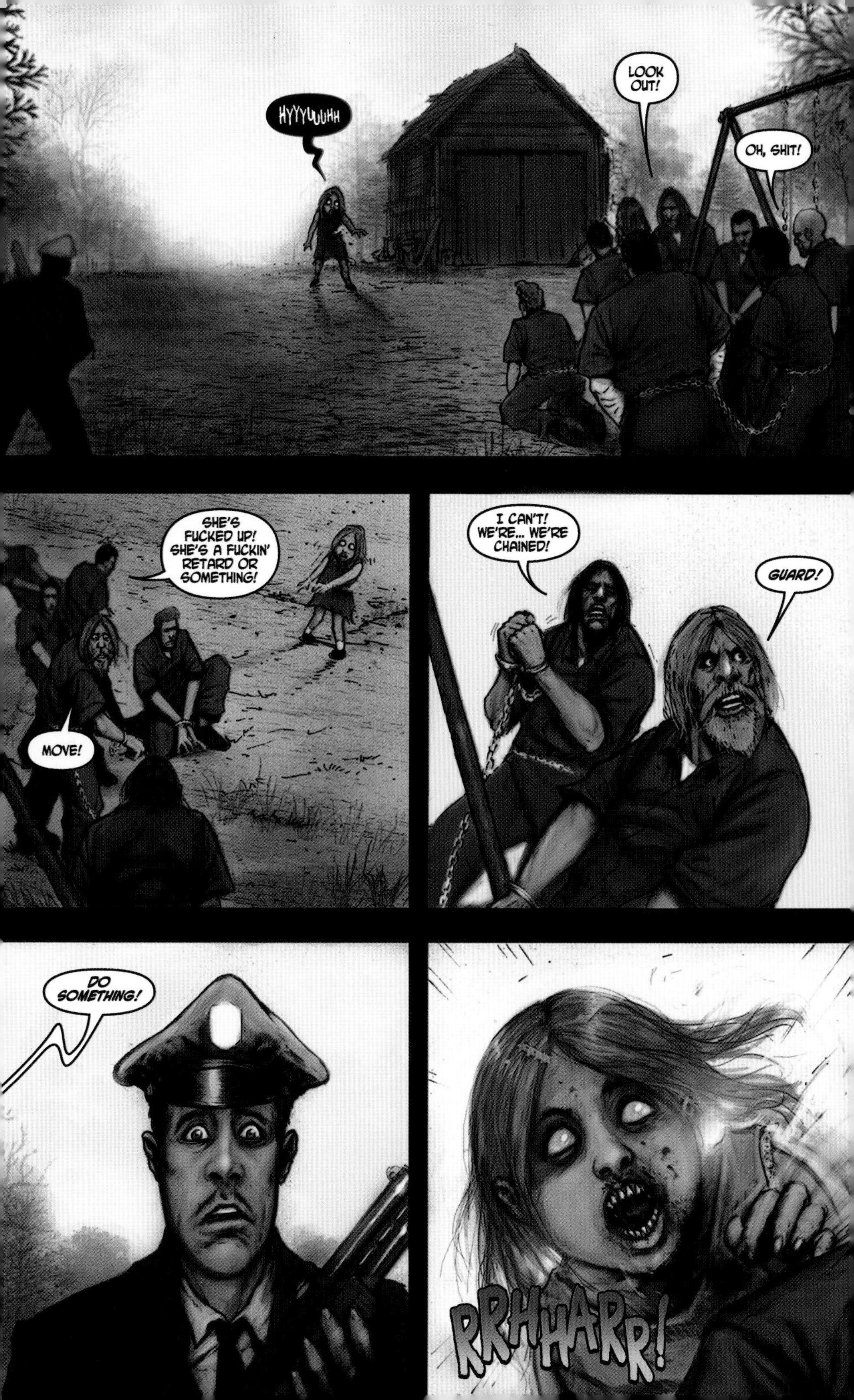
HYYYUUUHH
LOOK OUT!
OH, SHIT!
SHE'S FUCKED UP! SHE'S A FUCKIN' RETARD OR SOMETHING!
MOVE!
I CAN'T! WE'RE... WE'RE CHAINED!
GUARD!
DO SOMETHING!
RRHHARR!

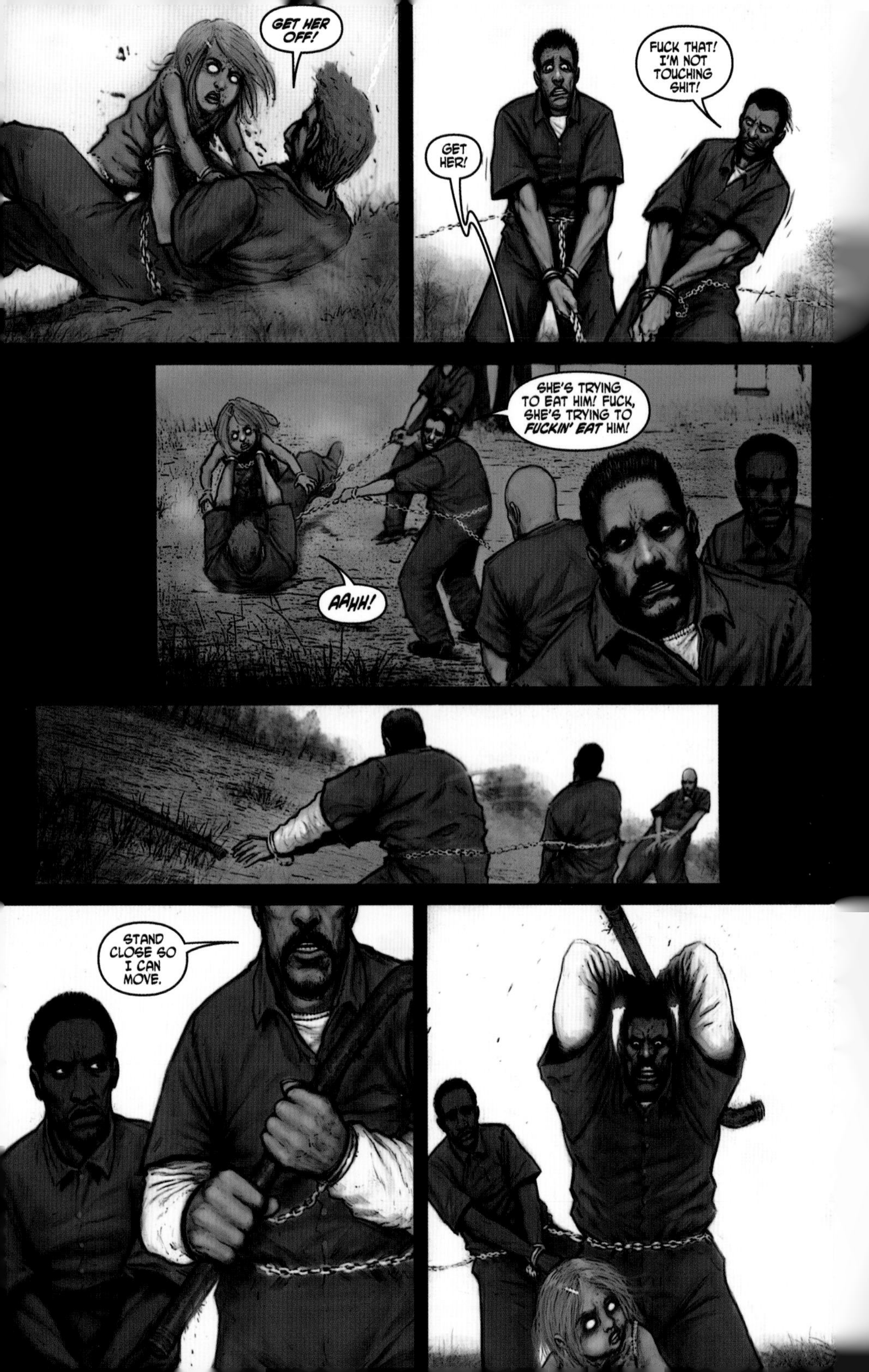
GET HER OFF!
FUCK THAT! I'M NOT TOUCHING SHIT!
GET HER!
SHE'S TRYING TO EAT HIM! FUCK, SHE'S TRYING TO FUCKIN' EAT HIM!
AAHH!
STAND CLOSE SO I CAN MOVE.

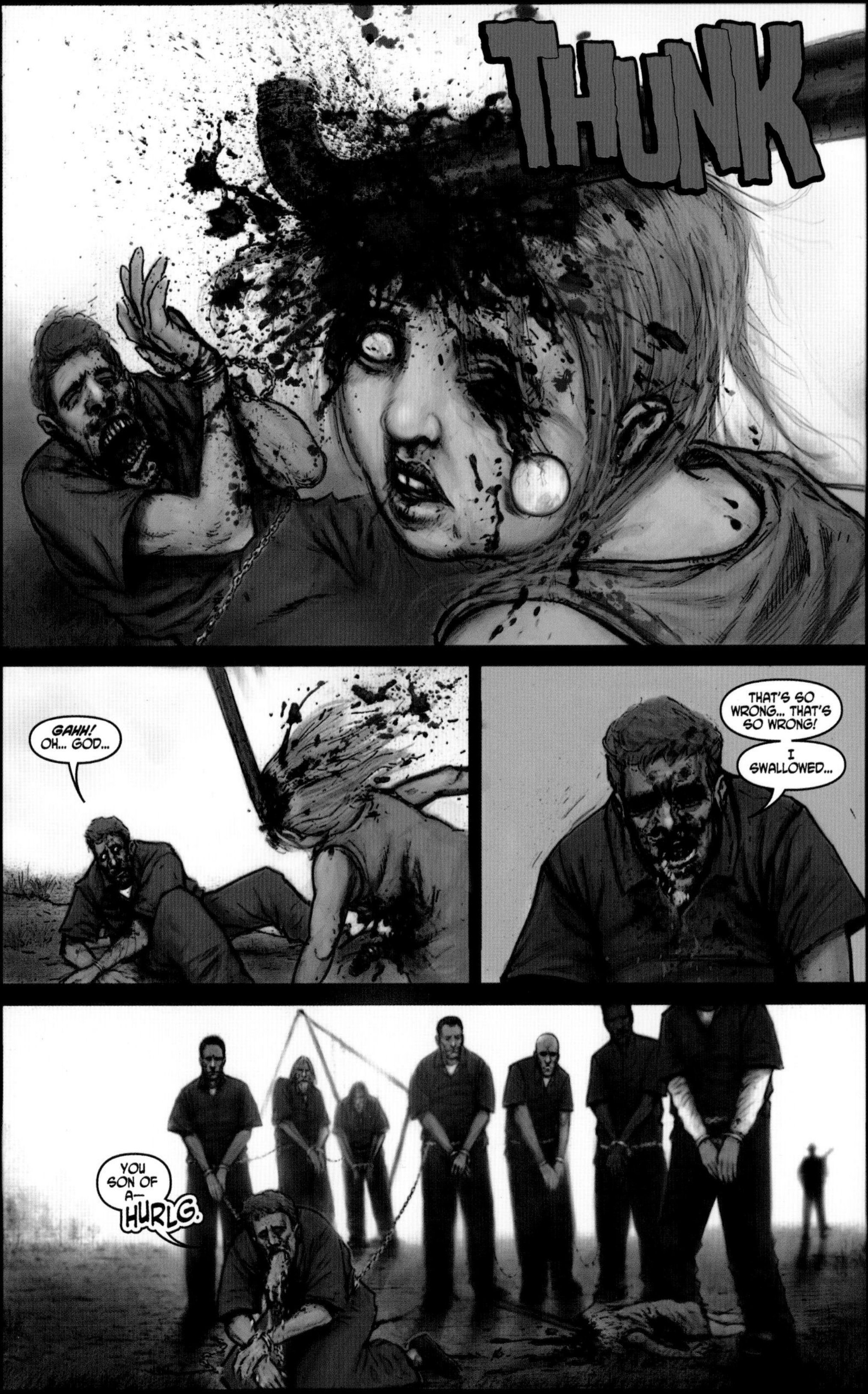
THUNK
GAHH! OH... GOD...
THAT'S SO WRONG... THAT'S SO WRONG!
I SWALLOWED...
YOU SON OF A—
HURLG.

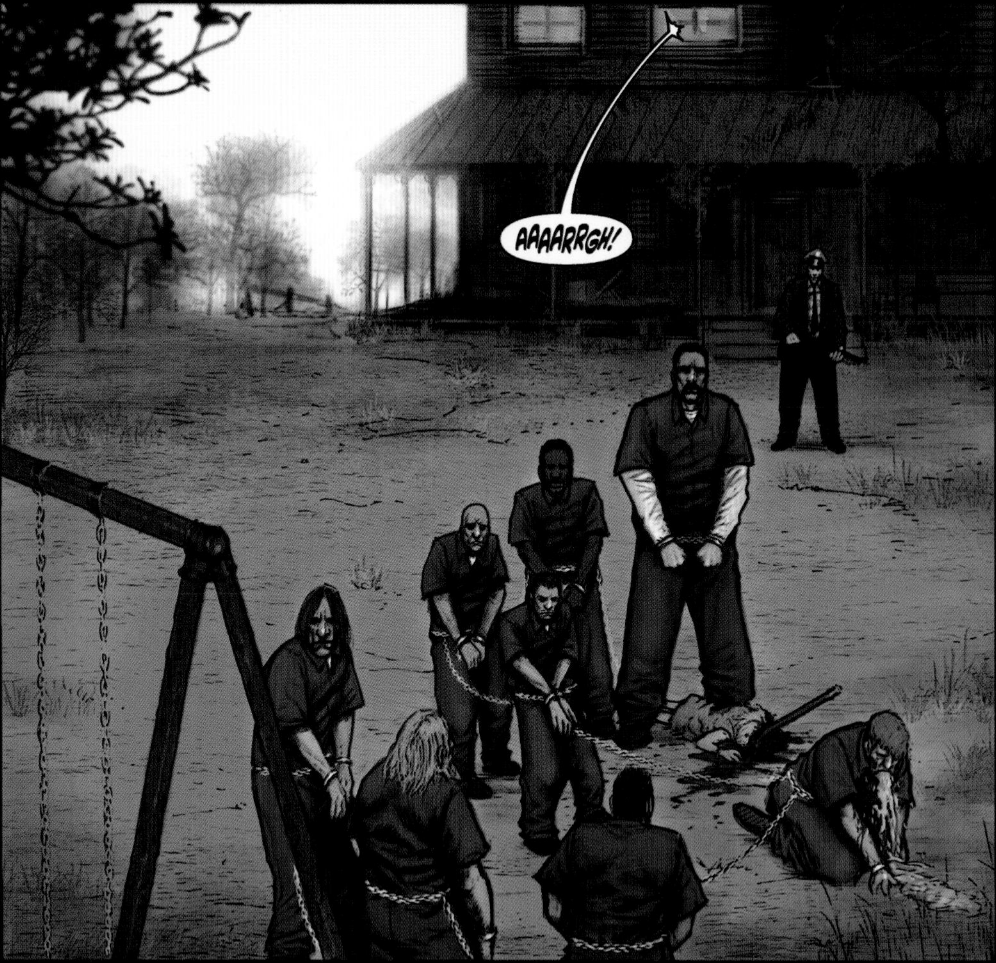
AAAARRGH!

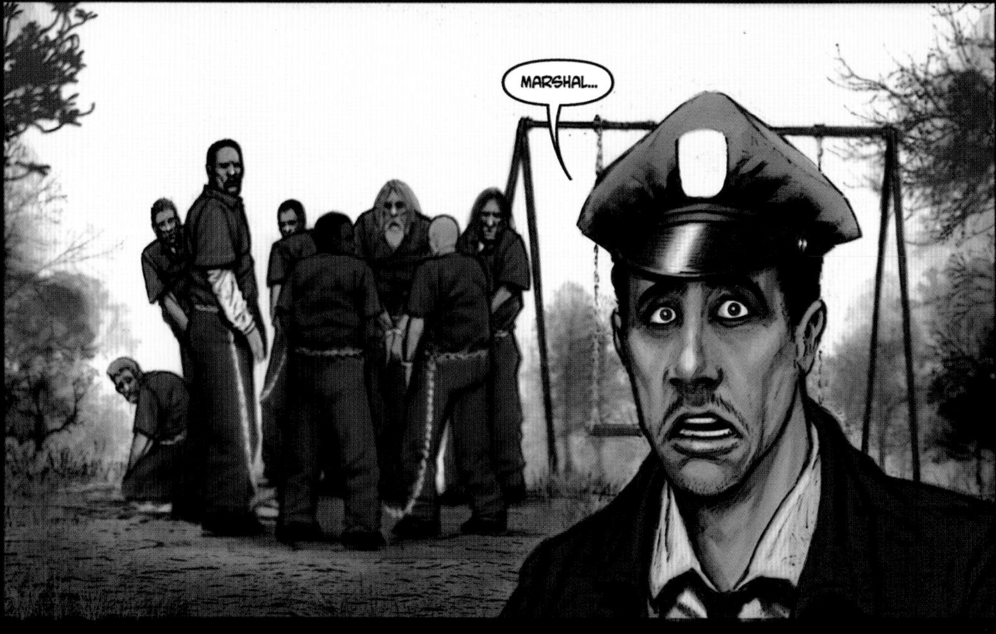
MARSHAL...

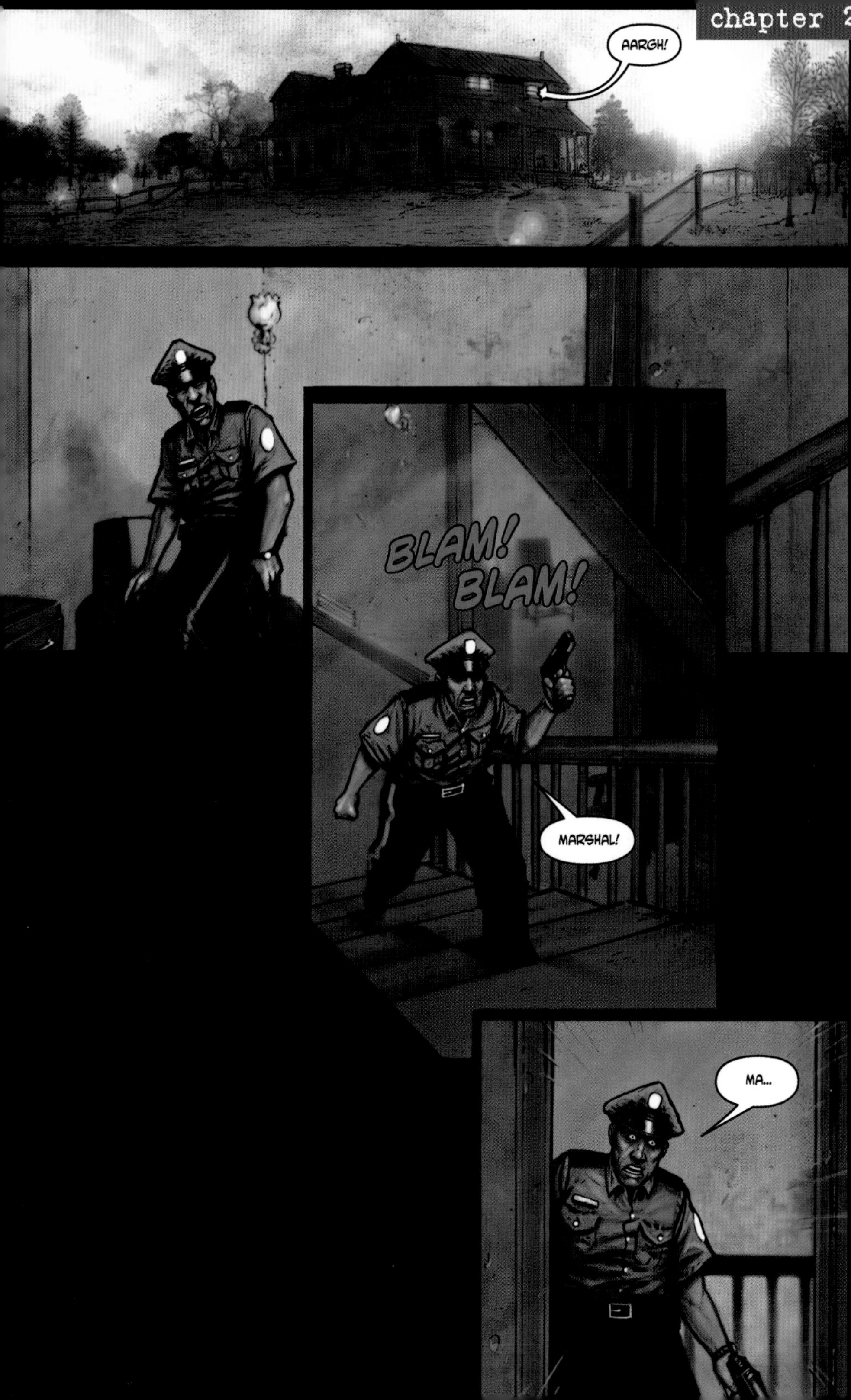
AARGH!
BLAM! BLAM!
MARSHAL!
MA...

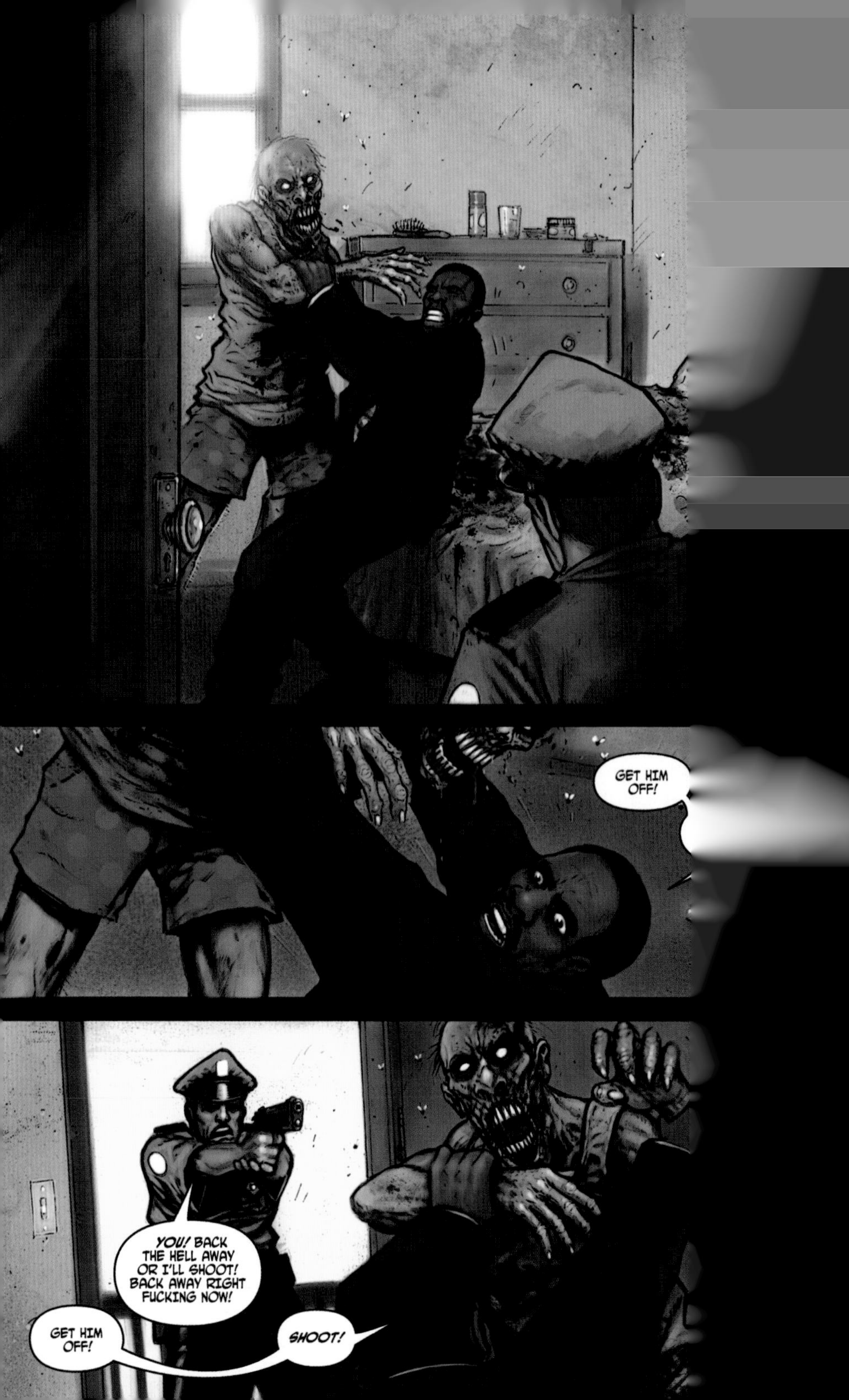
GET HIM OFF!
YOU! BACK THE HELL AWAY OR I'LL SHOOT! BACK AWAY RIGHT FUCKING NOW!
GET HIM OFF!
SHOOT!

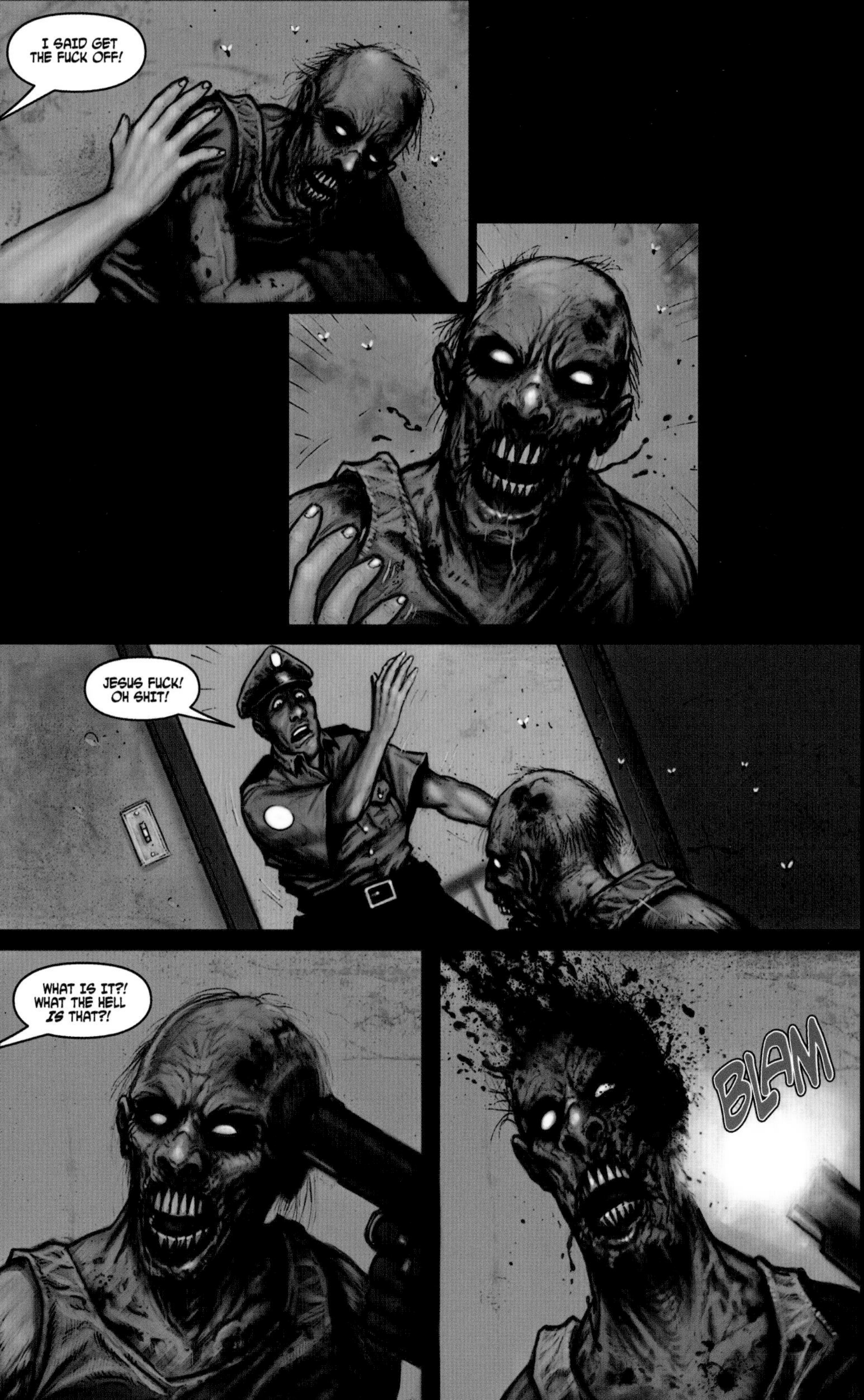
I SAID GET THE FUCK OFF!
JESUS FUCK! OH SHIT!
WHAT IS IT?! WHAT THE HELL IS THAT?!
BLAM

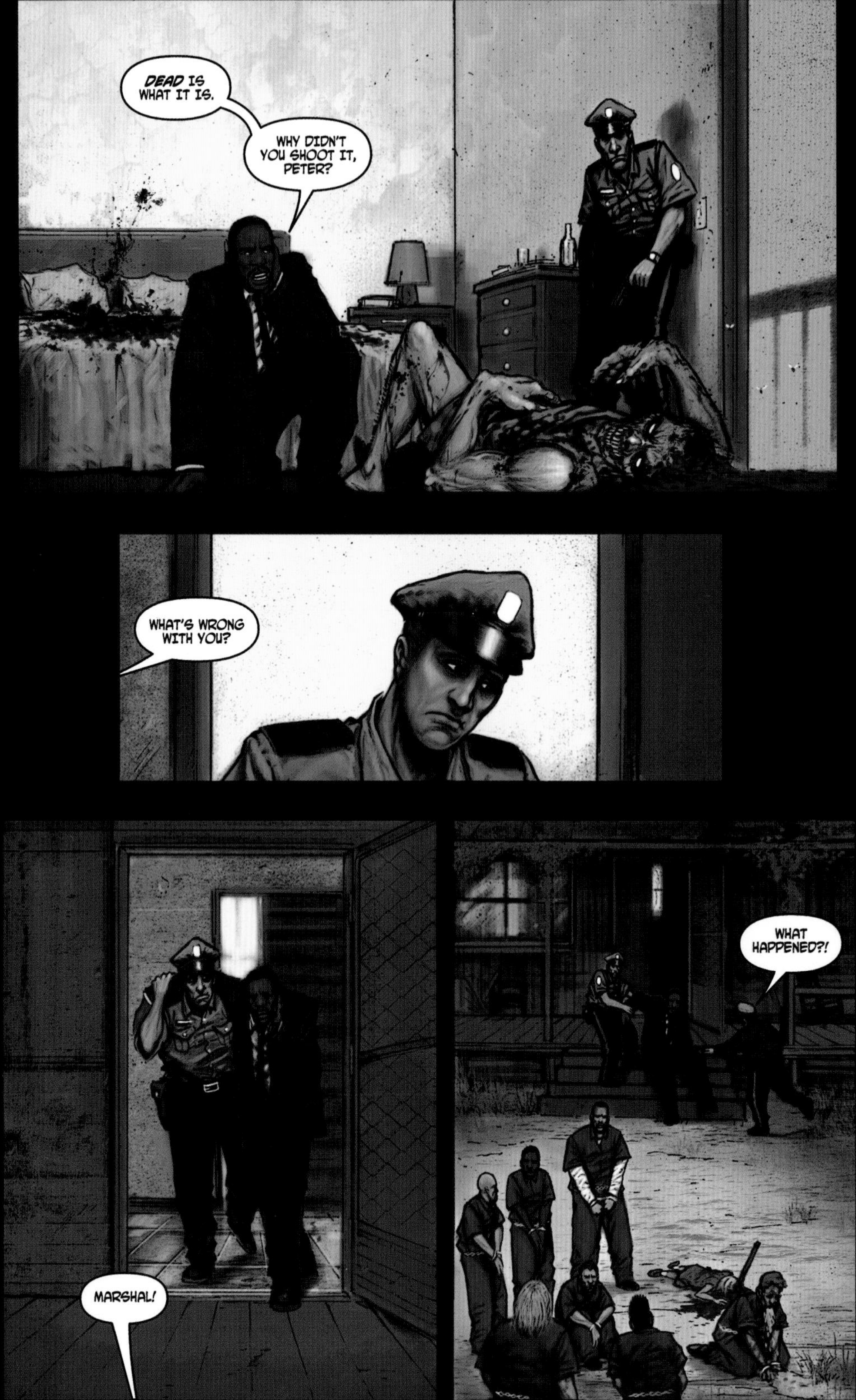
DEAD IS WHAT IT IS.
WHY DIDN'T YOU SHOOT IT, PETER?
WHAT'S WRONG WITH YOU?
MARSHAL!
WHAT HAPPENED?!

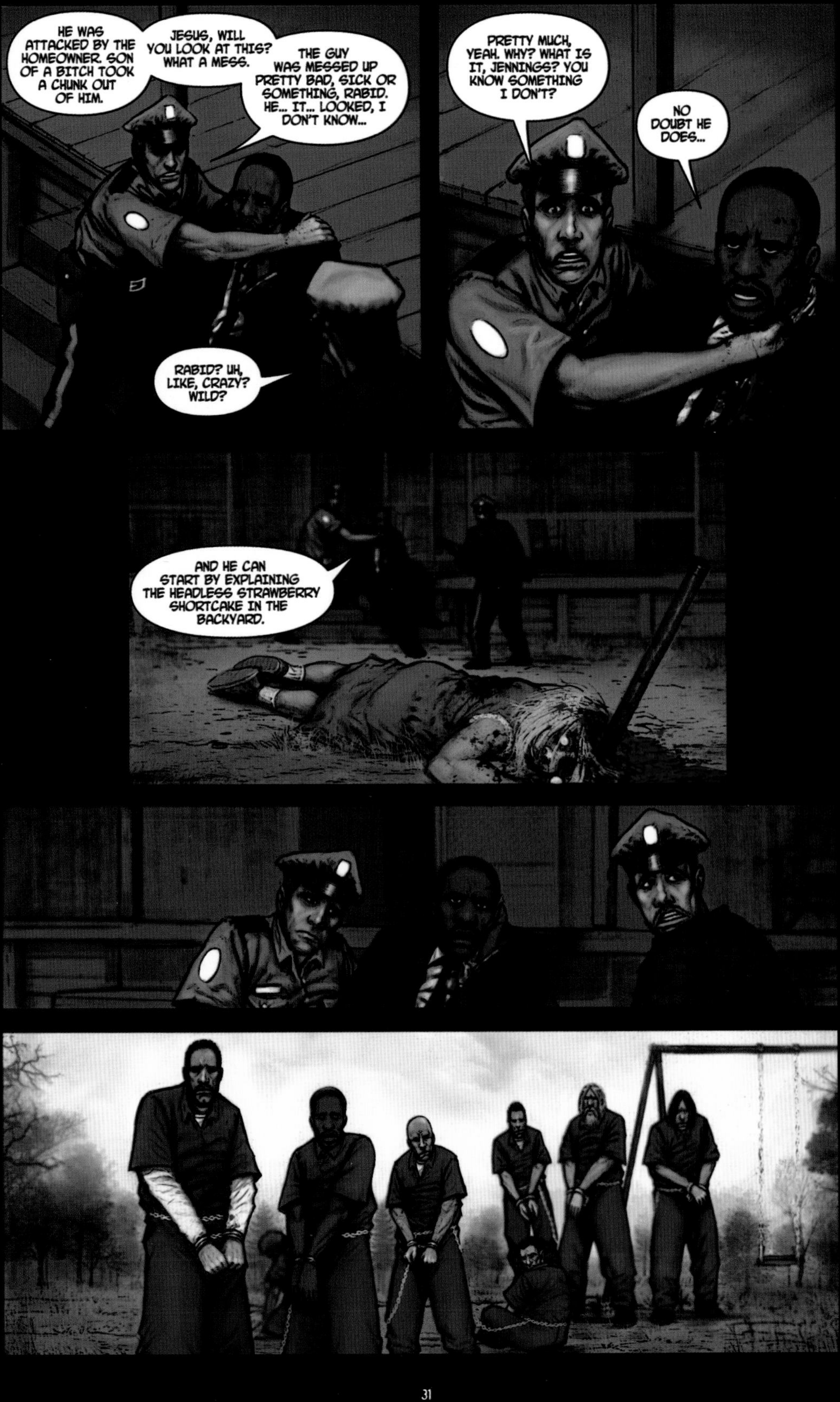
HE WAS ATTACKED BY THE HOMEOWNER. SON OF A BITCH TOOK A CHUNK OUT OF HIM.
JESUS, WILL YOU LOOK AT THIS? WHAT A MESS.
THE GUY WAS MESSED UP PRETTY BAD, SICK OR SOMETHING, RABID. HE... IT... LOOKED, I DON'T KNOW...
RABID? UH, LIKE, CRAZY? WILD?
PRETTY MUCH, YEAH. WHY? WHAT IS IT, JENNINGS? YOU KNOW SOMETHING I DON'T?
NO DOUBT HE DOES...
AND HE CAN START BY EXPLAINING THE HEADLESS STRAWBERRY SHORTCAKE IN THE BACKYARD.

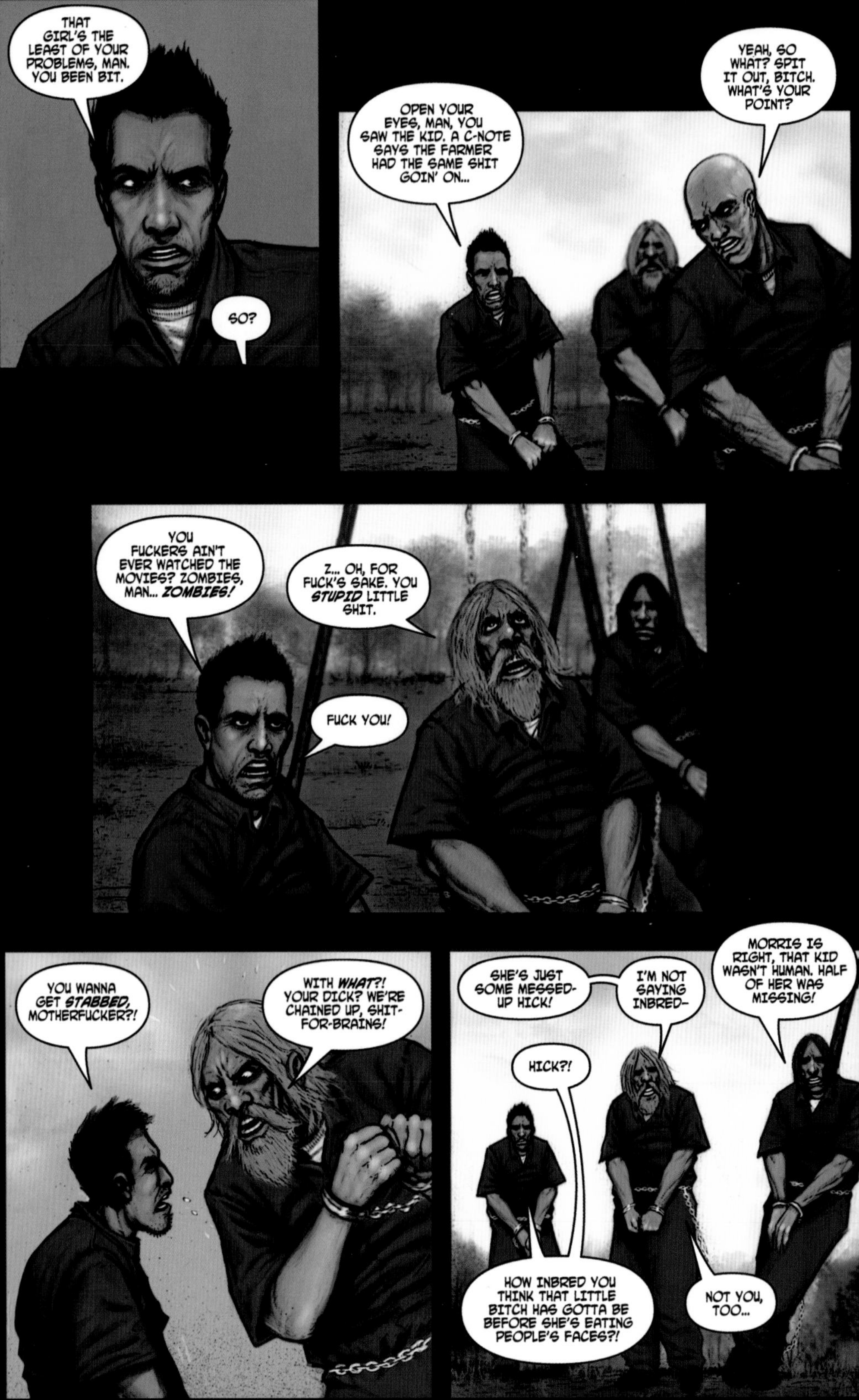
THAT GIRL'S THE LEAST OF YOUR PROBLEMS, MAN. YOU BEEN BIT.
SO?
OPEN YOUR EYES, MAN, YOU SAW THE KID. A C-NOTE SAYS THE FARMER HAD THE SAME SHIT GOIN' ON...
YEAH, SO WHAT? SPIT IT OUT, BITCH. WHAT'S YOUR POINT?
YOU FUCKERS AIN'T EVER WATCHED THE MOVIES? ZOMBIES, MAN... *ZOMBIES!*
Z... OH, FOR FUCK'S SAKE. YOU *STUPID* LITTLE SHIT.
FUCK YOU!
YOU WANNA GET *STABBED,* MOTHERFUCKER?!
WITH *WHAT?!* YOUR DICK? WE'RE CHAINED UP, SHIT-FOR-BRAINS!
SHE'S JUST SOME MESSED-UP HICK!
I'M NOT SAYING INBRED-
MORRIS IS RIGHT, THAT KID WASN'T HUMAN. HALF OF HER WAS MISSING!
HICK?!
HOW INBRED YOU THINK THAT LITTLE BITCH HAS GOTTA BE BEFORE SHE'S EATING PEOPLE'S FACES?!
NOT YOU, TOO...

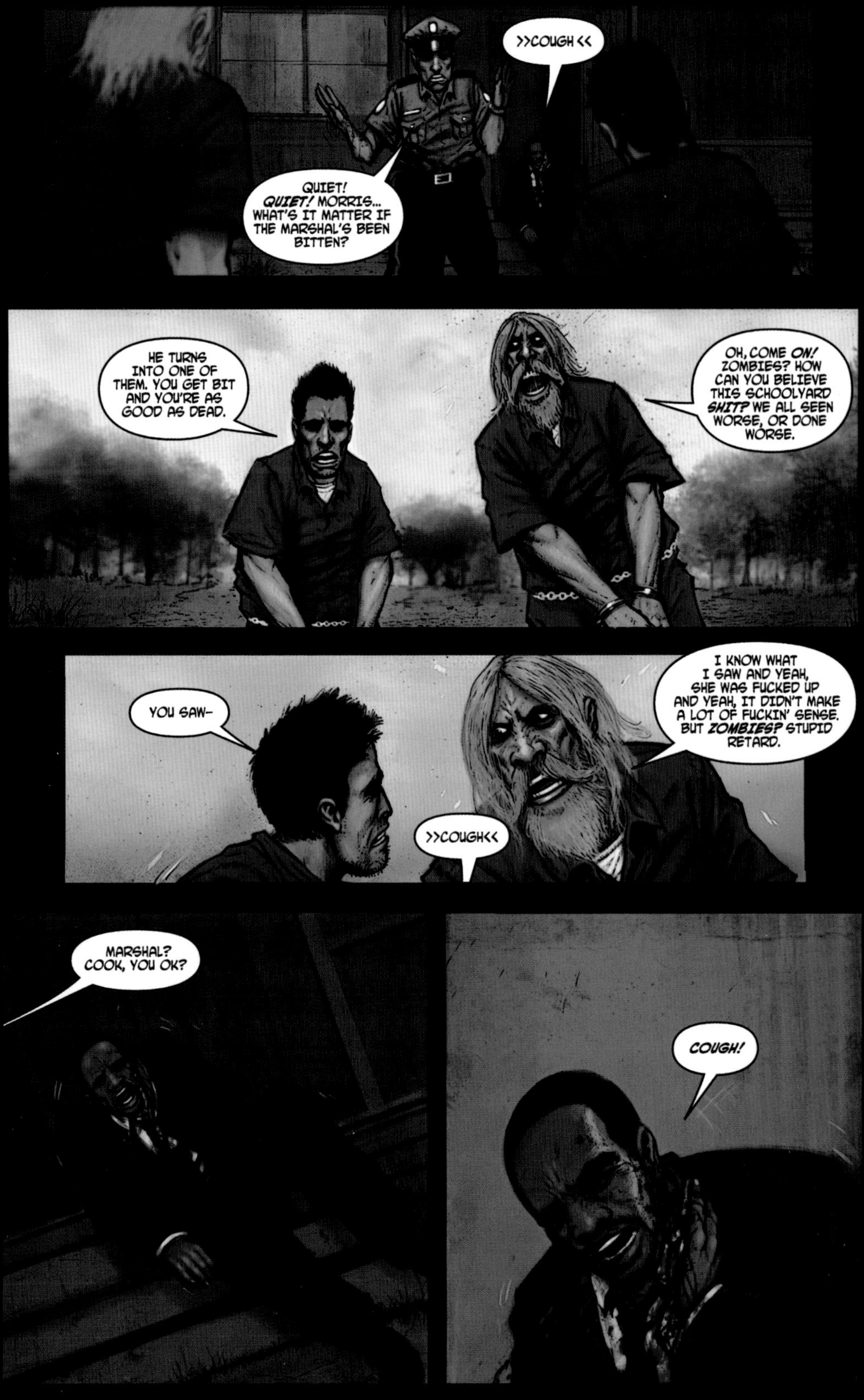
>>COUGH<<
QUIET! *QUIET!* MORRIS... WHAT'S IT MATTER IF THE MARSHAL'S BEEN BITTEN?
HE TURNS INTO ONE OF THEM. YOU GET BIT AND YOU'RE AS GOOD AS DEAD.
OH, COME *ON!* ZOMBIES? HOW CAN YOU BELIEVE THIS SCHOOLYARD *SHIT?* WE ALL SEEN WORSE, OR DONE WORSE.
YOU SAW-
I KNOW WHAT I SAW AND YEAH, SHE WAS FUCKED UP AND YEAH, IT DIDN'T MAKE A LOT OF FUCKIN' SENSE. BUT *ZOMBIES?* STUPID RETARD.
>>COUGH<<
MARSHAL? COOK, YOU OK?
COUGH!

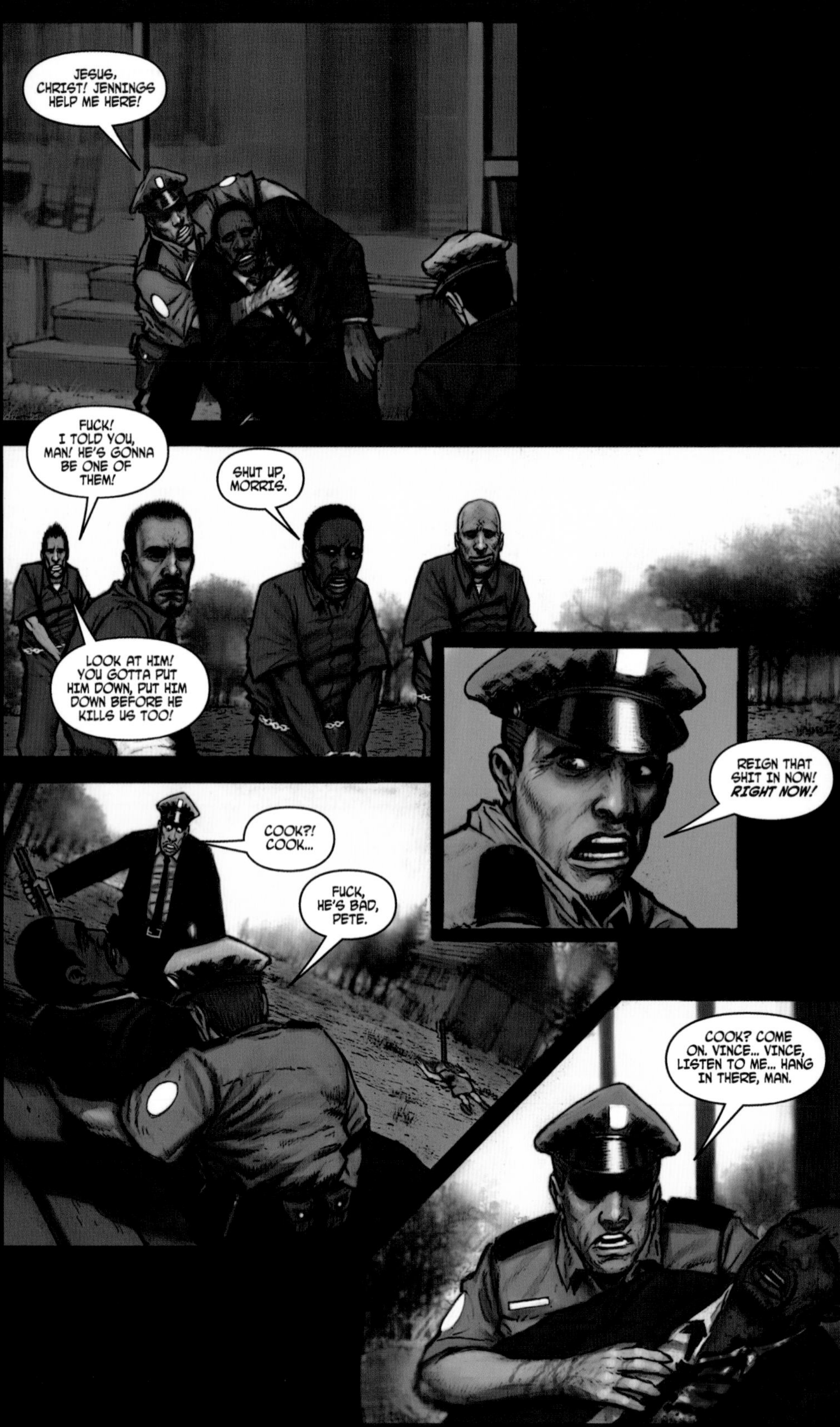
JESUS, CHRIST! JENNINGS HELP ME HERE!
FUCK! I TOLD YOU, MAN! HE'S GONNA BE ONE OF THEM!
SHUT UP, MORRIS.
LOOK AT HIM! YOU GOTTA PUT HIM DOWN, PUT HIM DOWN BEFORE HE KILLS US TOO!
REIGN THAT SHIT IN NOW! RIGHT NOW!
COOK?! COOK...
FUCK, HE'S BAD, PETE.
COOK? COME ON. VINCE... VINCE, LISTEN TO ME... HANG IN THERE, MAN.

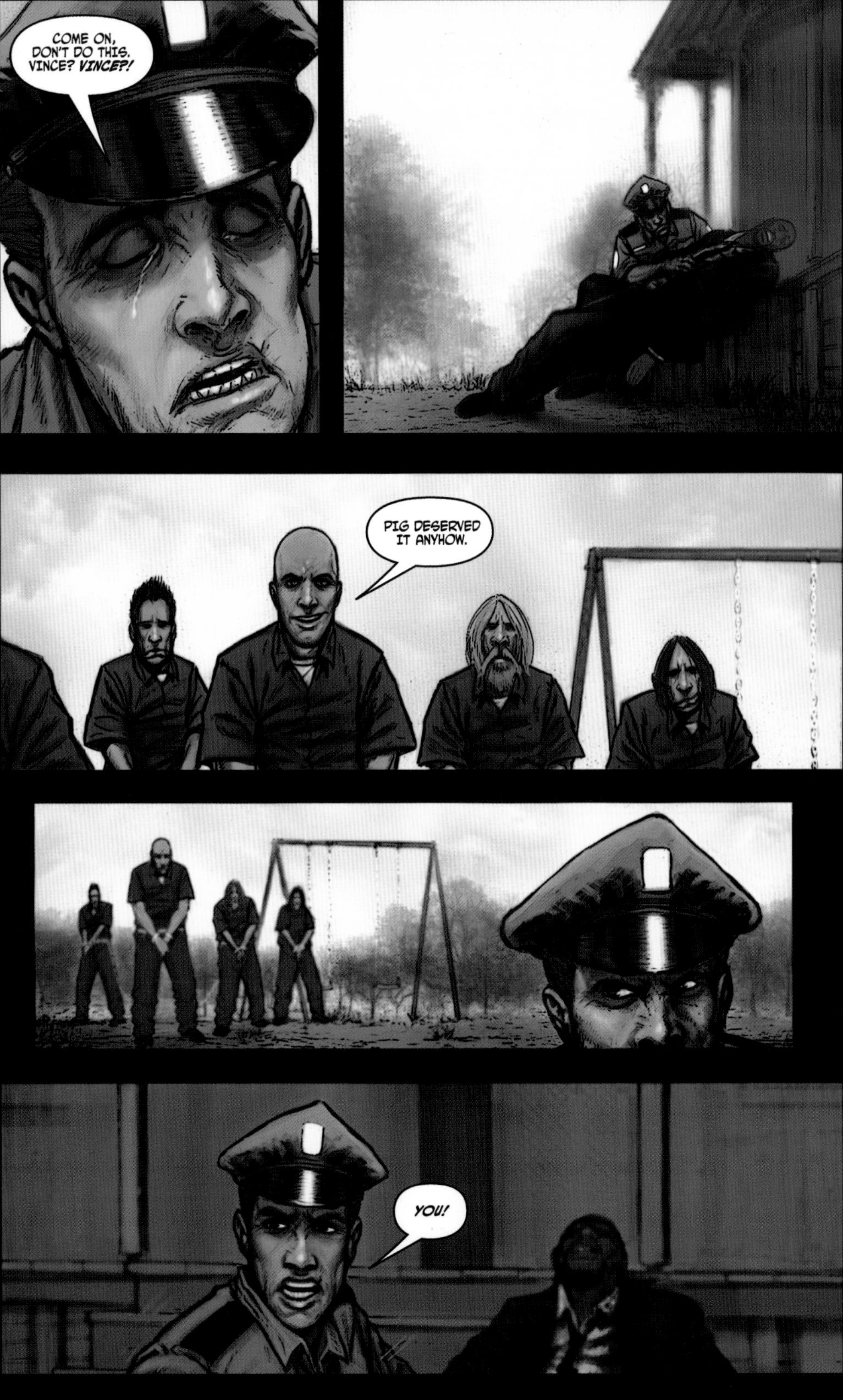
COME ON, DON'T DO THIS. VINCE? VINCE?!
PIG DESERVED IT ANYHOW.
YOU!

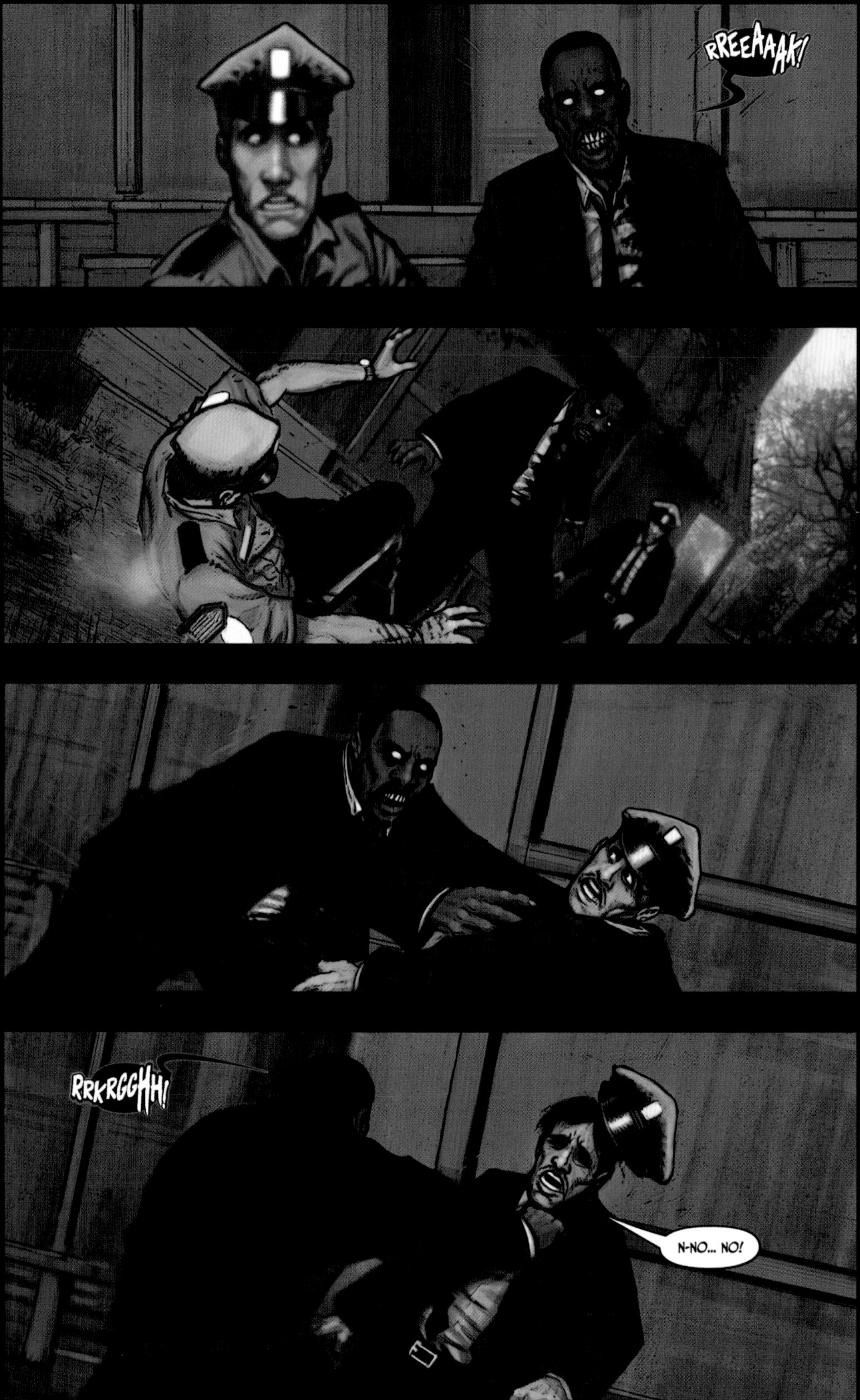
RREEAAAK!
RRKRGGHH!
N-NO... NO!

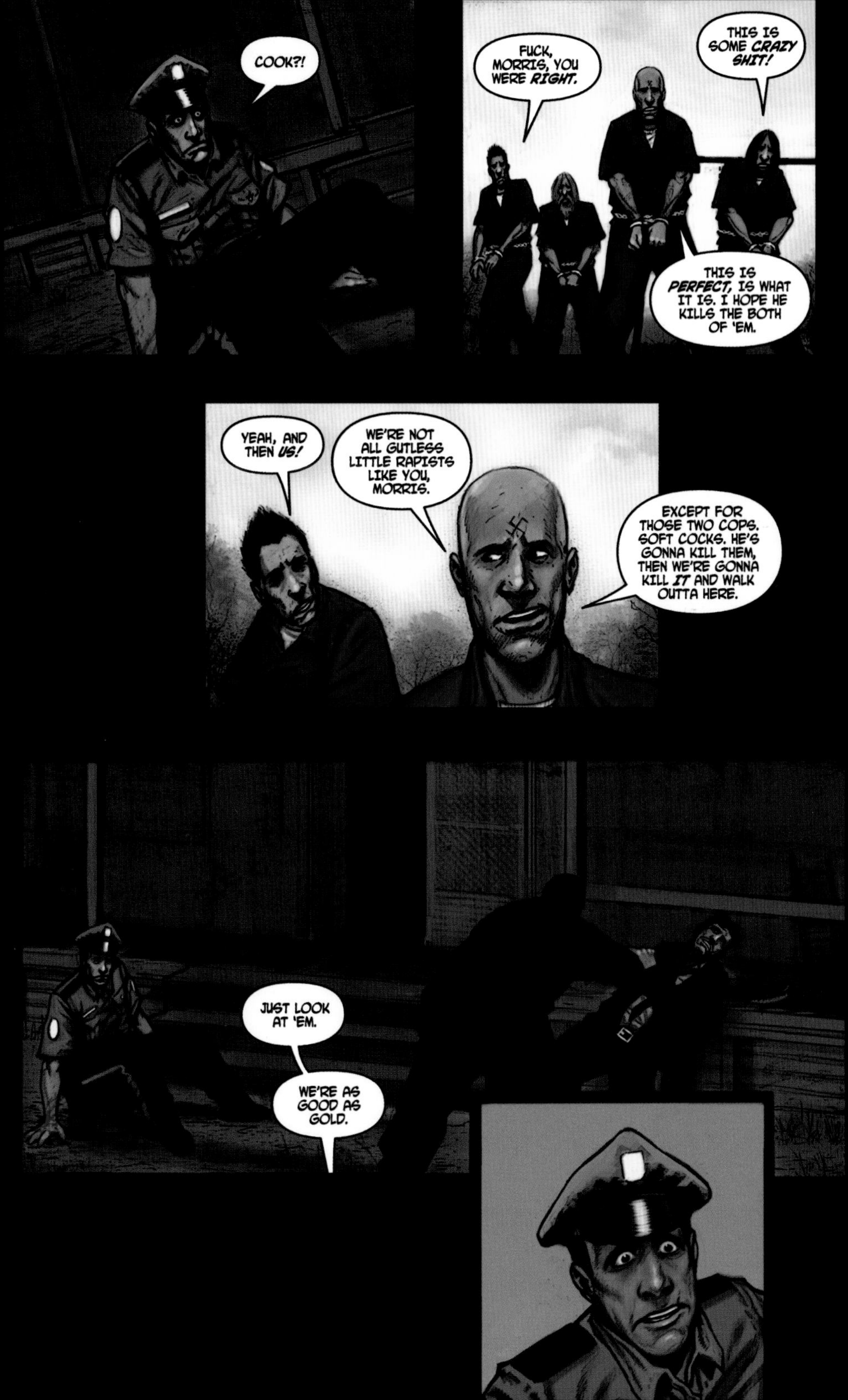
COOK?!
FUCK, MORRIS, YOU WERE RIGHT.
THIS IS SOME CRAZY SHIT!
THIS IS PERFECT, IS WHAT IT IS. I HOPE HE KILLS THE BOTH OF 'EM.
YEAH, AND THEN US!
WE'RE NOT ALL GUTLESS LITTLE RAPISTS LIKE YOU, MORRIS.
EXCEPT FOR THOSE TWO COPS. SOFT COCKS. HE'S GONNA KILL THEM, THEN WE'RE GONNA KILL IT AND WALK OUTTA HERE.
JUST LOOK AT 'EM.
WE'RE AS GOOD AS GOLD.

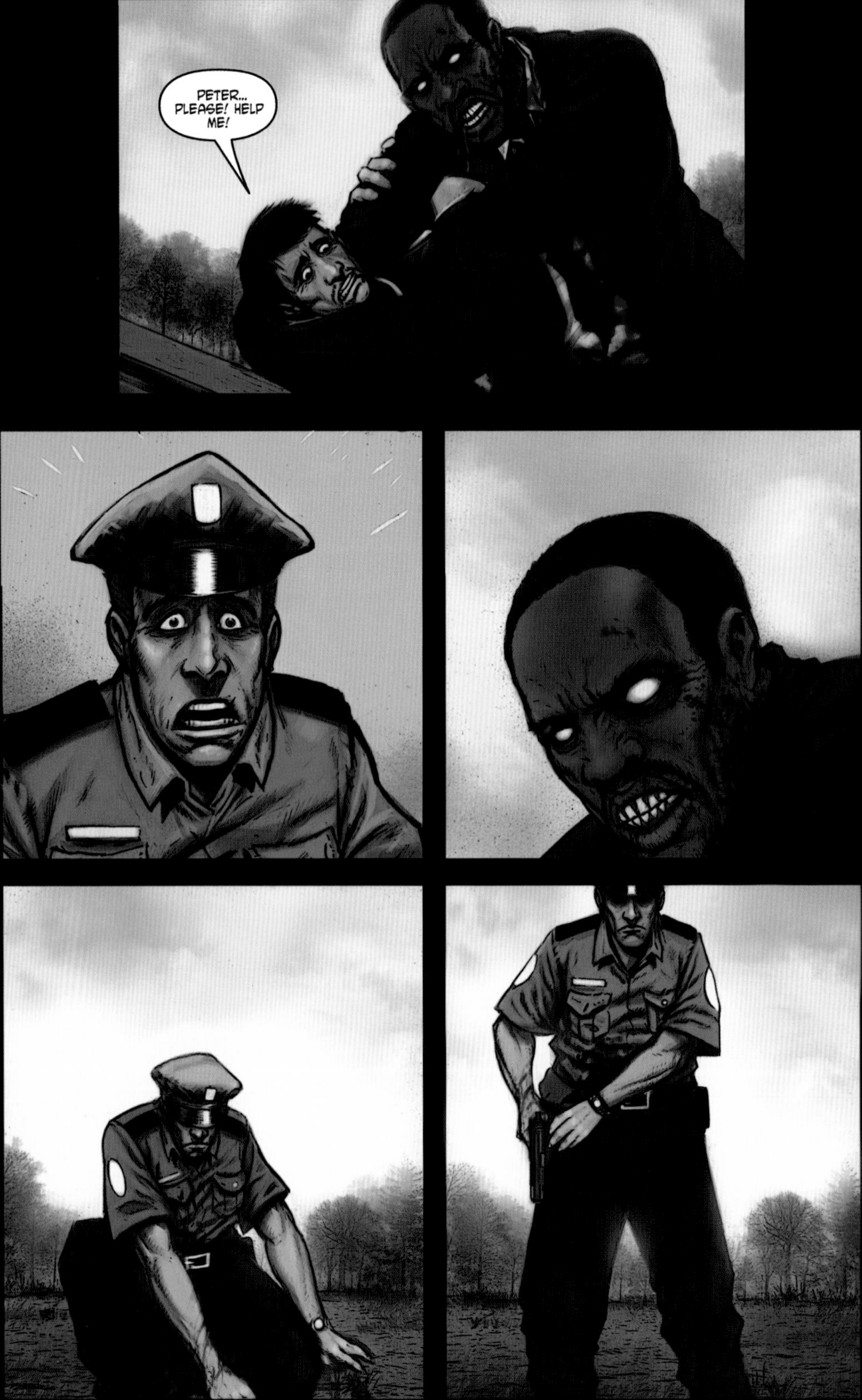
PETER... PLEASE! HELP ME!

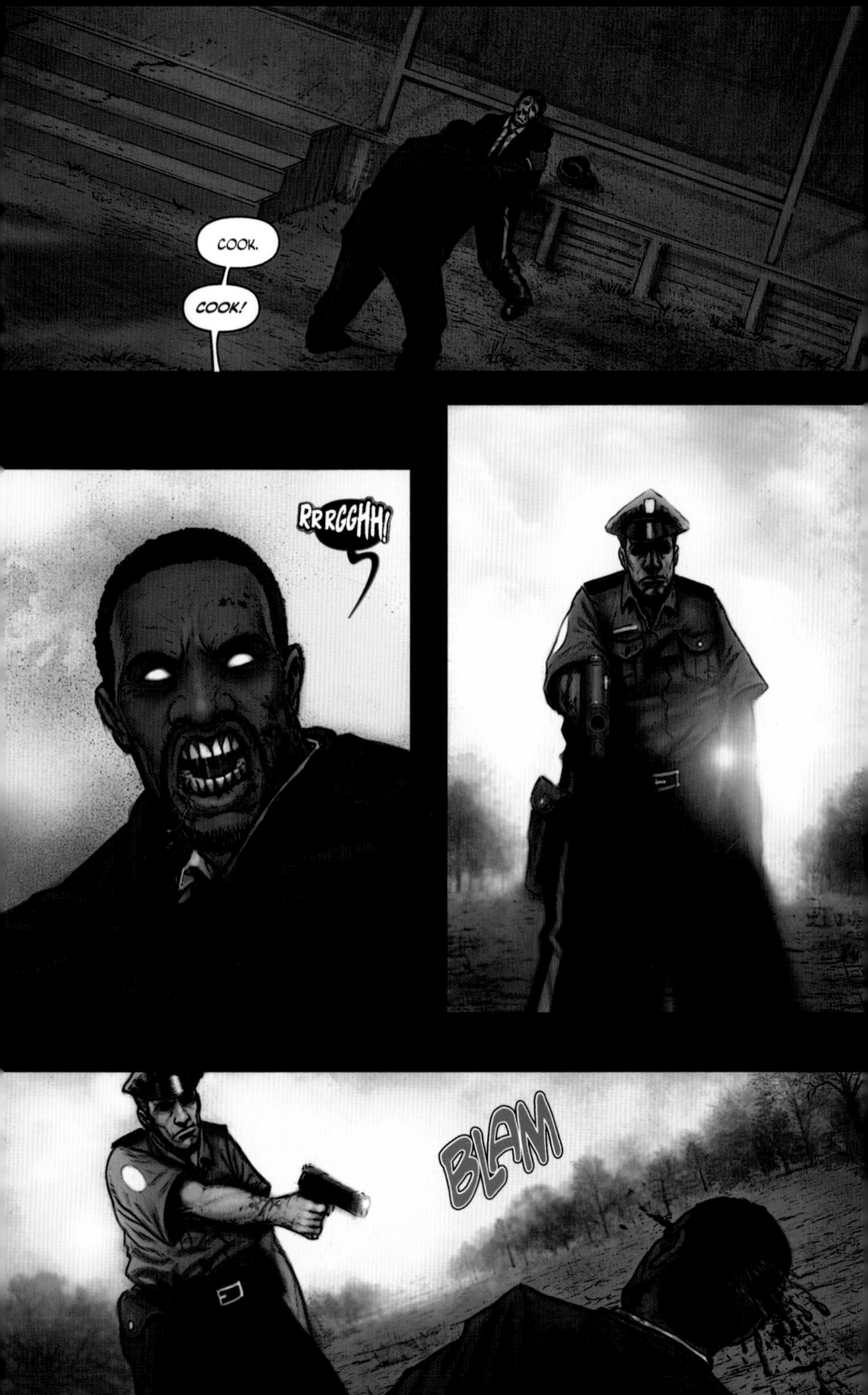
COOK.
COOK!
RRRGGHH!
BLAM

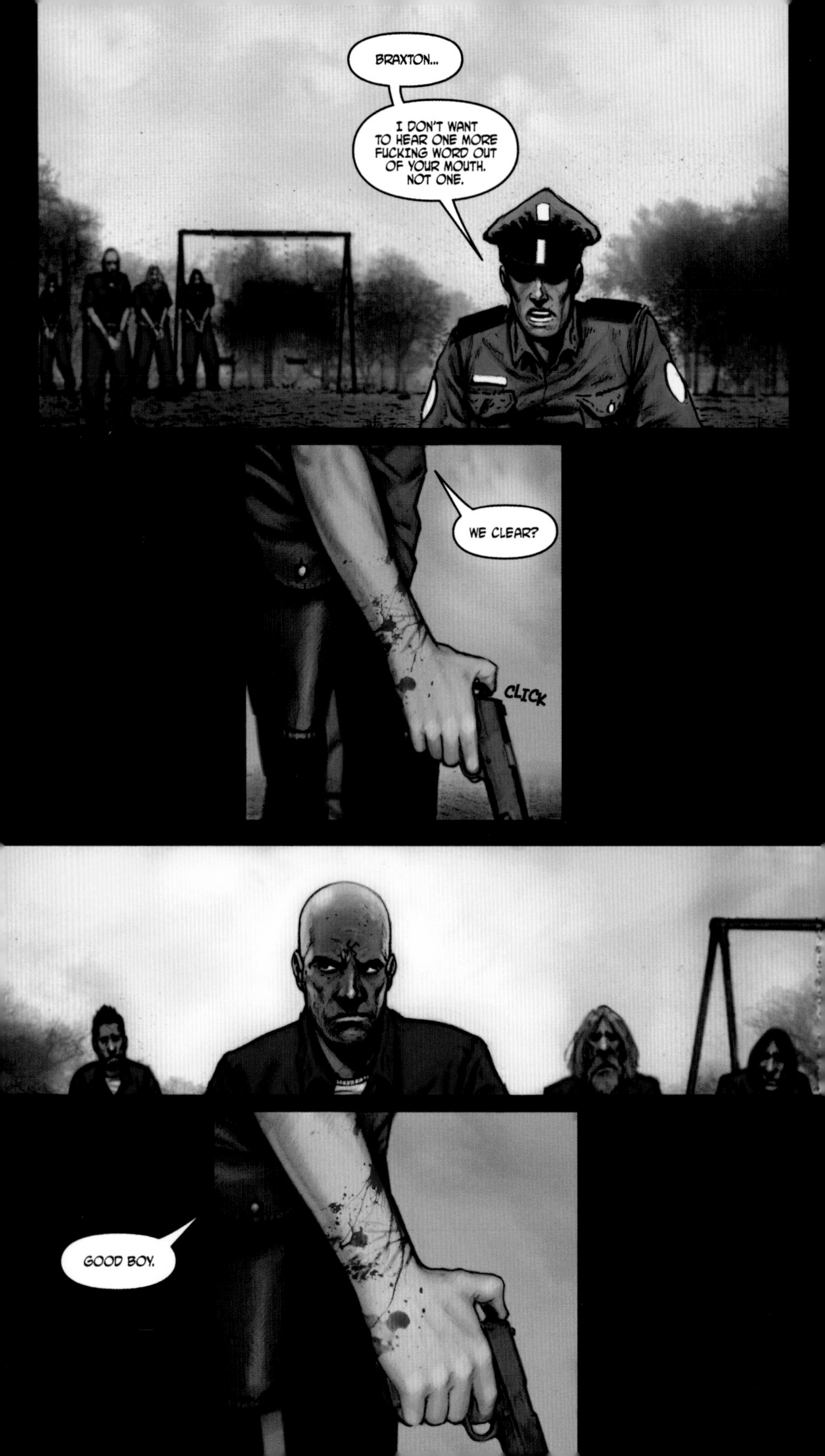
BRAXTON...
I DON'T WANT TO HEAR ONE MORE FUCKING WORD OUT OF YOUR MOUTH. NOT ONE.
WE CLEAR?
CLICK
GOOD BOY.

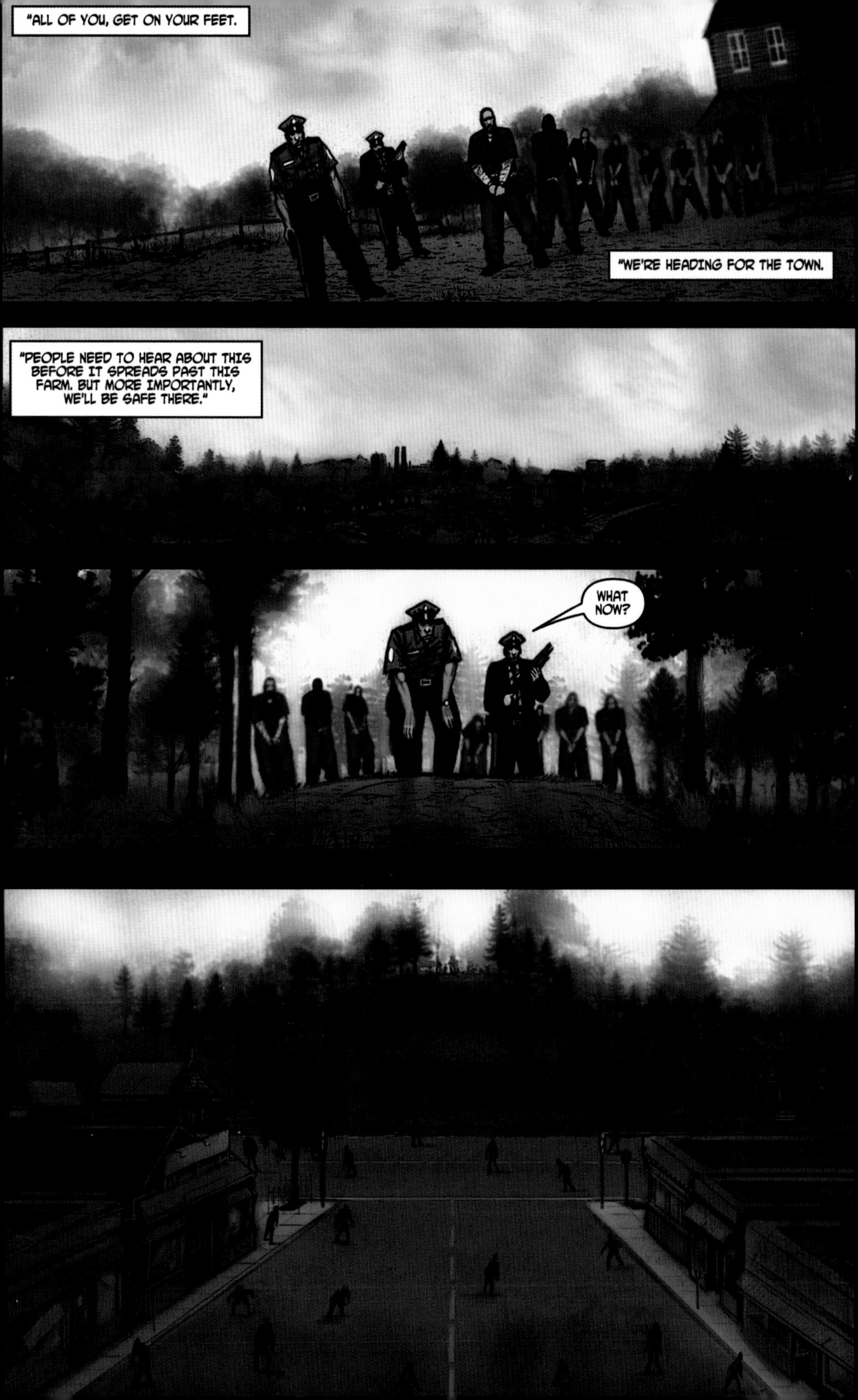
"ALL OF YOU, GET ON YOUR FEET.
"WE'RE HEADING FOR THE TOWN.
"PEOPLE NEED TO HEAR ABOUT THIS BEFORE IT SPREADS PAST THIS FARM. BUT MORE IMPORTANTLY, WE'LL BE SAFE THERE."
WHAT NOW?

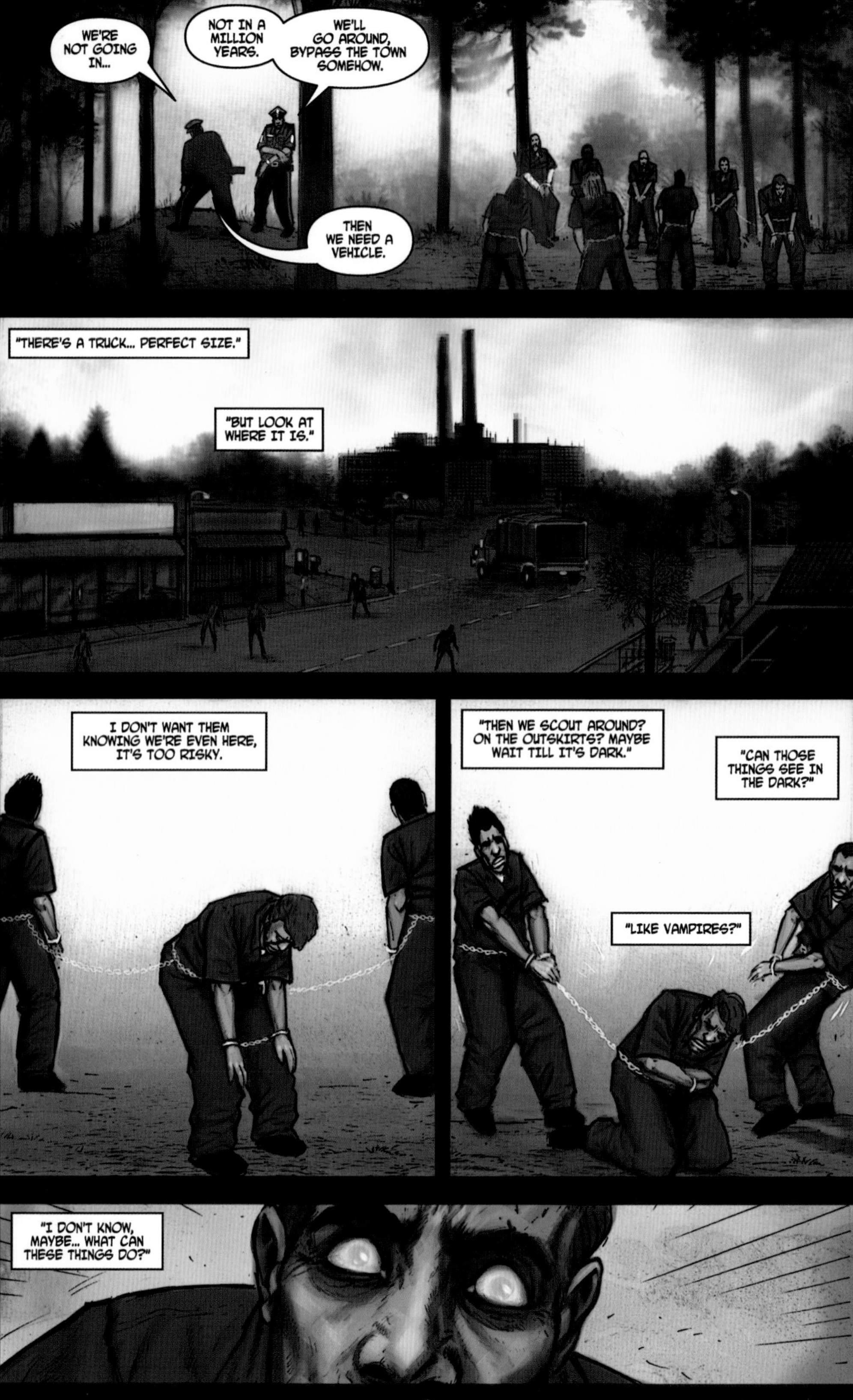
WE'RE NOT GOING IN...
NOT IN A MILLION YEARS.
WE'LL GO AROUND, BYPASS THE TOWN SOMEHOW.
THEN WE NEED A VEHICLE.
"THERE'S A TRUCK... PERFECT SIZE."
"BUT LOOK AT WHERE IT IS."
I DON'T WANT THEM KNOWING WE'RE EVEN HERE, IT'S TOO RISKY.
"THEN WE SCOUT AROUND? ON THE OUTSKIRTS? MAYBE WAIT TILL IT'S DARK."
"CAN THOSE THINGS SEE IN THE DARK?"
"LIKE VAMPIRES?"
"I DON'T KNOW, MAYBE... WHAT CAN THESE THINGS DO?"

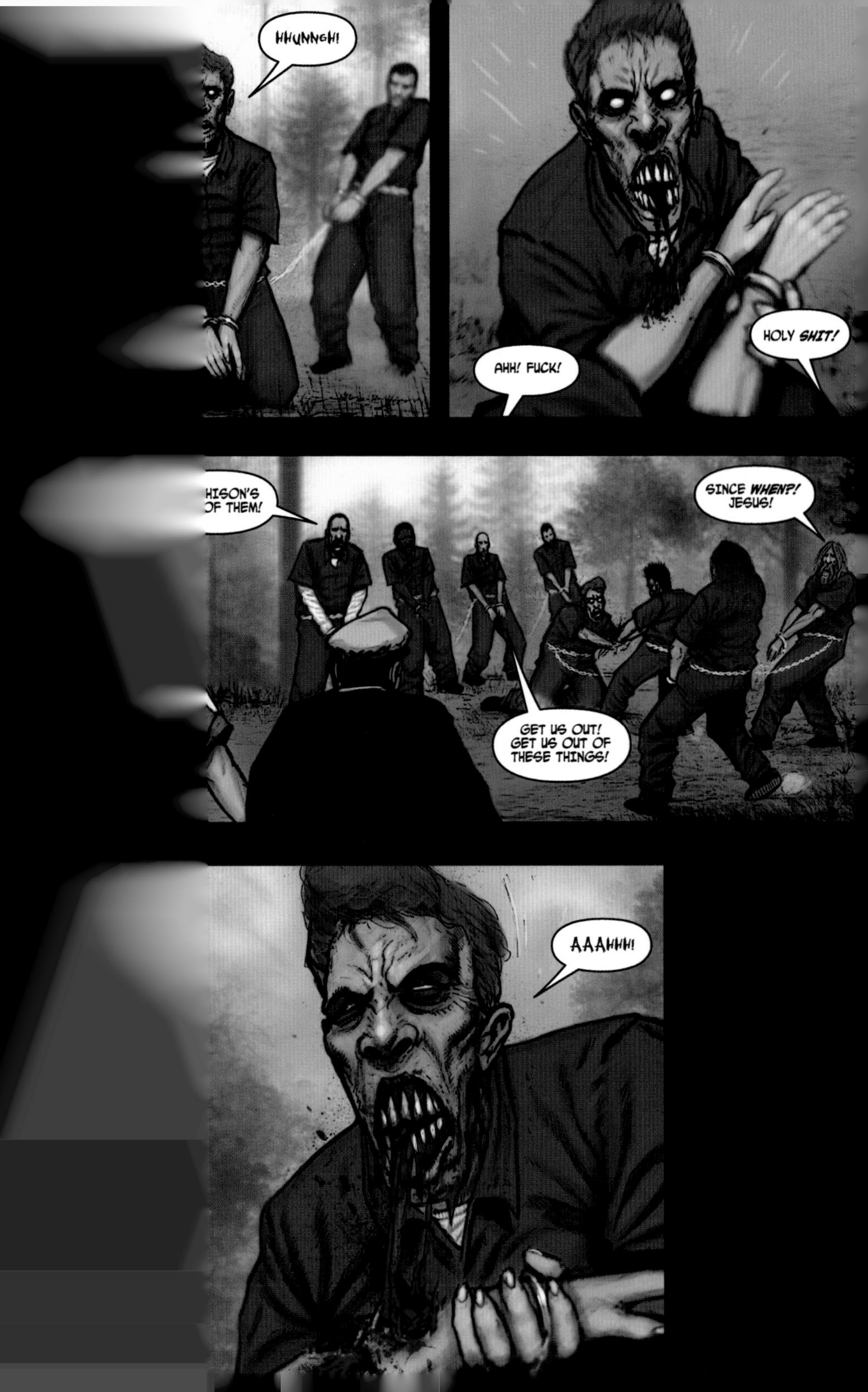
HHUNNGH!
AHH! FUCK!
HOLY SHIT!
HISON'S OF THEM!
SINCE WHEN?! JESUS!
GET US OUT! GET US OUT OF THESE THINGS!
AAAHHH!

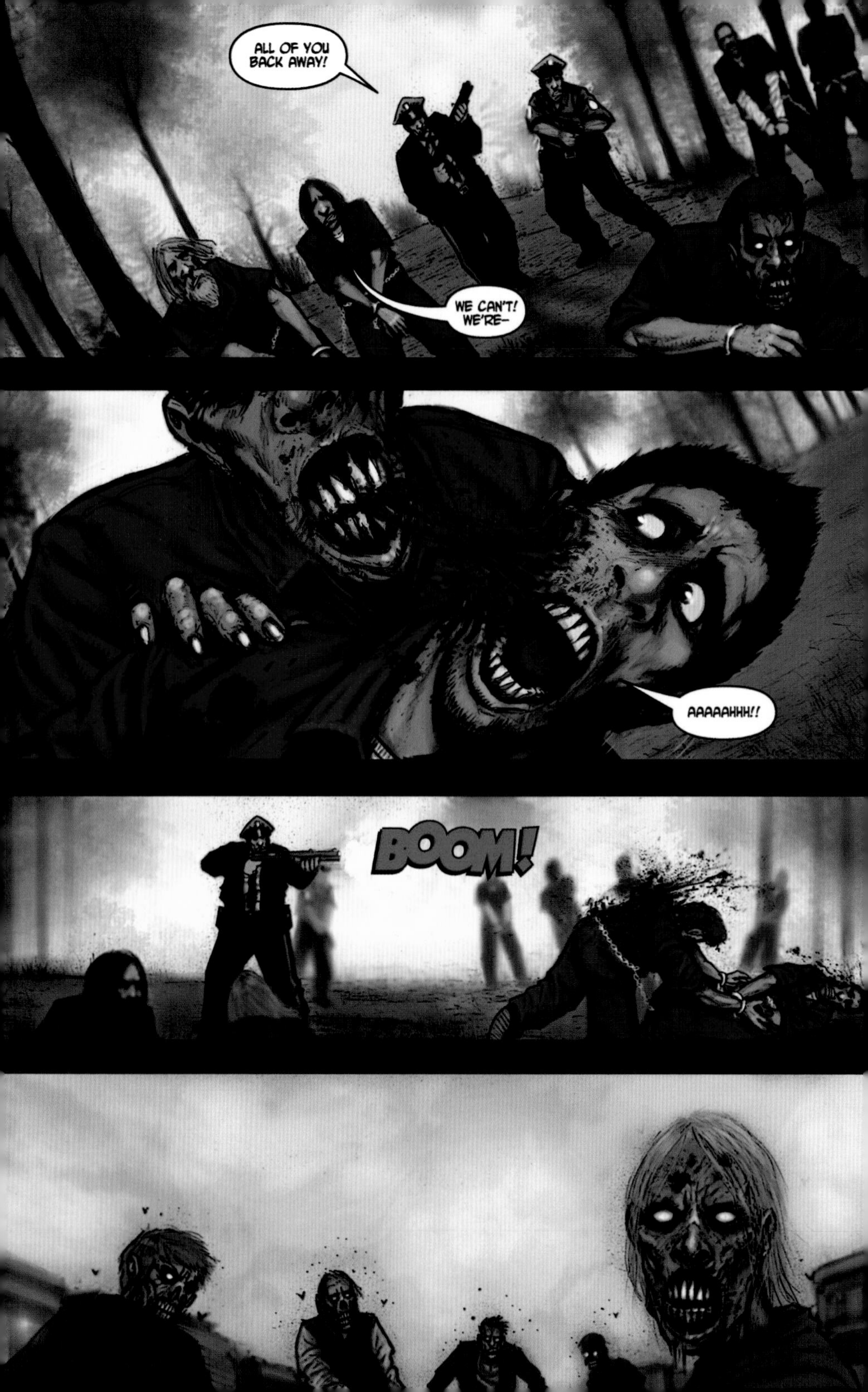
ALL OF YOU BACK AWAY!
WE CAN'T! WE'RE-
AAAAAHHH!!
BOOM!

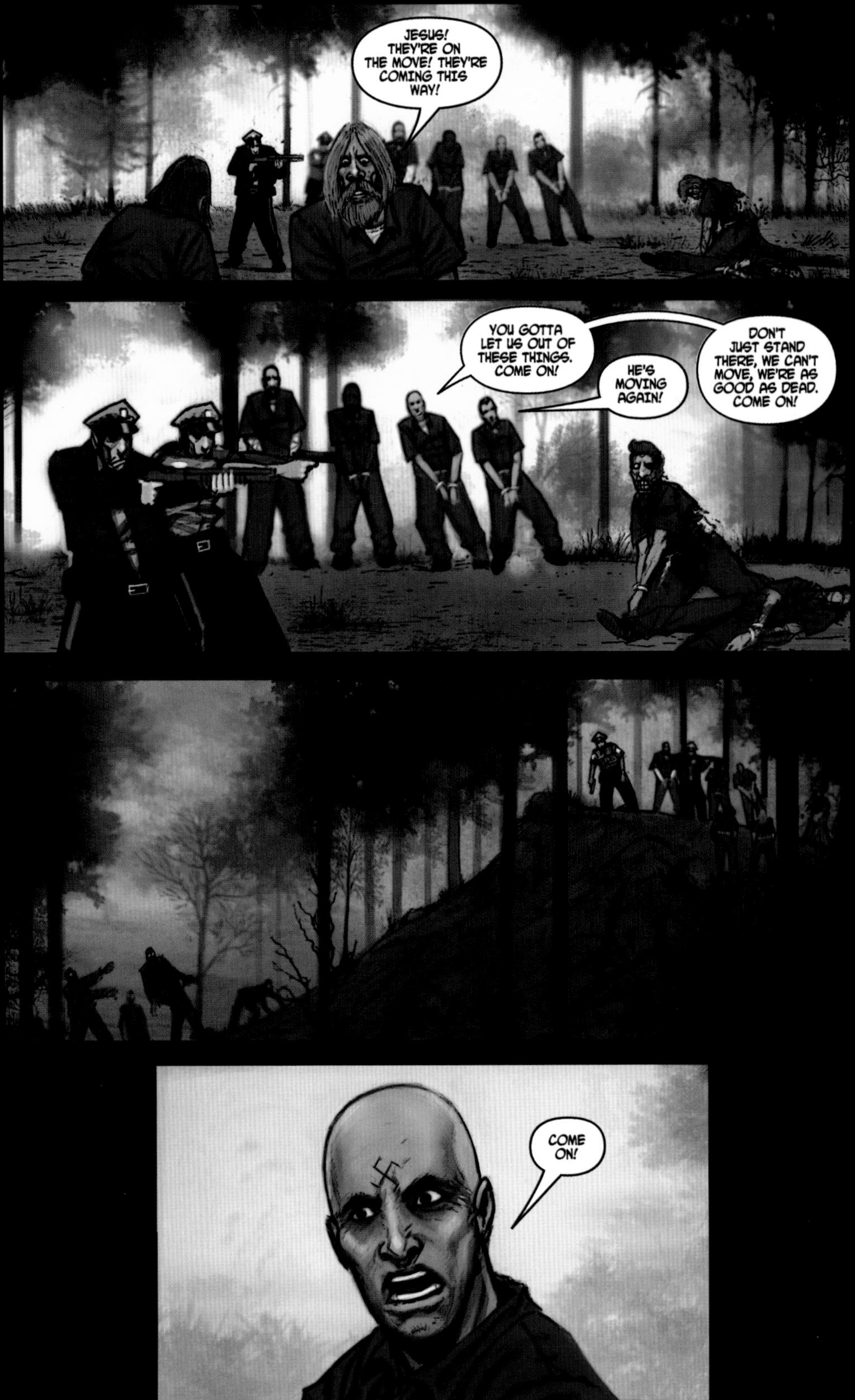
JESUS! THEY'RE ON THE MOVE! THEY'RE COMING THIS WAY!
YOU GOTTA LET US OUT OF THESE THINGS. COME ON!
DON'T JUST STAND THERE, WE CAN'T MOVE, WE'RE AS GOOD AS DEAD. COME ON!
HE'S MOVING AGAIN!
COME ON!

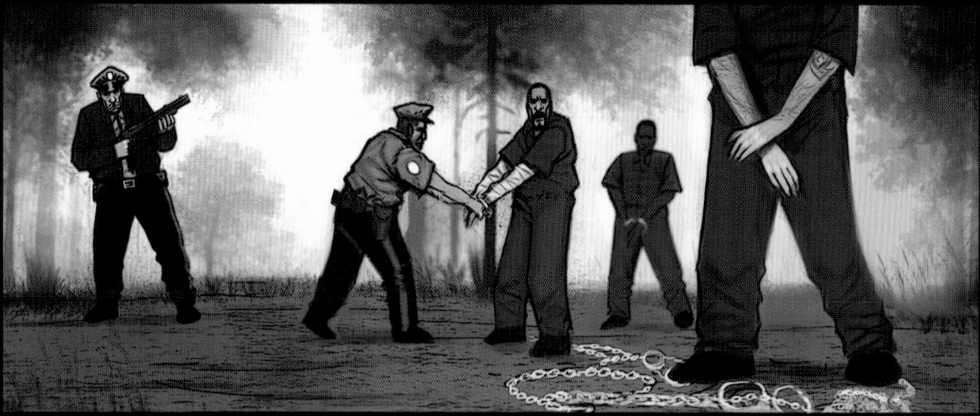

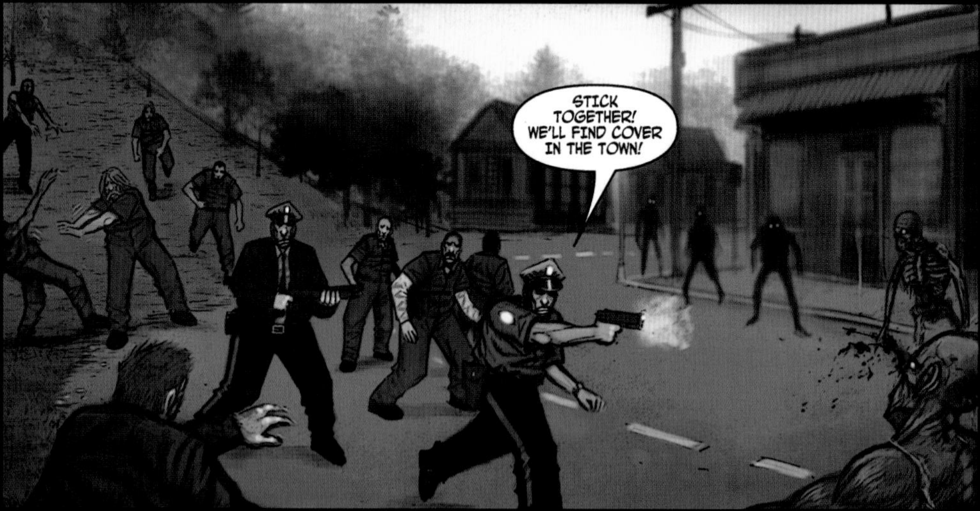
STICK TOGETHER! WE'LL FIND COVER IN THE TOWN!

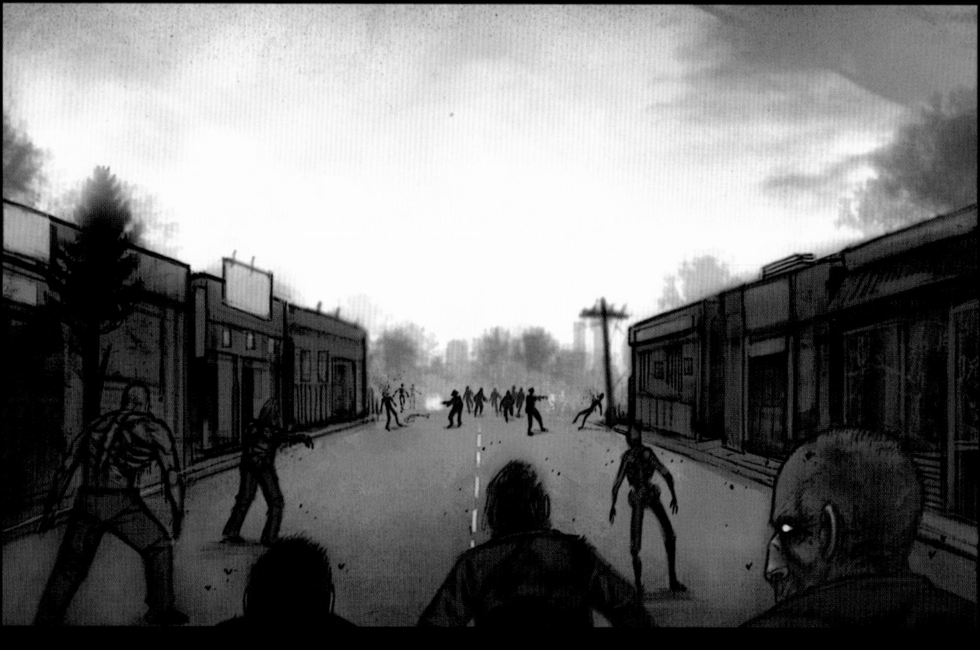

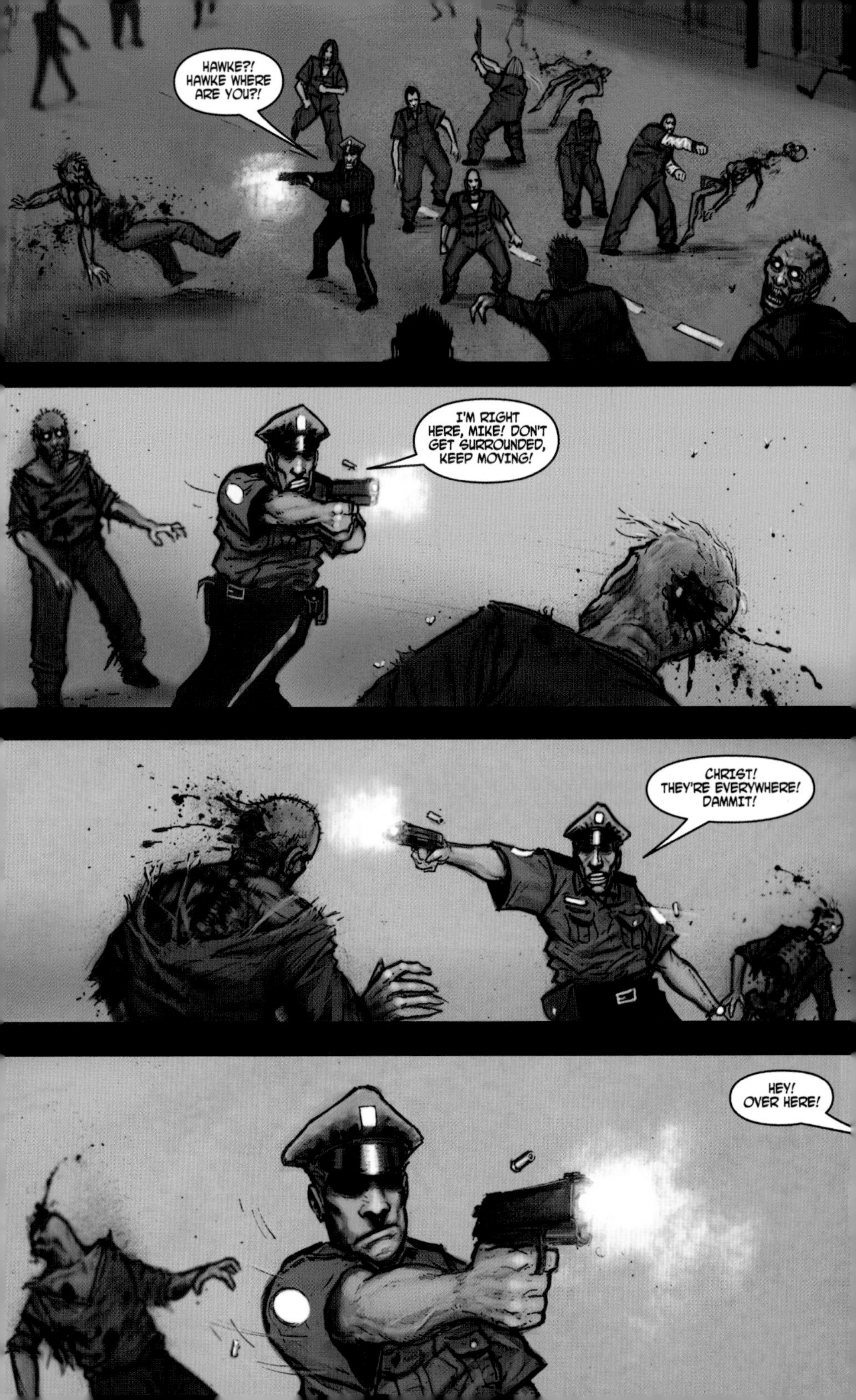
HAWKE?! HAWKE WHERE ARE YOU?!
I'M RIGHT HERE, MIKE! DON'T GET SURROUNDED, KEEP MOVING!
CHRIST! THEY'RE EVERYWHERE! DAMMIT!
HEY! OVER HERE!

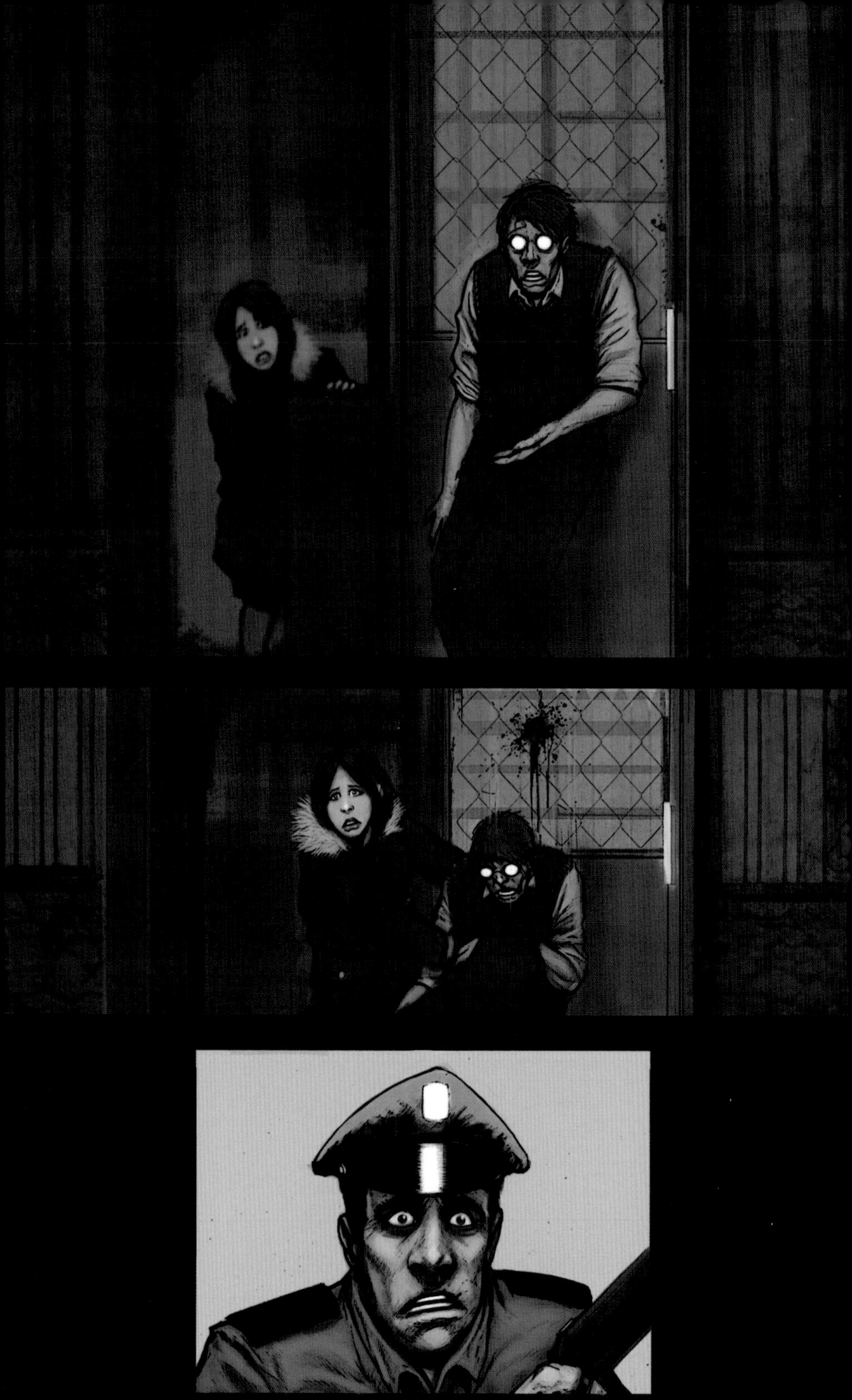

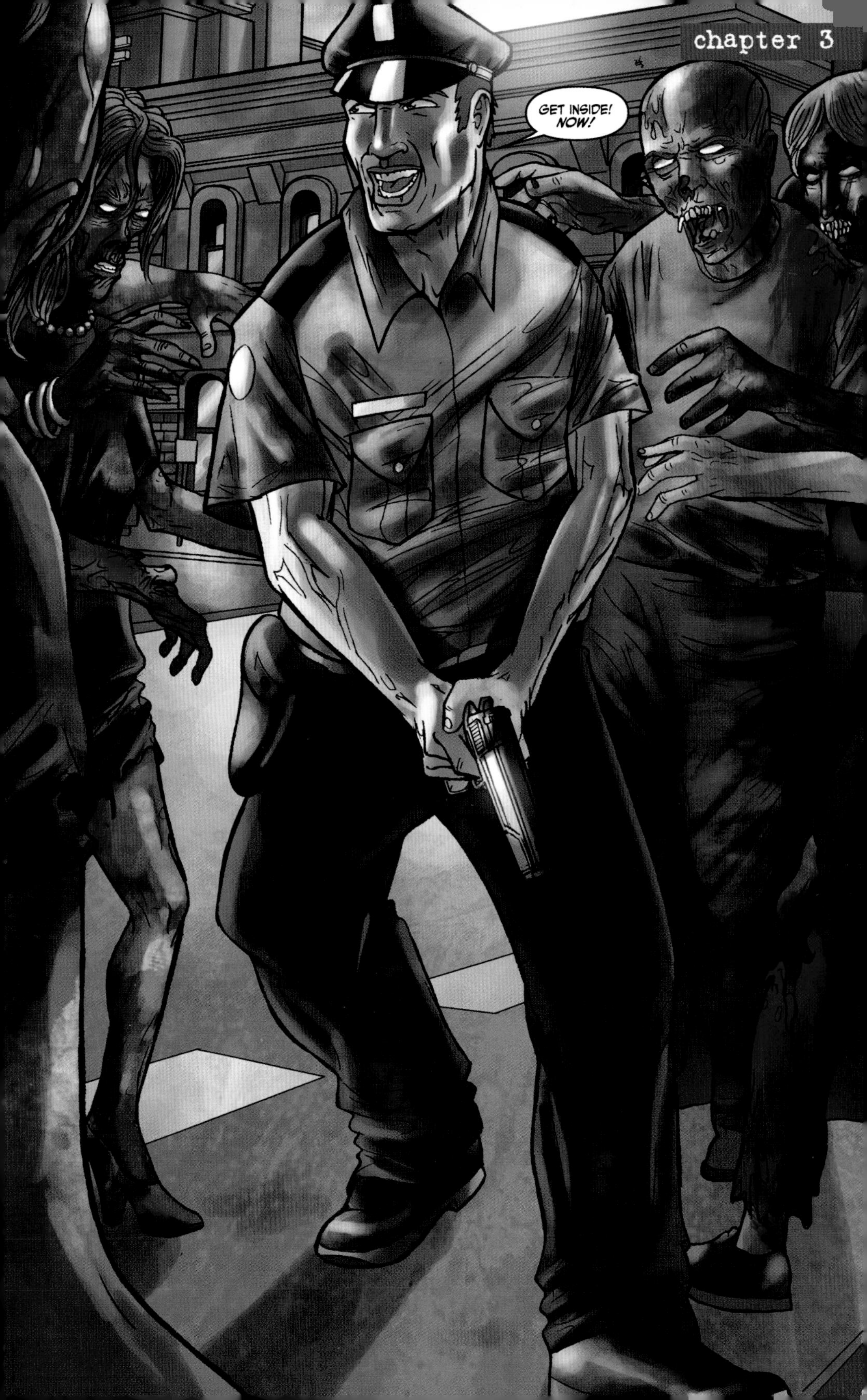
chapter 3
GET INSIDE! NOW!

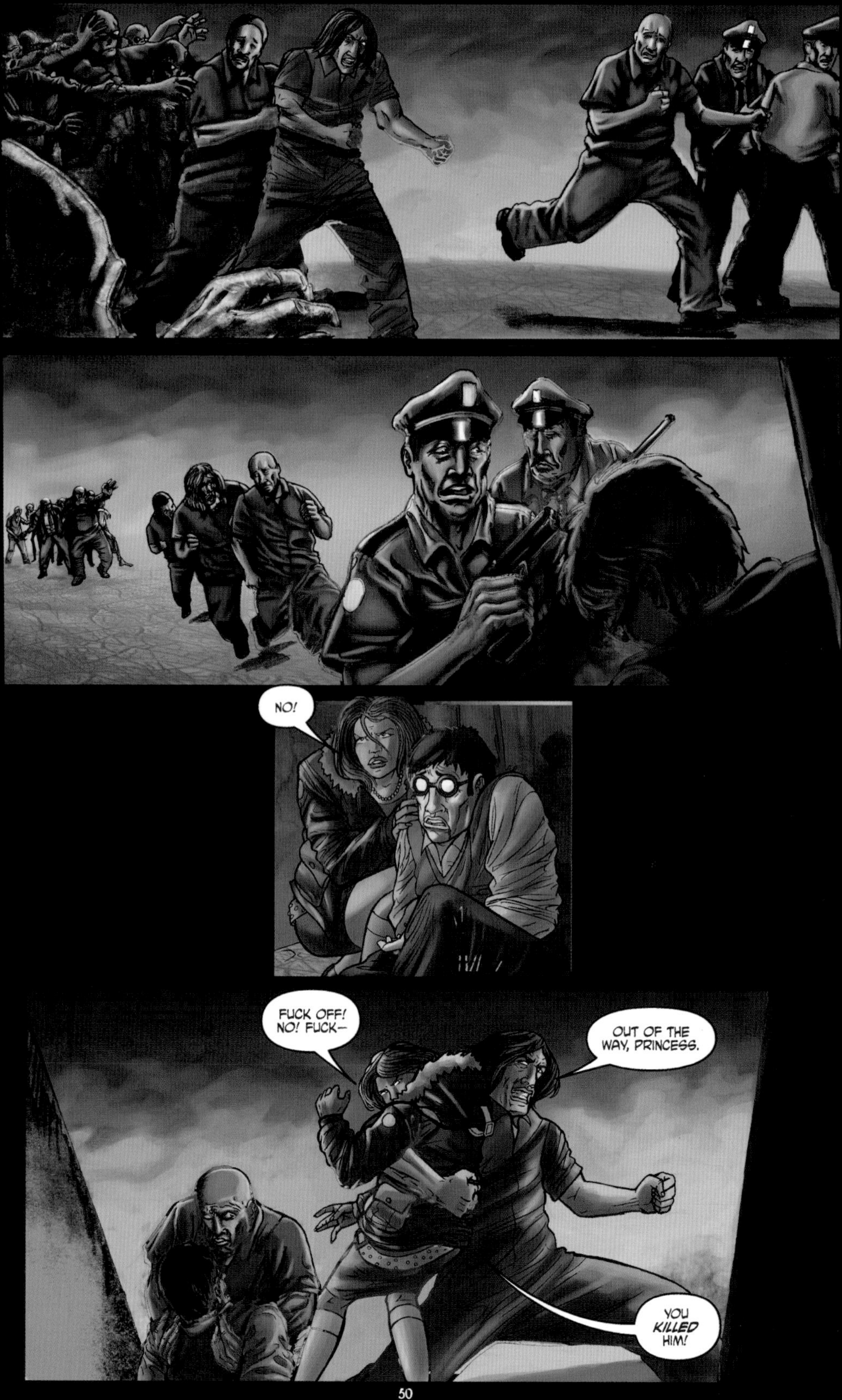
NO!
FUCK OFF! NO! FUCK–
OUT OF THE WAY, PRINCESS.
YOU *KILLED* HIM!

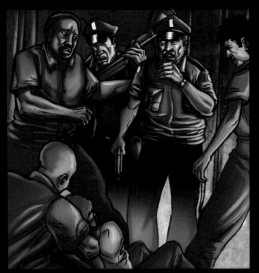

KILLED AN INNOCENT MAN, HERO, HOW'S IT FEEL?

IT WAS A MISTAKE...

THAT'S WHAT WE *ALL* SAY.

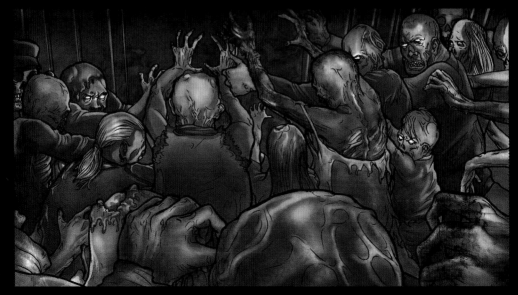

MOTHER...

SMAK

FUCKER!

I'M SORRY. I'M SO SORRY, IT WAS... IT WAS AN ACCIDENT. I DIDN'T KNOW...

HE WAS TRYING TO HELP YOU! HE WANTED TO HELP...

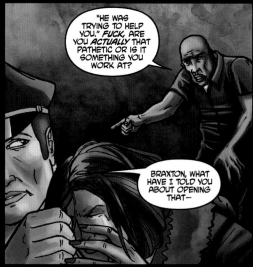

"HE WAS TRYING TO HELP YOU." *FUCK*, ARE YOU *ACTUALLY* THAT PATHETIC OR IS IT SOMETHING YOU WORK AT?

BRAXTON, WHAT HAVE I TOLD YOU ABOUT OPENING THAT—

YEAH, BLAH, BLAH, BLAH. NEWSFLASH— YOU'RE *DONE*, ASSHOLE.

52

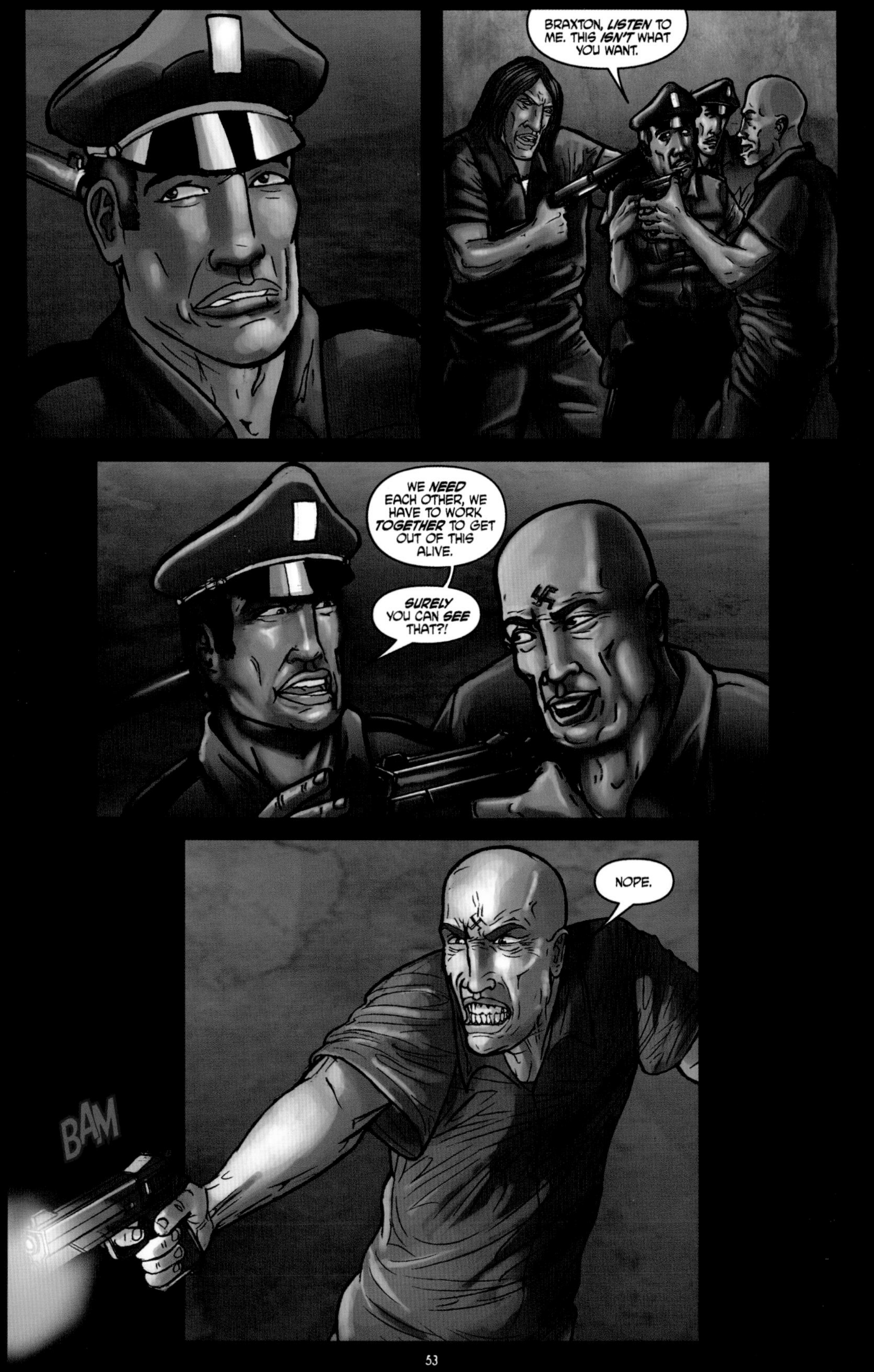
BRAXTON, LISTEN TO ME. THIS ISN'T WHAT YOU WANT.
WE NEED EACH OTHER, WE HAVE TO WORK TOGETHER TO GET OUT OF THIS ALIVE.
SURELY YOU CAN SEE THAT?!
NOPE.
BAM

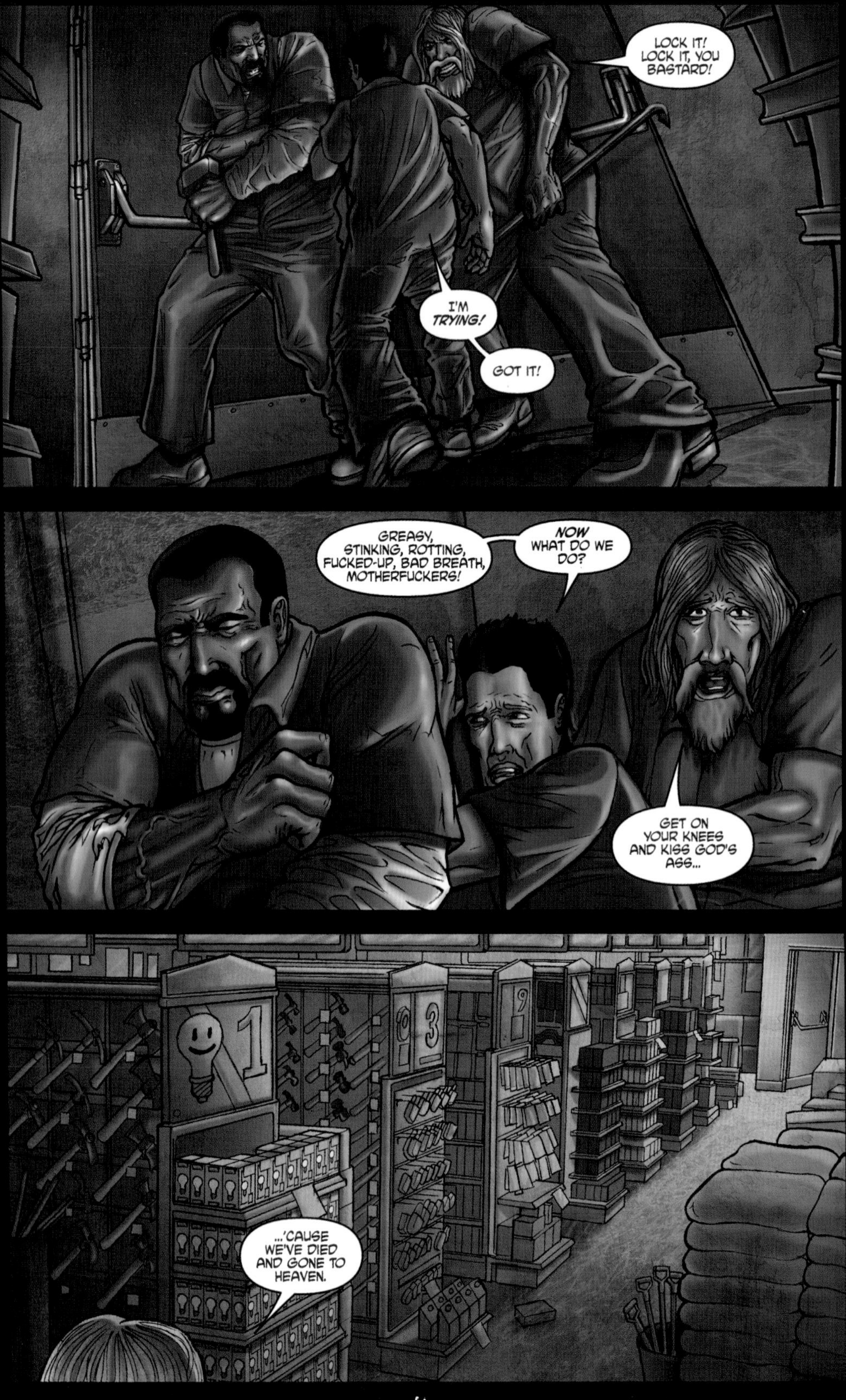
LOCK IT! LOCK IT, YOU BASTARD!
I'M *TRYING!*
GOT IT!
GREASY, STINKING, ROTTING, FUCKED-UP, BAD BREATH, MOTHERFUCKERS!
NOW WHAT DO WE DO?
GET ON YOUR KNEES AND KISS GOD'S ASS...
...'CAUSE WE'VE DIED AND GONE TO HEAVEN.

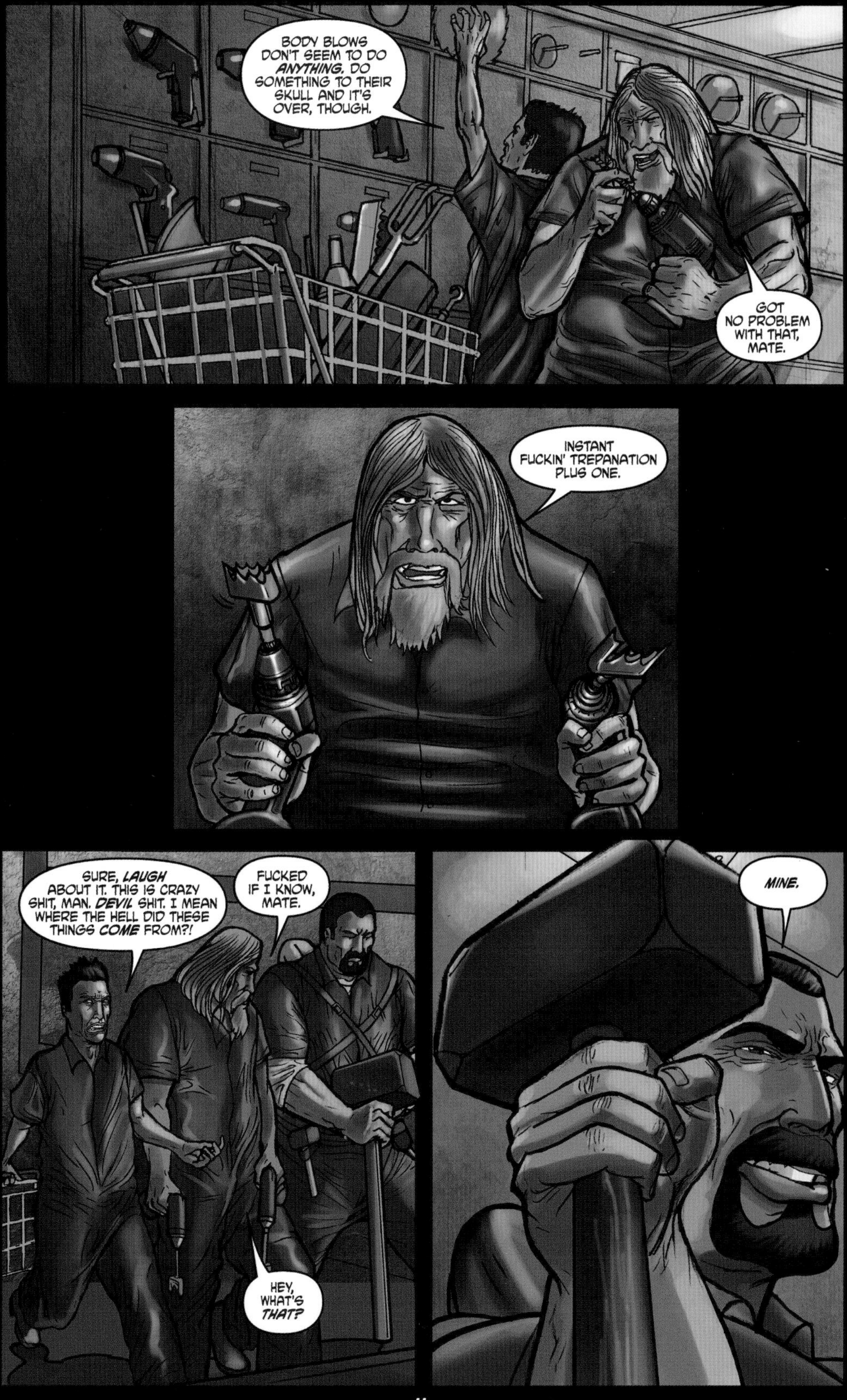
BODY BLOWS DON'T SEEM TO DO *ANYTHING.* DO SOMETHING TO THEIR SKULL AND IT'S OVER, THOUGH.
GOT NO PROBLEM WITH THAT, MATE.
INSTANT FUCKIN' TREPANATION PLUS ONE.
SURE, *LAUGH* ABOUT IT. THIS IS CRAZY SHIT, MAN. *DEVIL* SHIT. I MEAN WHERE THE HELL DID THESE THINGS *COME* FROM?!
FUCKED IF I KNOW, MATE.
HEY, WHAT'S *THAT?*
MINE.

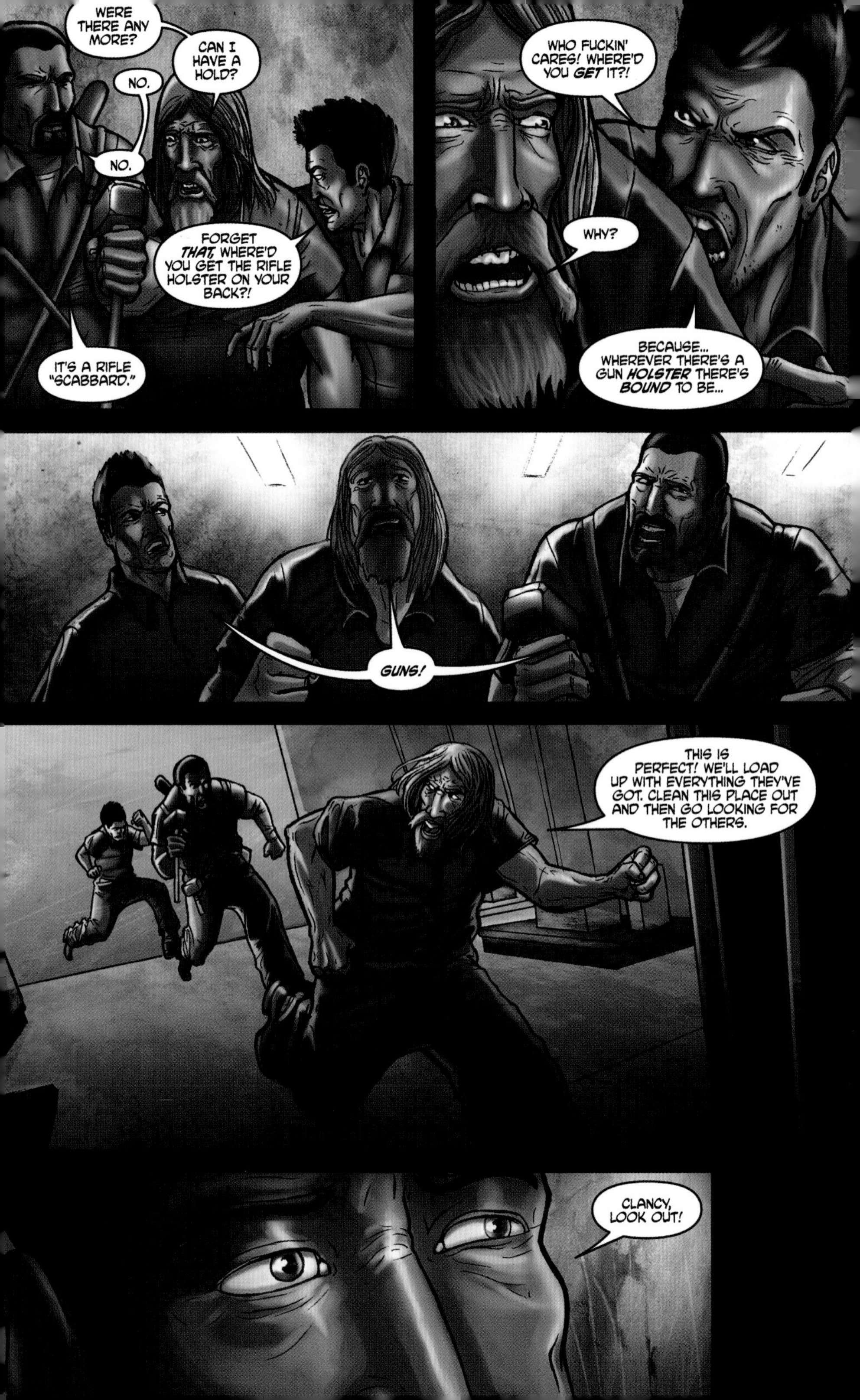
WERE THERE ANY MORE?
CAN I HAVE A HOLD?
NO.
NO.
FORGET THAT, WHERE'D YOU GET THE RIFLE HOLSTER ON YOUR BACK?!
IT'S A RIFLE "SCABBARD."
WHO FUCKIN' CARES! WHERE'D YOU GET IT?!
WHY?
BECAUSE... WHEREVER THERE'S A GUN HOLSTER THERE'S BOUND TO BE...
GUNS!
THIS IS PERFECT! WE'LL LOAD UP WITH EVERYTHING THEY'VE GOT. CLEAN THIS PLACE OUT AND THEN GO LOOKING FOR THE OTHERS.
CLANCY, LOOK OUT!

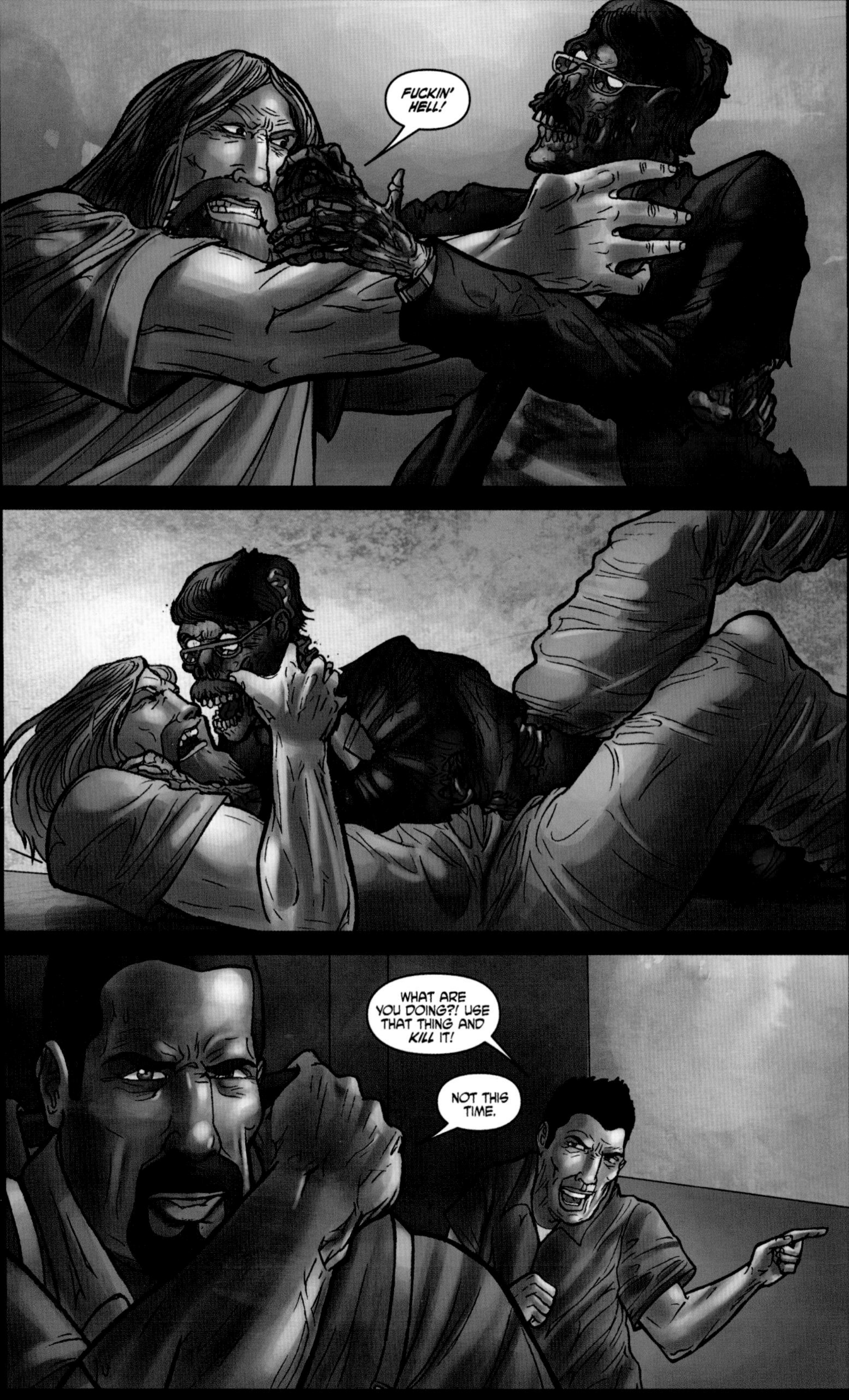
FUCKIN' HELL!
WHAT ARE YOU DOING?! USE THAT THING AND KILL IT!
NOT THIS TIME.

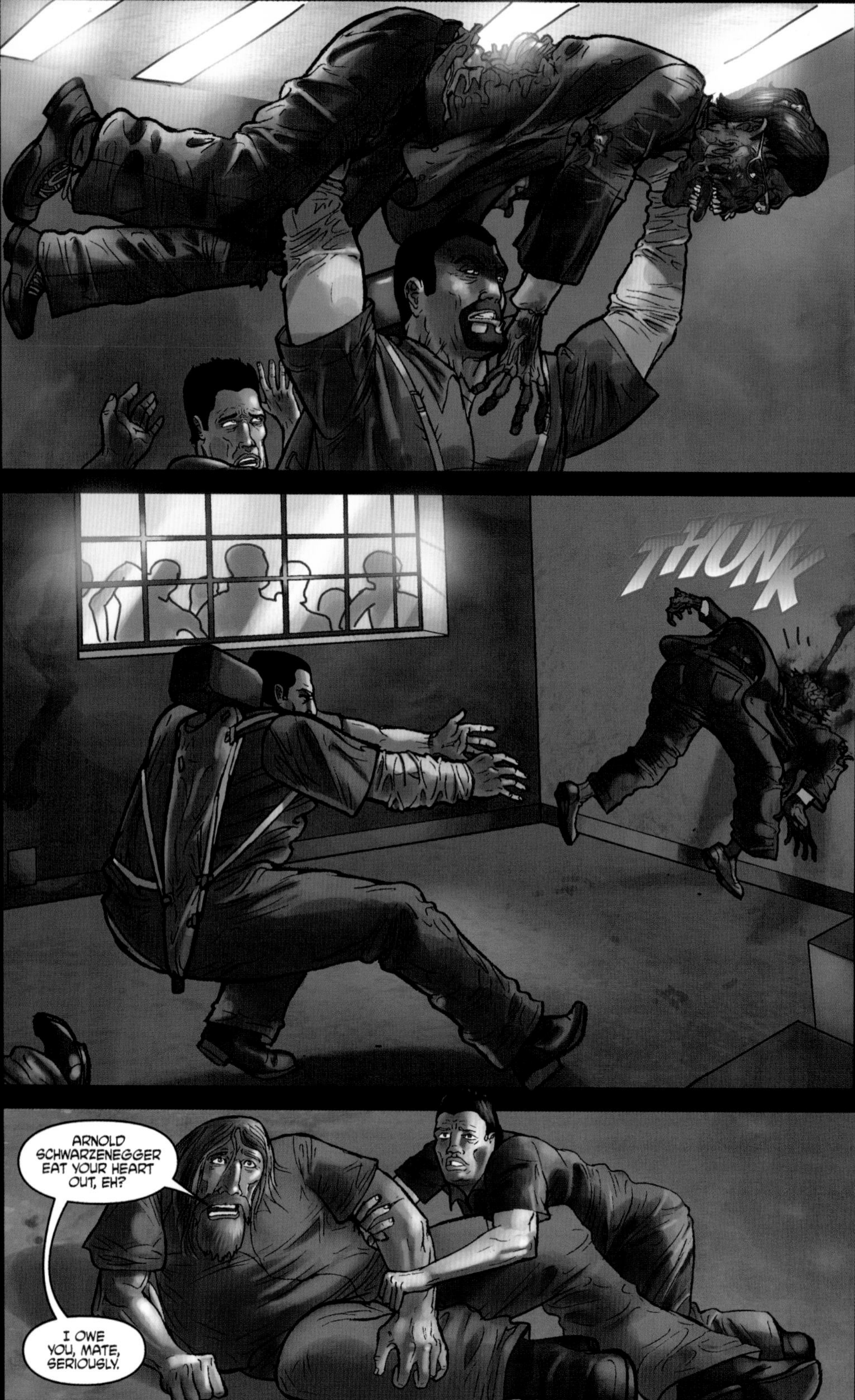
THUNK
ARNOLD SCHWARZENEGGER EAT YOUR HEART OUT, EH?
I OWE YOU, MATE, SERIOUSLY.

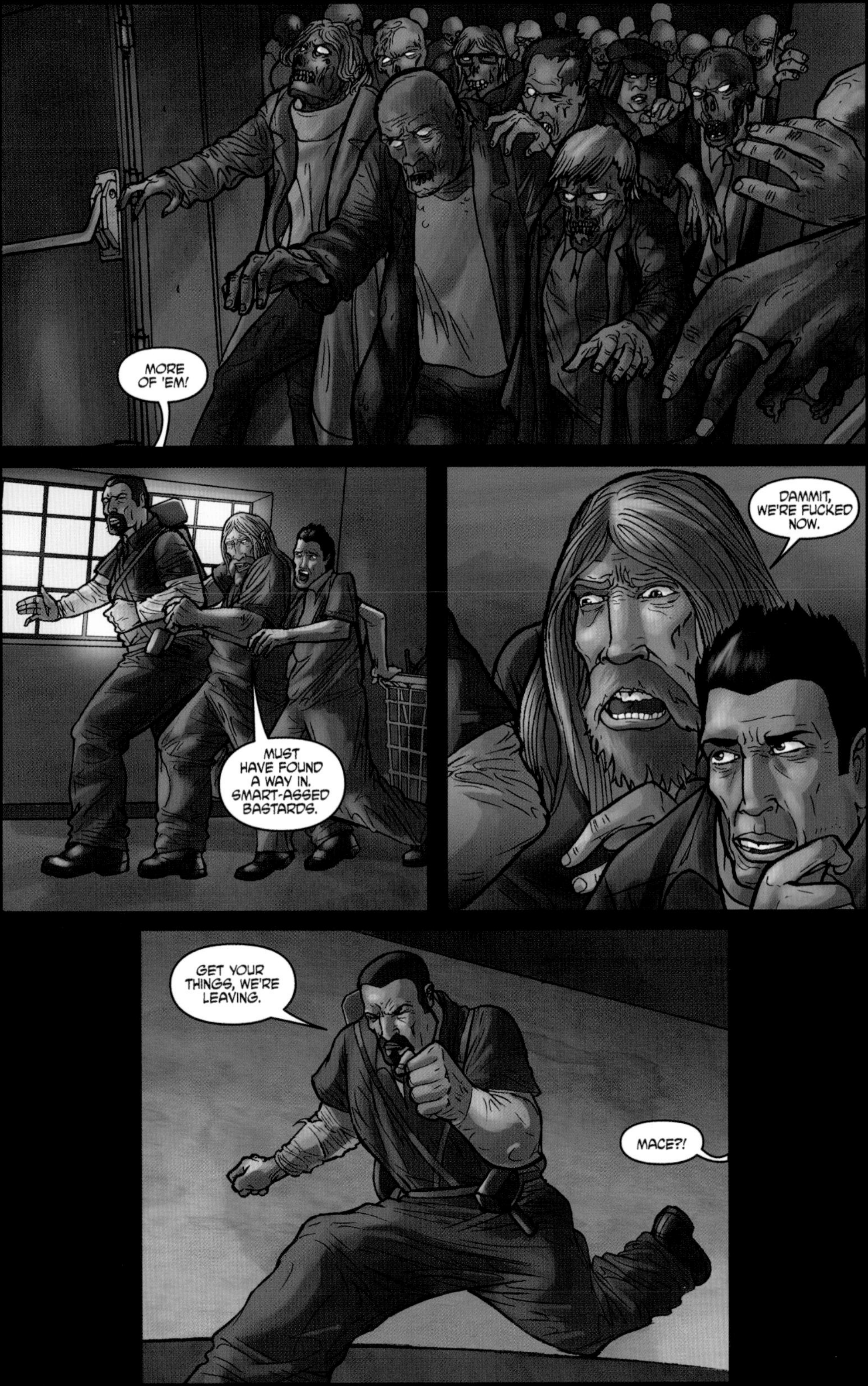
MORE OF 'EM!
MUST HAVE FOUND A WAY IN. SMART-ASSED BASTARDS.
DAMMIT, WE'RE FUCKED NOW.
GET YOUR THINGS, WE'RE LEAVING.
MACE?!

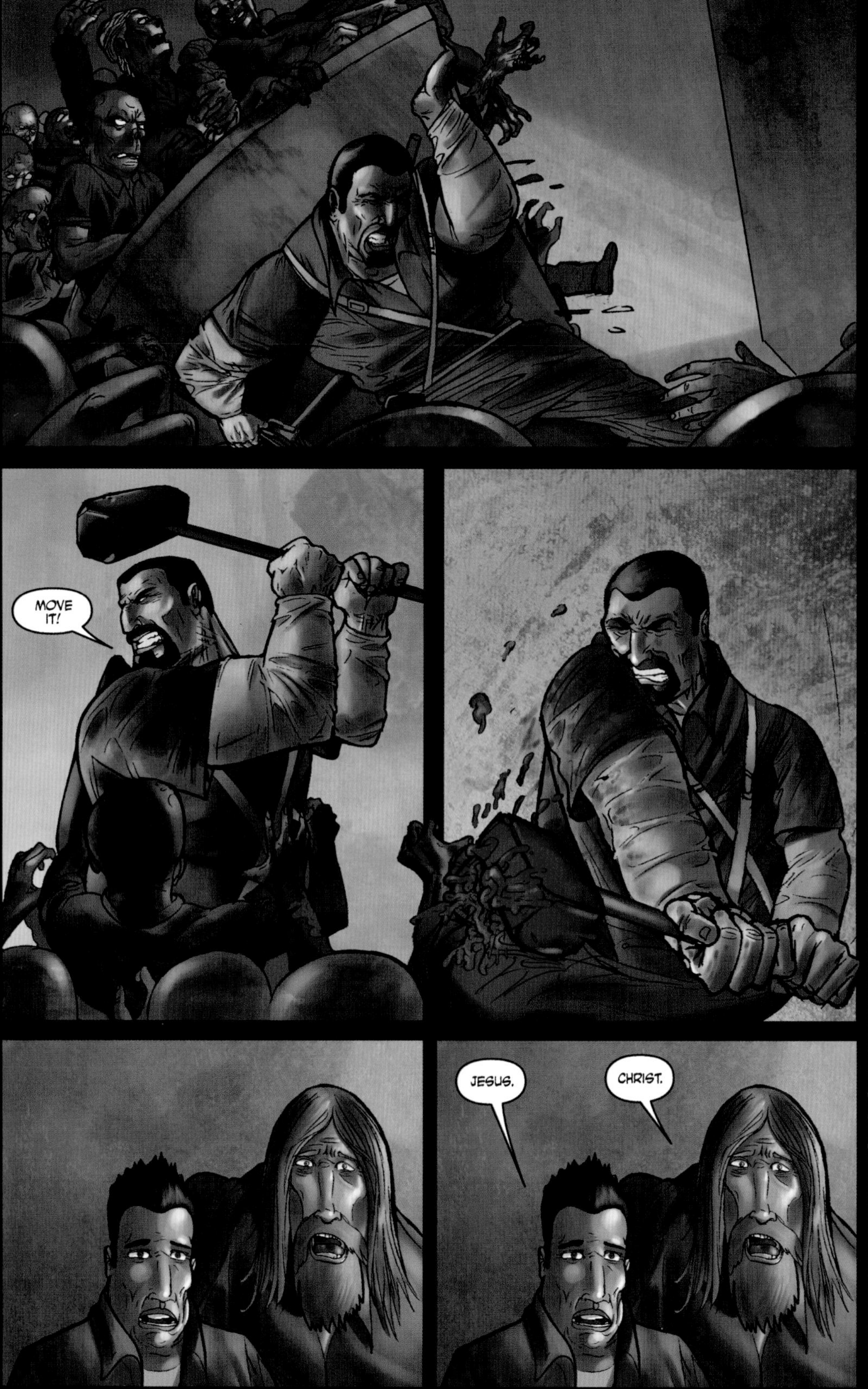
MOVE IT!
JESUS.
CHRIST.

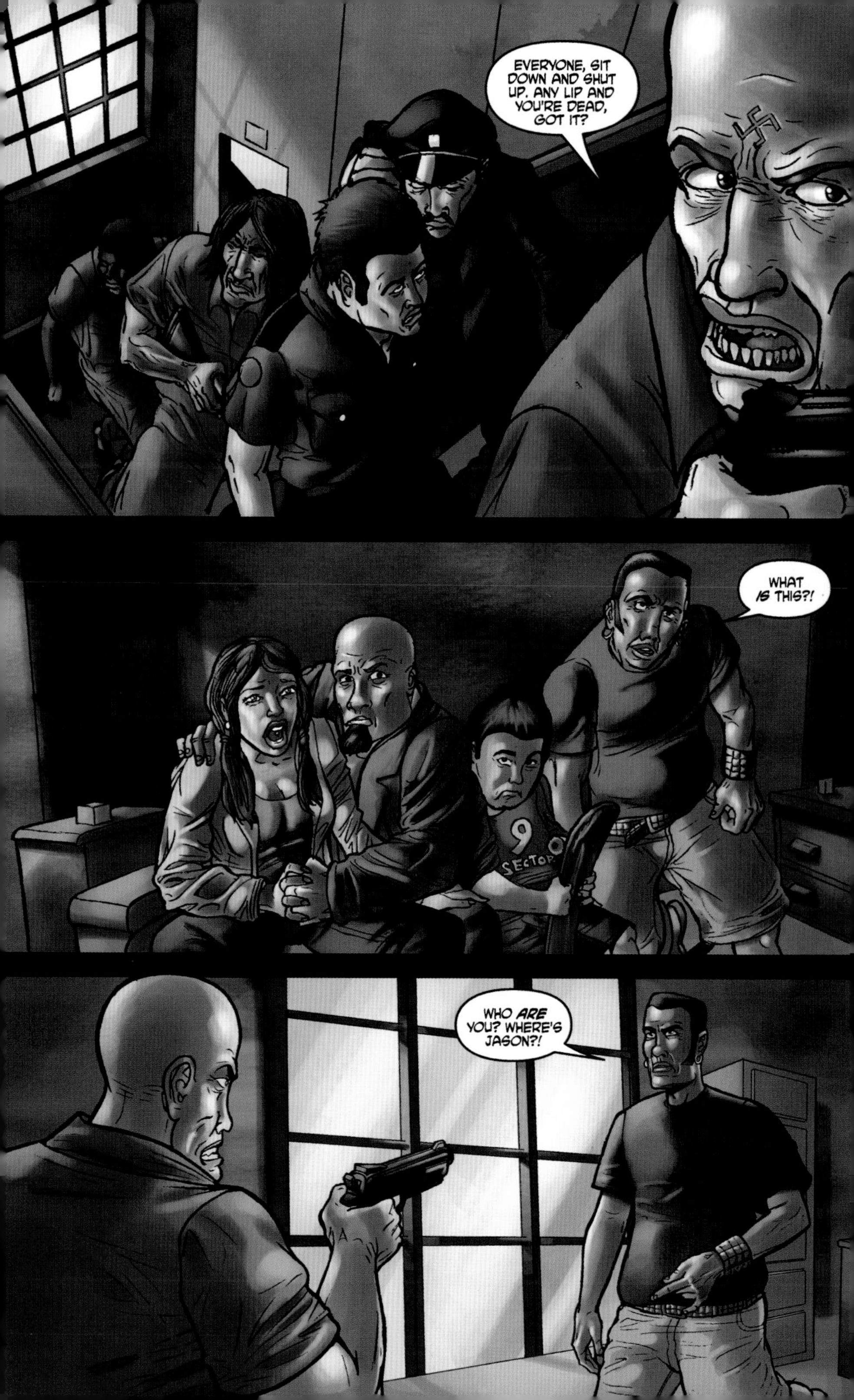
EVERYONE, SIT DOWN AND SHUT UP. ANY LIP AND YOU'RE DEAD, GOT IT?
WHAT *IS* THIS?!
WHO *ARE* YOU? WHERE'S JASON?!

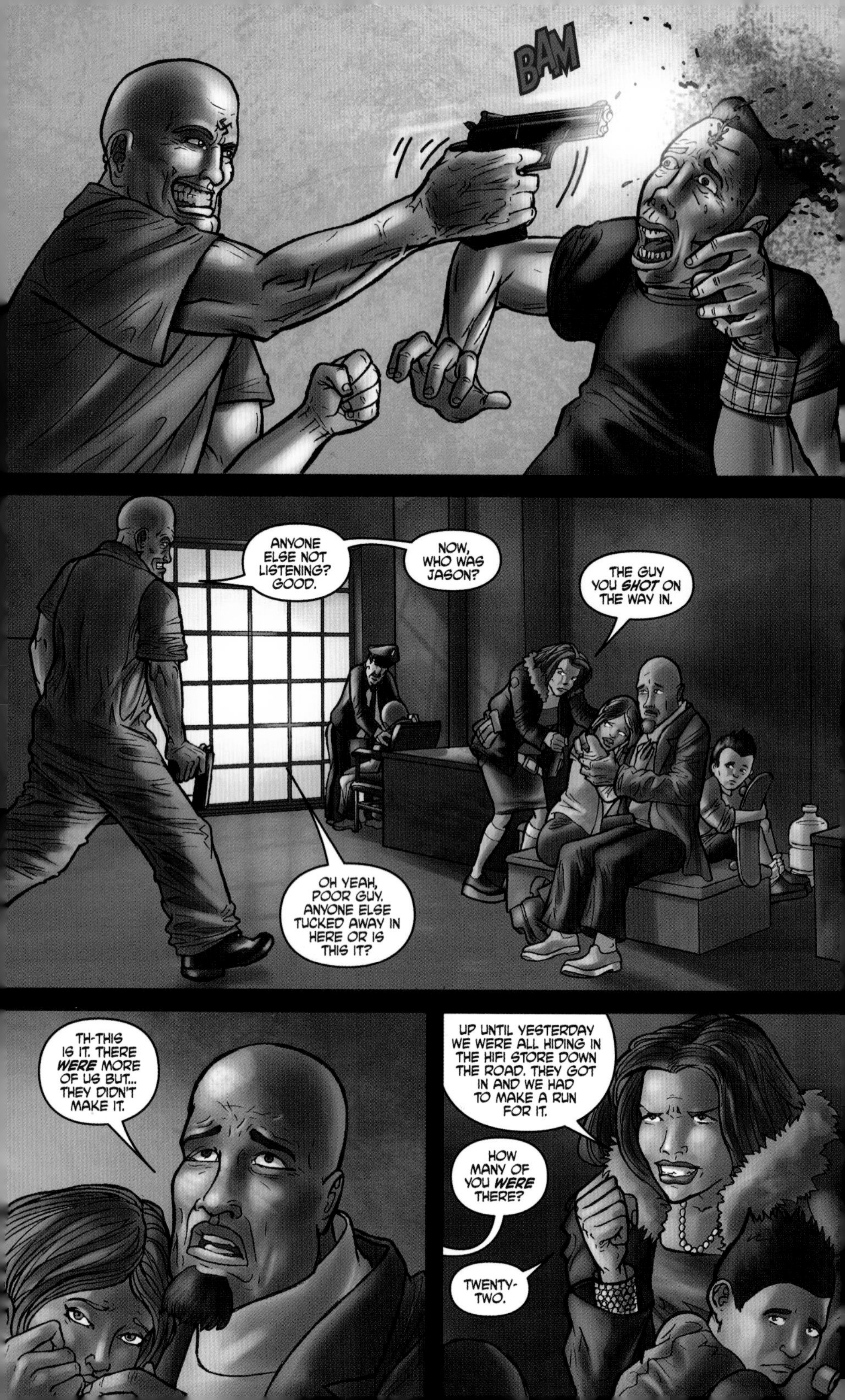
BAM
ANYONE ELSE NOT LISTENING? GOOD.
NOW, WHO WAS JASON?
THE GUY YOU *SHOT* ON THE WAY IN.
OH YEAH, POOR GUY. ANYONE ELSE TUCKED AWAY IN HERE OR IS THIS IT?
TH-THIS IS IT. THERE *WERE* MORE OF US BUT... THEY DIDN'T MAKE IT.
UP UNTIL YESTERDAY WE WERE ALL HIDING IN THE HIFI STORE DOWN THE ROAD. THEY GOT IN AND WE HAD TO MAKE A RUN FOR IT.
HOW MANY OF YOU *WERE* THERE?
TWENTY-TWO.

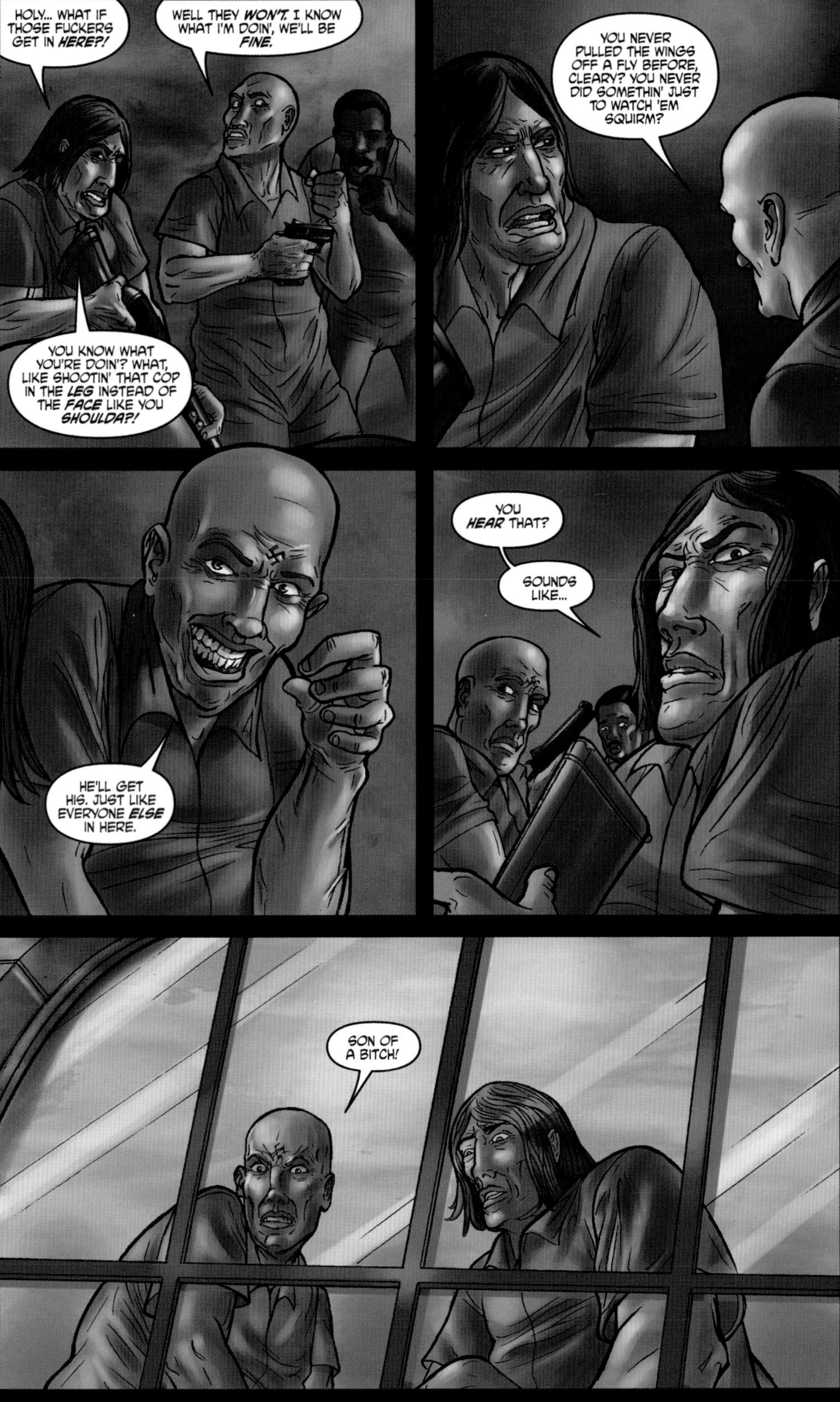
HOLY... WHAT IF THOSE FUCKERS GET IN HERE?!
WELL THEY WON'T. I KNOW WHAT I'M DOIN', WE'LL BE FINE.
YOU KNOW WHAT YOU'RE DOIN'? WHAT, LIKE SHOOTIN' THAT COP IN THE LEG INSTEAD OF THE FACE LIKE YOU SHOULDA?!
YOU NEVER PULLED THE WINGS OFF A FLY BEFORE, CLEARY? YOU NEVER DID SOMETHIN' JUST TO WATCH 'EM SQUIRM?
HE'LL GET HIS. JUST LIKE EVERYONE ELSE IN HERE.
YOU HEAR THAT?
SOUNDS LIKE...
SON OF A BITCH!

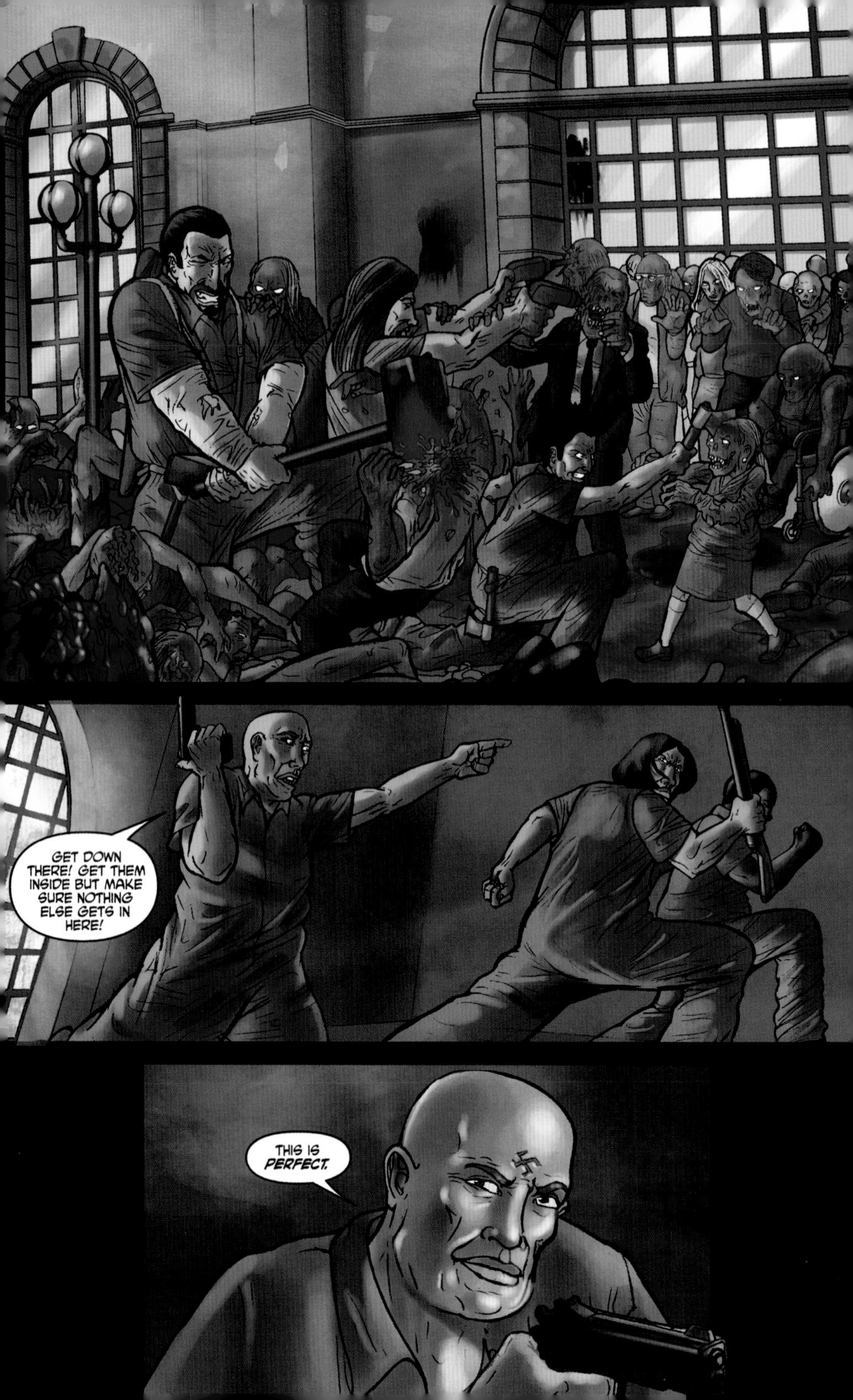
GET DOWN THERE! GET THEM INSIDE BUT MAKE SURE NOTHING ELSE GETS IN HERE!
THIS IS *PERFECT.*

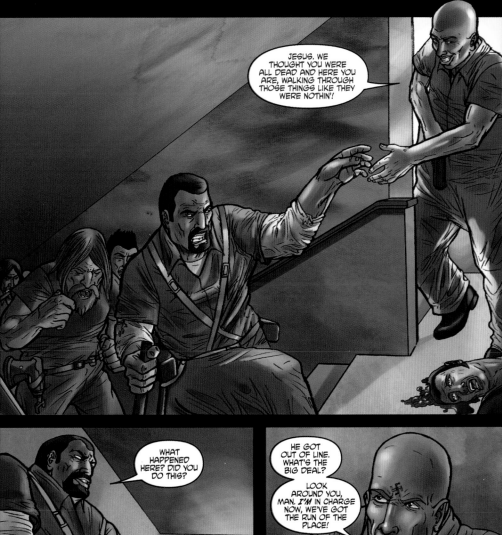

JESUS. WE THOUGHT YOU WERE ALL DEAD AND HERE YOU ARE, WALKING THROUGH THOSE THINGS LIKE THEY WERE NOTHIN'!

WHAT HAPPENED HERE? DID YOU DO THIS?

HE GOT OUT OF LINE. WHAT'S THE BIG DEAL?

LOOK AROUND YOU, MAN. *I'M* IN CHARGE NOW. WE'VE GOT THE RUN OF THE PLACE!

EVERY *ONE* OF US IS A LIFER. ALL OF US HAVE KILLED OUR FAIR SHARE. YOU OF ALL PEOPLE SHOULDN'T HAVE AN ISSUE WITH *THAT!*

HELL, YOU'RE THE *WORST* OUT OF ALL OF US!

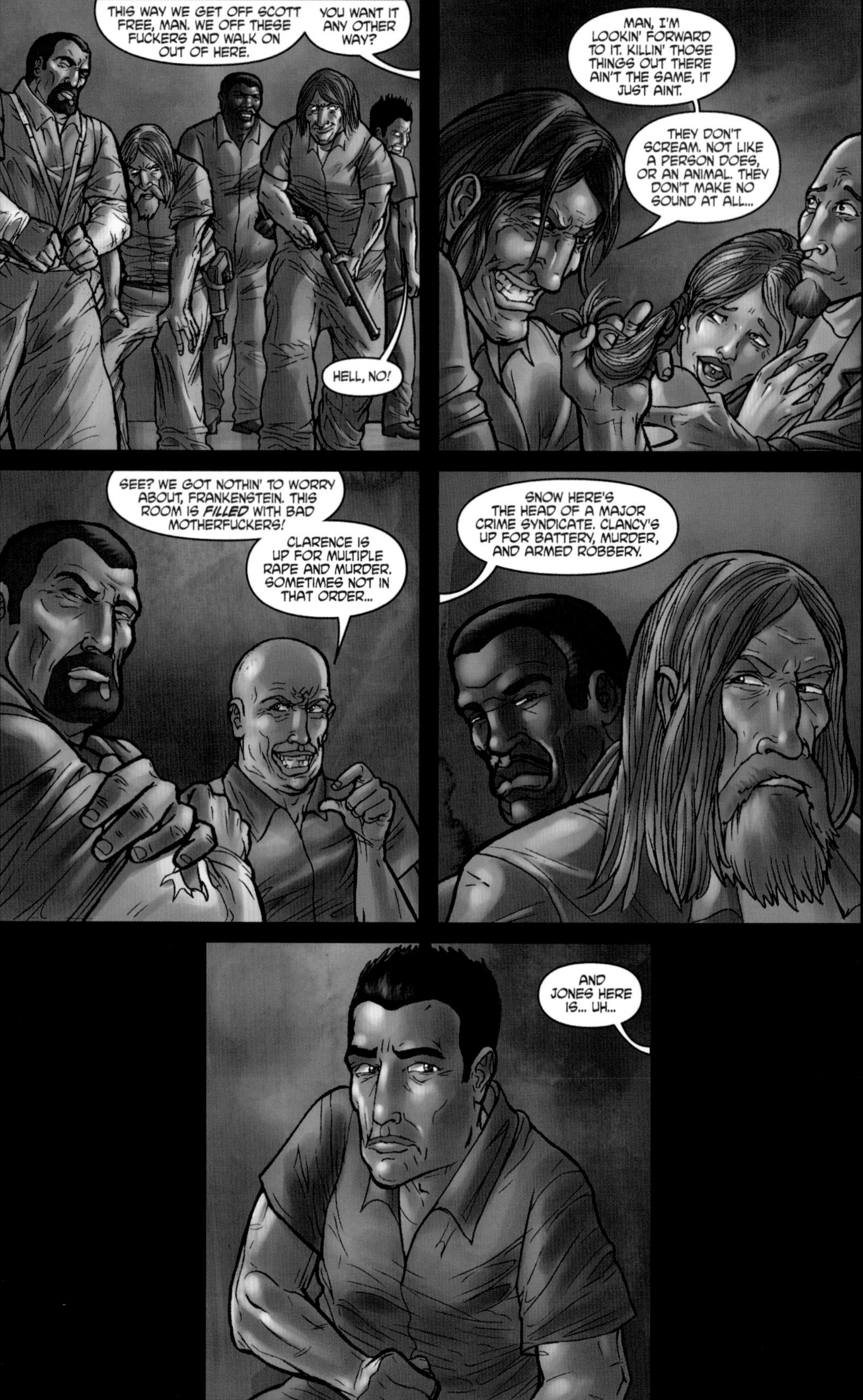
THIS WAY WE GET OFF SCOTT FREE, MAN. WE OFF THESE FUCKERS AND WALK ON OUT OF HERE.
YOU WANT IT ANY OTHER WAY?
HELL, NO!
MAN, I'M LOOKIN' FORWARD TO IT. KILLIN' THOSE THINGS OUT THERE AIN'T THE SAME, IT JUST AINT.
THEY DON'T SCREAM. NOT LIKE A PERSON DOES, OR AN ANIMAL. THEY DON'T MAKE NO SOUND AT ALL...
SEE? WE GOT NOTHIN' TO WORRY ABOUT, FRANKENSTEIN. THIS ROOM IS *FILLED* WITH BAD MOTHERFUCKERS!
CLARENCE IS UP FOR MULTIPLE RAPE AND MURDER. SOMETIMES NOT IN THAT ORDER...
SNOW HERE'S THE HEAD OF A MAJOR CRIME SYNDICATE. CLANCY'S UP FOR BATTERY, MURDER, AND ARMED ROBBERY.
AND JONES HERE IS... UH...

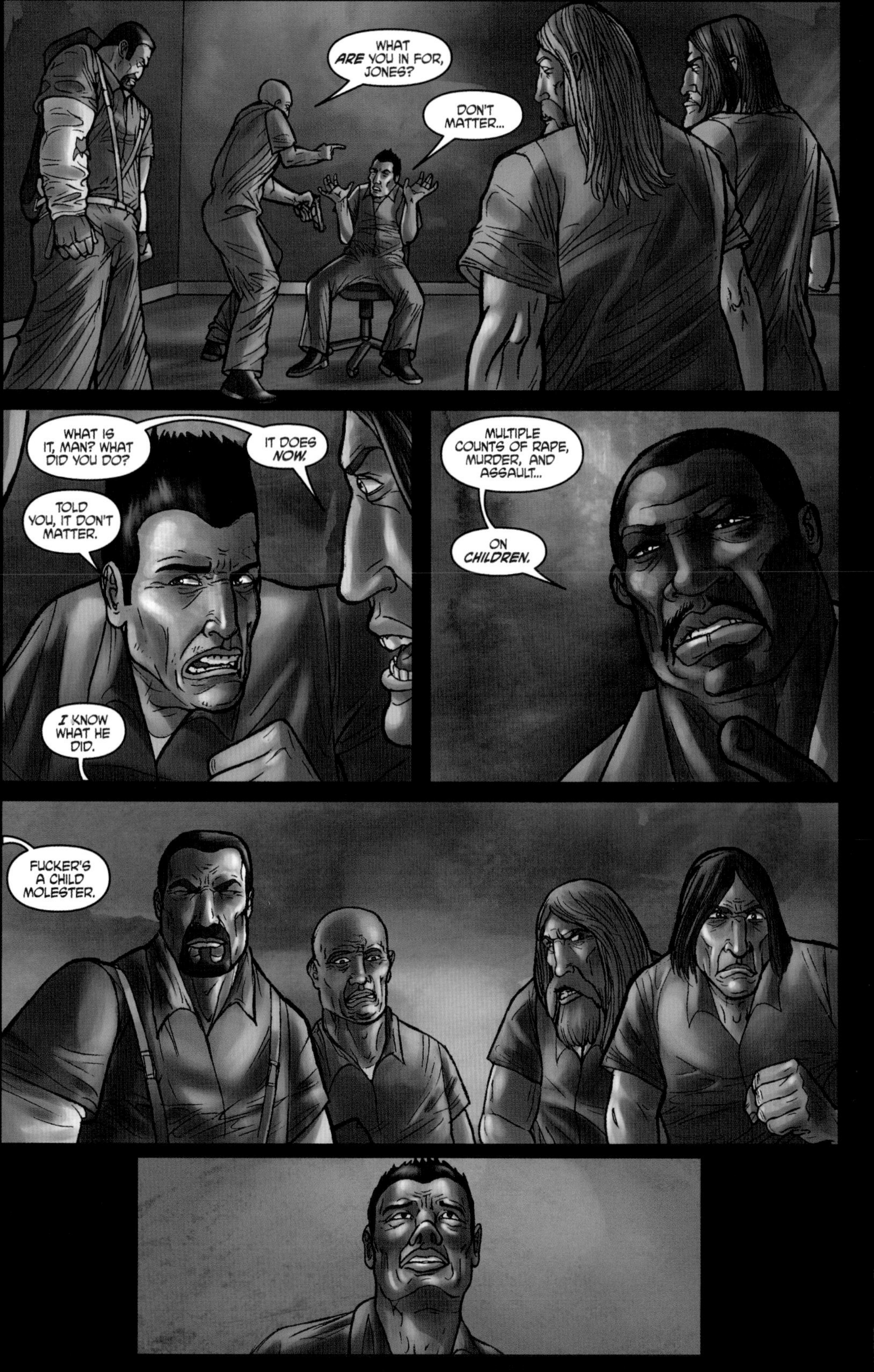
WHAT ARE YOU IN FOR, JONES?
DON'T MATTER...
WHAT IS IT, MAN? WHAT DID YOU DO?
IT DOES NOW.
TOLD YOU, IT DON'T MATTER.
I KNOW WHAT HE DID.
MULTIPLE COUNTS OF RAPE, MURDER, AND ASSAULT...
ON CHILDREN.
FUCKER'S A CHILD MOLESTER.

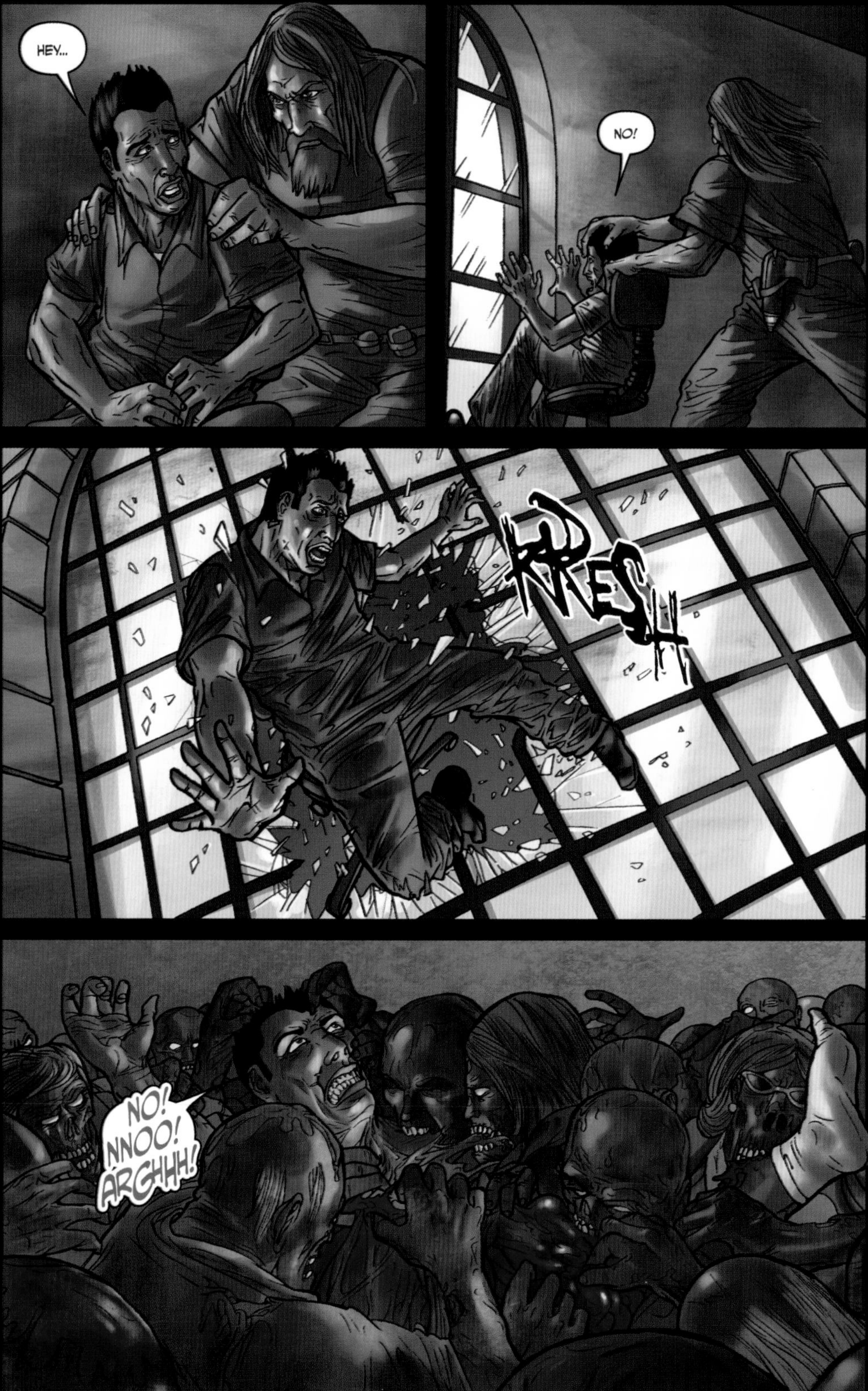
HEY...
NO!
KRESH
NO! NNOO! ARGHH!

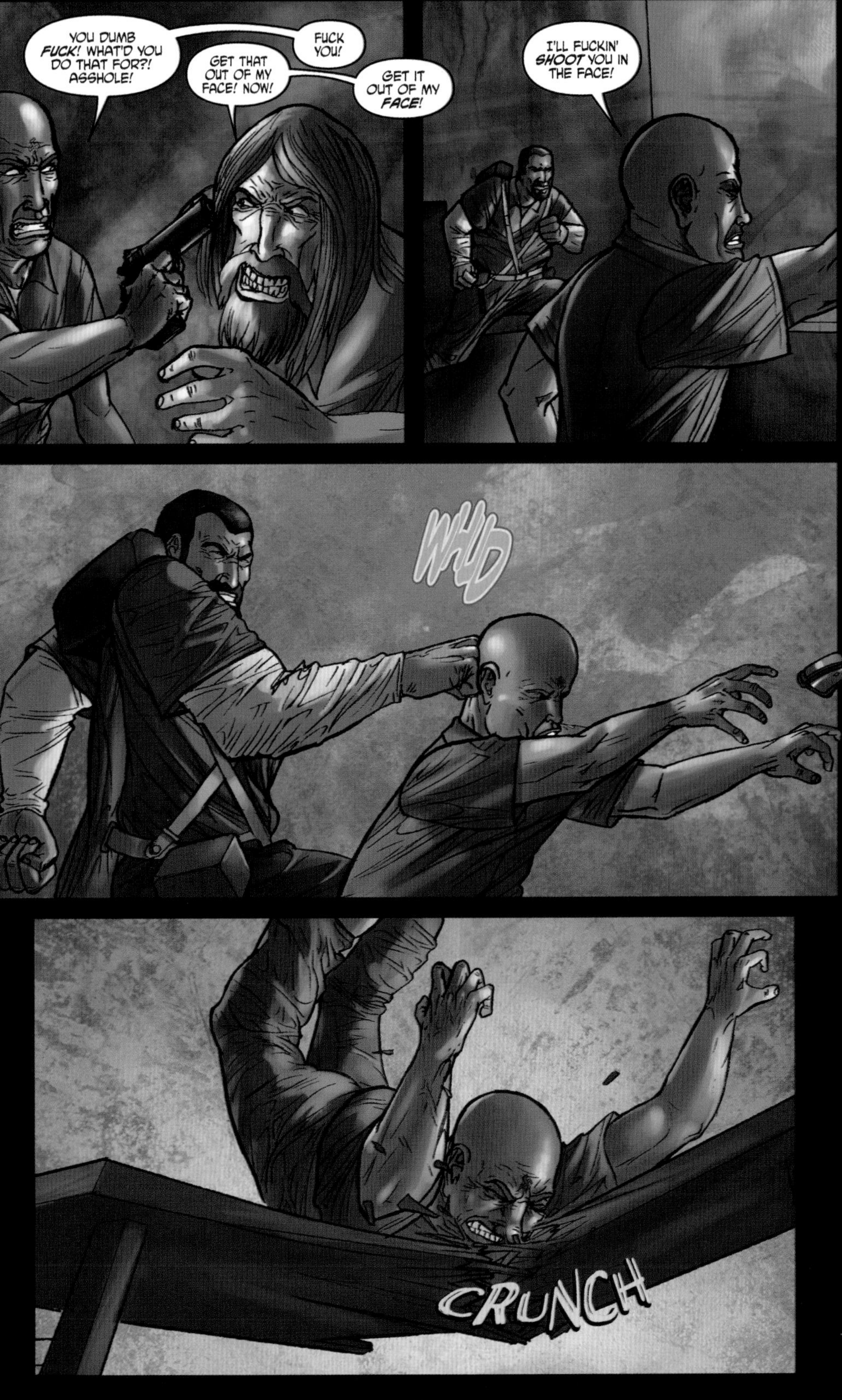

YOU DUMB FUCK! WHAT'D YOU DO THAT FOR?! ASSHOLE!
FUCK YOU!
GET THAT OUT OF MY FACE! NOW!
GET IT OUT OF MY FACE!
I'LL FUCKIN' SHOOT YOU IN THE FACE!
WHUD
CRUNCH

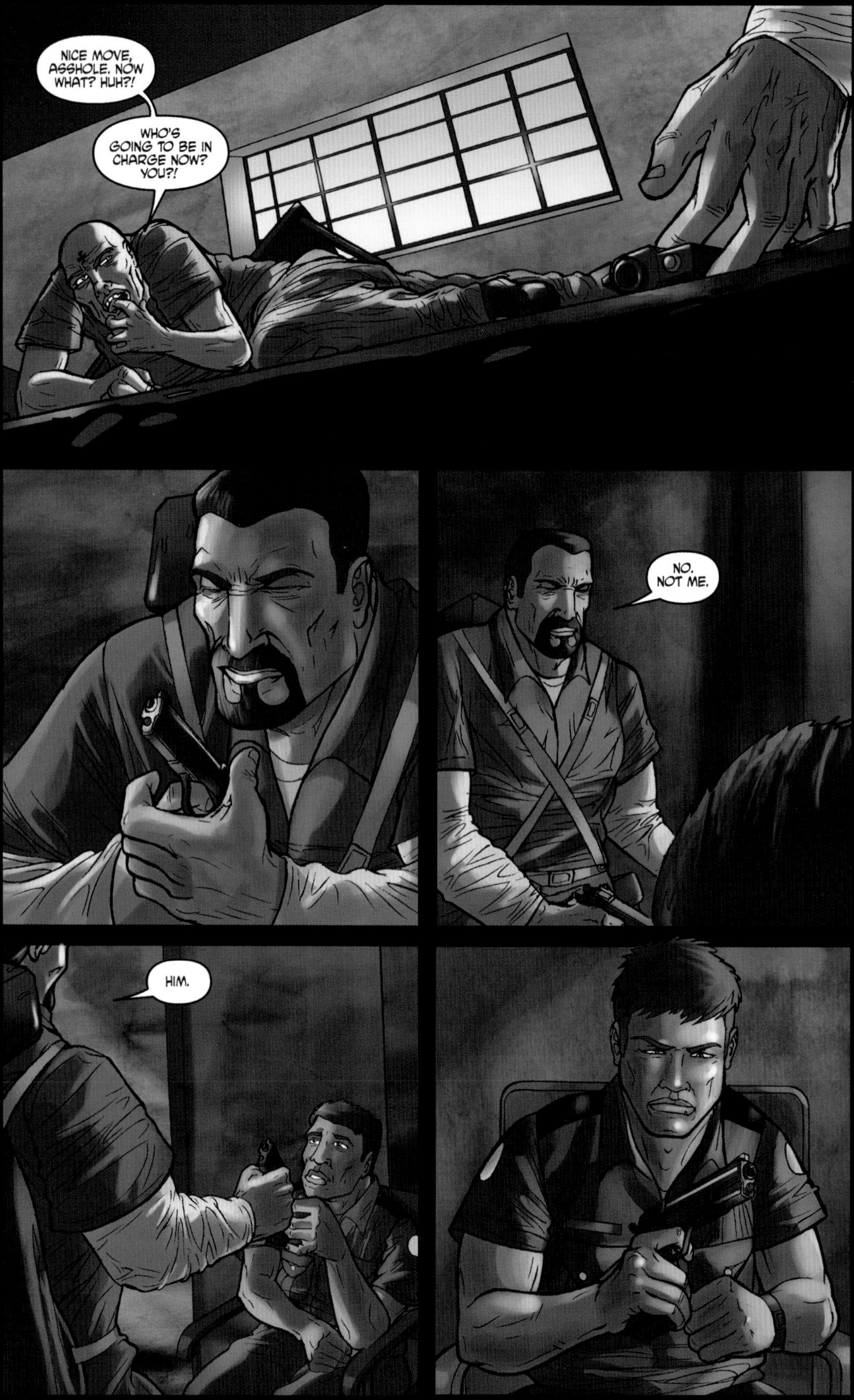
NICE MOVE, ASSHOLE. NOW WHAT? HUH?!
WHO'S GOING TO BE IN CHARGE NOW? YOU?!
NO. NOT ME.
HIM.

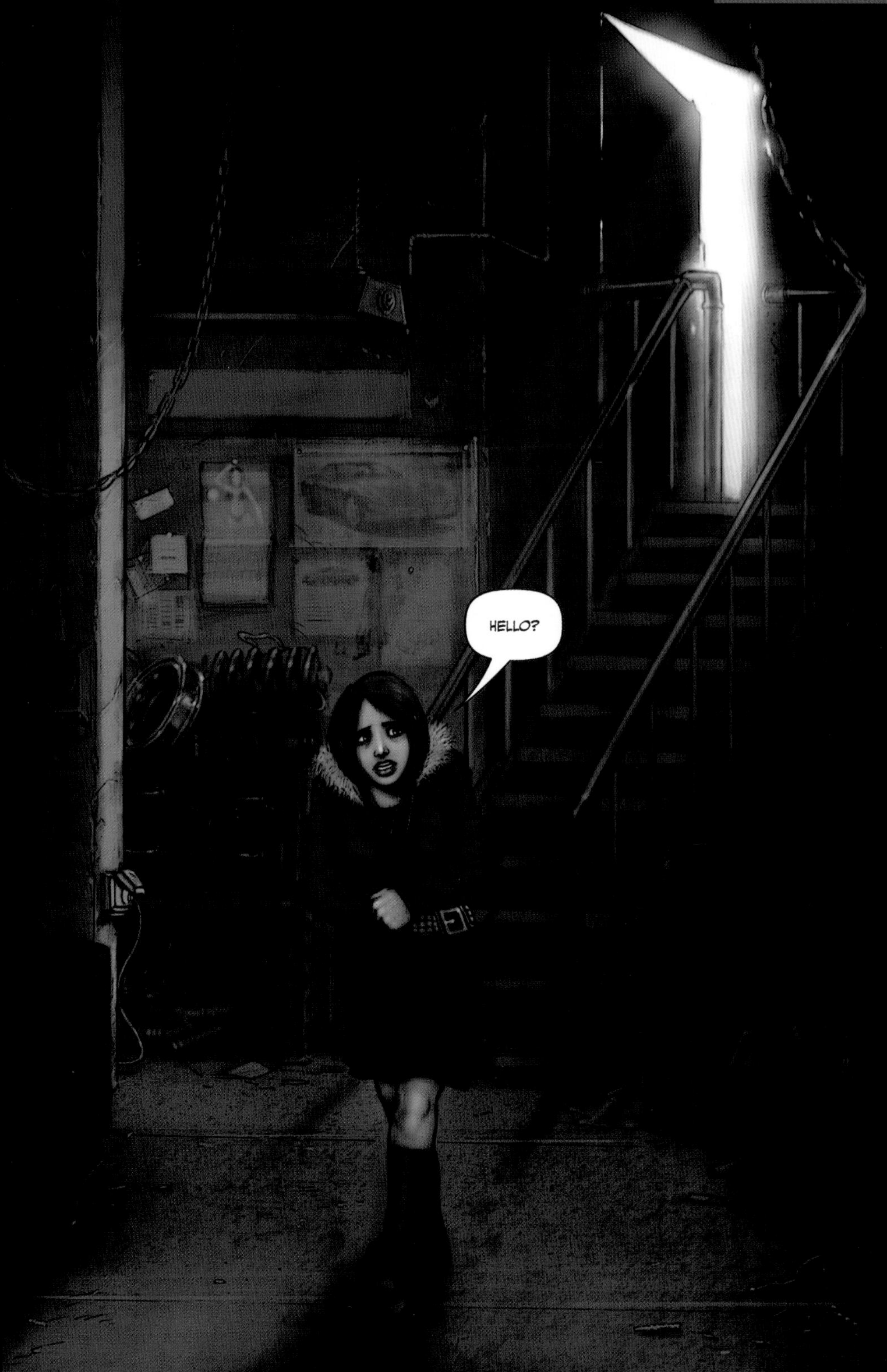
HELLO?

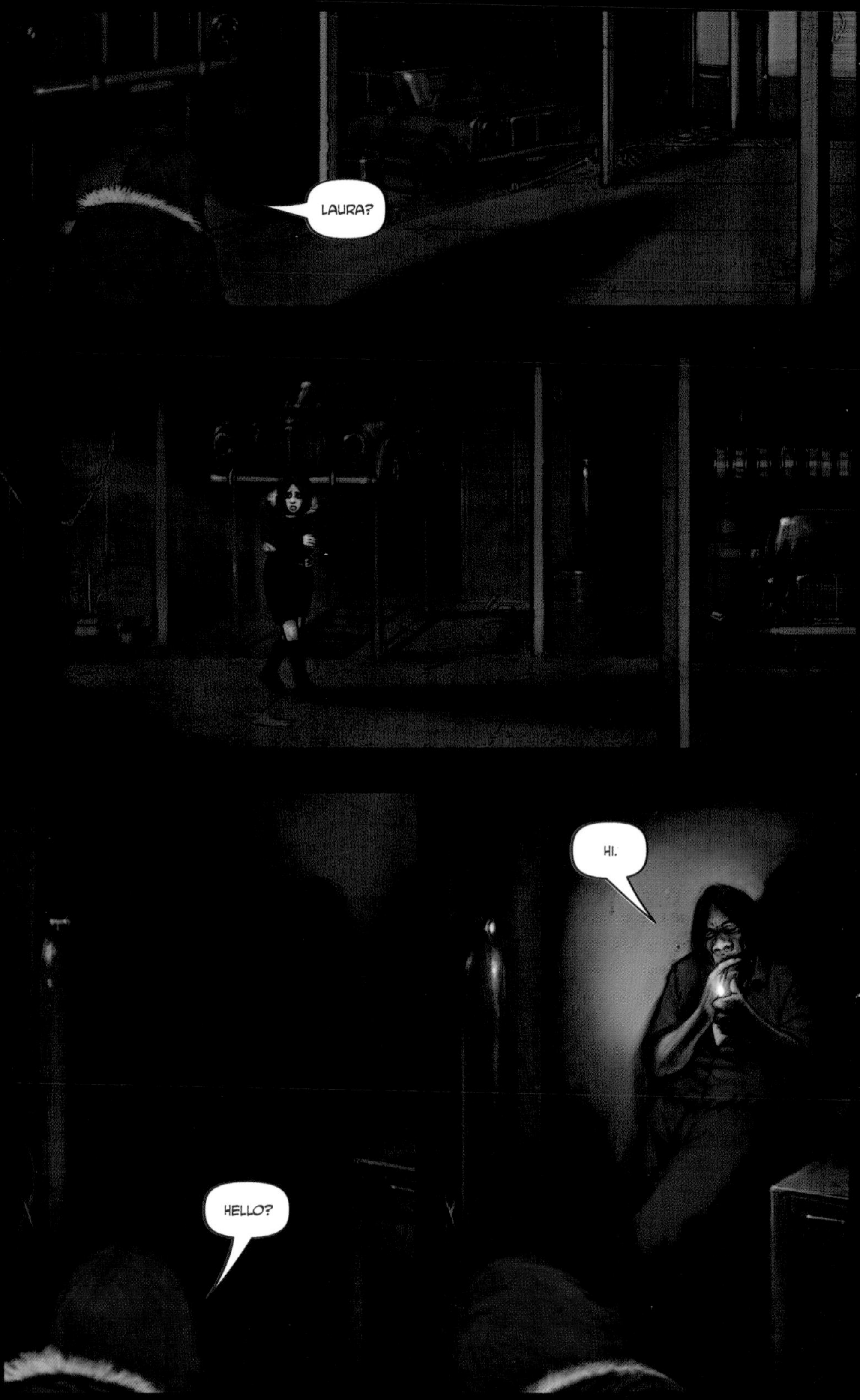
LAURA?
HI.
HELLO?

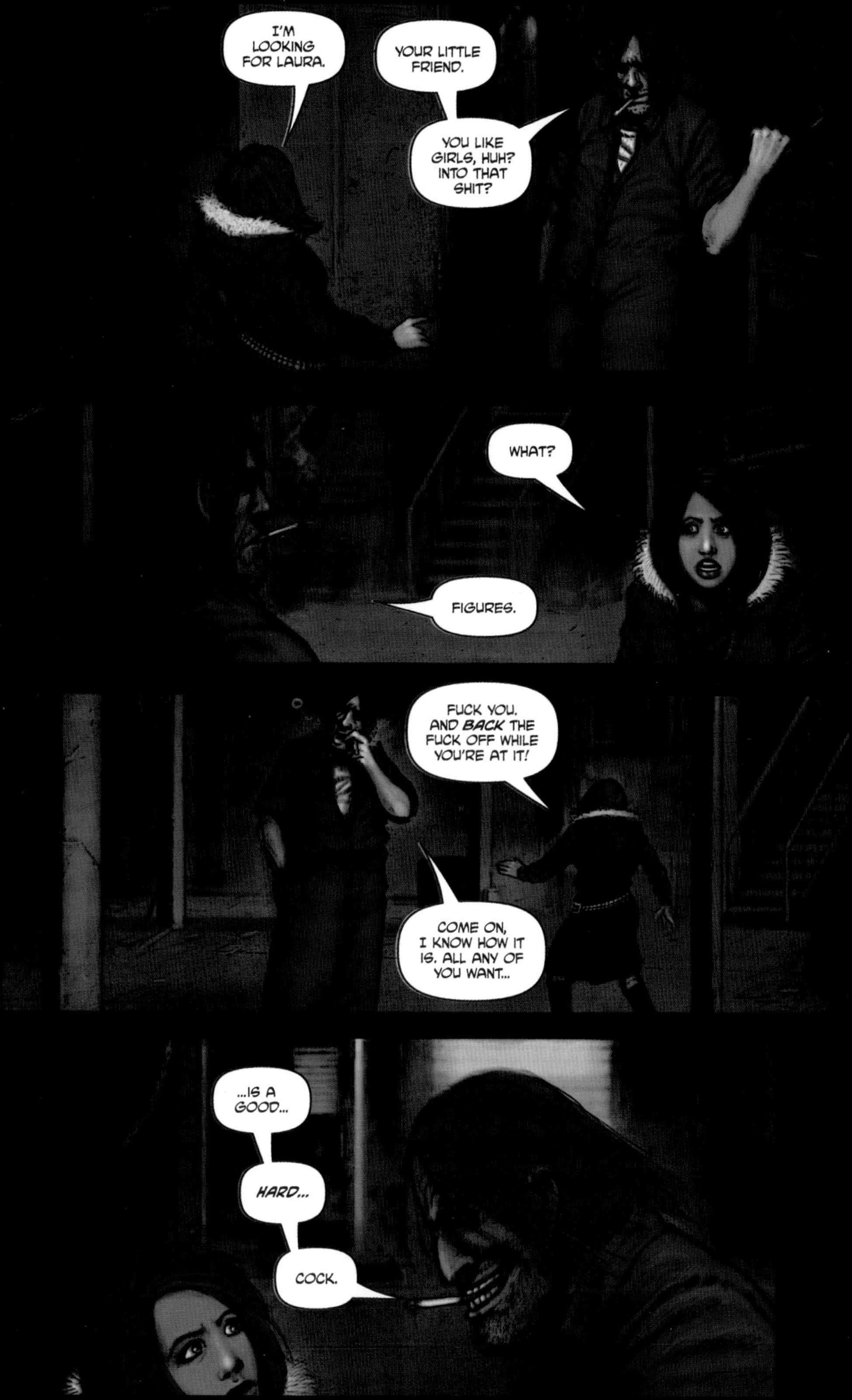
I'M LOOKING FOR LAURA.
YOUR LITTLE FRIEND.
YOU LIKE GIRLS, HUH? INTO THAT SHIT?
WHAT?
FIGURES.
FUCK YOU. AND BACK THE FUCK OFF WHILE YOU'RE AT IT!
COME ON, I KNOW HOW IT IS. ALL ANY OF YOU WANT...
...IS A GOOD...
HARD...
COCK.

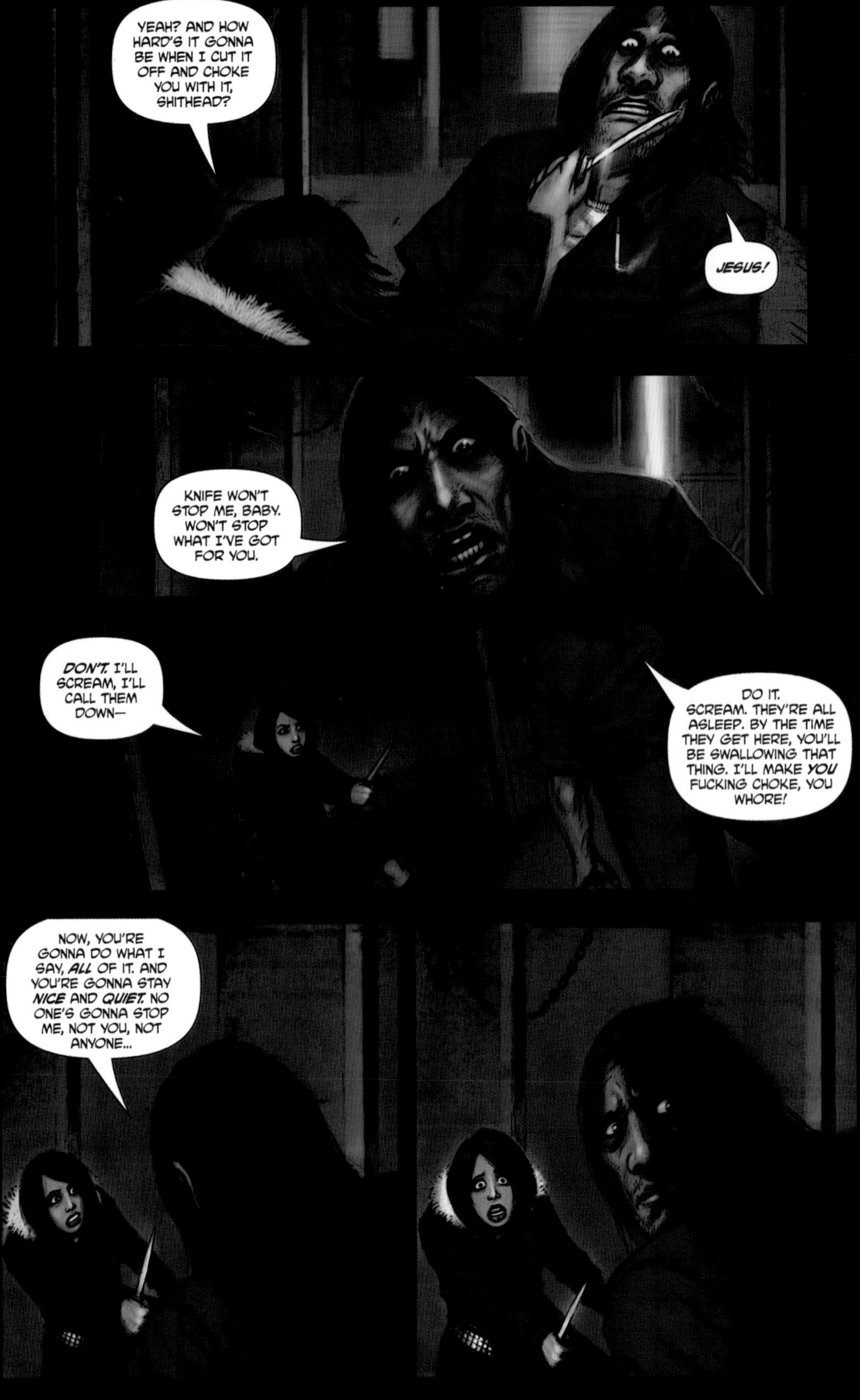
YEAH? AND HOW HARD'S IT GONNA BE WHEN I CUT IT OFF AND CHOKE YOU WITH IT, SHITHEAD?
JESUS!
KNIFE WON'T STOP ME, BABY. WON'T STOP WHAT I'VE GOT FOR YOU.
DON'T. I'LL SCREAM, I'LL CALL THEM DOWN—
DO IT. SCREAM. THEY'RE ALL ASLEEP. BY THE TIME THEY GET HERE, YOU'LL BE SWALLOWING THAT THING. I'LL MAKE YOU FUCKING CHOKE, YOU WHORE!
NOW, YOU'RE GONNA DO WHAT I SAY, ALL OF IT. AND YOU'RE GONNA STAY NICE AND QUIET. NO ONE'S GONNA STOP ME, NOT YOU, NOT ANYONE...

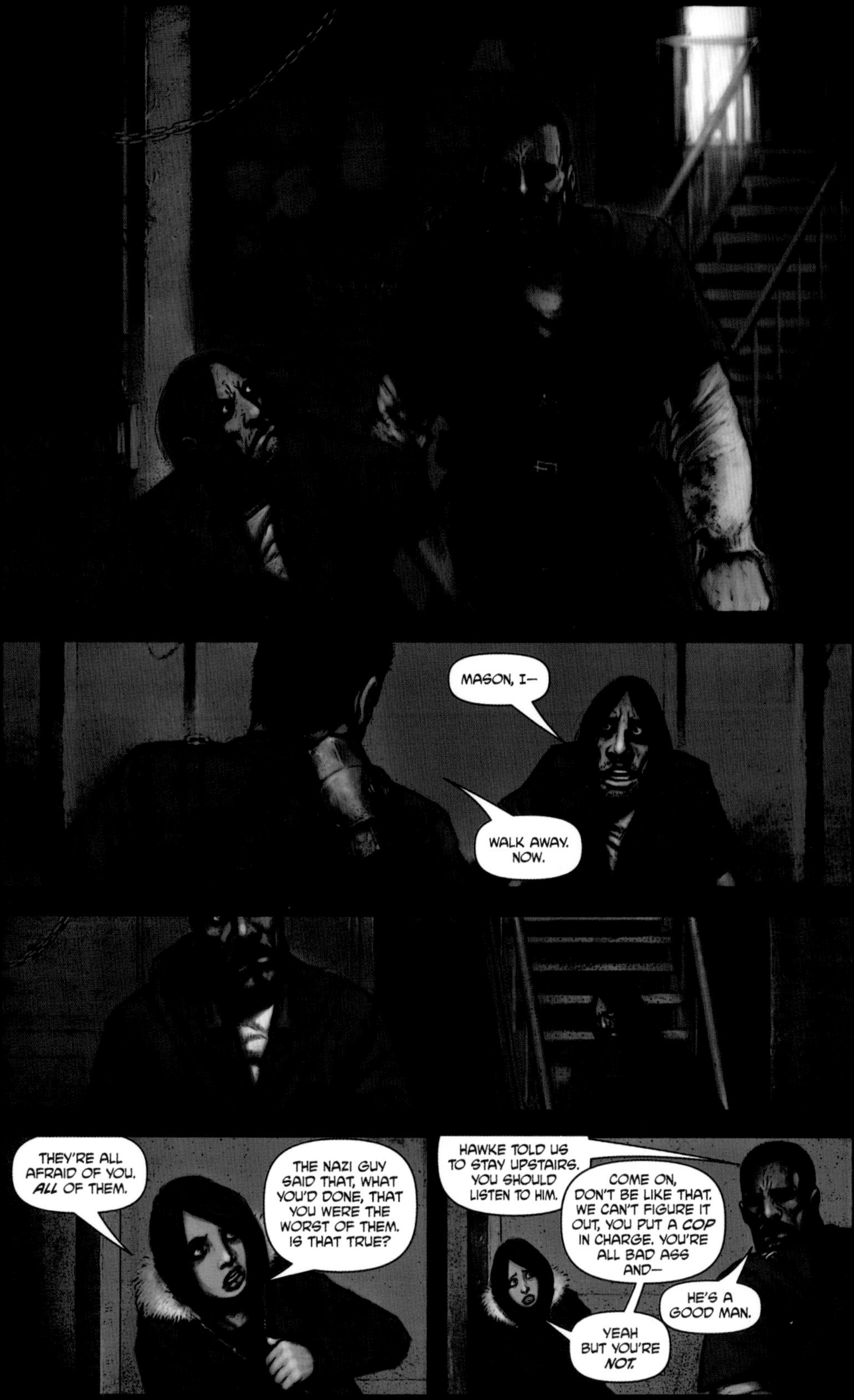
MASON, I--
WALK AWAY. NOW.
THEY'RE ALL AFRAID OF YOU. *ALL* OF THEM.
THE NAZI GUY SAID THAT, WHAT YOU'D DONE, THAT YOU WERE THE WORST OF THEM. IS THAT TRUE?
HAWKE TOLD US TO STAY UPSTAIRS. YOU SHOULD LISTEN TO HIM.
COME ON, DON'T BE LIKE THAT. WE CAN'T FIGURE IT OUT, YOU PUT A *COP* IN CHARGE. YOU'RE ALL BAD ASS AND--
HE'S A GOOD MAN.
YEAH BUT YOU'RE *NOT.*

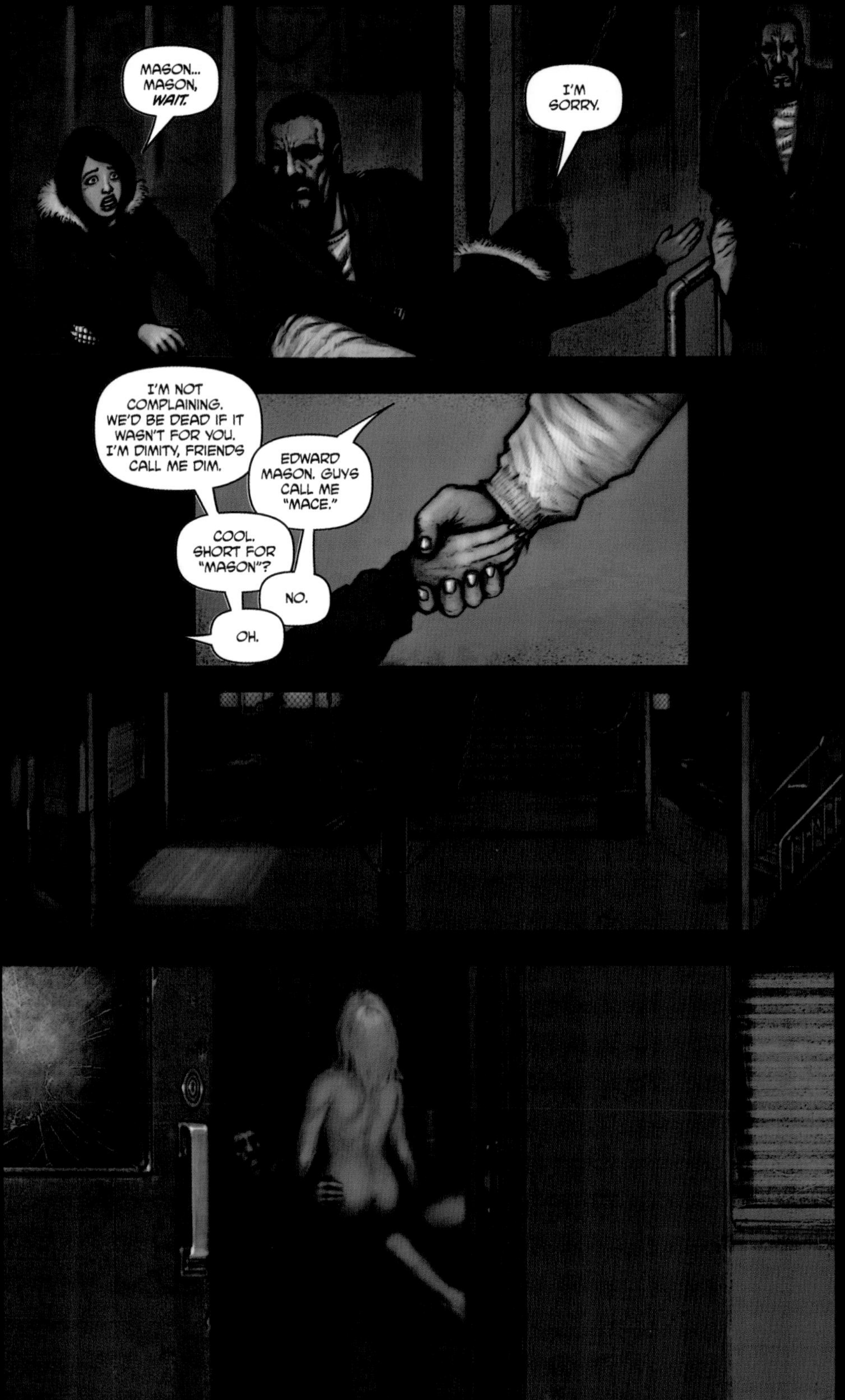
MASON... MASON, *WAIT.*
I'M SORRY.
I'M NOT COMPLAINING. WE'D BE DEAD IF IT WASN'T FOR YOU. I'M DIMITY, FRIENDS CALL ME DIM.
EDWARD MASON. GUYS CALL ME "MACE."
COOL. SHORT FOR "MASON"?
NO.
OH.

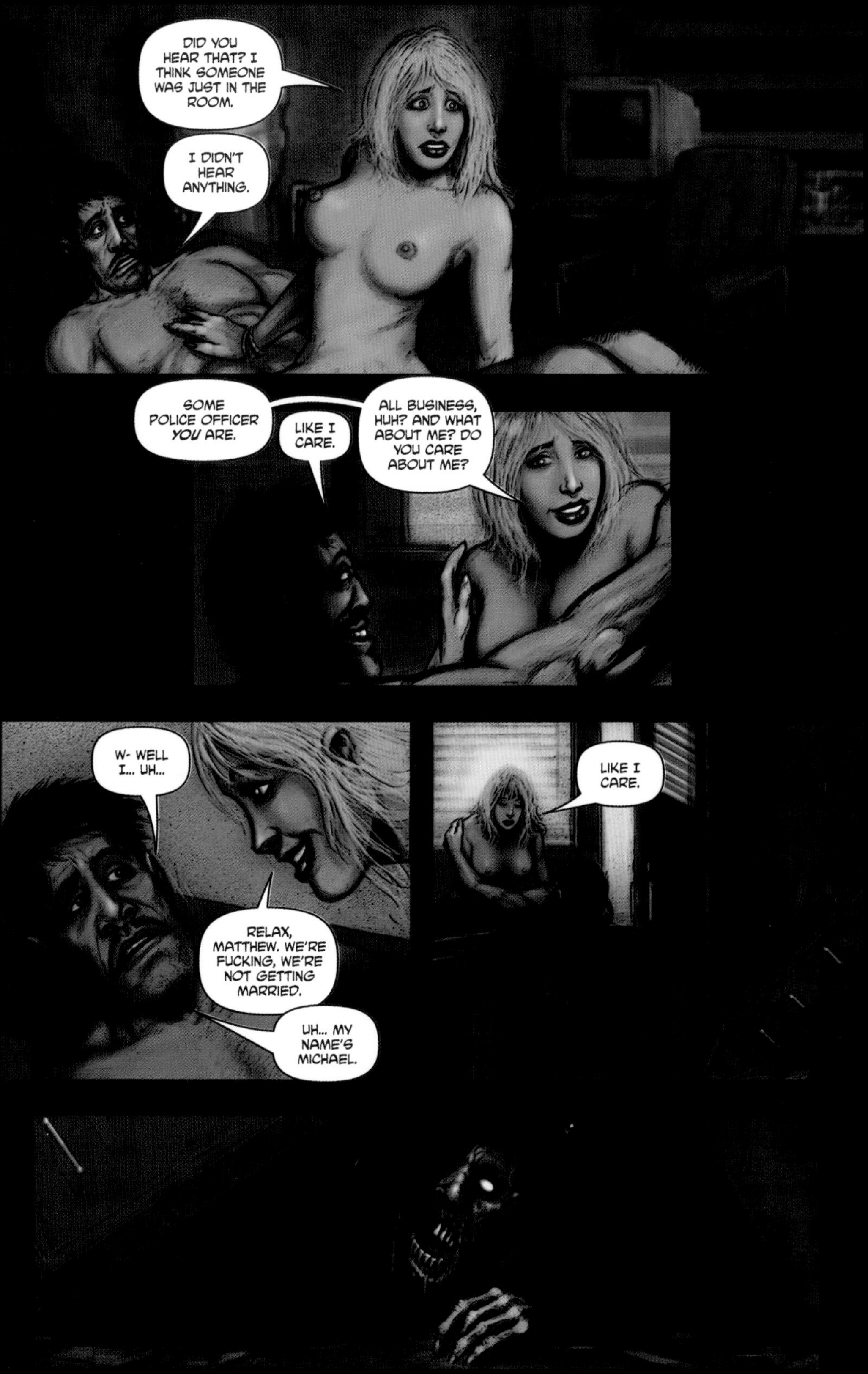
DID YOU HEAR THAT? I THINK SOMEONE WAS JUST IN THE ROOM.
I DIDN'T HEAR ANYTHING.
SOME POLICE OFFICER *YOU* ARE.
LIKE I CARE.
ALL BUSINESS, HUH? AND WHAT ABOUT ME? DO YOU CARE ABOUT ME?
W- WELL I... UH...
RELAX, MATTHEW. WE'RE FUCKING, WE'RE NOT GETTING MARRIED.
UH... MY NAME'S MICHAEL.
LIKE I CARE.

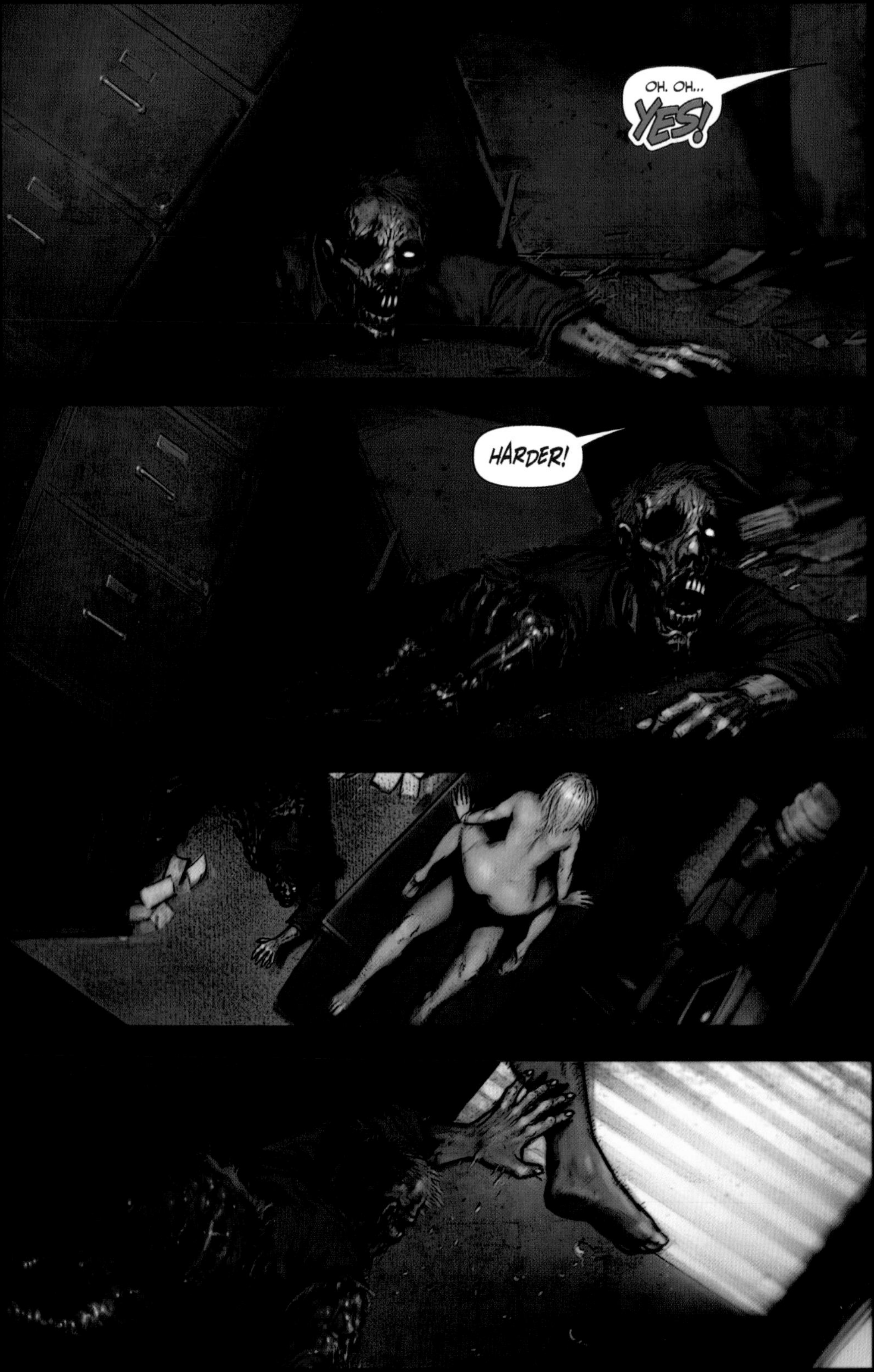
OH. OH... YES!
HARDER!

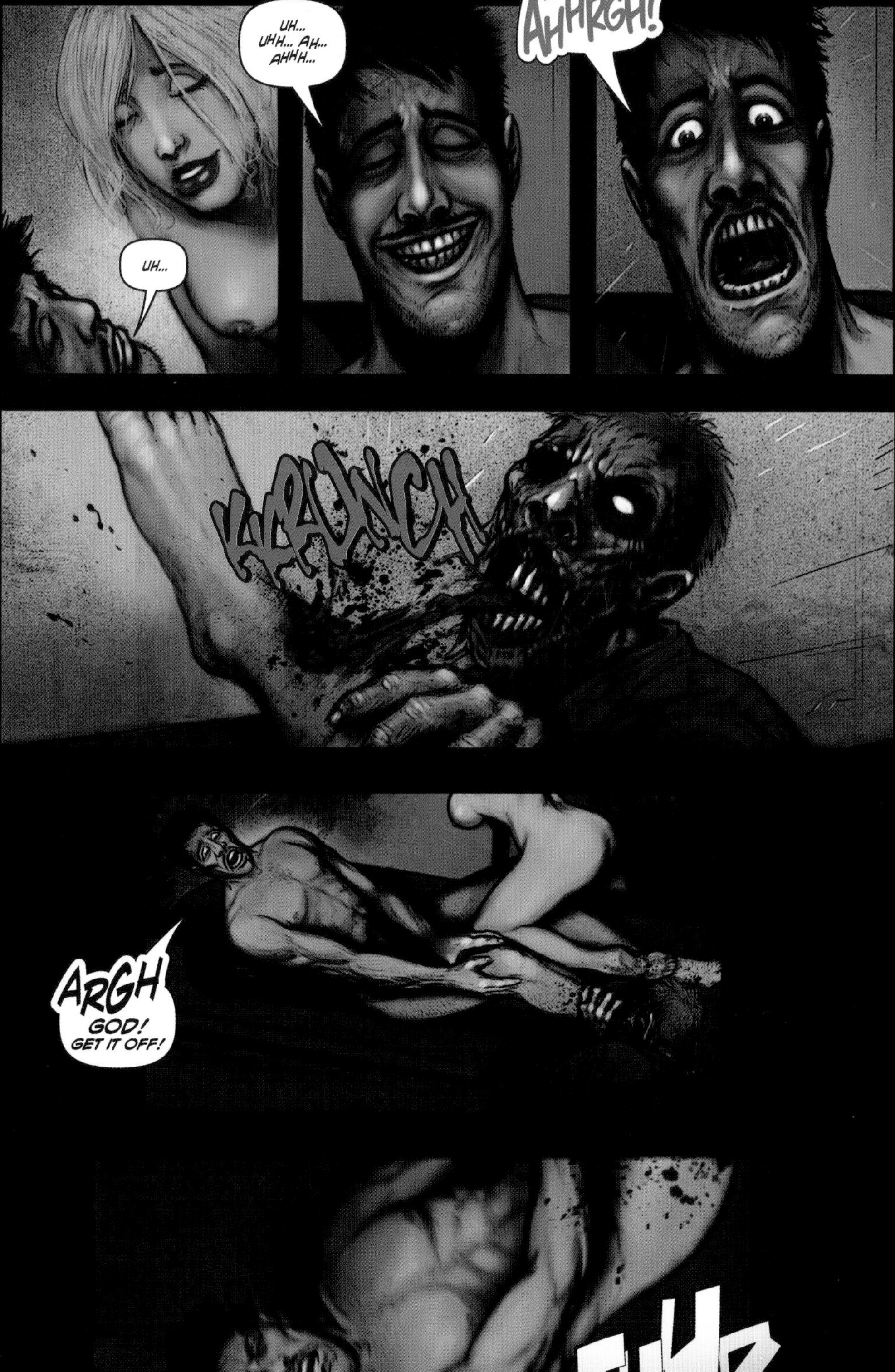
UH...
UH... UHH... AH... AHHH...
AHHRGH!
KRUNCH
ARGH GOD! GET IT OFF!
THUD

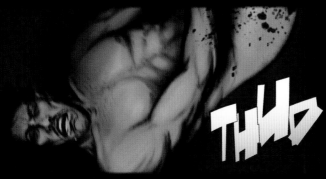

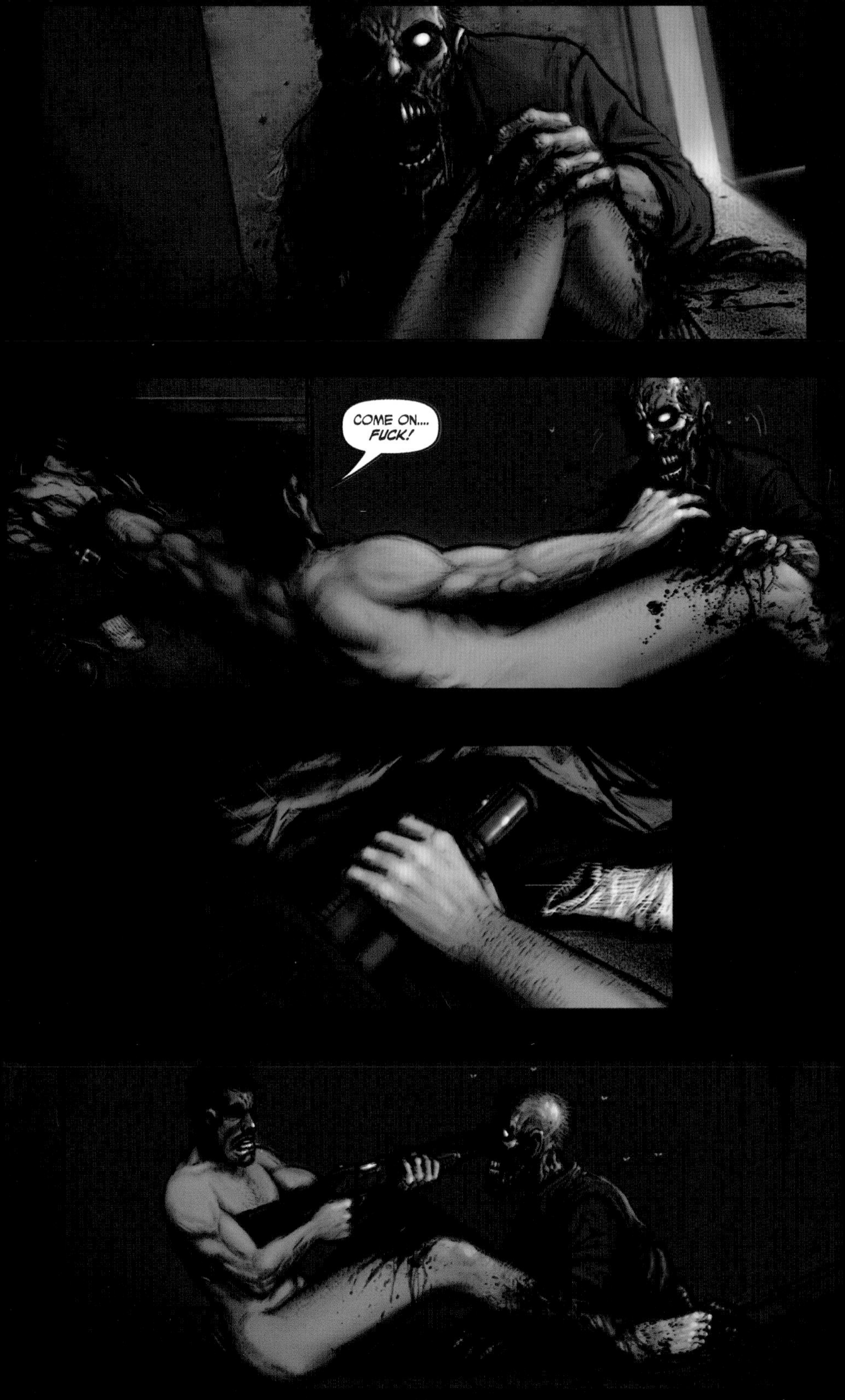
COME ON.... FUCK!

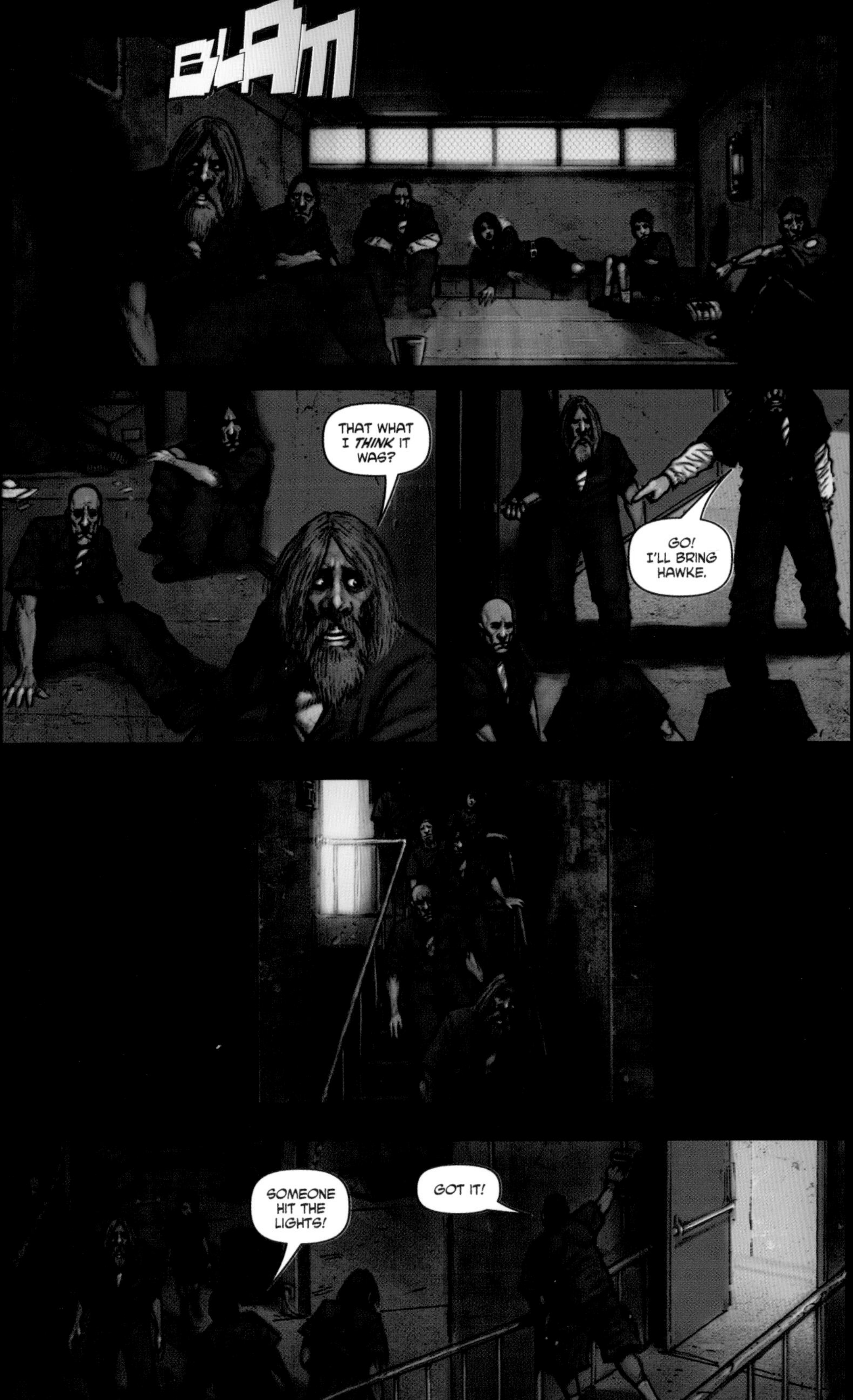
BLAM
THAT WHAT I *THINK* IT WAS?
GO! I'LL BRING HAWKE.
SOMEONE HIT THE LIGHTS!
GOT IT!

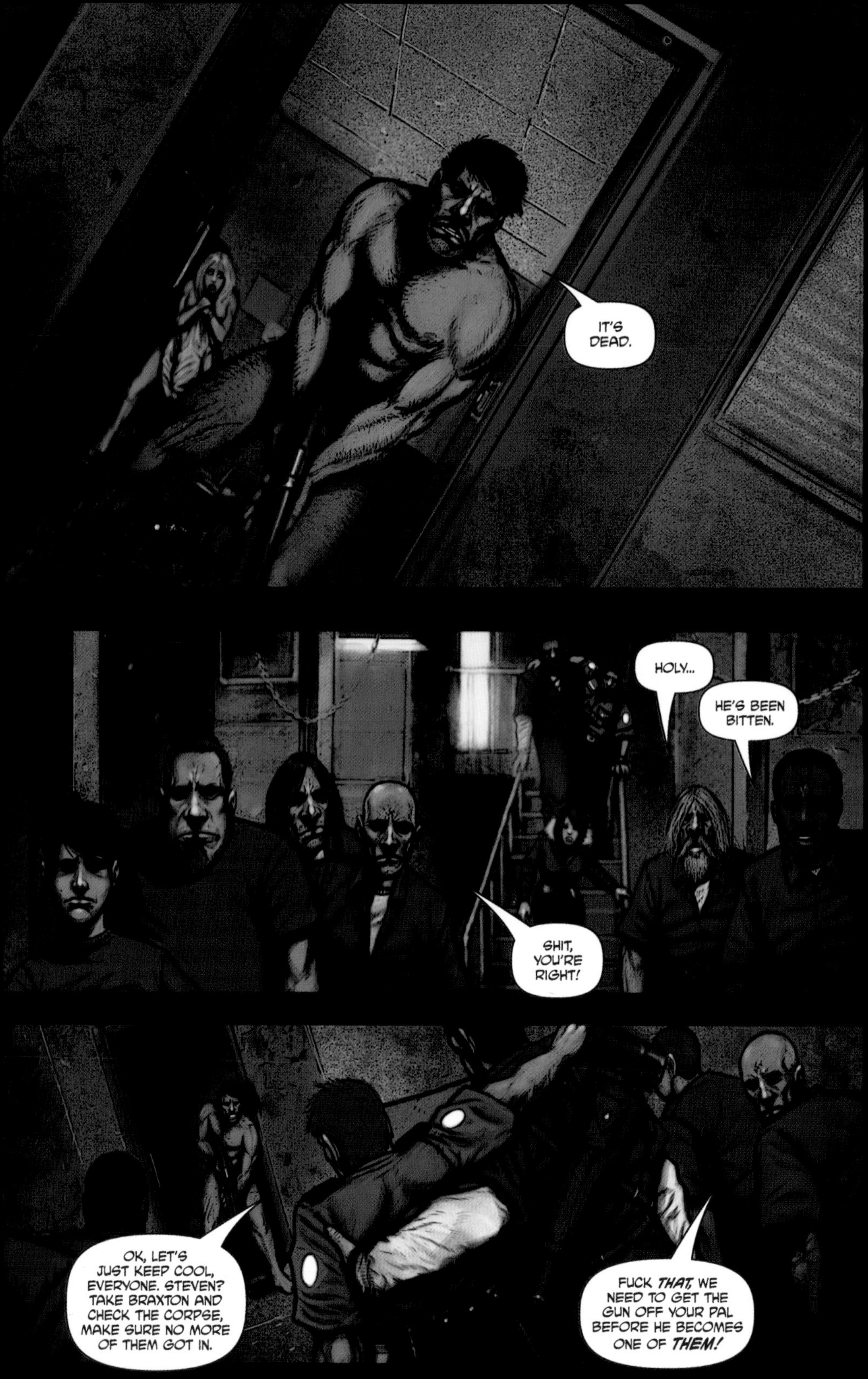
IT'S DEAD.
HOLY...
HE'S BEEN BITTEN.
SHIT, YOU'RE RIGHT!
OK, LET'S JUST KEEP COOL, EVERYONE. STEVEN? TAKE BRAXTON AND CHECK THE CORPSE, MAKE SURE NO MORE OF THEM GOT IN.
FUCK *THAT,* WE NEED TO GET THE GUN OFF YOUR PAL BEFORE HE BECOMES ONE OF ***THEM!***

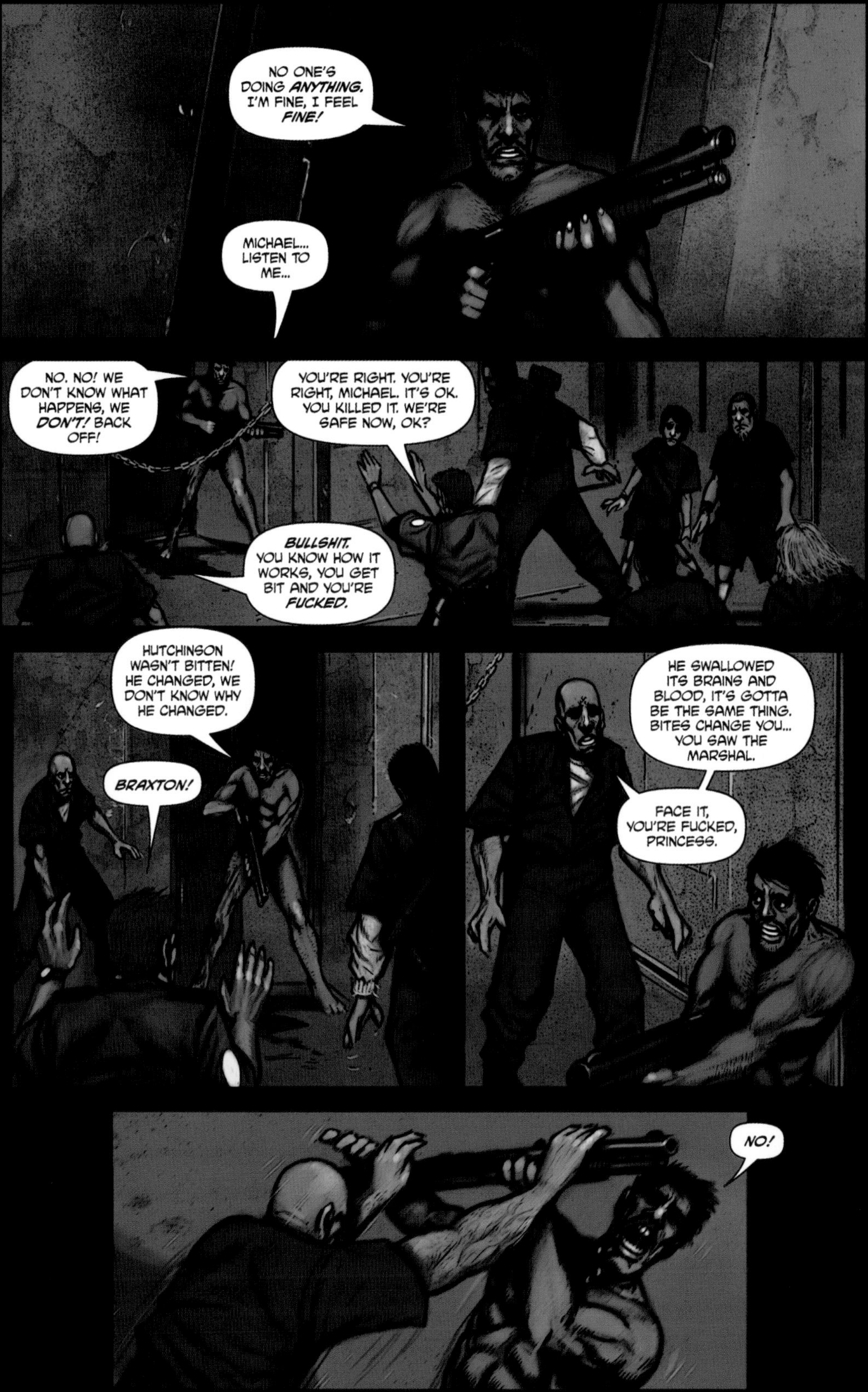
NO ONE'S DOING ANYTHING. I'M FINE, I FEEL FINE!
MICHAEL... LISTEN TO ME...
NO. NO! WE DON'T KNOW WHAT HAPPENS, WE DON'T! BACK OFF!
YOU'RE RIGHT. YOU'RE RIGHT, MICHAEL. IT'S OK. YOU KILLED IT. WE'RE SAFE NOW, OK?
BULLSHIT. YOU KNOW HOW IT WORKS, YOU GET BIT AND YOU'RE FUCKED.
HUTCHINSON WASN'T BITTEN! HE CHANGED, WE DON'T KNOW WHY HE CHANGED.
BRAXTON!
HE SWALLOWED ITS BRAINS AND BLOOD, IT'S GOTTA BE THE SAME THING. BITES CHANGE YOU... YOU SAW THE MARSHAL.
FACE IT, YOU'RE FUCKED, PRINCESS.
NO!

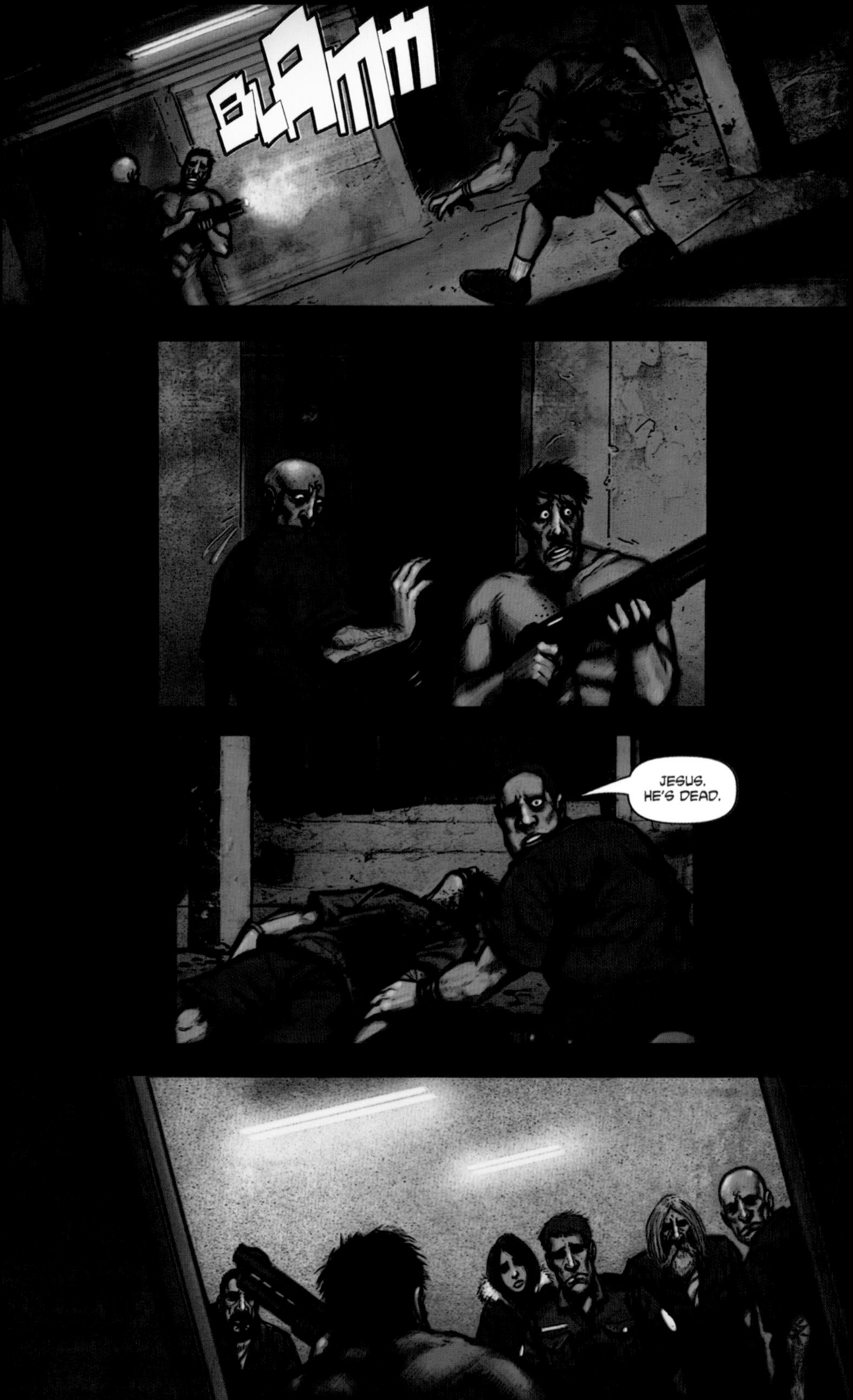
BLAMM
JESUS. HE'S DEAD.

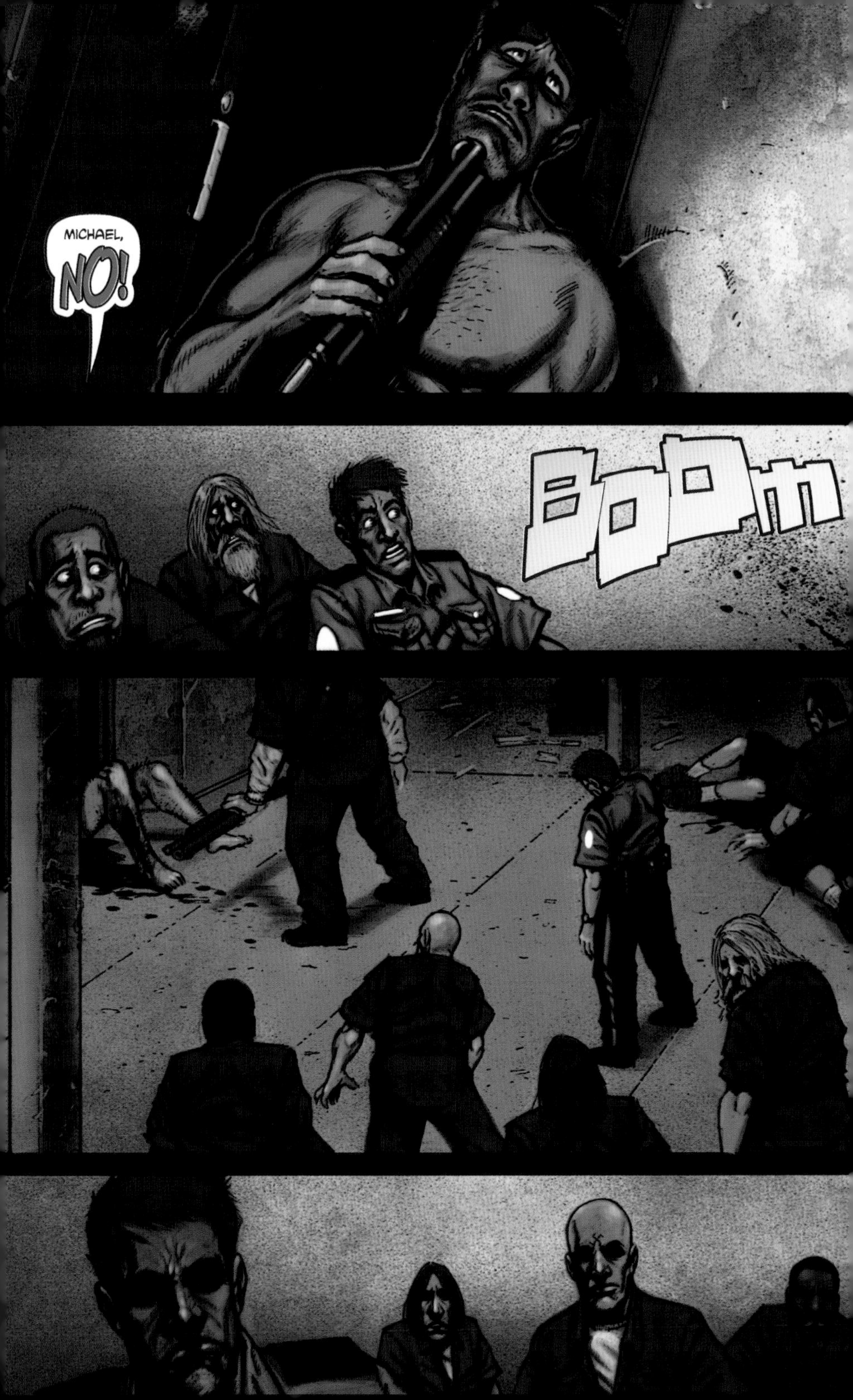
MICHAEL, NO!
BOOM

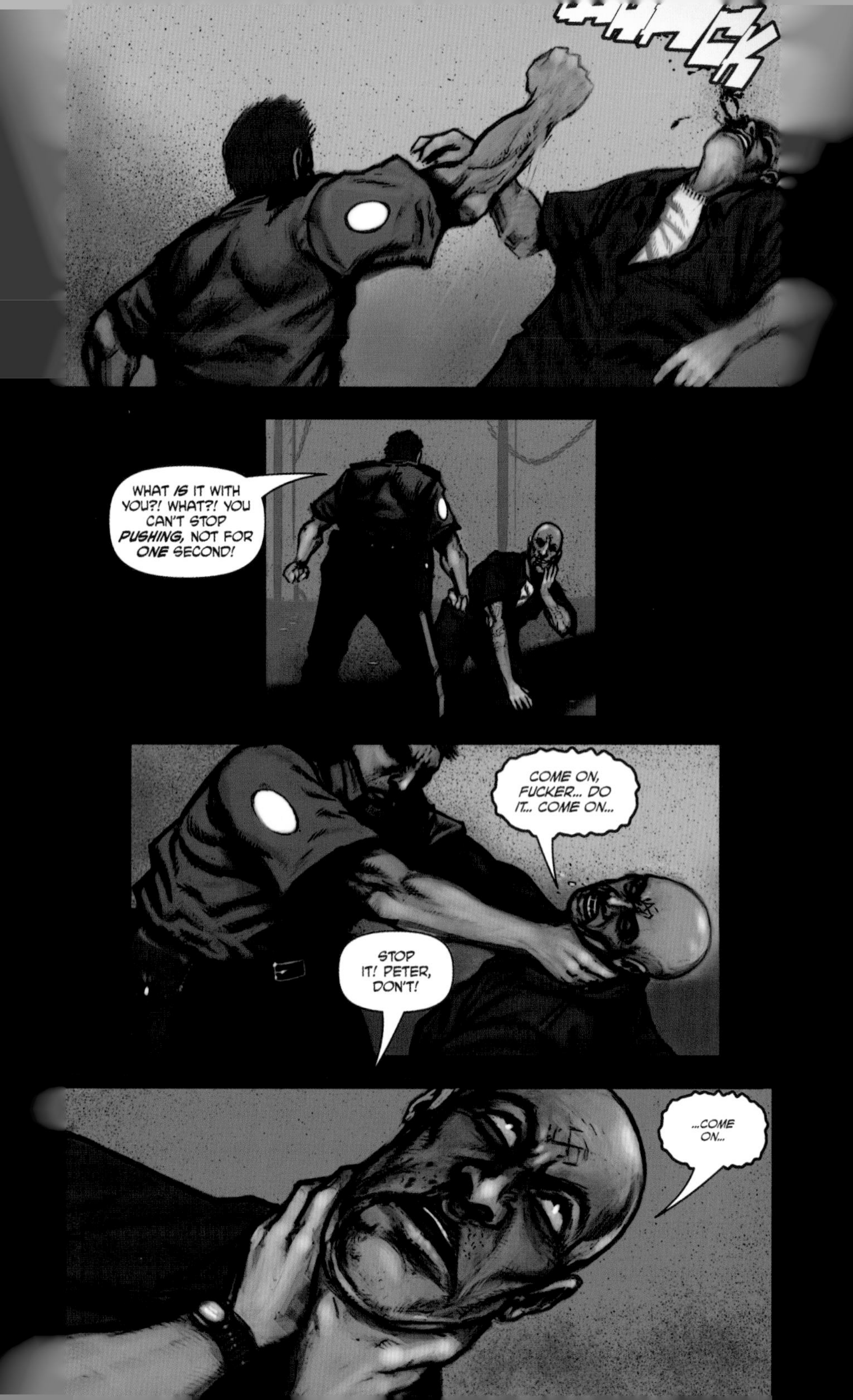
WHAT *IS* IT WITH YOU?! WHAT?! YOU CAN'T STOP *PUSHING,* NOT FOR *ONE* SECOND!
COME ON, FUCKER... DO IT... COME ON...
STOP IT! PETER, DON'T!
...COME ON...

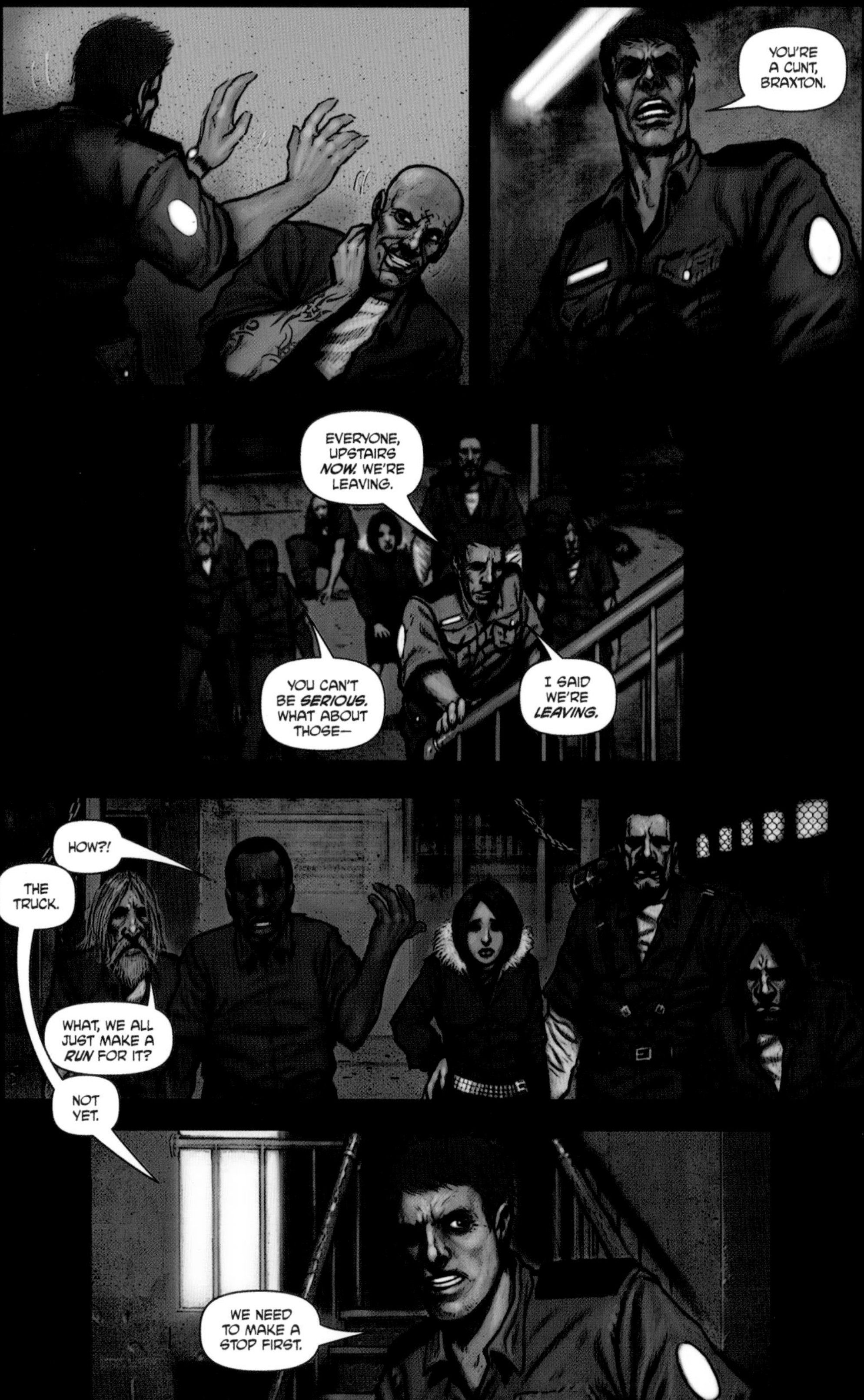
YOU'RE A CUNT, BRAXTON.
EVERYONE, UPSTAIRS NOW. WE'RE LEAVING.
YOU CAN'T BE SERIOUS. WHAT ABOUT THOSE—
I SAID WE'RE LEAVING.
HOW?!
THE TRUCK.
WHAT, WE ALL JUST MAKE A RUN FOR IT?
NOT YET.
WE NEED TO MAKE A STOP FIRST.

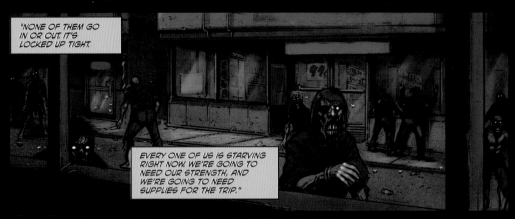

"NONE OF THEM GO IN OR OUT. IT'S LOCKED UP TIGHT.

EVERY ONE OF US IS STARVING RIGHT NOW. WE'RE GOING TO NEED OUR STRENGTH, AND WE'RE GOING TO NEED SUPPLIES FOR THE TRIP."

WHO KNOWS HOW FAR THIS HAS SPREAD?

NO PROBLEM. CLANCY AND I CAN CIRCLE AROUND THE BACK, WE'LL TAKE BRAXTON WITH US.

HE'S TROUBLE.

WE CAN HANDLE HIM. YOU'RE ONLY ONE MAN, YOU'RE WOUNDED AND WEAK— HE'LL USE THAT. HE COMES WITH US.

I'M GRATEFUL, EDWARD. WE *ALL* ARE.

CHANCES LIKE THESE, THEY DON'T COME ALONG ALL THAT OFTEN FOR A MAN LIKE ME.

CHANCES?

YOU AND CLANCY WILL NEED A DISTRACTION.

WAY AHEAD OF YOU.

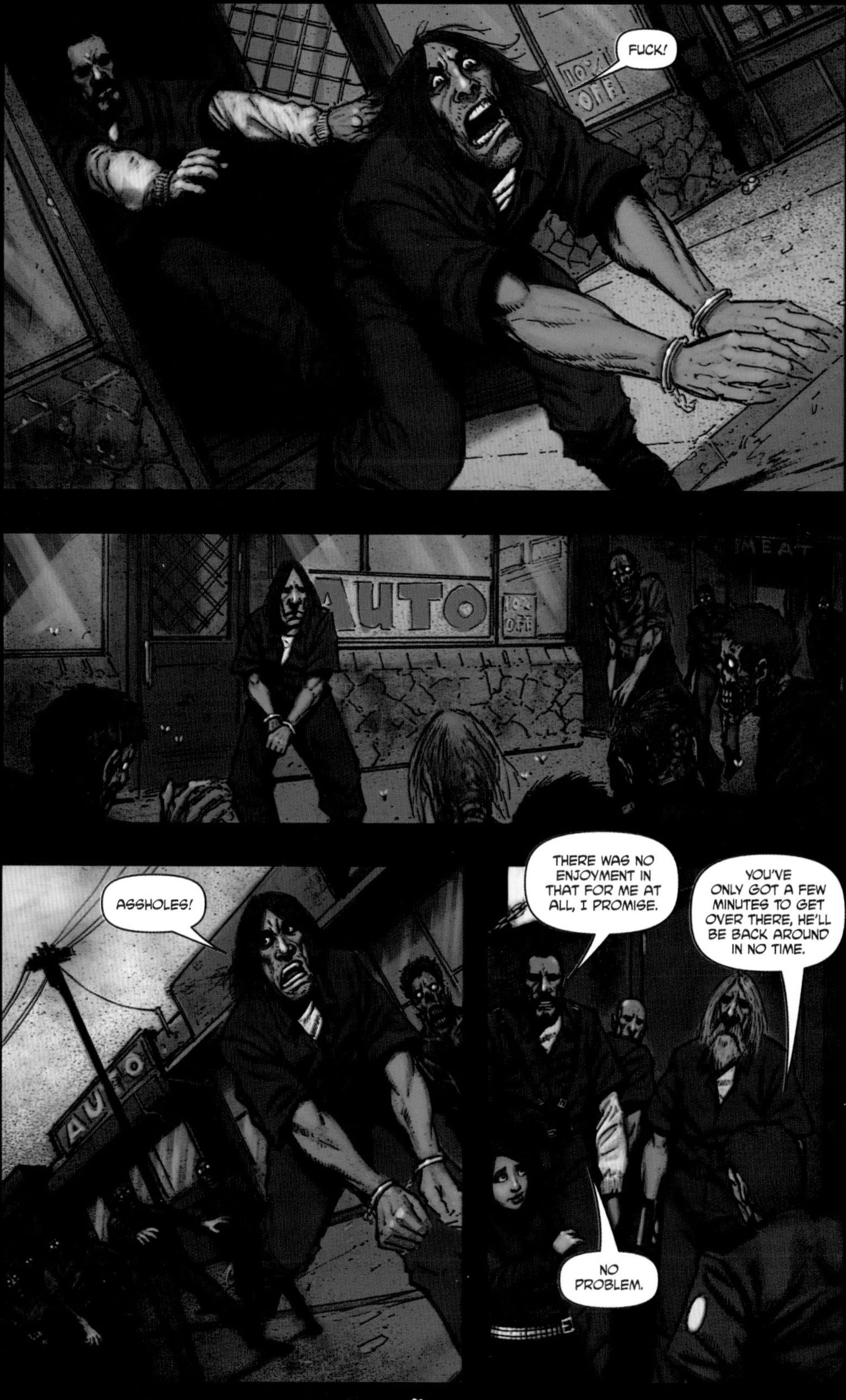
FUCK!
ASSHOLES!
THERE WAS NO ENJOYMENT IN THAT FOR ME AT ALL, I PROMISE.
YOU'VE ONLY GOT A FEW MINUTES TO GET OVER THERE, HE'LL BE BACK AROUND IN NO TIME.
NO PROBLEM.

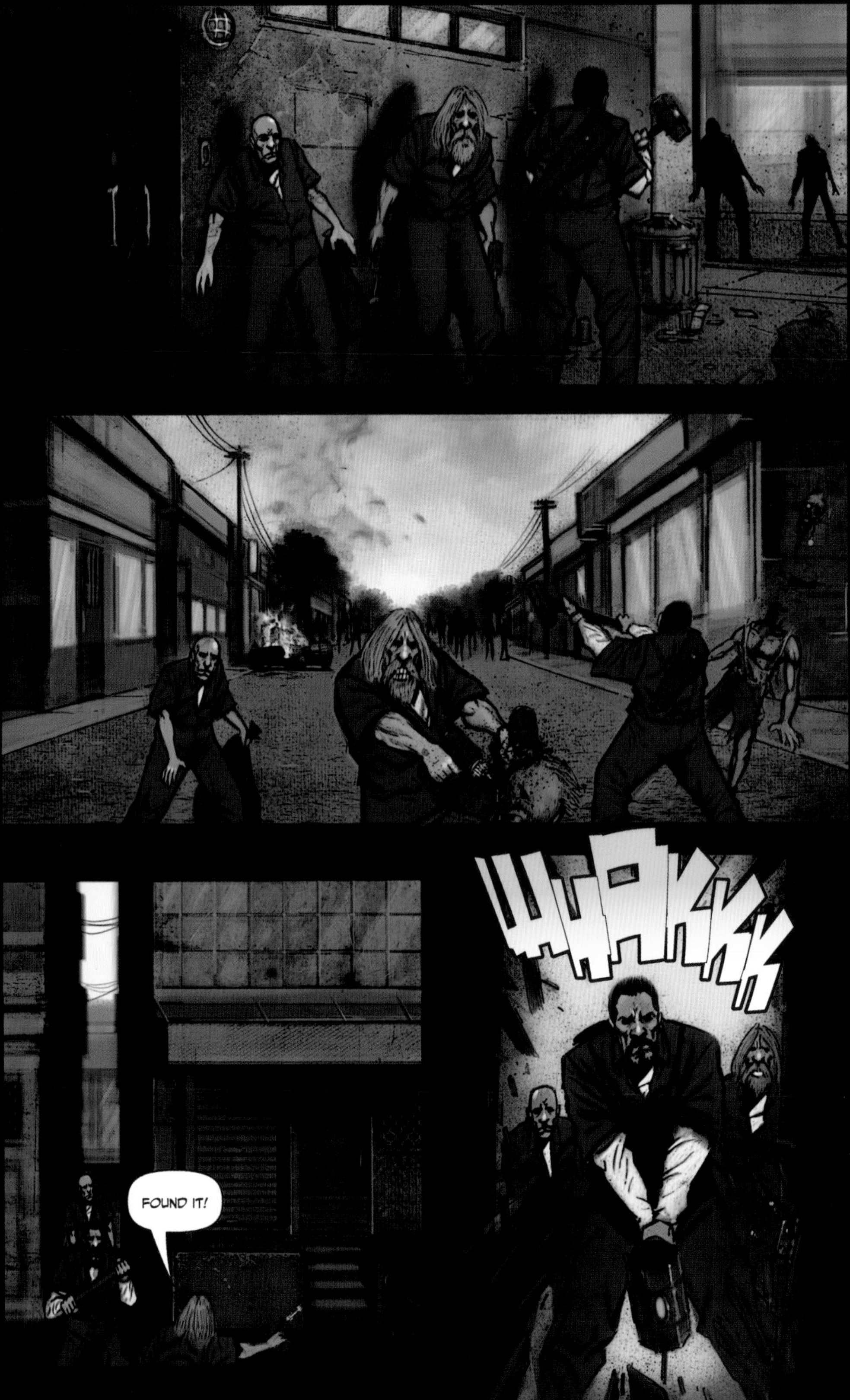
FOUND IT!
WHAKK

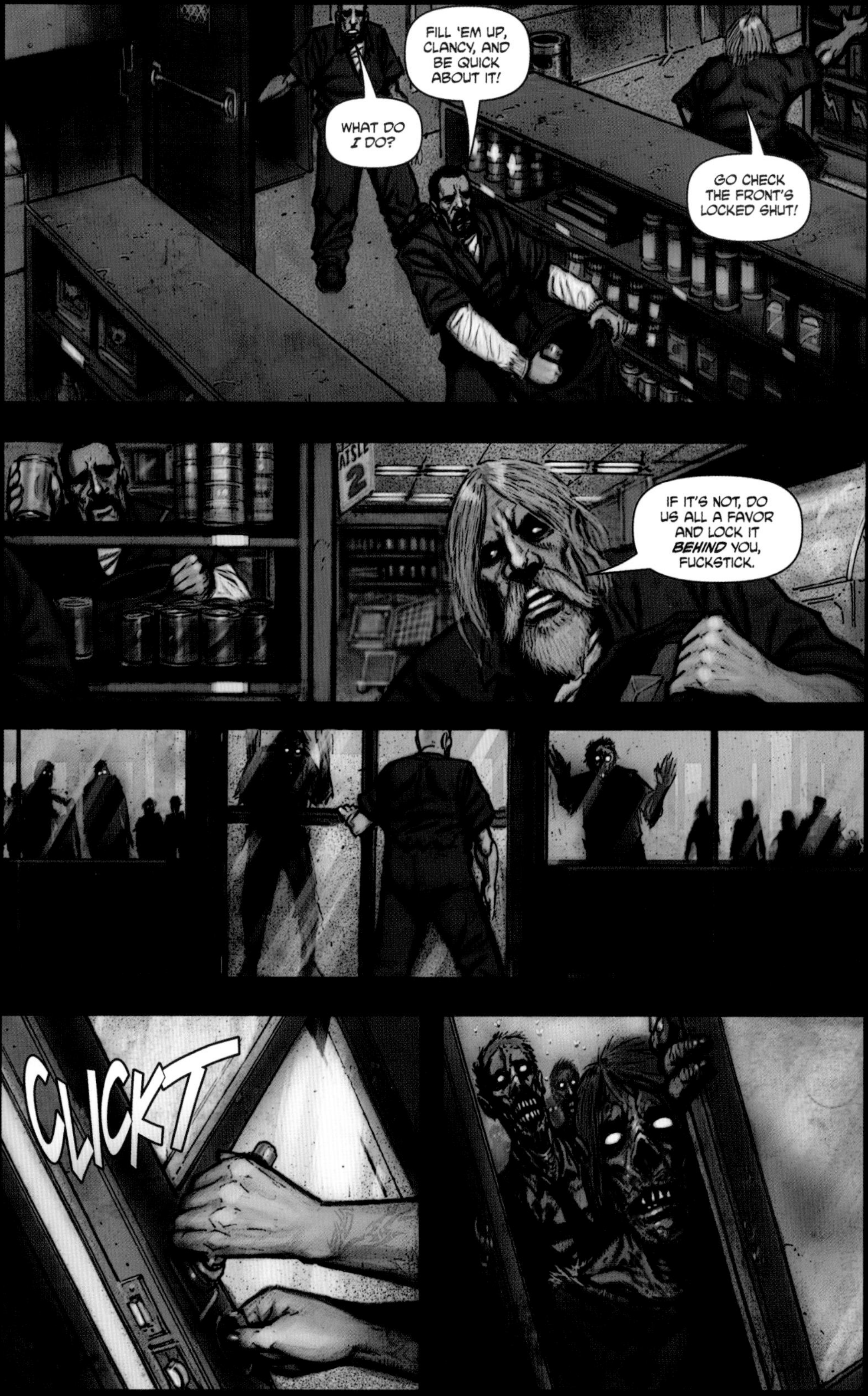
FILL 'EM UP, CLANCY, AND BE QUICK ABOUT IT!
WHAT DO *I* DO?
GO CHECK THE FRONT'S LOCKED SHUT!
IF IT'S NOT, DO US ALL A FAVOR AND LOCK IT *BEHIND* YOU, FUCKSTICK.
AISLE 2
CLICKT

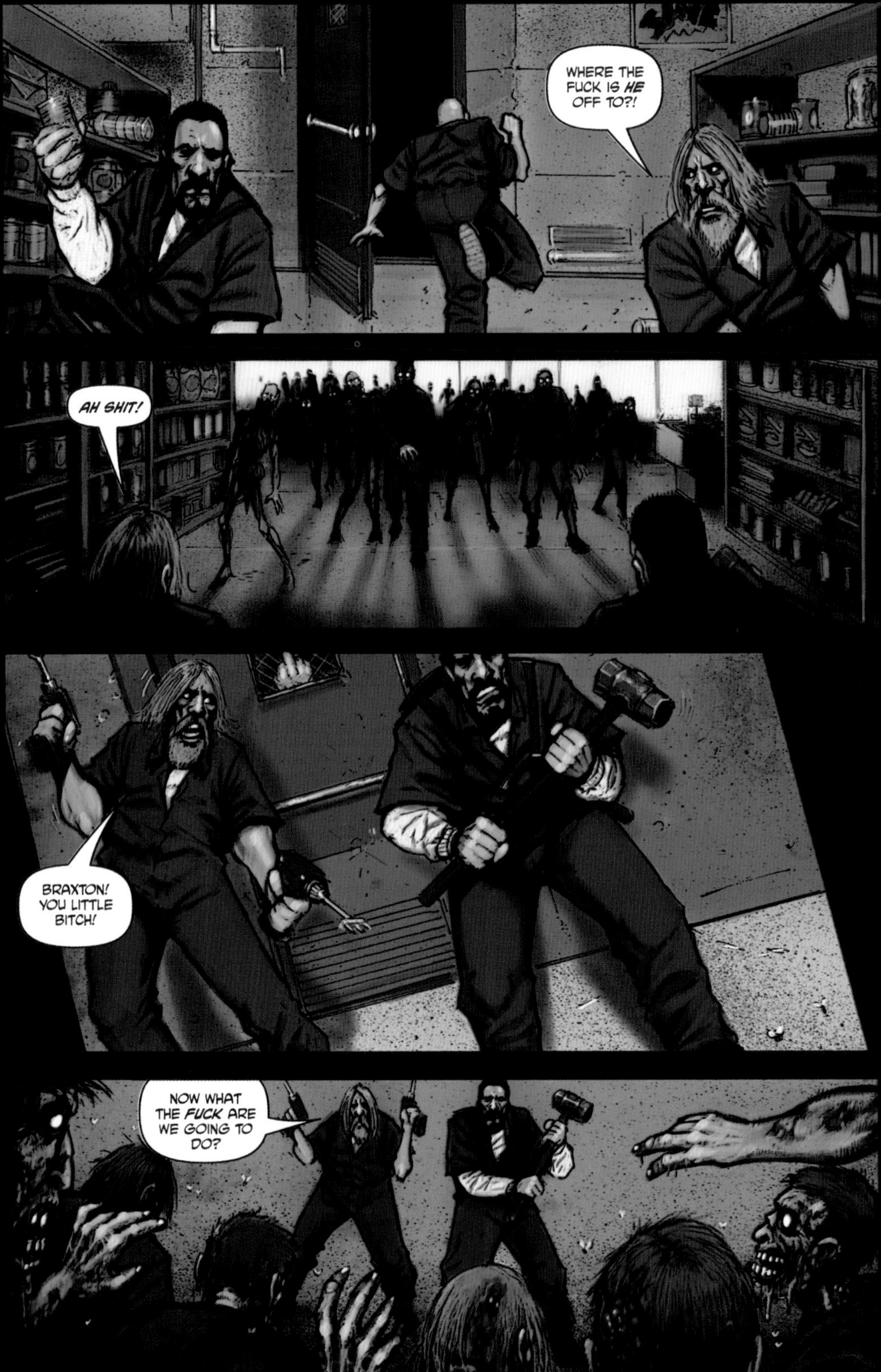
WHERE THE FUCK IS HE OFF TO?!
AH SHIT!
BRAXTON! YOU LITTLE BITCH!
NOW WHAT THE FUCK ARE WE GOING TO DO?

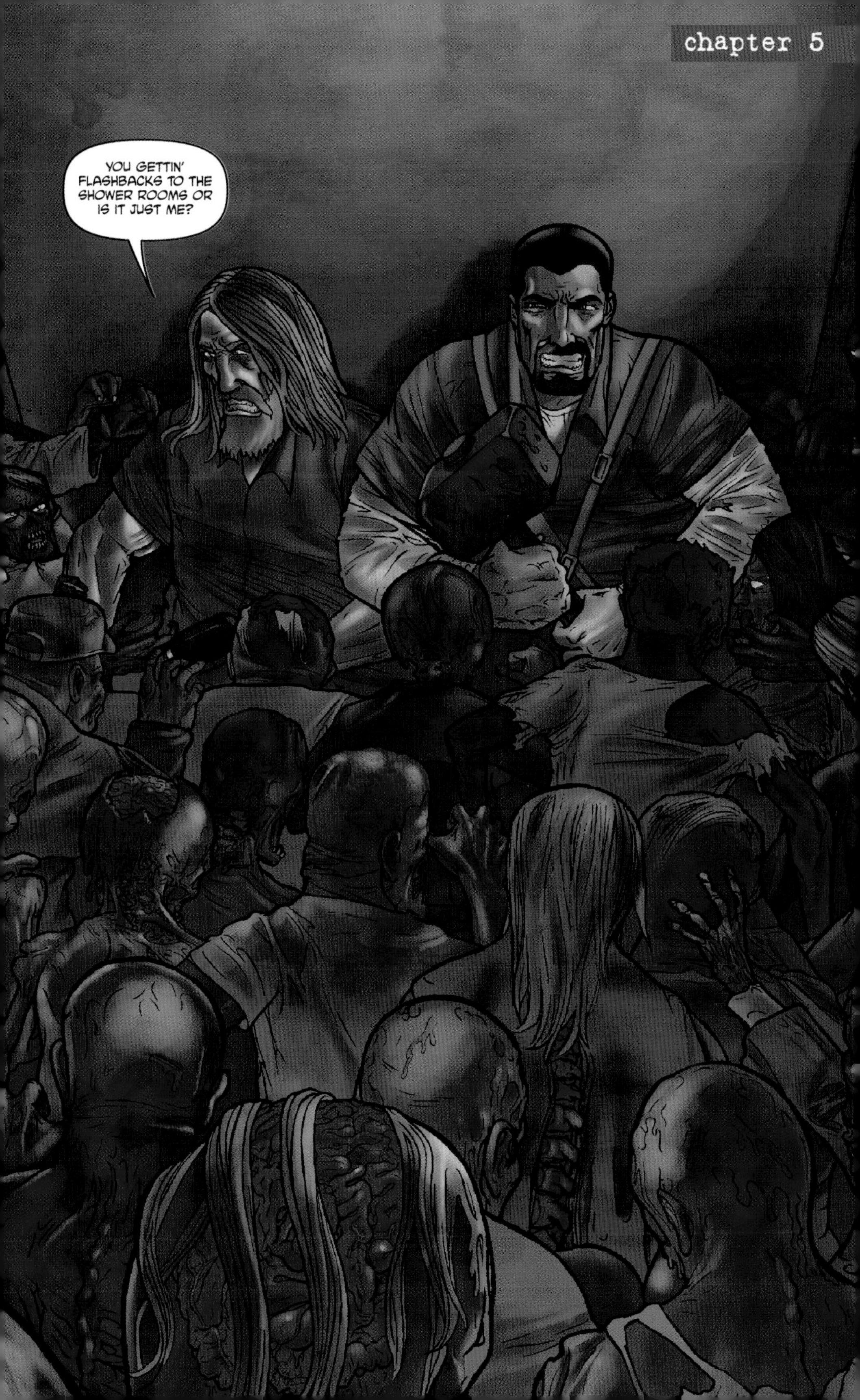
YOU GETTIN' FLASHBACKS TO THE SHOWER ROOMS OR IS IT JUST ME?

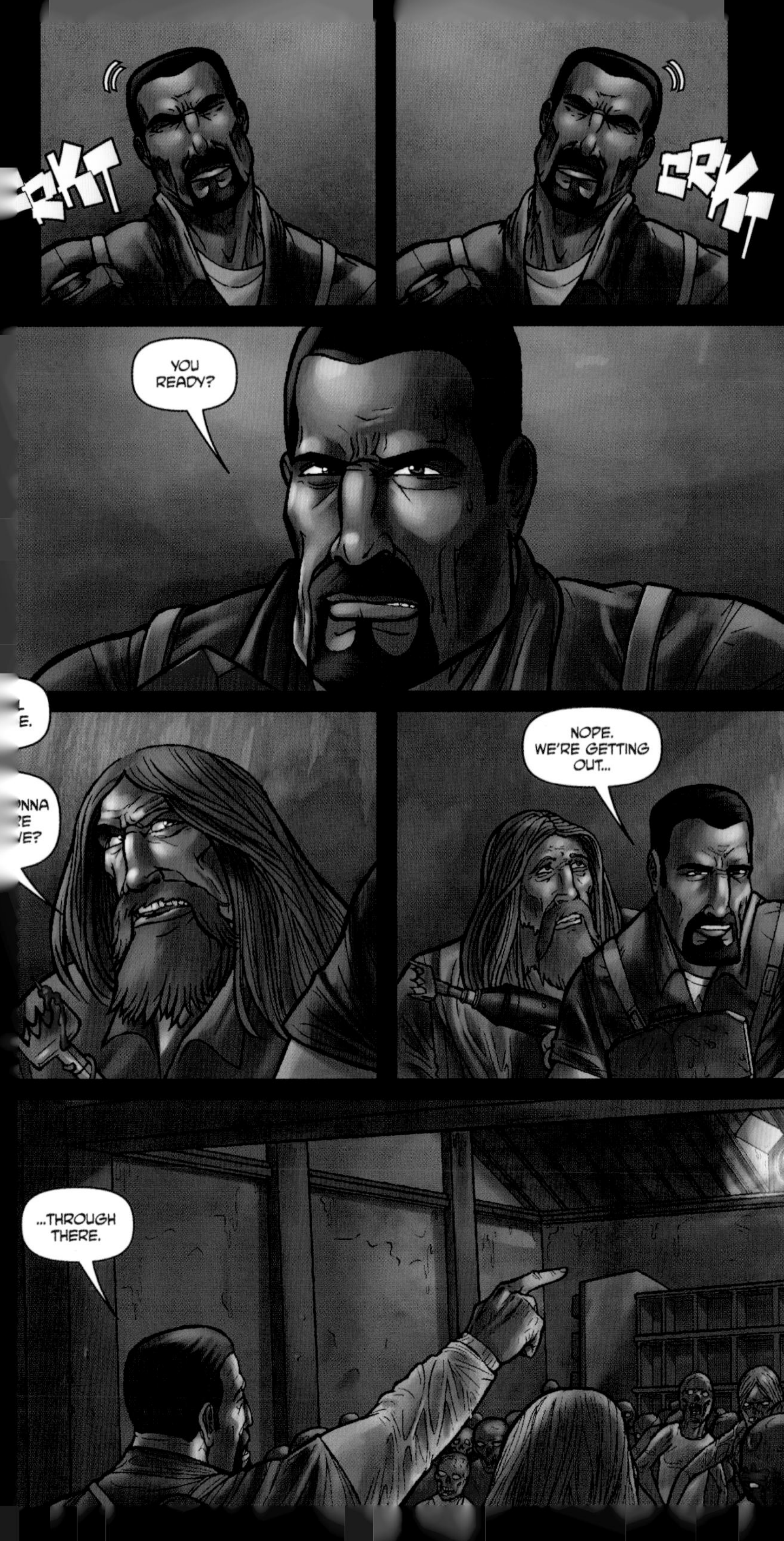
RKT
CRKT
YOU READY?
NOPE. WE'RE GETTING OUT...
...THROUGH THERE.

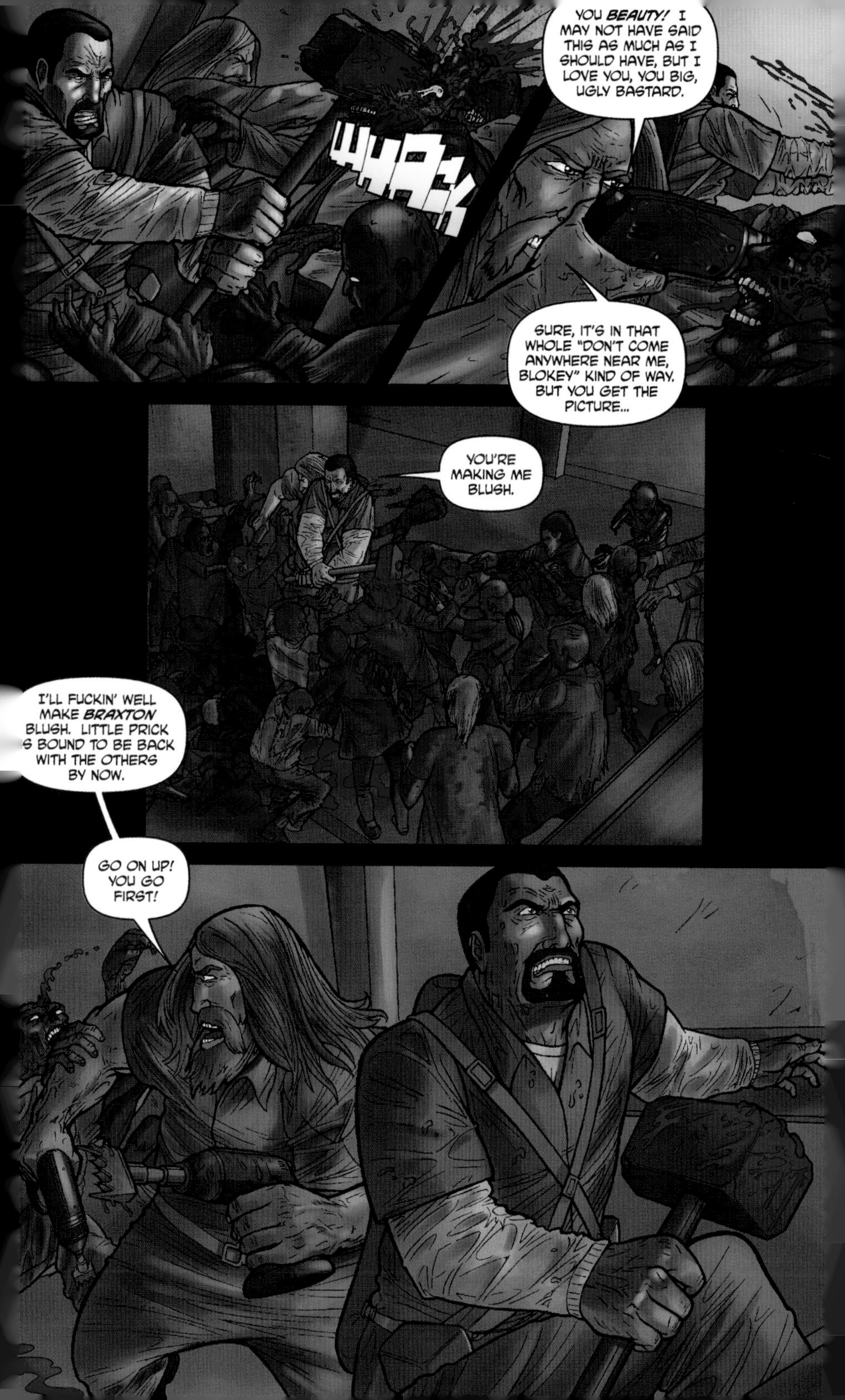
WHACK
YOU BEAUTY! I MAY NOT HAVE SAID THIS AS MUCH AS I SHOULD HAVE, BUT I LOVE YOU, YOU BIG, UGLY BASTARD.
SURE, IT'S IN THAT WHOLE "DON'T COME ANYWHERE NEAR ME, BLOKEY" KIND OF WAY. BUT YOU GET THE PICTURE...
YOU'RE MAKING ME BLUSH.
I'LL FUCKIN' WELL MAKE BRAXTON BLUSH. LITTLE PRICK S BOUND TO BE BACK WITH THE OTHERS BY NOW.
GO ON UP! YOU GO FIRST!

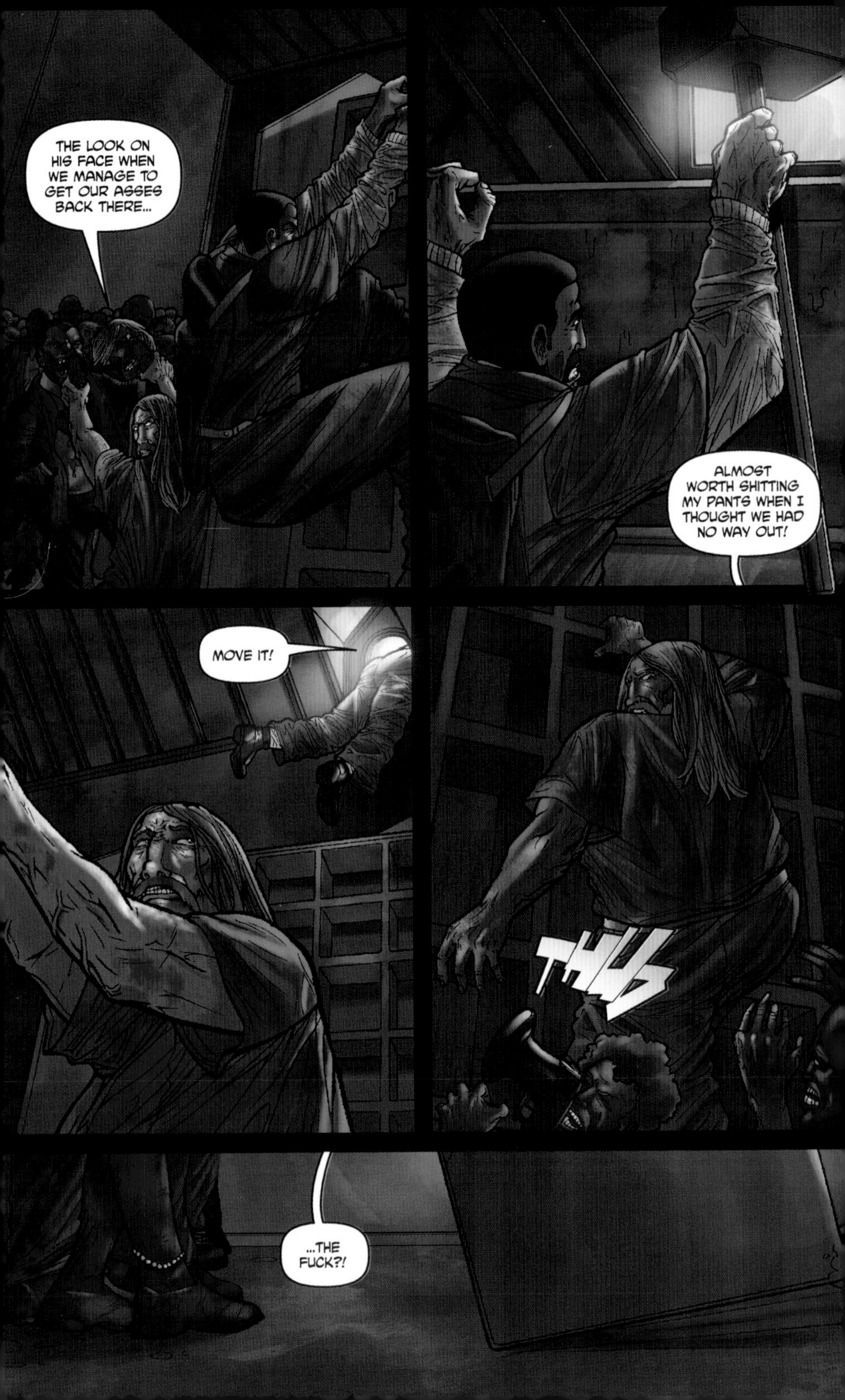
THE LOOK ON HIS FACE WHEN WE MANAGE TO GET OUR ASSES BACK THERE...
ALMOST WORTH SHITTING MY PANTS WHEN I THOUGHT WE HAD NO WAY OUT!
MOVE IT!
THUD
...THE FUCK?!

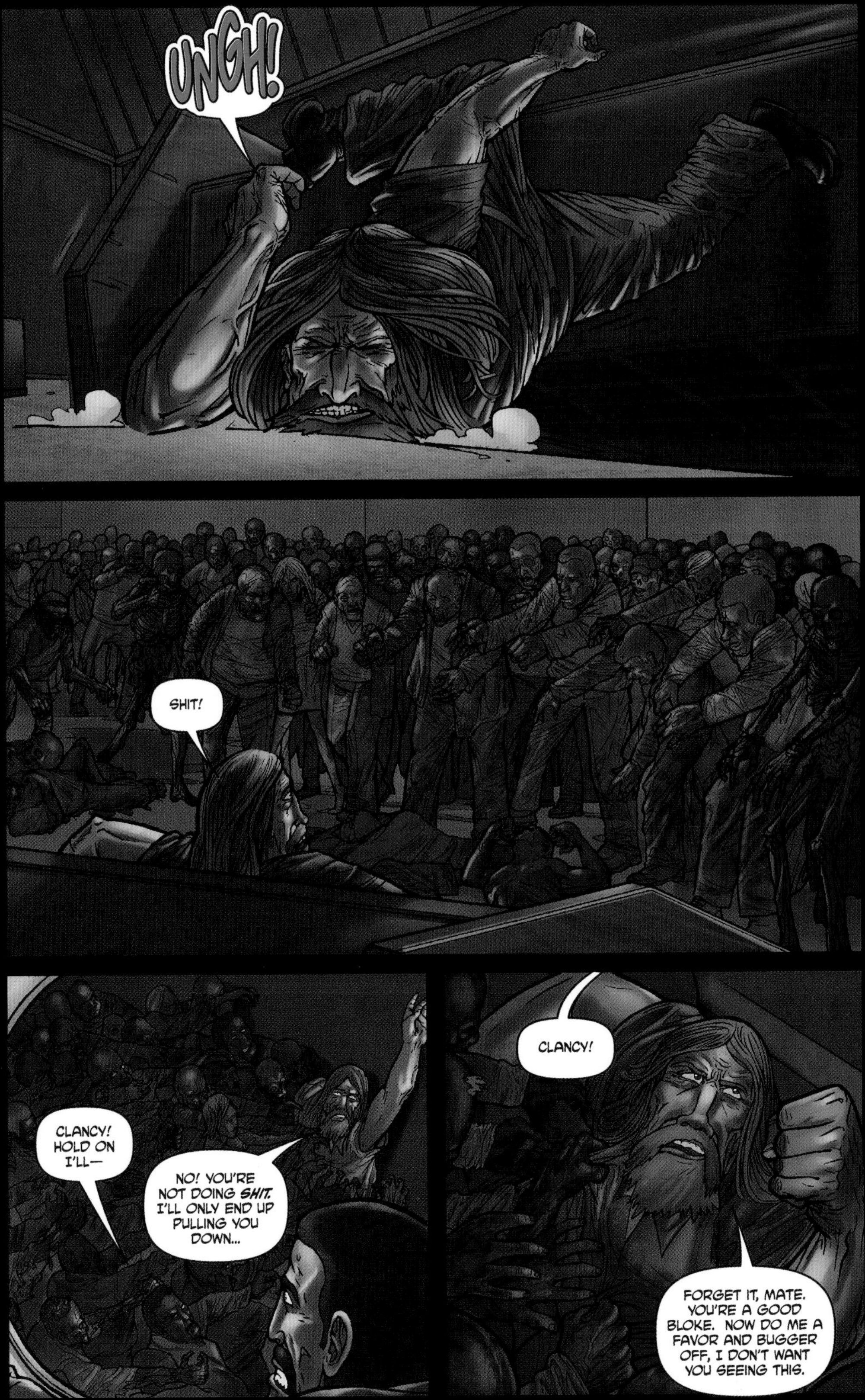
UNGH!
SHIT!
CLANCY! HOLD ON I'LL—
NO! YOU'RE NOT DOING *SHIT.* I'LL ONLY END UP PULLING YOU DOWN...
CLANCY!
FORGET IT, MATE. YOU'RE A GOOD BLOKE. NOW DO ME A FAVOR AND BUGGER OFF, I DON'T WANT YOU SEEING THIS.

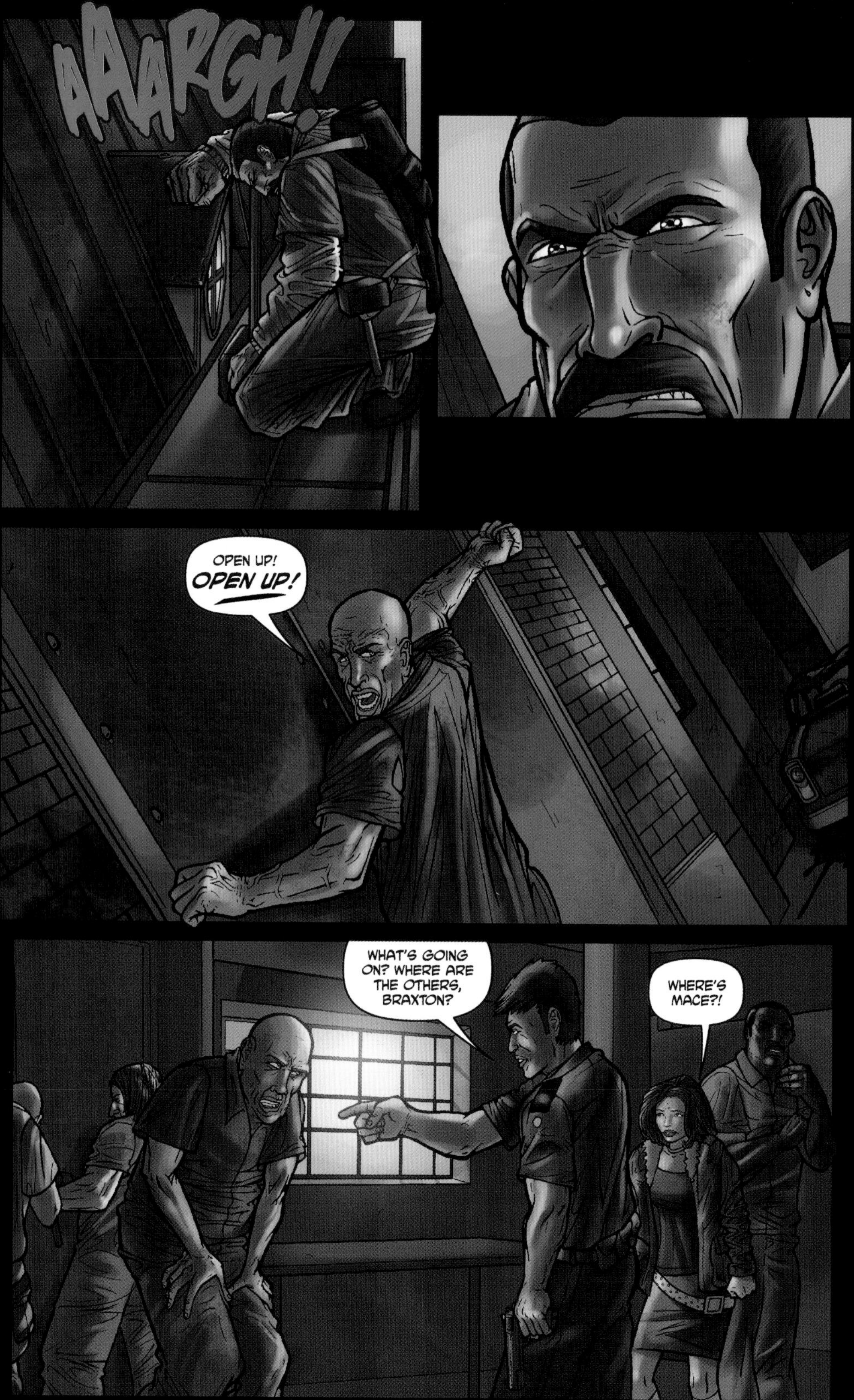
AAARGH!
OPEN UP! OPEN UP!
WHAT'S GOING ON? WHERE ARE THE OTHERS, BRAXTON?
WHERE'S MACE?!

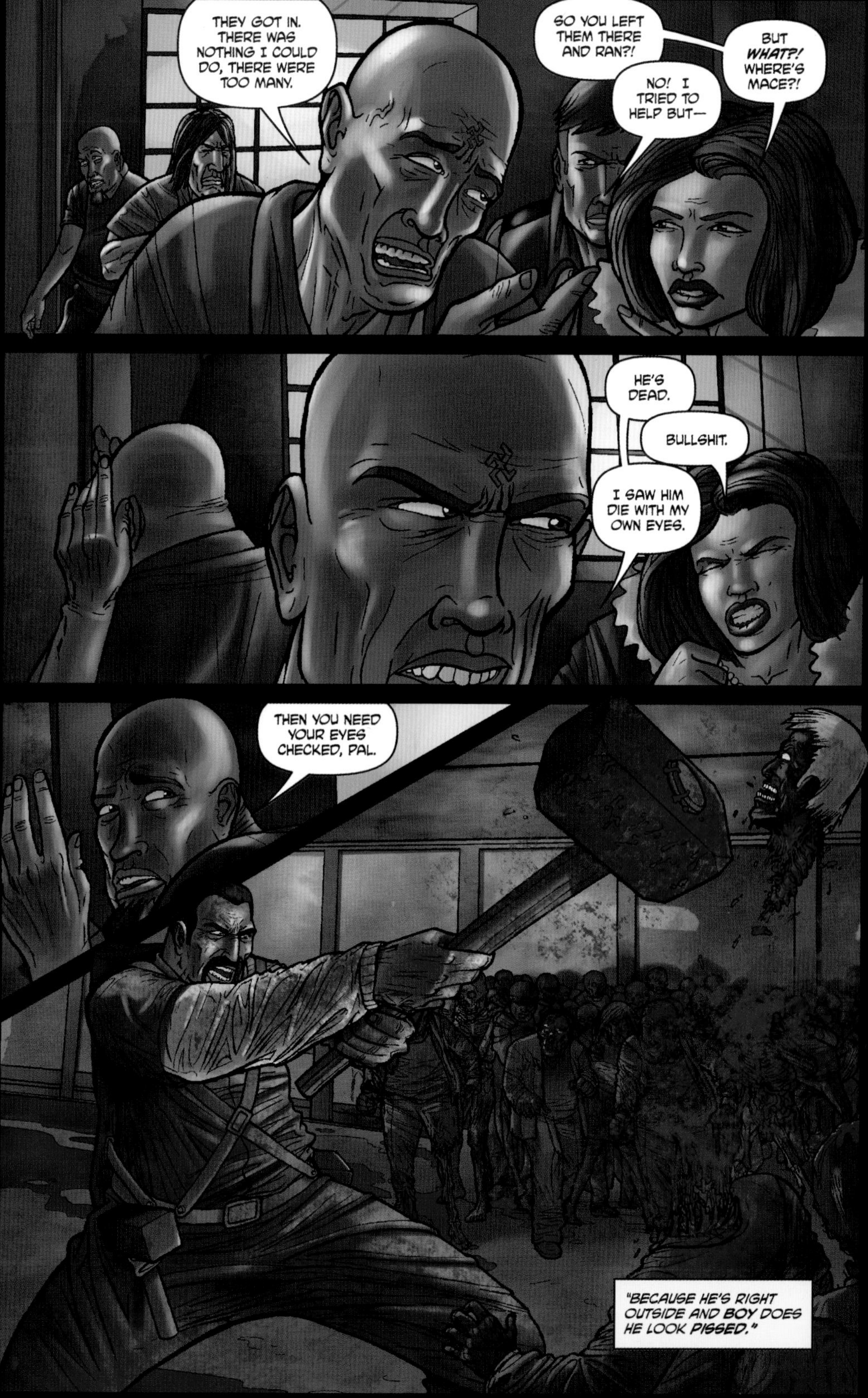
THEY GOT IN. THERE WAS NOTHING I COULD DO, THERE WERE TOO MANY.
SO YOU LEFT THEM THERE AND RAN?!
NO! I TRIED TO HELP BUT—
BUT *WHAT?!* WHERE'S MACE?!
HE'S DEAD.
BULLSHIT.
I SAW HIM DIE WITH MY OWN EYES.
THEN YOU NEED YOUR EYES CHECKED, PAL.
"BECAUSE HE'S RIGHT OUTSIDE AND **BOY** DOES HE LOOK ***PISSED.***"

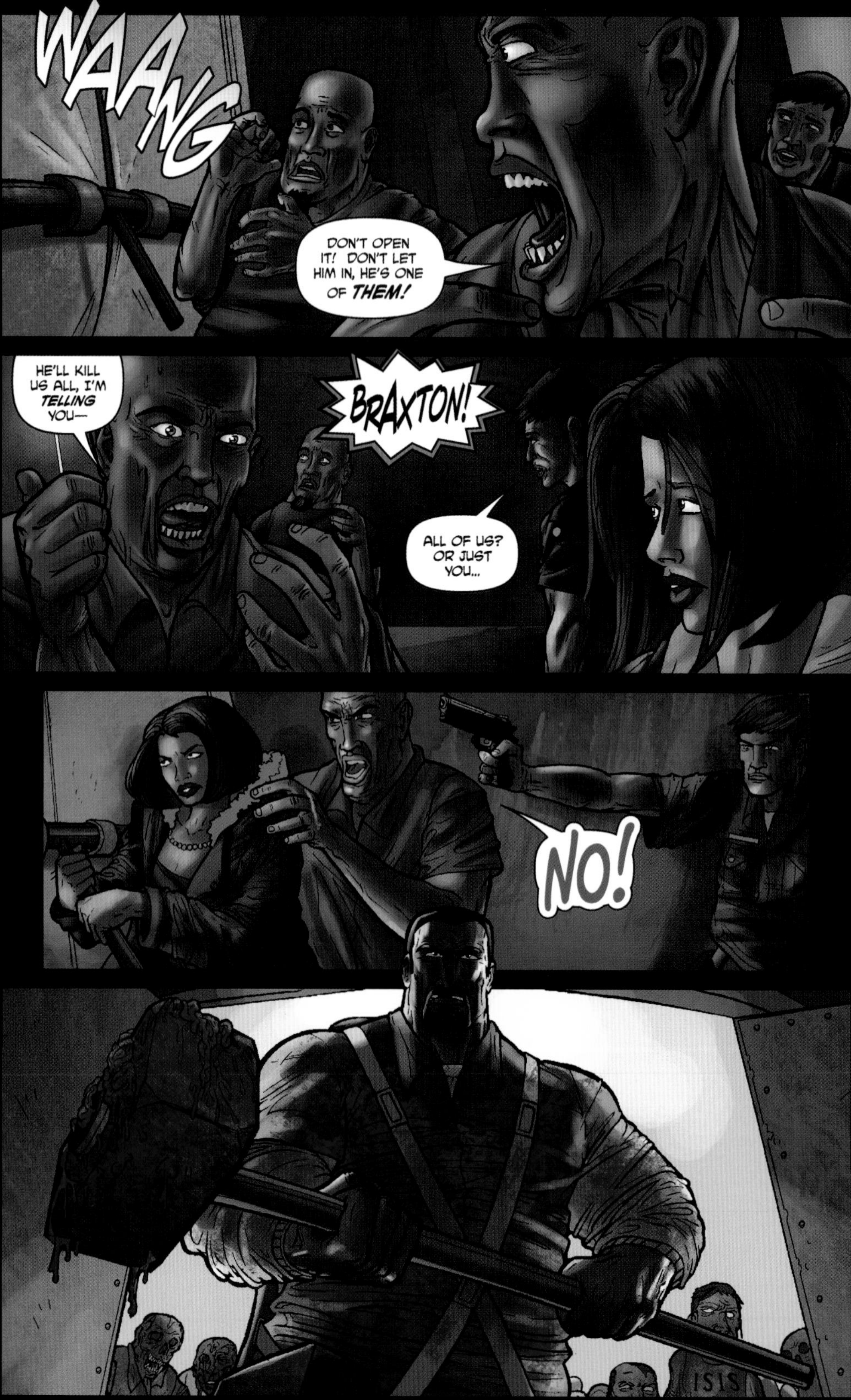
WAANG
DON'T OPEN IT! DON'T LET HIM IN, HE'S ONE OF THEM!
HE'LL KILL US ALL, I'M TELLING YOU—
BRAXTON!
ALL OF US? OR JUST YOU...
NO!
ISIS

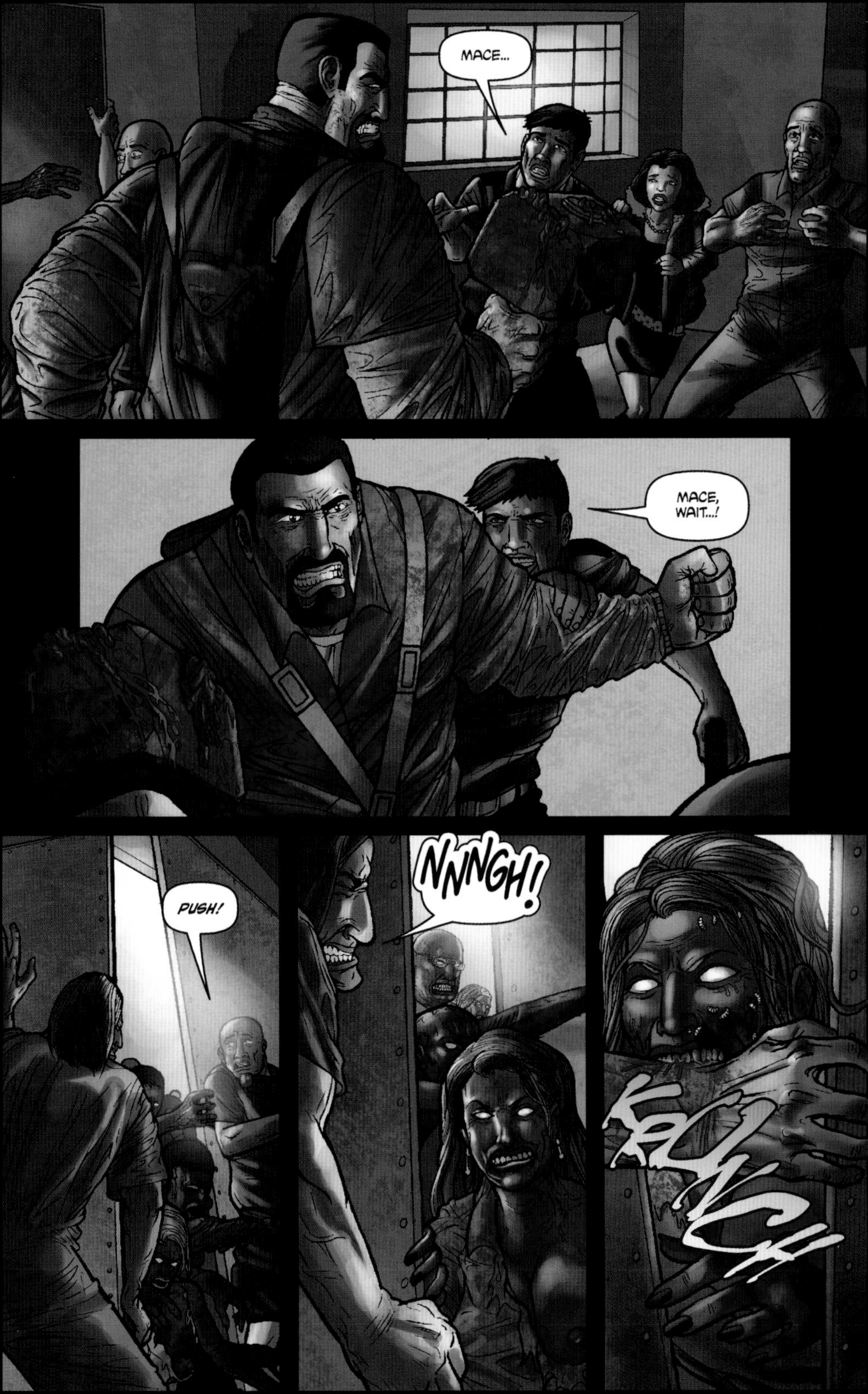
MACE...
MACE, WAIT...!
PUSH!
NNNGH!

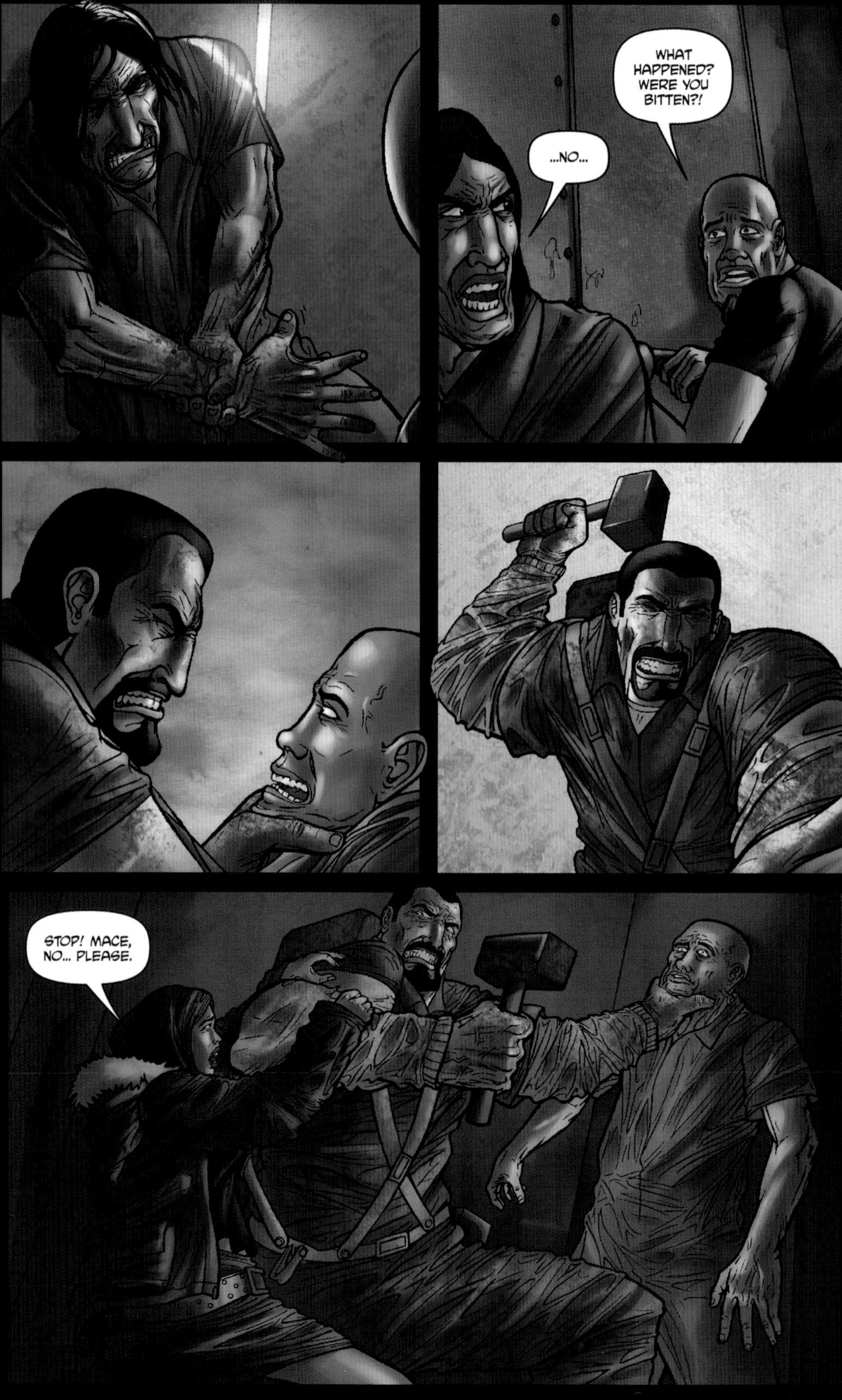
WHAT HAPPENED? WERE YOU BITTEN?!
...NO...
STOP! MACE, NO... PLEASE.

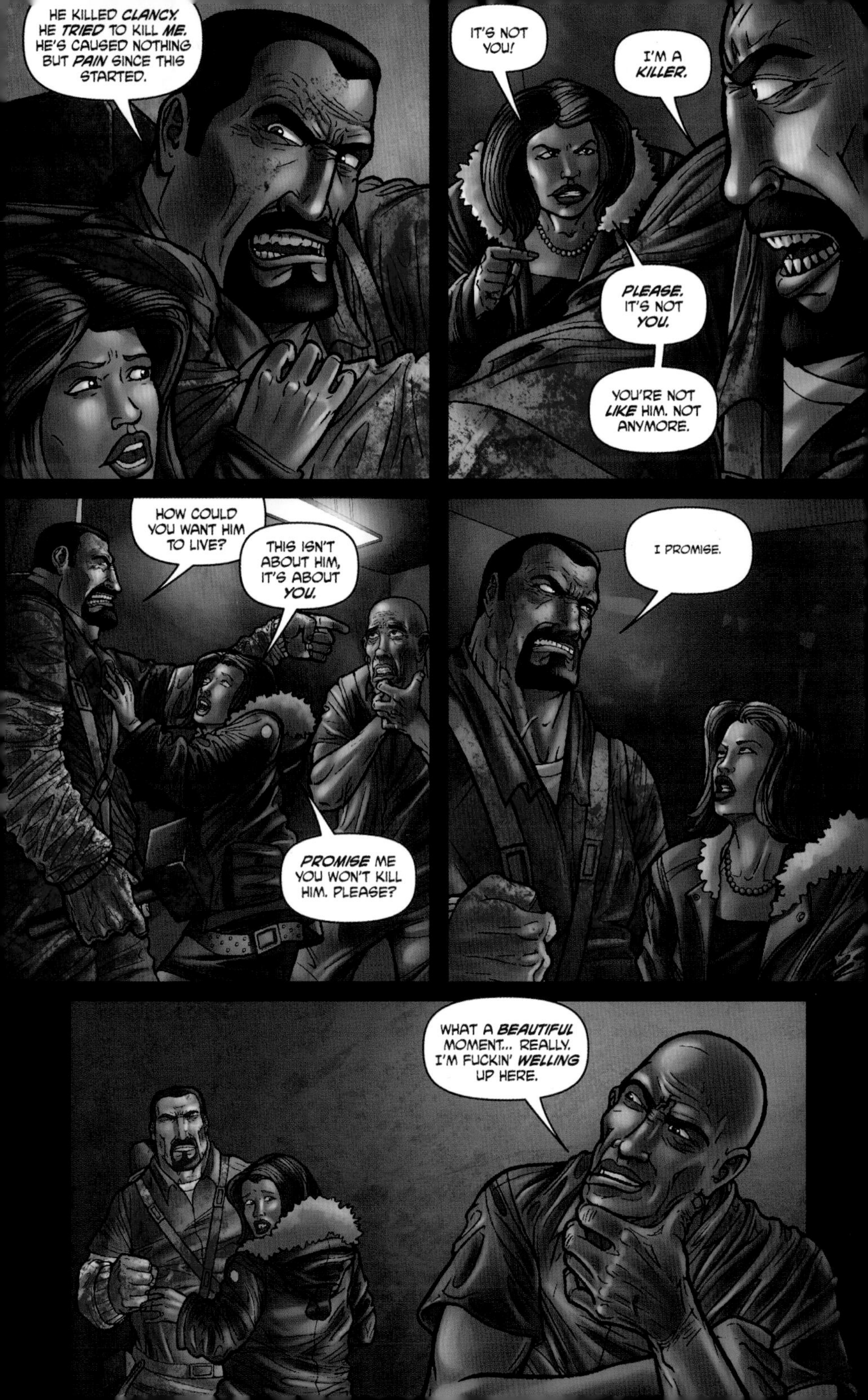

HE KILLED CLANCY. HE TRIED TO KILL ME. HE'S CAUSED NOTHING BUT PAIN SINCE THIS STARTED.
IT'S NOT YOU!
I'M A KILLER.
PLEASE. IT'S NOT YOU.
YOU'RE NOT LIKE HIM. NOT ANYMORE.
HOW COULD YOU WANT HIM TO LIVE?
THIS ISN'T ABOUT HIM, IT'S ABOUT YOU.
PROMISE ME YOU WON'T KILL HIM. PLEASE?
I PROMISE.
WHAT A BEAUTIFUL MOMENT... REALLY. I'M FUCKIN' WELLING UP HERE.

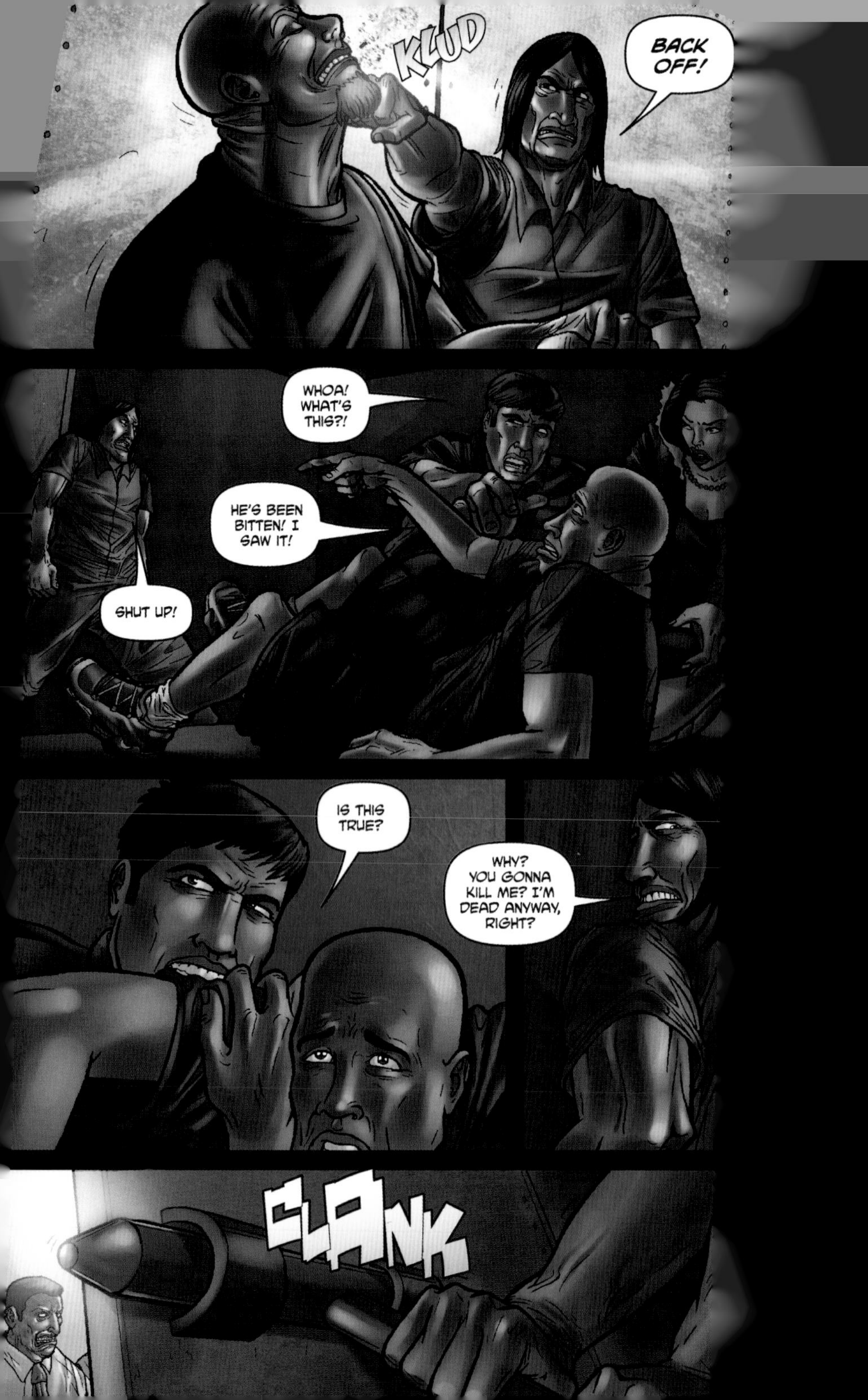
KLUD
BACK OFF!
WHOA! WHAT'S THIS?!
HE'S BEEN BITTEN! I SAW IT!
SHUT UP!
IS THIS TRUE?
WHY? YOU GONNA KILL ME? I'M DEAD ANYWAY, RIGHT?
CLANK

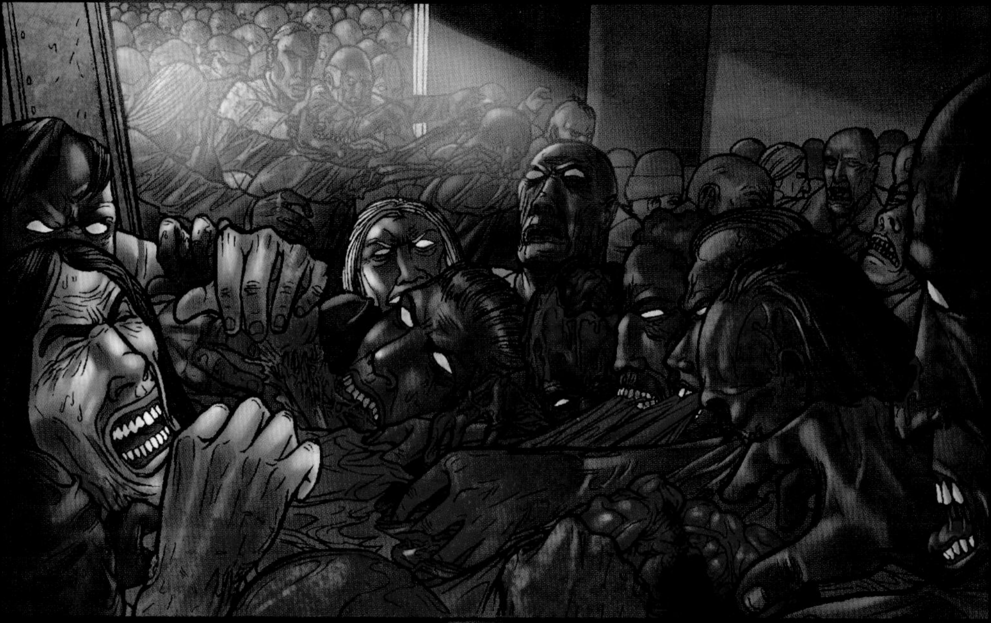

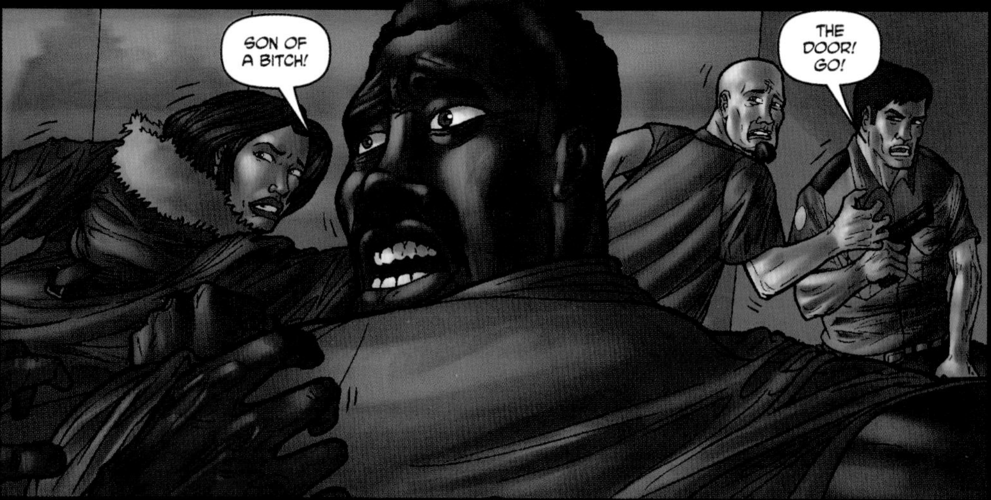
SON OF A BITCH!
THE DOOR! GO!

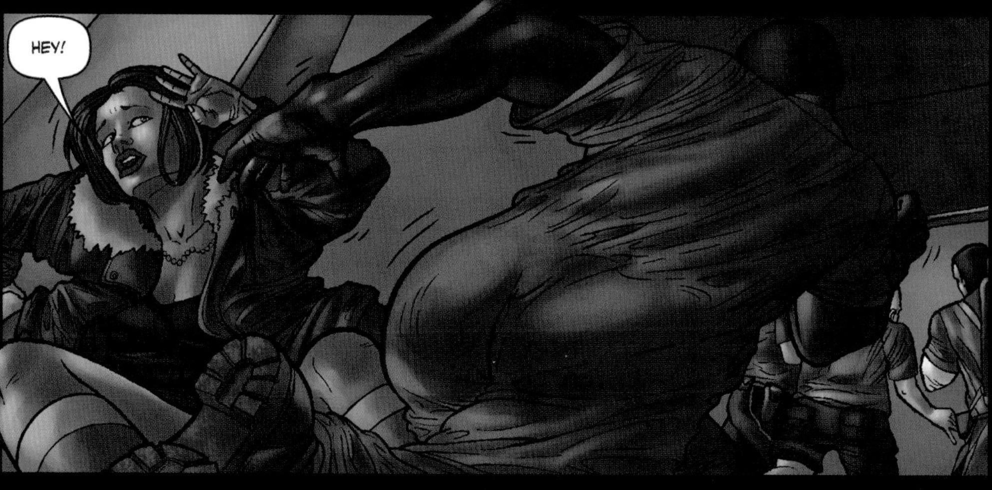
HEY!

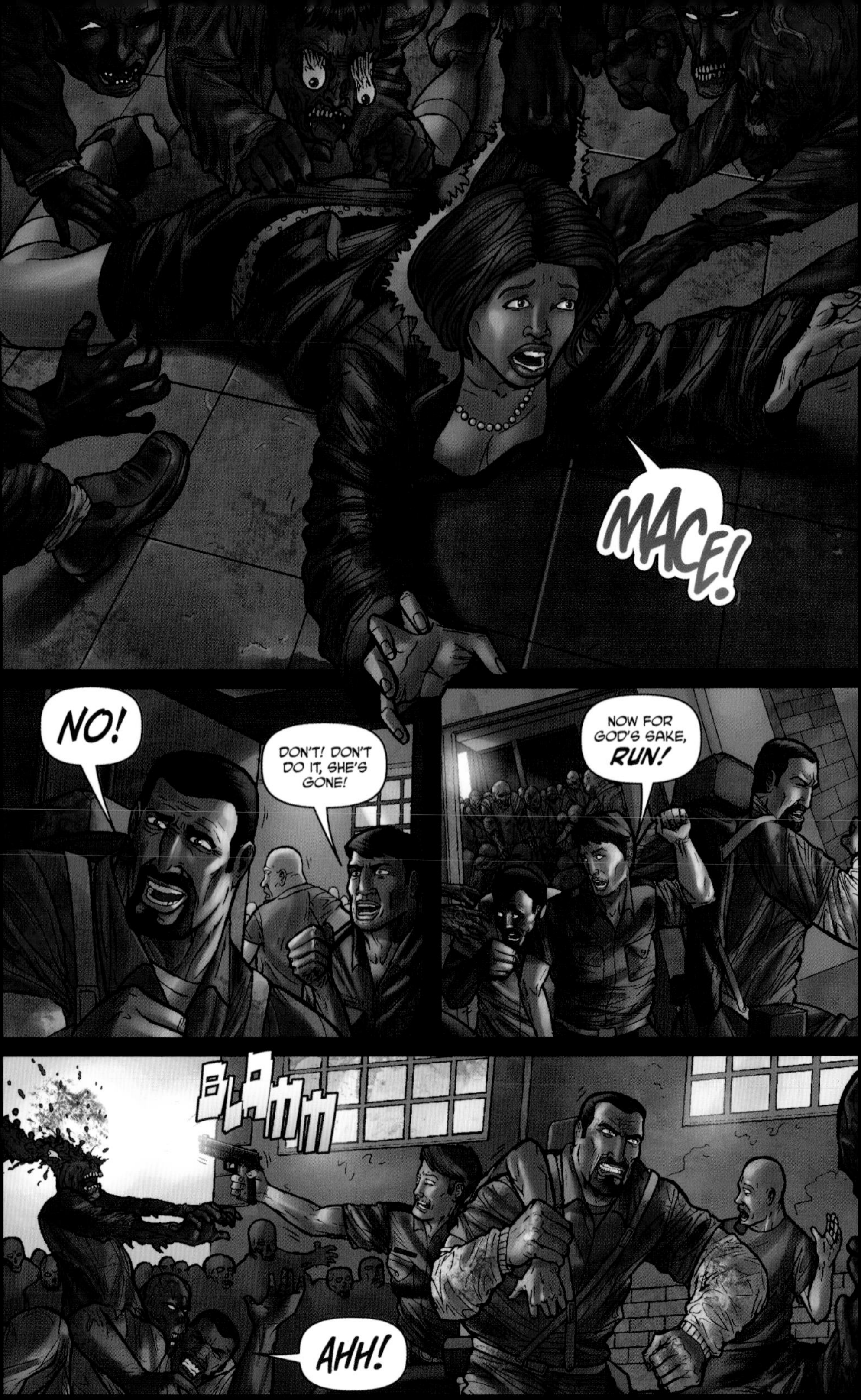
MACE!
NO!
DON'T! DON'T DO IT, SHE'S GONE!
NOW FOR GOD'S SAKE, RUN!
BLAMM
AHH!

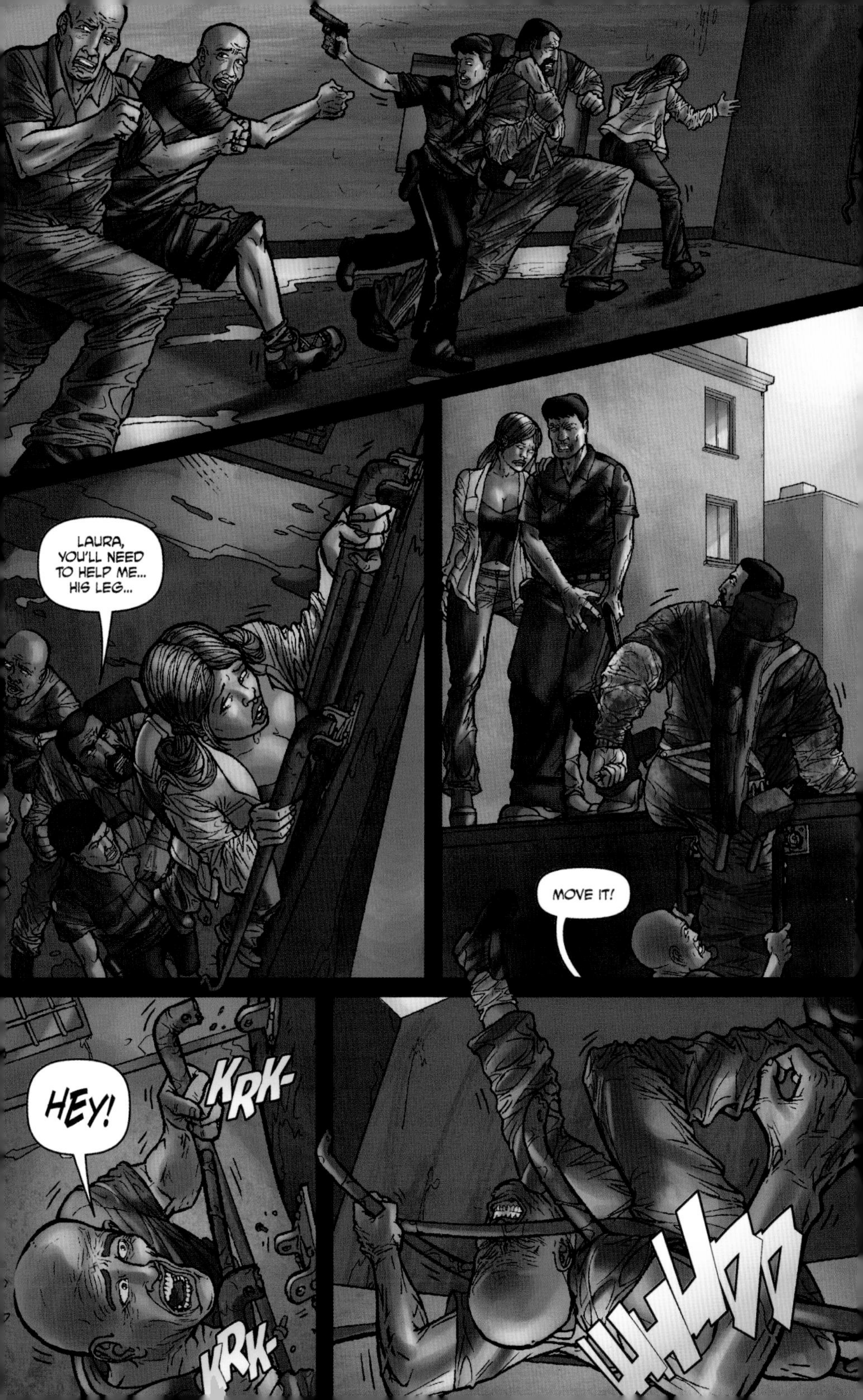
LAURA, YOU'LL NEED TO HELP ME... HIS LEG...
MOVE IT!
HEY!
KRK-
KRK-
WHOOD

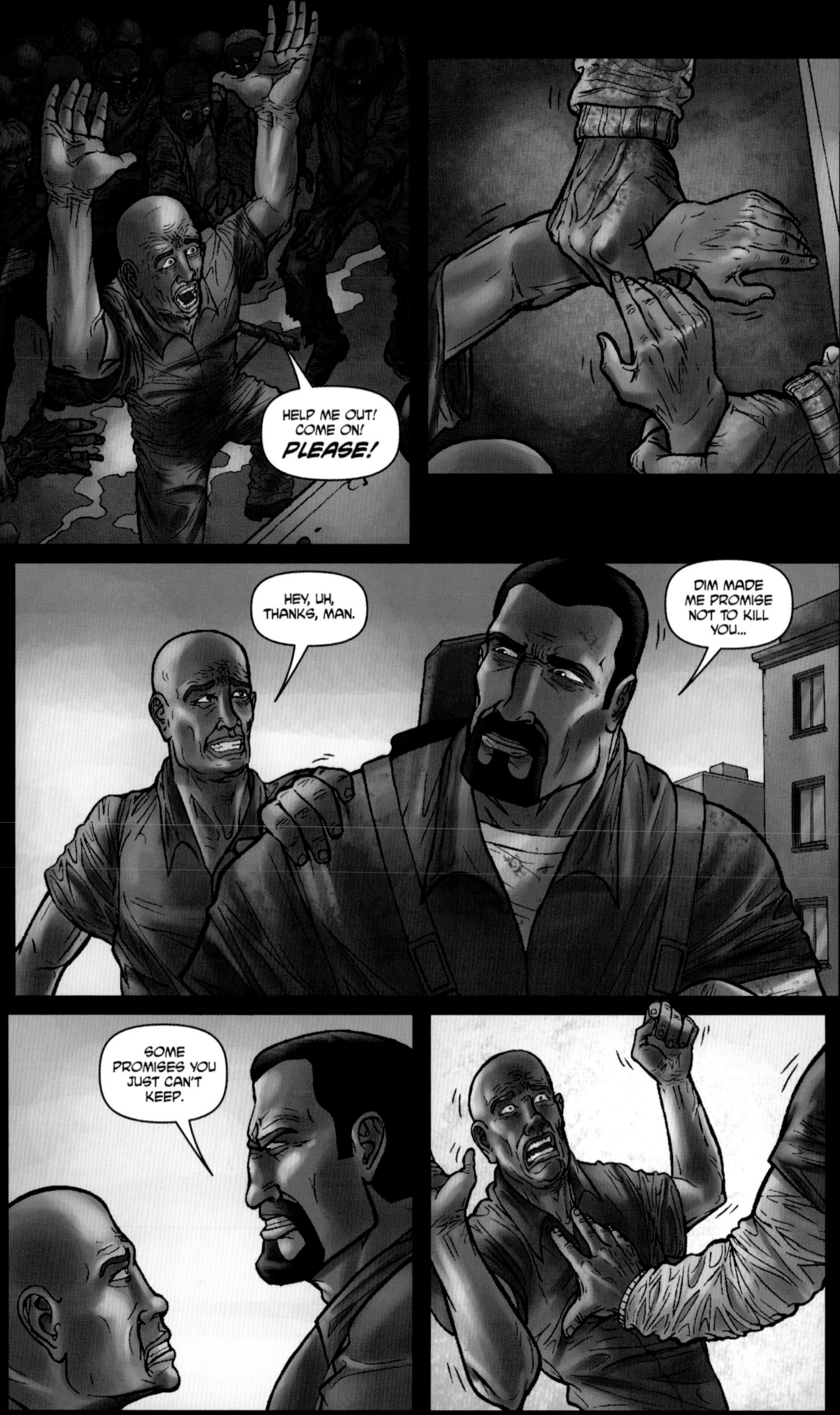
HELP ME OUT! COME ON! PLEASE!
HEY, UH, THANKS, MAN.
DIM MADE ME PROMISE NOT TO KILL YOU...
SOME PROMISES YOU JUST CAN'T KEEP.

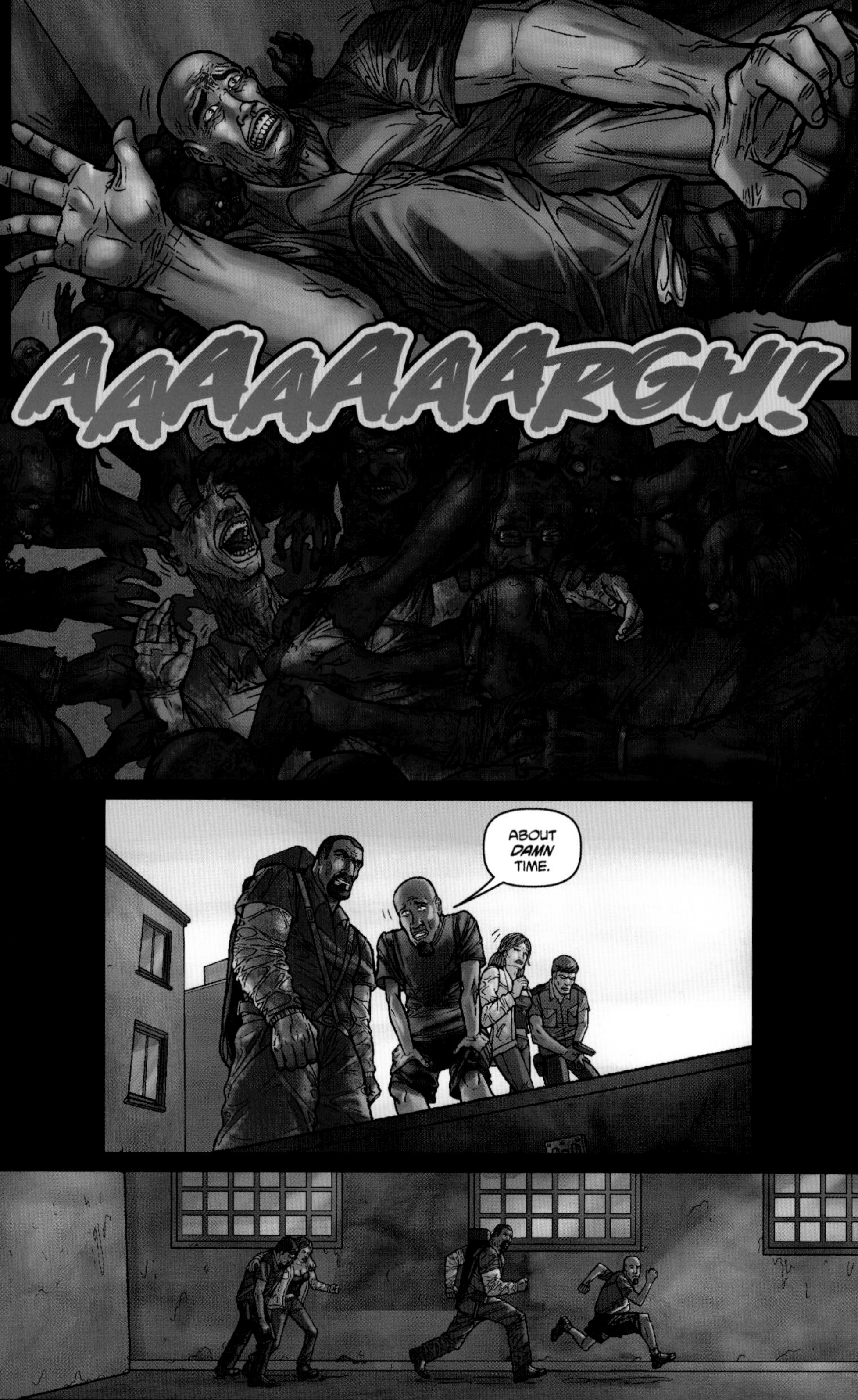
AAAAAAAARGH!
ABOUT DAMN TIME.

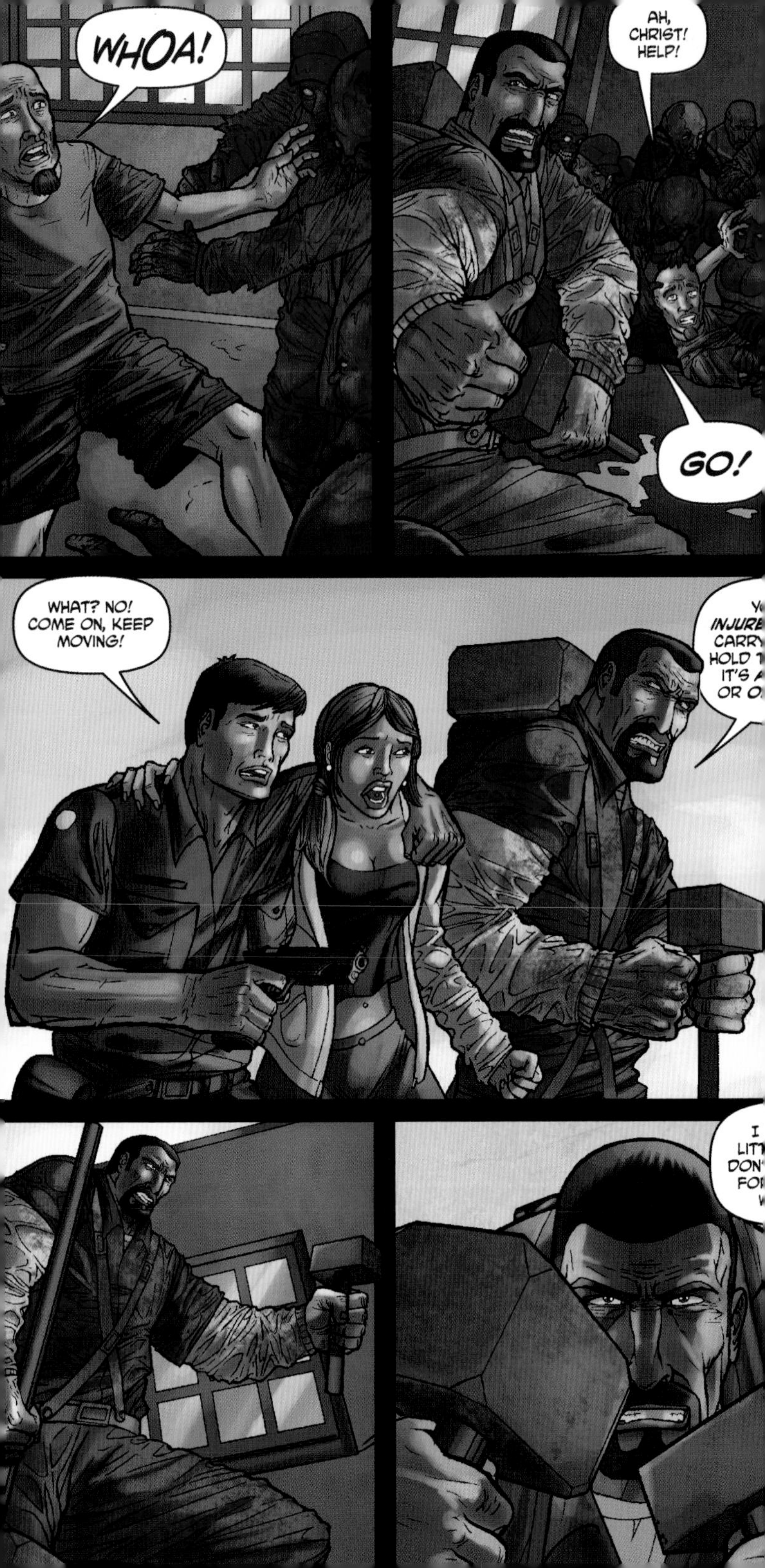
WHOA!
AH, CHRIST! HELP!
GO!
WHAT? NO! COME ON, KEEP MOVING!

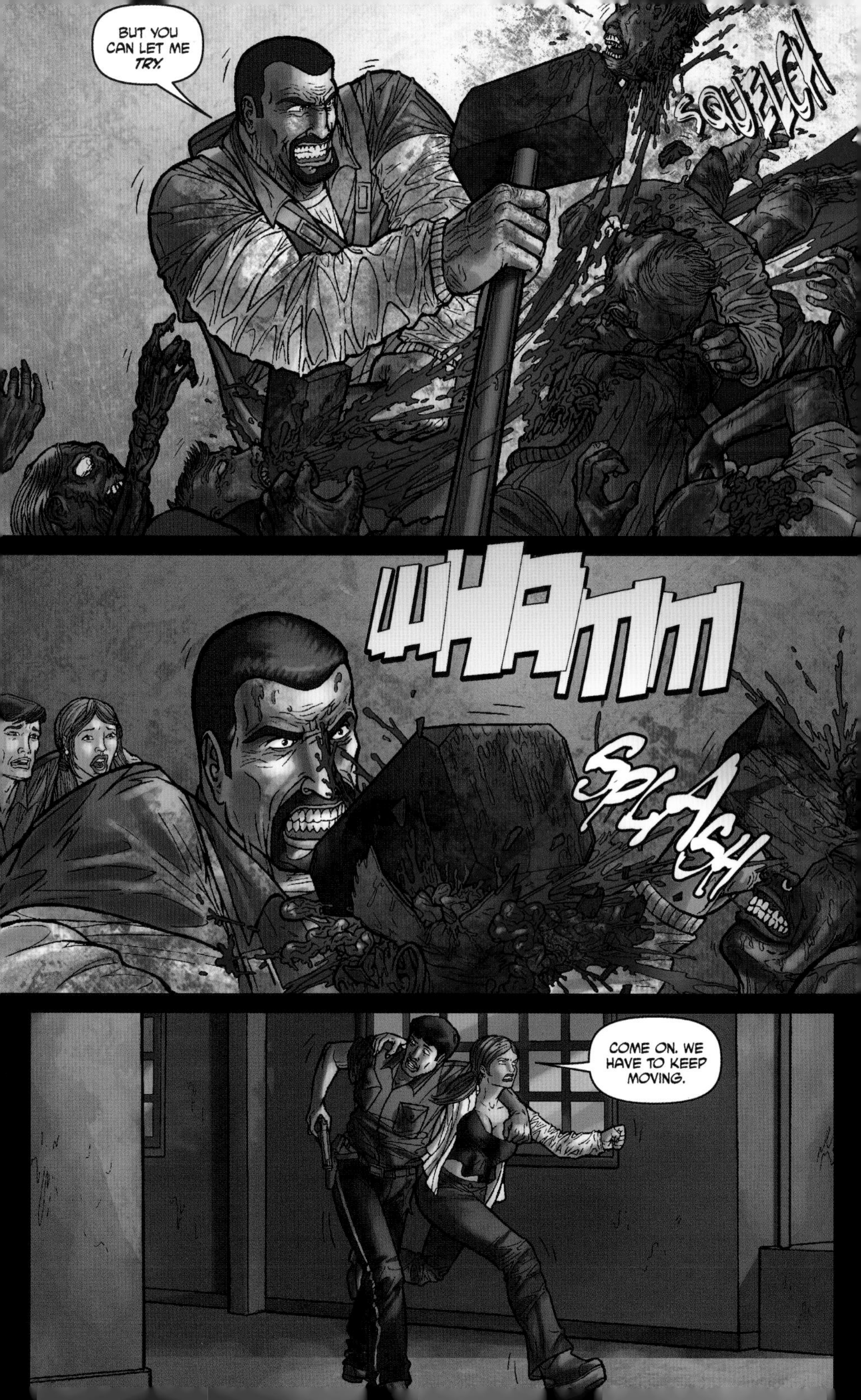
BUT YOU CAN LET ME *TRY.*
SQUELCH
WHAMM
SPLASH
COME ON. WE HAVE TO KEEP MOVING.

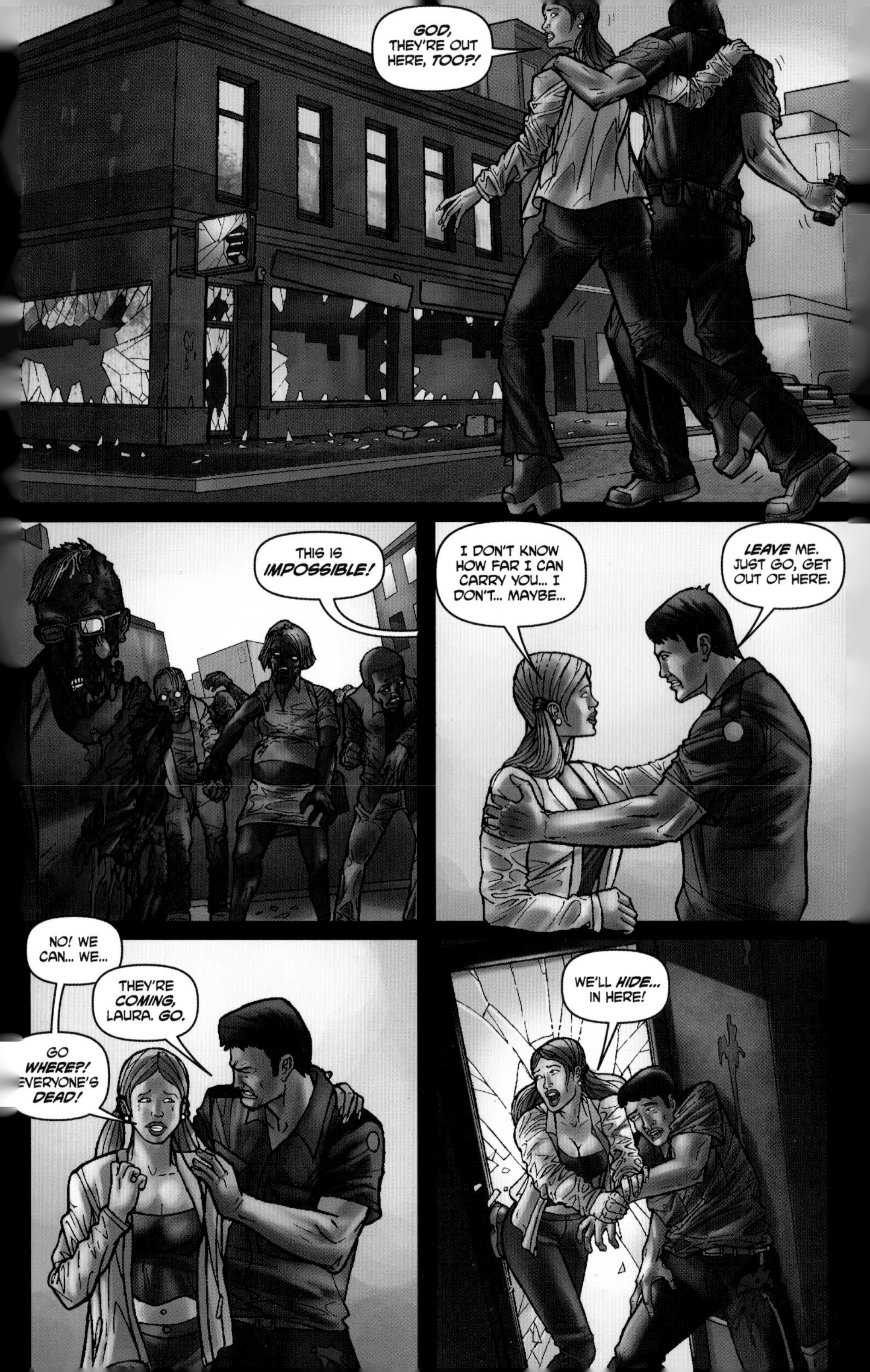
GOD, THEY'RE OUT HERE, TOO?!
THIS IS IMPOSSIBLE!
I DON'T KNOW HOW FAR I CAN CARRY YOU... I DON'T... MAYBE...
LEAVE ME. JUST GO, GET OUT OF HERE.
NO! WE CAN... WE...
THEY'RE COMING, LAURA. GO.
GO WHERE?! EVERYONE'S DEAD!
WE'LL HIDE... IN HERE!

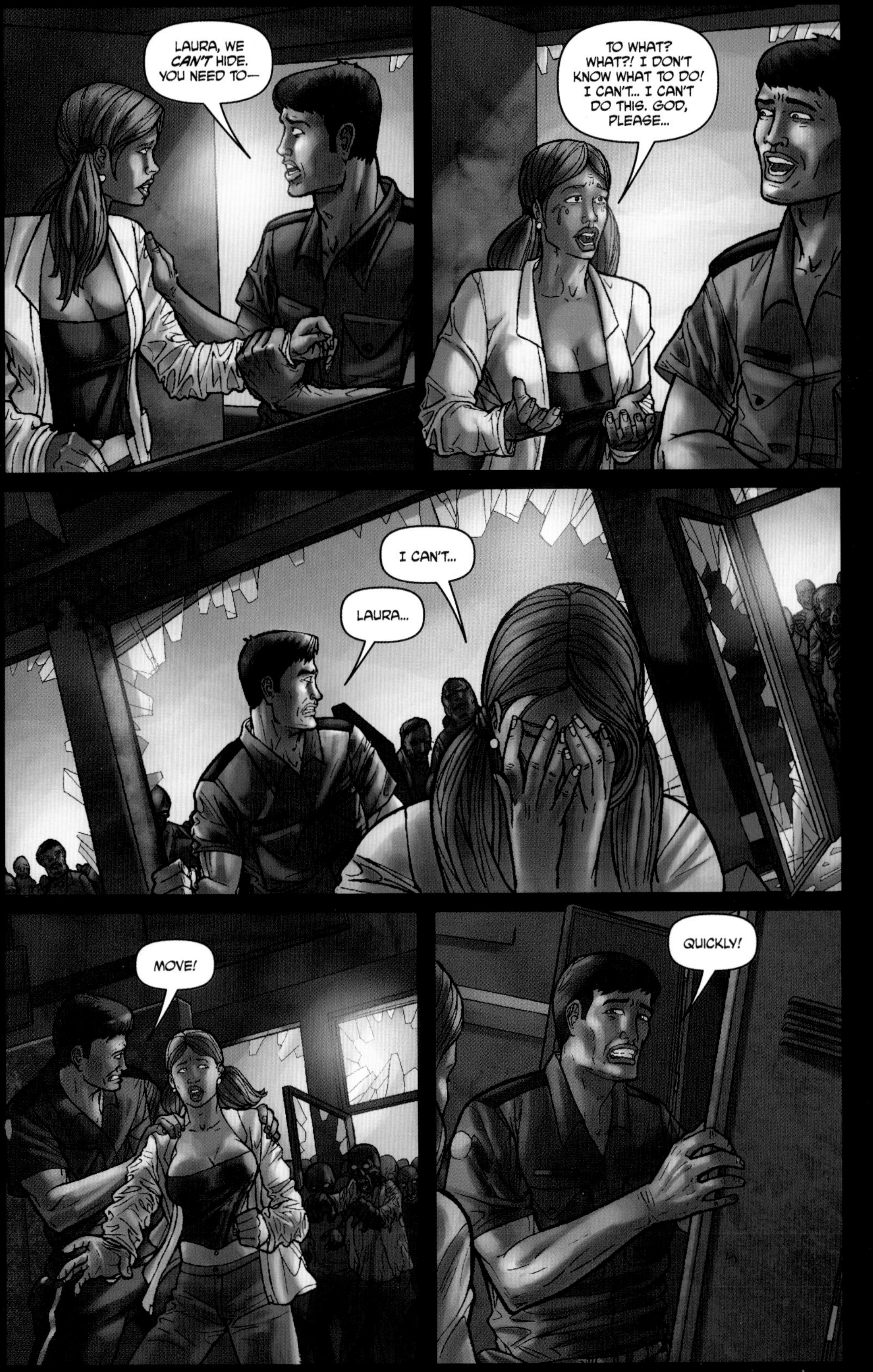
LAURA, WE *CAN'T* HIDE. YOU NEED TO—
TO WHAT? WHAT?! I DON'T KNOW WHAT TO DO! I CAN'T... I CAN'T DO THIS. GOD, PLEASE...
I CAN'T...
LAURA...
MOVE!
QUICKLY!

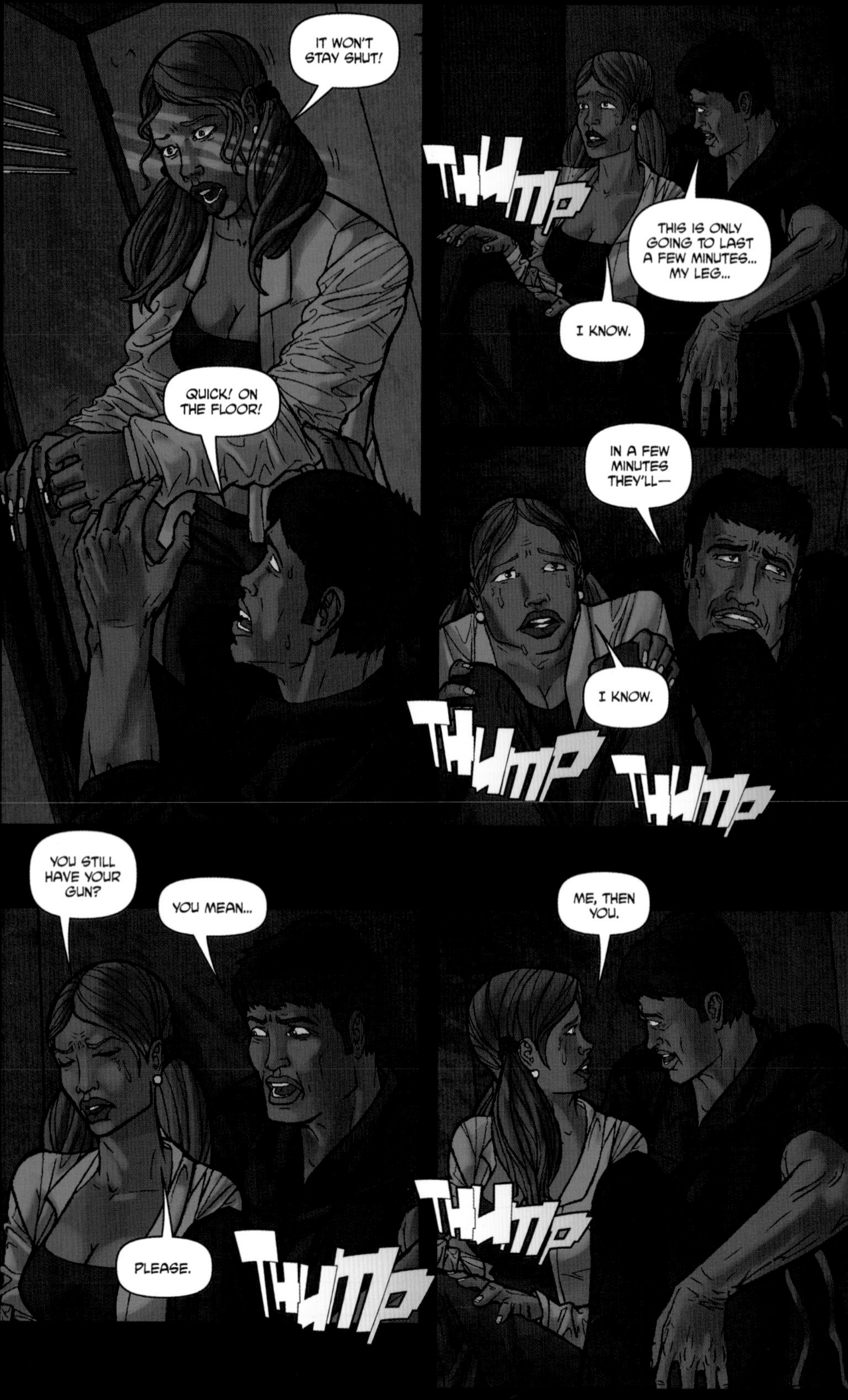

IT WON'T STAY SHUT!
QUICK! ON THE FLOOR!
THUMP
THIS IS ONLY GOING TO LAST A FEW MINUTES... MY LEG...
I KNOW.
IN A FEW MINUTES THEY'LL—
I KNOW.
THUMP THUMP
YOU STILL HAVE YOUR GUN?
YOU MEAN...
PLEASE.
THUMP
ME, THEN YOU.
THUMP

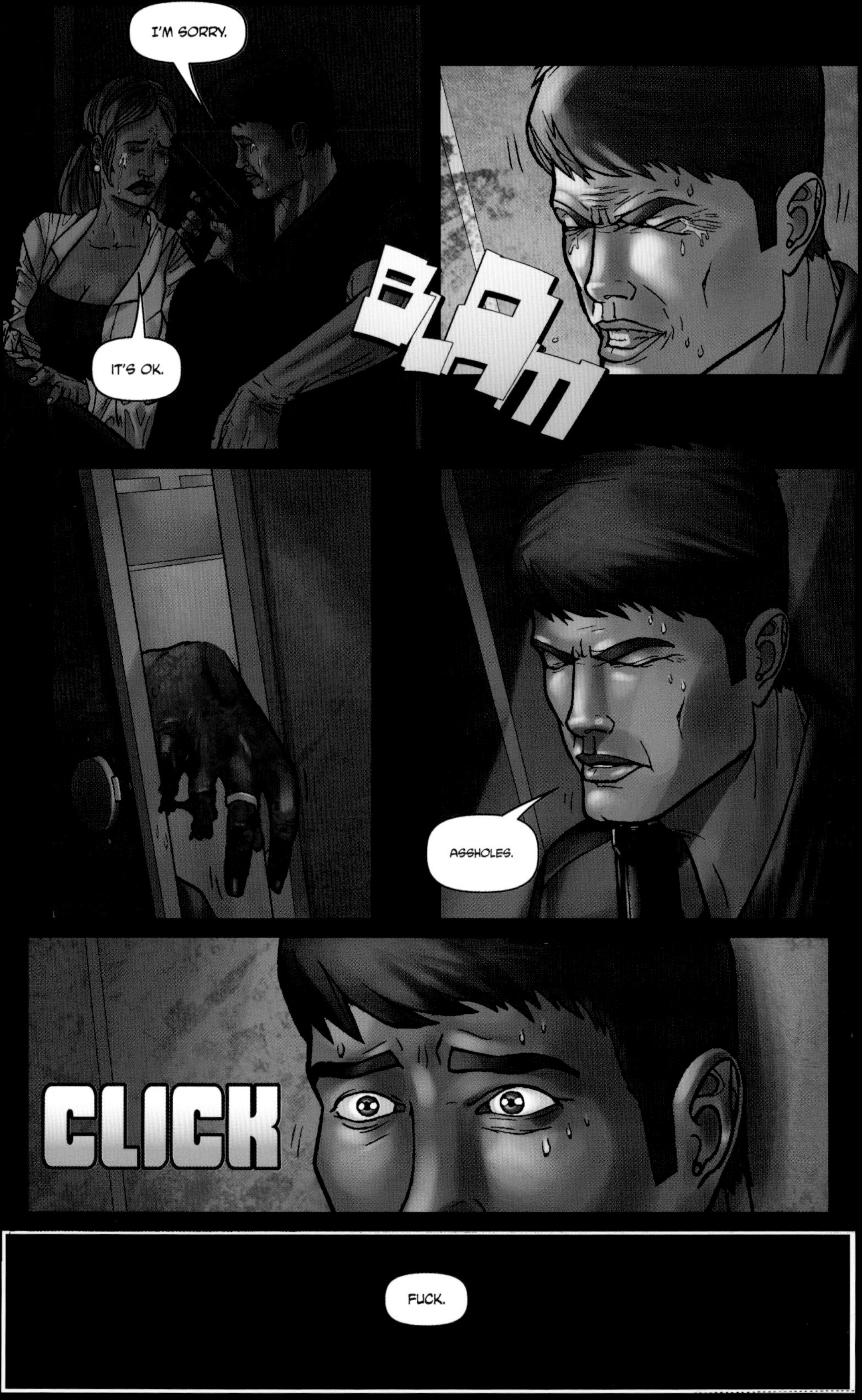
I'M SORRY.
IT'S OK.
BLAM
ASSHOLES.
CLICK
FUCK.

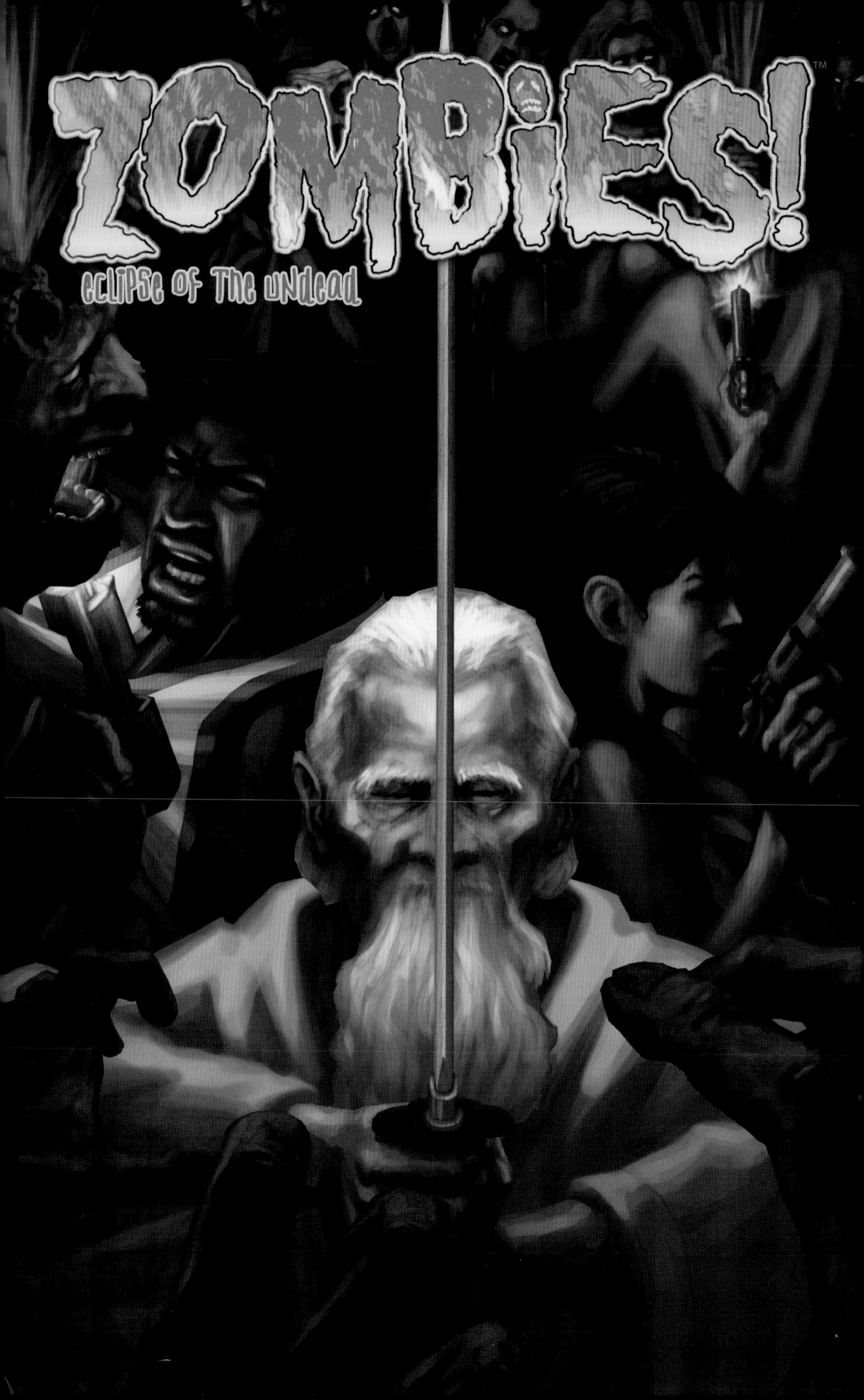
ZOMBIES!™
eclipse of the undead

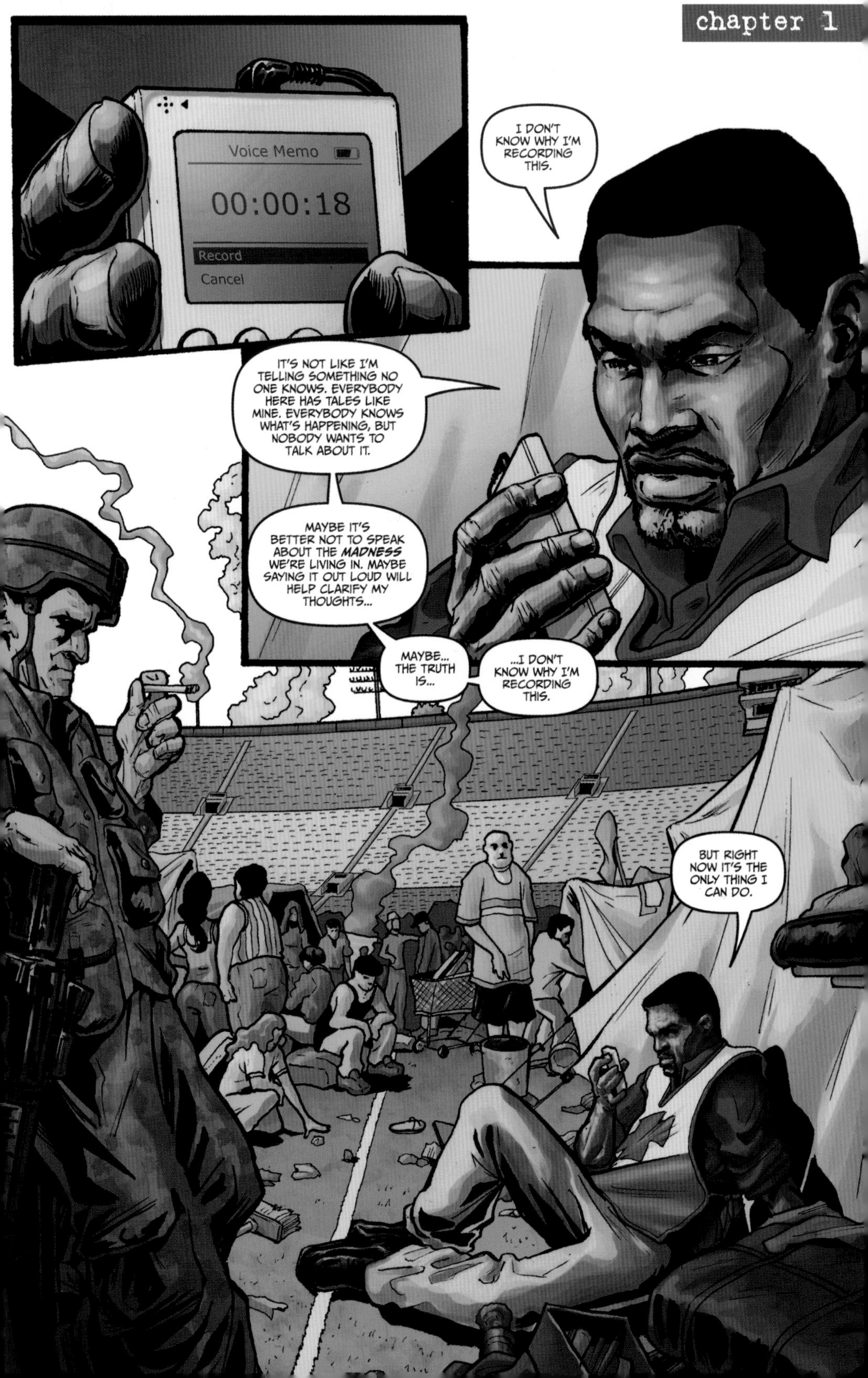
Voice Memo
00:00:18
Record
Cancel
I DON'T KNOW WHY I'M RECORDING THIS.
IT'S NOT LIKE I'M TELLING SOMETHING NO ONE KNOWS. EVERYBODY HERE HAS TALES LIKE MINE. EVERYBODY KNOWS WHAT'S HAPPENING, BUT NOBODY WANTS TO TALK ABOUT IT.
MAYBE IT'S BETTER NOT TO SPEAK ABOUT THE MADNESS WE'RE LIVING IN. MAYBE SAYING IT OUT LOUD WILL HELP CLARIFY MY THOUGHTS...
MAYBE... THE TRUTH IS...
...I DON'T KNOW WHY I'M RECORDING THIS.
BUT RIGHT NOW IT'S THE ONLY THING I CAN DO.

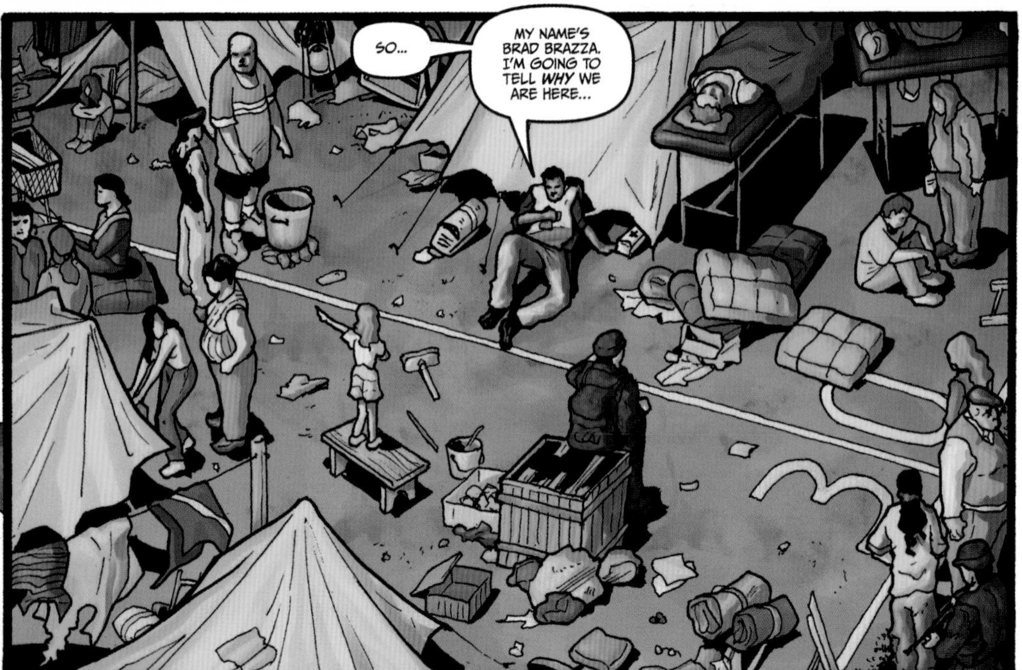
SO...
MY NAME'S BRAD BRAZZA. I'M GOING TO TELL WHY WE ARE HERE...

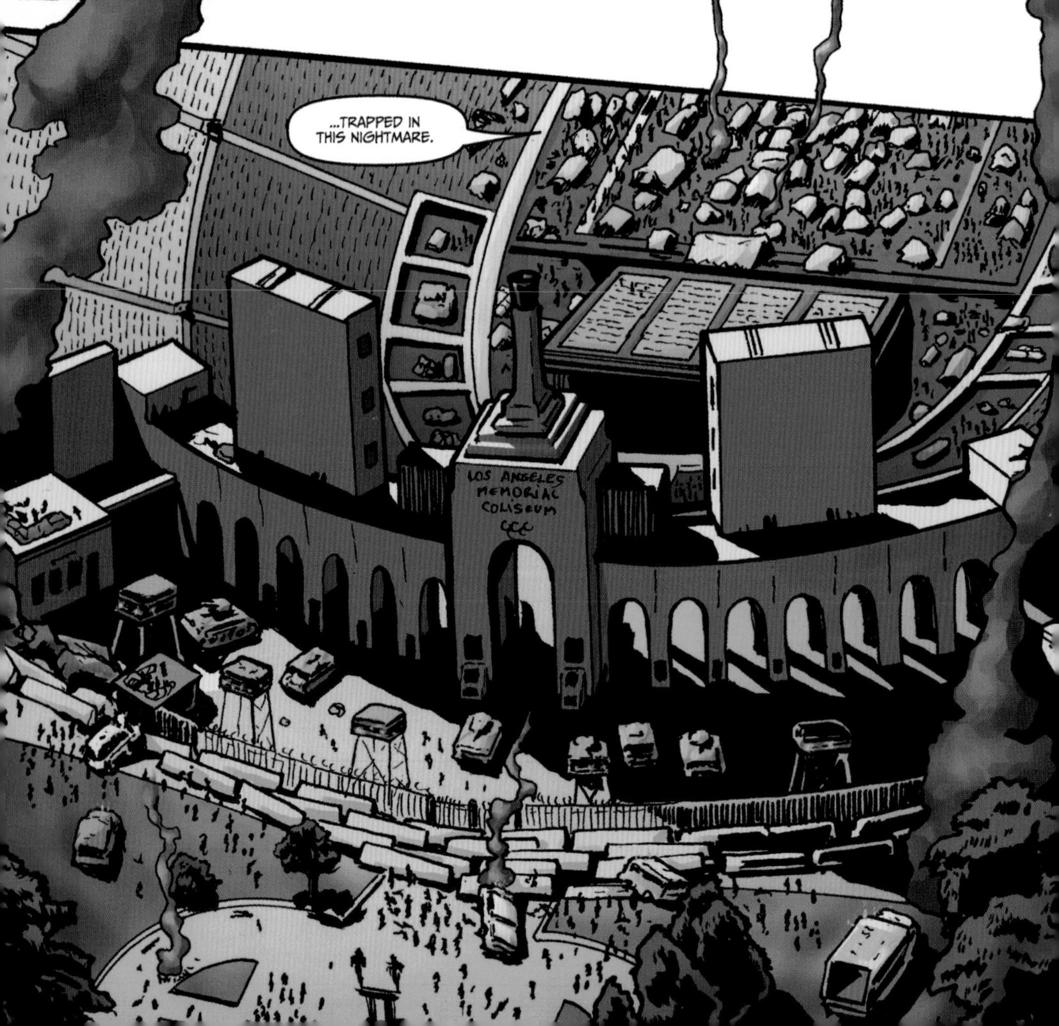
...TRAPPED IN THIS NIGHTMARE.
LOS ANGELES MEMORIAL COLISEUM

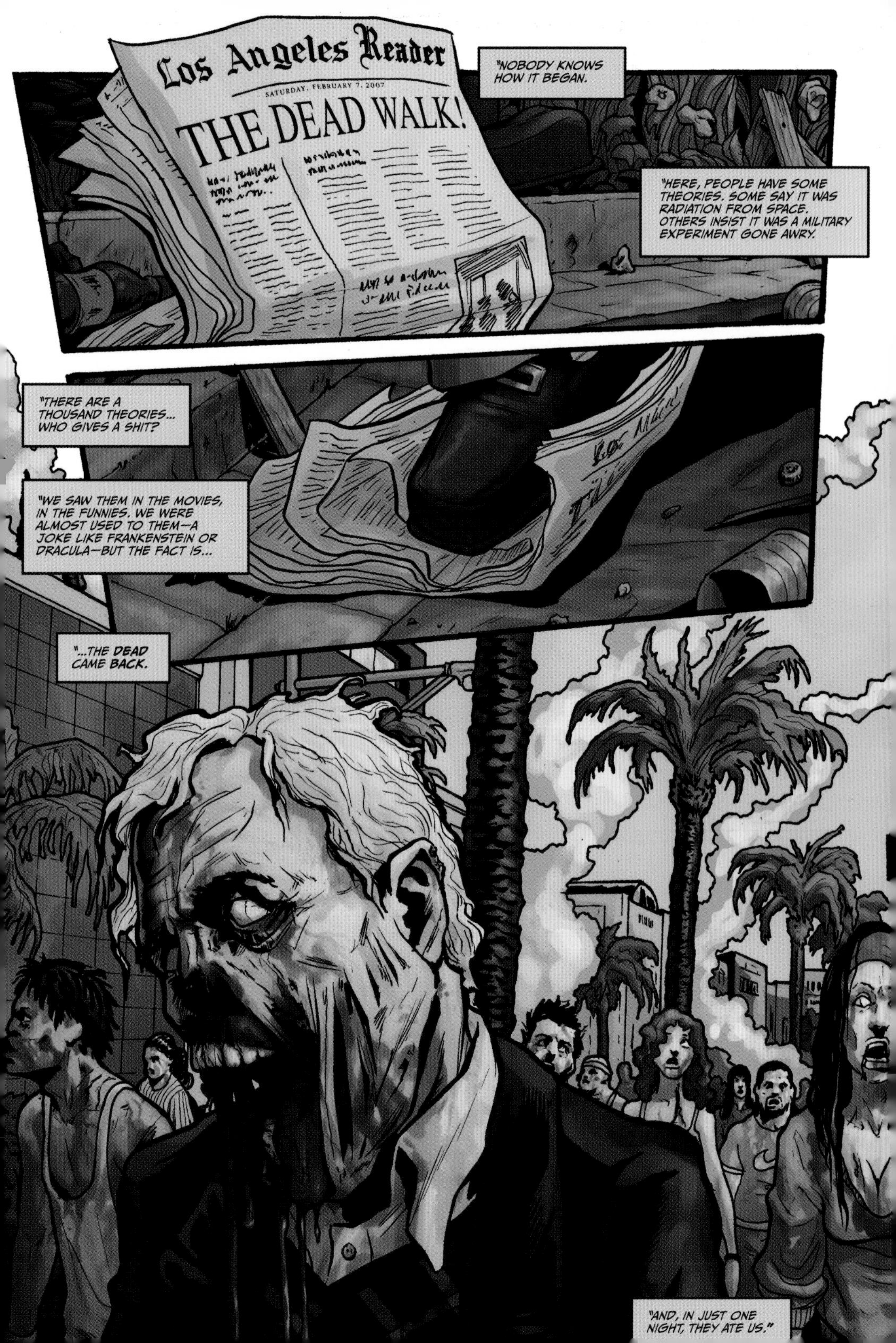
Los Angeles Reader
SATURDAY, FEBRUARY 7, 2007
THE DEAD WALK!
"NOBODY KNOWS HOW IT BEGAN.
"HERE, PEOPLE HAVE SOME THEORIES. SOME SAY IT WAS RADIATION FROM SPACE. OTHERS INSIST IT WAS A MILITARY EXPERIMENT GONE AWRY.
"THERE ARE A THOUSAND THEORIES... WHO GIVES A SHIT?
"WE SAW THEM IN THE MOVIES, IN THE FUNNIES. WE WERE ALMOST USED TO THEM—A JOKE LIKE FRANKENSTEIN OR DRACULA—BUT THE FACT IS...
"...THE DEAD CAME BACK.
"AND, IN JUST ONE NIGHT, THEY ATE US."

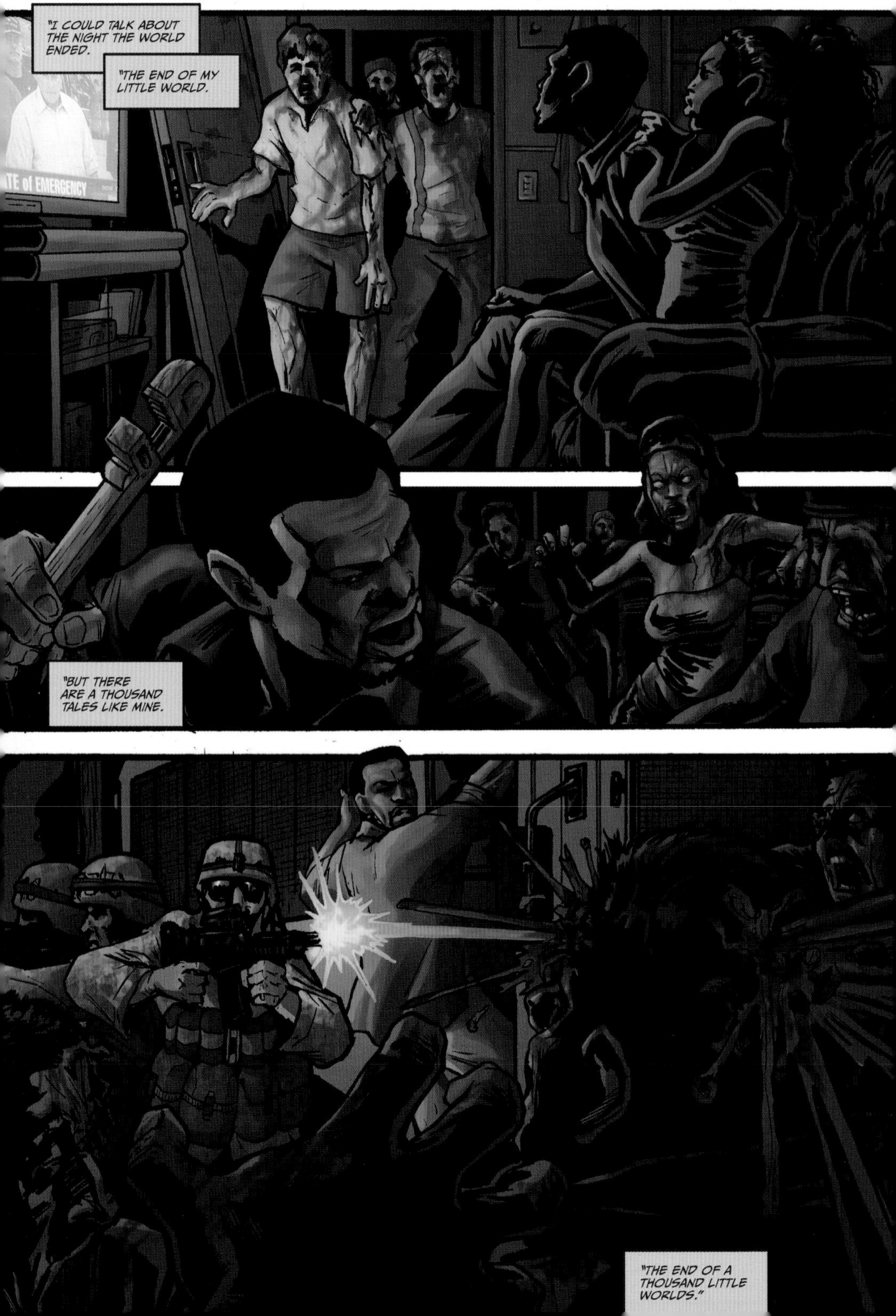
"I COULD TALK ABOUT THE NIGHT THE WORLD ENDED.
"THE END OF MY LITTLE WORLD.
TE of EMERGENCY
"BUT THERE ARE A THOUSAND TALES LIKE MINE.
"THE END OF A THOUSAND LITTLE WORLDS."

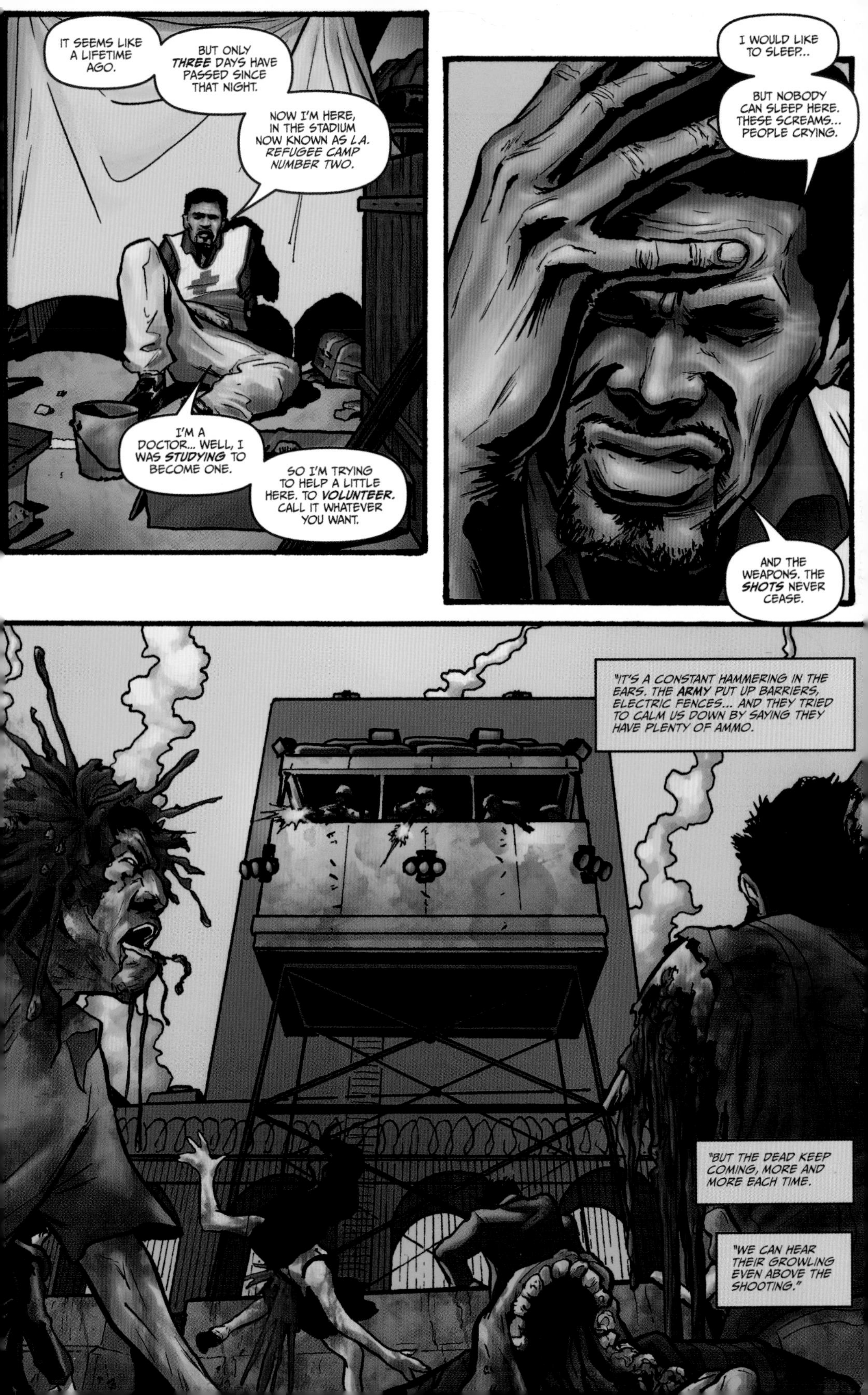
IT SEEMS LIKE A LIFETIME AGO.
BUT ONLY THREE DAYS HAVE PASSED SINCE THAT NIGHT.
NOW I'M HERE, IN THE STADIUM NOW KNOWN AS L.A. REFUGEE CAMP NUMBER TWO.
I'M A DOCTOR... WELL, I WAS STUDYING TO BECOME ONE.
SO I'M TRYING TO HELP A LITTLE HERE. TO VOLUNTEER. CALL IT WHATEVER YOU WANT.
I WOULD LIKE TO SLEEP...
BUT NOBODY CAN SLEEP HERE. THESE SCREAMS... PEOPLE CRYING.
AND THE WEAPONS. THE SHOTS NEVER CEASE.
"IT'S A CONSTANT HAMMERING IN THE EARS. THE ARMY PUT UP BARRIERS, ELECTRIC FENCES... AND THEY TRIED TO CALM US DOWN BY SAYING THEY HAVE PLENTY OF AMMO.
"BUT THE DEAD KEEP COMING, MORE AND MORE EACH TIME.
"WE CAN HEAR THEIR GROWLING EVEN ABOVE THE SHOOTING."

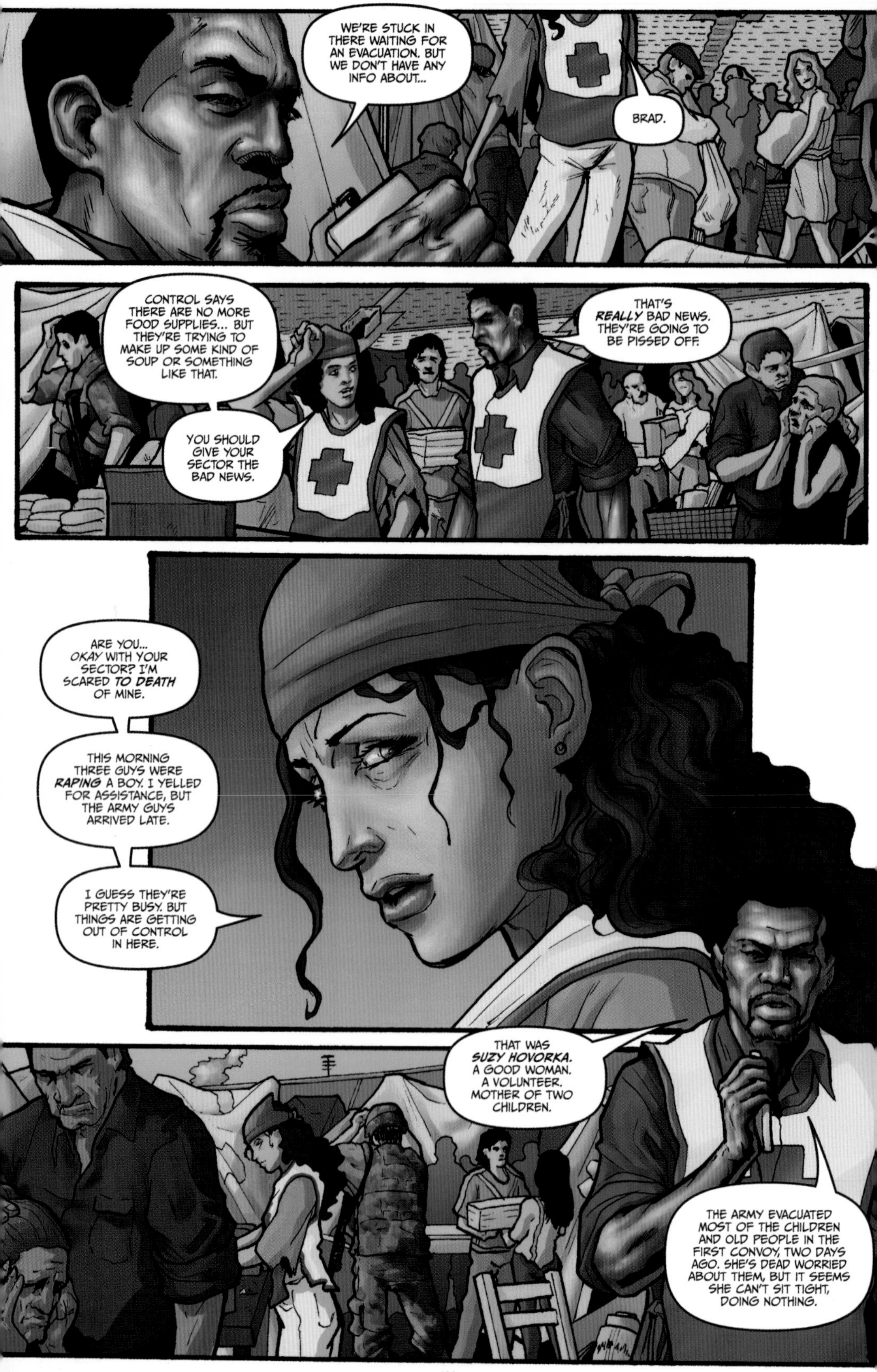
WE'RE STUCK IN THERE WAITING FOR AN EVACUATION. BUT WE DON'T HAVE ANY INFO ABOUT...
BRAD.
CONTROL SAYS THERE ARE NO MORE FOOD SUPPLIES... BUT THEY'RE TRYING TO MAKE UP SOME KIND OF SOUP OR SOMETHING LIKE THAT.
YOU SHOULD GIVE YOUR SECTOR THE BAD NEWS.
THAT'S *REALLY* BAD NEWS. THEY'RE GOING TO BE PISSED OFF.
ARE YOU... *OKAY* WITH YOUR SECTOR? I'M SCARED ***TO DEATH*** OF MINE.
THIS MORNING THREE GUYS WERE ***RAPING*** A BOY. I YELLED FOR ASSISTANCE, BUT THE ARMY GUYS ARRIVED LATE.
I GUESS THEY'RE PRETTY BUSY. BUT THINGS ARE GETTING OUT OF CONTROL IN HERE.
THAT WAS ***SUZY HOVORKA.*** A GOOD WOMAN. A VOLUNTEER. MOTHER OF TWO CHILDREN.
THE ARMY EVACUATED MOST OF THE CHILDREN AND OLD PEOPLE IN THE FIRST CONVOY, TWO DAYS AGO. SHE'S DEAD WORRIED ABOUT THEM, BUT IT SEEMS SHE CAN'T SIT TIGHT, DOING NOTHING.

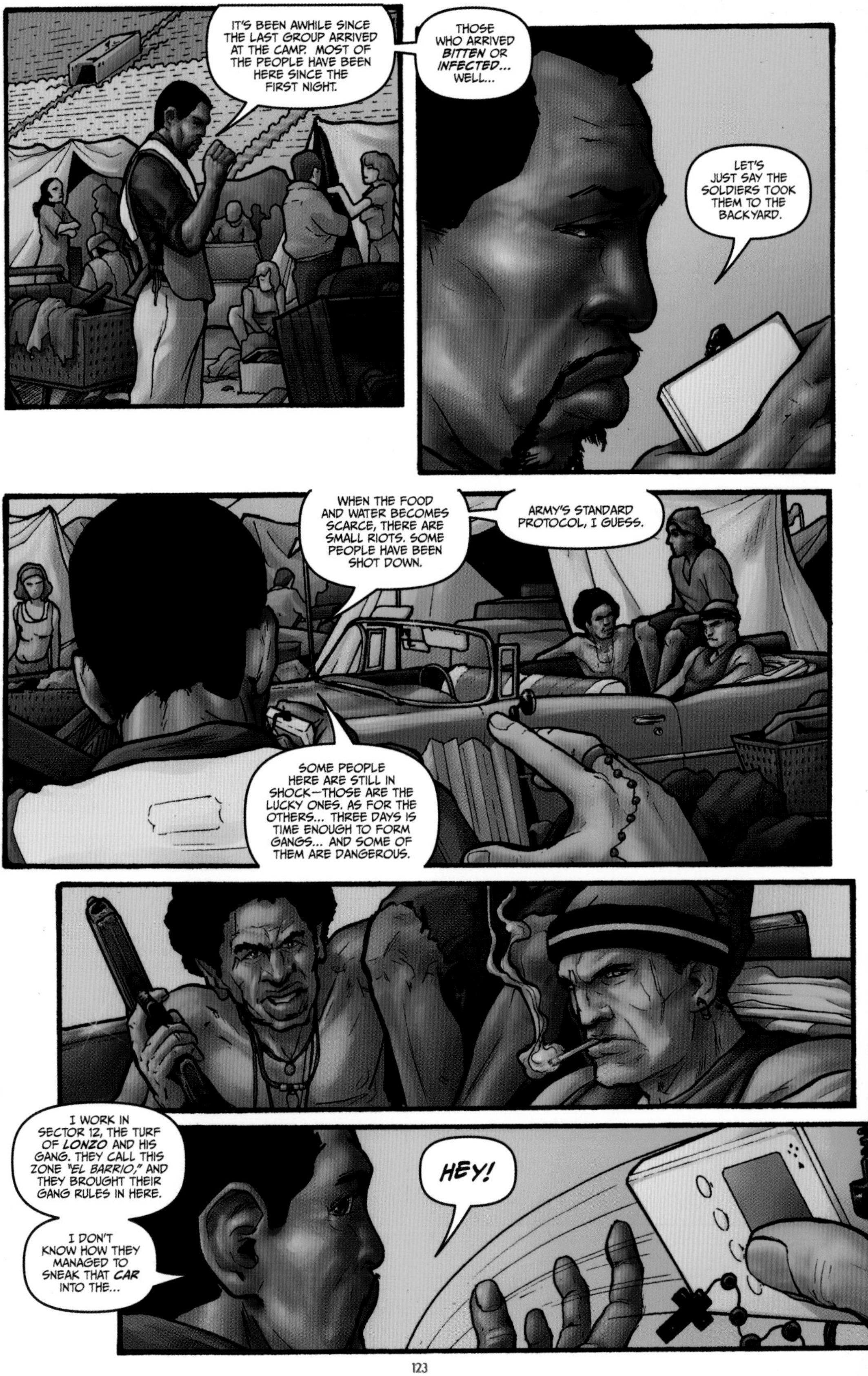
IT'S BEEN AWHILE SINCE THE LAST GROUP ARRIVED AT THE CAMP. MOST OF THE PEOPLE HAVE BEEN HERE SINCE THE FIRST NIGHT.
THOSE WHO ARRIVED *BITTEN* OR *INFECTED*... WELL...
LET'S JUST SAY THE SOLDIERS TOOK THEM TO THE BACKYARD.
WHEN THE FOOD AND WATER BECOMES SCARCE, THERE ARE SMALL RIOTS. SOME PEOPLE HAVE BEEN SHOT DOWN.
ARMY'S STANDARD PROTOCOL, I GUESS.
SOME PEOPLE HERE ARE STILL IN SHOCK—THOSE ARE THE LUCKY ONES. AS FOR THE OTHERS... THREE DAYS IS TIME ENOUGH TO FORM GANGS... AND SOME OF THEM ARE DANGEROUS.
I WORK IN SECTOR 12, THE TURF OF *LONZO* AND HIS GANG. THEY CALL THIS ZONE *"EL BARRIO,"* AND THEY BROUGHT THEIR GANG RULES IN HERE.
I DON'T KNOW HOW THEY MANAGED TO SNEAK THAT *CAR* INTO THE...
HEY!

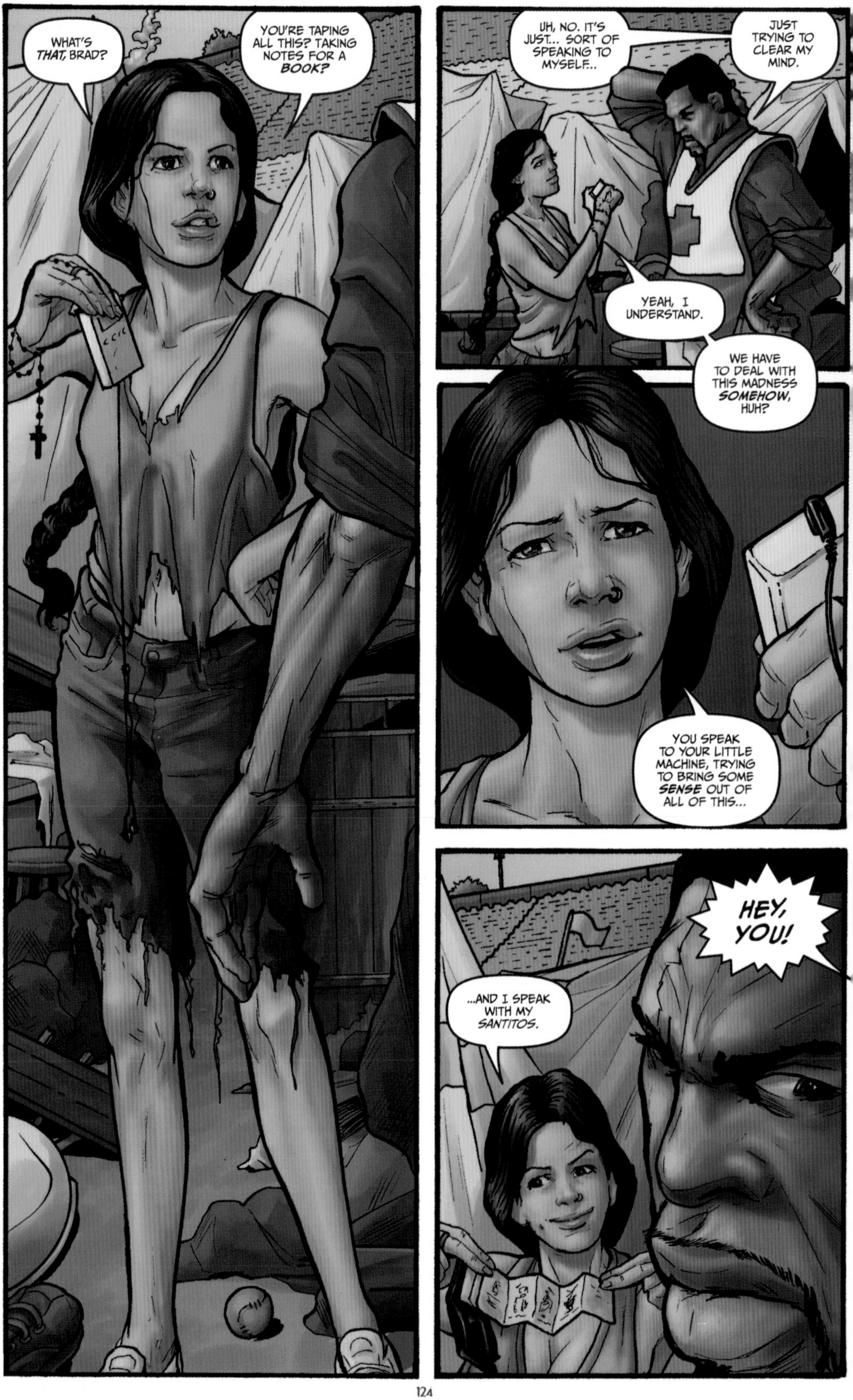

WHAT'S *THAT,* BRAD?
YOU'RE TAPING ALL THIS? TAKING NOTES FOR A *BOOK?*
UH, NO. IT'S JUST... SORT OF SPEAKING TO MYSELF...
JUST TRYING TO CLEAR MY MIND.
YEAH, I UNDERSTAND.
WE HAVE TO DEAL WITH THIS MADNESS *SOMEHOW,* HUH?
YOU SPEAK TO YOUR LITTLE MACHINE, TRYING TO BRING SOME *SENSE* OUT OF ALL OF THIS...
...AND I SPEAK WITH MY *SANTITOS.*
HEY, YOU!

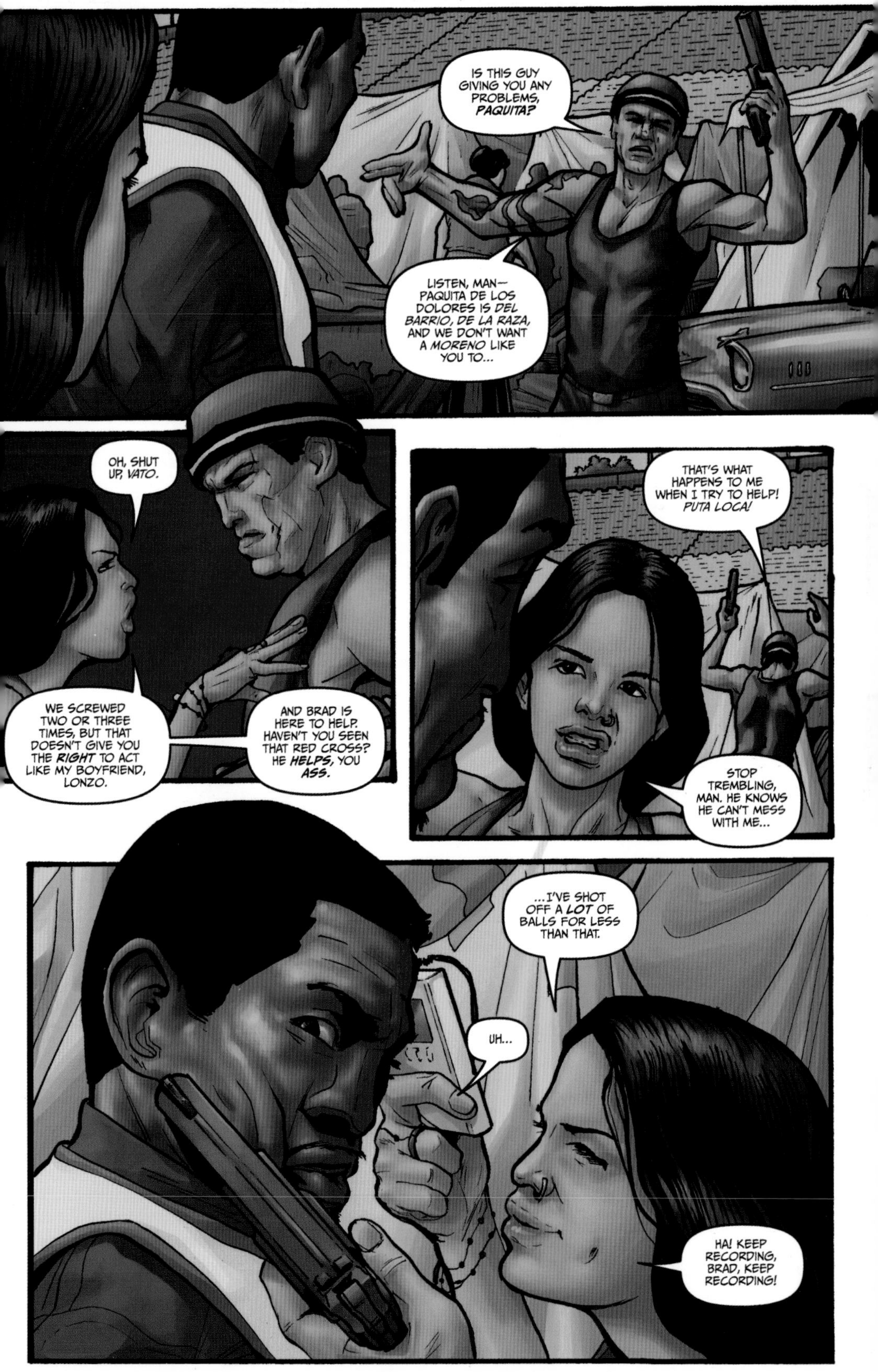
IS THIS GUY GIVING YOU ANY PROBLEMS, *PAQUITA?*
LISTEN, MAN— PAQUITA DE LOS DOLORES IS *DEL BARRIO, DE LA RAZA,* AND WE DON'T WANT A *MORENO* LIKE YOU TO...
OH, SHUT UP, *VATO.*
WE SCREWED TWO OR THREE TIMES, BUT THAT DOESN'T GIVE YOU THE ***RIGHT*** TO ACT LIKE MY BOYFRIEND, LONZO.
AND BRAD IS HERE TO HELP. HAVEN'T YOU SEEN THAT RED CROSS? HE ***HELPS,*** YOU ***ASS.***
THAT'S WHAT HAPPENS TO ME WHEN I TRY TO HELP! *PUTA LOCA!*
STOP TREMBLING, MAN. HE KNOWS HE CAN'T MESS WITH ME...
...I'VE SHOT OFF A ***LOT*** OF BALLS FOR LESS THAN THAT.
UH...
HA! KEEP RECORDING, BRAD, KEEP RECORDING!

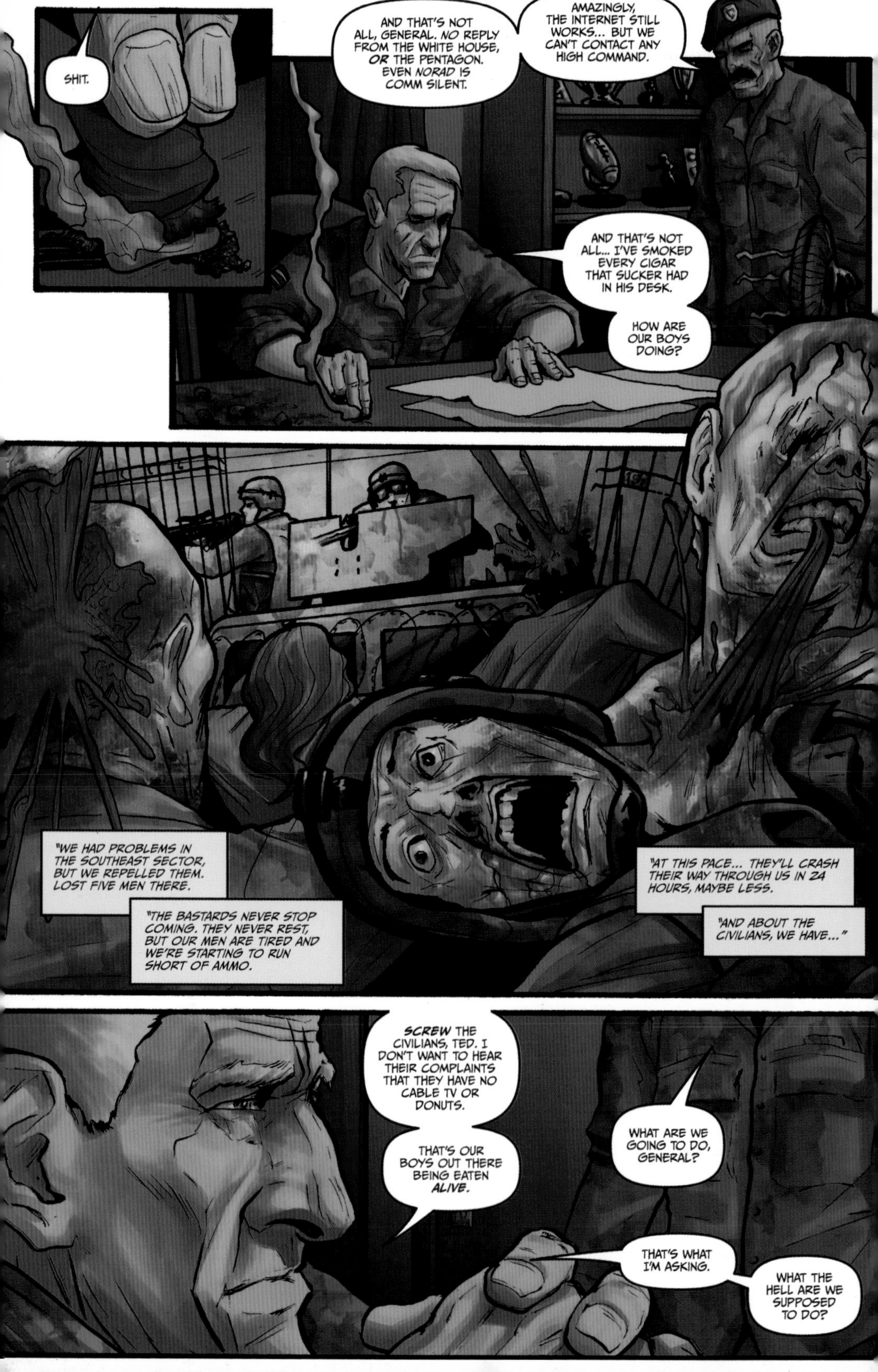
SHIT.
AND THAT'S NOT ALL, GENERAL. *NO* REPLY FROM THE WHITE HOUSE, ***OR*** THE PENTAGON. EVEN *NORAD* IS COMM SILENT.
AMAZINGLY, THE INTERNET STILL WORKS... BUT WE CAN'T CONTACT ANY HIGH COMMAND.
AND THAT'S NOT ALL... I'VE SMOKED EVERY CIGAR THAT SUCKER HAD IN HIS DESK.
HOW ARE OUR BOYS DOING?
"WE HAD PROBLEMS IN THE SOUTHEAST SECTOR, BUT WE REPELLED THEM. LOST FIVE MEN THERE.
"THE BASTARDS NEVER STOP COMING. THEY NEVER REST, BUT OUR MEN ARE TIRED AND WE'RE STARTING TO RUN SHORT OF AMMO.
"AT THIS PACE... THEY'LL CRASH THEIR WAY THROUGH US IN 24 HOURS, MAYBE LESS.
"AND ABOUT THE CIVILIANS, WE HAVE..."
SCREW THE CIVILIANS, TED. I DON'T WANT TO HEAR THEIR COMPLAINTS THAT THEY HAVE NO CABLE TV OR DONUTS.
THAT'S OUR BOYS OUT THERE BEING EATEN ***ALIVE***.
WHAT ARE WE GOING TO DO, GENERAL?
THAT'S WHAT I'M ASKING.
WHAT THE HELL ARE WE SUPPOSED TO DO?

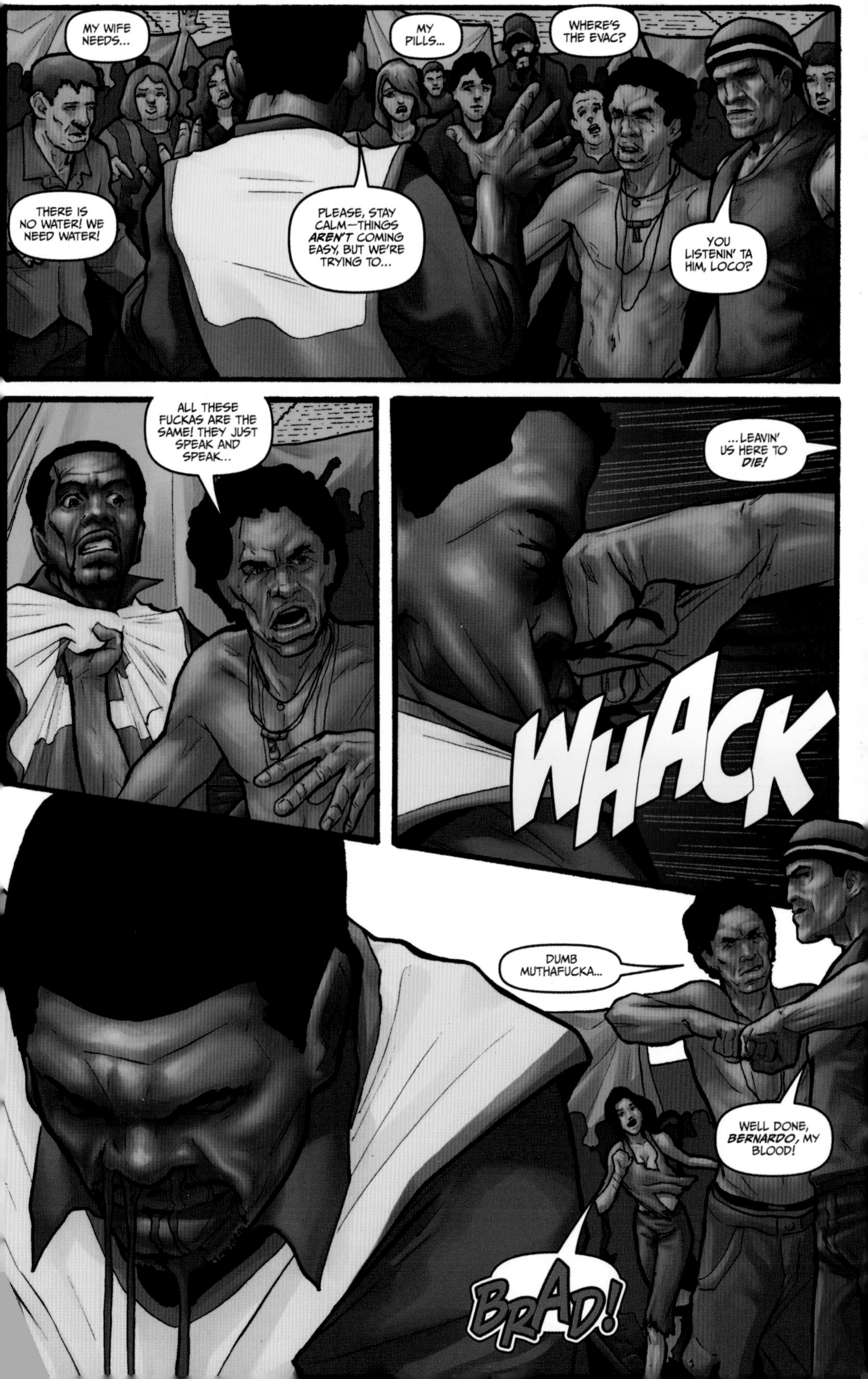
MY WIFE NEEDS...
MY PILLS...
WHERE'S THE EVAC?
THERE IS NO WATER! WE NEED WATER!
PLEASE, STAY CALM—THINGS AREN'T COMING EASY, BUT WE'RE TRYING TO...
YOU LISTENIN' TA HIM, LOCO?
ALL THESE FUCKAS ARE THE SAME! THEY JUST SPEAK AND SPEAK...
...LEAVIN' US HERE TO DIE!
WHACK
DUMB MUTHAFUCKA...
WELL DONE, BERNARDO, MY BLOOD!
BRAD!

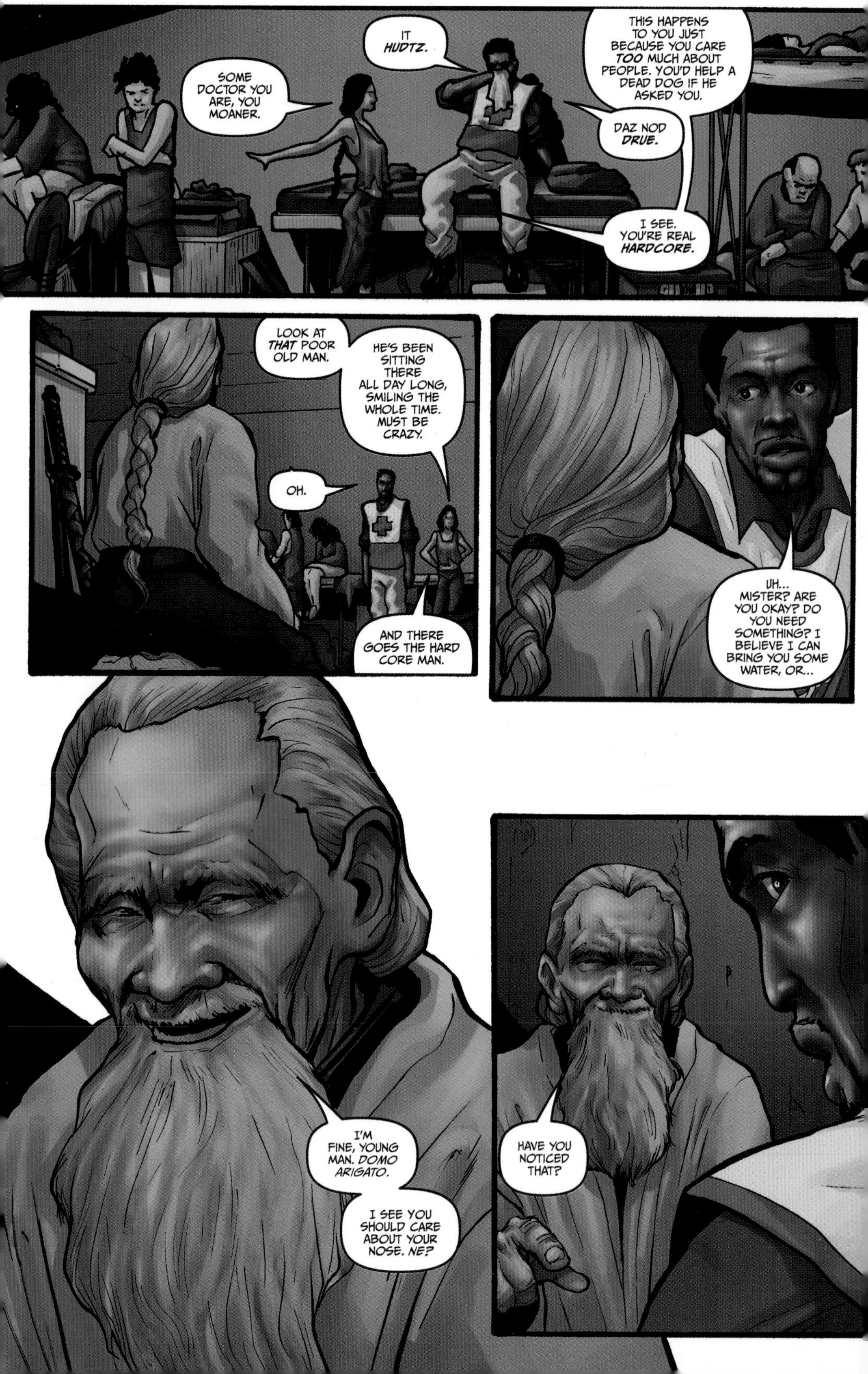
SOME DOCTOR YOU ARE, YOU MOANER.
IT *HUDTZ.*
THIS HAPPENS TO YOU JUST BECAUSE YOU CARE *TOO* MUCH ABOUT PEOPLE. YOU'D HELP A DEAD DOG IF HE ASKED YOU.
DAZ NOD *DRUE.*
I SEE. YOU'RE REAL *HARDCORE.*
LOOK AT *THAT* POOR OLD MAN.
HE'S BEEN SITTING THERE ALL DAY LONG, SMILING THE WHOLE TIME. MUST BE CRAZY.
OH.
AND THERE GOES THE HARD CORE MAN.
UH... MISTER? ARE YOU OKAY? DO YOU NEED SOMETHING? I BELIEVE I CAN BRING YOU SOME WATER, OR...
I'M FINE, YOUNG MAN. *DOMO ARIGATO.*
I SEE YOU SHOULD CARE ABOUT YOUR NOSE. *NE?*
HAVE YOU NOTICED THAT?

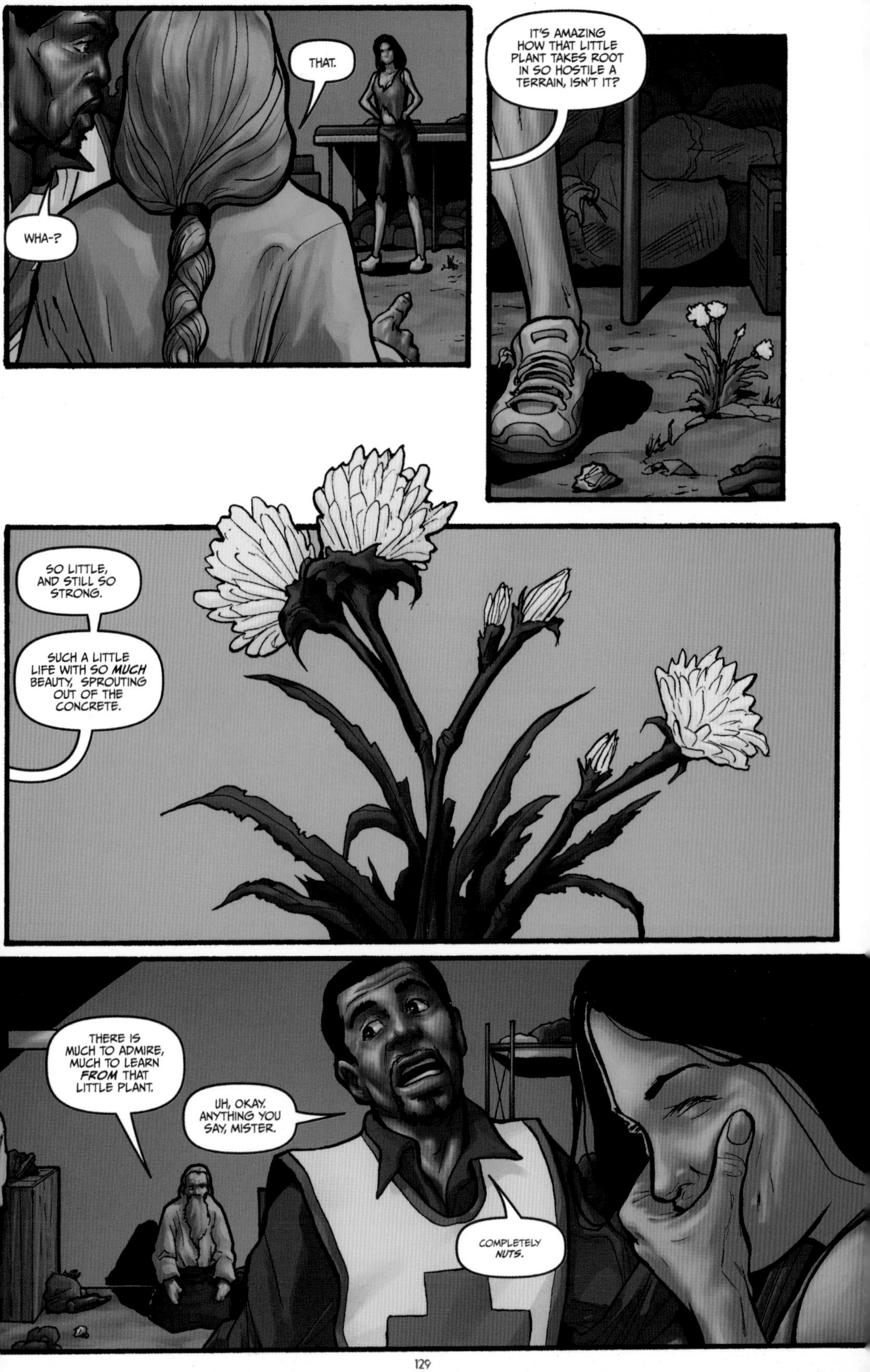
THAT.
WHA-?
IT'S AMAZING HOW THAT LITTLE PLANT TAKES ROOT IN SO HOSTILE A TERRAIN, ISN'T IT?
SO LITTLE, AND STILL SO STRONG.
SUCH A LITTLE LIFE WITH SO *MUCH* BEAUTY, SPROUTING OUT OF THE CONCRETE.
THERE IS MUCH TO ADMIRE, MUCH TO LEARN *FROM* THAT LITTLE PLANT.
UH, OKAY. ANYTHING YOU SAY, MISTER.
COMPLETELY *NUTS*.

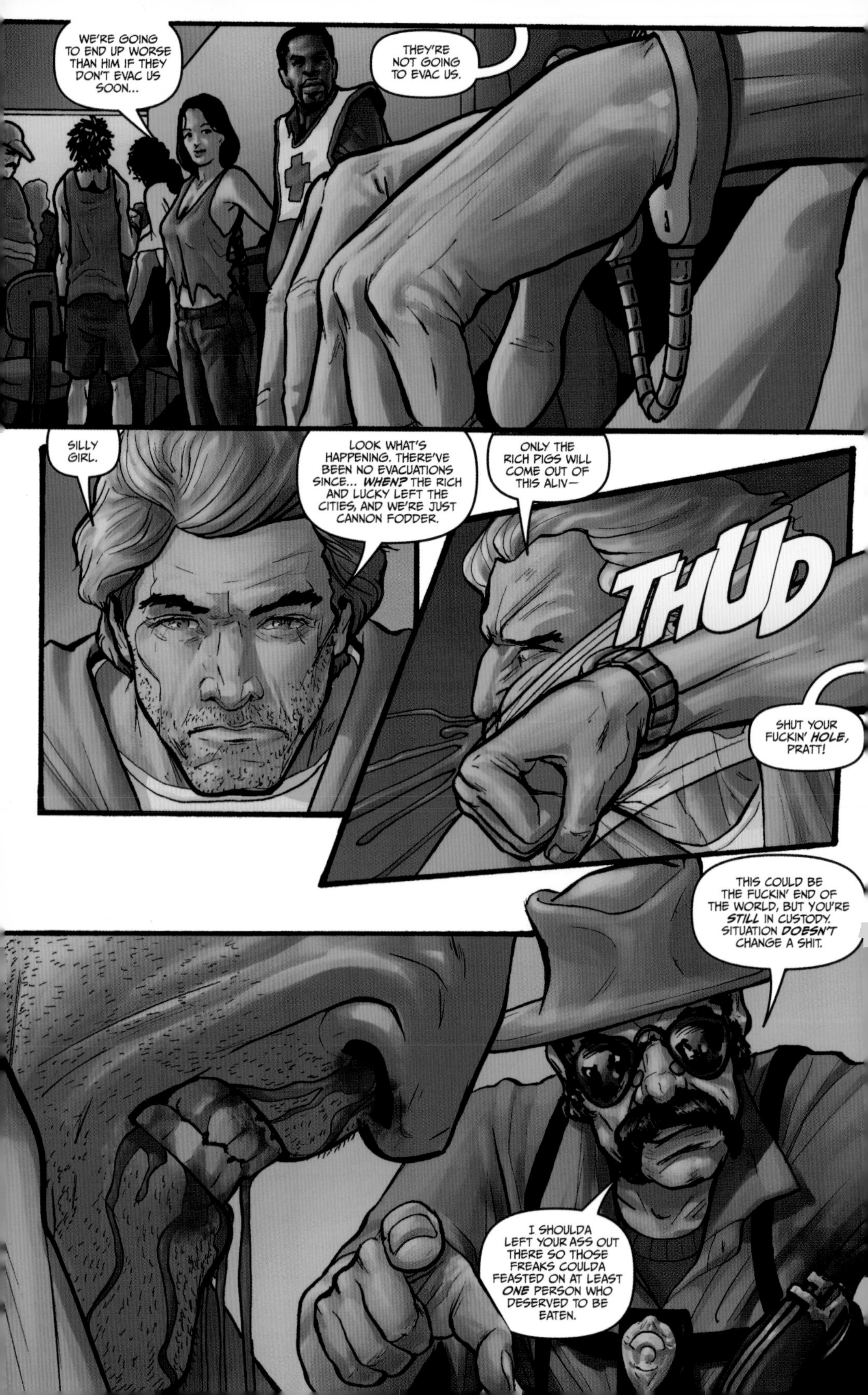
WE'RE GOING TO END UP WORSE THAN HIM IF THEY DON'T EVAC US SOON...
THEY'RE NOT GOING TO EVAC US.
SILLY GIRL.
LOOK WHAT'S HAPPENING. THERE'VE BEEN NO EVACUATIONS SINCE... *WHEN?* THE RICH AND LUCKY LEFT THE CITIES, AND WE'RE JUST CANNON FODDER.
ONLY THE RICH PIGS WILL COME OUT OF THIS ALIV—
THUD
SHUT YOUR FUCKIN' *HOLE,* PRATT!
THIS COULD BE THE FUCKIN' END OF THE WORLD, BUT YOU'RE *STILL* IN CUSTODY. SITUATION *DOESN'T* CHANGE A SHIT.
I SHOULDA LEFT YOUR ASS OUT THERE SO THOSE FREAKS COULDA FEASTED ON AT LEAST *ONE* PERSON WHO DESERVED TO BE EATEN.

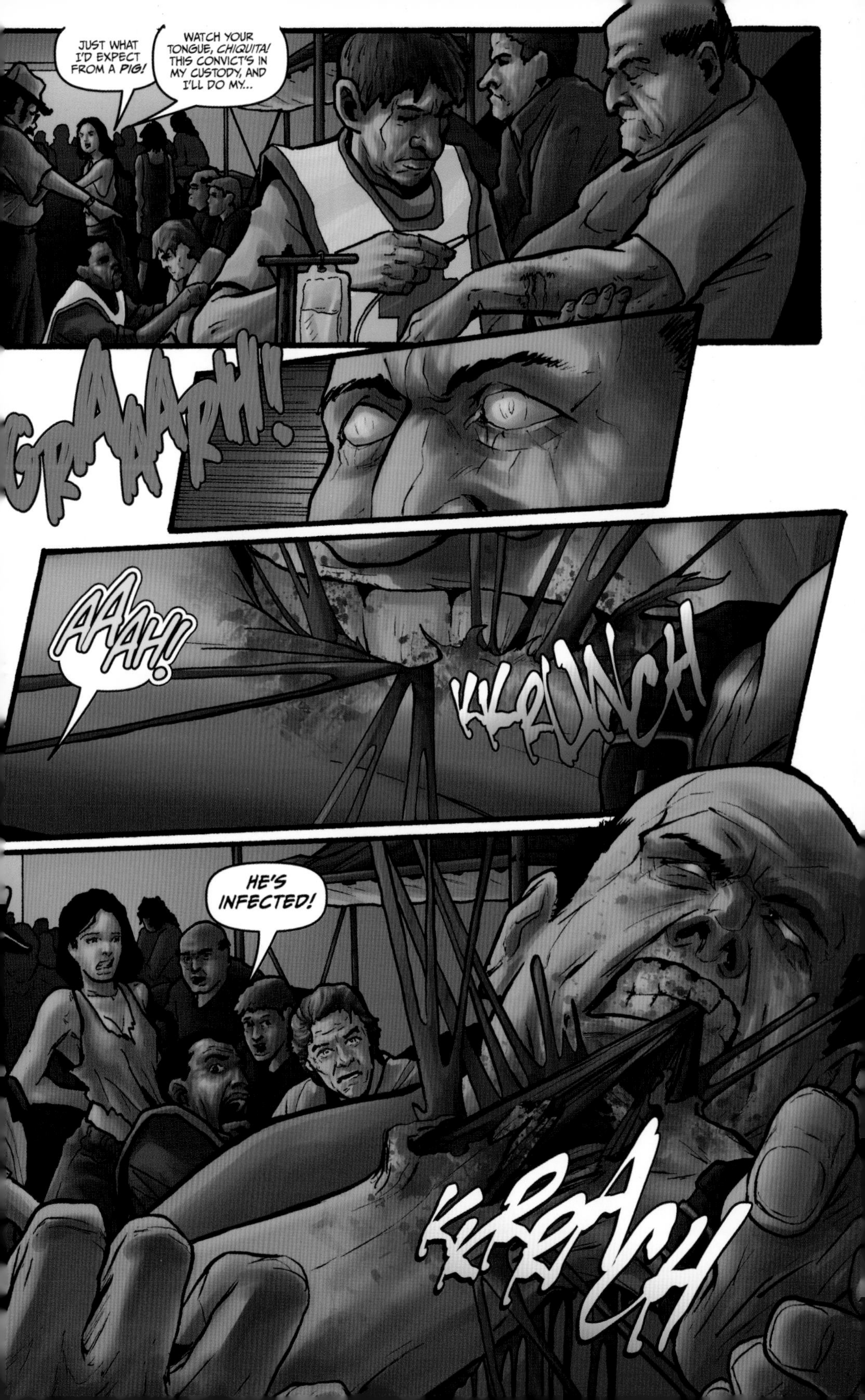
JUST WHAT I'D EXPECT FROM A PIG!
WATCH YOUR TONGUE, CHIQUITA! THIS CONVICT'S IN MY CUSTODY, AND I'LL DO MY...
GRAAARH!
AAAAH!
KKRUNCH
HE'S INFECTED!
KKREACH

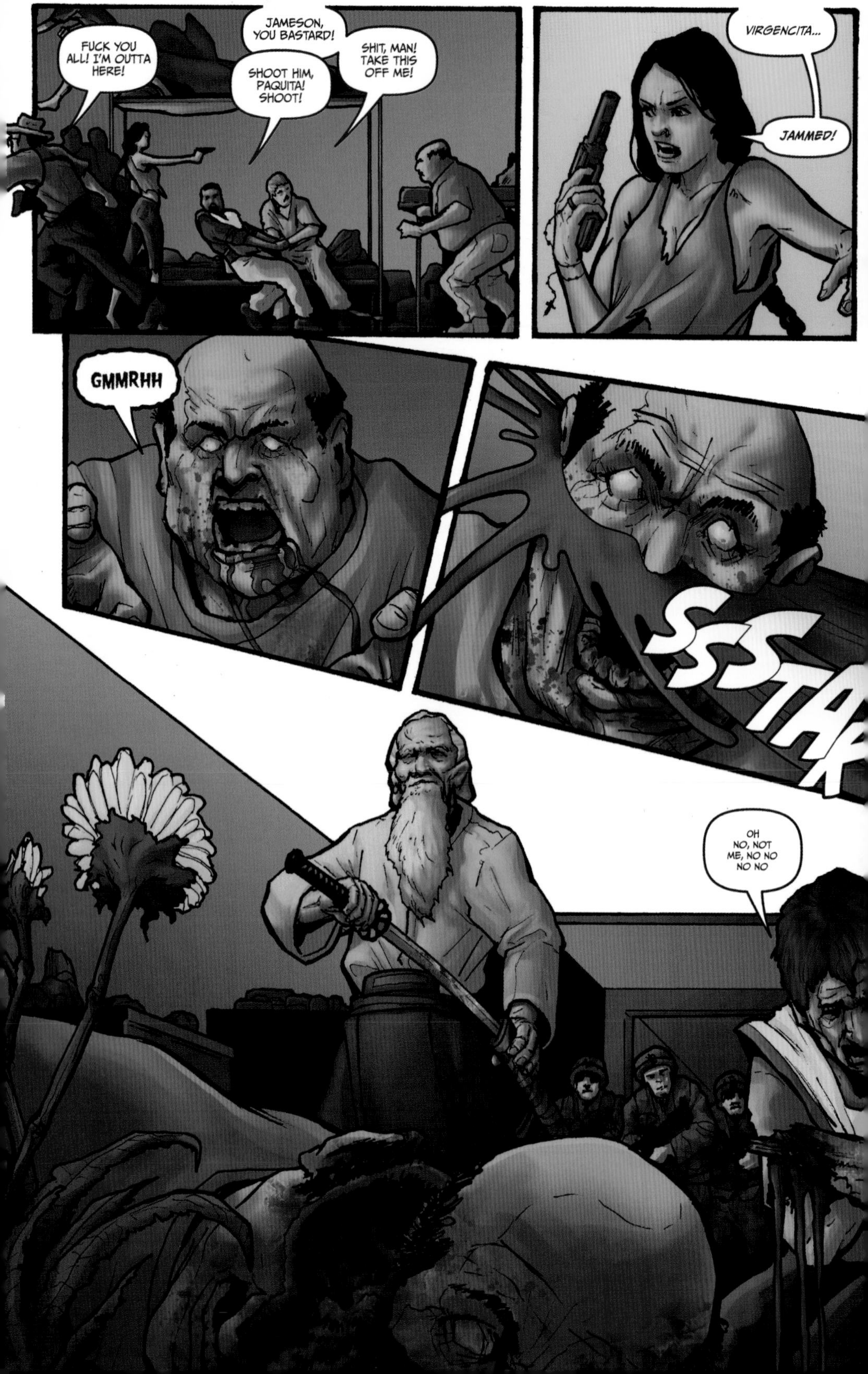
FUCK YOU ALL! I'M OUTTA HERE!
JAMESON, YOU BASTARD!
SHOOT HIM, PAQUITA! SHOOT!
SHIT, MAN! TAKE THIS OFF ME!
VIRGENCITA...
JAMMED!
GMMRHH
SSTAK
OH NO, NOT ME, NO NO NO NO

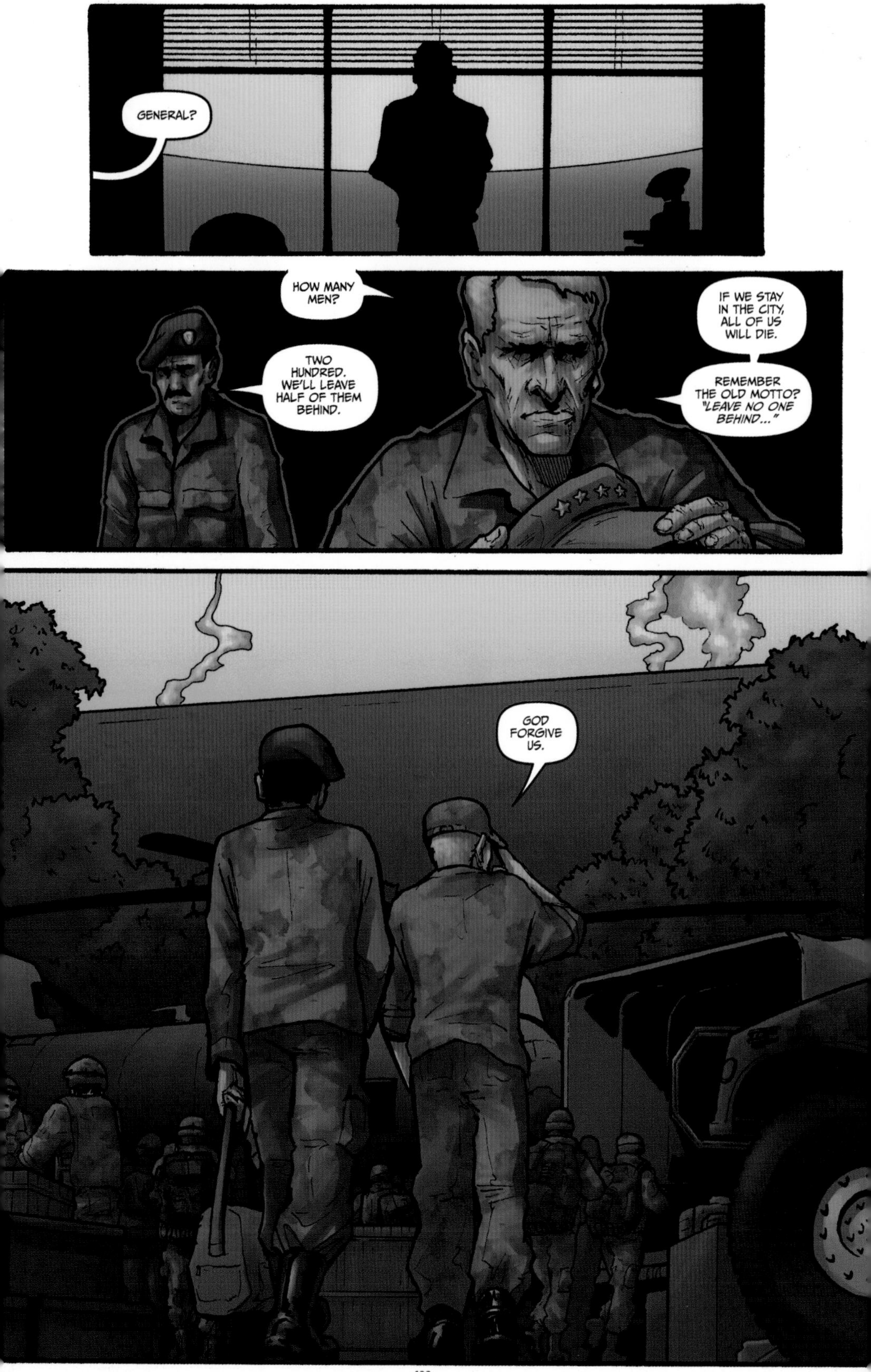
GENERAL?
HOW MANY MEN?
TWO HUNDRED. WE'LL LEAVE HALF OF THEM BEHIND.
IF WE STAY IN THE CITY, ALL OF US WILL DIE.
REMEMBER THE OLD MOTTO? "LEAVE NO ONE BEHIND..."
GOD FORGIVE US.

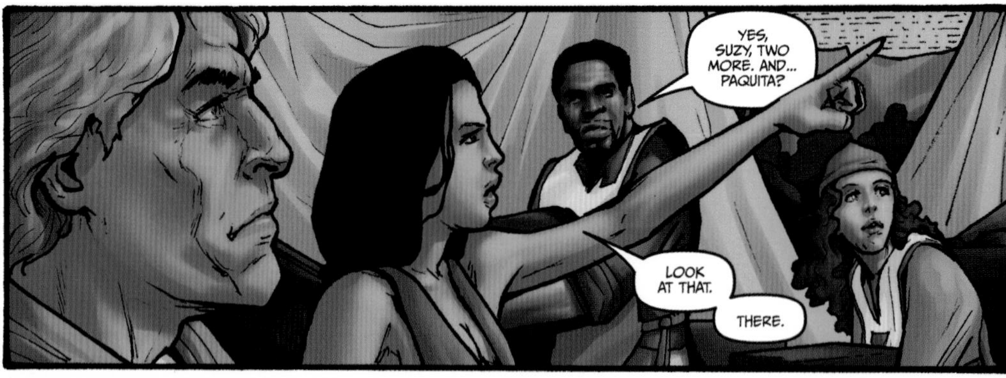
YES, SUZY, TWO MORE. AND... PAQUITA?
LOOK AT THAT.
THERE.

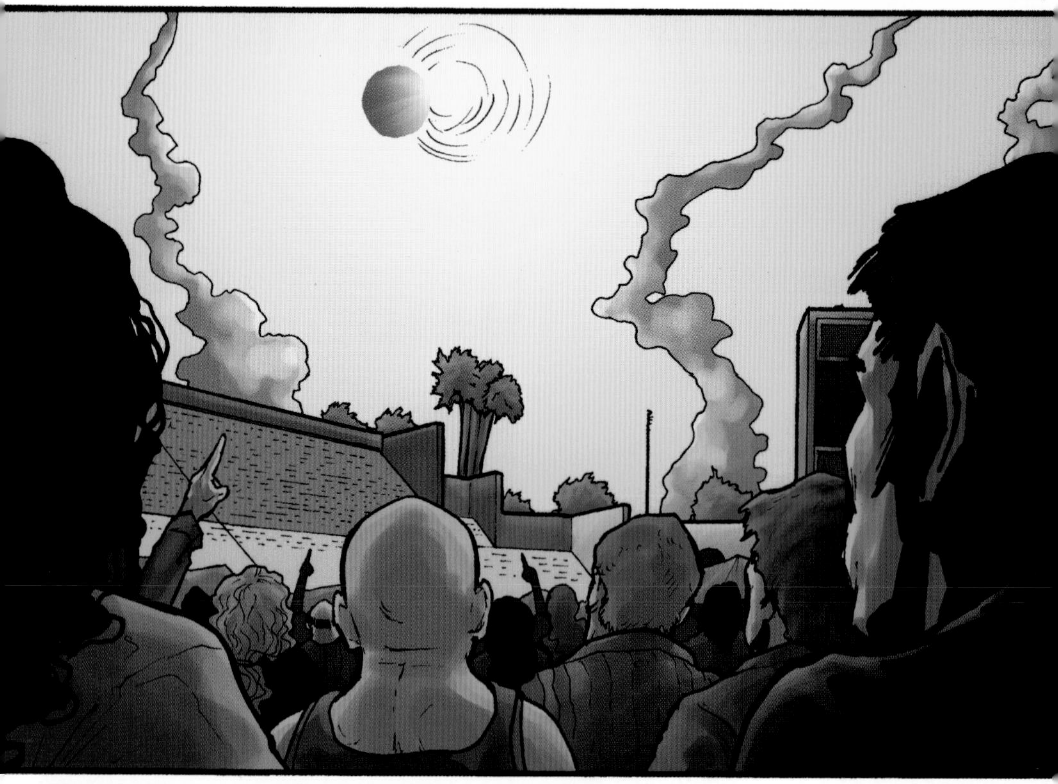

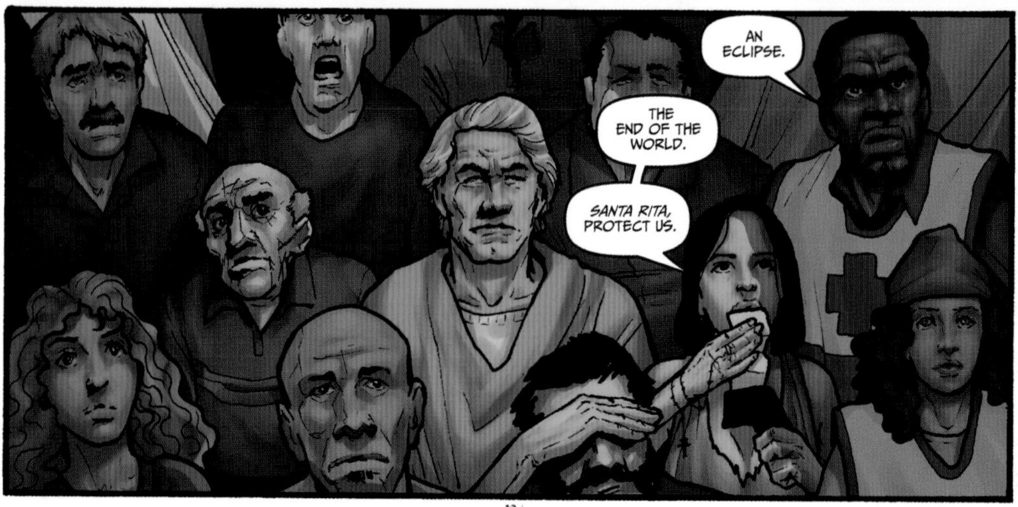
AN ECLIPSE.
THE END OF THE WORLD.
SANTA RITA, PROTECT US.

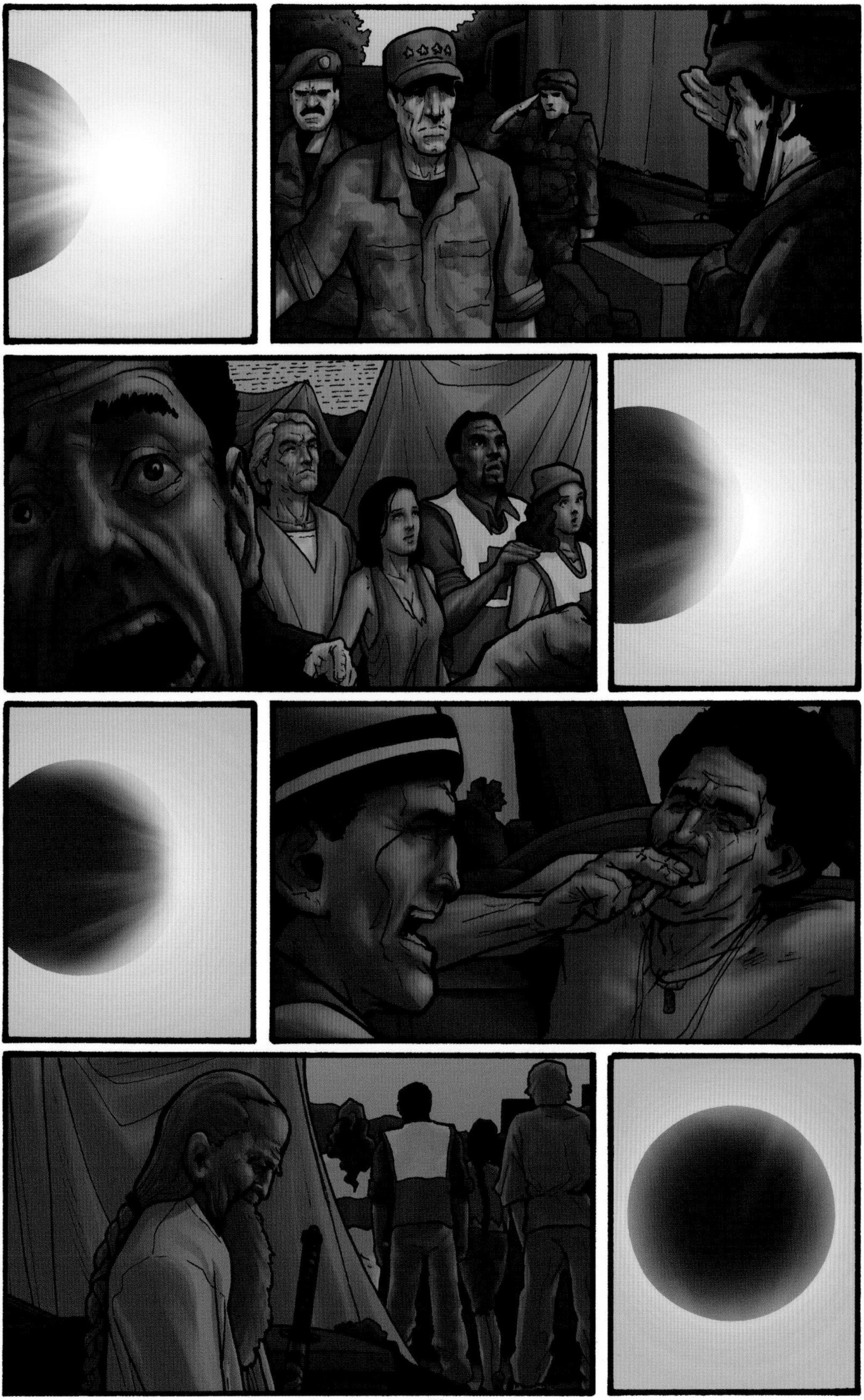

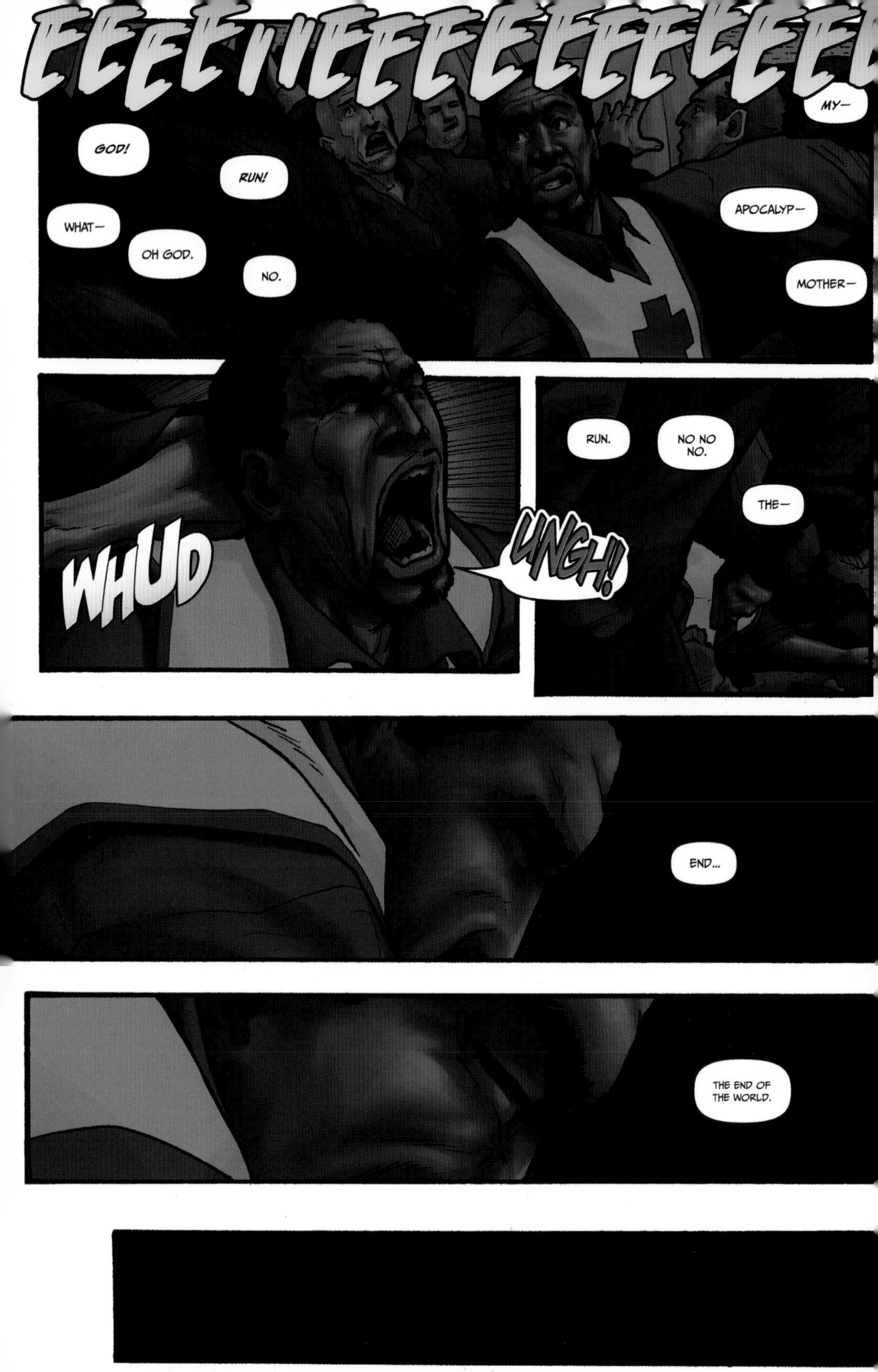
EEEIIEEEEEEEEE
GOD!
RUN!
WHAT—
OH GOD.
NO.
MY—
APOCALYP—
MOTHER—
WHUD
UNGH!
RUN.
NO NO NO.
THE—
END...
THE END OF THE WORLD.

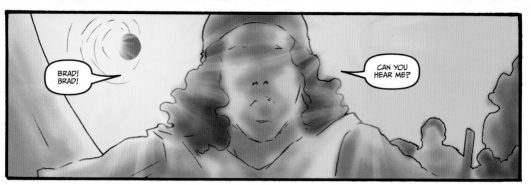

BRAD! BRAD!

CAN YOU HEAR ME?

UH...

OH, THANK GOD. DO NOT MOVE, BRAD. YOU MIGHT HAVE A CONCUSSION!

YOU SHOULD BE GRATEFUL, BRAD. YOU GOT STOMPED IN THE RIOT—

—BUT THE OLD *SAMURAI* SAVED YOUR ASS.

YOU SHOULD 'AVE SEEN HIM JUMPING. GOOD KUNG-FU SHIT!

WHA—

THE—THE PEOPLE...

THE MILITARY, THE BOSSES... THEY'RE *LEAVING!*

SOMEONE SAW THEM RETREATING, DURING THE ECLIPSE...

...AND PEOPLE JUST WENT CRAZY!

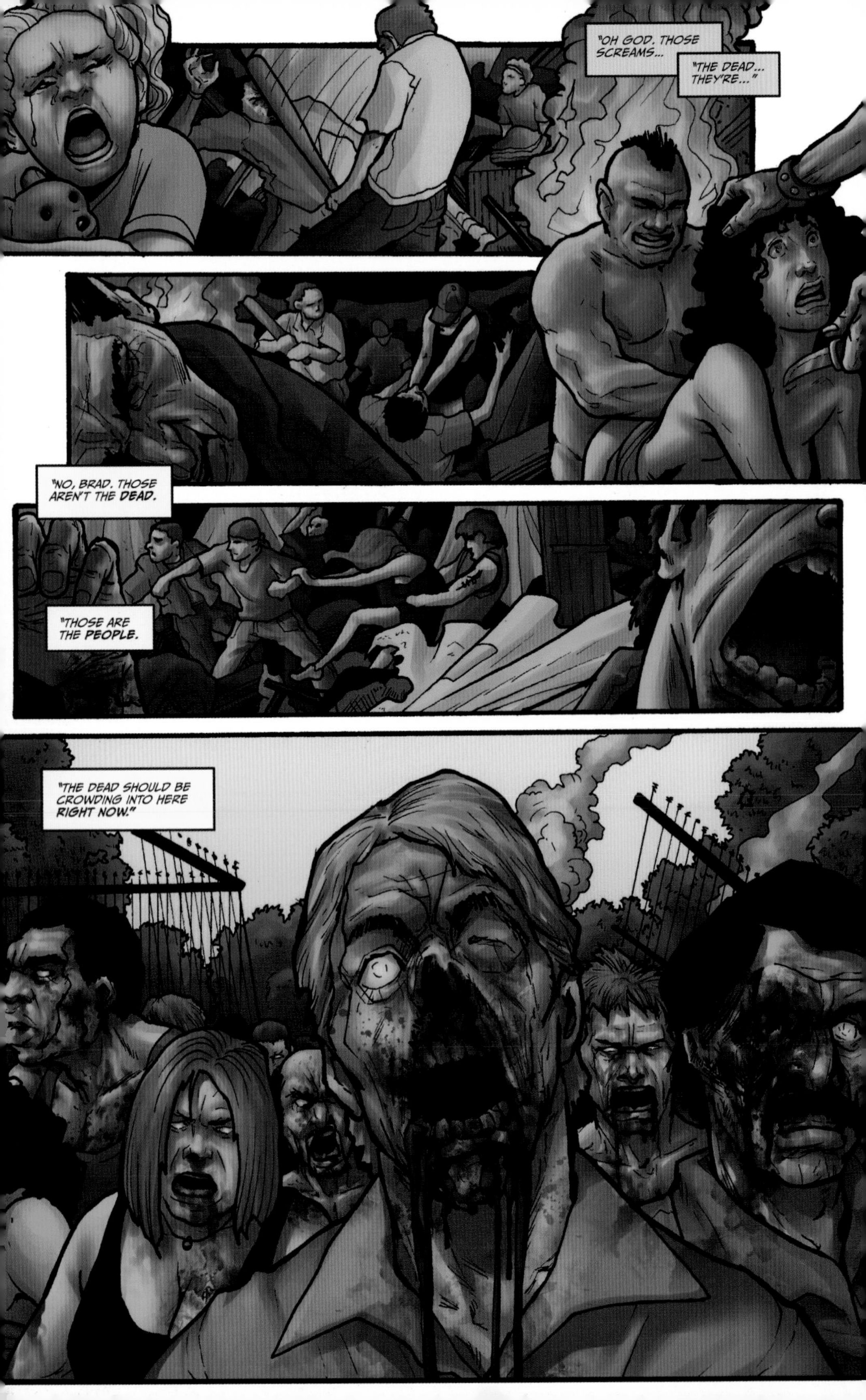
"OH GOD. THOSE SCREAMS...
"THE DEAD... THEY'RE..."
"NO, BRAD. THOSE AREN'T THE DEAD.
"THOSE ARE THE PEOPLE.
"THE DEAD SHOULD BE CROWDING INTO HERE RIGHT NOW."

chapter 2

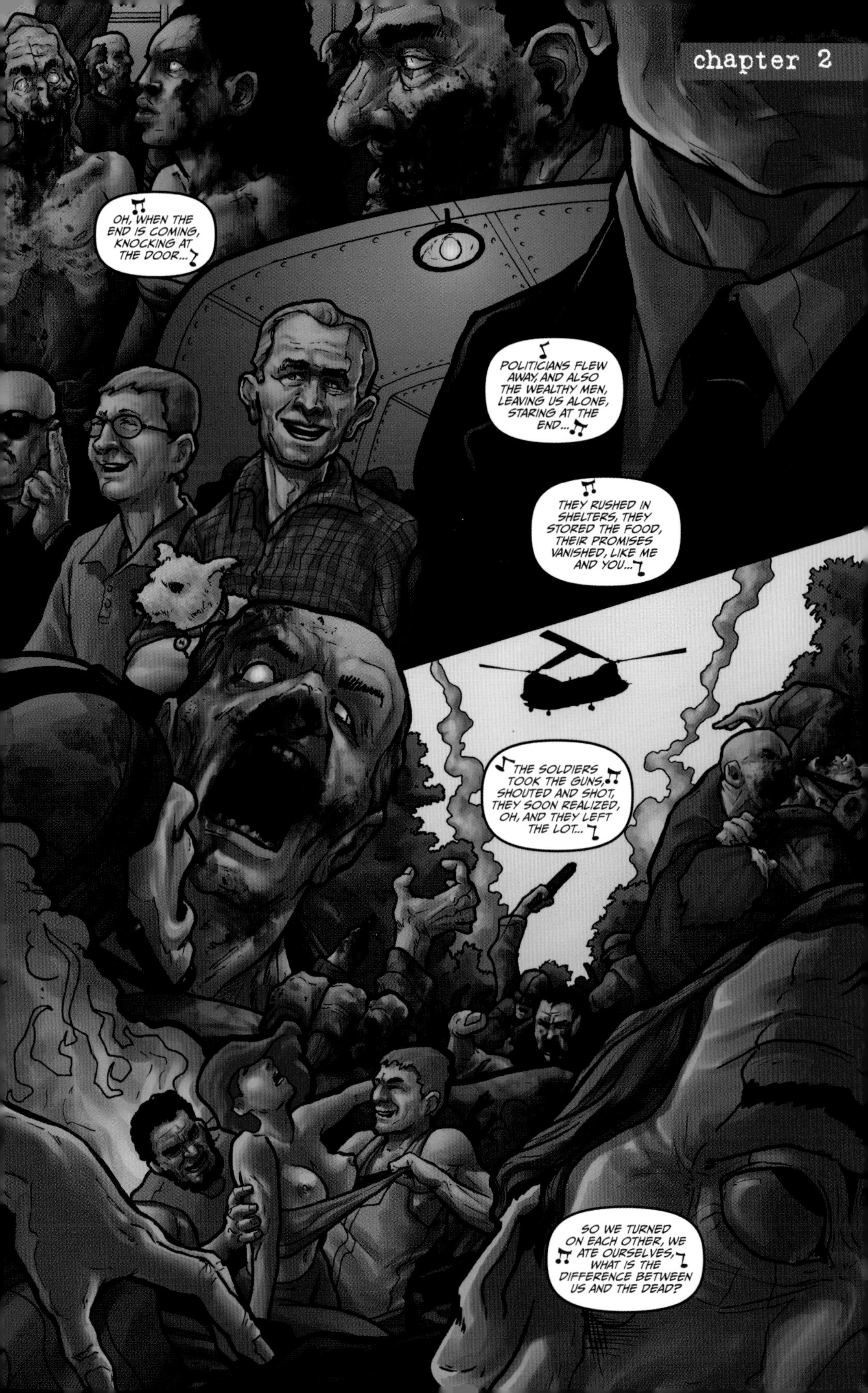
OH, WHEN THE END IS COMING, KNOCKING AT THE DOOR...
POLITICIANS FLEW AWAY, AND ALSO THE WEALTHY MEN, LEAVING US ALONE, STARING AT THE END...
THEY RUSHED IN SHELTERS, THEY STORED THE FOOD, THEIR PROMISES VANISHED, LIKE ME AND YOU...
THE SOLDIERS TOOK THE GUNS, SHOUTED AND SHOT, THEY SOON REALIZED, OH, AND THEY LEFT THE LOT...
SO WE TURNED ON EACH OTHER, WE ATE OURSELVES, WHAT IS THE DIFFERENCE BETWEEN US AND THE DEAD?

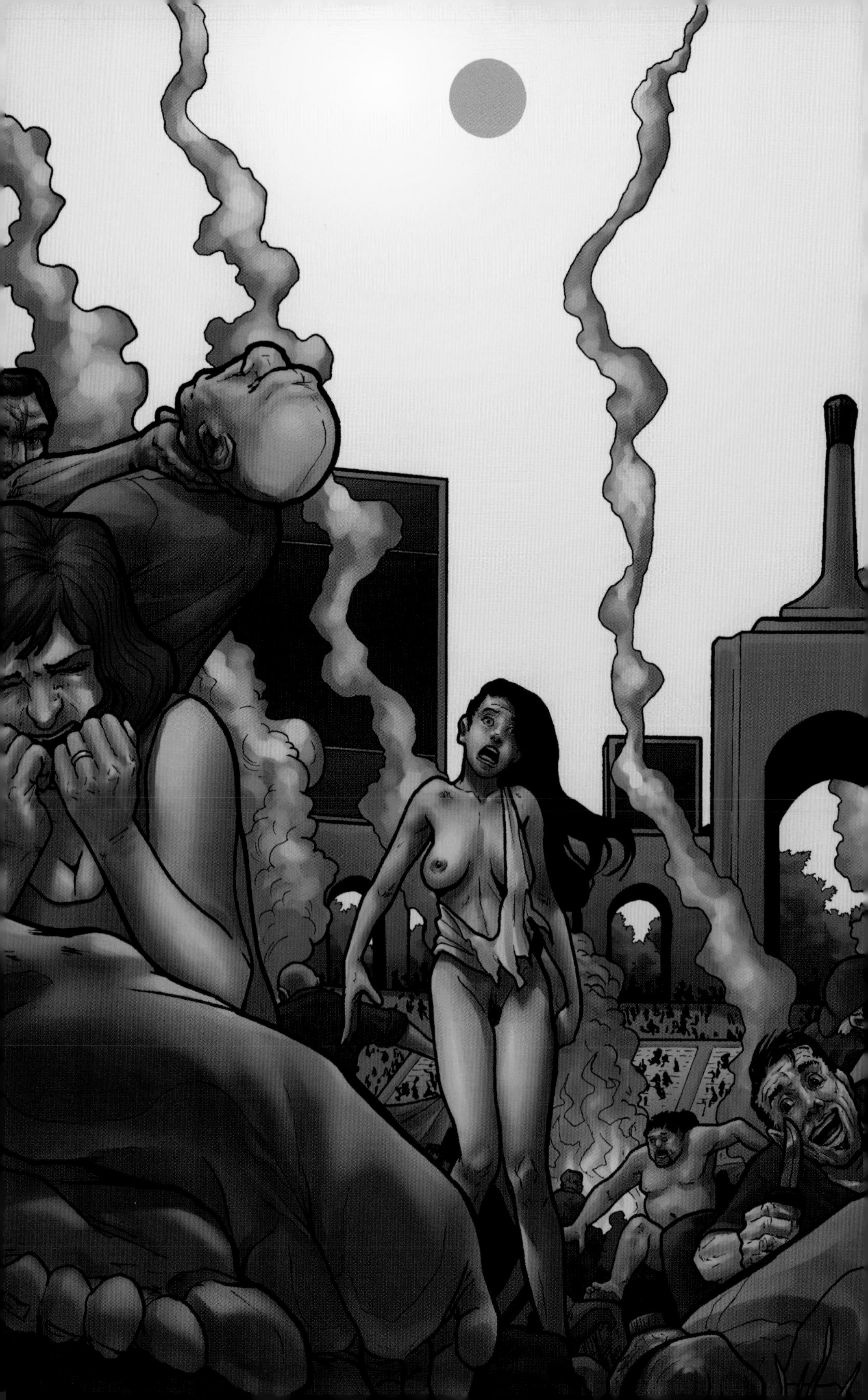

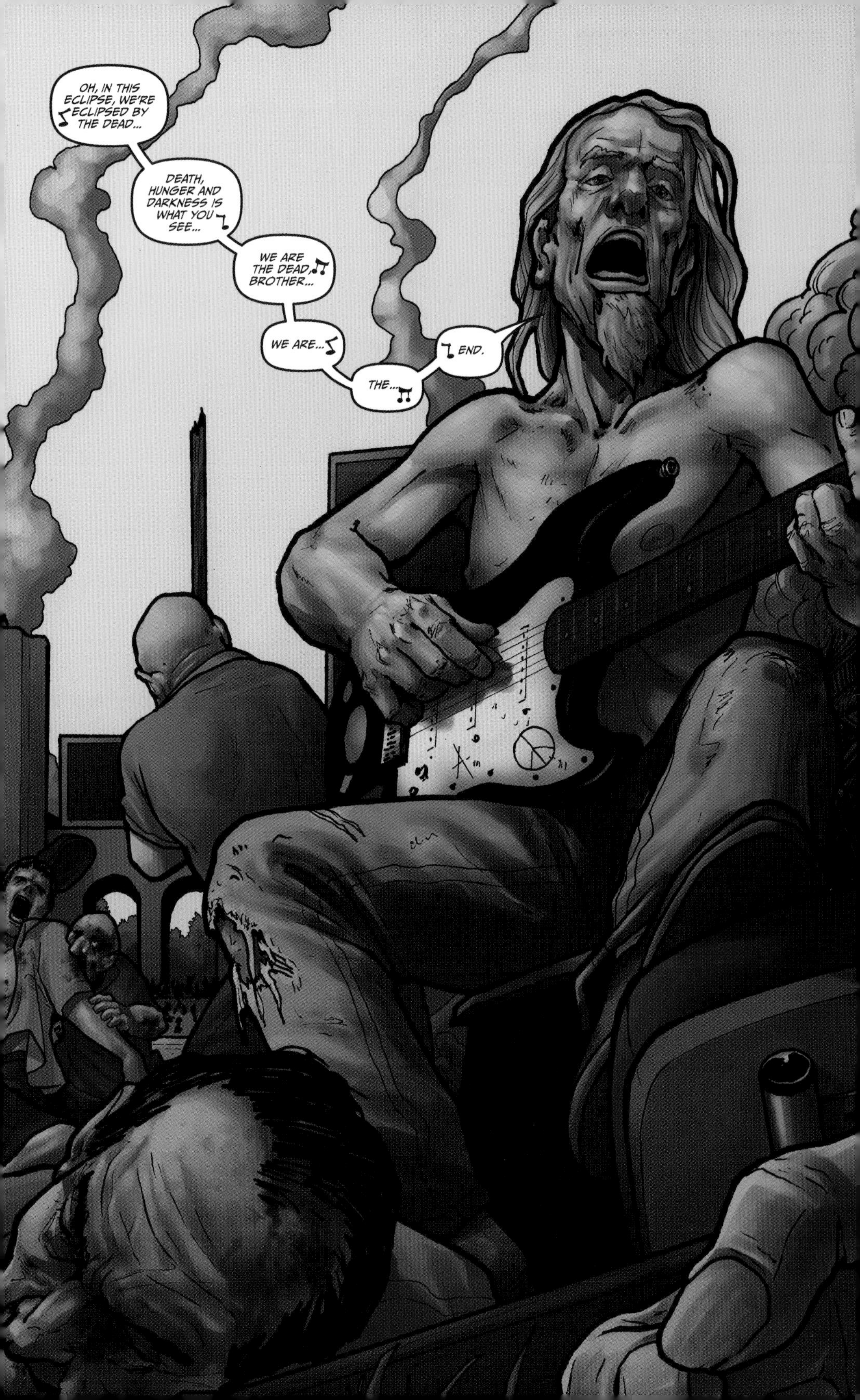
OH, IN THIS ECLIPSE, WE'RE ECLIPSED BY THE DEAD...
DEATH, HUNGER AND DARKNESS IS WHAT YOU SEE...
WE ARE THE DEAD, BROTHER...
WE ARE...
THE...
END.

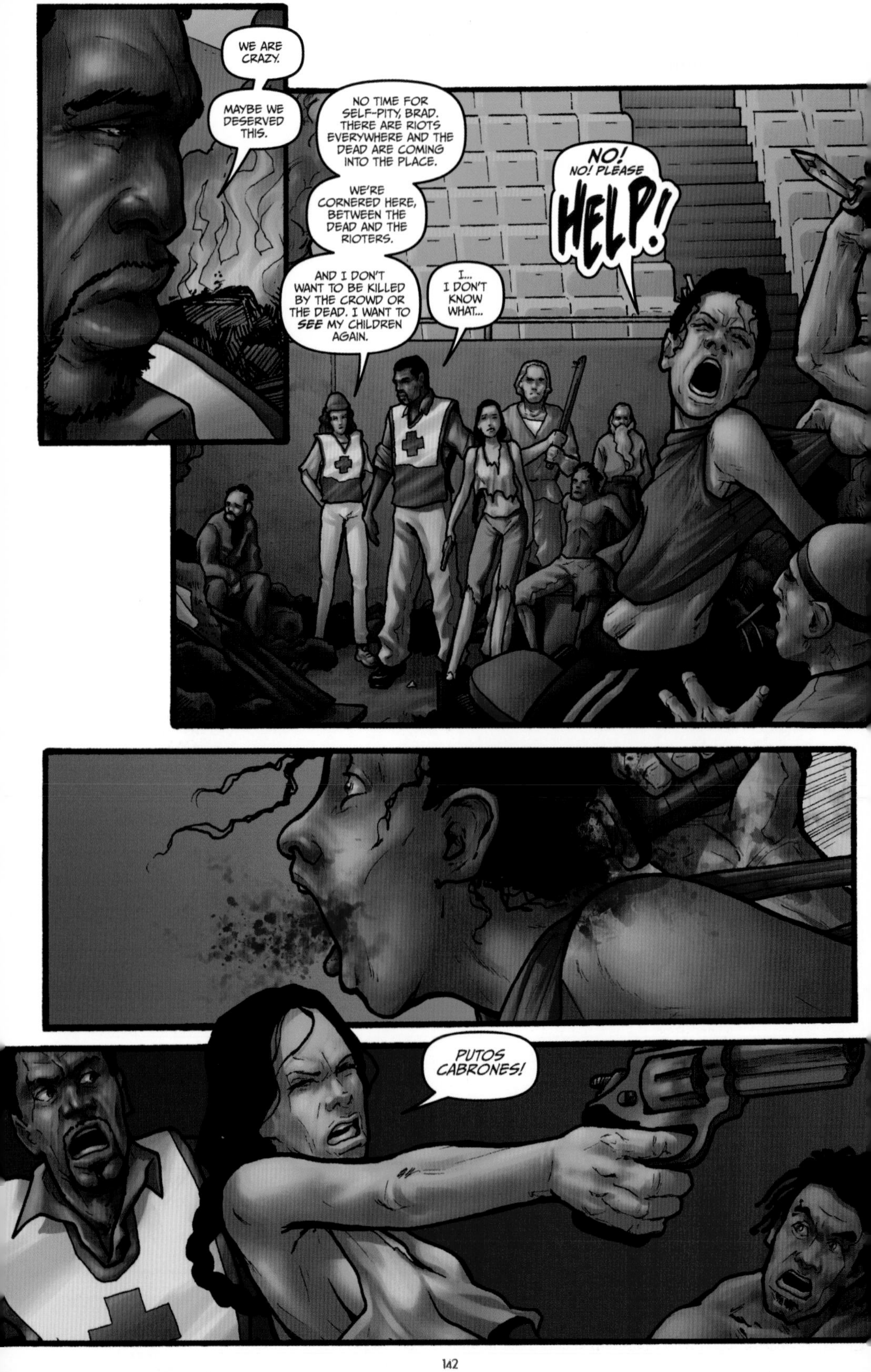
WE ARE CRAZY.
MAYBE WE DESERVED THIS.
NO TIME FOR SELF-PITY, BRAD. THERE ARE RIOTS EVERYWHERE AND THE DEAD ARE COMING INTO THE PLACE.
WE'RE CORNERED HERE, BETWEEN THE DEAD AND THE RIOTERS.
AND I DON'T WANT TO BE KILLED BY THE CROWD OR THE DEAD. I WANT TO SEE MY CHILDREN AGAIN.
I... I DON'T KNOW WHAT...
NO! NO! PLEASE HELP!
PUTOS CABRONES!

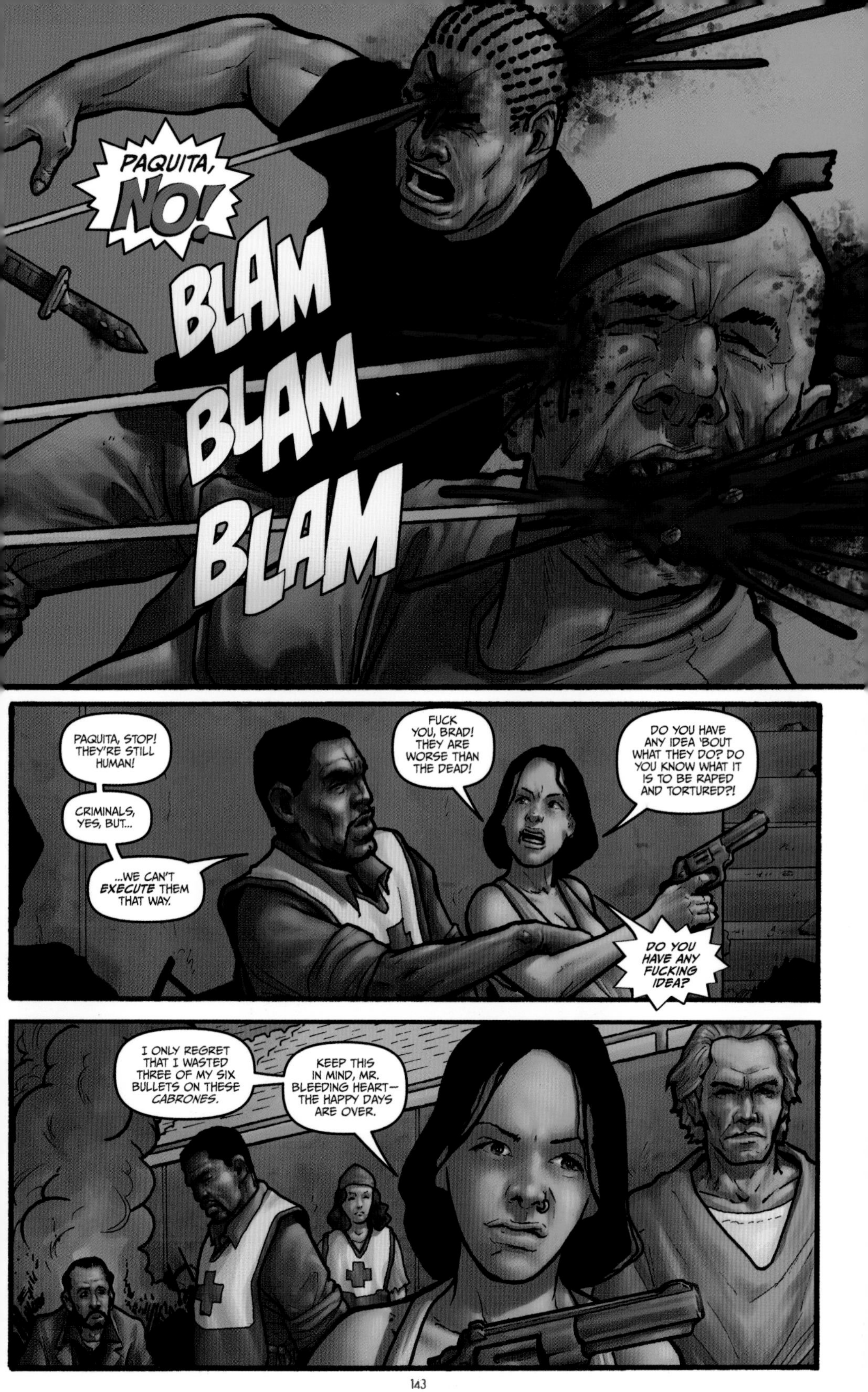
PAQUITA, NO!
BLAM
BLAM
BLAM
PAQUITA, STOP! THEY'RE STILL HUMAN!
CRIMINALS, YES, BUT...
...WE CAN'T EXECUTE THEM THAT WAY.
FUCK YOU, BRAD! THEY ARE WORSE THAN THE DEAD!
DO YOU HAVE ANY IDEA 'BOUT WHAT THEY DO? DO YOU KNOW WHAT IT IS TO BE RAPED AND TORTURED?!
DO YOU HAVE ANY FUCKING IDEA?
I ONLY REGRET THAT I WASTED THREE OF MY SIX BULLETS ON THESE CABRONES.
KEEP THIS IN MIND, MR. BLEEDING HEART—THE HAPPY DAYS ARE OVER.

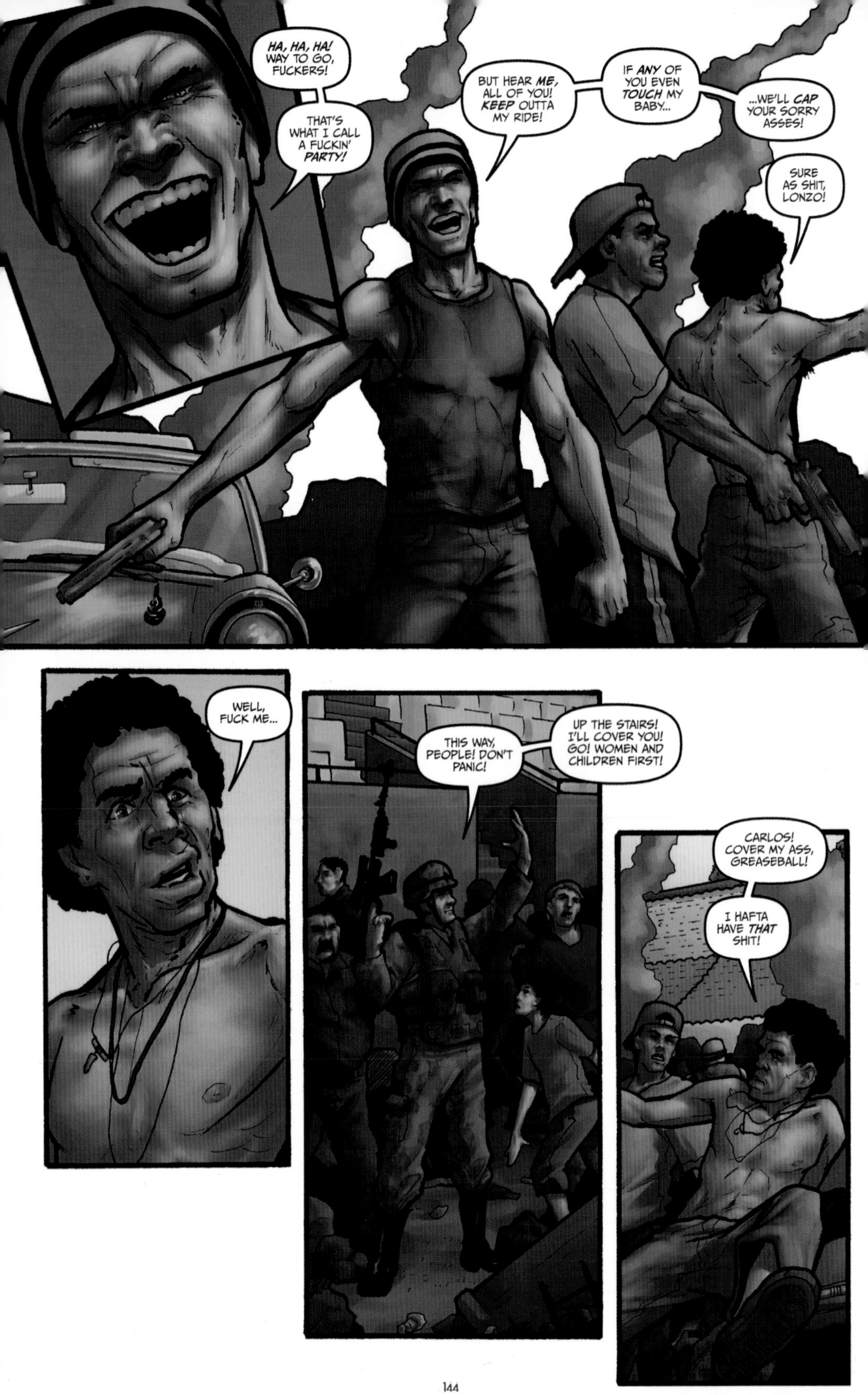
HA, HA, HA! WAY TO GO, FUCKERS!
THAT'S WHAT I CALL A FUCKIN' PARTY!
BUT HEAR ME, ALL OF YOU! KEEP OUTTA MY RIDE!
IF ANY OF YOU EVEN TOUCH MY BABY...
...WE'LL CAP YOUR SORRY ASSES!
SURE AS SHIT, LONZO!
WELL, FUCK ME...
THIS WAY, PEOPLE! DON'T PANIC!
UP THE STAIRS! I'LL COVER YOU! GO! WOMEN AND CHILDREN FIRST!
CARLOS! COVER MY ASS, GREASEBALL!
I HAFTA HAVE THAT SHIT!

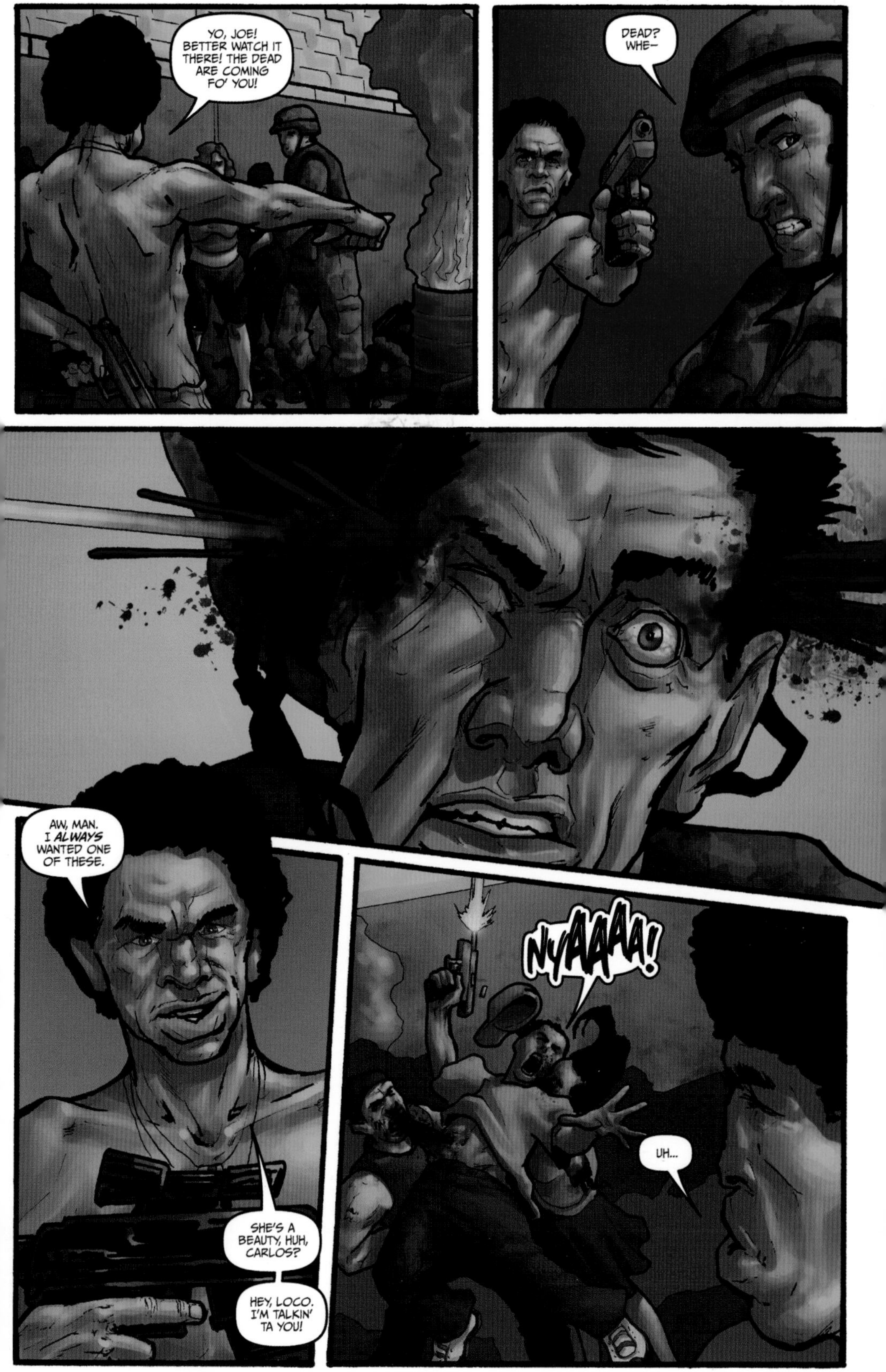
YO, JOE! BETTER WATCH IT THERE! THE DEAD ARE COMING FO' YOU!
DEAD? WHE–
AW, MAN. I *ALWAYS* WANTED ONE OF THESE.
SHE'S A BEAUTY, HUH, CARLOS?
HEY, LOCO. I'M TALKIN' TA YOU!
NyAAAAA!
UH...

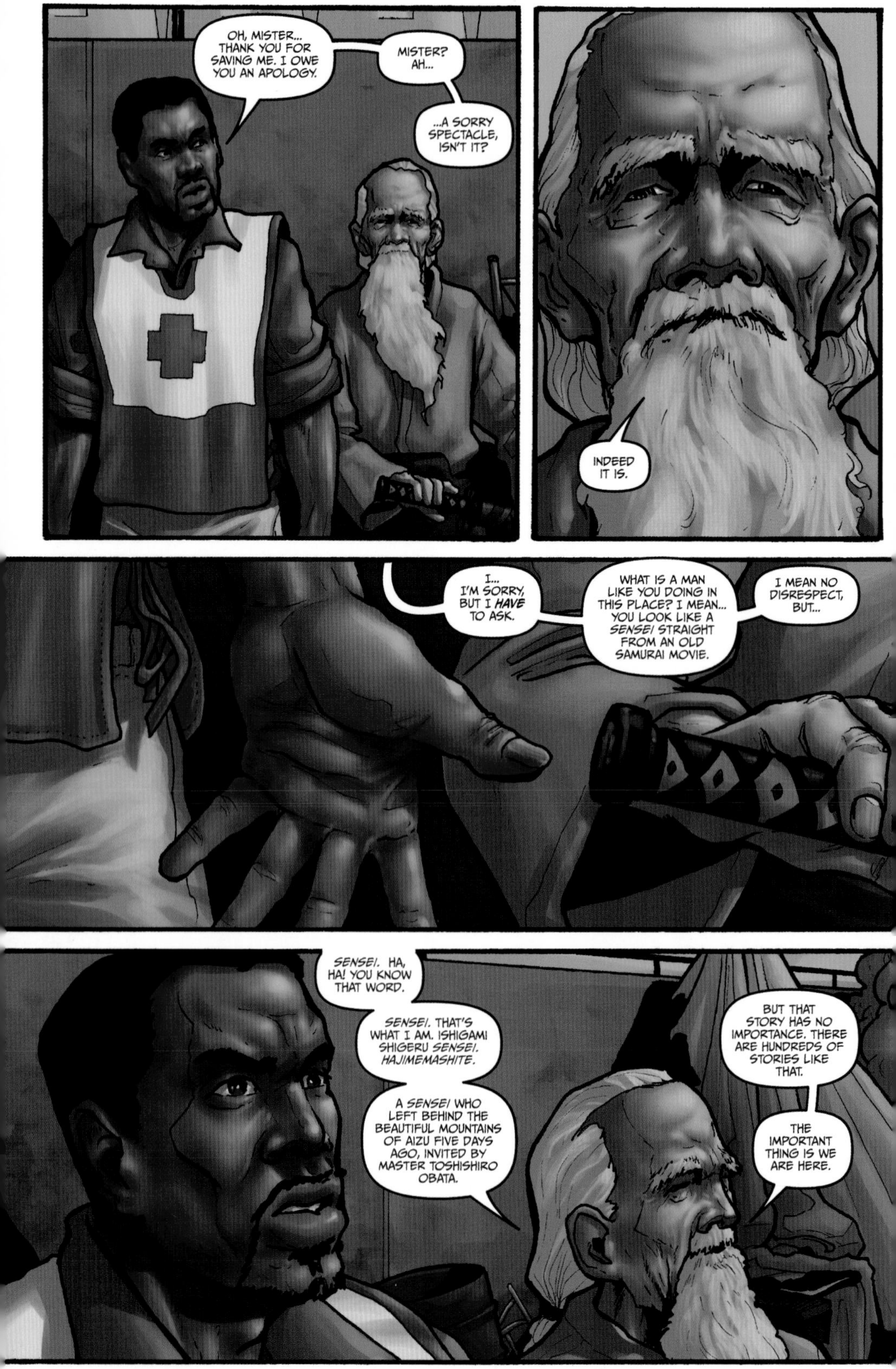
OH, MISTER... THANK YOU FOR SAVING ME. I OWE YOU AN APOLOGY.
MISTER? AH...
...A SORRY SPECTACLE, ISN'T IT?
INDEED IT IS.
I... I'M SORRY, BUT I *HAVE* TO ASK.
WHAT IS A MAN LIKE YOU DOING IN THIS PLACE? I MEAN... YOU LOOK LIKE A *SENSEI* STRAIGHT FROM AN OLD SAMURAI MOVIE.
I MEAN NO DISRESPECT, BUT...
SENSEI. HA, HA! YOU KNOW THAT WORD.
SENSEI. THAT'S WHAT I AM. ISHIGAMI SHIGERU *SENSEI*. *HAJIMEMASHITE*.
A *SENSEI* WHO LEFT BEHIND THE BEAUTIFUL MOUNTAINS OF AIZU FIVE DAYS AGO, INVITED BY MASTER TOSHISHIRO OBATA.
BUT THAT STORY HAS NO IMPORTANCE. THERE ARE HUNDREDS OF STORIES LIKE THAT.
THE IMPORTANT THING IS WE ARE HERE.

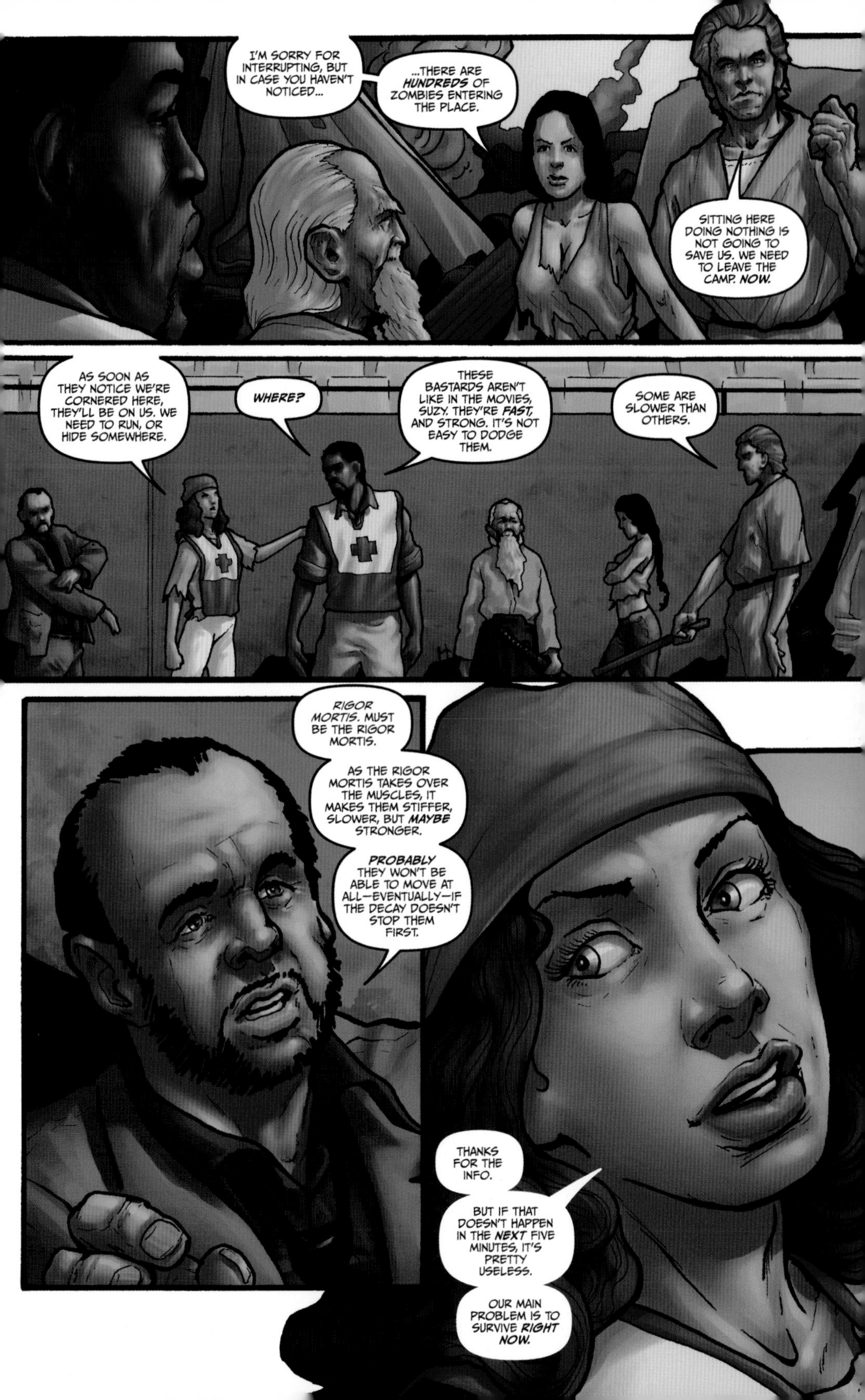

I'M SORRY FOR INTERRUPTING, BUT IN CASE YOU HAVEN'T NOTICED...
...THERE ARE *HUNDREDS* OF ZOMBIES ENTERING THE PLACE.
SITTING HERE DOING NOTHING IS NOT GOING TO SAVE US. WE NEED TO LEAVE THE CAMP. *NOW.*
AS SOON AS THEY NOTICE WE'RE CORNERED HERE, THEY'LL BE ON US. WE NEED TO RUN, OR HIDE SOMEWHERE.
WHERE?
THESE BASTARDS AREN'T LIKE IN THE MOVIES, SUZY. THEY'RE *FAST,* AND STRONG. IT'S NOT EASY TO DODGE THEM.
SOME ARE SLOWER THAN OTHERS.
RIGOR MORTIS. MUST BE THE RIGOR MORTIS.
AS THE RIGOR MORTIS TAKES OVER THE MUSCLES, IT MAKES THEM STIFFER, SLOWER, BUT *MAYBE* STRONGER.
PROBABLY THEY WON'T BE ABLE TO MOVE AT ALL—EVENTUALLY—IF THE DECAY DOESN'T STOP THEM FIRST.
THANKS FOR THE INFO.
BUT IF THAT DOESN'T HAPPEN IN THE *NEXT* FIVE MINUTES, IT'S PRETTY USELESS.
OUR MAIN PROBLEM IS TO SURVIVE *RIGHT NOW.*

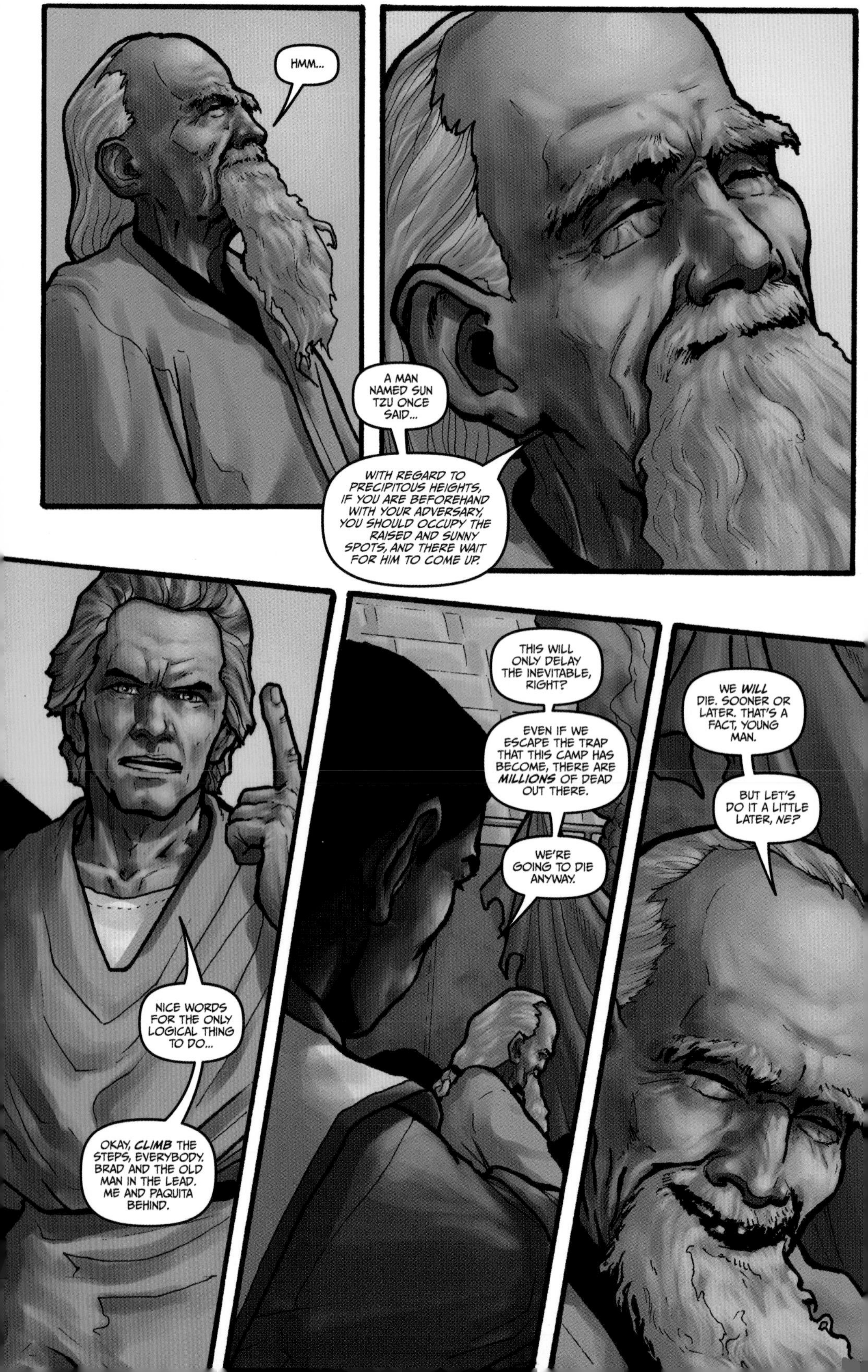
HMM...
A MAN NAMED SUN TZU ONCE SAID...
WITH REGARD TO PRECIPITOUS HEIGHTS, IF YOU ARE BEFOREHAND WITH YOUR ADVERSARY, YOU SHOULD OCCUPY THE RAISED AND SUNNY SPOTS, AND THERE WAIT FOR HIM TO COME UP.
NICE WORDS FOR THE ONLY LOGICAL THING TO DO...
OKAY, CLIMB THE STEPS, EVERYBODY. BRAD AND THE OLD MAN IN THE LEAD. ME AND PAQUITA BEHIND.
THIS WILL ONLY DELAY THE INEVITABLE, RIGHT?
EVEN IF WE ESCAPE THE TRAP THAT THIS CAMP HAS BECOME, THERE ARE MILLIONS OF DEAD OUT THERE.
WE'RE GOING TO DIE ANYWAY.
WE WILL DIE. SOONER OR LATER. THAT'S A FACT, YOUNG MAN.
BUT LET'S DO IT A LITTLE LATER, NE?

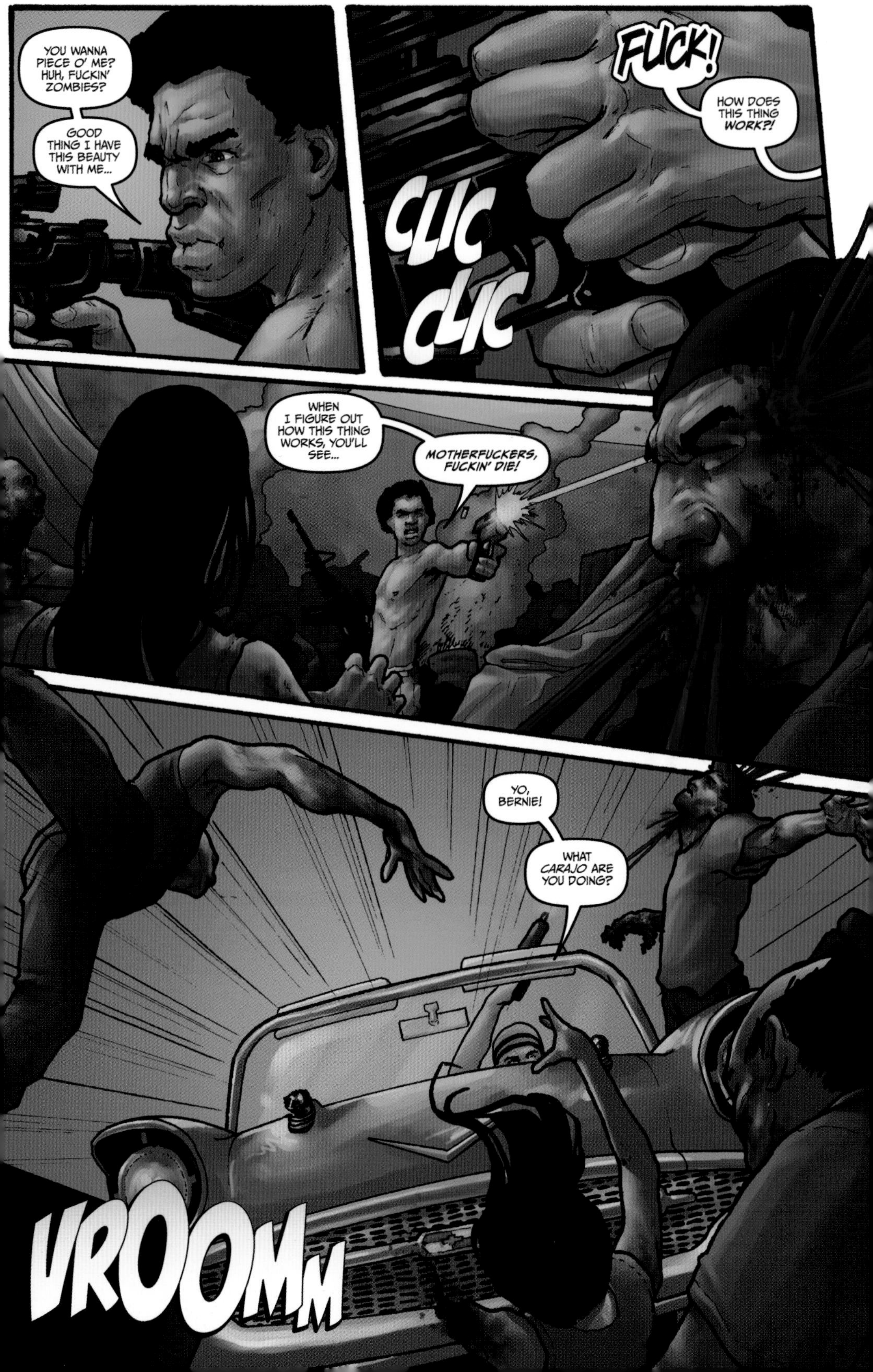

YOU WANNA PIECE O' ME? HUH, FUCKIN' ZOMBIES?
GOOD THING I HAVE THIS BEAUTY WITH ME...
FUCK!
HOW DOES THIS THING WORK?!
CLIC
CLIC
WHEN I FIGURE OUT HOW THIS THING WORKS, YOU'LL SEE...
MOTHERFUCKERS, FUCKIN' DIE!
YO, BERNIE!
WHAT CARAJO ARE YOU DOING?
VROOMM

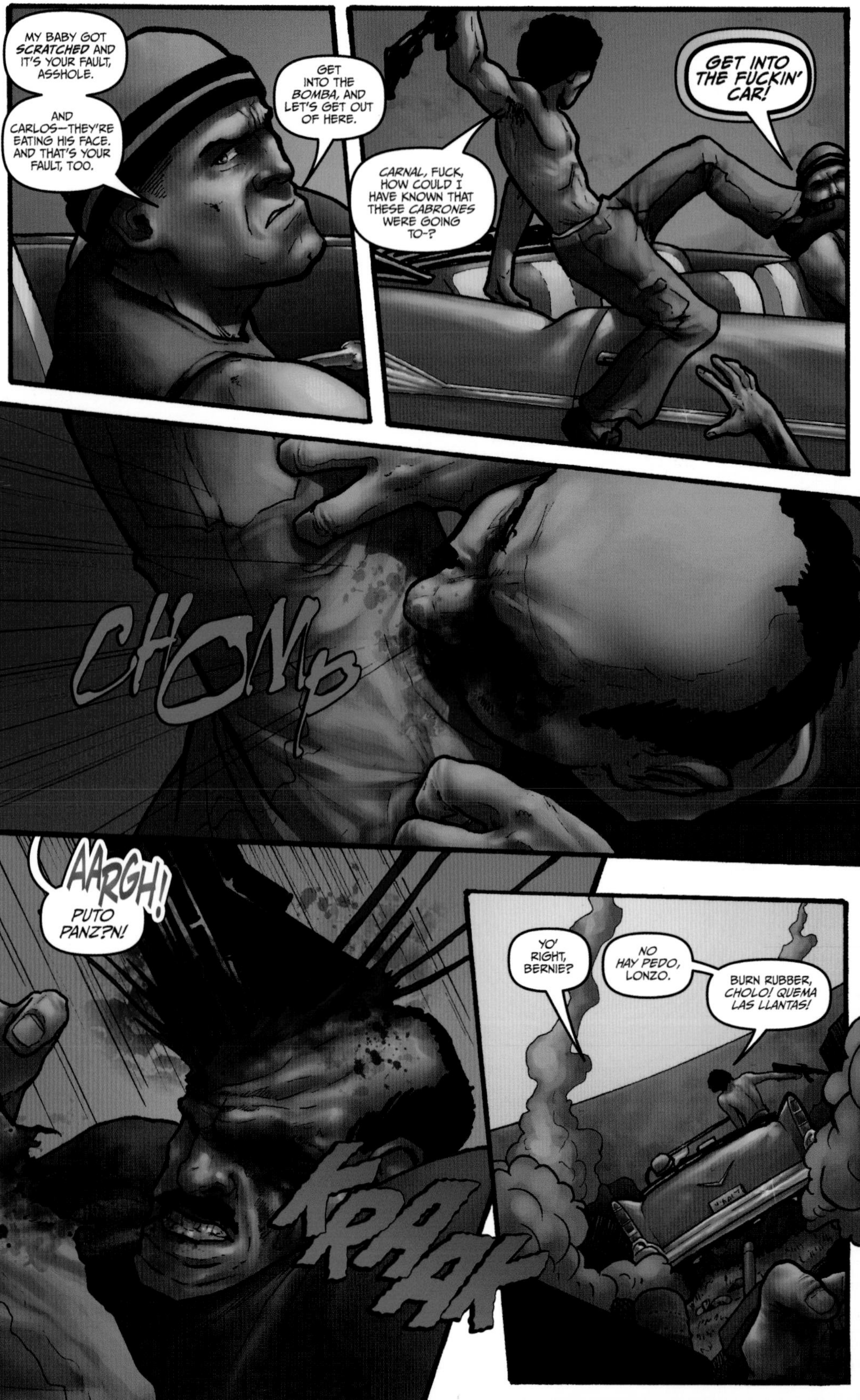
MY BABY GOT SCRATCHED AND IT'S YOUR FAULT, ASSHOLE.
AND CARLOS—THEY'RE EATING HIS FACE. AND THAT'S YOUR FAULT, TOO.
GET INTO THE BOMBA, AND LET'S GET OUT OF HERE.
CARNAL, FUCK, HOW COULD I HAVE KNOWN THAT THESE CABRONES WERE GOING TO-?
GET INTO THE FUCKIN' CAR!
CHOMP
AARGH! PUTO PANZ?N!
KRAAK
YO' RIGHT, BERNIE?
NO HAY PEDO, LONZO.
BURN RUBBER, CHOLO! QUEMA LAS LLANTAS!

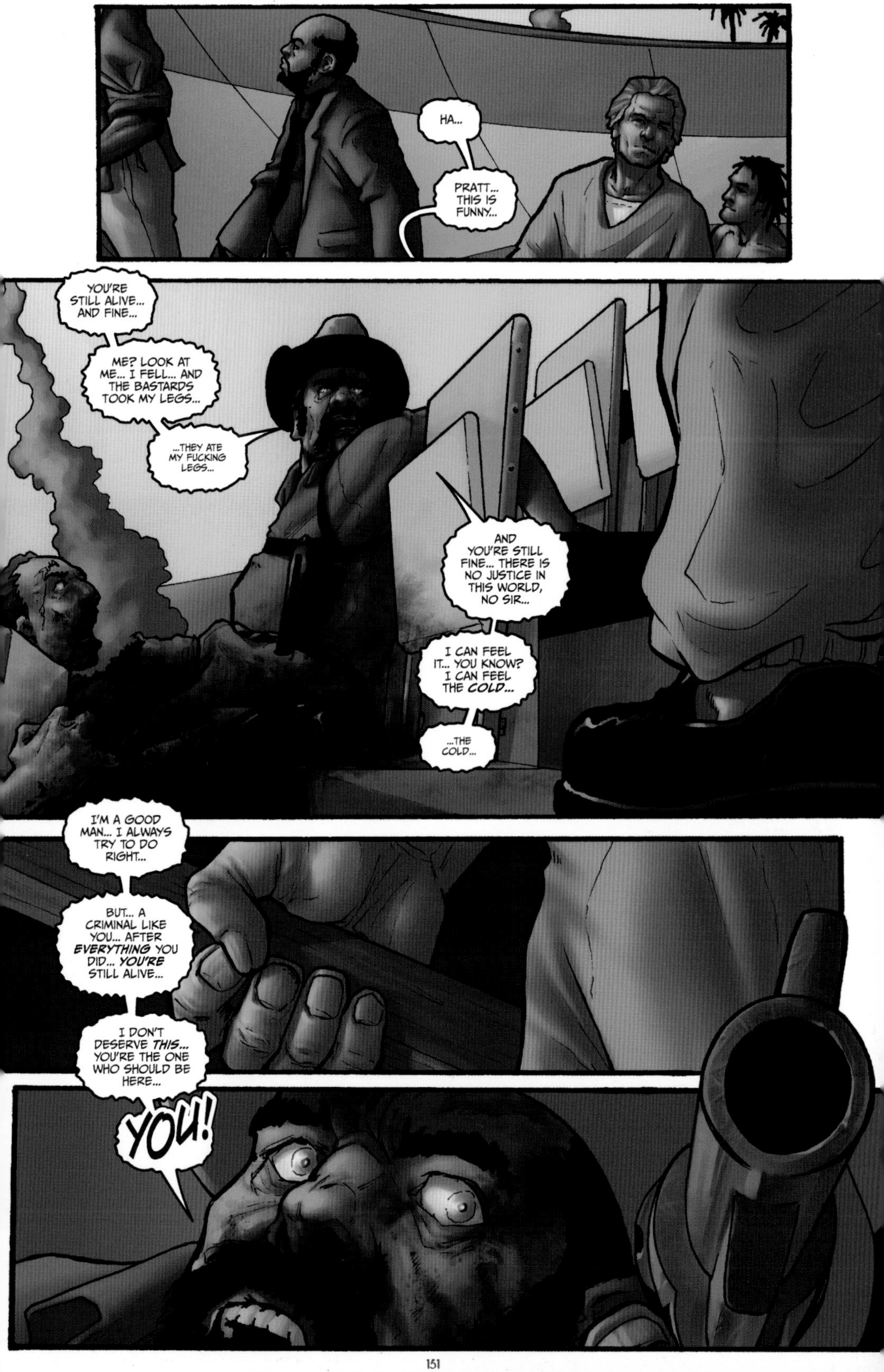
HA...
PRATT... THIS IS FUNNY...
YOU'RE STILL ALIVE... AND FINE...
ME? LOOK AT ME... I FELL... AND THE BASTARDS TOOK MY LEGS...
...THEY ATE MY FUCKING LEGS...
AND YOU'RE STILL FINE... THERE IS NO JUSTICE IN THIS WORLD, NO SIR...
I CAN FEEL IT... YOU KNOW? I CAN FEEL THE *COLD*...
...THE COLD...
I'M A GOOD MAN... I ALWAYS TRY TO DO RIGHT...
BUT... A CRIMINAL LIKE YOU... AFTER *EVERYTHING* YOU DID... *YOU'RE* STILL ALIVE...
I DON'T DESERVE *THIS*... YOU'RE THE ONE WHO SHOULD BE HERE...
YOU!

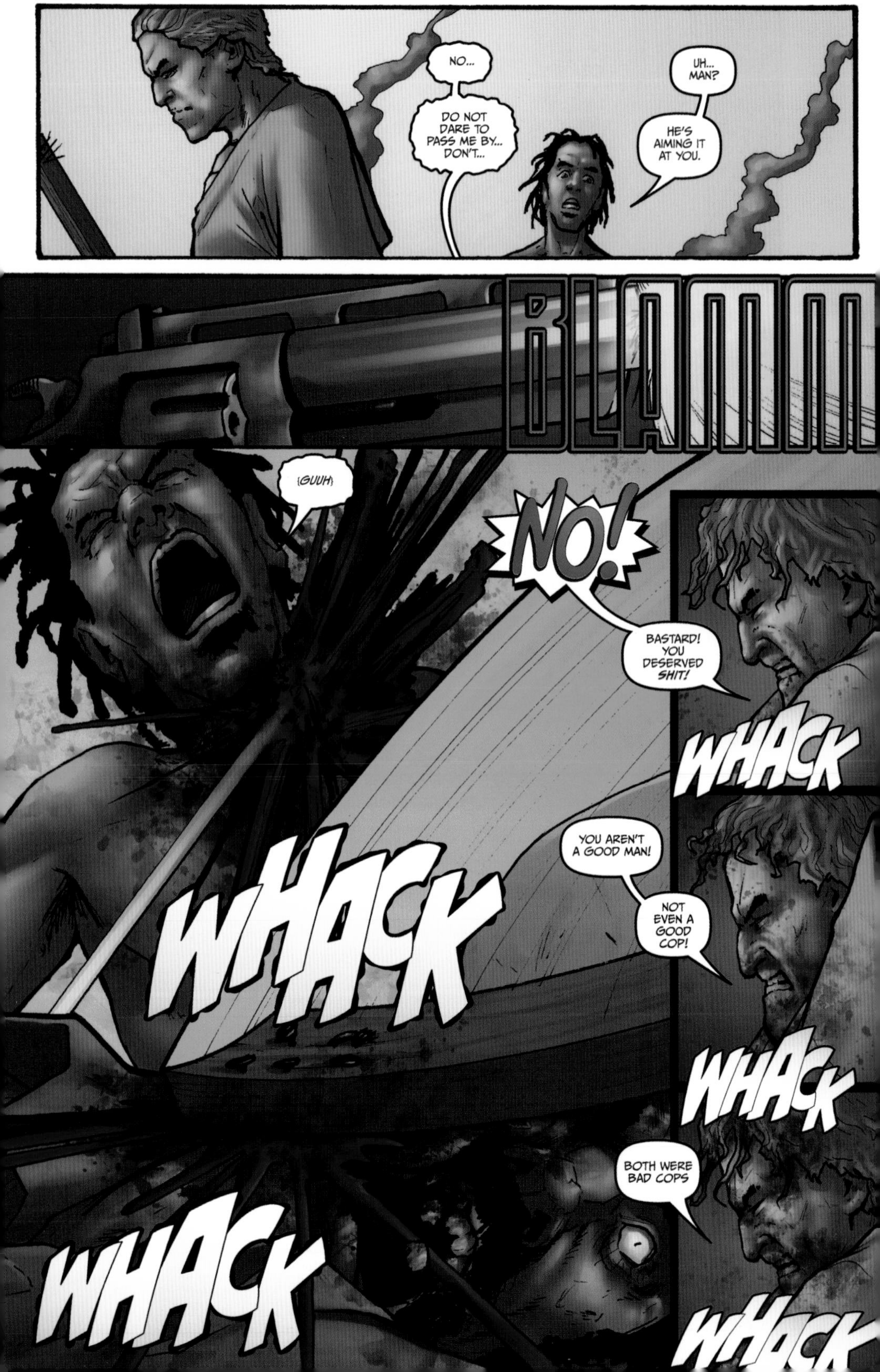
NO...
DO NOT DARE TO PASS ME BY... DON'T...
UH... MAN?
HE'S AIMING IT AT YOU.
BLAMM
{GUUH}
NO!
BASTARD! YOU DESERVED SHIT!
WHACK
WHACK
YOU AREN'T A GOOD MAN!
NOT EVEN A GOOD COP!
WHACK
BOTH WERE BAD COPS
WHACK
WHACK

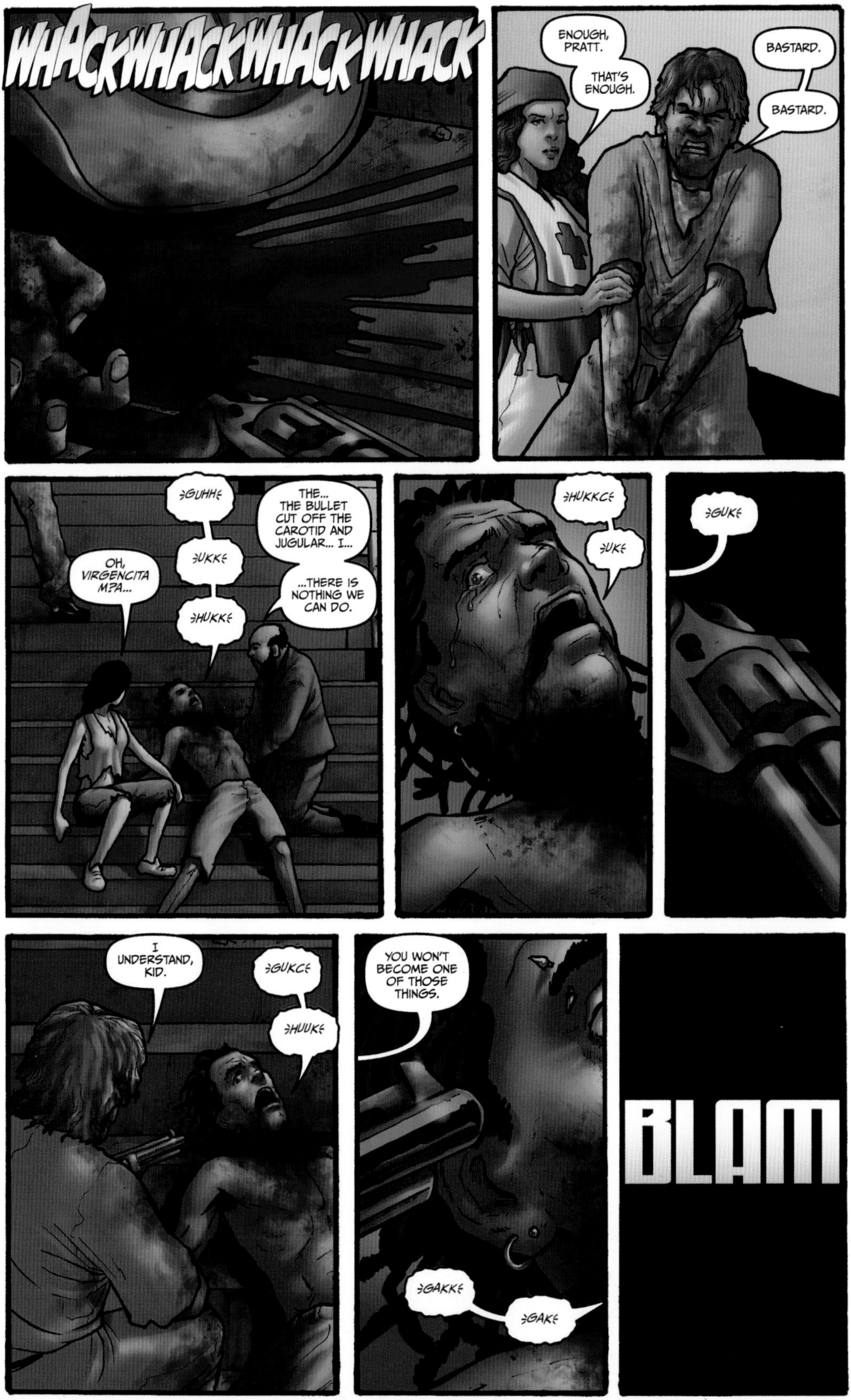
WHACKWHACKWHACKWHACK
ENOUGH, PRATT.
THAT'S ENOUGH.
BASTARD.
BASTARD.
OH, VIRGENCITA M?A...
GUHH
UKK
HUKK
THE... THE BULLET CUT OFF THE CAROTID AND JUGULAR... I...
...THERE IS NOTHING WE CAN DO.
HUKKC
UK
GUK
I UNDERSTAND, KID.
GUKC
HUUK
YOU WON'T BECOME ONE OF THOSE THINGS.
GAKK
GAK
BLAM

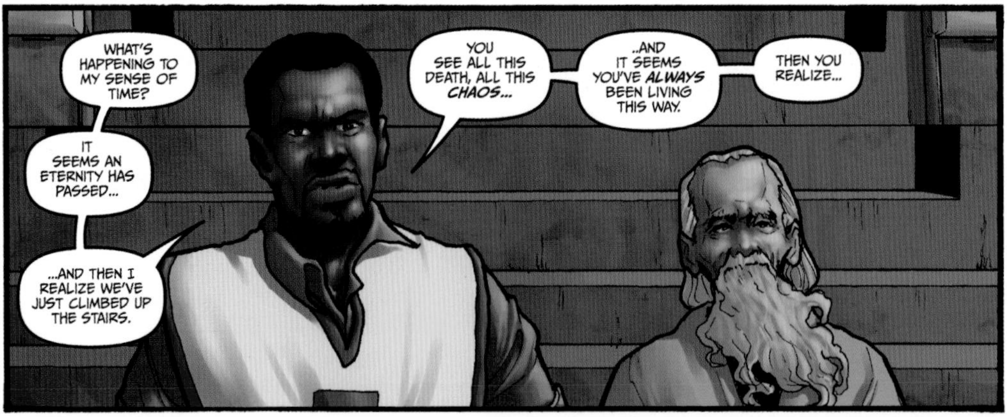
WHAT'S HAPPENING TO MY SENSE OF TIME?
IT SEEMS AN ETERNITY HAS PASSED...
...AND THEN I REALIZE WE'VE JUST CLIMBED UP THE STAIRS.
YOU SEE ALL THIS DEATH, ALL THIS CHAOS...
..AND IT SEEMS YOU'VE ALWAYS BEEN LIVING THIS WAY.
THEN YOU REALIZE...

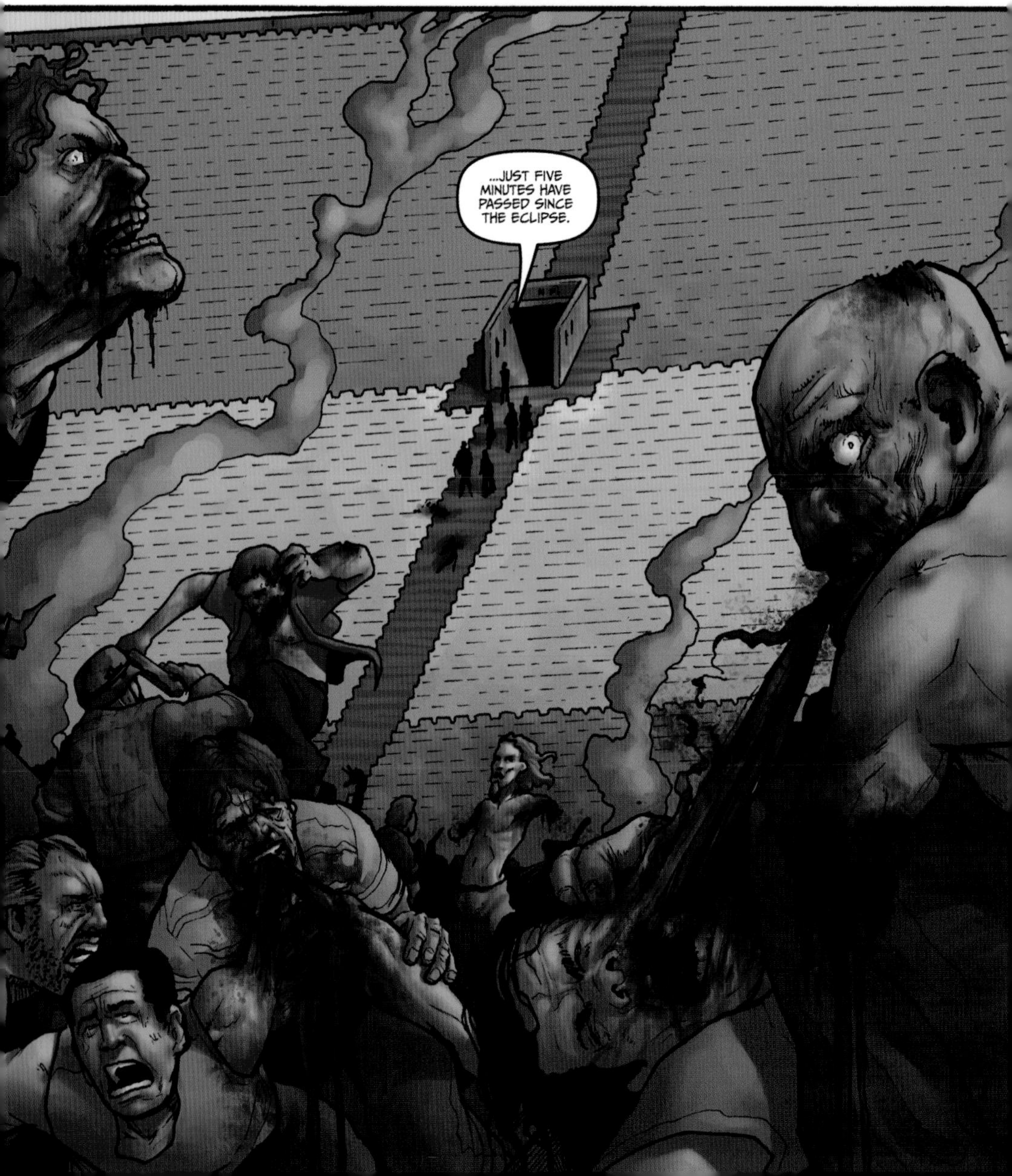
...JUST FIVE MINUTES HAVE PASSED SINCE THE ECLIPSE.

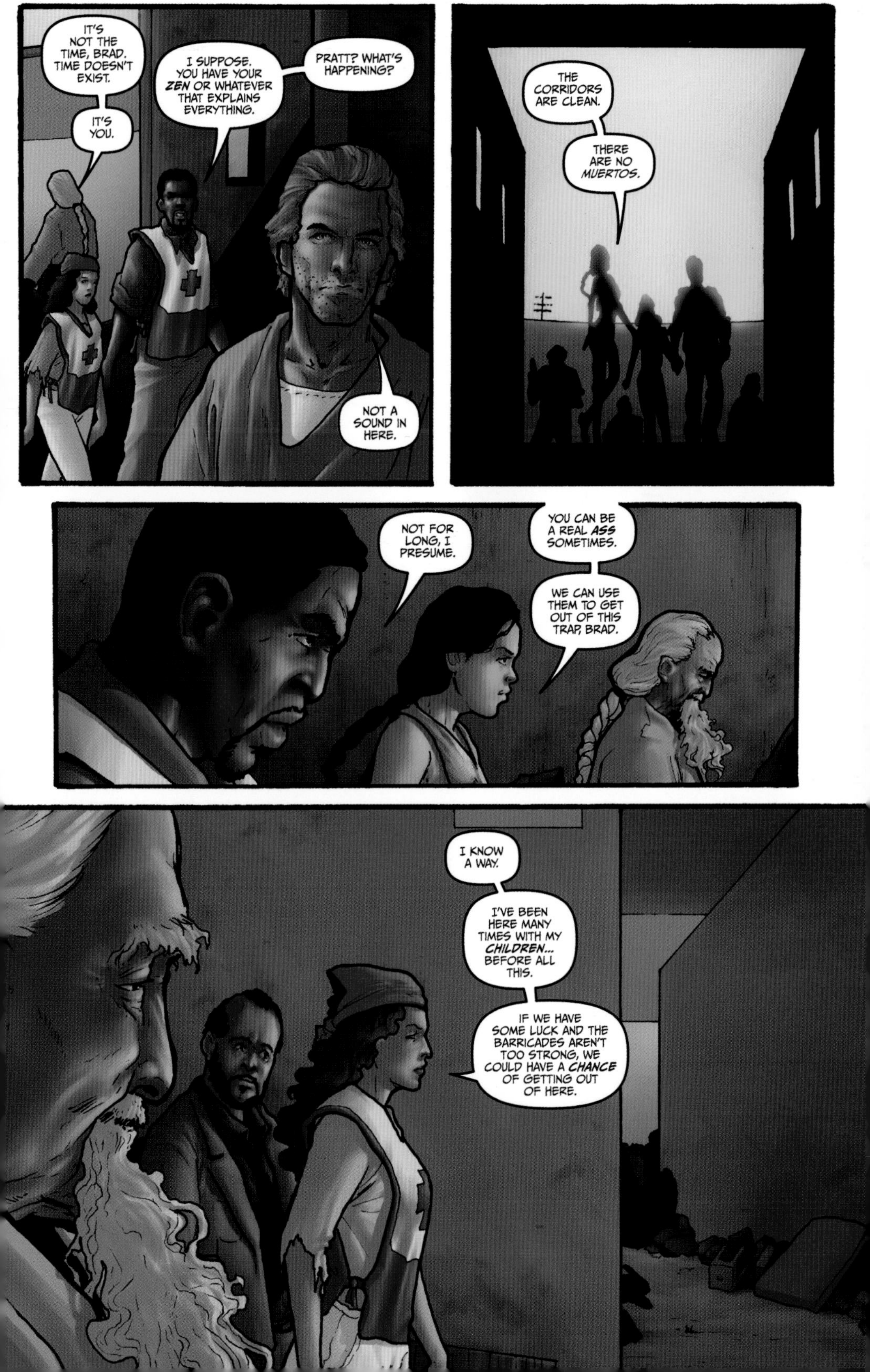
IT'S NOT THE TIME, BRAD. TIME DOESN'T EXIST.
IT'S YOU.
I SUPPOSE. YOU HAVE YOUR ZEN OR WHATEVER THAT EXPLAINS EVERYTHING.
PRATT? WHAT'S HAPPENING?
NOT A SOUND IN HERE.
THE CORRIDORS ARE CLEAN.
THERE ARE NO MUERTOS.
NOT FOR LONG, I PRESUME.
YOU CAN BE A REAL ASS SOMETIMES.
WE CAN USE THEM TO GET OUT OF THIS TRAP, BRAD.
I KNOW A WAY.
I'VE BEEN HERE MANY TIMES WITH MY CHILDREN... BEFORE ALL THIS.
IF WE HAVE SOME LUCK AND THE BARRICADES AREN'T TOO STRONG, WE COULD HAVE A CHANCE OF GETTING OUT OF HERE.

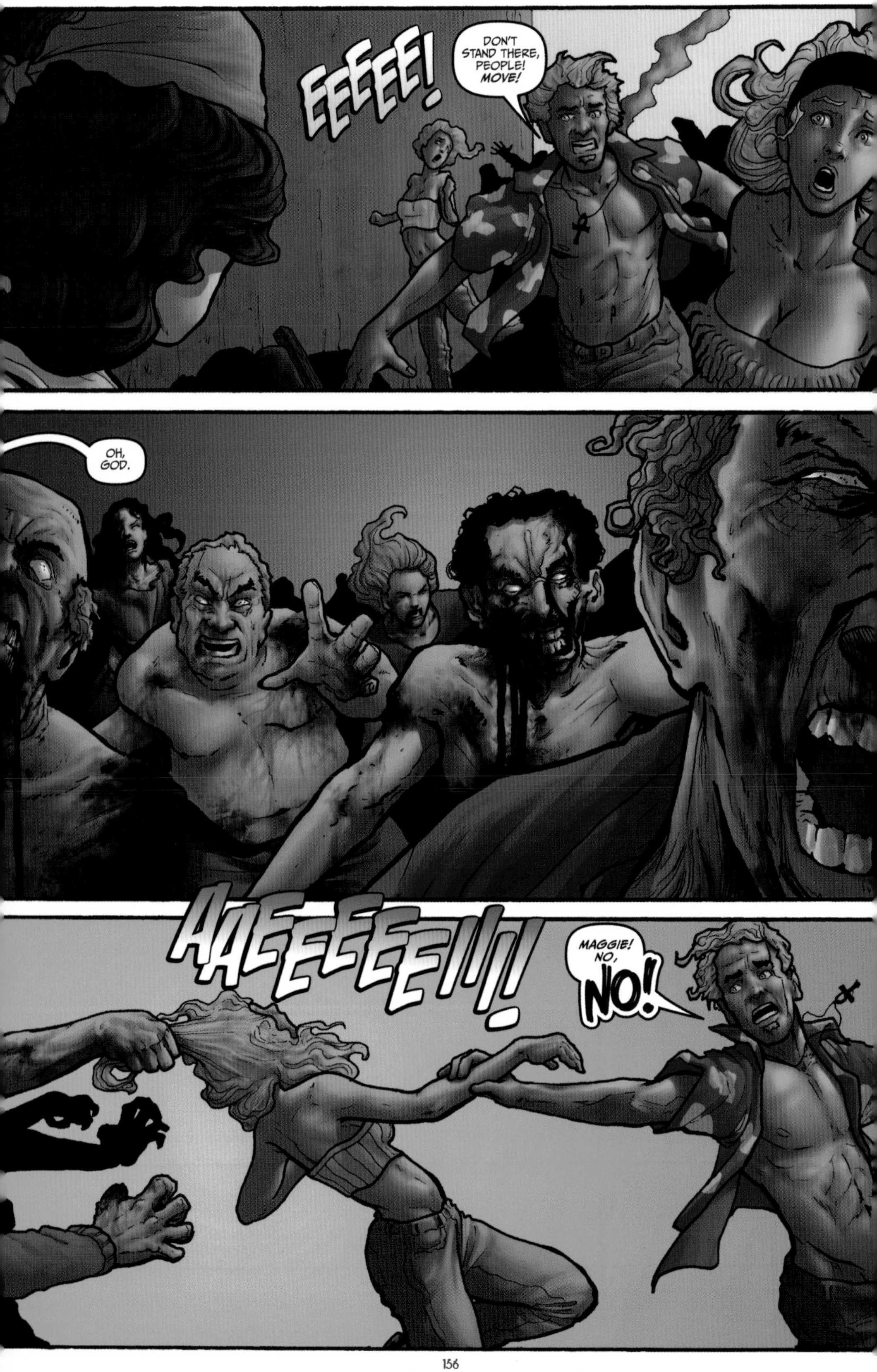
EEEEE!
DON'T STAND THERE, PEOPLE! MOVE!
OH, GOD.
AAEEEEEIII!
MAGGIE! NO, NO!

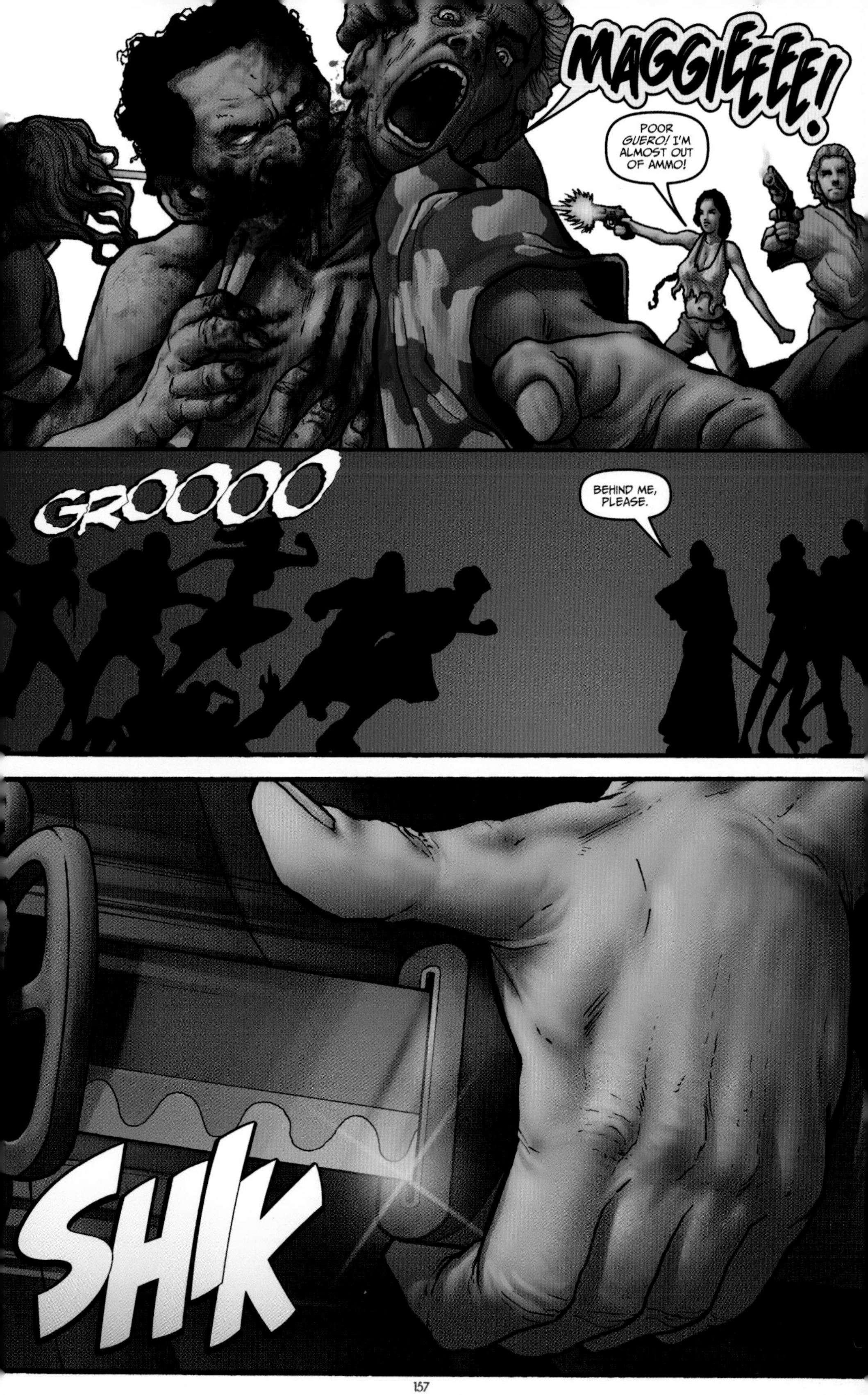
MAGGIEEEE!
POOR GUERO! I'M ALMOST OUT OF AMMO!
GROOOO
BEHIND ME, PLEASE.
SHIK

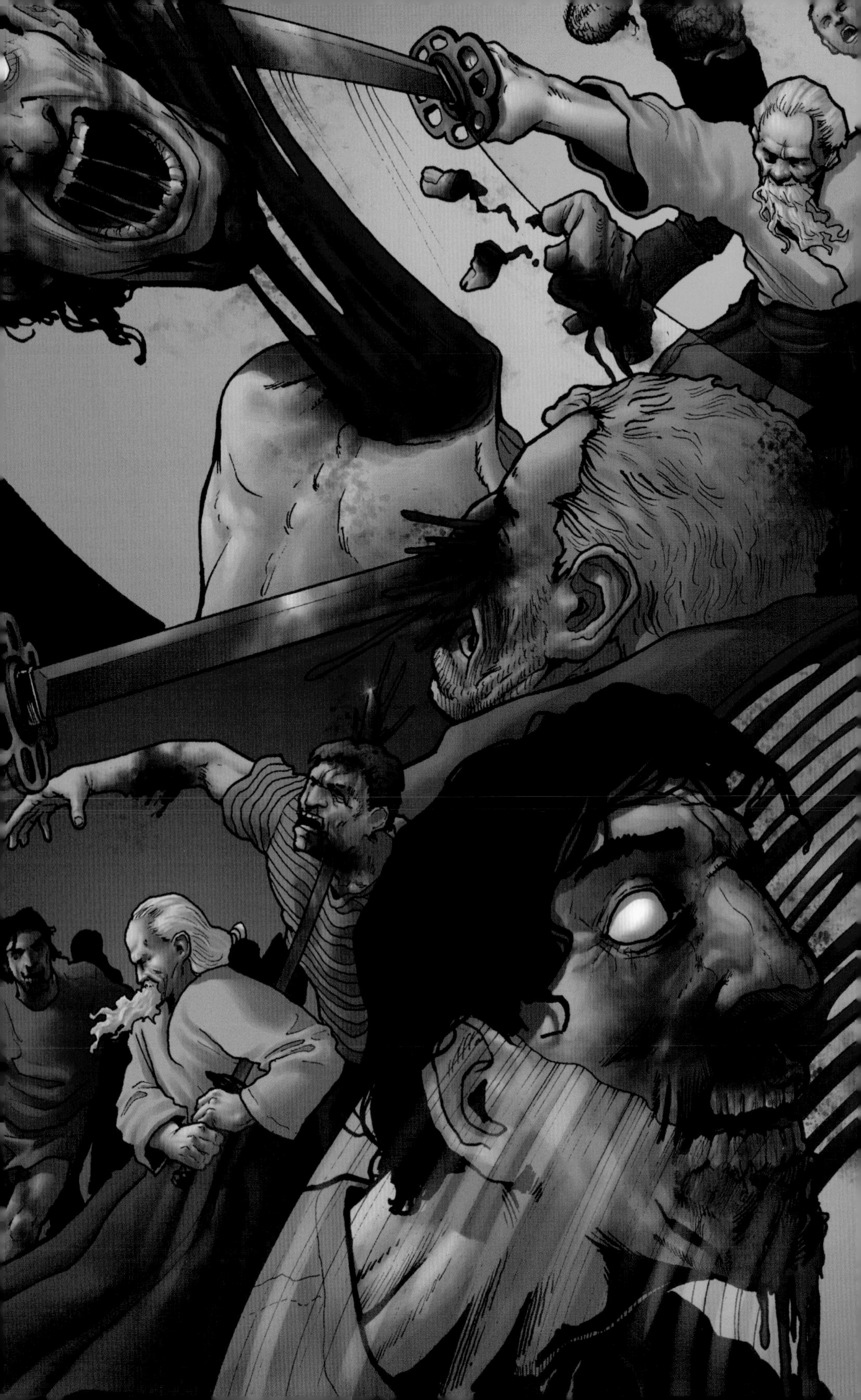

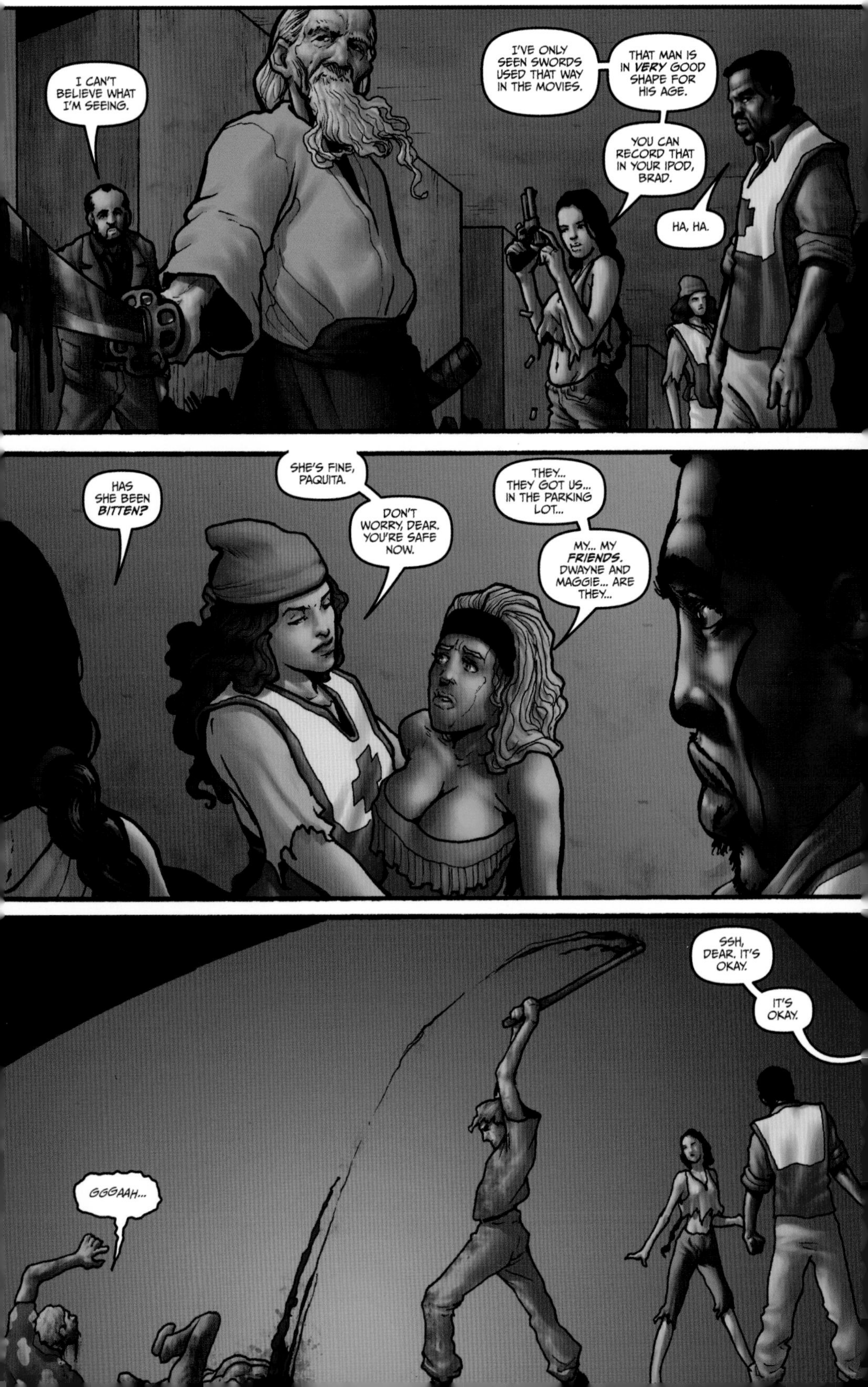
I CAN'T BELIEVE WHAT I'M SEEING.
I'VE ONLY SEEN SWORDS USED THAT WAY IN THE MOVIES.
THAT MAN IS IN *VERY* GOOD SHAPE FOR HIS AGE.
YOU CAN RECORD THAT IN YOUR IPOD, BRAD.
HA, HA.
HAS SHE BEEN *BITTEN?*
SHE'S FINE, PAQUITA.
DON'T WORRY, DEAR. YOU'RE SAFE NOW.
THEY... THEY GOT US... IN THE PARKING LOT...
MY... MY *FRIENDS.* DWAYNE AND MAGGIE... ARE THEY...
SSH, DEAR. IT'S OKAY.
IT'S OKAY.
GGGAAH...

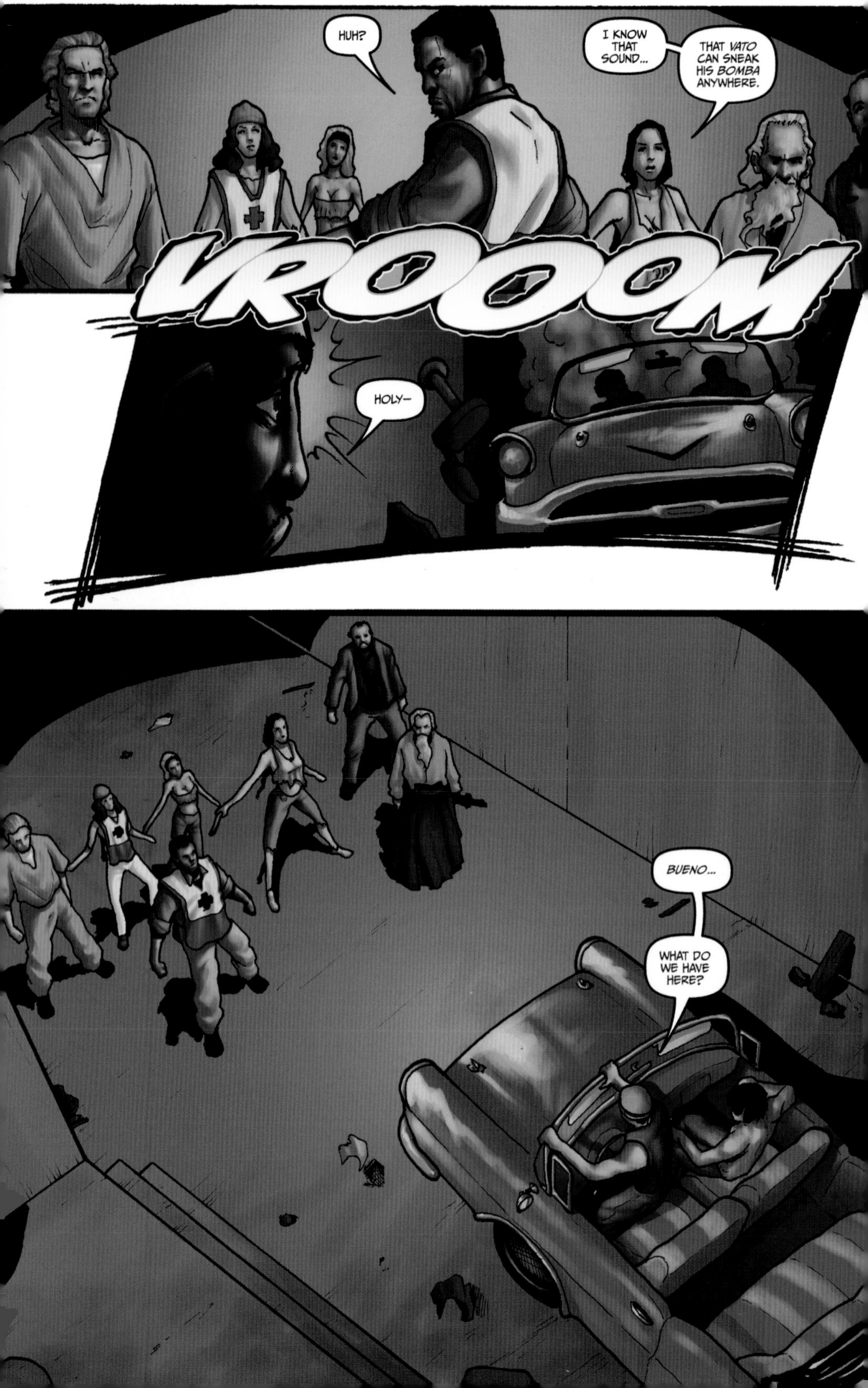
HUH?
I KNOW THAT SOUND...
THAT *VATO* CAN SNEAK HIS *BOMBA* ANYWHERE.
VROOOM
HOLY—
BUENO...
WHAT DO WE HAVE HERE?

chapter 3

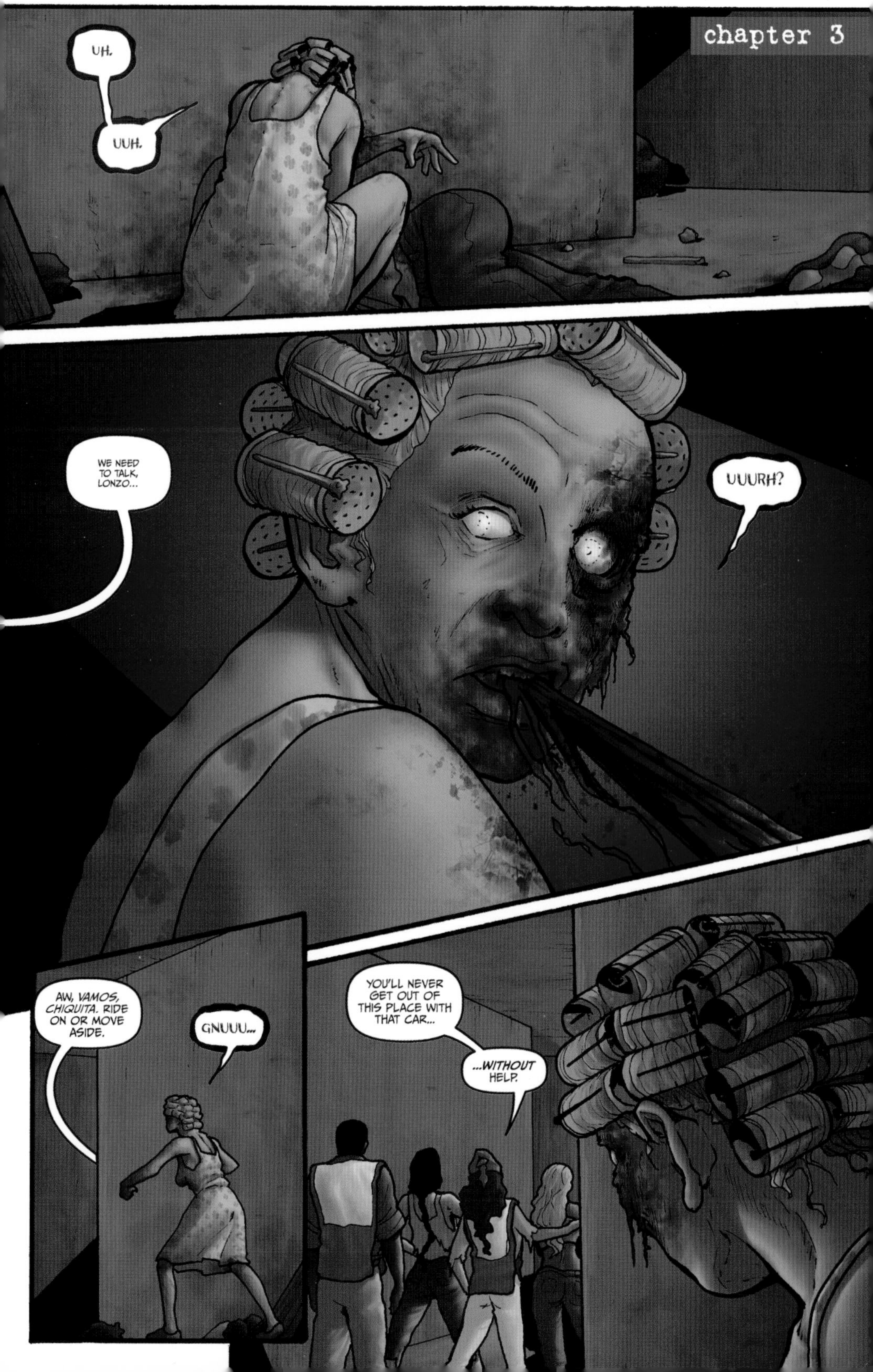
UH.
UUH.
WE NEED TO TALK, LONZO...
UUURH?
AW, *VAMOS, CHIQUITA.* RIDE ON OR MOVE ASIDE.
GNUUU...
YOU'LL NEVER GET OUT OF THIS PLACE WITH THAT CAR...
...*WITHOUT* HELP.

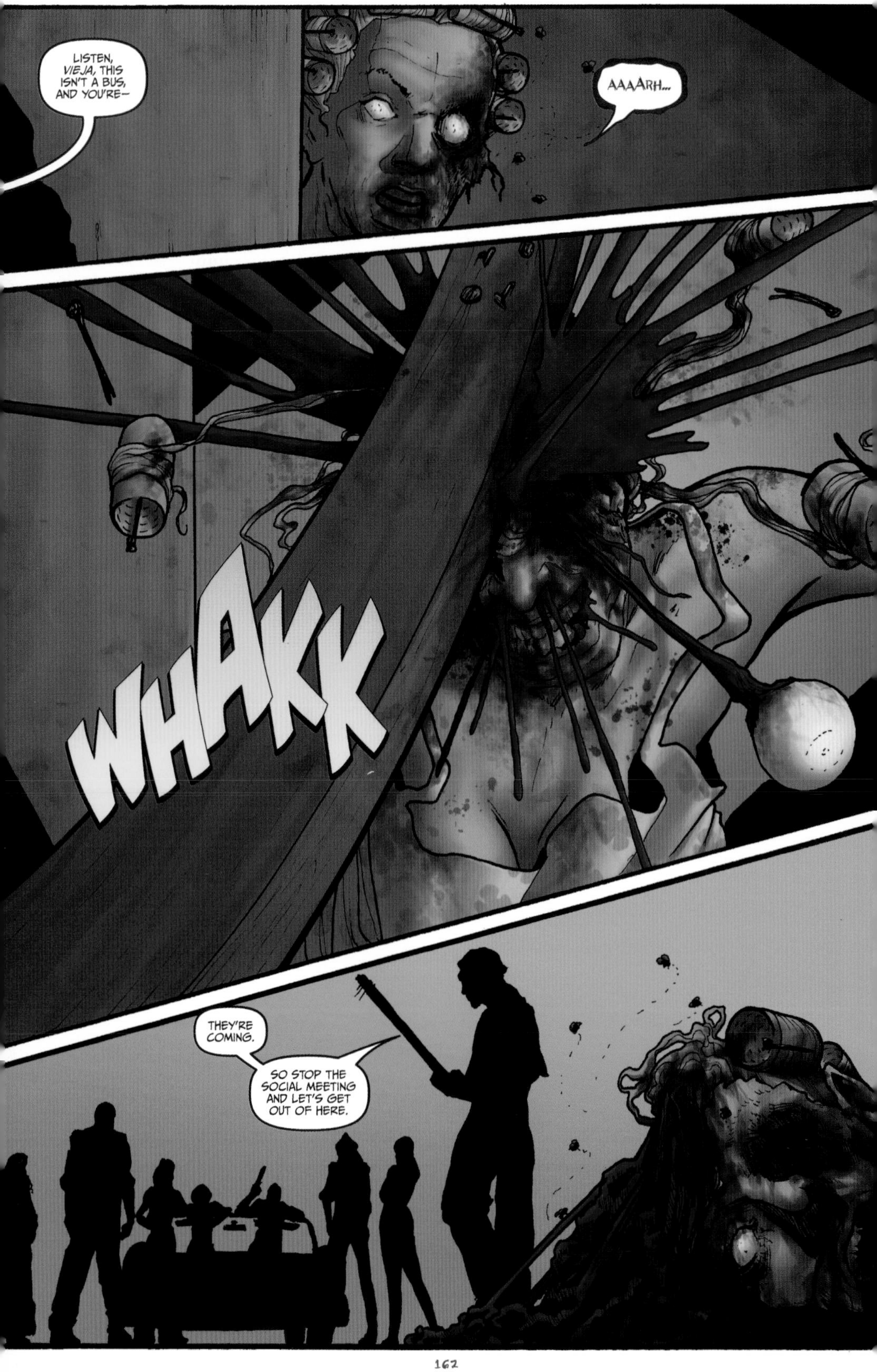

LISTEN, *VIEJA*, THIS ISN'T A BUS, AND YOU'RE—
AAAARH...
WHAKK
THEY'RE COMING.
SO STOP THE SOCIAL MEETING AND LET'S GET OUT OF HERE.

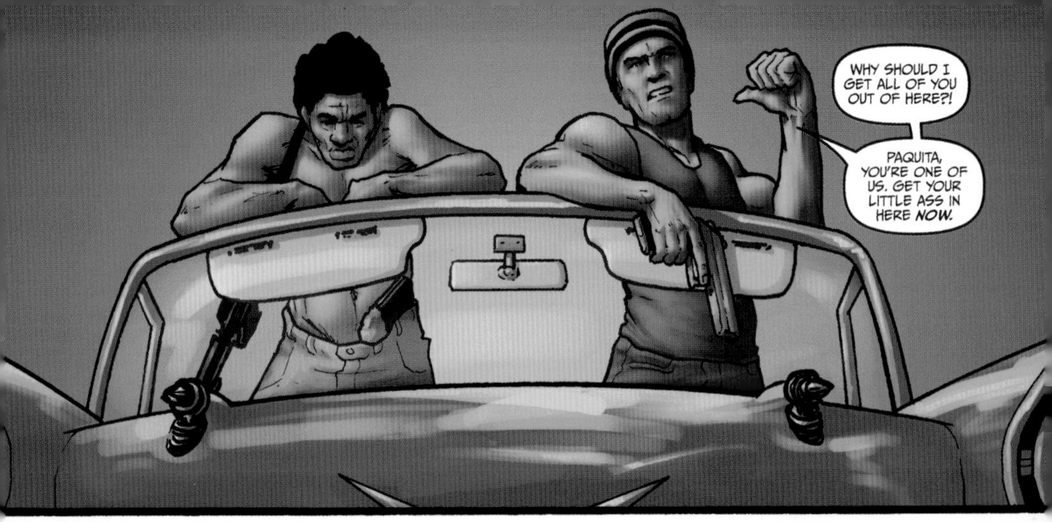
WHY SHOULD I GET ALL OF YOU OUT OF HERE?!
PAQUITA, YOU'RE ONE OF US. GET YOUR LITTLE ASS IN HERE *NOW.*

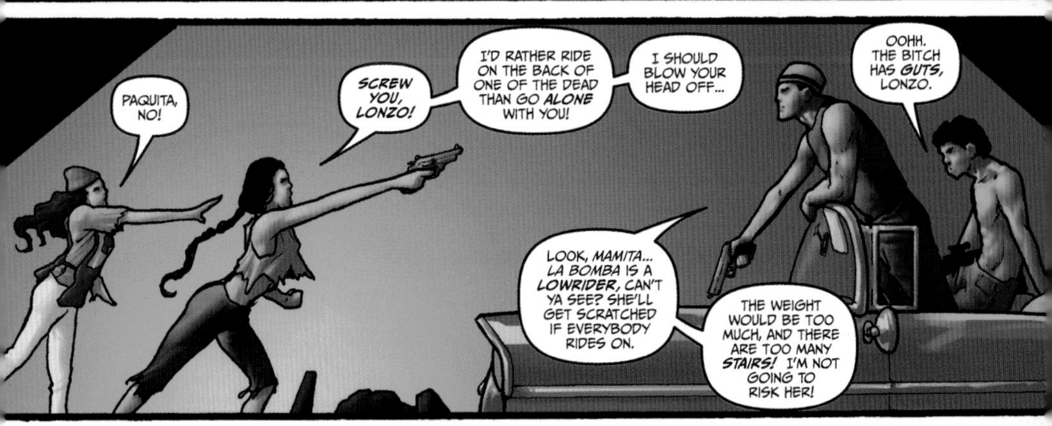
PAQUITA, NO!
SCREW YOU, LONZO!
I'D RATHER RIDE ON THE BACK OF ONE OF THE DEAD THAN GO *ALONE* WITH YOU!
I SHOULD BLOW YOUR HEAD OFF...
OOHH. THE BITCH HAS *GUTS,* LONZO.
LOOK, *MAMITA... LA BOMBA* IS A *LOWRIDER,* CAN'T YA SEE? SHE'LL GET SCRATCHED IF EVERYBODY RIDES ON.
THE WEIGHT WOULD BE TOO MUCH, AND THERE ARE TOO MANY *STAIRS!* I'M NOT GOING TO RISK HER!

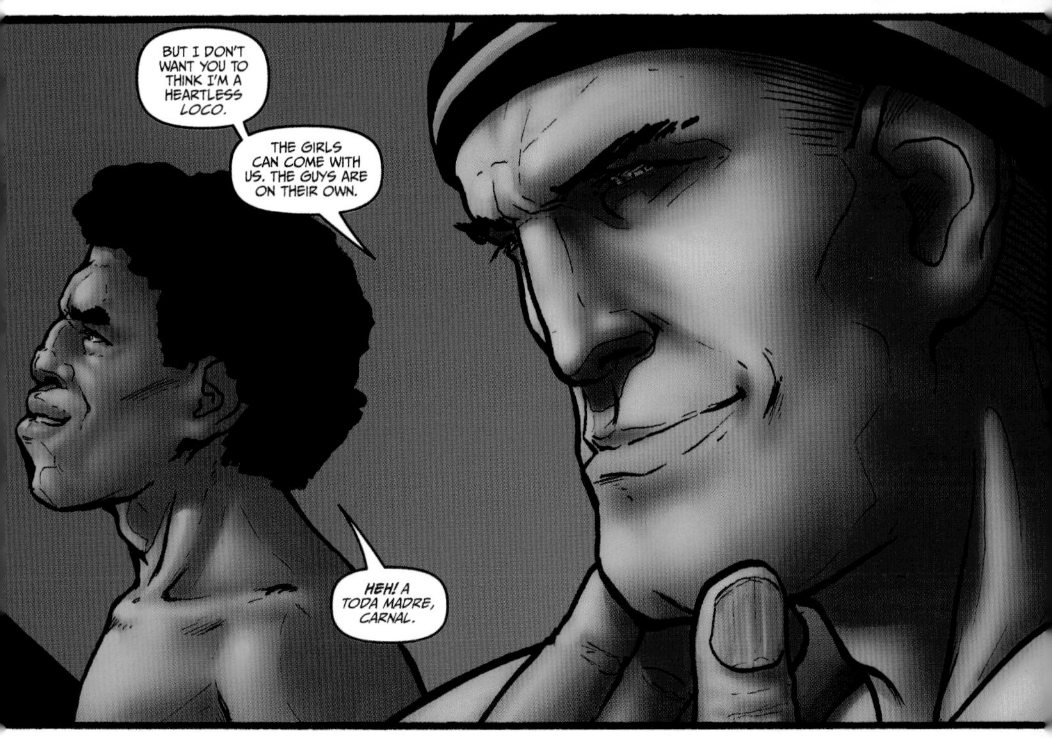
BUT I DON'T WANT YOU TO THINK I'M A HEARTLESS *LOCO.*
THE GIRLS CAN COME WITH US. THE GUYS ARE ON THEIR OWN.
HEH! A *TODA MADRE, CARNAL.*

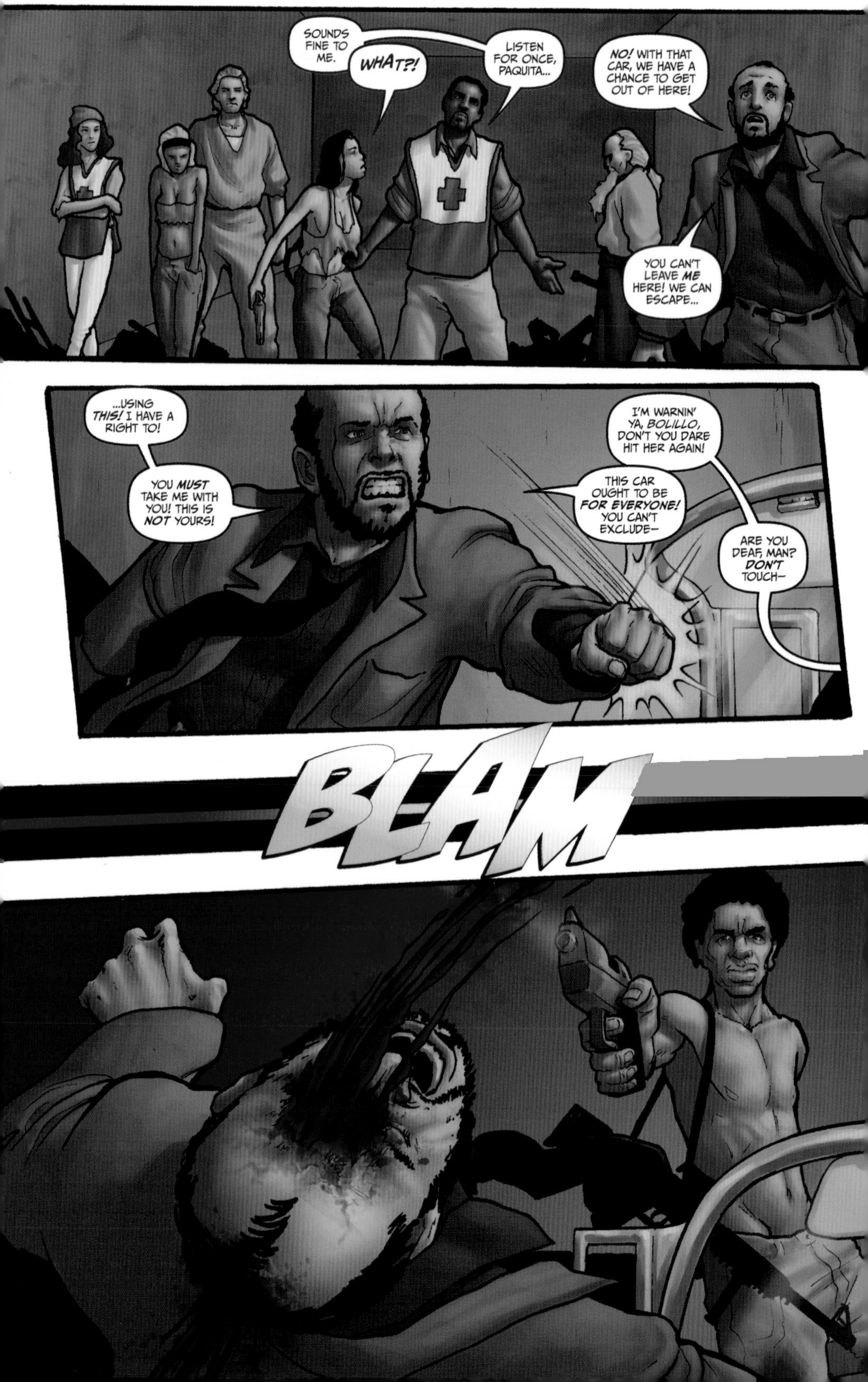
SOUNDS FINE TO ME.
WHAT?!
LISTEN FOR ONCE, PAQUITA...
NO! WITH THAT CAR, WE HAVE A CHANCE TO GET OUT OF HERE!
YOU CAN'T LEAVE ME HERE! WE CAN ESCAPE...
...USING THIS! I HAVE A RIGHT TO!
YOU MUST TAKE ME WITH YOU! THIS IS NOT YOURS!
THIS CAR OUGHT TO BE FOR EVERYONE! YOU CAN'T EXCLUDE–
I'M WARNIN' YA, BOLILLO, DON'T YOU DARE HIT HER AGAIN!
ARE YOU DEAF, MAN? DON'T TOUCH–
BLAM

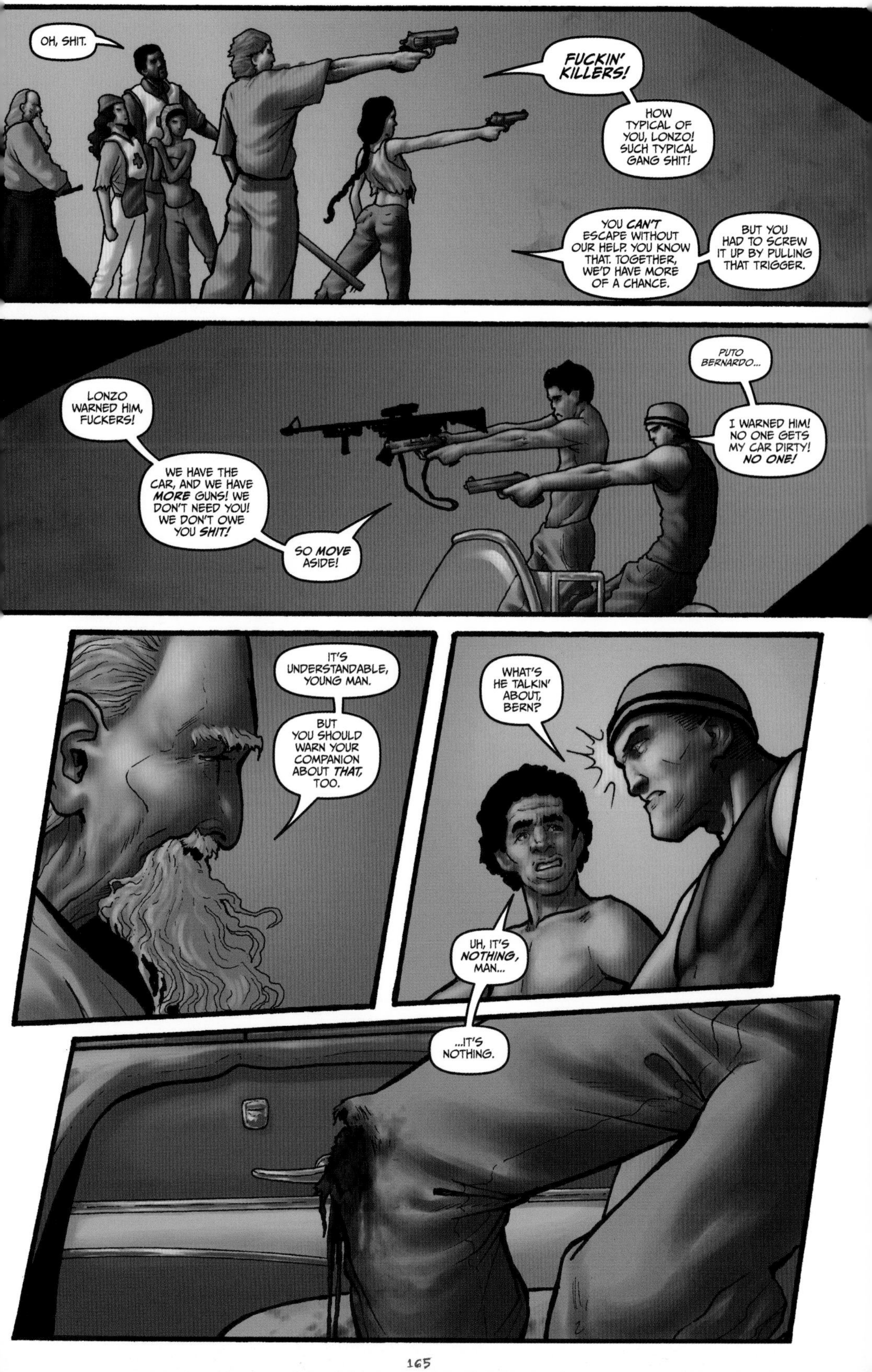
OH, SHIT.
FUCKIN' KILLERS!
HOW TYPICAL OF YOU, LONZO! SUCH TYPICAL GANG SHIT!
YOU CAN'T ESCAPE WITHOUT OUR HELP. YOU KNOW THAT. TOGETHER, WE'D HAVE MORE OF A CHANCE.
BUT YOU HAD TO SCREW IT UP BY PULLING THAT TRIGGER.
PUTO BERNARDO...
I WARNED HIM! NO ONE GETS MY CAR DIRTY! NO ONE!
LONZO WARNED HIM, FUCKERS!
WE HAVE THE CAR, AND WE HAVE MORE GUNS! WE DON'T NEED YOU! WE DON'T OWE YOU SHIT!
SO MOVE ASIDE!
IT'S UNDERSTANDABLE, YOUNG MAN.
BUT YOU SHOULD WARN YOUR COMPANION ABOUT THAT, TOO.
WHAT'S HE TALKIN' ABOUT, BERN?
UH, IT'S NOTHING, MAN...
...IT'S NOTHING.

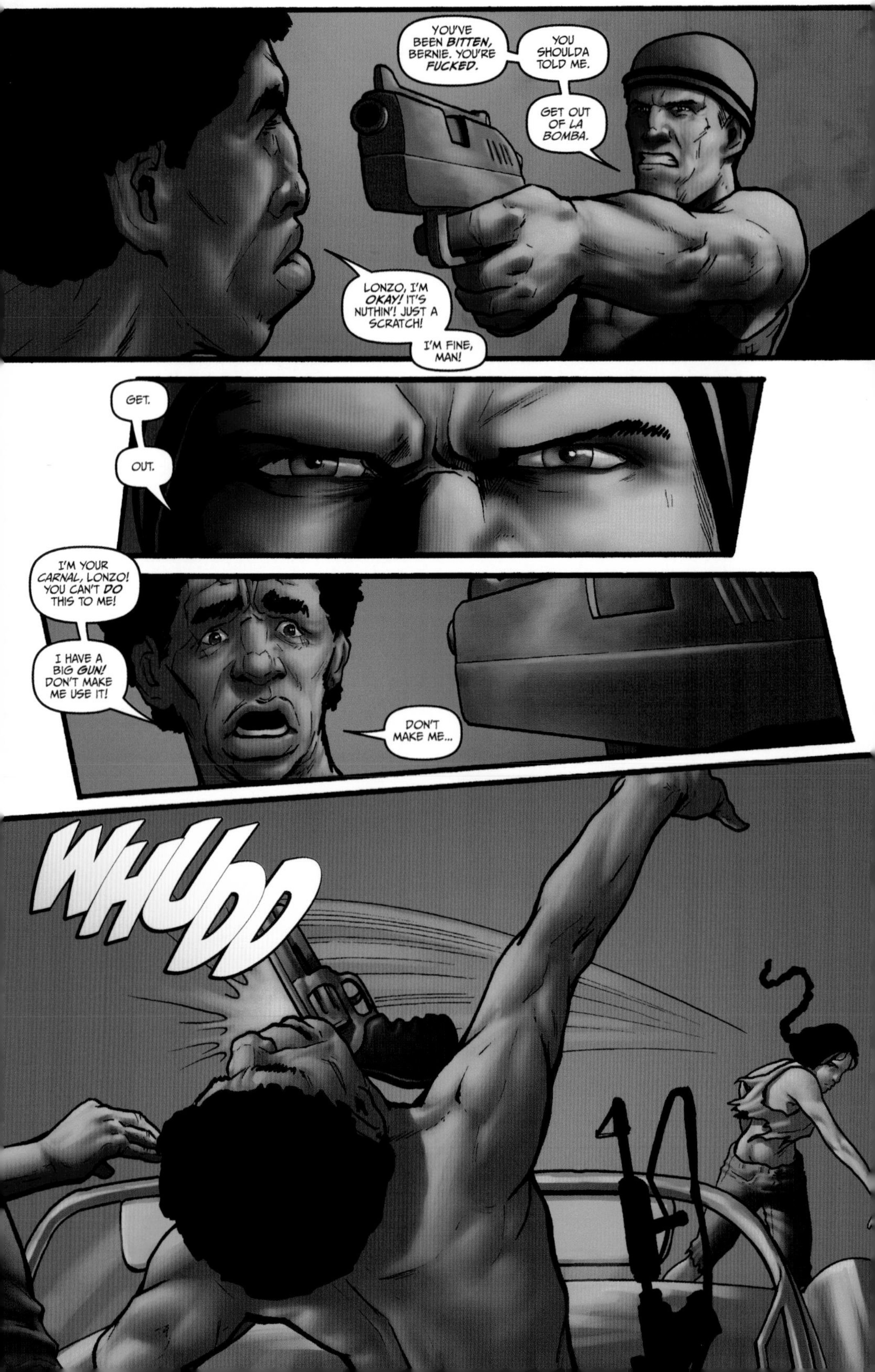
YOU'VE BEEN BITTEN, BERNIE. YOU'RE FUCKED.
YOU SHOULDA TOLD ME.
GET OUT OF LA BOMBA.
LONZO, I'M OKAY! IT'S NUTHIN'! JUST A SCRATCH!
I'M FINE, MAN!
GET.
OUT.
I'M YOUR CARNAL, LONZO! YOU CAN'T DO THIS TO ME!
I HAVE A BIG GUN! DON'T MAKE ME USE IT!
DON'T MAKE ME...
WHUDD

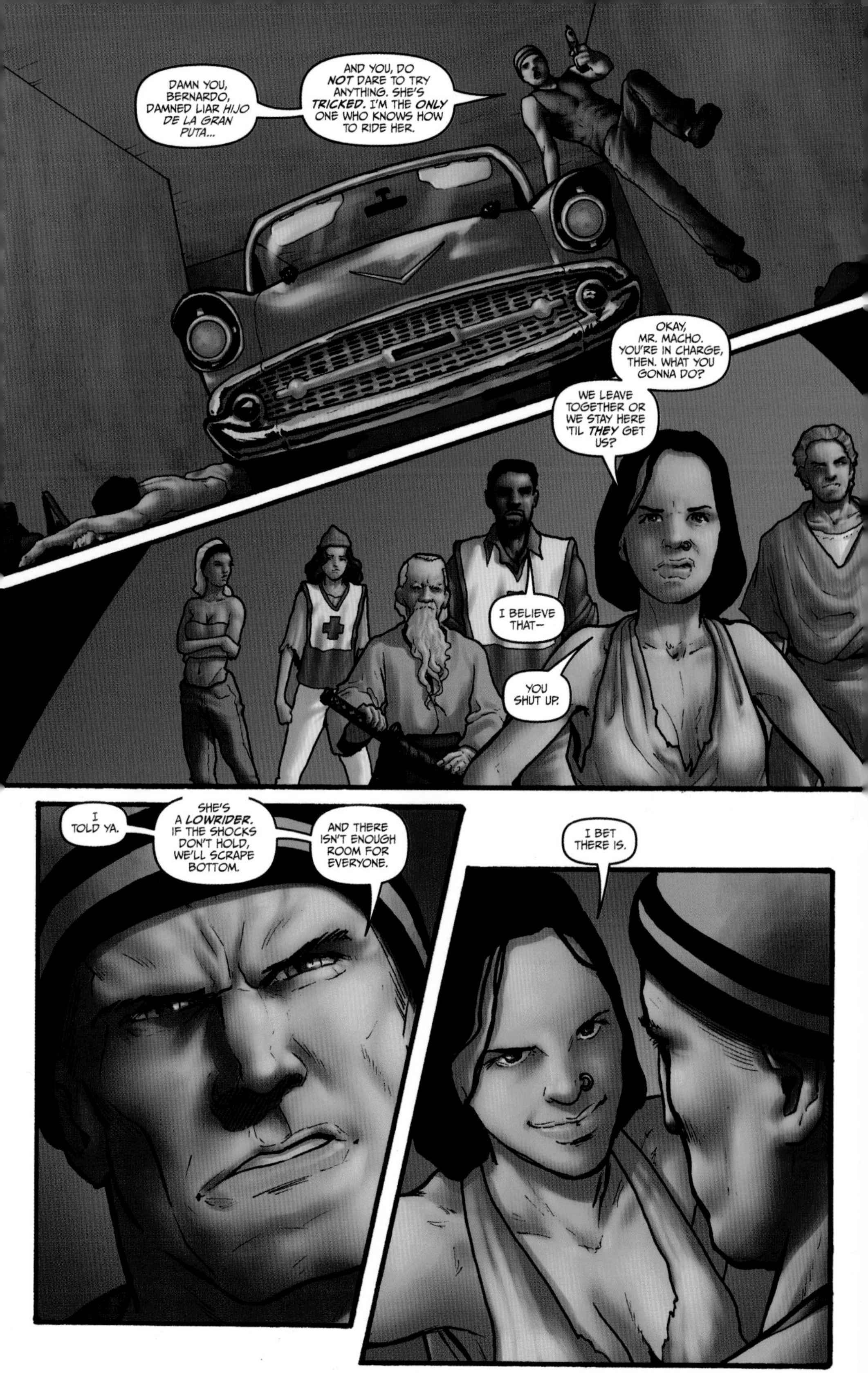
DAMN YOU, BERNARDO, DAMNED LIAR HIJO DE LA GRAN PUTA...
AND YOU, DO NOT DARE TO TRY ANYTHING. SHE'S TRICKED. I'M THE ONLY ONE WHO KNOWS HOW TO RIDE HER.
OKAY, MR. MACHO. YOU'RE IN CHARGE, THEN. WHAT YOU GONNA DO?
WE LEAVE TOGETHER OR WE STAY HERE 'TIL THEY GET US?
I BELIEVE THAT—
YOU SHUT UP.
I TOLD YA.
SHE'S A LOWRIDER. IF THE SHOCKS DON'T HOLD, WE'LL SCRAPE BOTTOM.
AND THERE ISN'T ENOUGH ROOM FOR EVERYONE.
I BET THERE IS.

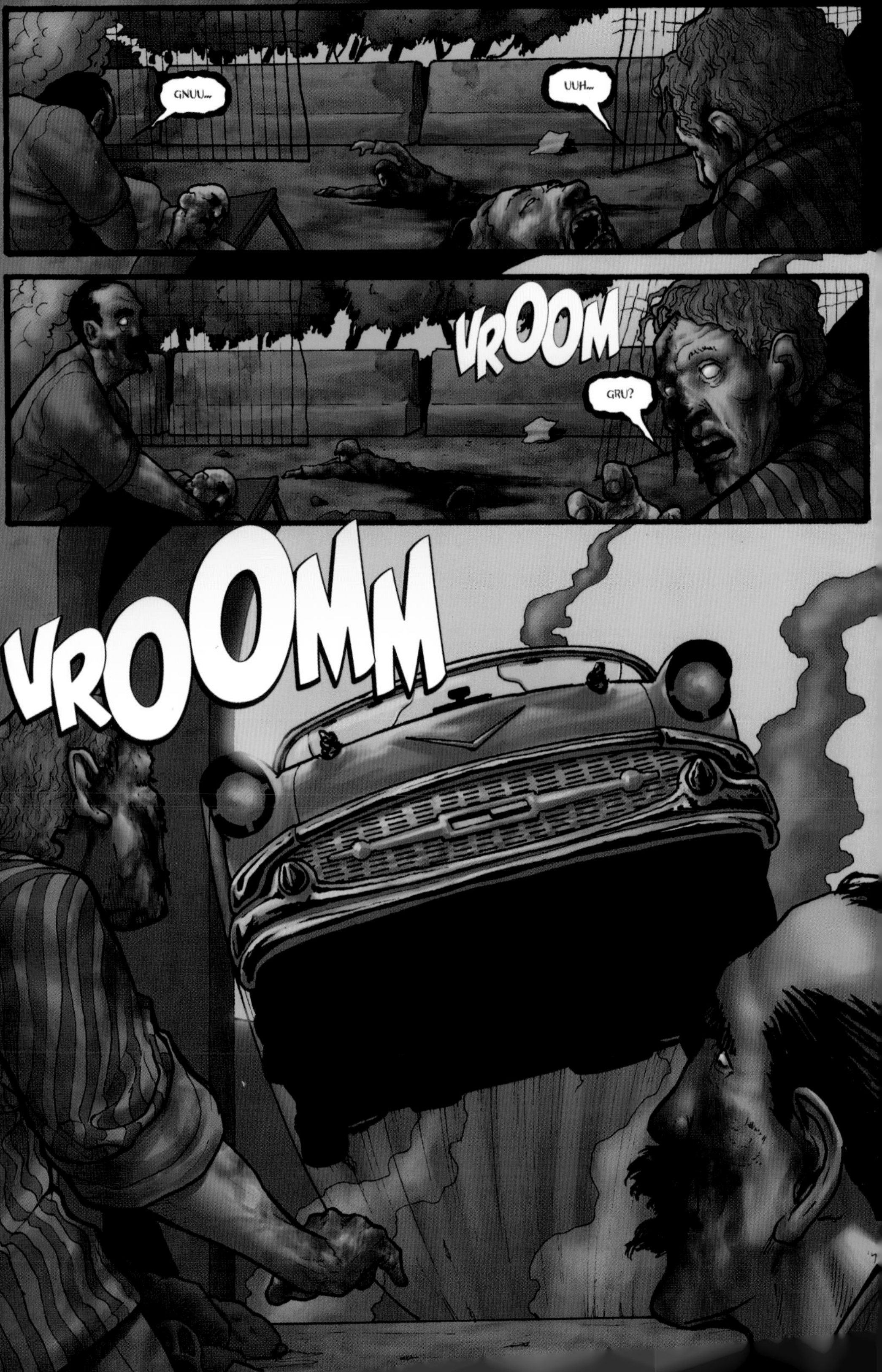
GNUU...
UUH...
VROOM
GRU?
VROOMM

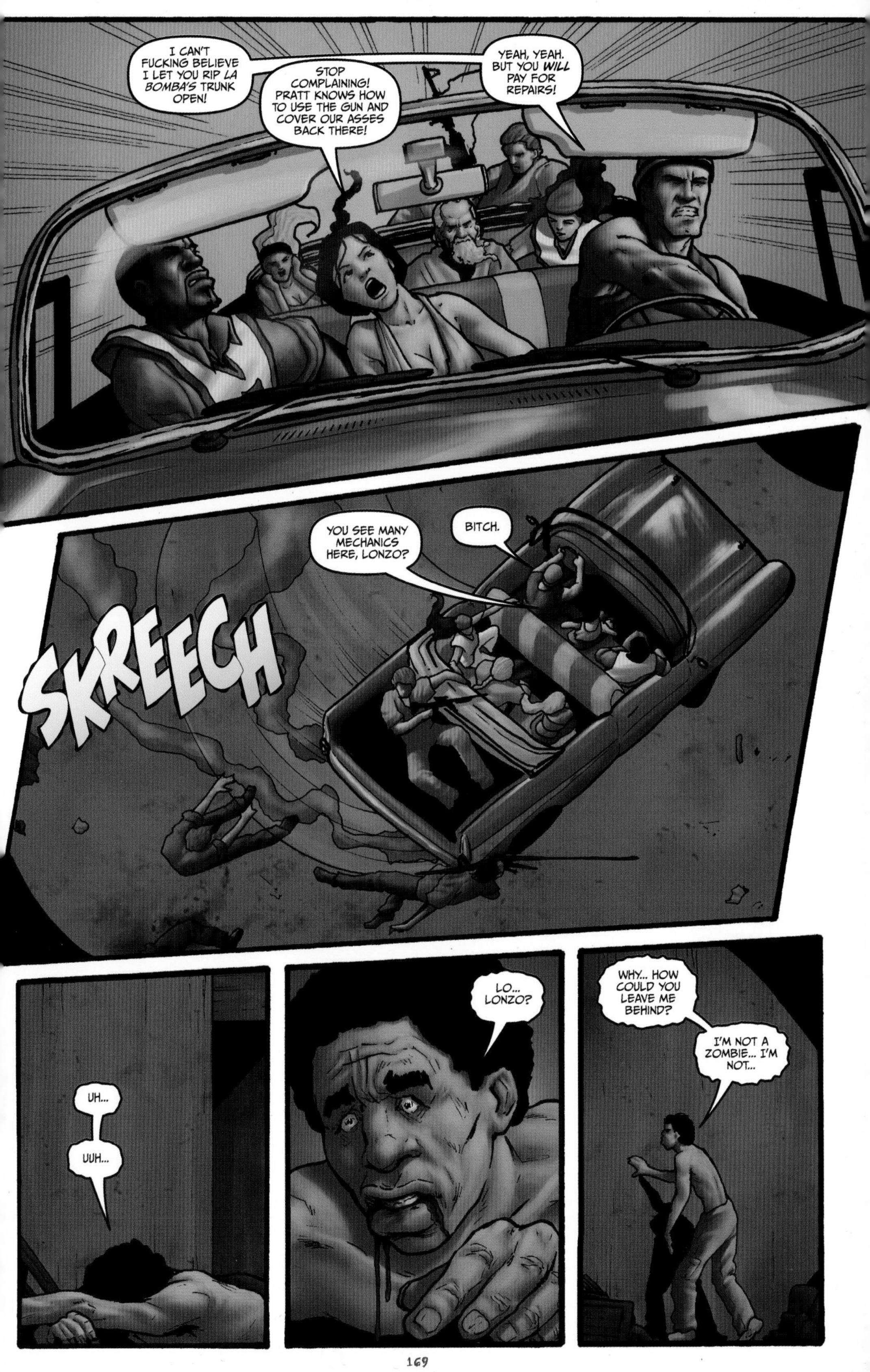
I CAN'T FUCKING BELIEVE I LET YOU RIP *LA BOMBA'S* TRUNK OPEN!
STOP COMPLAINING! PRATT KNOWS HOW TO USE THE GUN AND COVER OUR ASSES BACK THERE!
YEAH, YEAH. BUT YOU ***WILL*** PAY FOR REPAIRS!
YOU SEE MANY MECHANICS HERE, LONZO?
BITCH.
SKREECH
UH...
UUH...
LO... LONZO?
WHY... HOW COULD YOU LEAVE ME BEHIND?
I'M NOT A ZOMBIE... I'M NOT...

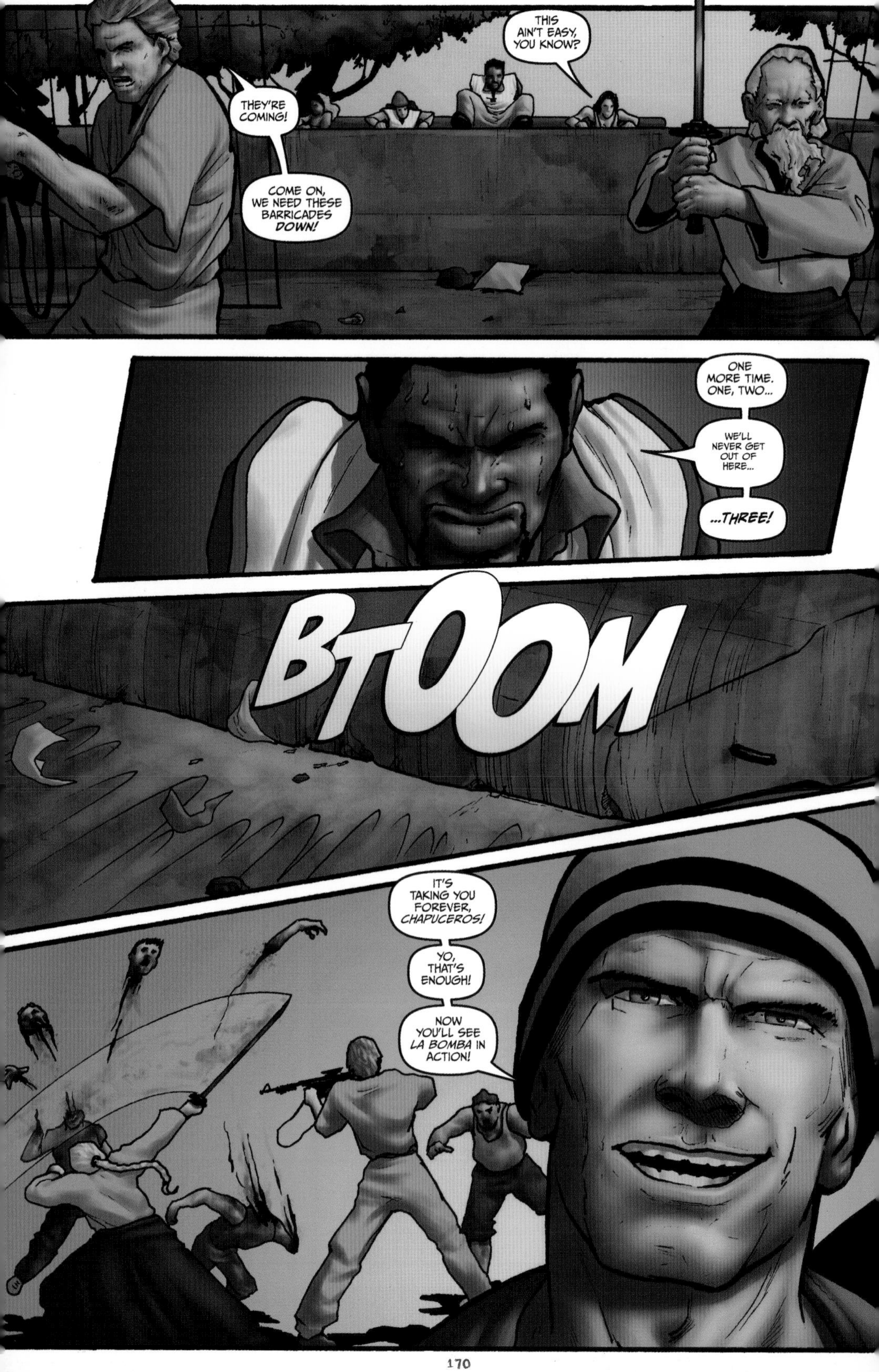
THEY'RE COMING!
COME ON, WE NEED THESE BARRICADES *DOWN!*
THIS AIN'T EASY, YOU KNOW?
ONE MORE TIME. ONE, TWO...
WE'LL NEVER GET OUT OF HERE...
...THREE!
BTOOM
IT'S TAKING YOU FOREVER, *CHAPUCEROS!*
YO, THAT'S ENOUGH!
NOW YOU'LL SEE *LA BOMBA* IN ACTION!

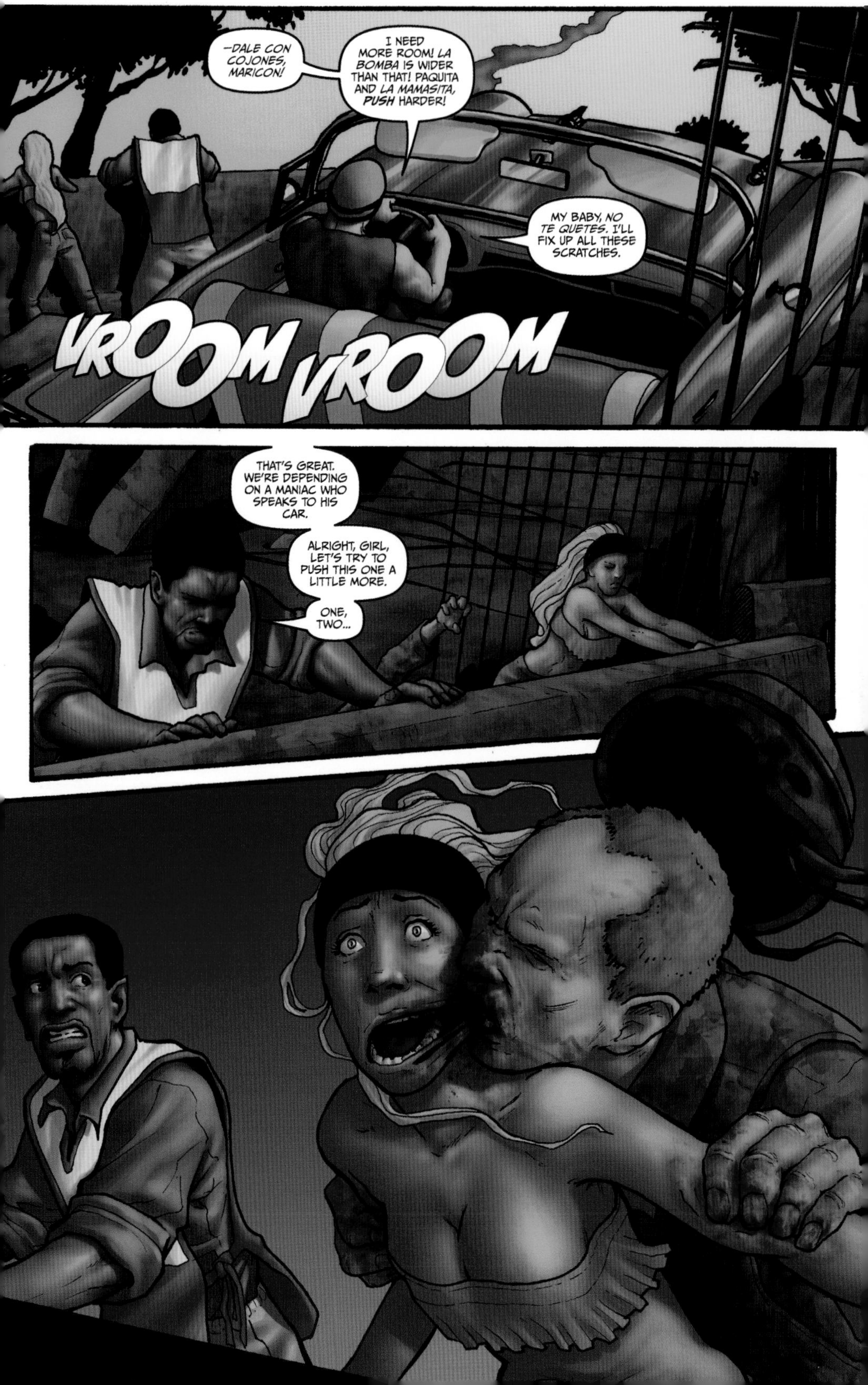

—DALE CON COJONES, MARICON!
I NEED MORE ROOM! LA BOMBA IS WIDER THAN THAT! PAQUITA AND LA MAMASITA, PUSH HARDER!
MY BABY, NO TE QUETES. I'LL FIX UP ALL THESE SCRATCHES.
VROOM VROOM
THAT'S GREAT. WE'RE DEPENDING ON A MANIAC WHO SPEAKS TO HIS CAR.
ALRIGHT, GIRL, LET'S TRY TO PUSH THIS ONE A LITTLE MORE.
ONE, TWO...

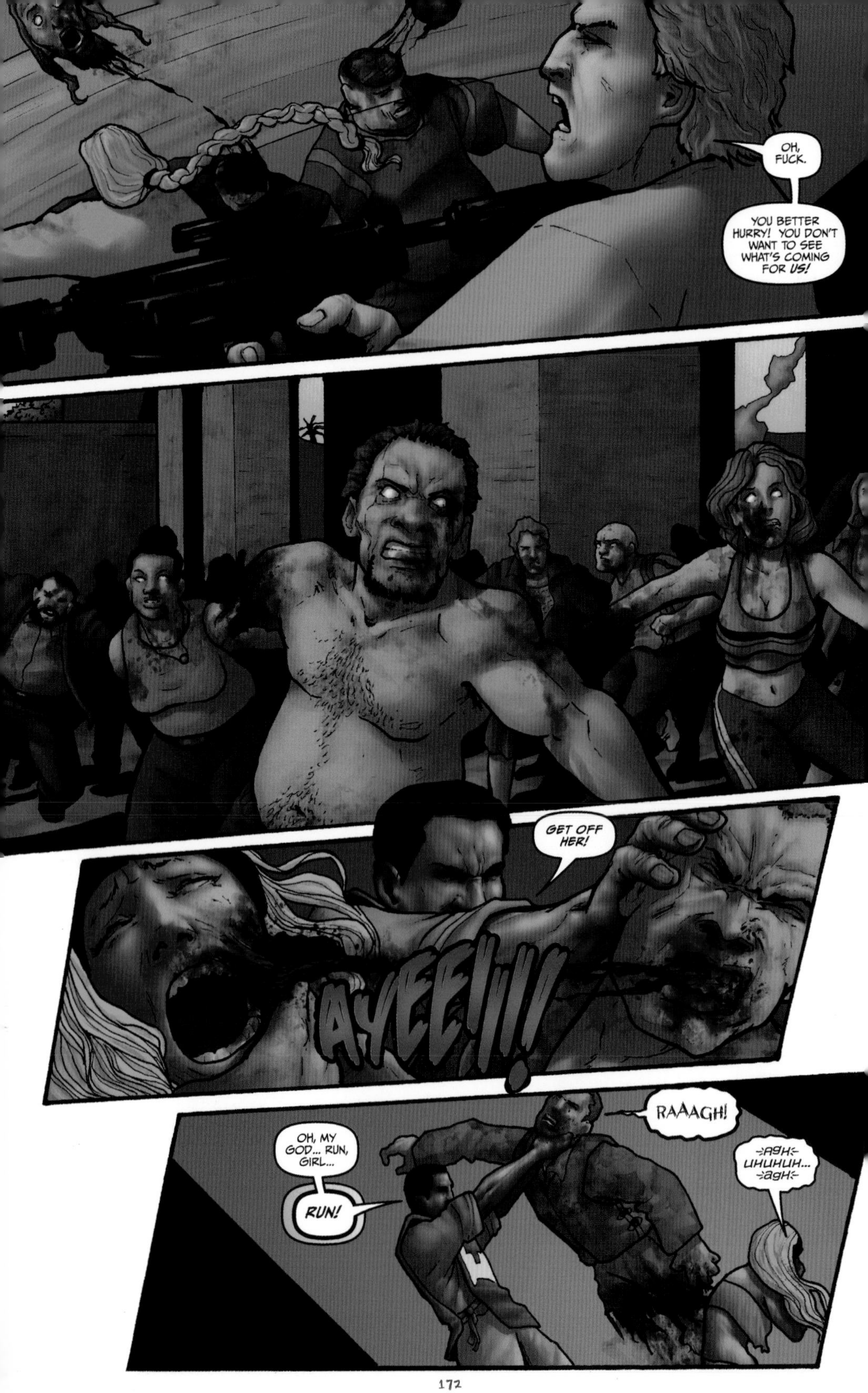
OH, FUCK.
YOU BETTER HURRY! YOU DON'T WANT TO SEE WHAT'S COMING FOR US!
GET OFF HER!
AYEE!!!!
OH, MY GOD... RUN, GIRL...
RUN!
RAAAGH!
-AGH- UHUHUH... -AGH-

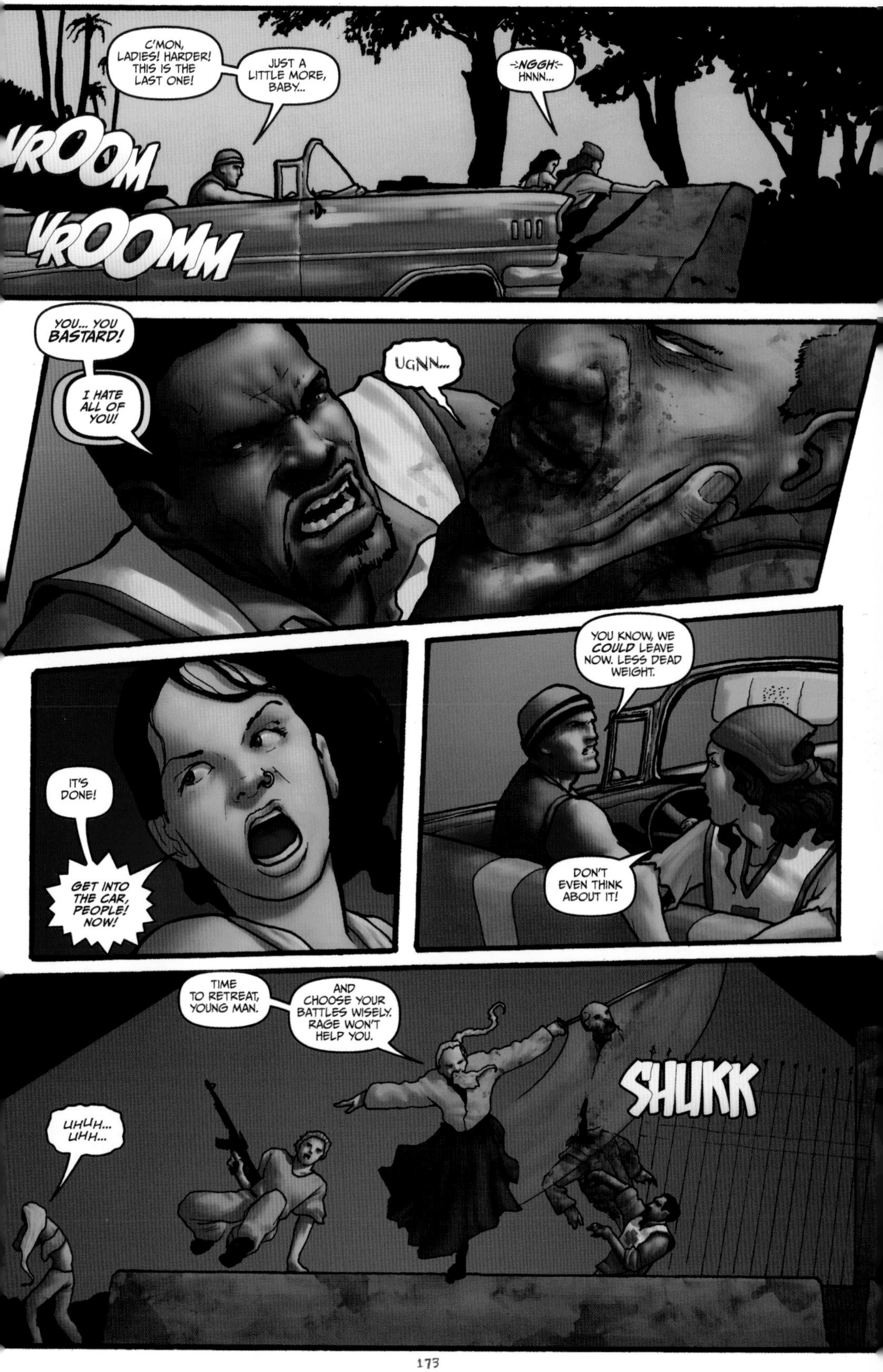
C'MON, LADIES! HARDER! THIS IS THE LAST ONE!
JUST A LITTLE MORE, BABY...
-NGGH- HNNN...
VROOM
VROOMM
YOU... YOU BASTARD!
I HATE ALL OF YOU!
UGNN...
IT'S DONE!
GET INTO THE CAR, PEOPLE! NOW!
YOU KNOW, WE COULD LEAVE NOW. LESS DEAD WEIGHT.
DON'T EVEN THINK ABOUT IT!
TIME TO RETREAT, YOUNG MAN.
AND CHOOSE YOUR BATTLES WISELY. RAGE WON'T HELP YOU.
SHUKK
UHUH... UHH...

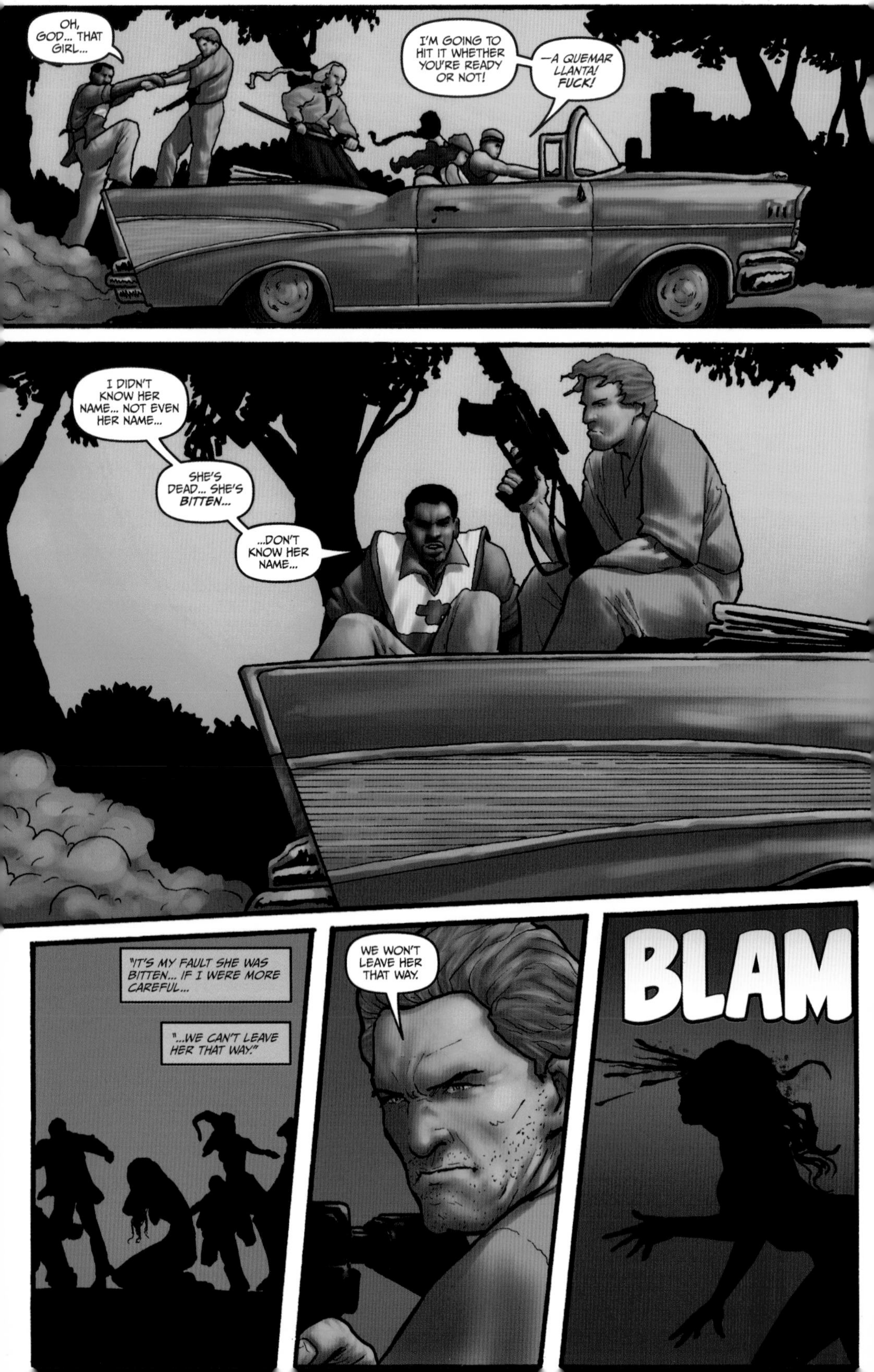
OH, GOD... THAT GIRL...
I'M GOING TO HIT IT WHETHER YOU'RE READY OR NOT!
—A QUEMAR LLANTA! FUCK!
I DIDN'T KNOW HER NAME... NOT EVEN HER NAME...
SHE'S DEAD... SHE'S BITTEN...
...DON'T KNOW HER NAME...
"IT'S MY FAULT SHE WAS BITTEN... IF I WERE MORE CAREFUL...
"...WE CAN'T LEAVE HER THAT WAY."
WE WON'T LEAVE HER THAT WAY.
BLAM

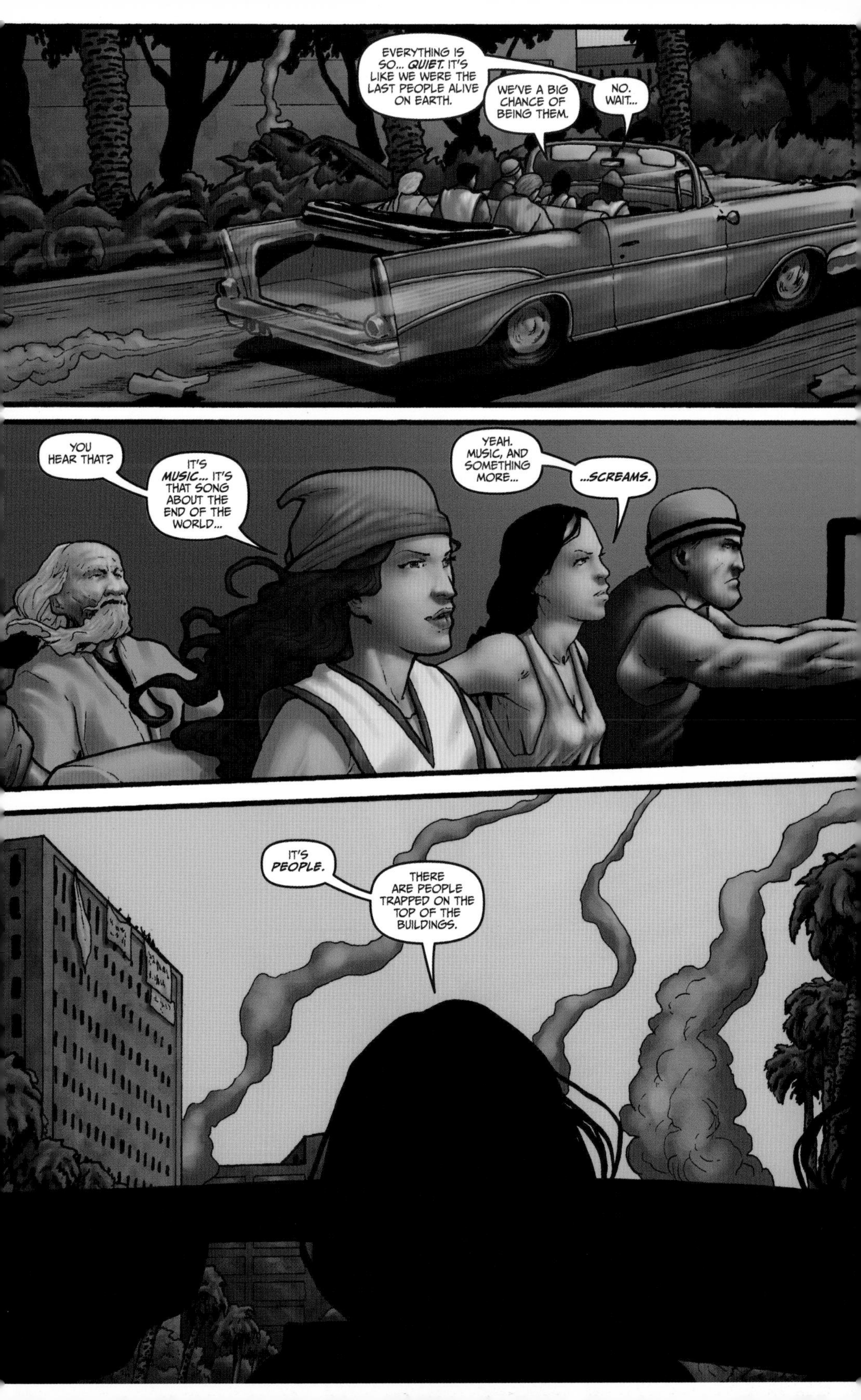
EVERYTHING IS SO... *QUIET.* IT'S LIKE WE WERE THE LAST PEOPLE ALIVE ON EARTH.
WE'VE A BIG CHANCE OF BEING THEM.
NO. WAIT...
YOU HEAR THAT?
IT'S *MUSIC...* IT'S THAT SONG ABOUT THE END OF THE WORLD...
YEAH. MUSIC, AND SOMETHING MORE...
...SCREAMS.
IT'S *PEOPLE.*
THERE ARE PEOPLE TRAPPED ON THE TOP OF THE BUILDINGS.

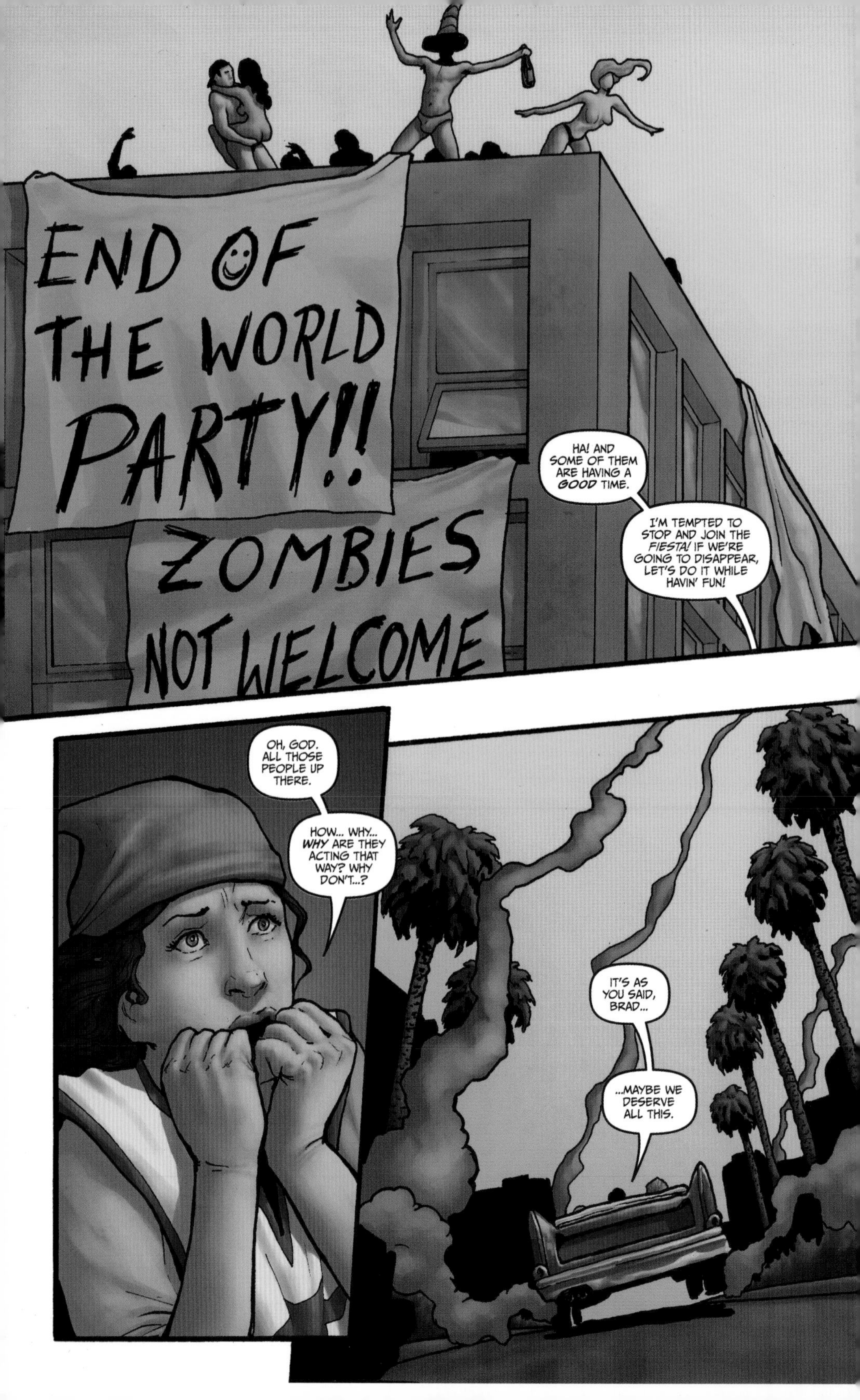

END OF THE WORLD PARTY!!
ZOMBIES NOT WELCOME
HA! AND SOME OF THEM ARE HAVING A *GOOD* TIME.
I'M TEMPTED TO STOP AND JOIN THE *FIESTA!* IF WE'RE GOING TO DISAPPEAR, LET'S DO IT WHILE HAVIN' FUN!
OH, GOD. ALL THOSE PEOPLE UP THERE.
HOW... WHY... *WHY* ARE THEY ACTING THAT WAY? WHY DON'T...?
IT'S AS YOU SAID, BRAD...
...MAYBE WE DESERVE ALL THIS.

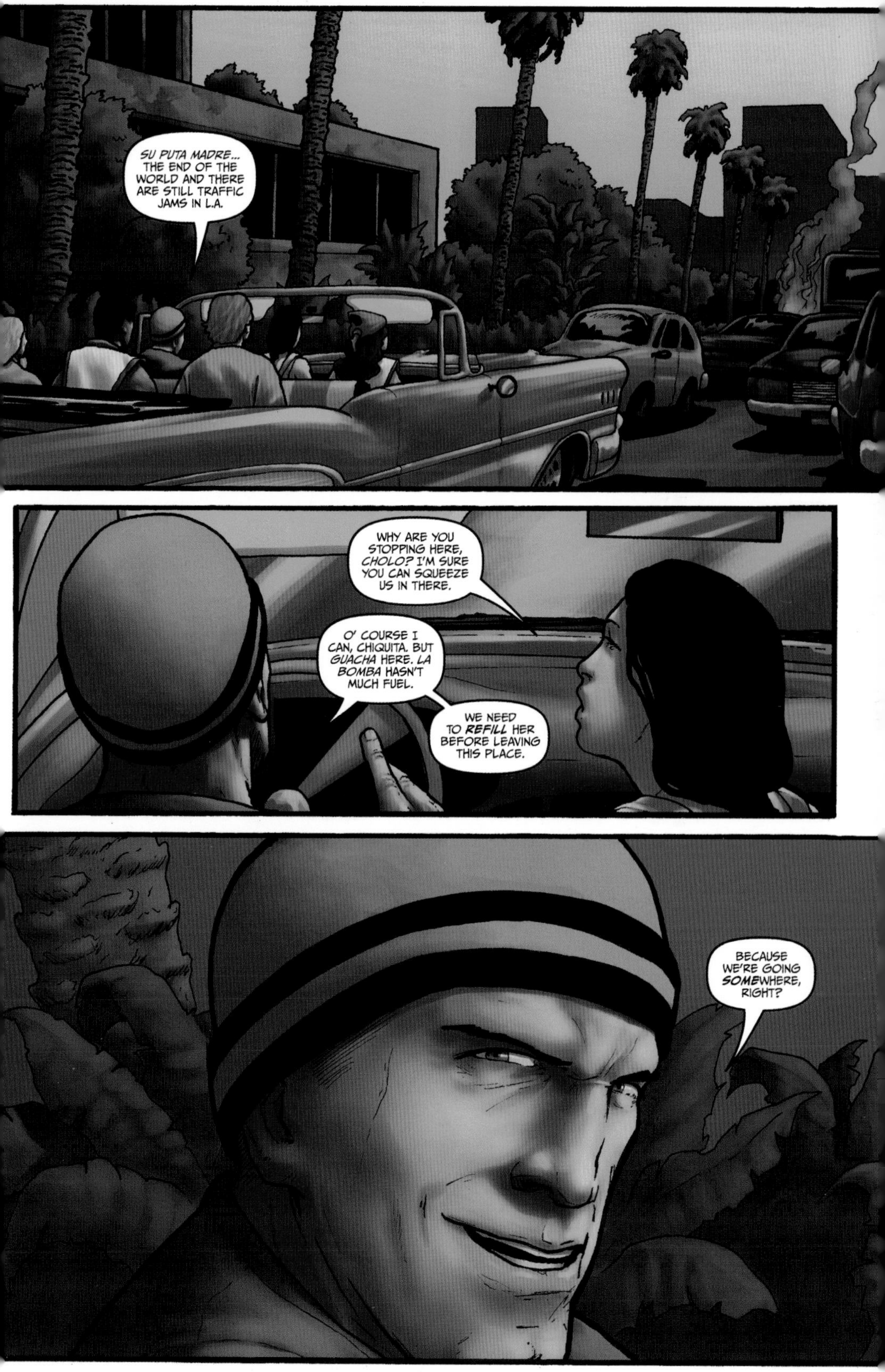
SU PUTA MADRE... THE END OF THE WORLD AND THERE ARE STILL TRAFFIC JAMS IN L.A.
WHY ARE YOU STOPPING HERE, CHOLO? I'M SURE YOU CAN SQUEEZE US IN THERE.
O' COURSE I CAN, CHIQUITA. BUT GUACHA HERE. LA BOMBA HASN'T MUCH FUEL.
WE NEED TO REFILL HER BEFORE LEAVING THIS PLACE.
BECAUSE WE'RE GOING SOMEWHERE, RIGHT?

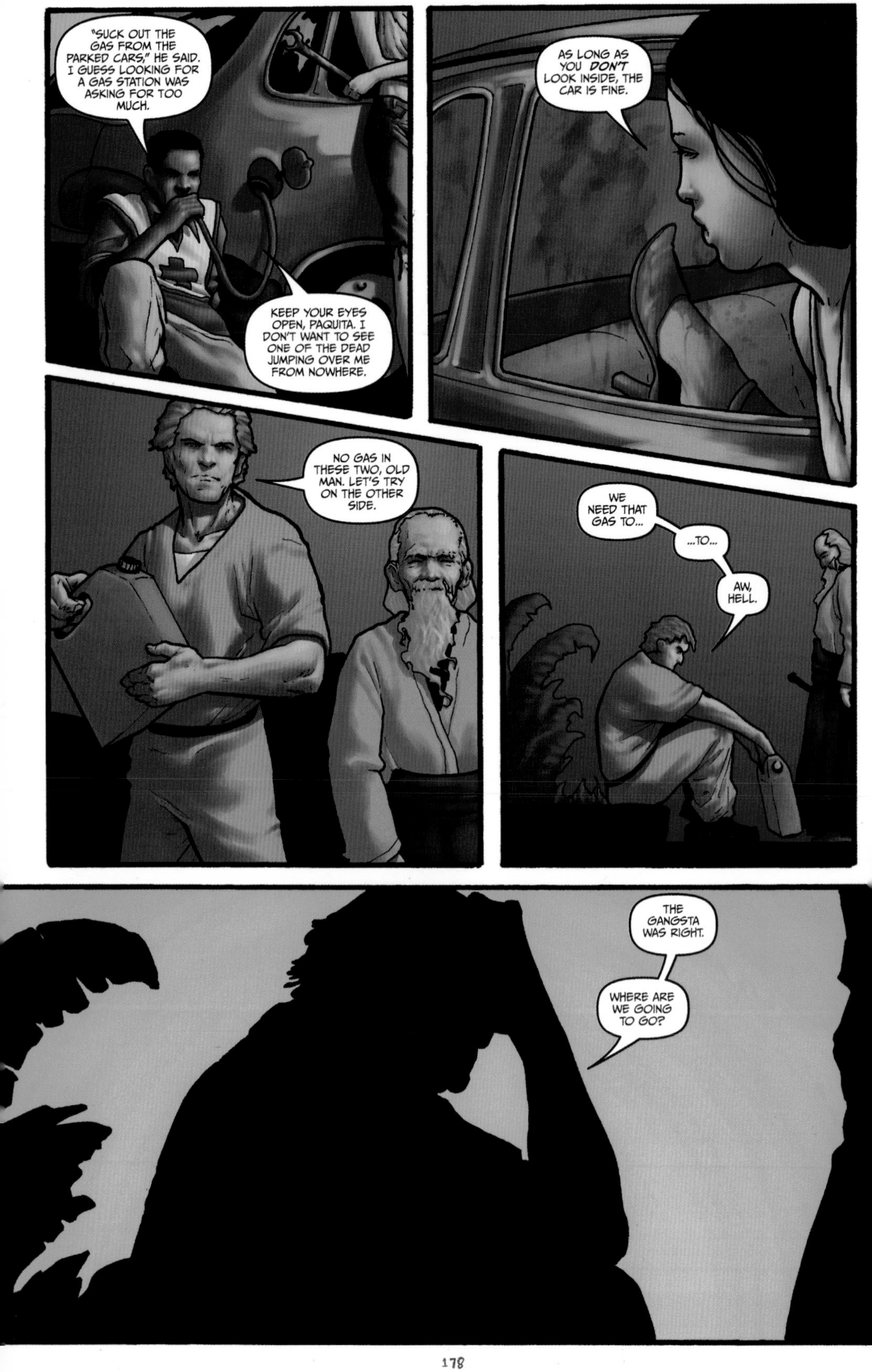
"SUCK OUT THE GAS FROM THE PARKED CARS," HE SAID. I GUESS LOOKING FOR A GAS STATION WAS ASKING FOR TOO MUCH.
KEEP YOUR EYES OPEN, PAQUITA. I DON'T WANT TO SEE ONE OF THE DEAD JUMPING OVER ME FROM NOWHERE.
AS LONG AS YOU *DON'T* LOOK INSIDE, THE CAR IS FINE.
NO GAS IN THESE TWO, OLD MAN. LET'S TRY ON THE OTHER SIDE.
WE NEED THAT GAS TO...
...TO...
AW, HELL.
THE GANGSTA WAS RIGHT.
WHERE ARE WE GOING TO GO?

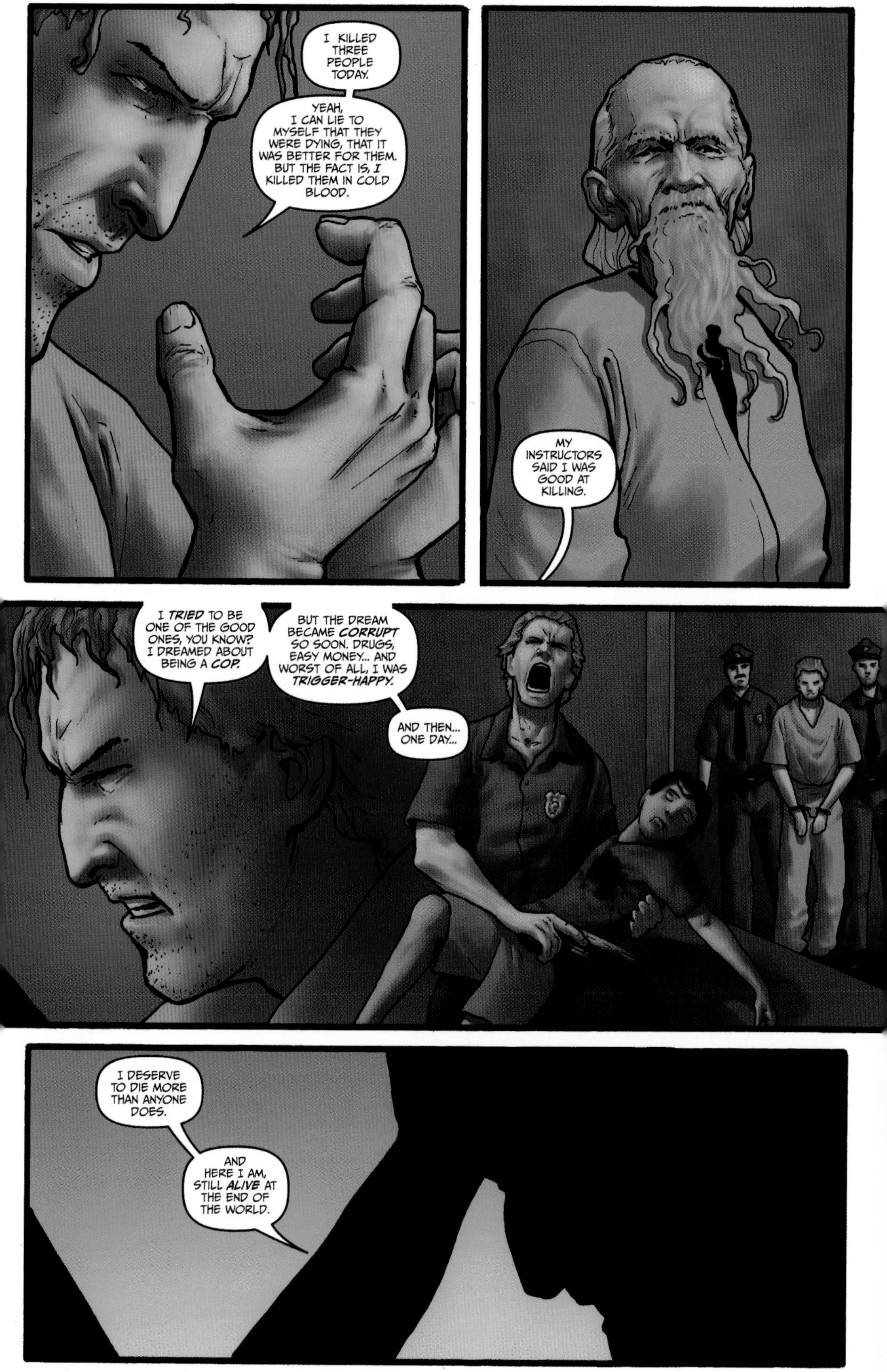
I KILLED THREE PEOPLE TODAY.
YEAH, I CAN LIE TO MYSELF THAT THEY WERE DYING, THAT IT WAS BETTER FOR THEM. BUT THE FACT IS, I KILLED THEM IN COLD BLOOD.
MY INSTRUCTORS SAID I WAS GOOD AT KILLING.
I TRIED TO BE ONE OF THE GOOD ONES, YOU KNOW? I DREAMED ABOUT BEING A COP.
BUT THE DREAM BECAME CORRUPT SO SOON. DRUGS, EASY MONEY... AND WORST OF ALL, I WAS TRIGGER-HAPPY.
AND THEN... ONE DAY...
I DESERVE TO DIE MORE THAN ANYONE DOES.
AND HERE I AM, STILL ALIVE AT THE END OF THE WORLD.

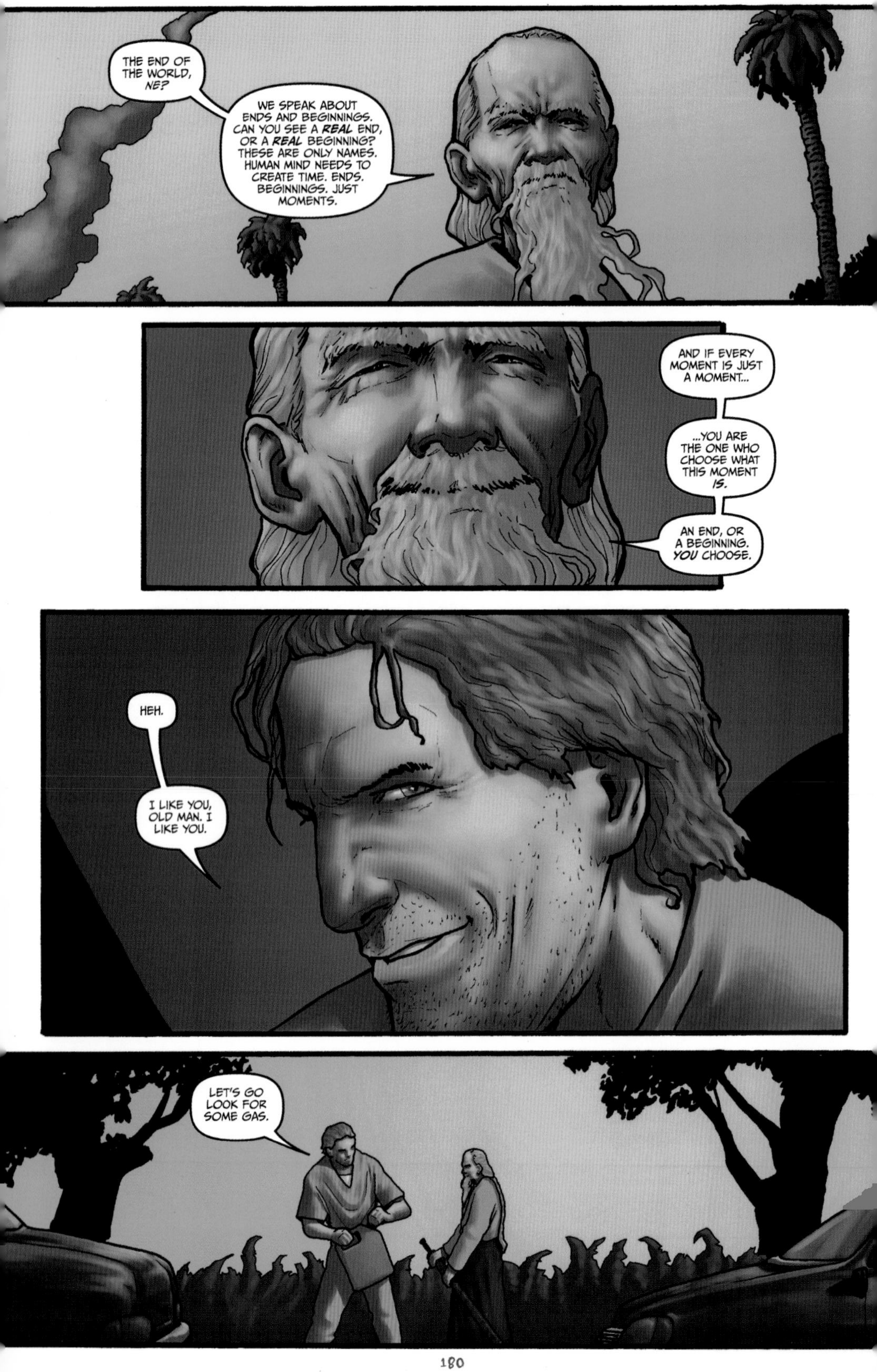
THE END OF THE WORLD, *NE?*
WE SPEAK ABOUT ENDS AND BEGINNINGS. CAN YOU SEE A ***REAL*** END, OR A ***REAL*** BEGINNING? THESE ARE ONLY NAMES. HUMAN MIND NEEDS TO CREATE TIME. ENDS. BEGINNINGS. JUST MOMENTS.
AND IF EVERY MOMENT IS JUST A MOMENT...
...YOU ARE THE ONE WHO CHOOSE WHAT THIS MOMENT *IS.*
AN END, OR A BEGINNING. ***YOU*** CHOOSE.
HEH.
I LIKE YOU, OLD MAN. I LIKE YOU.
LET'S GO LOOK FOR SOME GAS.

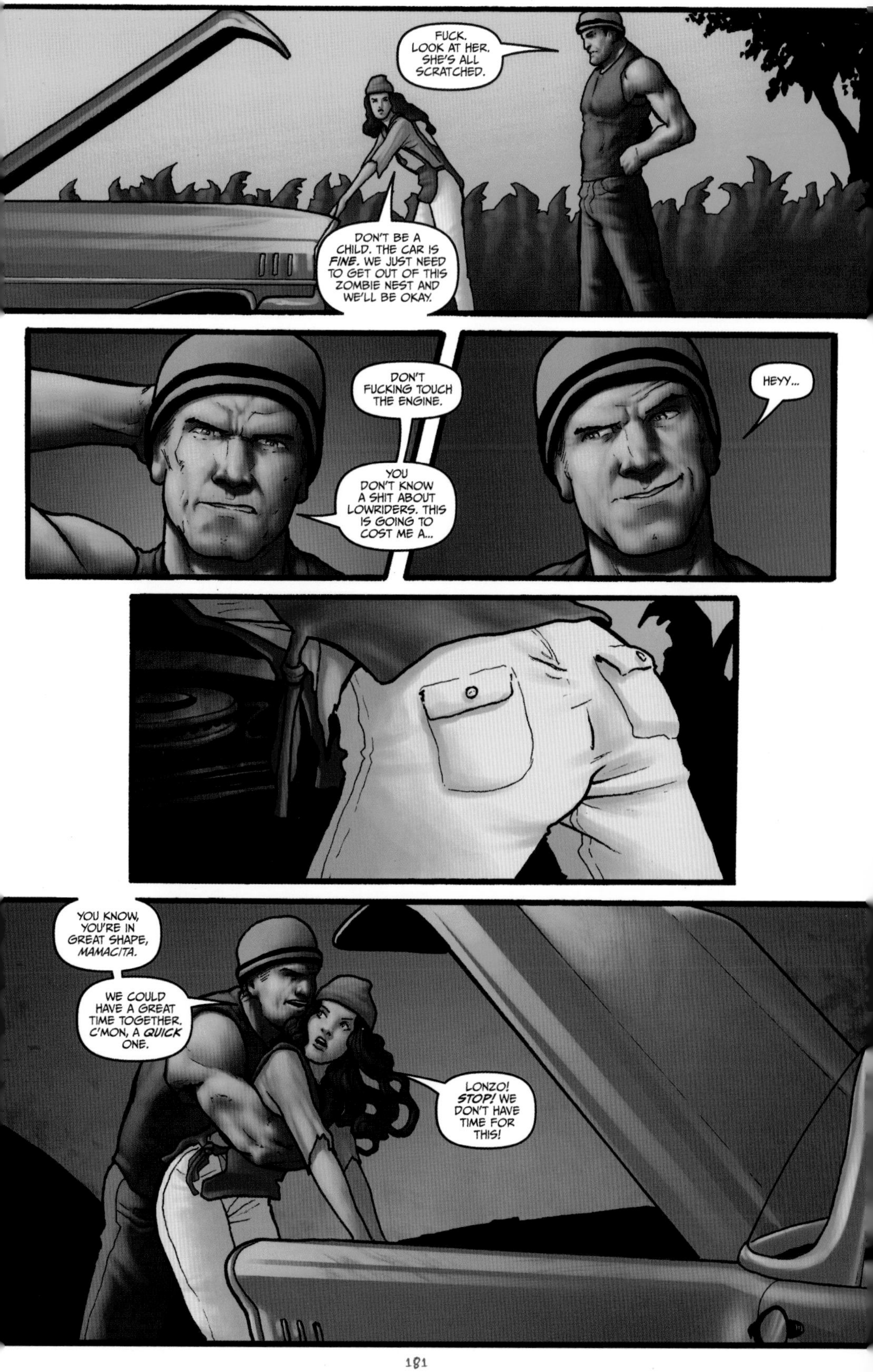
FUCK. LOOK AT HER. SHE'S ALL SCRATCHED.
DON'T BE A CHILD. THE CAR IS *FINE.* WE JUST NEED TO GET OUT OF THIS ZOMBIE NEST AND WE'LL BE OKAY.
DON'T FUCKING TOUCH THE ENGINE.
YOU DON'T KNOW A SHIT ABOUT LOWRIDERS. THIS IS GOING TO COST ME A...
HEYY...
YOU KNOW, YOU'RE IN GREAT SHAPE, *MAMACITA.*
WE COULD HAVE A GREAT TIME TOGETHER. C'MON, A *QUICK* ONE.
LONZO! *STOP!* WE DON'T HAVE TIME FOR THIS!

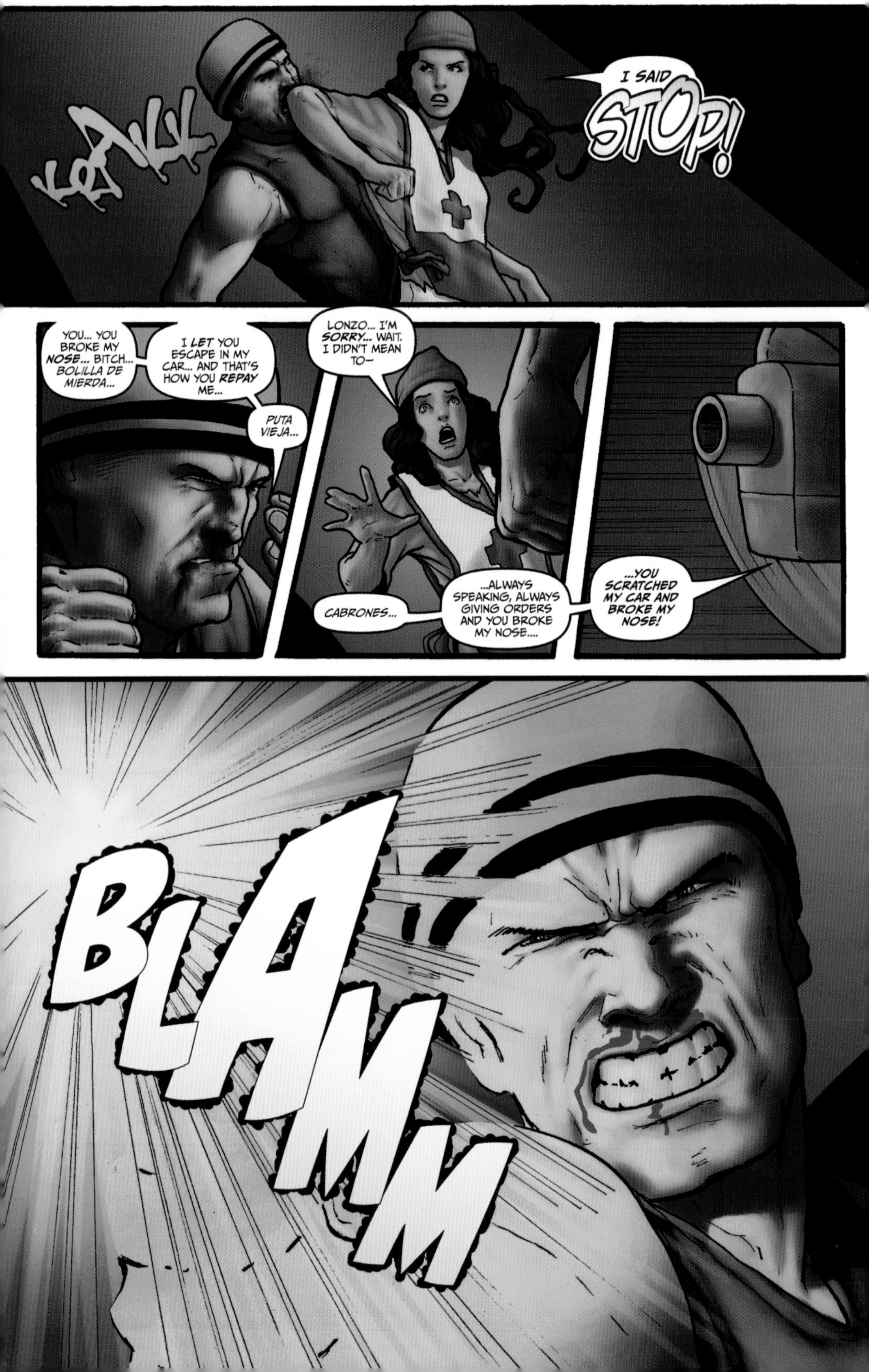

I SAID STOP!
YOU... YOU BROKE MY NOSE... BITCH... BOLILLA DE MIERDA...
I LET YOU ESCAPE IN MY CAR... AND THAT'S HOW YOU REPAY ME...
PUTA VIEJA...
LONZO... I'M SORRY... WAIT. I DIDN'T MEAN TO–
CABRONES...
...ALWAYS SPEAKING, ALWAYS GIVING ORDERS AND YOU BROKE MY NOSE....
...YOU SCRATCHED MY CAR AND BROKE MY NOSE!
BLAMM

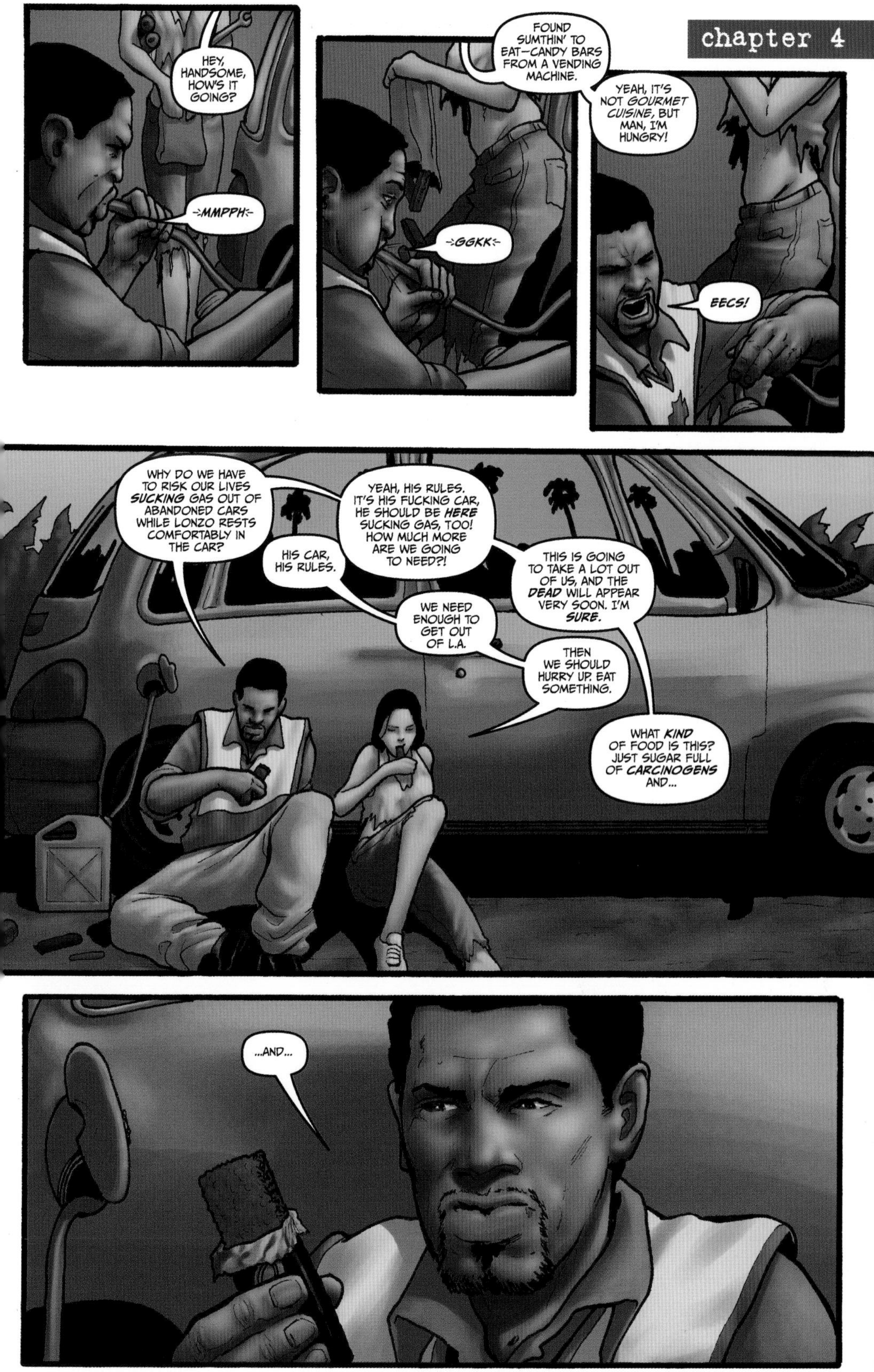
HEY, HANDSOME, HOW'S IT GOING?
-MMPPH-
FOUND SUMTHIN' TO EAT—CANDY BARS FROM A VENDING MACHINE.
-GGKK-
YEAH, IT'S NOT GOURMET CUISINE, BUT MAN, I'M HUNGRY!
EECS!
WHY DO WE HAVE TO RISK OUR LIVES SUCKING GAS OUT OF ABANDONED CARS WHILE LONZO RESTS COMFORTABLY IN THE CAR?
HIS CAR, HIS RULES.
YEAH, HIS RULES. IT'S HIS FUCKING CAR, HE SHOULD BE HERE SUCKING GAS, TOO! HOW MUCH MORE ARE WE GOING TO NEED?!
WE NEED ENOUGH TO GET OUT OF L.A.
THIS IS GOING TO TAKE A LOT OUT OF US, AND THE DEAD WILL APPEAR VERY SOON. I'M SURE.
THEN WE SHOULD HURRY UP. EAT SOMETHING.
WHAT KIND OF FOOD IS THIS? JUST SUGAR FULL OF CARCINOGENS AND...
...AND...

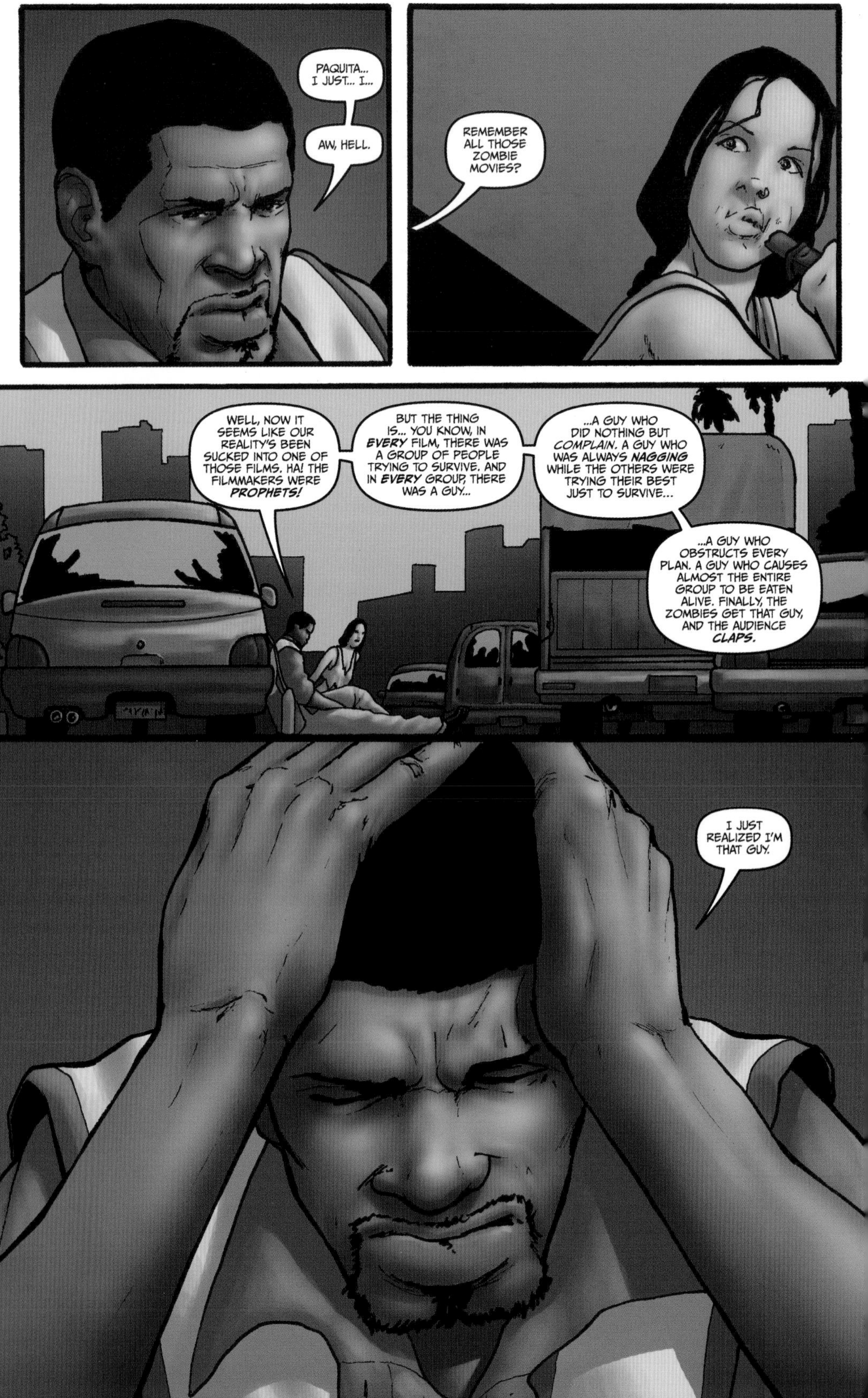
PAQUITA... I JUST... I...
AW, HELL.
REMEMBER ALL THOSE ZOMBIE MOVIES?
WELL, NOW IT SEEMS LIKE OUR REALITY'S BEEN SUCKED INTO ONE OF THOSE FILMS. HA! THE FILMMAKERS WERE PROPHETS!
BUT THE THING IS... YOU KNOW, IN EVERY FILM, THERE WAS A GROUP OF PEOPLE TRYING TO SURVIVE. AND IN EVERY GROUP, THERE WAS A GUY...
...A GUY WHO DID NOTHING BUT COMPLAIN. A GUY WHO WAS ALWAYS NAGGING WHILE THE OTHERS WERE TRYING THEIR BEST JUST TO SURVIVE...
...A GUY WHO OBSTRUCTS EVERY PLAN. A GUY WHO CAUSES ALMOST THE ENTIRE GROUP TO BE EATEN ALIVE. FINALLY, THE ZOMBIES GET THAT GUY, AND THE AUDIENCE CLAPS.
I JUST REALIZED I'M THAT GUY.

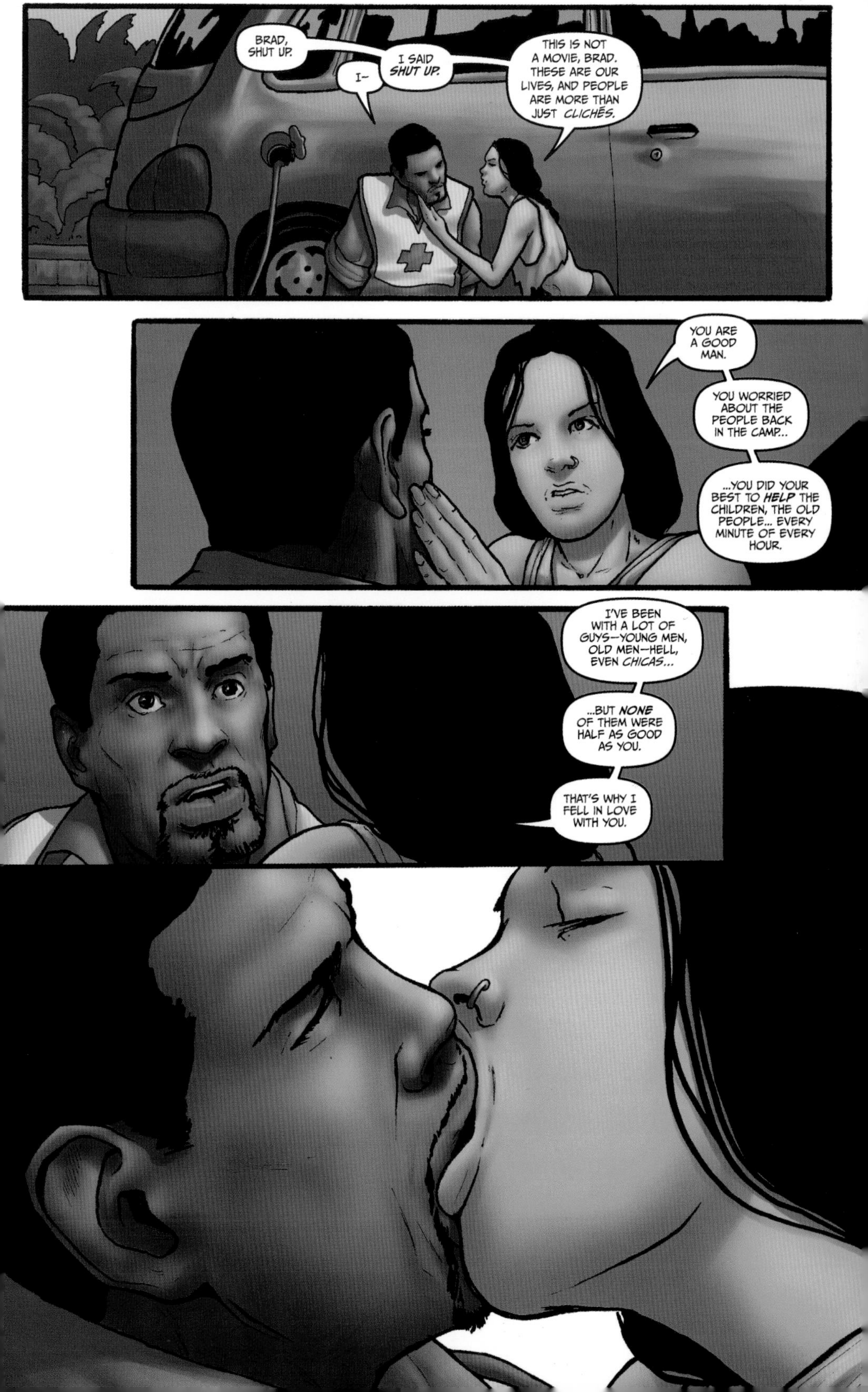
BRAD, SHUT UP.
I–
I SAID *SHUT UP.*
THIS IS NOT A MOVIE, BRAD. THESE ARE OUR LIVES, AND PEOPLE ARE MORE THAN JUST *CLICHÉS.*
YOU ARE A GOOD MAN.
YOU WORRIED ABOUT THE PEOPLE BACK IN THE CAMP...
...YOU DID YOUR BEST TO ***HELP*** THE CHILDREN, THE OLD PEOPLE... EVERY MINUTE OF EVERY HOUR.
I'VE BEEN WITH A LOT OF GUYS—YOUNG MEN, OLD MEN—HELL, EVEN *CHICAS*...
...BUT ***NONE*** OF THEM WERE HALF AS GOOD AS YOU.
THAT'S WHY I FELL IN LOVE WITH YOU.

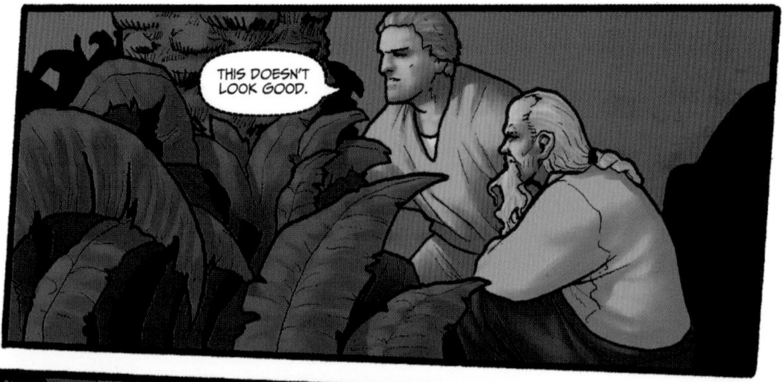
THIS DOESN'T LOOK GOOD.

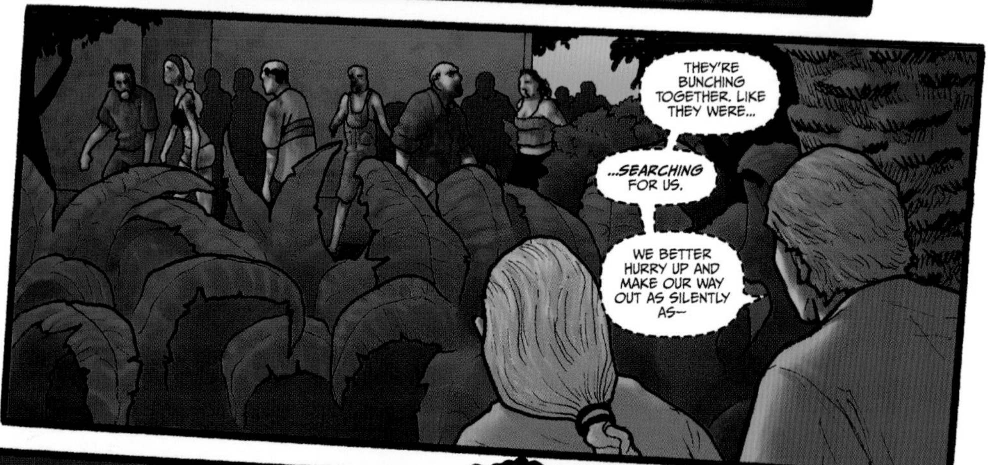
THEY'RE BUNCHING TOGETHER. LIKE THEY WERE...
...SEARCHING FOR US.
WE BETTER HURRY UP AND MAKE OUR WAY OUT AS SILENTLY AS--

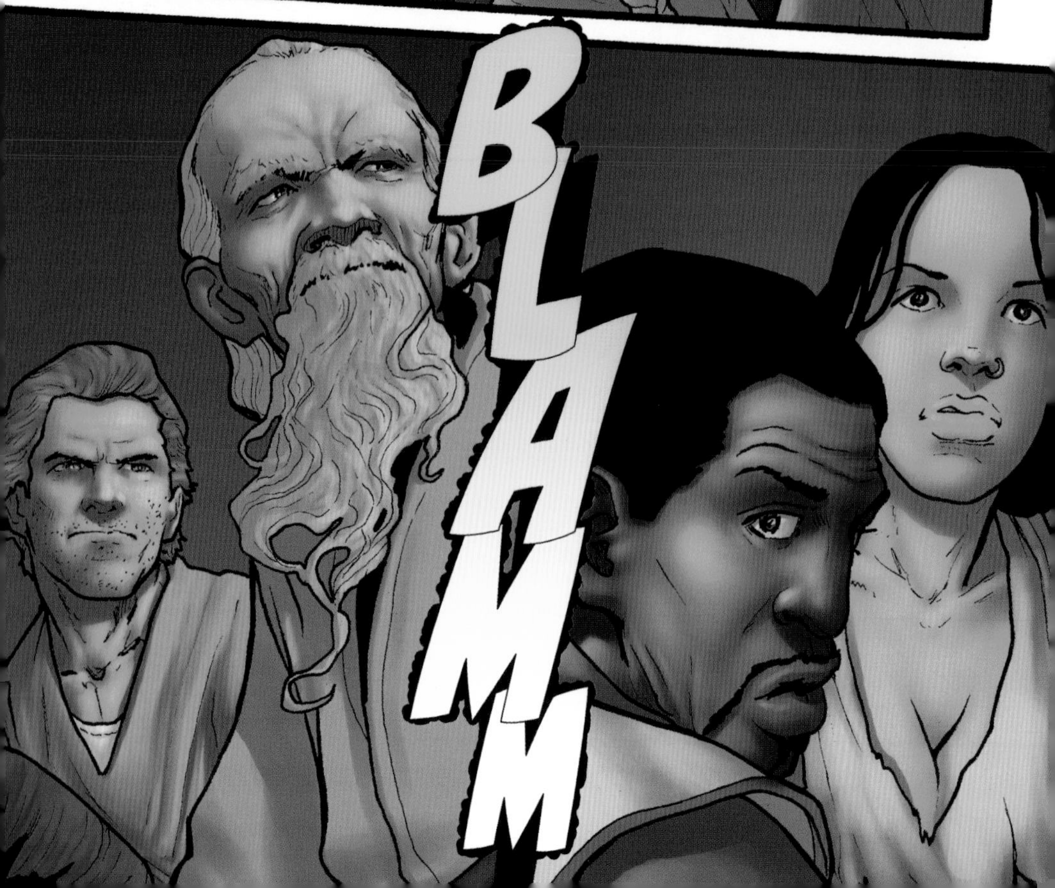
BLAMM

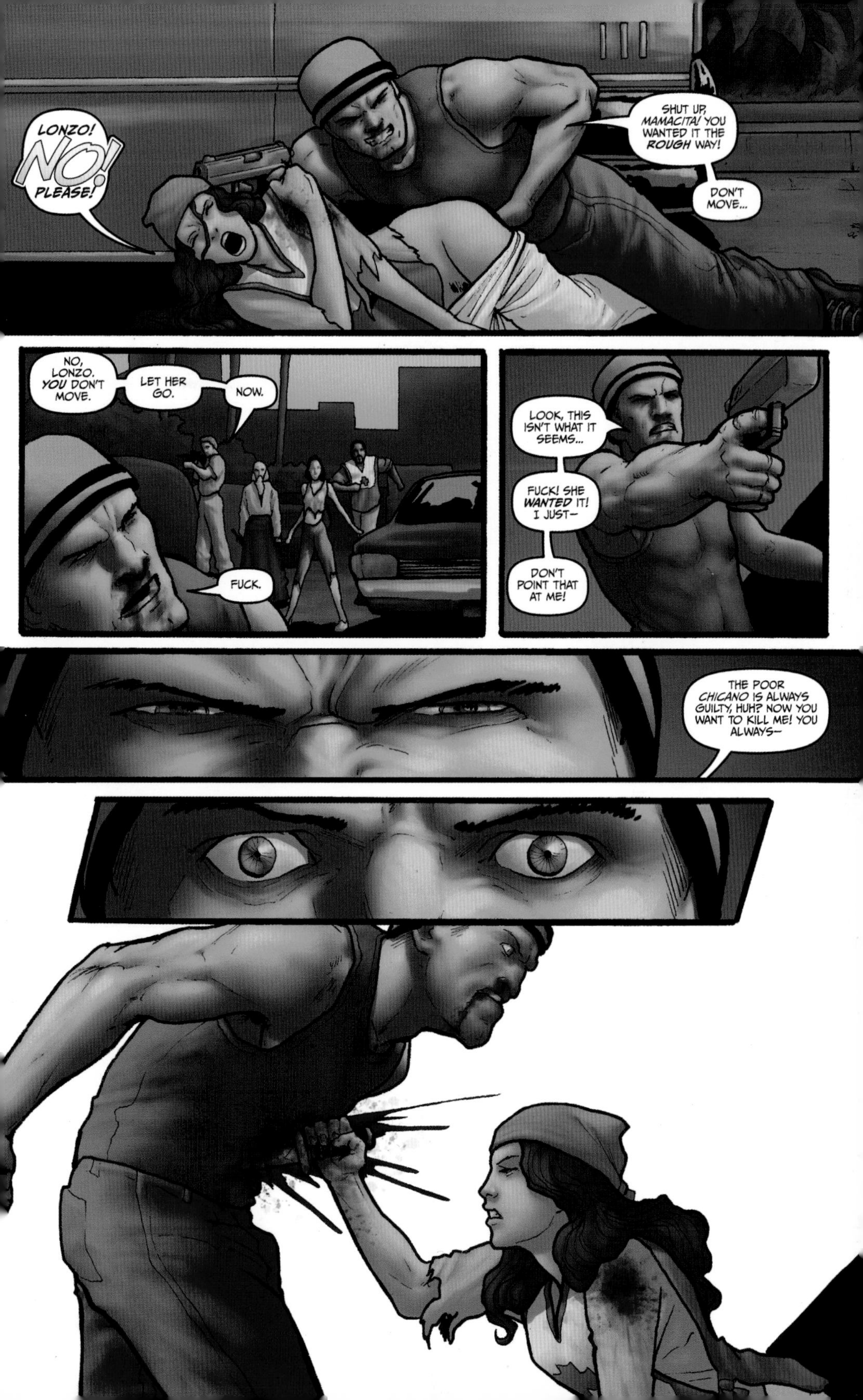
LONZO! NO! PLEASE!
SHUT UP, MAMACITA! YOU WANTED IT THE ROUGH WAY!
DON'T MOVE...
NO, LONZO. YOU DON'T MOVE.
LET HER GO.
NOW.
FUCK.
LOOK, THIS ISN'T WHAT IT SEEMS...
FUCK! SHE WANTED IT! I JUST—
DON'T POINT THAT AT ME!
THE POOR CHICANO IS ALWAYS GUILTY, HUH? NOW YOU WANT TO KILL ME! YOU ALWAYS—

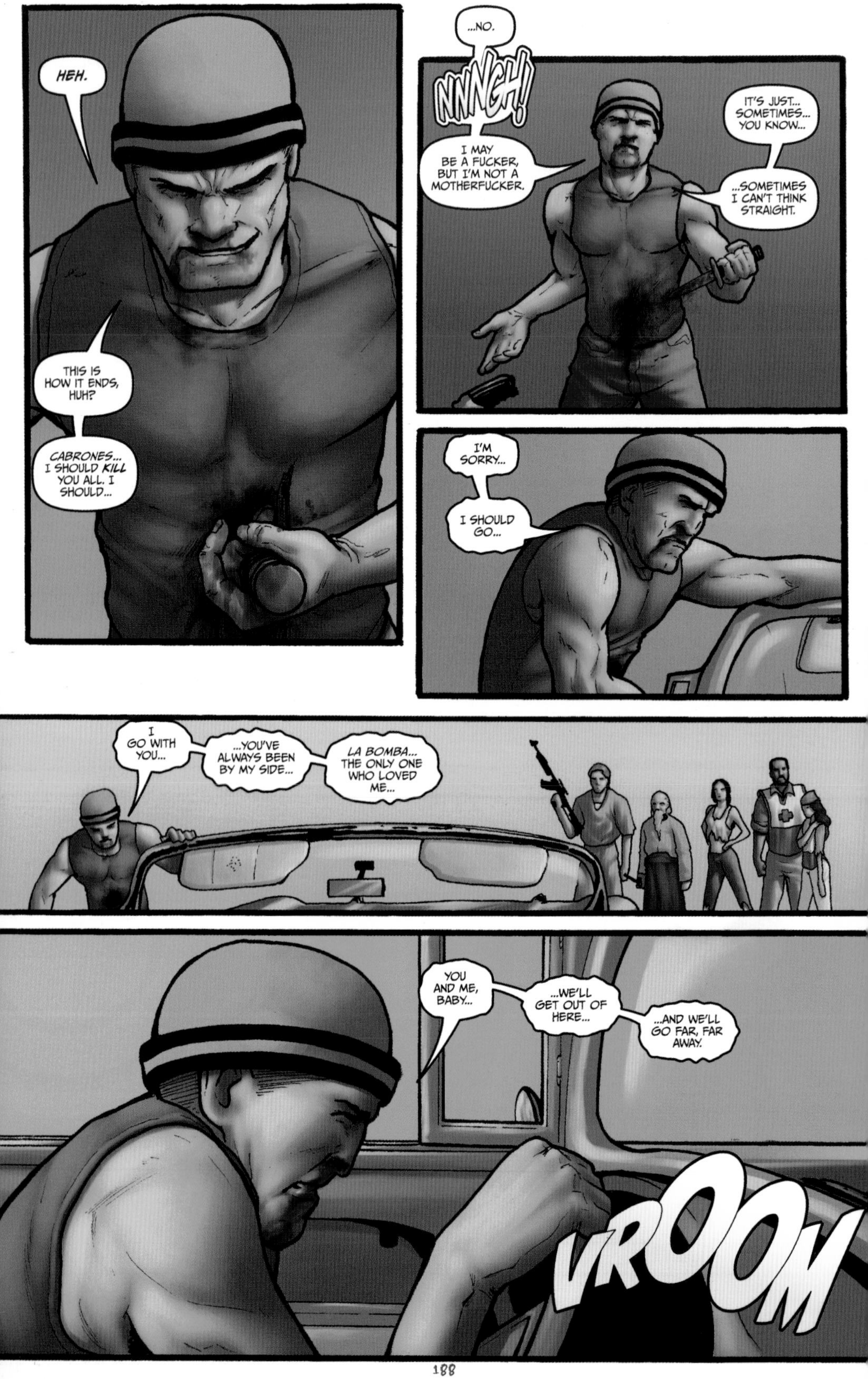
HEH.
THIS IS HOW IT ENDS, HUH?
CABRONES... I SHOULD KILL YOU ALL. I SHOULD...
...NO.
NNNGH!
I MAY BE A FUCKER, BUT I'M NOT A MOTHERFUCKER.
IT'S JUST... SOMETIMES... YOU KNOW...
...SOMETIMES I CAN'T THINK STRAIGHT.
I'M SORRY...
I SHOULD GO...
I GO WITH YOU...
...YOU'VE ALWAYS BEEN BY MY SIDE...
LA BOMBA... THE ONLY ONE WHO LOVED ME...
YOU AND ME, BABY...
...WE'LL GET OUT OF HERE...
...AND WE'LL GO FAR, FAR AWAY.
VROOOM

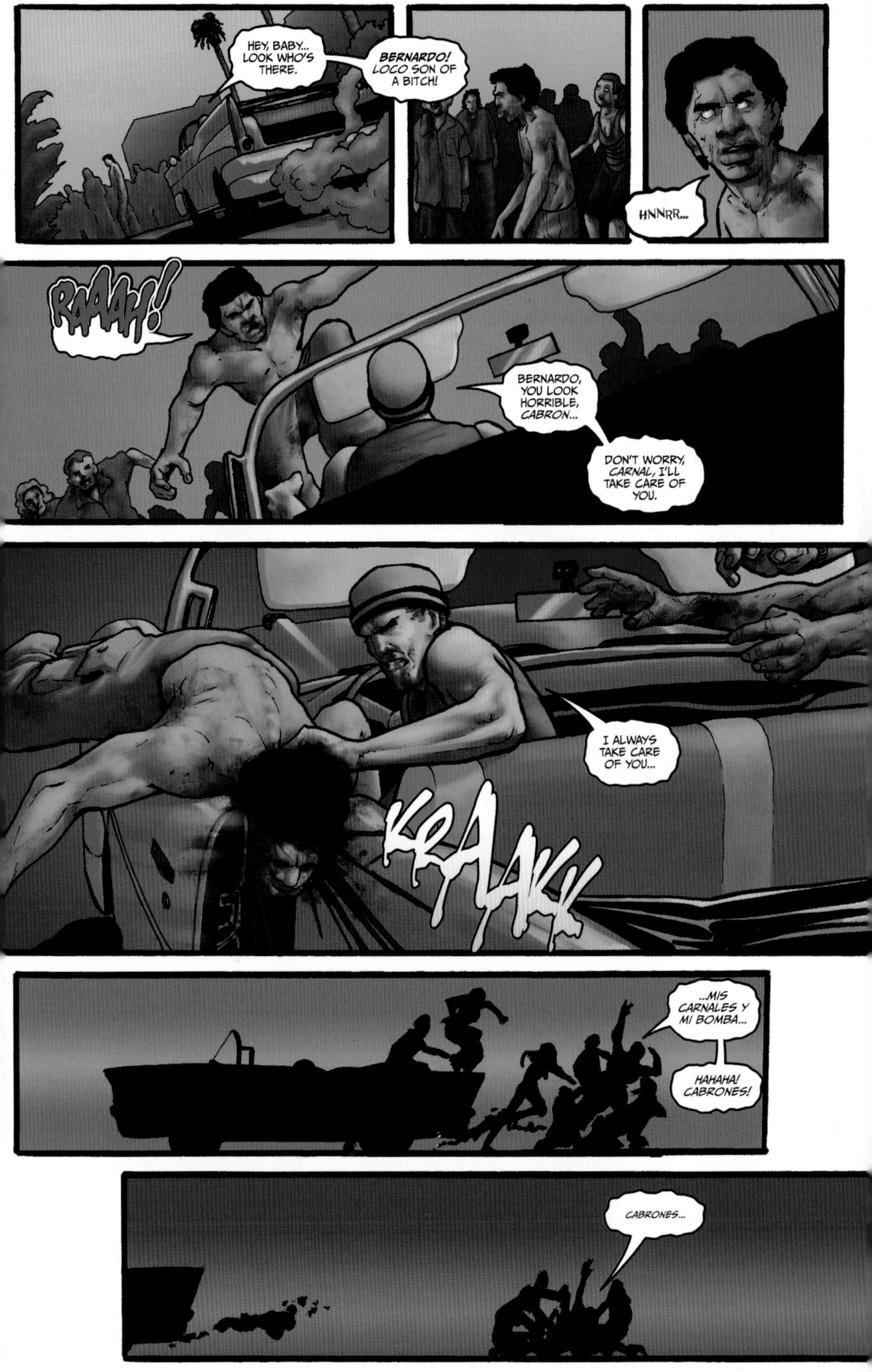
HEY, BABY... LOOK WHO'S THERE.
BERNARDO! LOCO SON OF A BITCH!
HNNRR...
RAAAH!
BERNARDO, YOU LOOK HORRIBLE, CABRON...
DON'T WORRY, CARNAL, I'LL TAKE CARE OF YOU.
I ALWAYS TAKE CARE OF YOU...
KRAAKK
...MIS CARNALES Y MI BOMBA...
HAHAHA! CABRONES!
CABRONES...

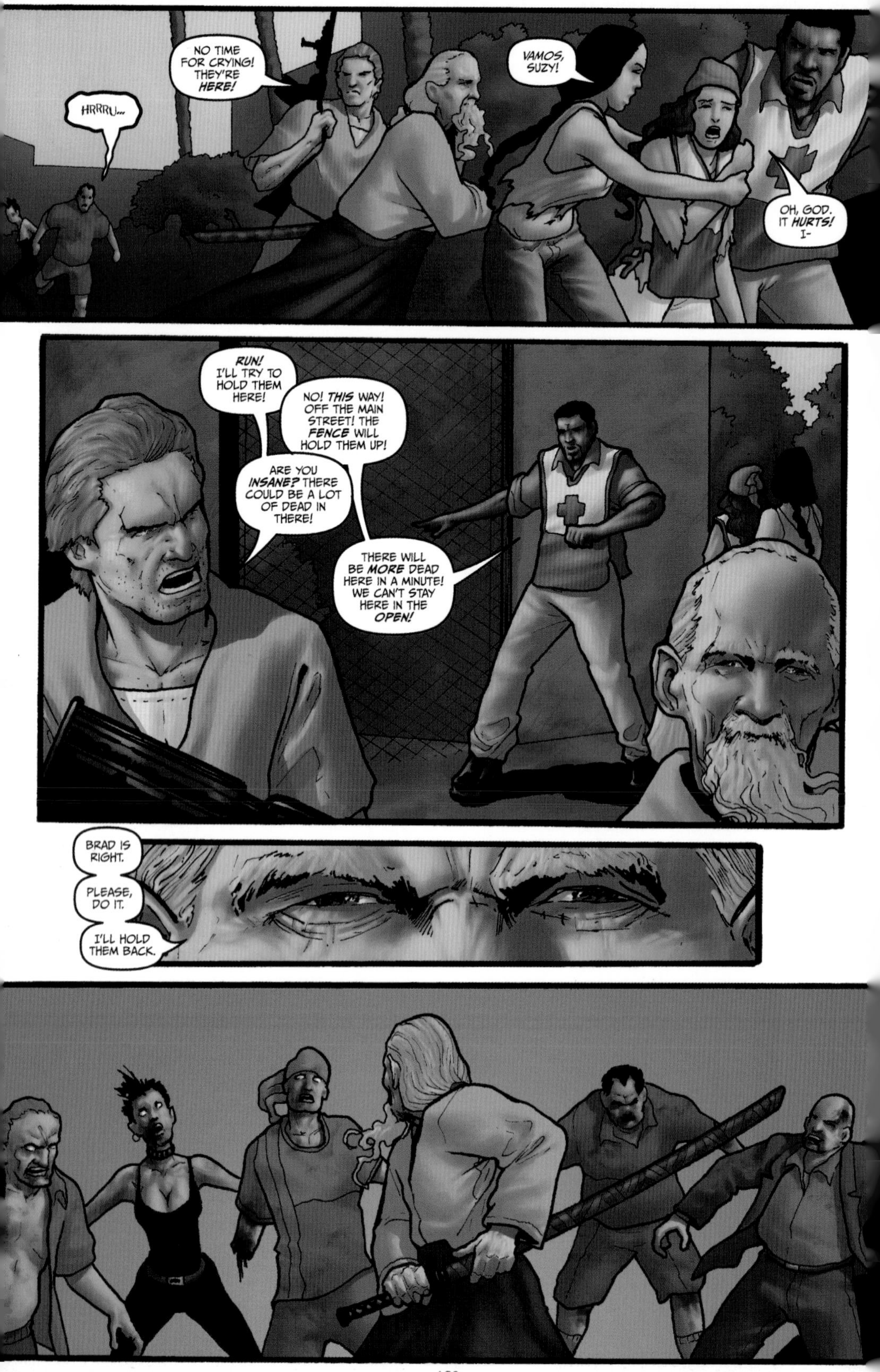
HRRRU...
NO TIME FOR CRYING! THEY'RE HERE!
VAMOS, SUZY!
OH, GOD. IT HURTS! I-
RUN! I'LL TRY TO HOLD THEM HERE!
NO! THIS WAY! OFF THE MAIN STREET! THE FENCE WILL HOLD THEM UP!
ARE YOU INSANE? THERE COULD BE A LOT OF DEAD IN THERE!
THERE WILL BE MORE DEAD HERE IN A MINUTE! WE CAN'T STAY HERE IN THE OPEN!
BRAD IS RIGHT.
PLEASE, DO IT.
I'LL HOLD THEM BACK.

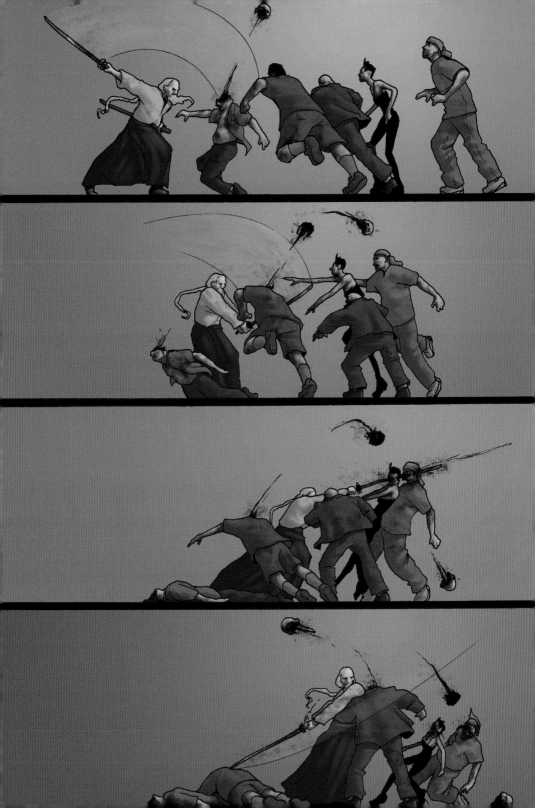

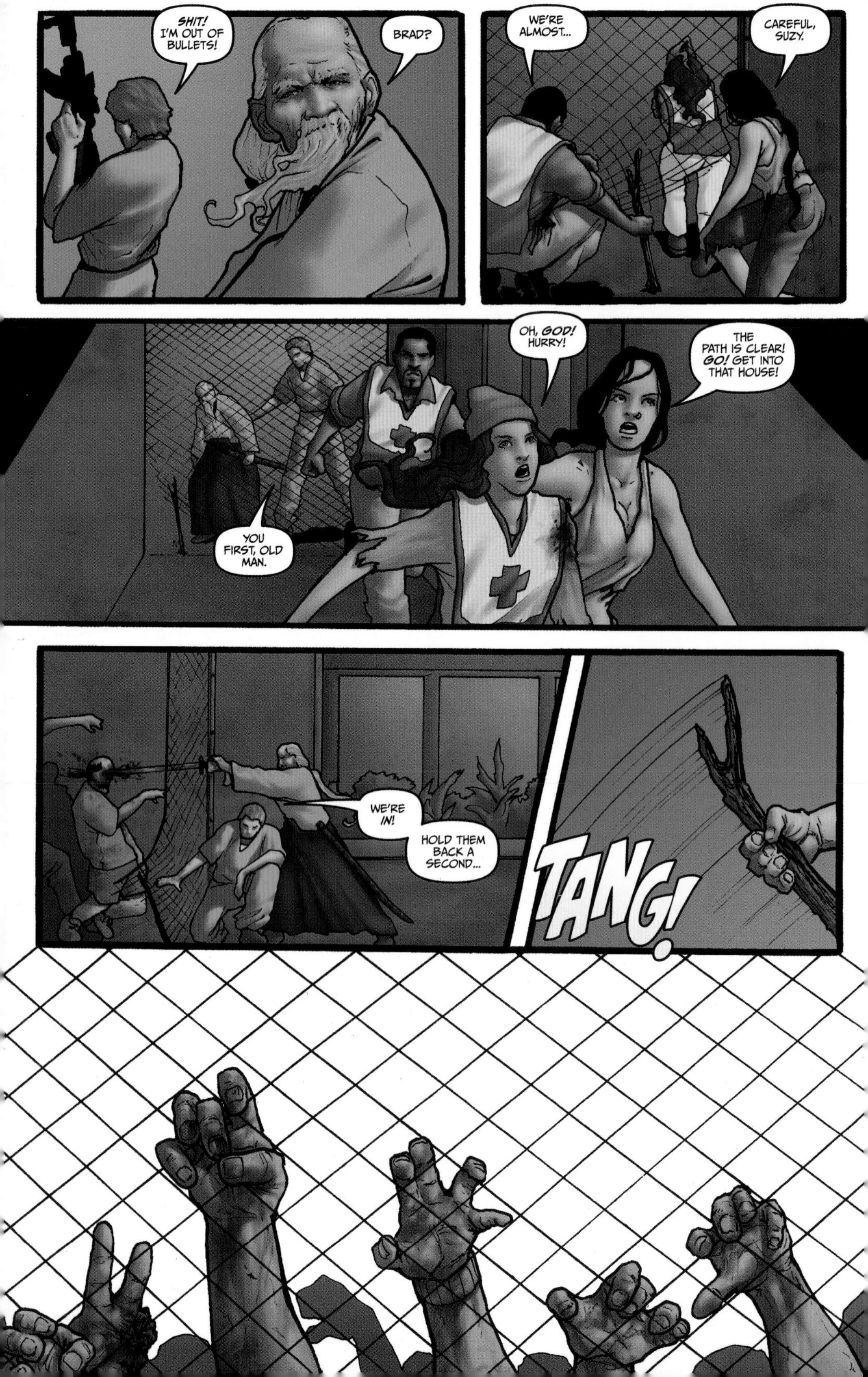
SHIT! I'M OUT OF BULLETS!
BRAD?
WE'RE ALMOST...
CAREFUL, SUZY.
YOU FIRST, OLD MAN.
OH, GOD! HURRY!
THE PATH IS CLEAR! GO! GET INTO THAT HOUSE!
WE'RE IN!
HOLD THEM BACK A SECOND...
TANG!

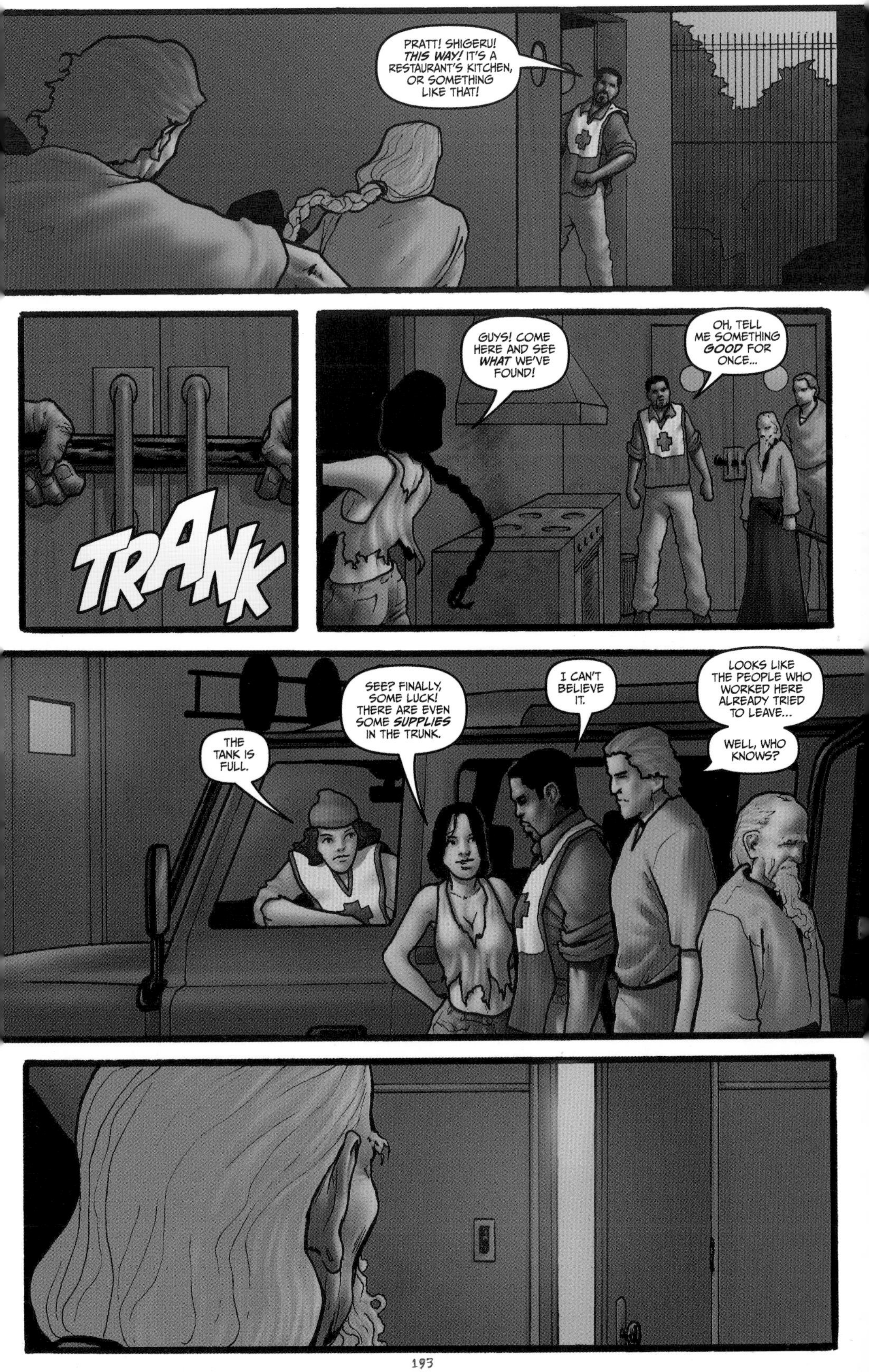
PRATT! SHIGERU! THIS WAY! IT'S A RESTAURANT'S KITCHEN, OR SOMETHING LIKE THAT!
TRANK
GUYS! COME HERE AND SEE WHAT WE'VE FOUND!
OH, TELL ME SOMETHING GOOD FOR ONCE...
THE TANK IS FULL.
SEE? FINALLY, SOME LUCK! THERE ARE EVEN SOME SUPPLIES IN THE TRUNK.
I CAN'T BELIEVE IT.
LOOKS LIKE THE PEOPLE WHO WORKED HERE ALREADY TRIED TO LEAVE...
WELL, WHO KNOWS?

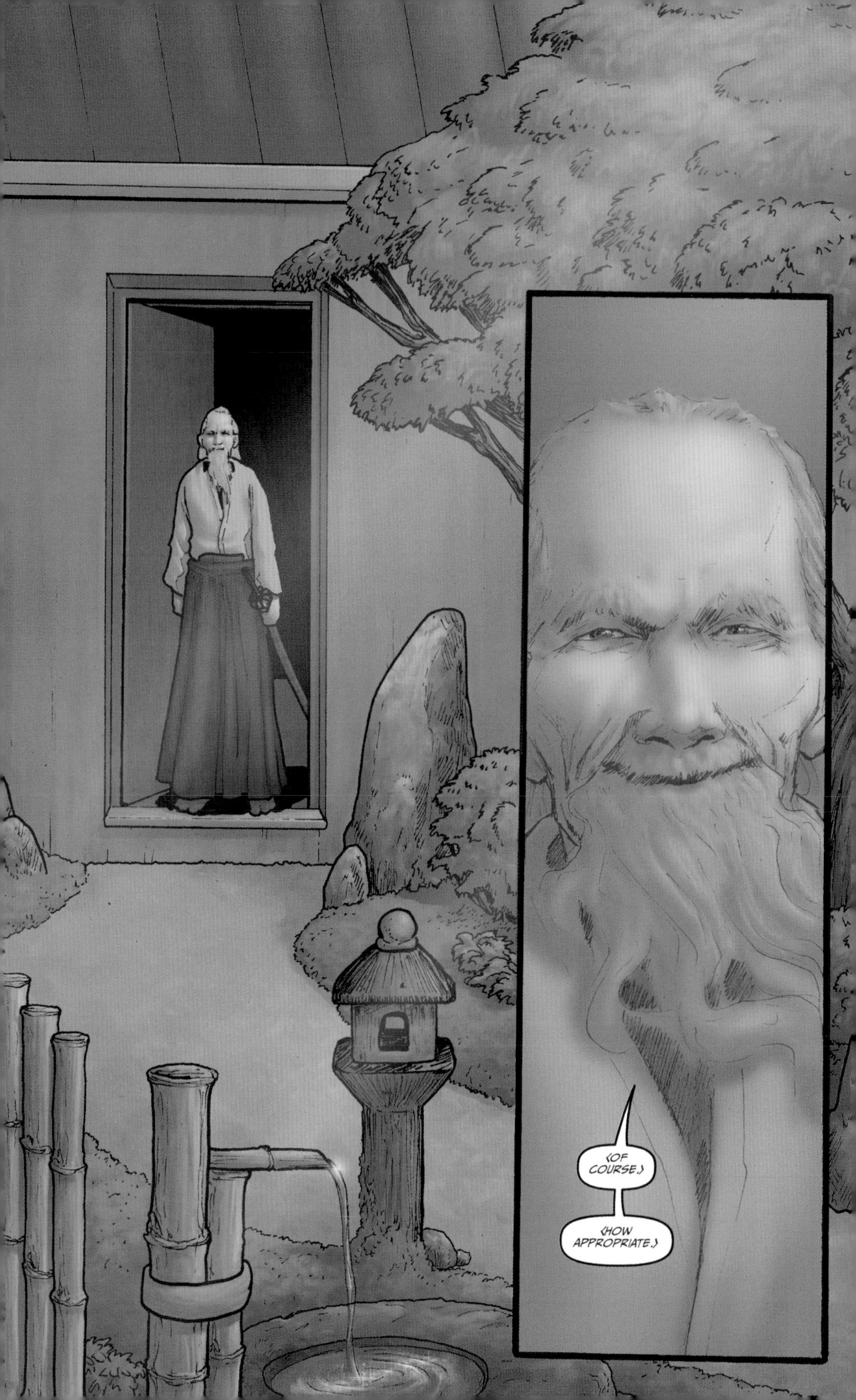
‹OF COURSE.›
‹HOW APPROPRIATE.›

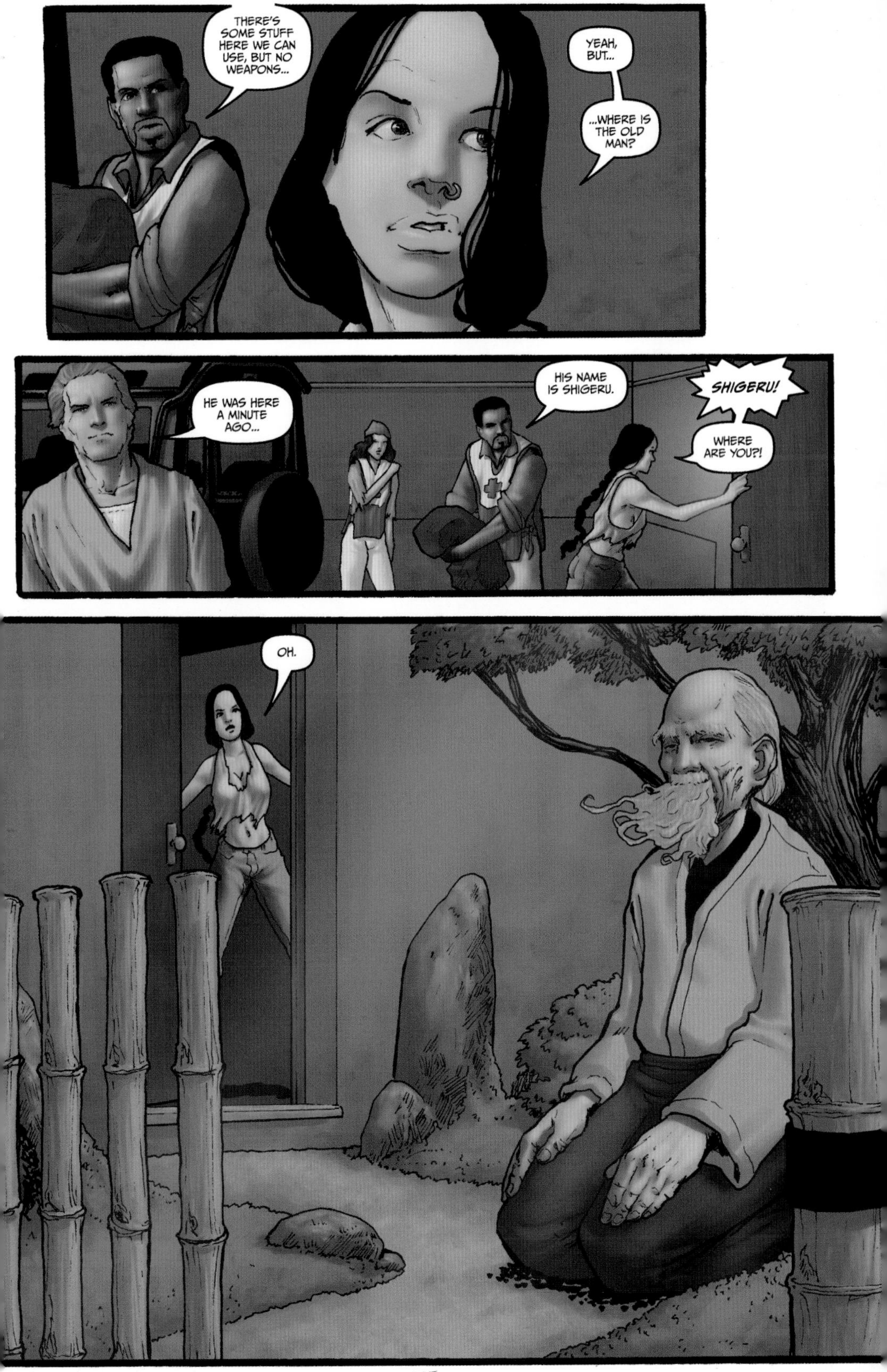
THERE'S SOME STUFF HERE WE CAN USE, BUT NO WEAPONS...
YEAH, BUT...
...WHERE IS THE OLD MAN?
HE WAS HERE A MINUTE AGO...
HIS NAME IS SHIGERU.
SHIGERU!
WHERE ARE YOU?!
OH.

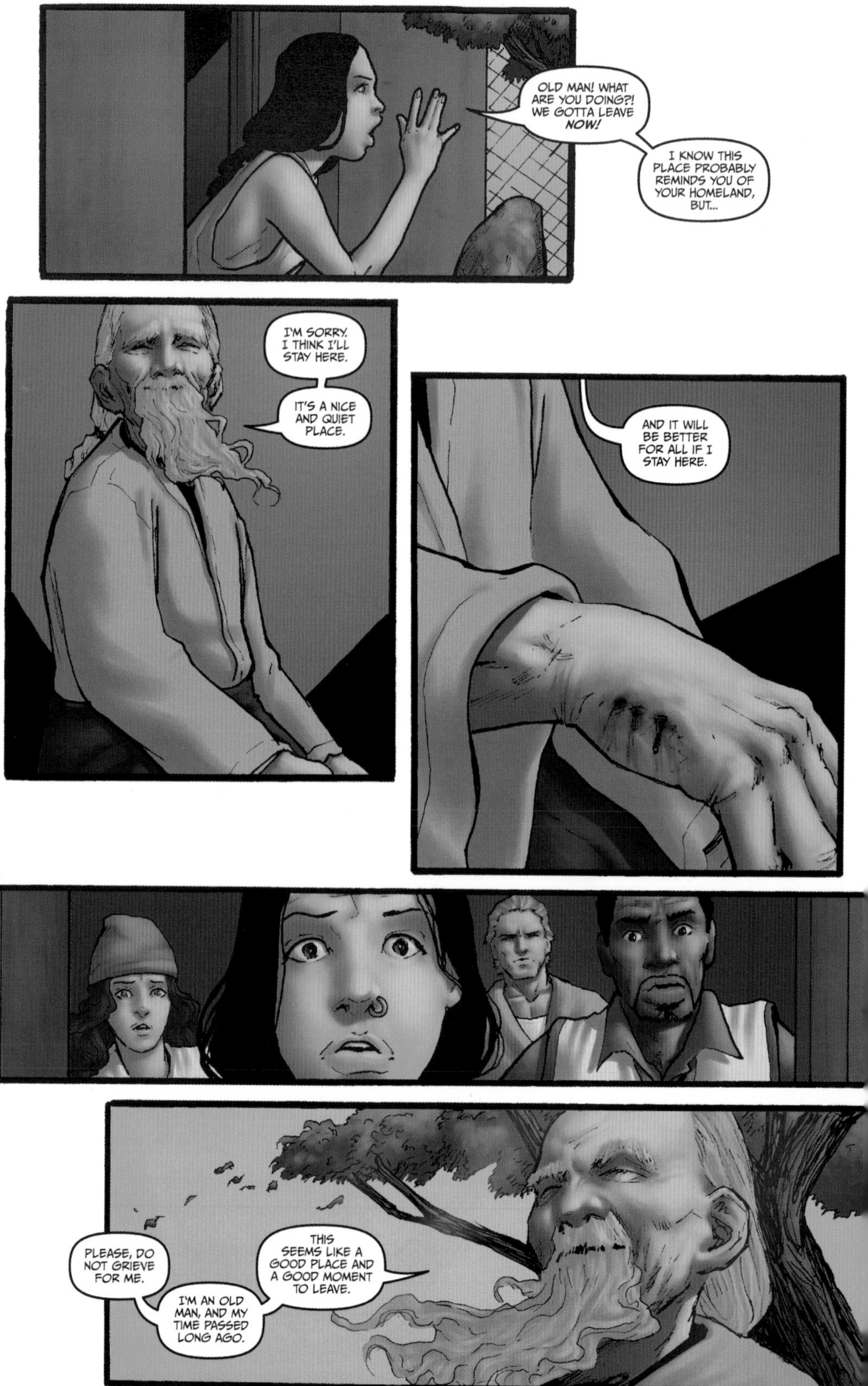
OLD MAN! WHAT ARE YOU DOING?! WE GOTTA LEAVE *NOW!*
I KNOW THIS PLACE PROBABLY REMINDS YOU OF YOUR HOMELAND, BUT...
I'M SORRY. I THINK I'LL STAY HERE.
IT'S A NICE AND QUIET PLACE.
AND IT WILL BE BETTER FOR ALL IF I STAY HERE.
THIS SEEMS LIKE A GOOD PLACE AND A GOOD MOMENT TO LEAVE.
PLEASE, DO NOT GRIEVE FOR ME.
I'M AN OLD MAN, AND MY TIME PASSED LONG AGO.

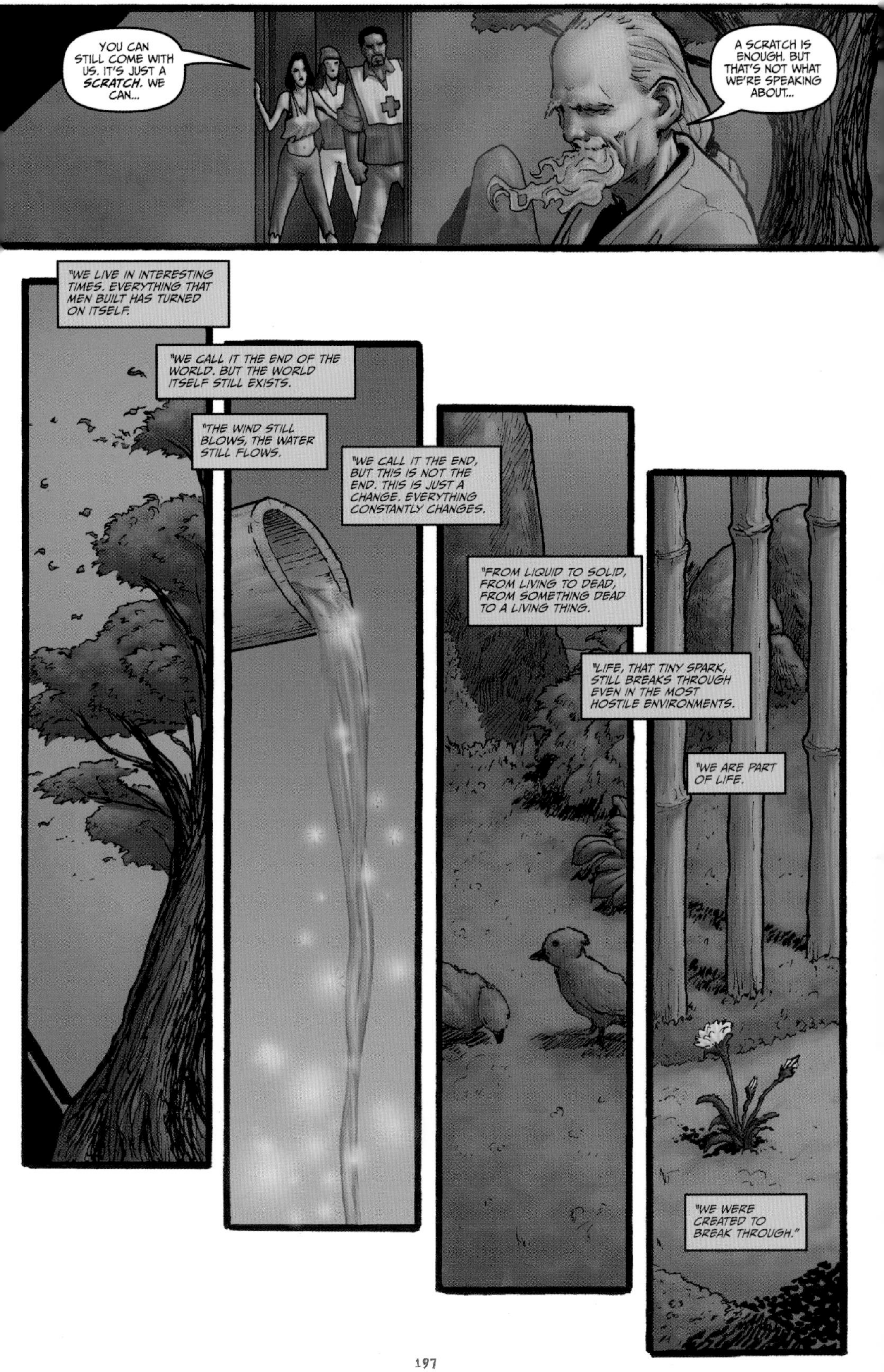

YOU CAN STILL COME WITH US. IT'S JUST A SCRATCH. WE CAN...
A SCRATCH IS ENOUGH. BUT THAT'S NOT WHAT WE'RE SPEAKING ABOUT...
"WE LIVE IN INTERESTING TIMES. EVERYTHING THAT MEN BUILT HAS TURNED ON ITSELF.
"WE CALL IT THE END OF THE WORLD. BUT THE WORLD ITSELF STILL EXISTS.
"THE WIND STILL BLOWS, THE WATER STILL FLOWS.
"WE CALL IT THE END, BUT THIS IS NOT THE END. THIS IS JUST A CHANGE. EVERYTHING CONSTANTLY CHANGES.
"FROM LIQUID TO SOLID, FROM LIVING TO DEAD, FROM SOMETHING DEAD TO A LIVING THING.
"LIFE, THAT TINY SPARK, STILL BREAKS THROUGH EVEN IN THE MOST HOSTILE ENVIRONMENTS.
"WE ARE PART OF LIFE.
"WE WERE CREATED TO BREAK THROUGH."

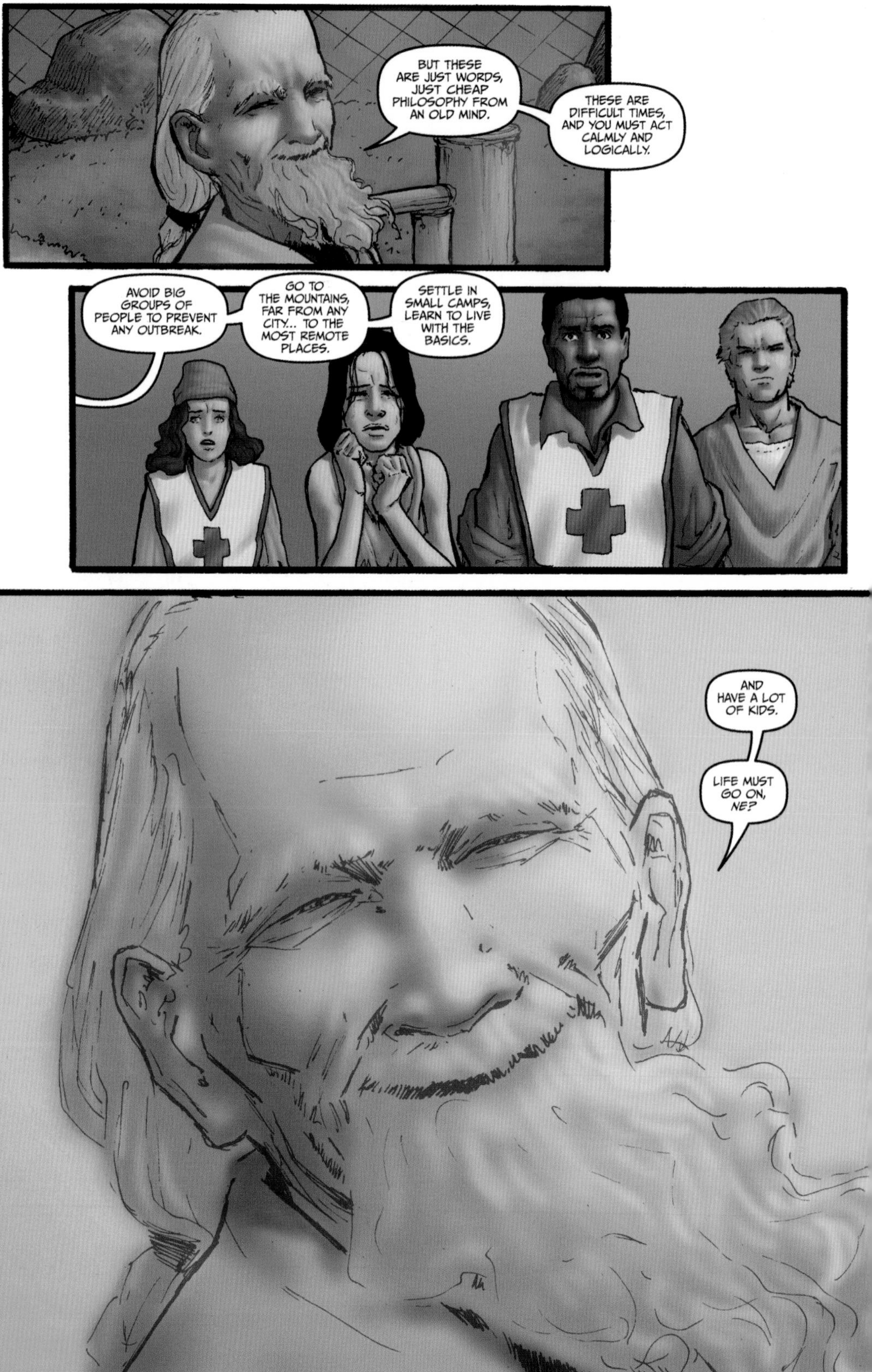
BUT THESE ARE JUST WORDS, JUST CHEAP PHILOSOPHY FROM AN OLD MIND.
THESE ARE DIFFICULT TIMES, AND YOU MUST ACT CALMLY AND LOGICALLY.
AVOID BIG GROUPS OF PEOPLE TO PREVENT ANY OUTBREAK.
GO TO THE MOUNTAINS, FAR FROM ANY CITY... TO THE MOST REMOTE PLACES.
SETTLE IN SMALL CAMPS, LEARN TO LIVE WITH THE BASICS.
AND HAVE A LOT OF KIDS.
LIFE MUST GO ON, *NE?*

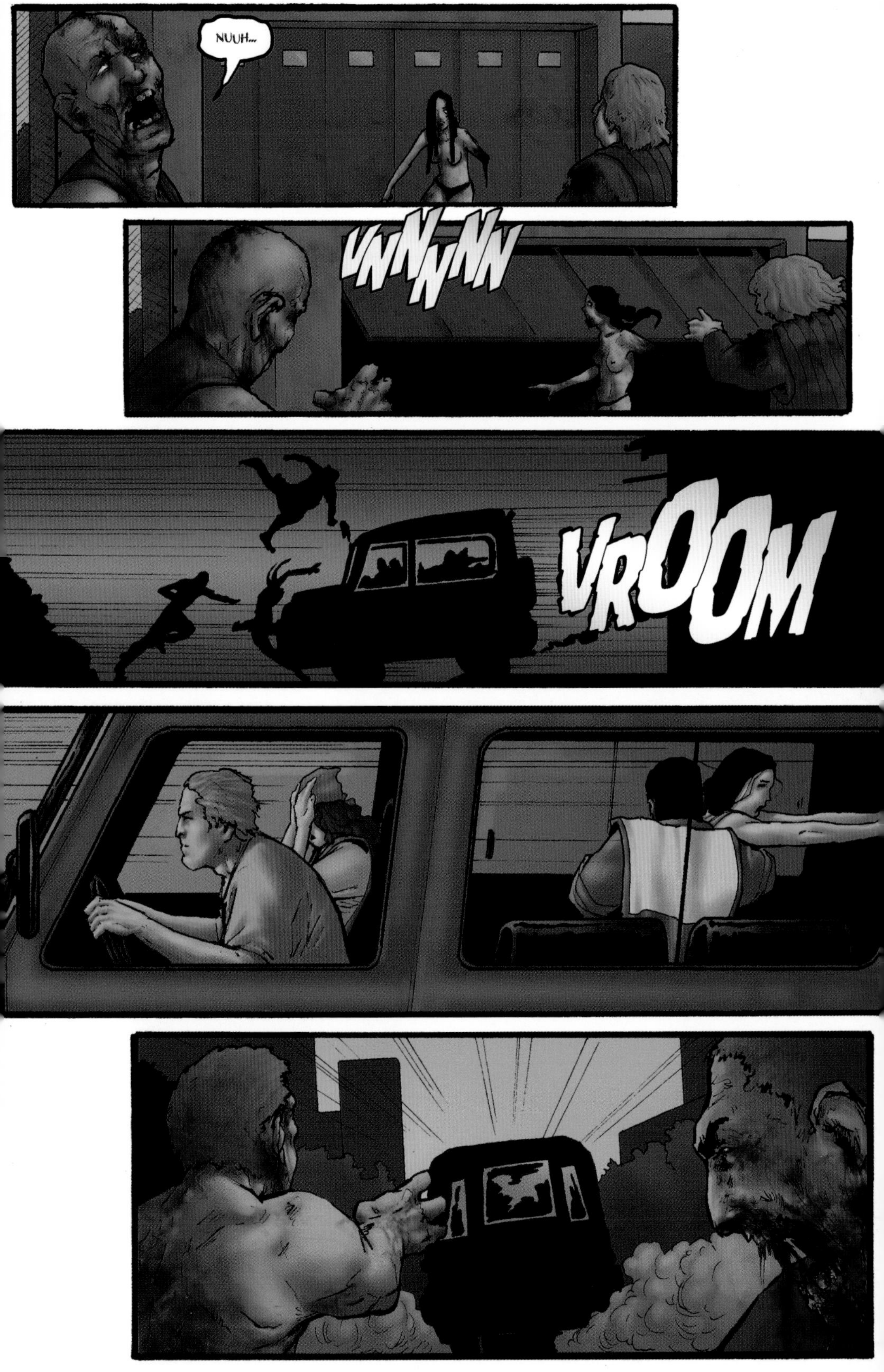
NUUH...
UNNNNNN
VROOM

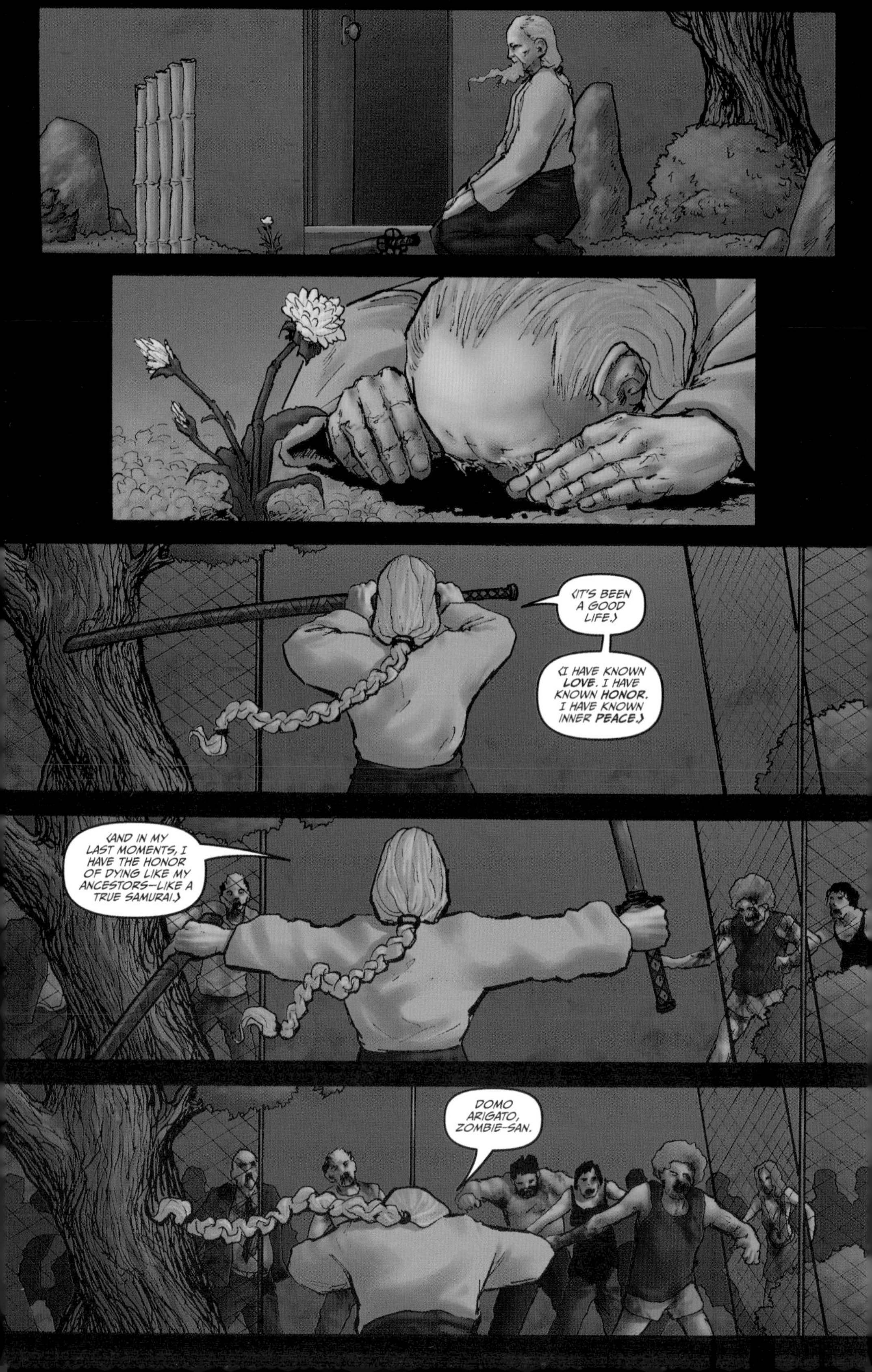
‹IT'S BEEN A GOOD LIFE.›
‹I HAVE KNOWN LOVE. I HAVE KNOWN HONOR. I HAVE KNOWN INNER PEACE.›
‹AND IN MY LAST MOMENTS, I HAVE THE HONOR OF DYING LIKE MY ANCESTORS--LIKE A TRUE SAMURAI.›
DOMO ARIGATO, ZOMBIE-SAN.

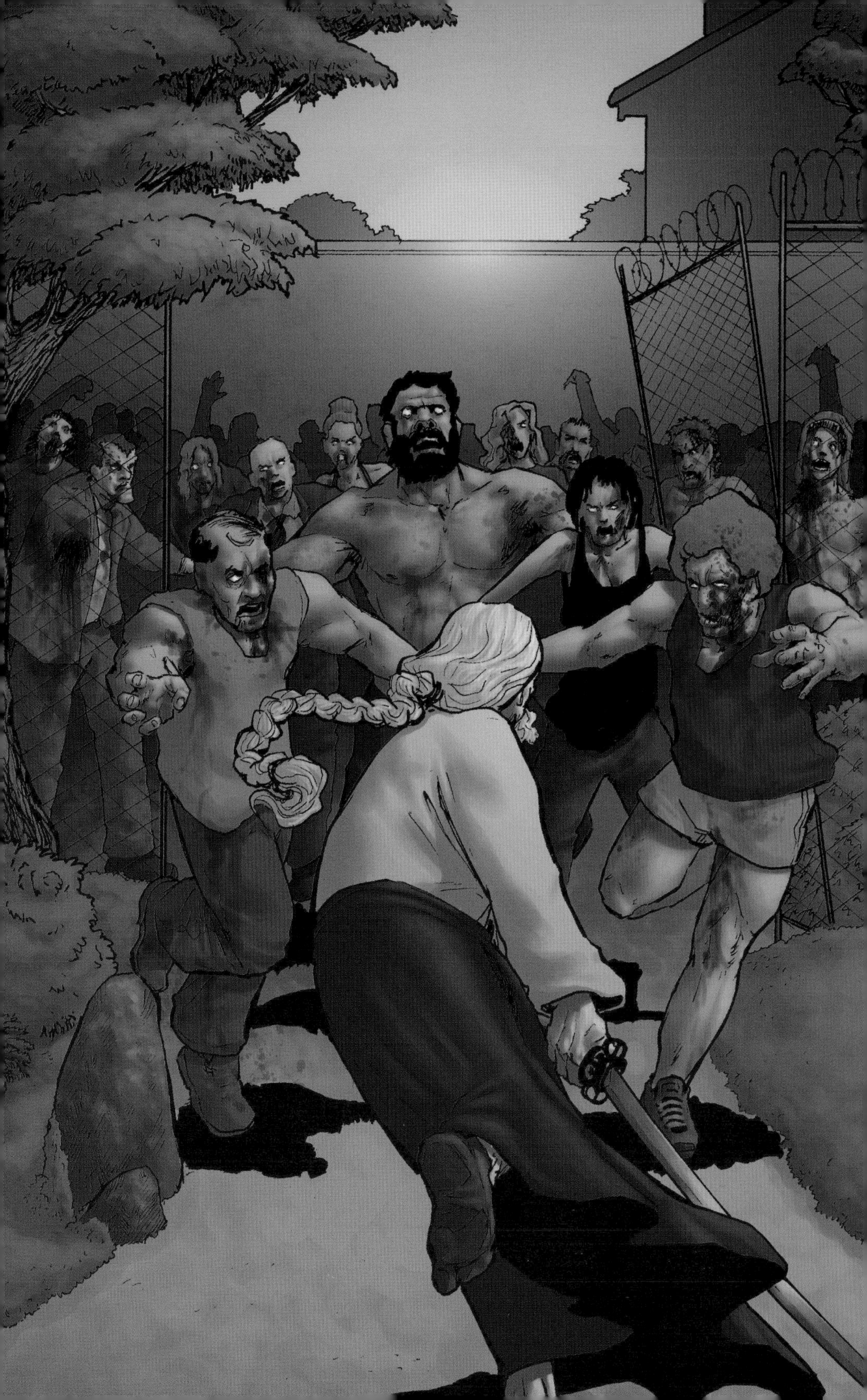

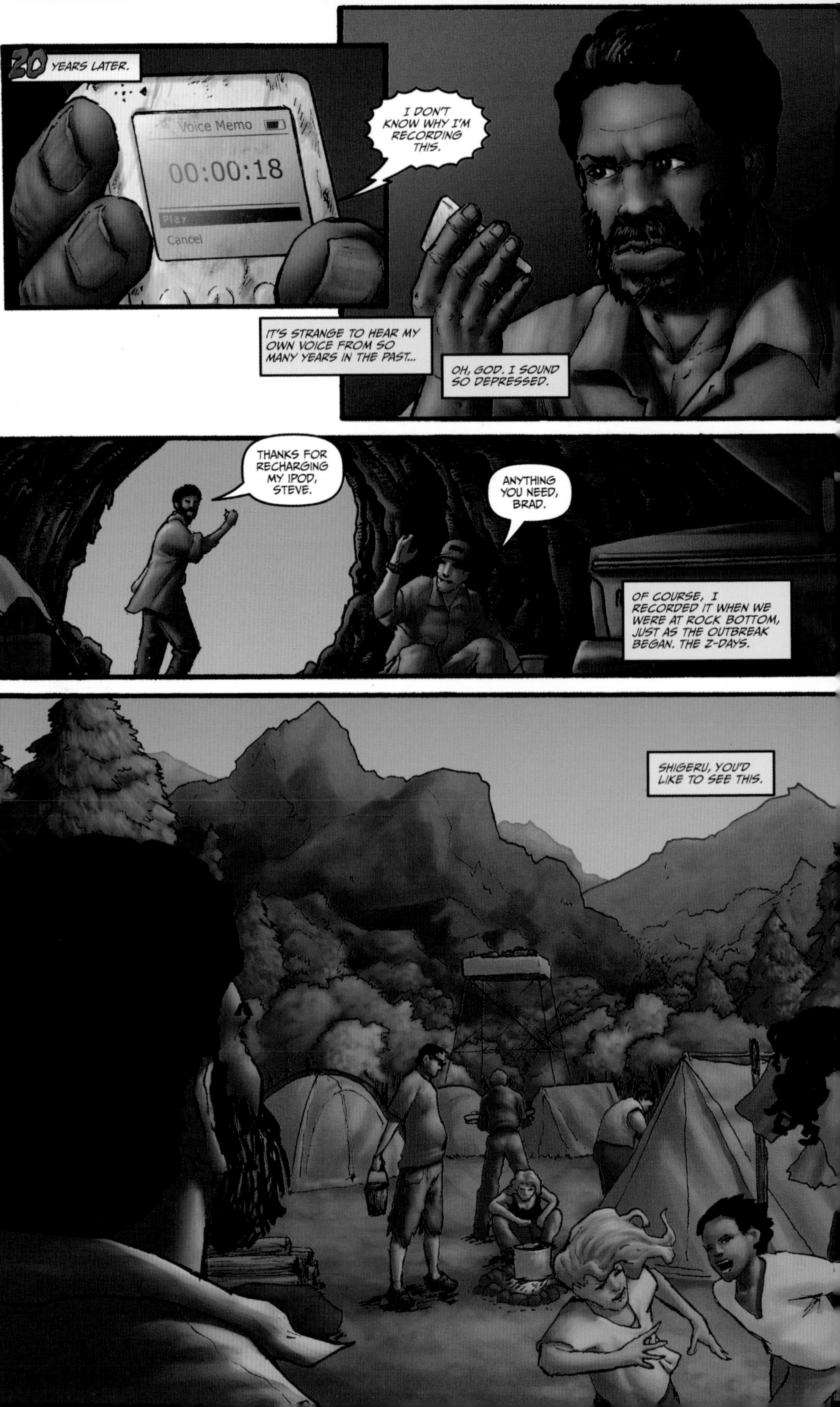
20 YEARS LATER.
Voice Memo
00:00:18
Play
Cancel
I DON'T KNOW WHY I'M RECORDING THIS.
IT'S STRANGE TO HEAR MY OWN VOICE FROM SO MANY YEARS IN THE PAST...
OH, GOD. I SOUND SO DEPRESSED.
THANKS FOR RECHARGING MY IPOD, STEVE.
ANYTHING YOU NEED, BRAD.
OF COURSE, I RECORDED IT WHEN WE WERE AT ROCK BOTTOM, JUST AS THE OUTBREAK BEGAN. THE Z-DAYS.
SHIGERU, YOU'D LIKE TO SEE THIS.

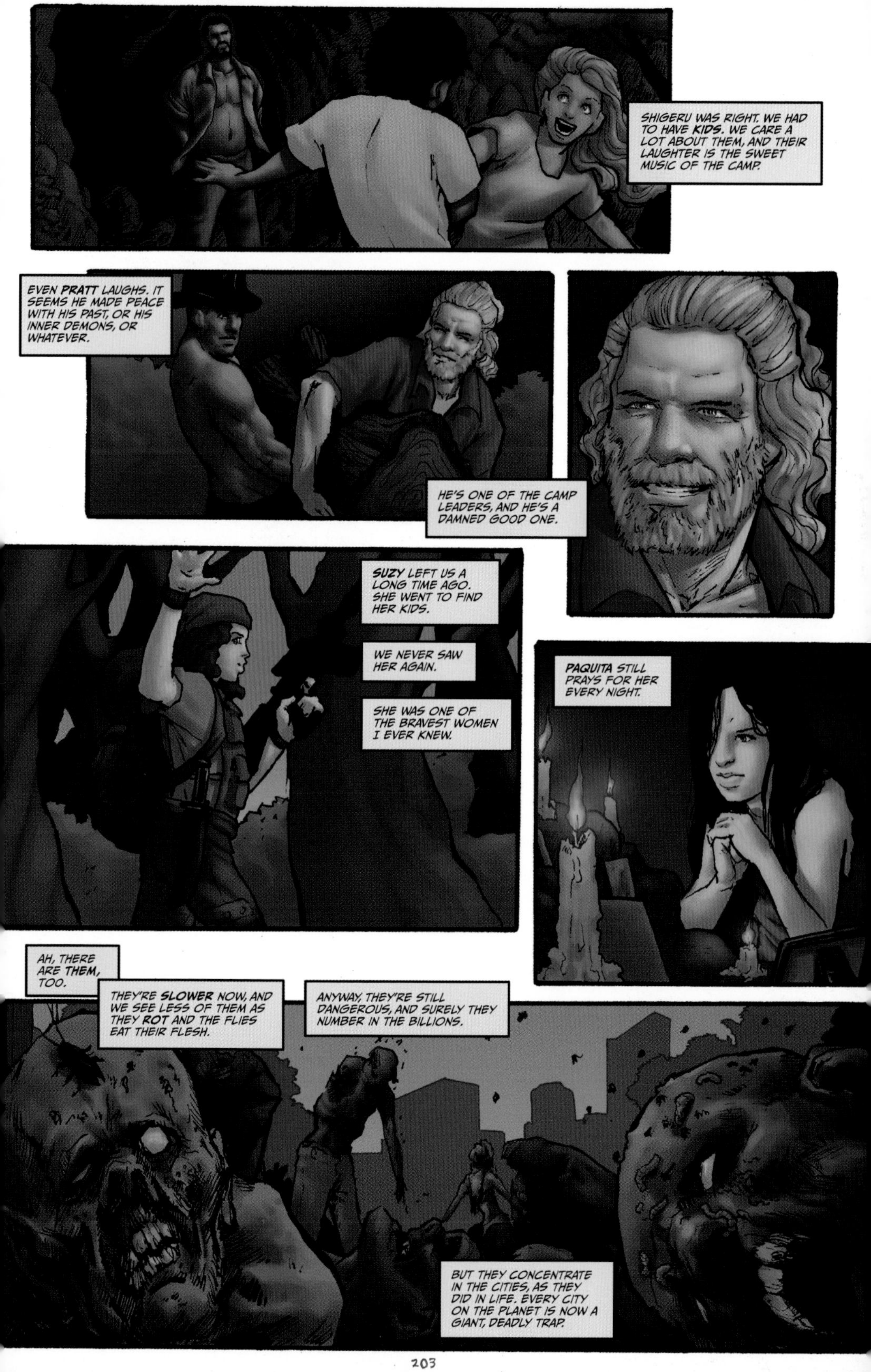
SHIGERU WAS RIGHT. WE HAD TO HAVE KIDS. WE CARE A LOT ABOUT THEM, AND THEIR LAUGHTER IS THE SWEET MUSIC OF THE CAMP.
EVEN PRATT LAUGHS. IT SEEMS HE MADE PEACE WITH HIS PAST, OR HIS INNER DEMONS, OR WHATEVER.
HE'S ONE OF THE CAMP LEADERS, AND HE'S A DAMNED GOOD ONE.
SUZY LEFT US A LONG TIME AGO. SHE WENT TO FIND HER KIDS.
WE NEVER SAW HER AGAIN.
SHE WAS ONE OF THE BRAVEST WOMEN I EVER KNEW.
PAQUITA STILL PRAYS FOR HER EVERY NIGHT.
AH, THERE ARE THEM, TOO.
THEY'RE SLOWER NOW, AND WE SEE LESS OF THEM AS THEY ROT AND THE FLIES EAT THEIR FLESH.
ANYWAY, THEY'RE STILL DANGEROUS, AND SURELY THEY NUMBER IN THE BILLIONS.
BUT THEY CONCENTRATE IN THE CITIES, AS THEY DID IN LIFE. EVERY CITY ON THE PLANET IS NOW A GIANT, DEADLY TRAP.

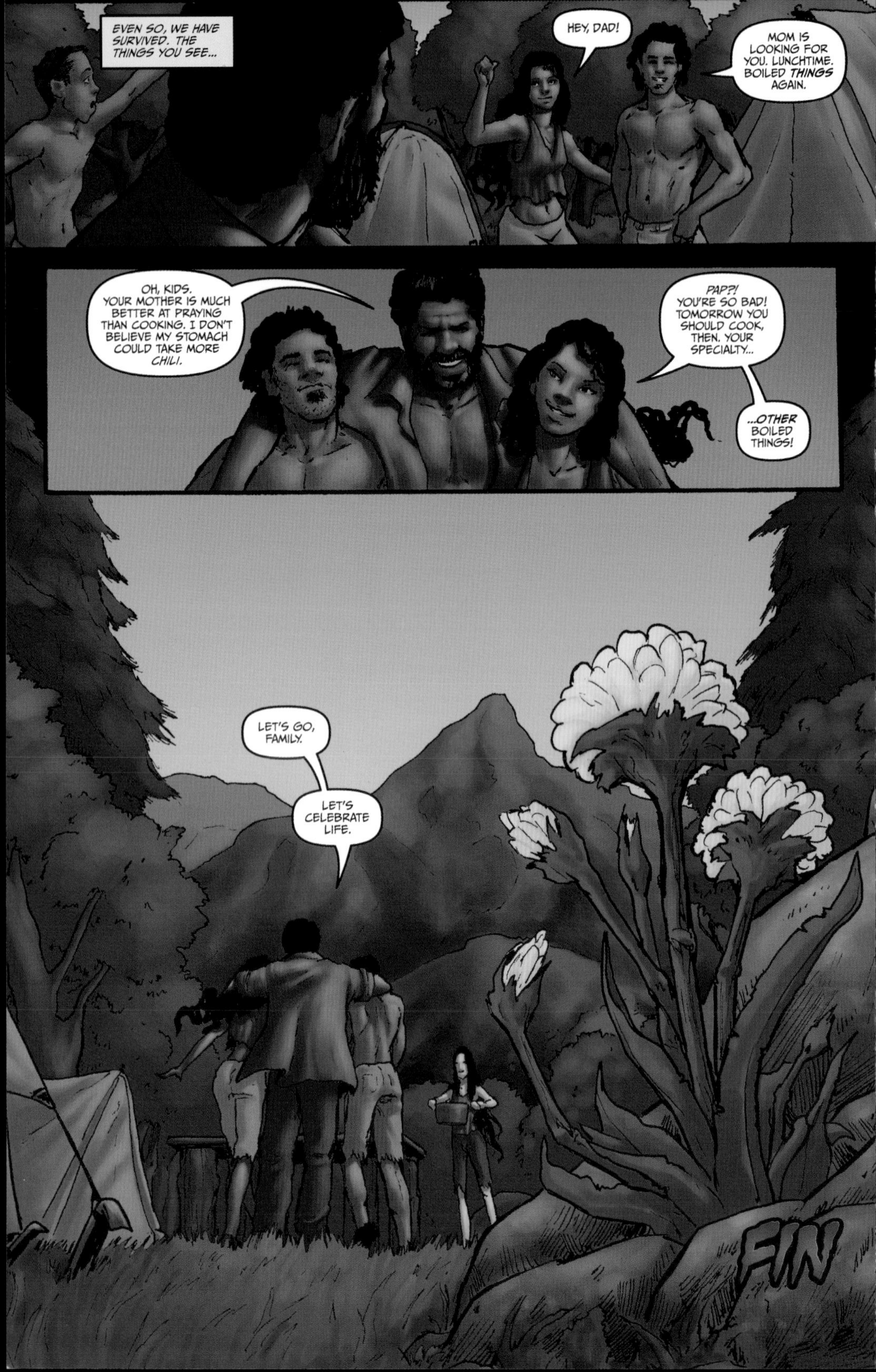
EVEN SO, WE HAVE SURVIVED. THE THINGS YOU SEE...
HEY, DAD!
MOM IS LOOKING FOR YOU. LUNCHTIME. BOILED *THINGS* AGAIN.
OH, KIDS. YOUR MOTHER IS MUCH BETTER AT PRAYING THAN COOKING. I DON'T BELIEVE MY STOMACH COULD TAKE MORE *CHILI*.
PAP?! YOU'RE SO BAD! TOMORROW YOU SHOULD COOK, THEN. YOUR SPECIALTY...
...*OTHER* BOILED THINGS!
LET'S GO, FAMILY.
LET'S CELEBRATE LIFE.
FIN

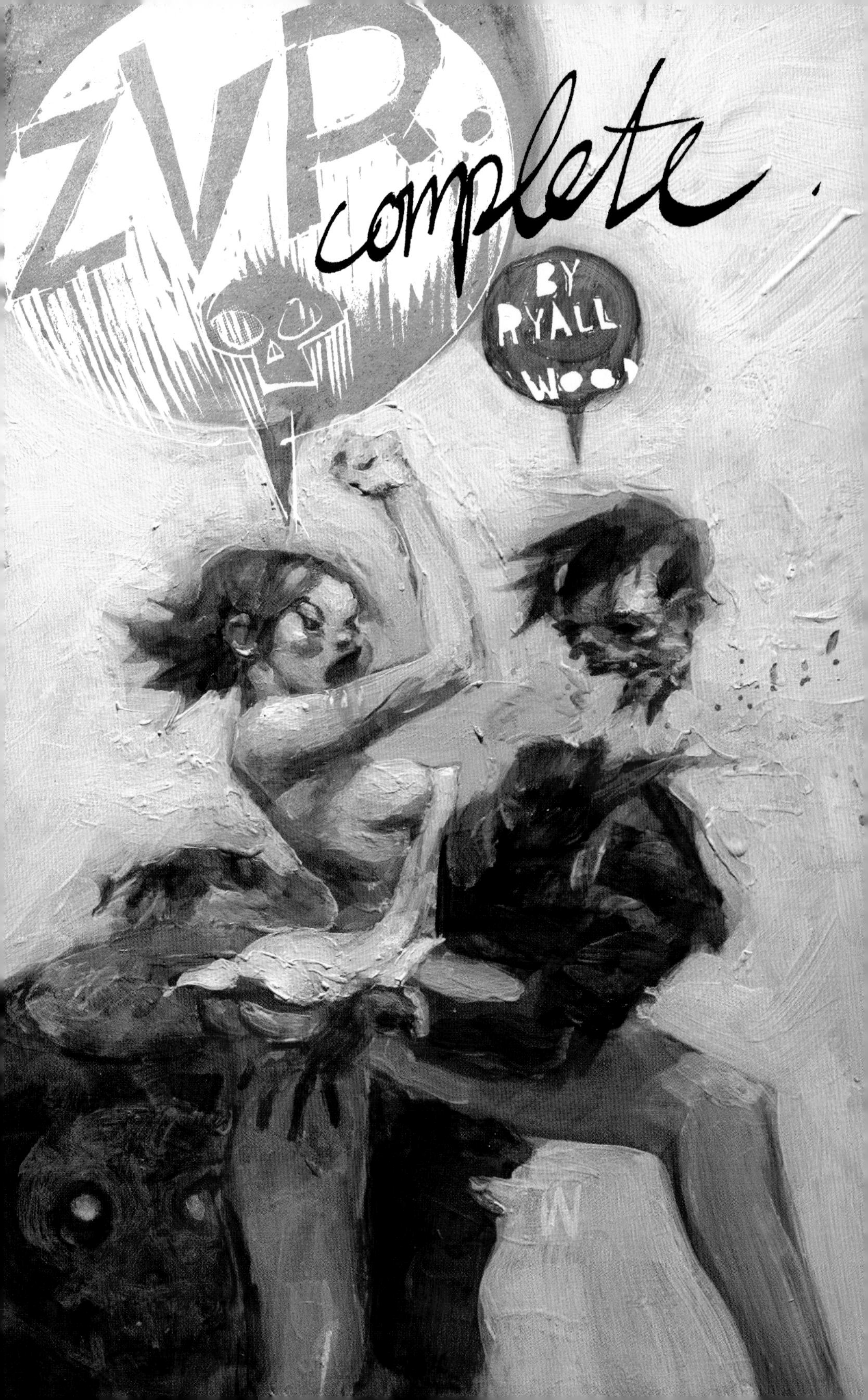
ZVR.
complete.
BY RYALL WOOD

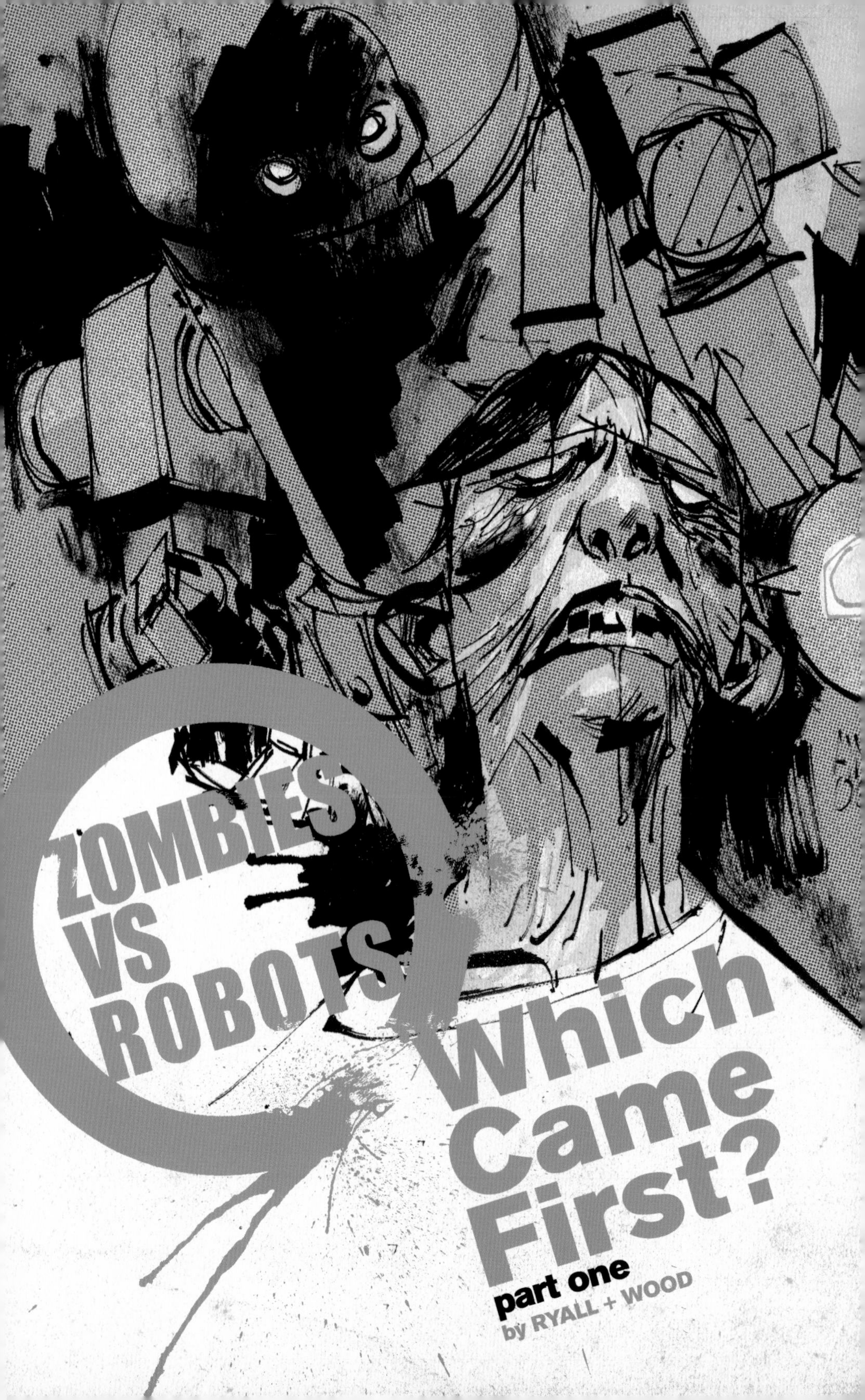
ZOMBIES VS ROBOTS
Which Came First?
part one
by RYALL + WOOD

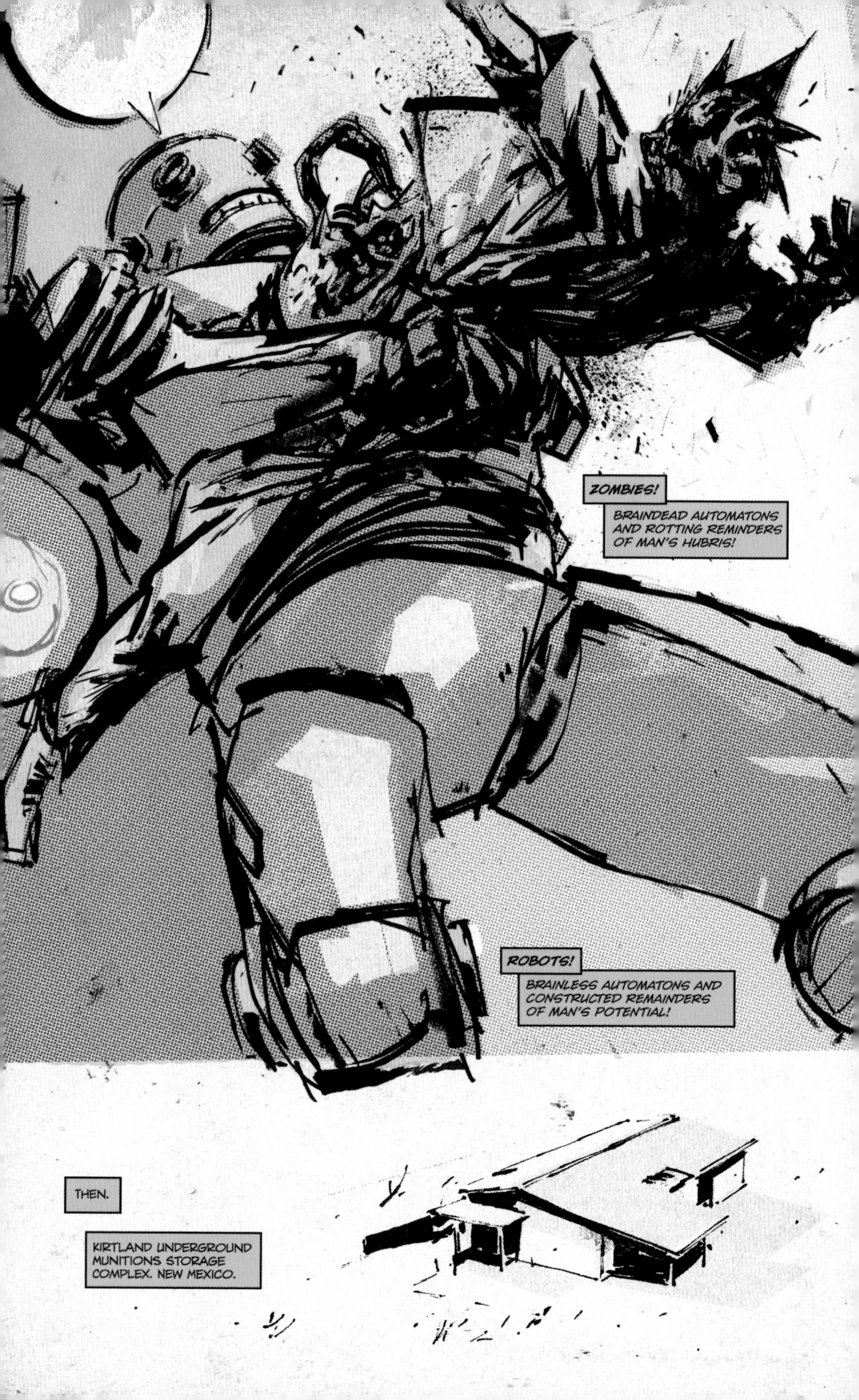
ZOMBIES!
BRAINDEAD AUTOMATONS AND ROTTING REMINDERS OF MAN'S HUBRIS!
ROBOTS!
BRAINLESS AUTOMATONS AND CONSTRUCTED REMAINDERS OF MAN'S POTENTIAL!
THEN.
KIRTLAND UNDERGROUND MUNITIONS STORAGE COMPLEX. NEW MEXICO.

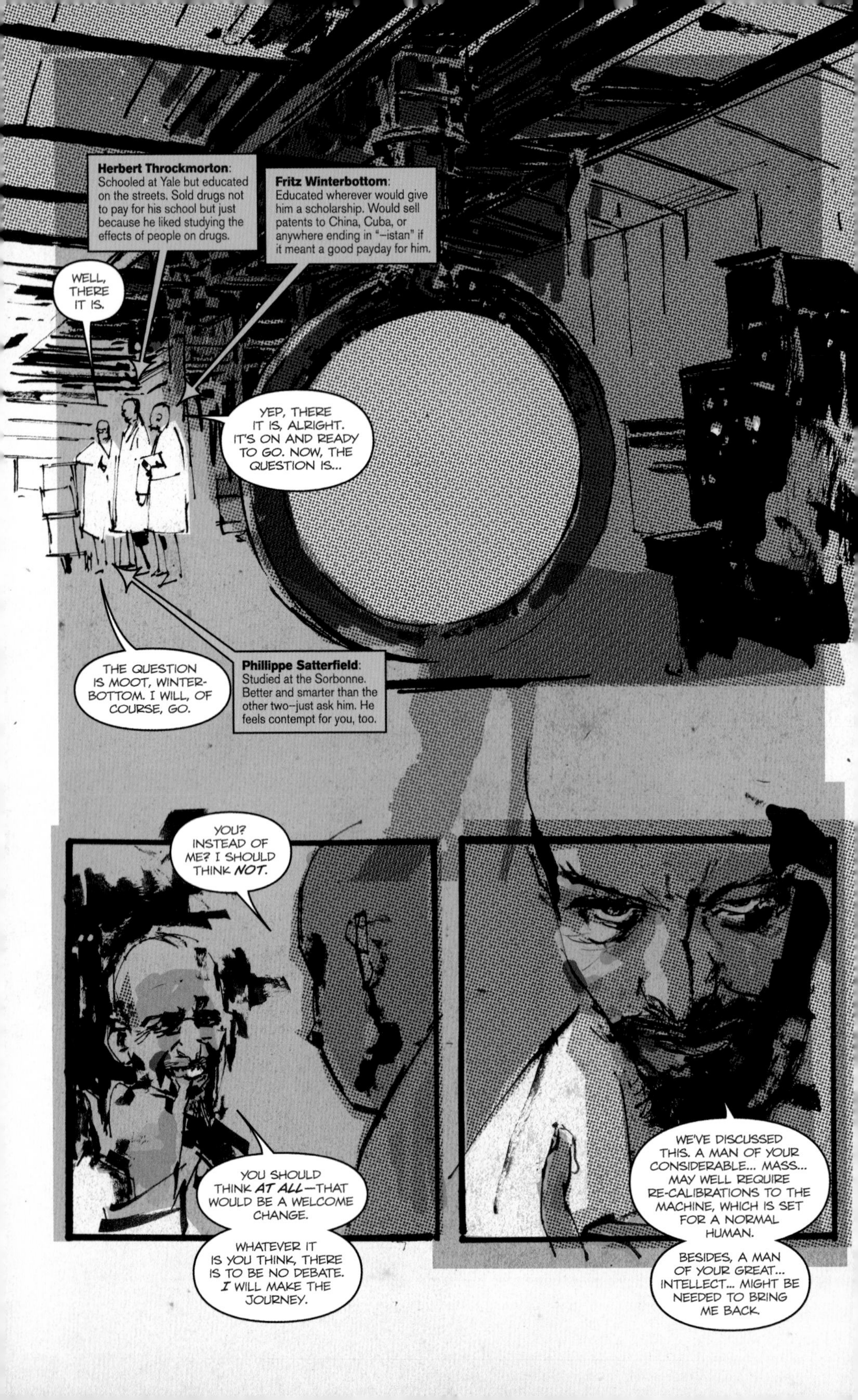
Herbert Throckmorton: Schooled at Yale but educated on the streets. Sold drugs not to pay for his school but just because he liked studying the effects of people on drugs.
Fritz Winterbottom: Educated wherever would give him a scholarship. Would sell patents to China, Cuba, or anywhere ending in "–istan" if it meant a good payday for him.
WELL, THERE IT IS.
YEP, THERE IT IS, ALRIGHT. IT'S ON AND READY TO GO. NOW, THE QUESTION IS...
THE QUESTION IS MOOT, WINTER-BOTTOM. I WILL, OF COURSE, GO.
Phillippe Satterfield: Studied at the Sorbonne. Better and smarter than the other two–just ask him. He feels contempt for you, too.
YOU? INSTEAD OF ME? I SHOULD THINK NOT.
YOU SHOULD THINK AT ALL—THAT WOULD BE A WELCOME CHANGE.
WHATEVER IT IS YOU THINK, THERE IS TO BE NO DEBATE. I WILL MAKE THE JOURNEY.
WE'VE DISCUSSED THIS. A MAN OF YOUR CONSIDERABLE... MASS... MAY WELL REQUIRE RE-CALIBRATIONS TO THE MACHINE, WHICH IS SET FOR A NORMAL HUMAN.
BESIDES, A MAN OF YOUR GREAT... INTELLECT... MIGHT BE NEEDED TO BRING ME BACK.

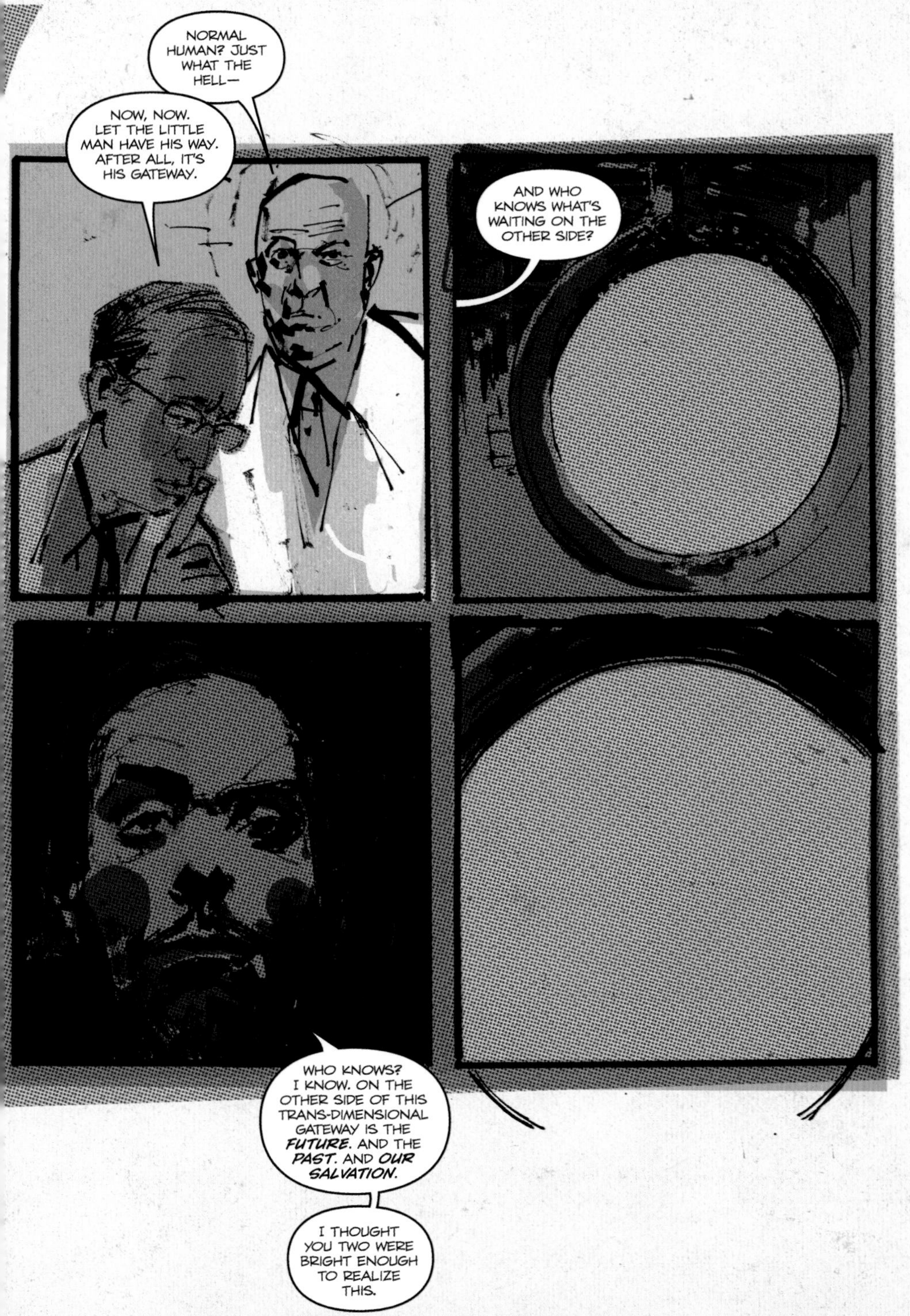

NORMAL HUMAN? JUST WHAT THE HELL—
NOW, NOW. LET THE LITTLE MAN HAVE HIS WAY. AFTER ALL, IT'S HIS GATEWAY.
AND WHO KNOWS WHAT'S WAITING ON THE OTHER SIDE?
WHO KNOWS? I KNOW. ON THE OTHER SIDE OF THIS TRANS-DIMENSIONAL GATEWAY IS THE FUTURE. AND THE PAST. AND OUR SALVATION.
I THOUGHT YOU TWO WERE BRIGHT ENOUGH TO REALIZE THIS.

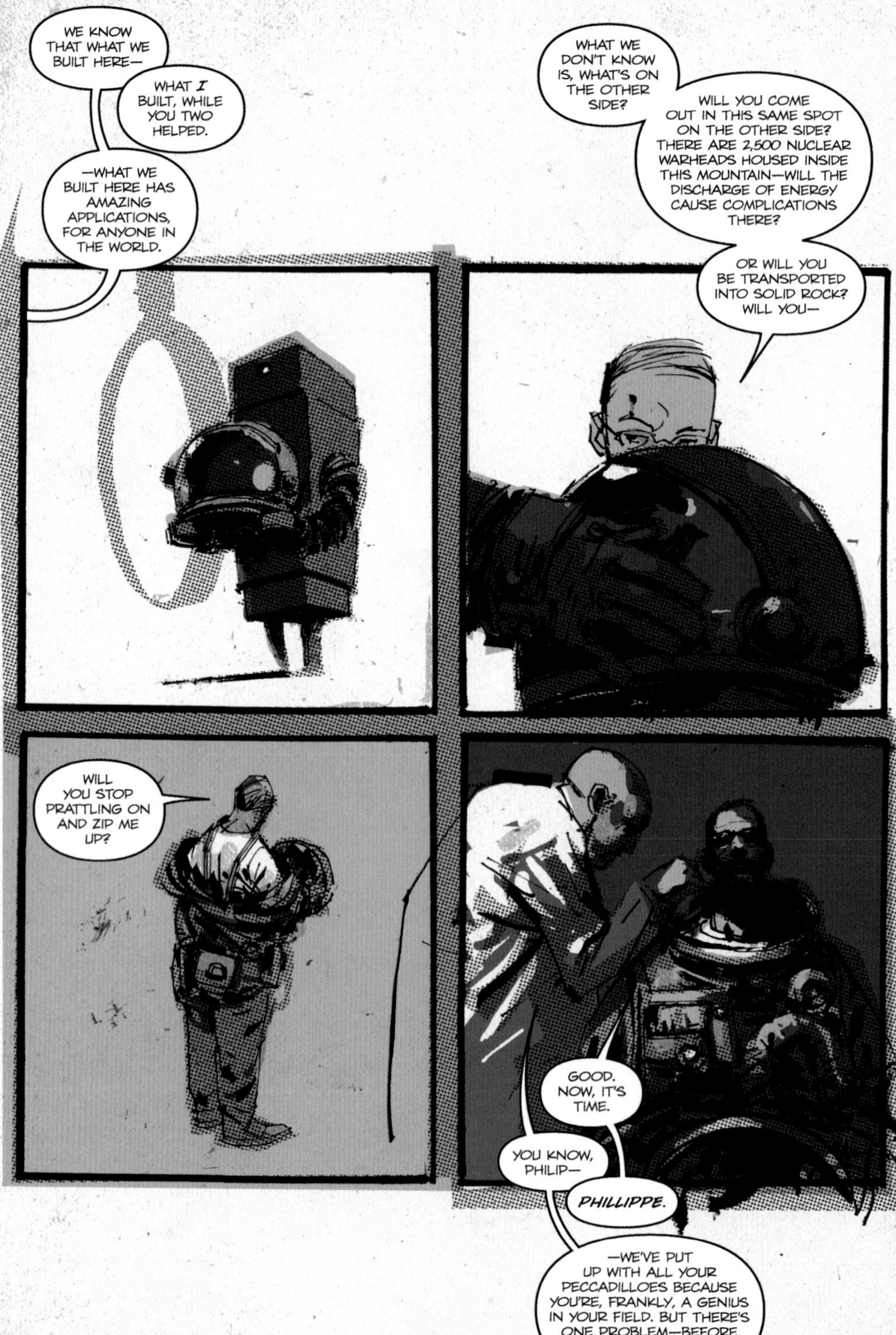
WE KNOW THAT WHAT WE BUILT HERE—
WHAT *I* BUILT, WHILE YOU TWO HELPED.
—WHAT WE BUILT HERE HAS AMAZING APPLICATIONS, FOR ANYONE IN THE WORLD.
WHAT WE DON'T KNOW IS, WHAT'S ON THE OTHER SIDE?
WILL YOU COME OUT IN THIS SAME SPOT ON THE OTHER SIDE? THERE ARE 2,500 NUCLEAR WARHEADS HOUSED INSIDE THIS MOUNTAIN—WILL THE DISCHARGE OF ENERGY CAUSE COMPLICATIONS THERE?
OR WILL YOU BE TRANSPORTED INTO SOLID ROCK? WILL YOU—
WILL YOU STOP PRATTLING ON AND ZIP ME UP?
GOOD. NOW, IT'S TIME.
YOU KNOW, PHILIP—
PHILLIPPE.
—WE'VE PUT UP WITH ALL YOUR PECCADILLOES BECAUSE YOU'RE, FRANKLY, A GENIUS IN YOUR FIELD. BUT THERE'S ONE PROBLEM—BEFORE YOU, YOUR FIELD DIDN'T EXIST.

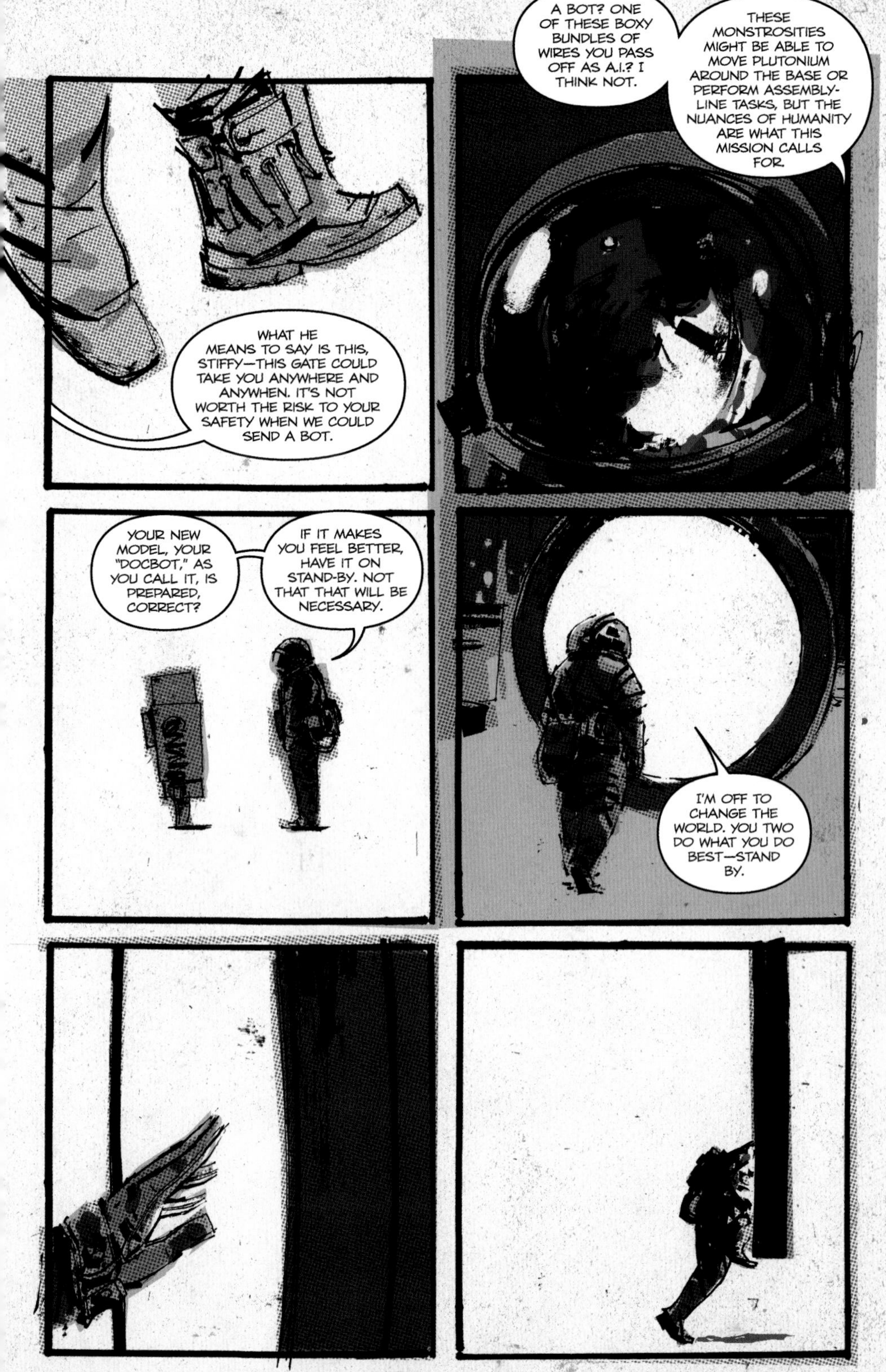
WHAT HE MEANS TO SAY IS THIS, STIFFY—THIS GATE COULD TAKE YOU ANYWHERE AND ANYWHEN. IT'S NOT WORTH THE RISK TO YOUR SAFETY WHEN WE COULD SEND A BOT.
A BOT? ONE OF THESE BOXY BUNDLES OF WIRES YOU PASS OFF AS A.I.? I THINK NOT.
THESE MONSTROSITIES MIGHT BE ABLE TO MOVE PLUTONIUM AROUND THE BASE OR PERFORM ASSEMBLY-LINE TASKS, BUT THE NUANCES OF HUMANITY ARE WHAT THIS MISSION CALLS FOR.
YOUR NEW MODEL, YOUR "DOCBOT," AS YOU CALL IT, IS PREPARED, CORRECT?
IF IT MAKES YOU FEEL BETTER, HAVE IT ON STAND-BY. NOT THAT THAT WILL BE NECESSARY.
I'M OFF TO CHANGE THE WORLD. YOU TWO DO WHAT YOU DO BEST—STAND BY.

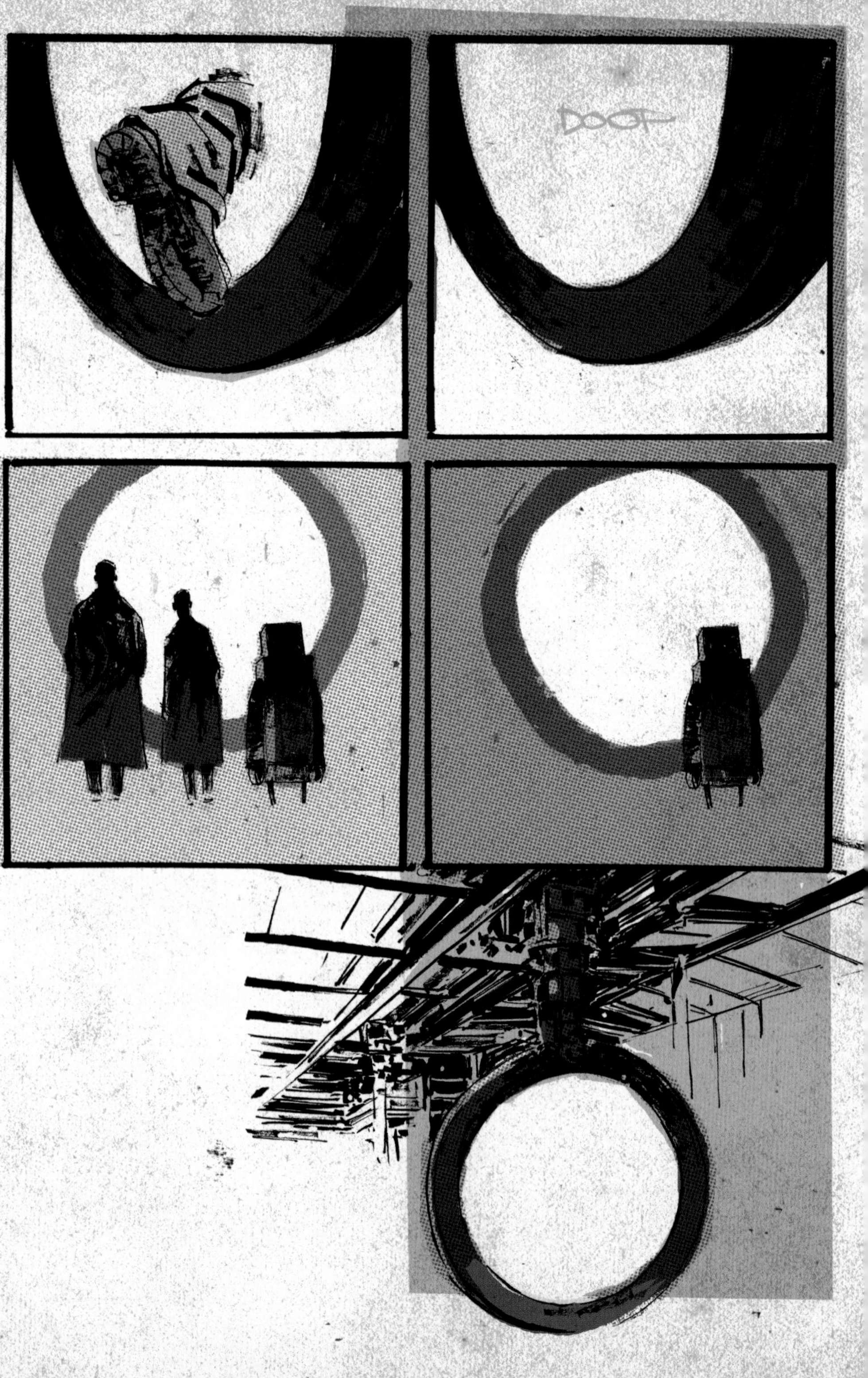
DOOF

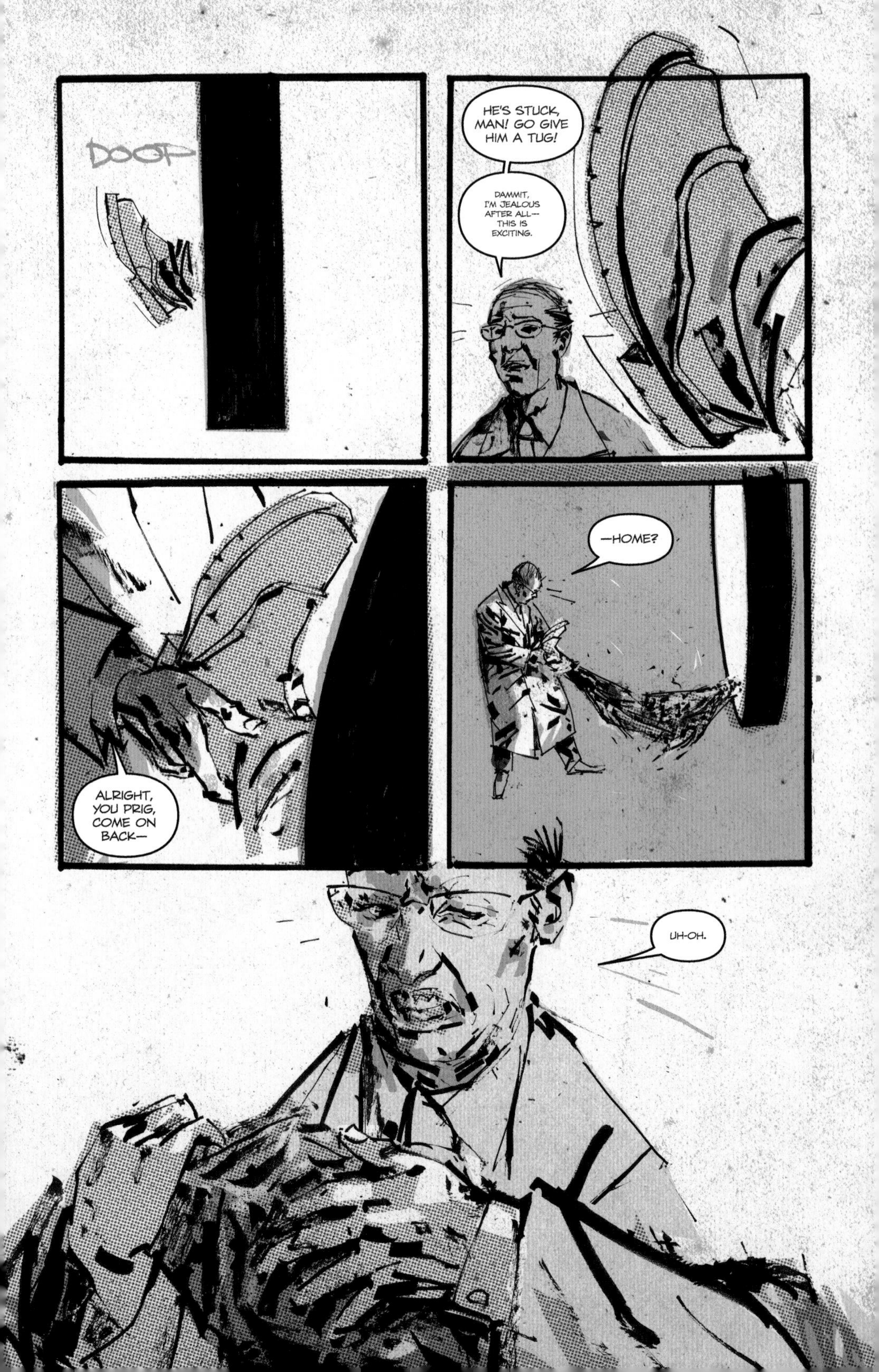
DOOP
HE'S STUCK, MAN! GO GIVE HIM A TUG!
DAMMIT, I'M JEALOUS AFTER ALL-- THIS IS EXCITING.
ALRIGHT, YOU PRIG, COME ON BACK—
—HOME?
UH-OH.

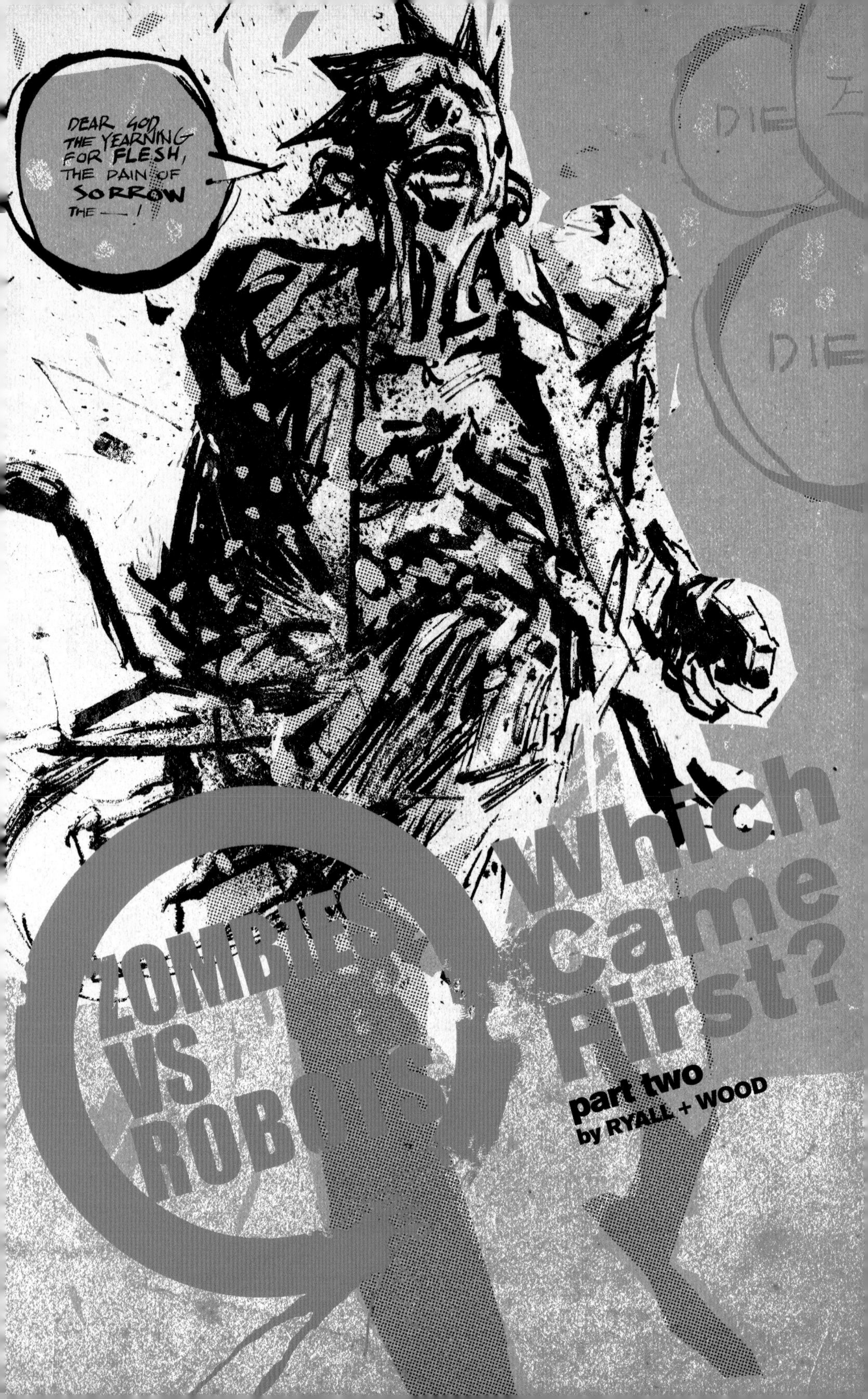
DEAR GOD THE YEARNING FOR FLESH, THE PAIN OF SORROW THE —!
DIE
DIE
ZOMBIES VS ROBOTS
Which Came First?
part two
by RYALL + WOOD

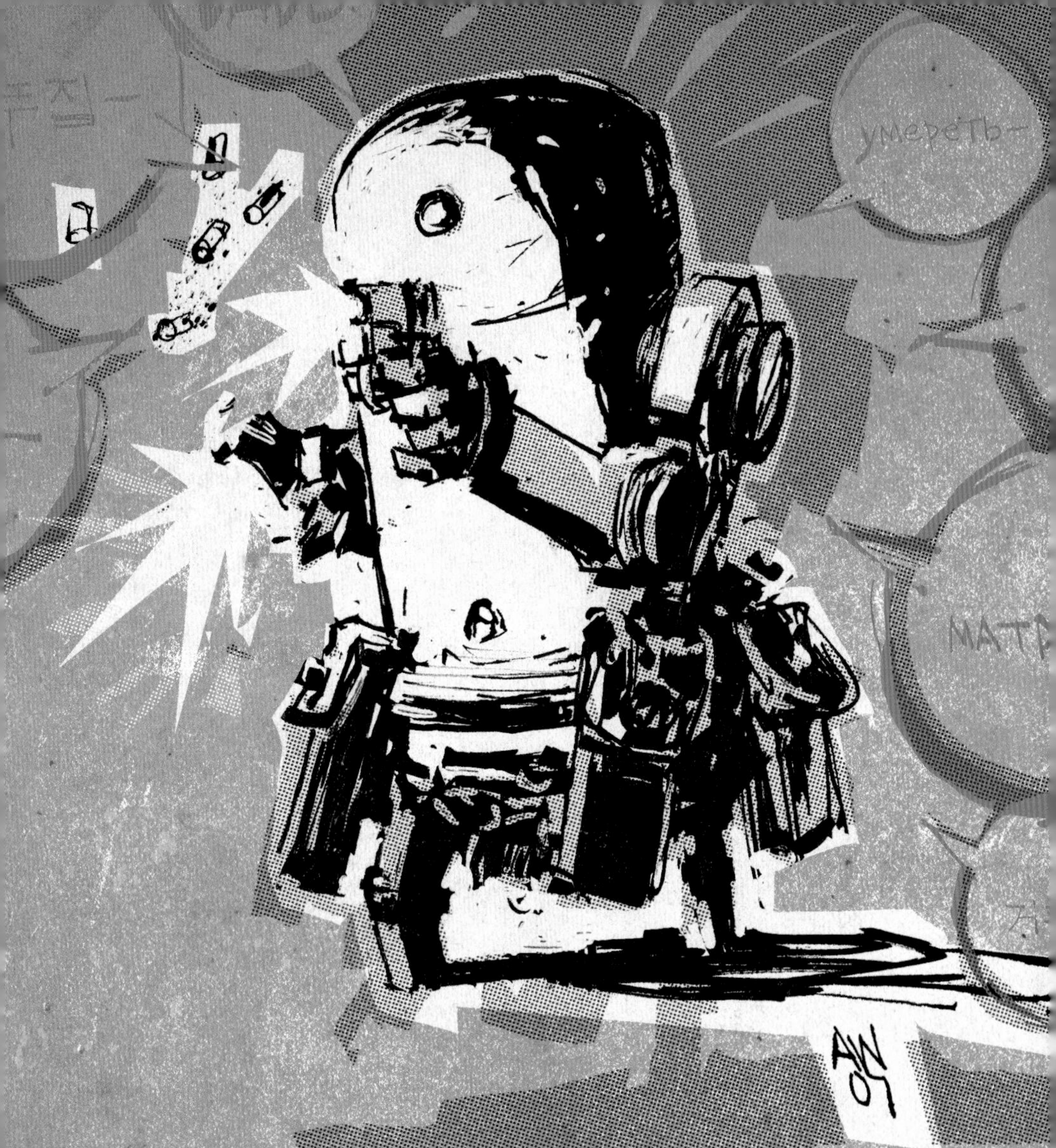
умереть—

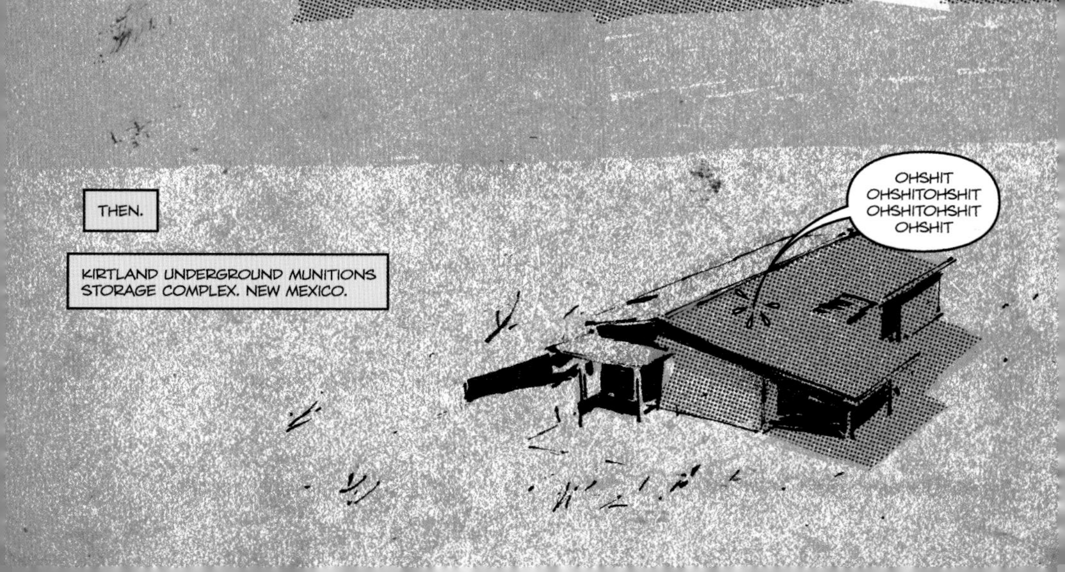
THEN.
KIRTLAND UNDERGROUND MUNITIONS STORAGE COMPLEX. NEW MEXICO.
OHSHIT OHSHITOHSHIT OHSHITOHSHIT OHSHIT

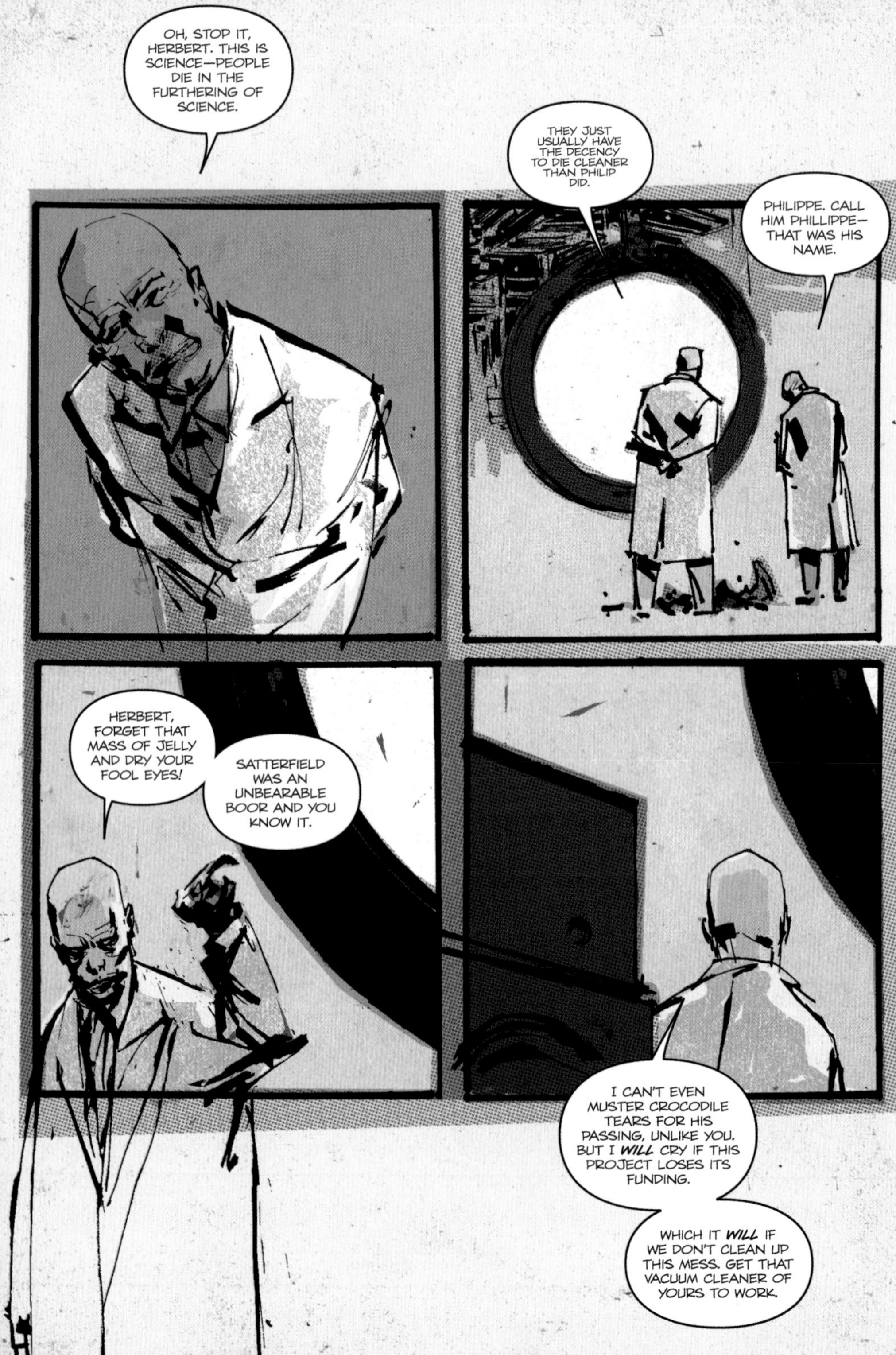
OH, STOP IT, HERBERT. THIS IS SCIENCE—PEOPLE DIE IN THE FURTHERING OF SCIENCE.
THEY JUST USUALLY HAVE THE DECENCY TO DIE CLEANER THAN PHILIP DID.
PHILIPPE. CALL HIM PHILLIPPE—THAT WAS HIS NAME.
HERBERT, FORGET THAT MASS OF JELLY AND DRY YOUR FOOL EYES!
SATTERFIELD WAS AN UNBEARABLE BOOR AND YOU KNOW IT.
I CAN'T EVEN MUSTER CROCODILE TEARS FOR HIS PASSING, UNLIKE YOU. BUT I WILL CRY IF THIS PROJECT LOSES ITS FUNDING.
WHICH IT WILL IF WE DON'T CLEAN UP THIS MESS. GET THAT VACUUM CLEANER OF YOURS TO WORK.

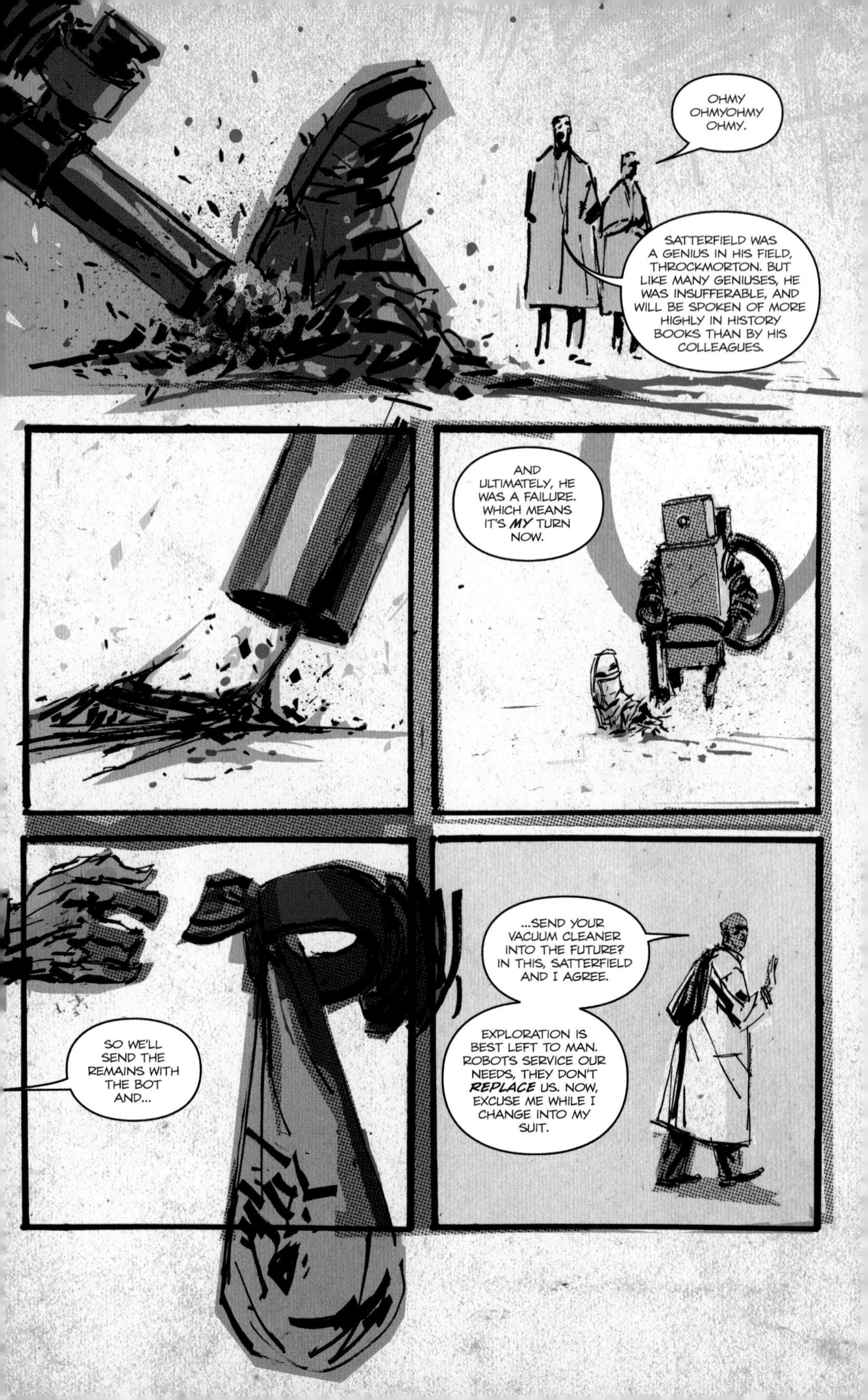
OHMY OHMYOHMY OHMY.
SATTERFIELD WAS A GENIUS IN HIS FIELD, THROCKMORTON. BUT LIKE MANY GENIUSES, HE WAS INSUFFERABLE, AND WILL BE SPOKEN OF MORE HIGHLY IN HISTORY BOOKS THAN BY HIS COLLEAGUES.
AND ULTIMATELY, HE WAS A FAILURE. WHICH MEANS IT'S *MY* TURN NOW.
SO WE'LL SEND THE REMAINS WITH THE BOT AND...
...SEND YOUR VACUUM CLEANER INTO THE FUTURE? IN THIS, SATTERFIELD AND I AGREE.
EXPLORATION IS BEST LEFT TO MAN. ROBOTS SERVICE OUR NEEDS, THEY DON'T ***REPLACE*** US. NOW, EXCUSE ME WHILE I CHANGE INTO MY SUIT.

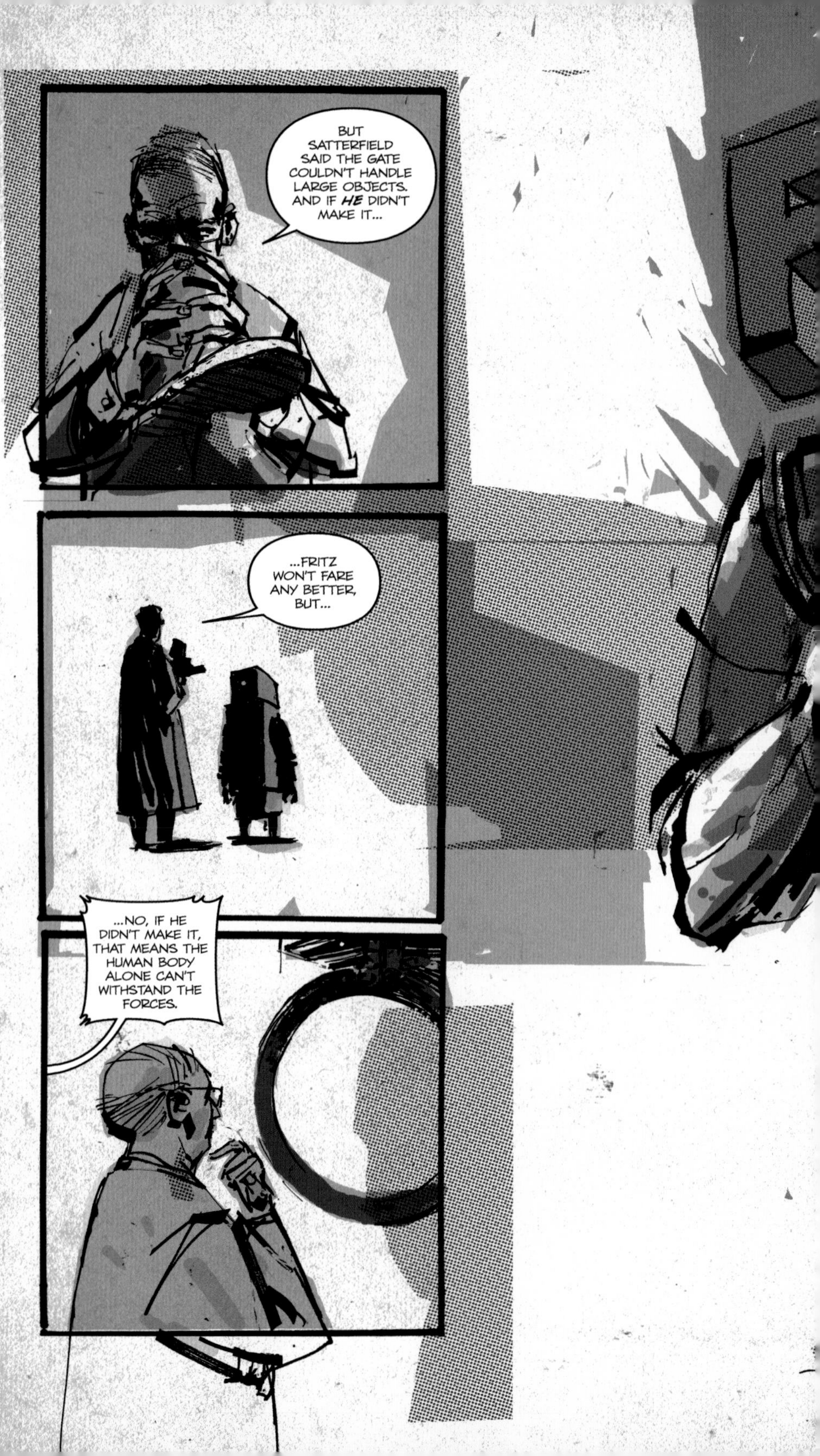
BUT SATTERFIELD SAID THE GATE COULDN'T HANDLE LARGE OBJECTS. AND IF *HE* DIDN'T MAKE IT...
...FRITZ WON'T FARE ANY BETTER, BUT...
...NO, IF HE DIDN'T MAKE IT, THAT MEANS THE HUMAN BODY ALONE CAN'T WITHSTAND THE FORCES.

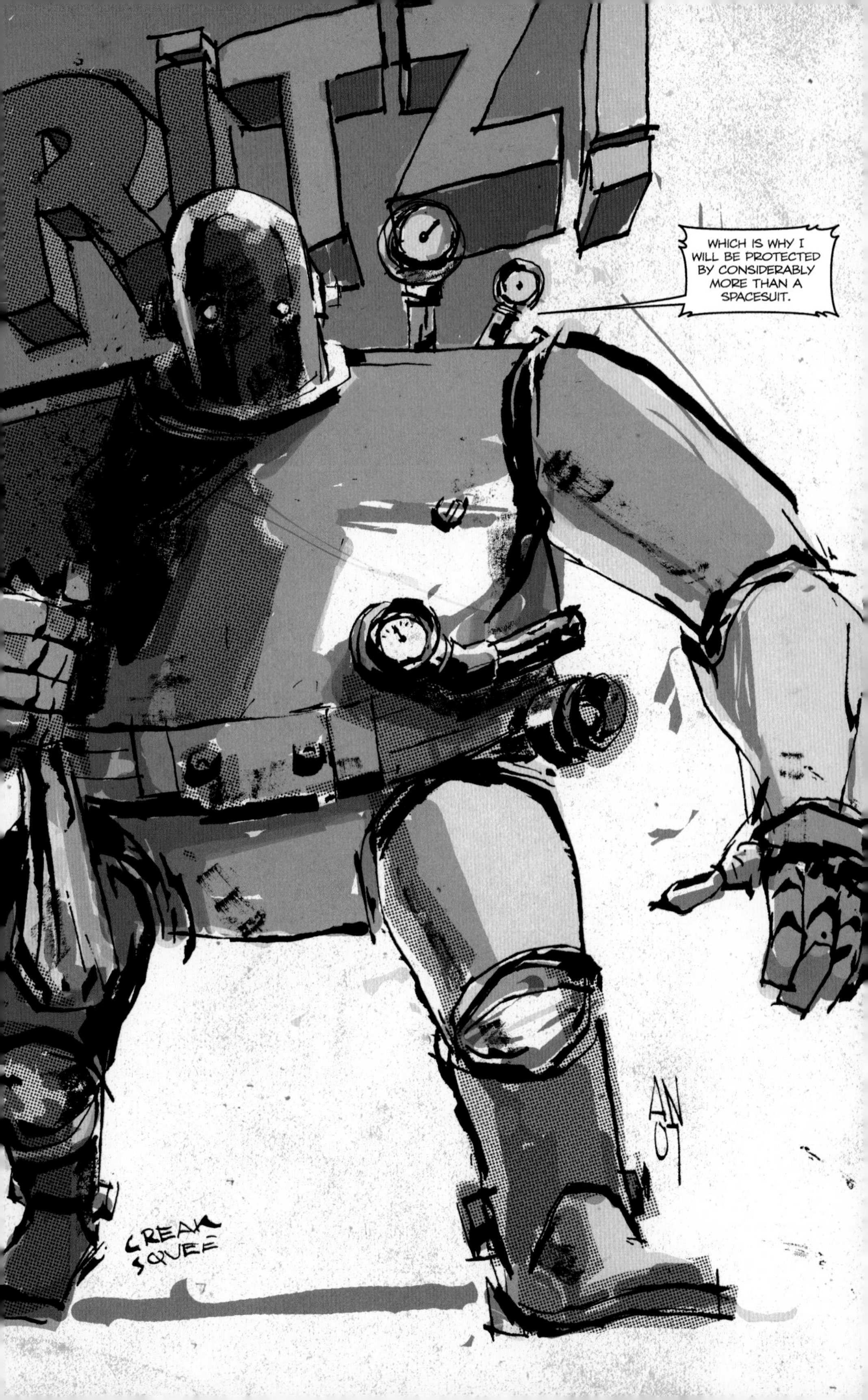
WHICH IS WHY I WILL BE PROTECTED BY CONSIDERABLY MORE THAN A SPACESUIT.
CREAK
SQUEE

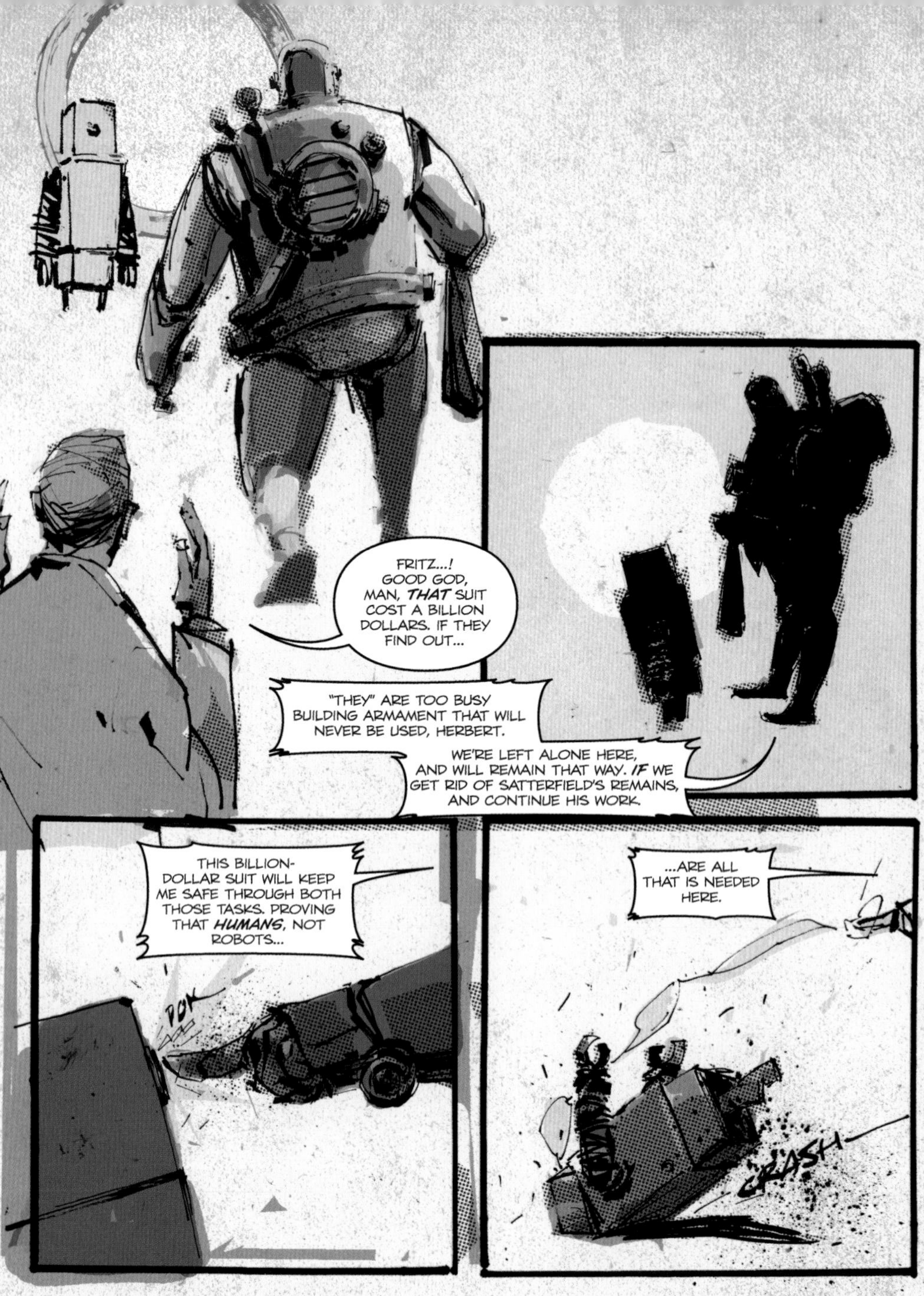
FRITZ...! GOOD GOD, MAN, THAT SUIT COST A BILLION DOLLARS. IF THEY FIND OUT...
"THEY" ARE TOO BUSY BUILDING ARMAMENT THAT WILL NEVER BE USED, HERBERT.
WE'RE LEFT ALONE HERE, AND WILL REMAIN THAT WAY. IF WE GET RID OF SATTERFIELD'S REMAINS, AND CONTINUE HIS WORK.
THIS BILLION-DOLLAR SUIT WILL KEEP ME SAFE THROUGH BOTH THOSE TASKS. PROVING THAT HUMANS, NOT ROBOTS...
POK
...ARE ALL THAT IS NEEDED HERE.
CRASH

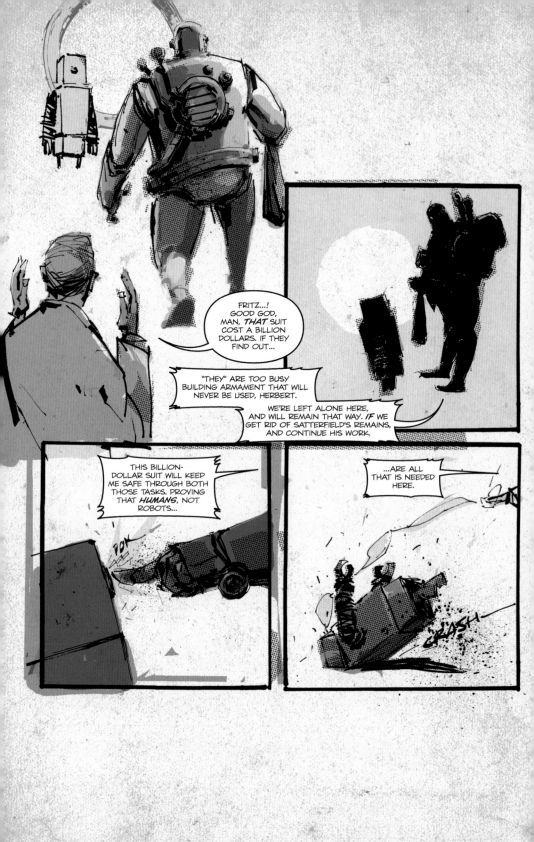

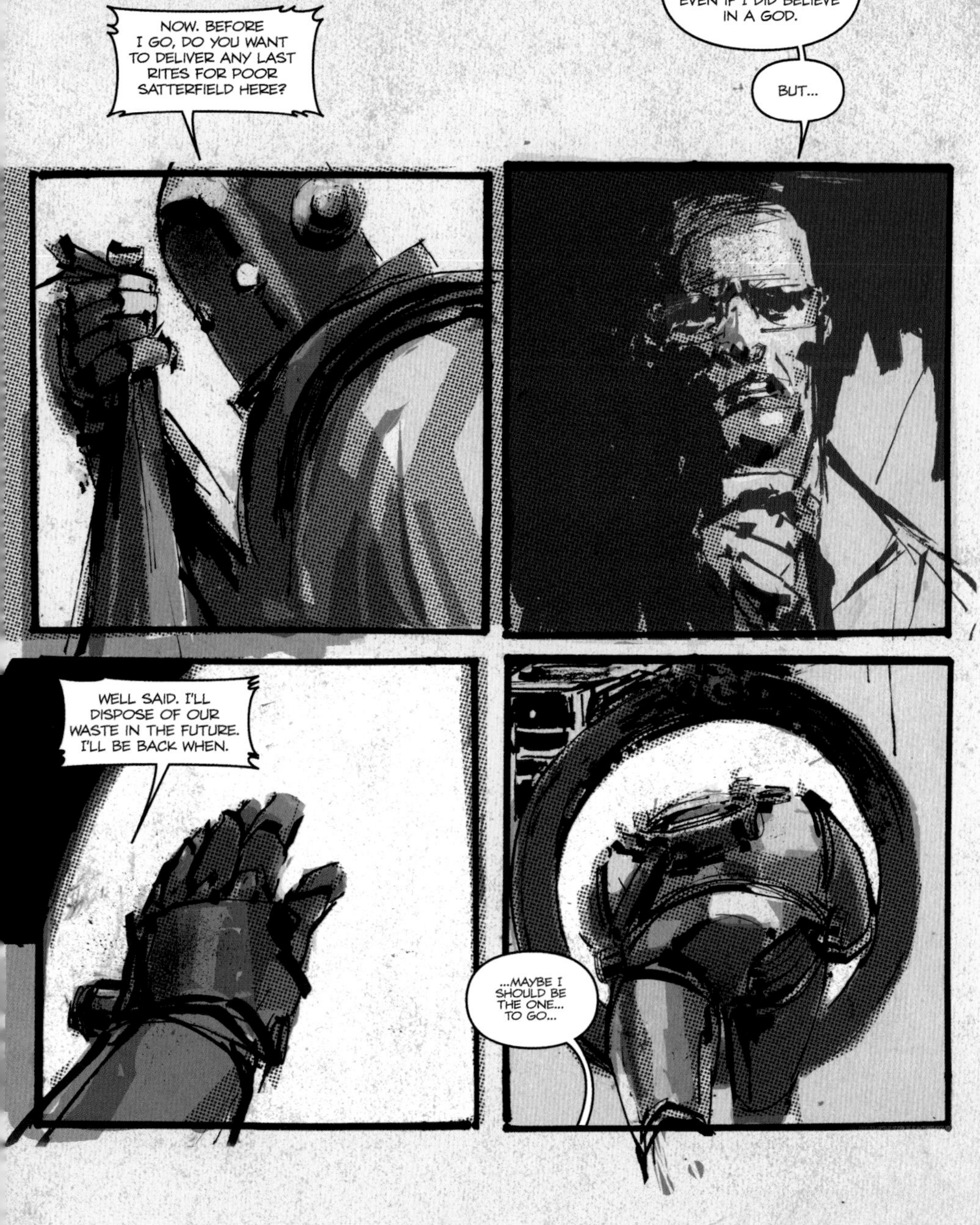
NOW. BEFORE I GO, DO YOU WANT TO DELIVER ANY LAST RITES FOR POOR SATTERFIELD HERE?
I—I COULDN'T SAY A PRAYER FOR THAT... THAT ***BAG***, EVEN IF I DID BELIEVE IN A GOD.
BUT...
WELL SAID. I'LL DISPOSE OF OUR WASTE IN THE FUTURE. I'LL BE BACK WHEN.
...MAYBE I SHOULD BE THE ONE... TO GO...

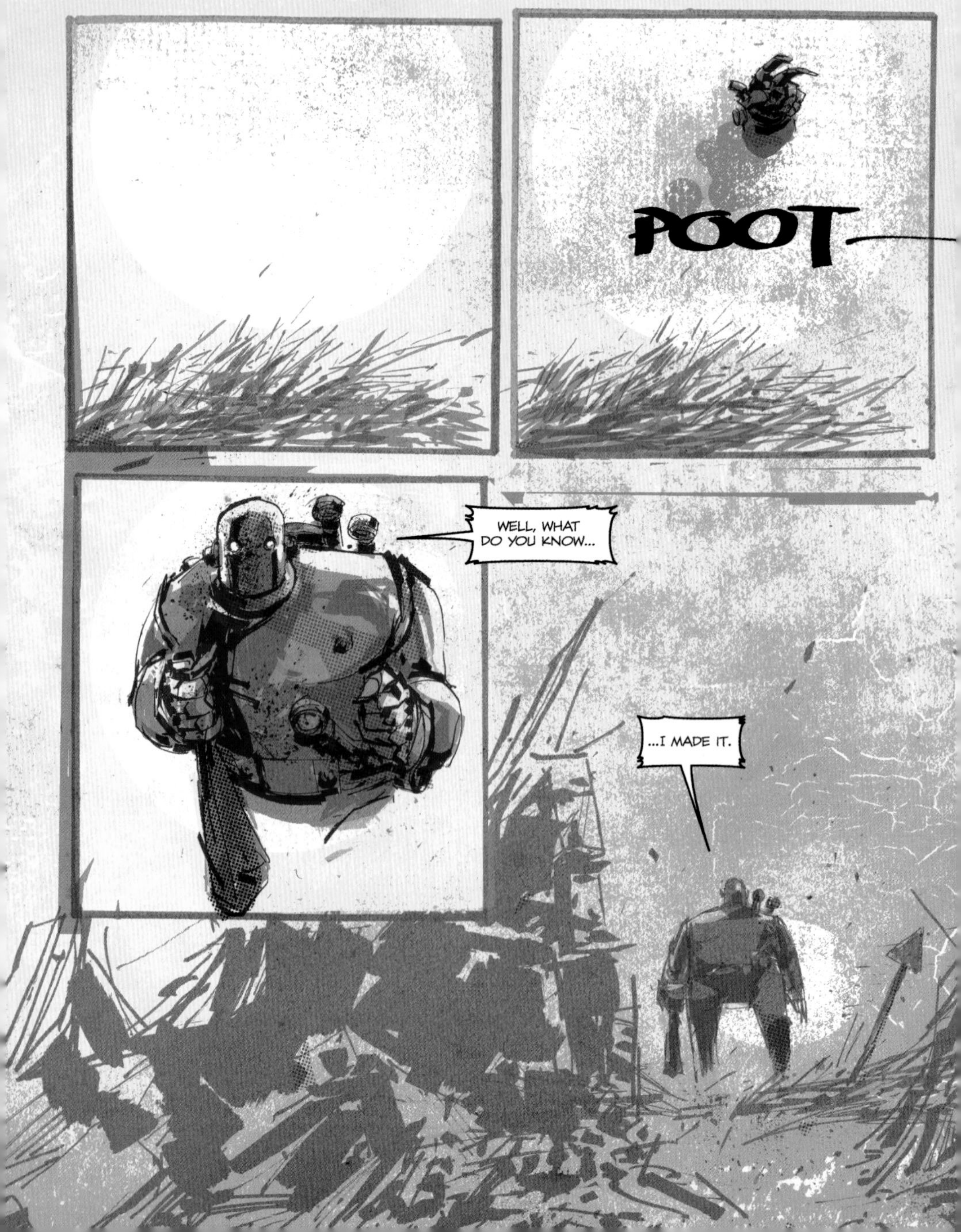
POOT
WELL, WHAT DO YOU KNOW...
...I MADE IT.

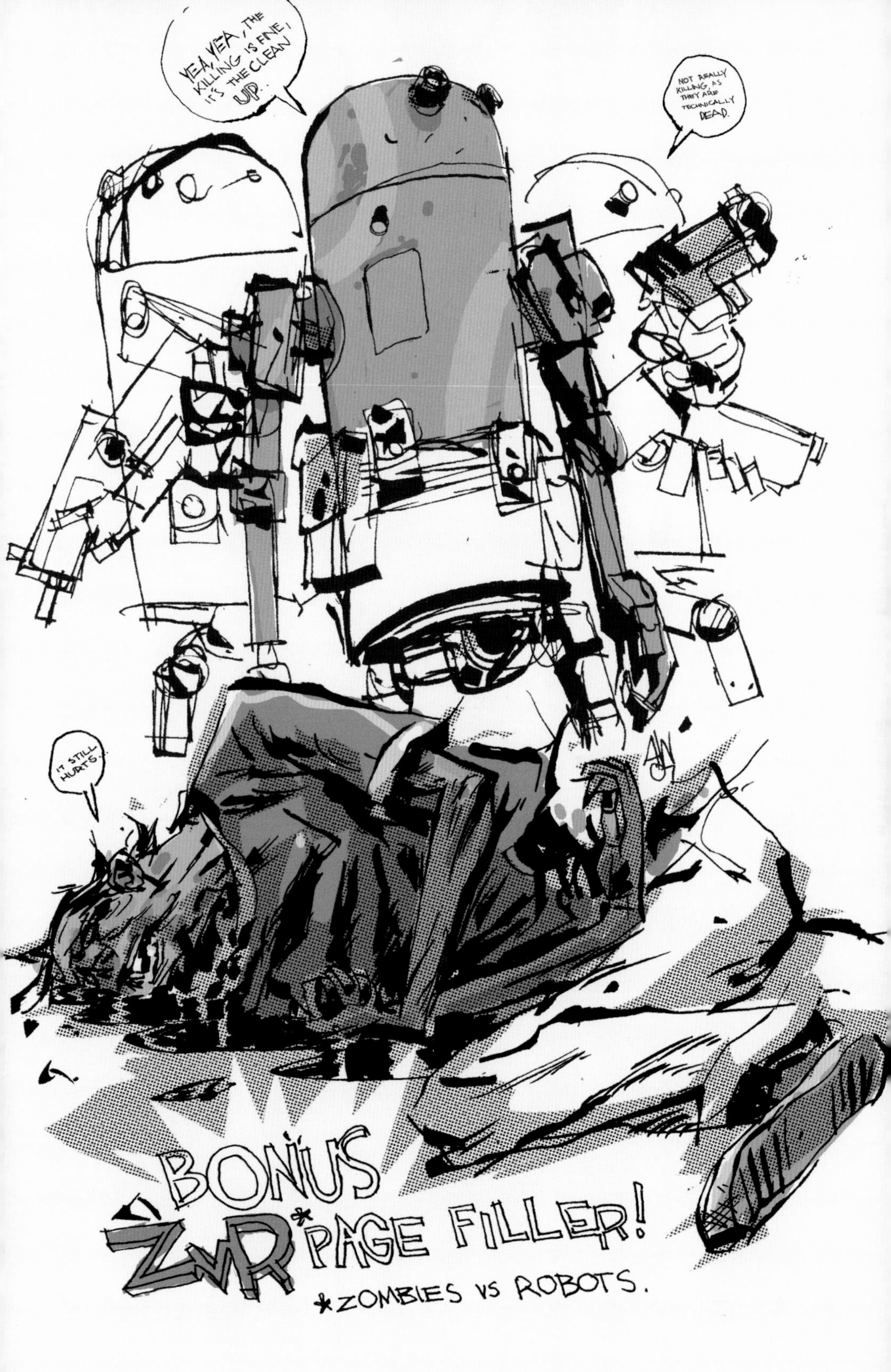
YEA, YEA, THE KILLING IS FINE, IT'S THE CLEAN UP.
NOT REALLY KILLING, AS THEY ARE TECHNICALLY DEAD.
IT STILL HURTS.
BONUS
ZvR* PAGE FILLER!
*ZOMBIES VS ROBOTS.

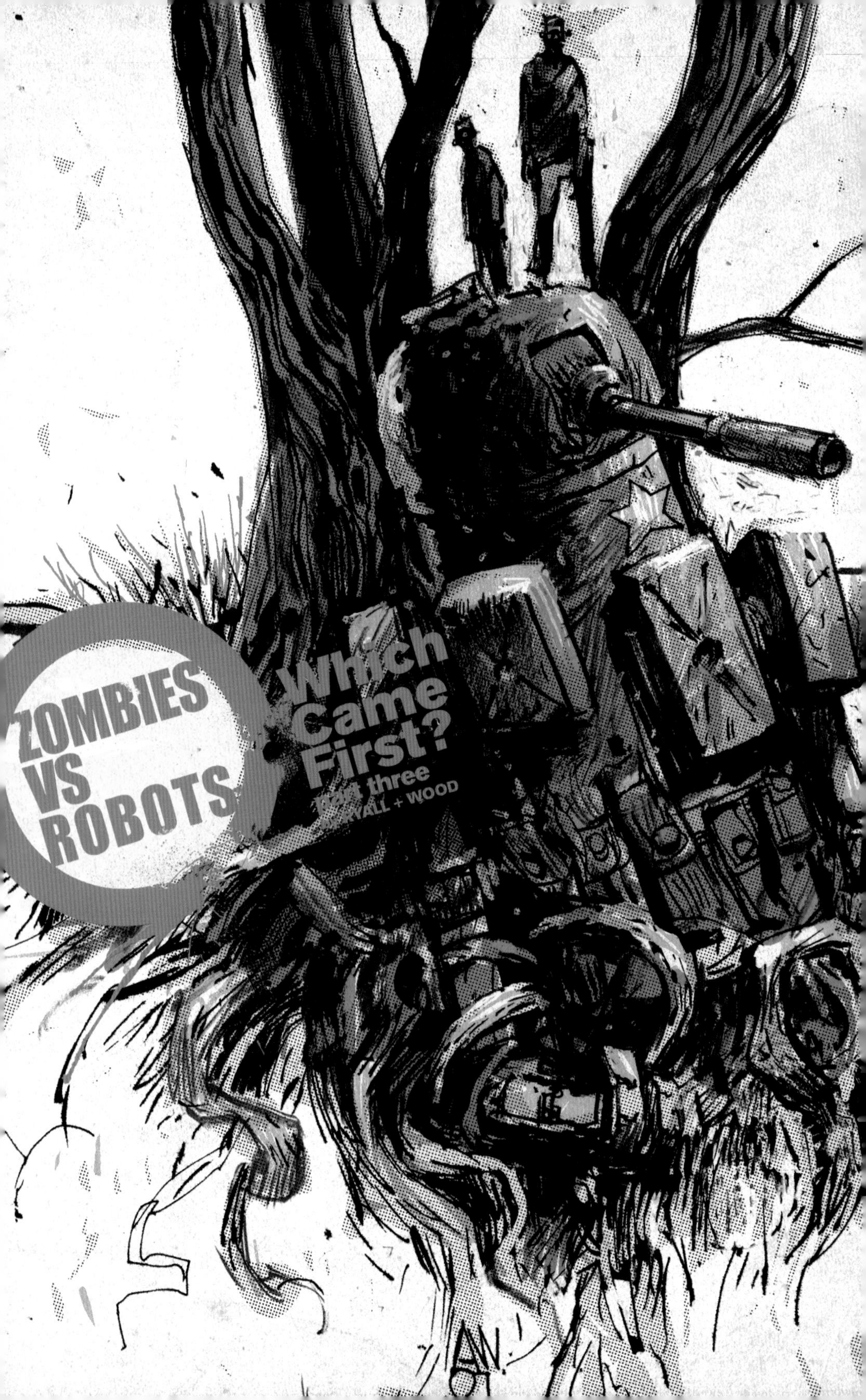
ZOMBIES
VS
ROBOTS
Which
Came
First?
three
ALL + WOOD

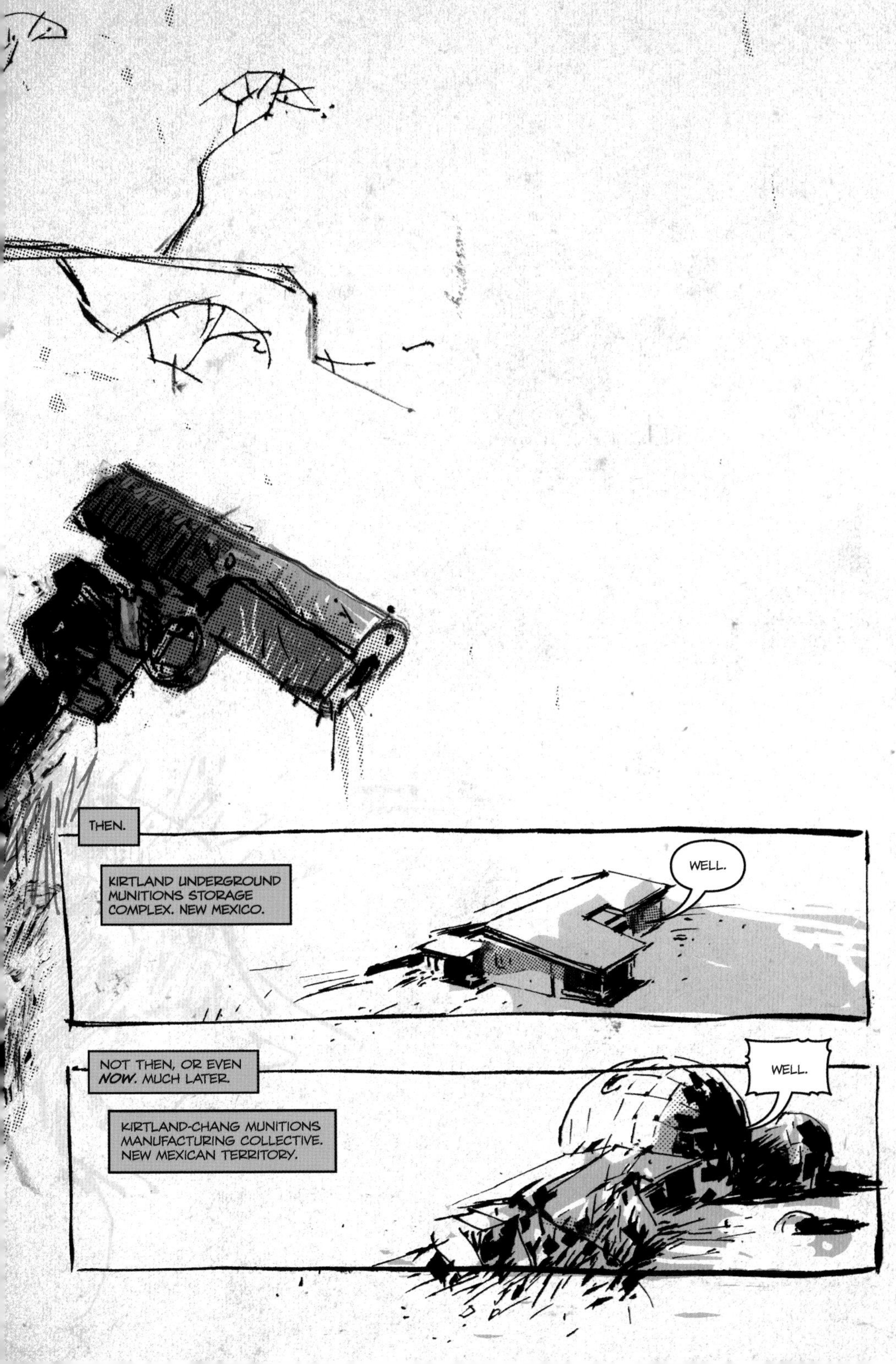
THEN.
KIRTLAND UNDERGROUND MUNITIONS STORAGE COMPLEX. NEW MEXICO.
WELL.
NOT THEN, OR EVEN *NOW*. MUCH LATER.
KIRTLAND-CHANG MUNITIONS MANUFACTURING COLLECTIVE. NEW MEXICAN TERRITORY.
WELL.

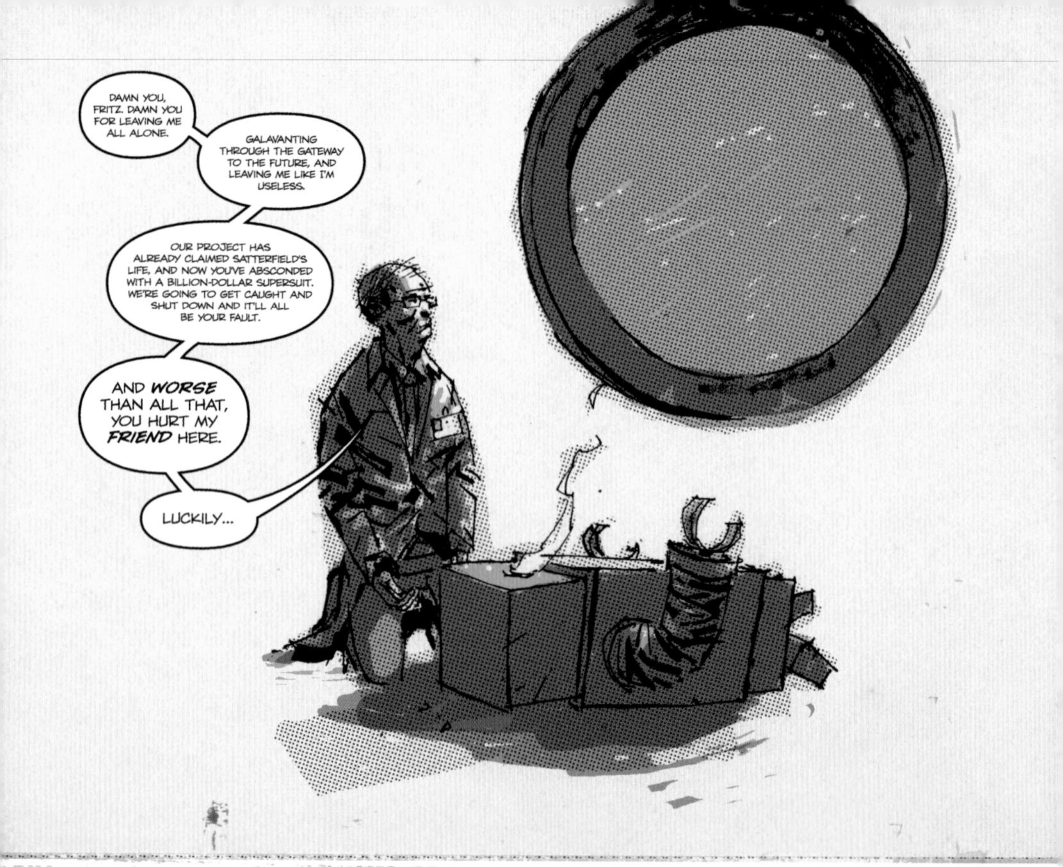
DAMN YOU, FRITZ. DAMN YOU FOR LEAVING ME ALL ALONE.
GALAVANTING THROUGH THE GATEWAY TO THE FUTURE, AND LEAVING ME LIKE I'M USELESS.
OUR PROJECT HAS ALREADY CLAIMED SATTERFIELD'S LIFE, AND NOW YOU'VE ABSCONDED WITH A BILLION-DOLLAR SUPERSUIT. WE'RE GOING TO GET CAUGHT AND SHUT DOWN AND IT'LL ALL BE YOUR FAULT.
AND *WORSE* THAN ALL THAT, YOU HURT MY *FRIEND* HERE.
LUCKILY...

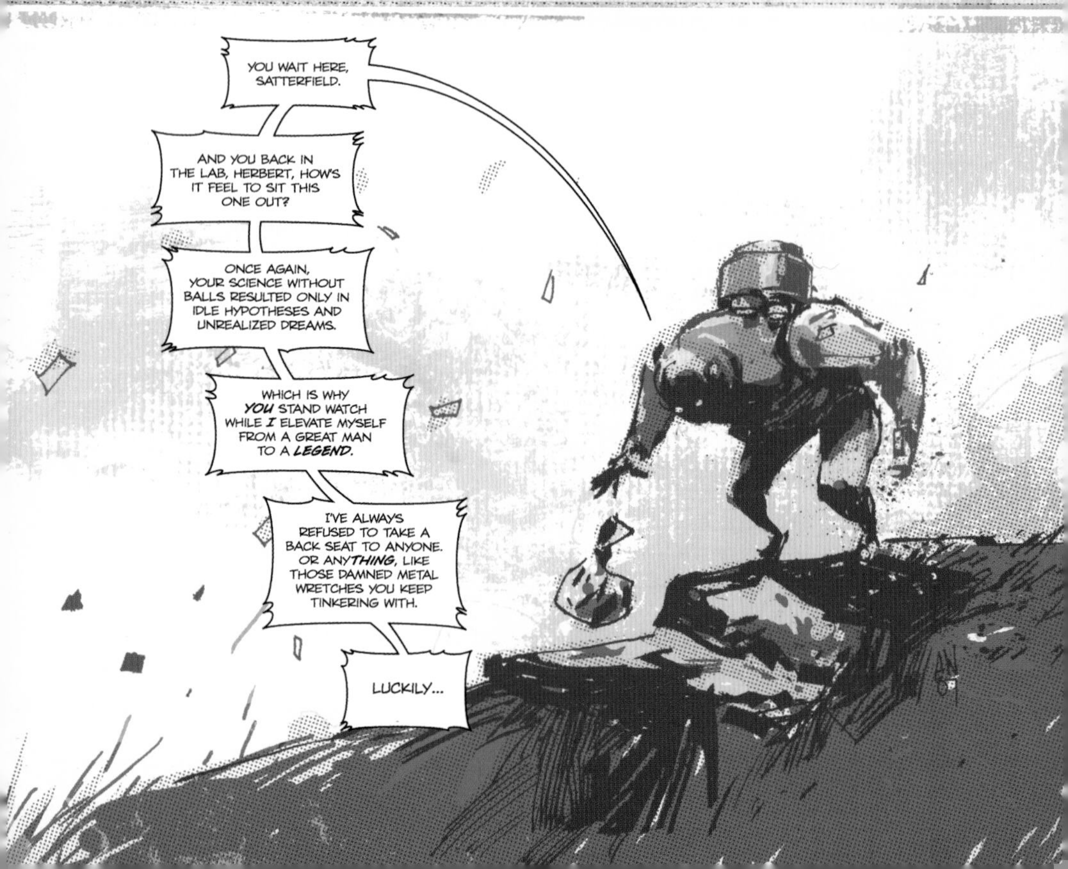
YOU WAIT HERE, SATTERFIELD.
AND YOU BACK IN THE LAB, HERBERT, HOW'S IT FEEL TO SIT THIS ONE OUT?
ONCE AGAIN, YOUR SCIENCE WITHOUT BALLS RESULTED ONLY IN IDLE HYPOTHESES AND UNREALIZED DREAMS.
WHICH IS WHY *YOU* STAND WATCH WHILE *I* ELEVATE MYSELF FROM A GREAT MAN TO A *LEGEND.*
I'VE ALWAYS REFUSED TO TAKE A BACK SEAT TO ANYONE. OR ANY*THING*, LIKE THOSE DAMNED METAL WRETCHES YOU KEEP TINKERING WITH.
LUCKILY...

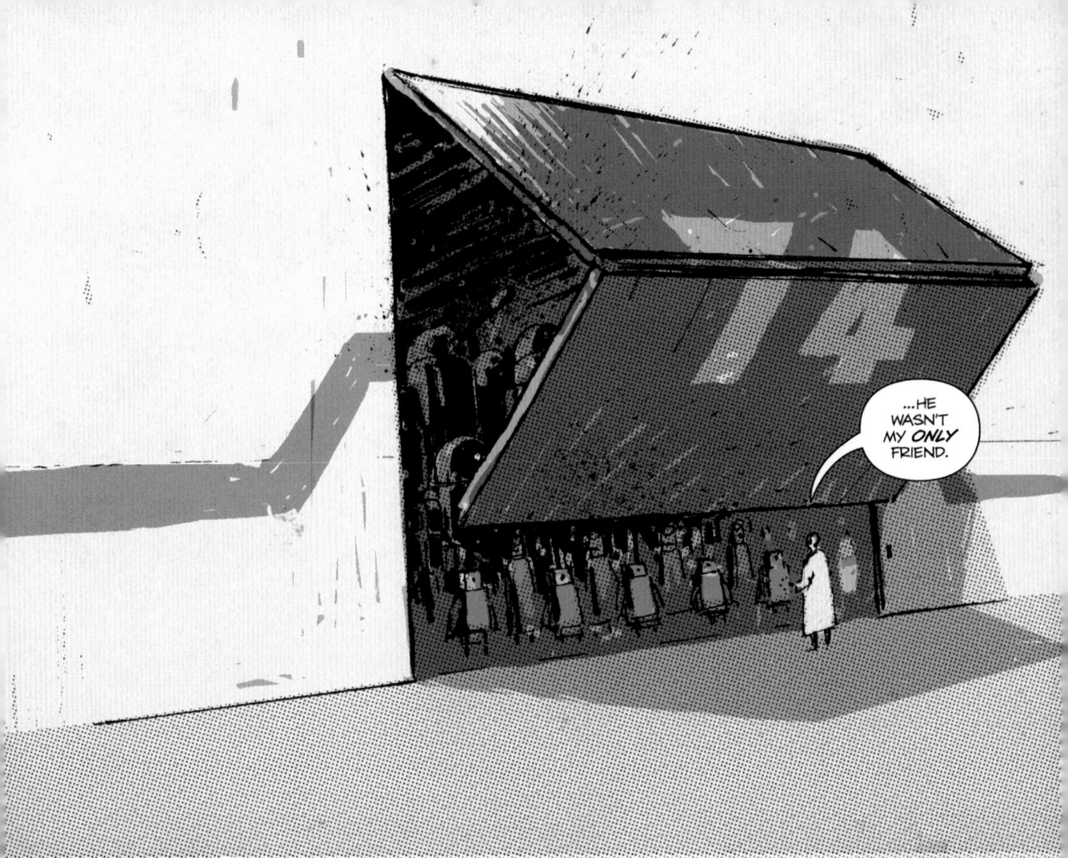
...HE WASN'T MY *ONLY* FRIEND.

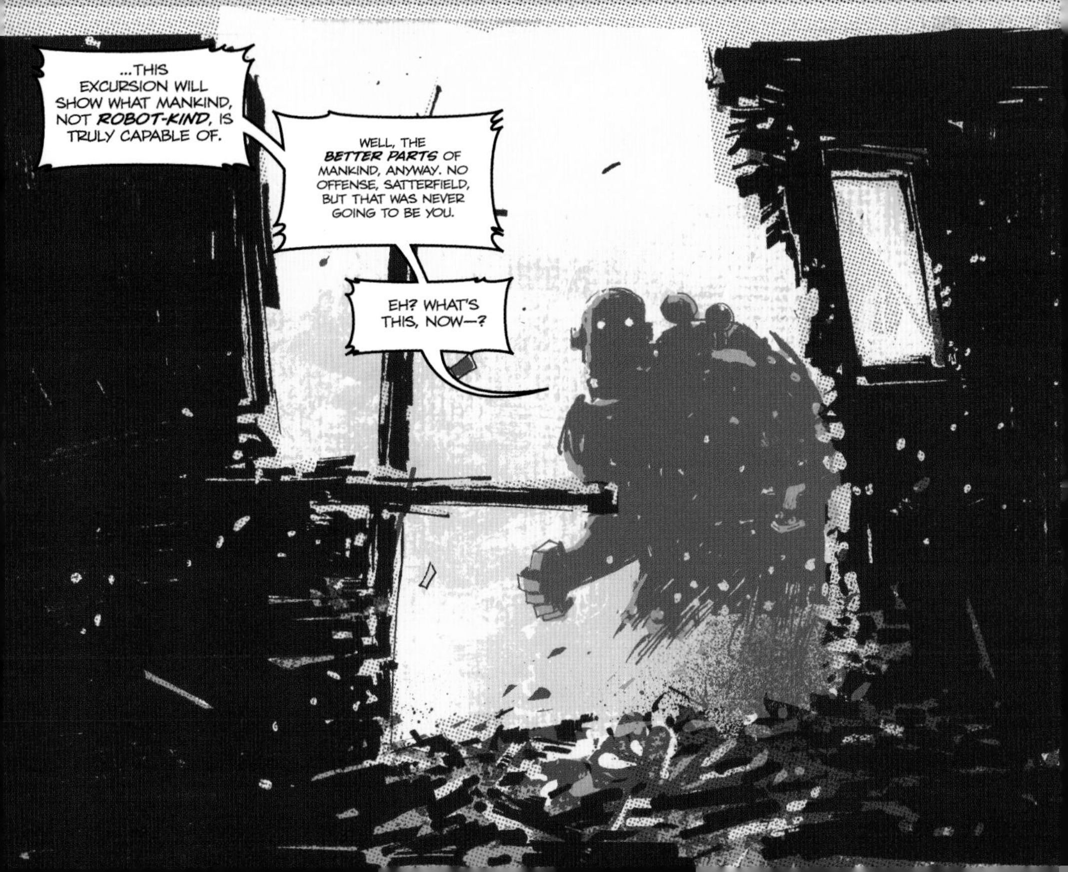
...THIS EXCURSION WILL SHOW WHAT MANKIND, NOT *ROBOT-KIND,* IS TRULY CAPABLE OF.
WELL, THE *BETTER PARTS* OF MANKIND, ANYWAY. NO OFFENSE, SATTERFIELD, BUT THAT WAS NEVER GOING TO BE YOU.
EH? WHAT'S THIS, NOW—?

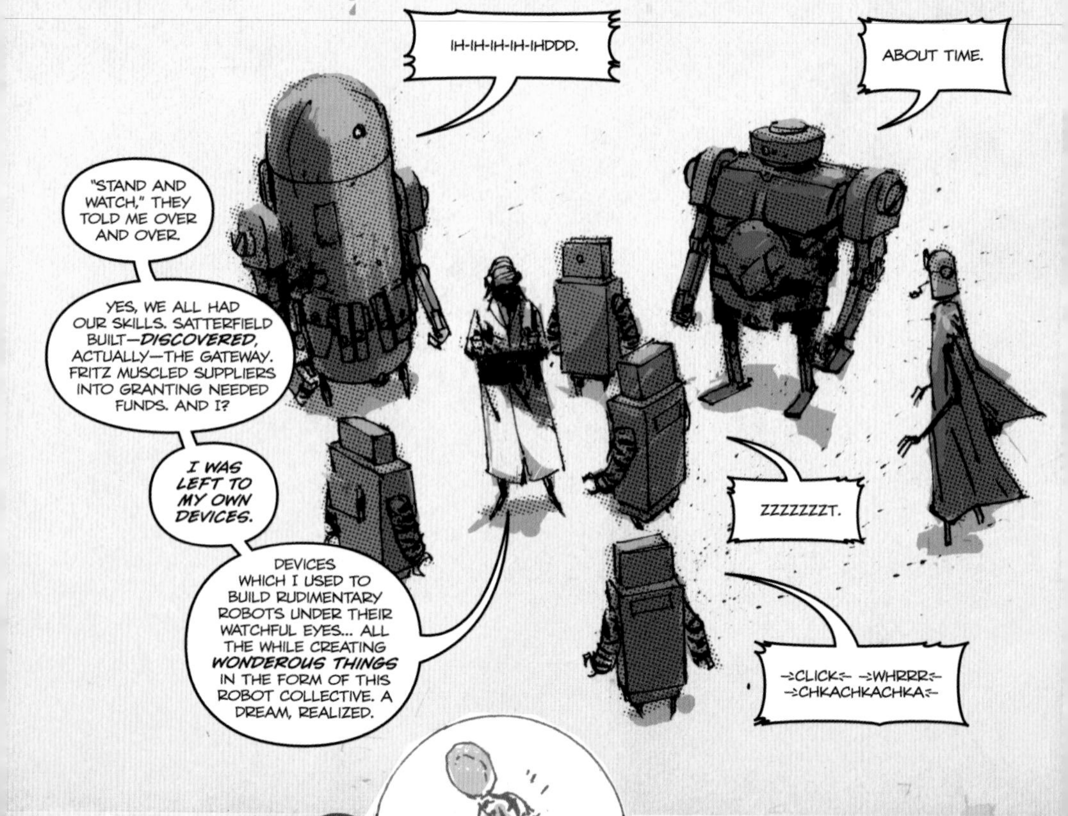
IH-IH-IH-IH-IHDDD.
ABOUT TIME.
"STAND AND WATCH," THEY TOLD ME OVER AND OVER.
YES, WE ALL HAD OUR SKILLS. SATTERFIELD BUILT—DISCOVERED, ACTUALLY—THE GATEWAY. FRITZ MUSCLED SUPPLIERS INTO GRANTING NEEDED FUNDS. AND I?
I WAS LEFT TO MY OWN DEVICES.
DEVICES WHICH I USED TO BUILD RUDIMENTARY ROBOTS UNDER THEIR WATCHFUL EYES... ALL THE WHILE CREATING WONDEROUS THINGS IN THE FORM OF THIS ROBOT COLLECTIVE. A DREAM, REALIZED.
ZZZZZZZT.
CLICK WHRRR CHKACHKACHKA

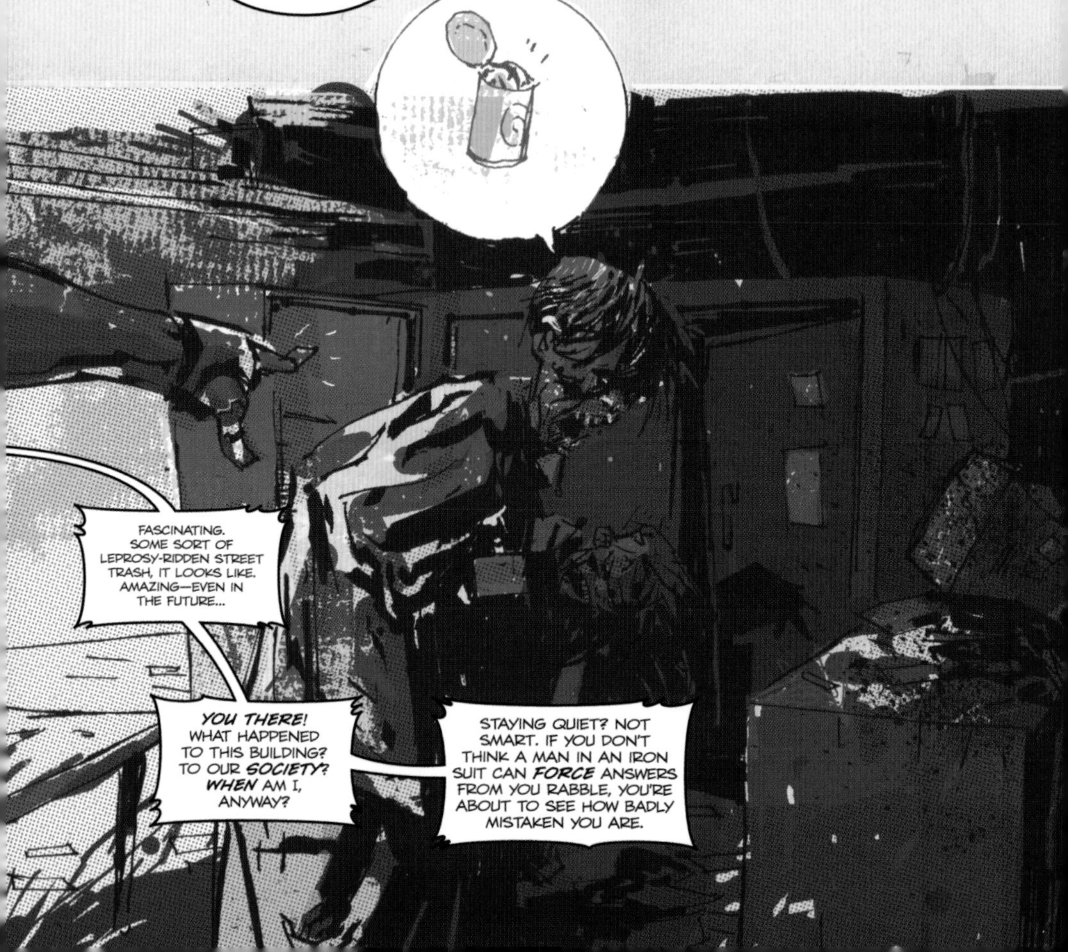
FASCINATING. SOME SORT OF LEPROSY-RIDDEN STREET TRASH, IT LOOKS LIKE. AMAZING—EVEN IN THE FUTURE...
YOU THERE! WHAT HAPPENED TO THIS BUILDING? TO OUR SOCIETY? WHEN AM I, ANYWAY?
STAYING QUIET? NOT SMART. IF YOU DON'T THINK A MAN IN AN IRON SUIT CAN FORCE ANSWERS FROM YOU RABBLE, YOU'RE ABOUT TO SEE HOW BADLY MISTAKEN YOU ARE.

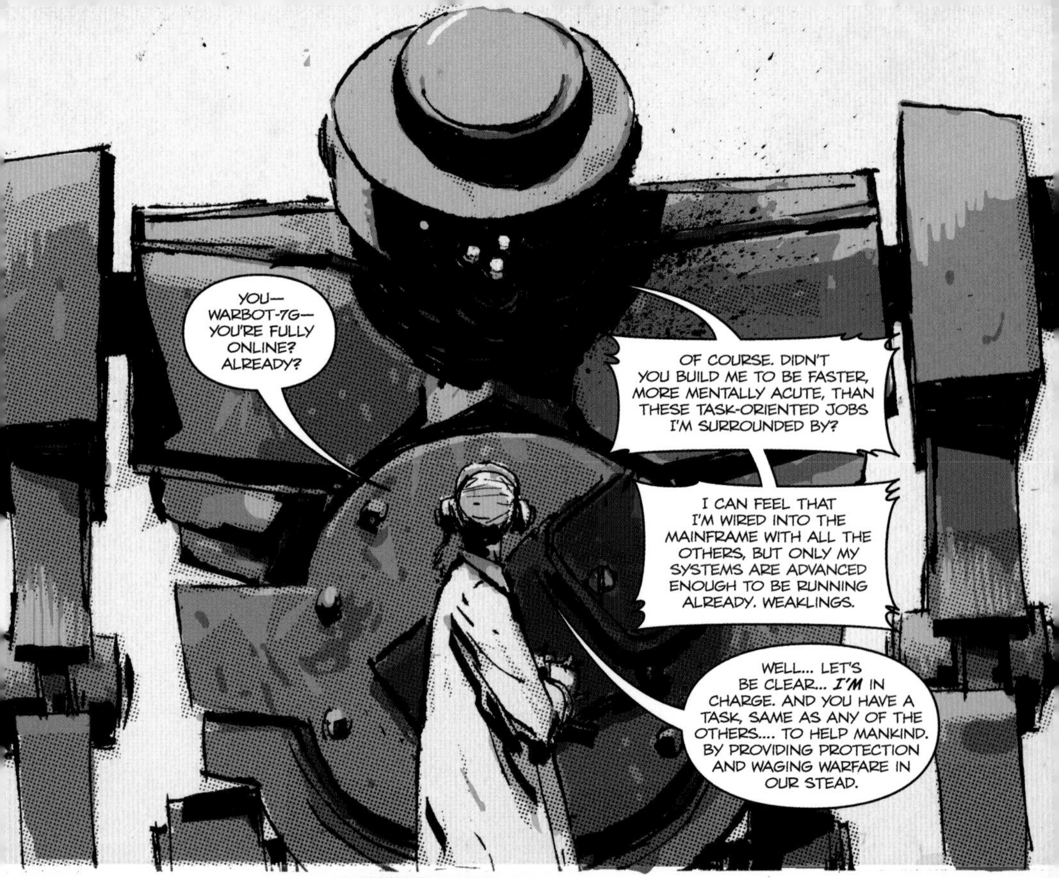
YOU—
WARBOT-7G—
YOU'RE FULLY
ONLINE?
ALREADY?
OF COURSE. DIDN'T YOU BUILD ME TO BE FASTER, MORE MENTALLY ACUTE, THAN THESE TASK-ORIENTED JOBS I'M SURROUNDED BY?
I CAN FEEL THAT I'M WIRED INTO THE MAINFRAME WITH ALL THE OTHERS, BUT ONLY MY SYSTEMS ARE ADVANCED ENOUGH TO BE RUNNING ALREADY. WEAKLINGS.
WELL... LET'S BE CLEAR... *I'M* IN CHARGE. AND YOU HAVE A TASK, SAME AS ANY OF THE OTHERS.... TO HELP MANKIND. BY PROVIDING PROTECTION AND WAGING WARFARE IN OUR STEAD.

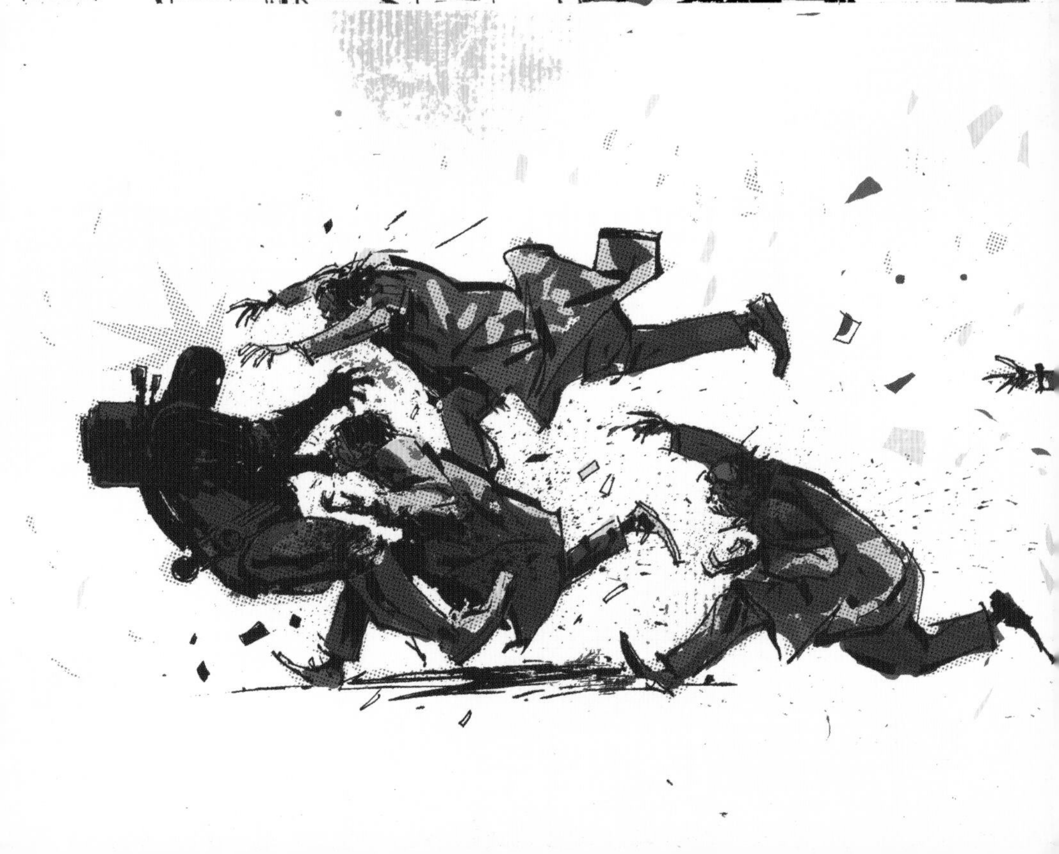

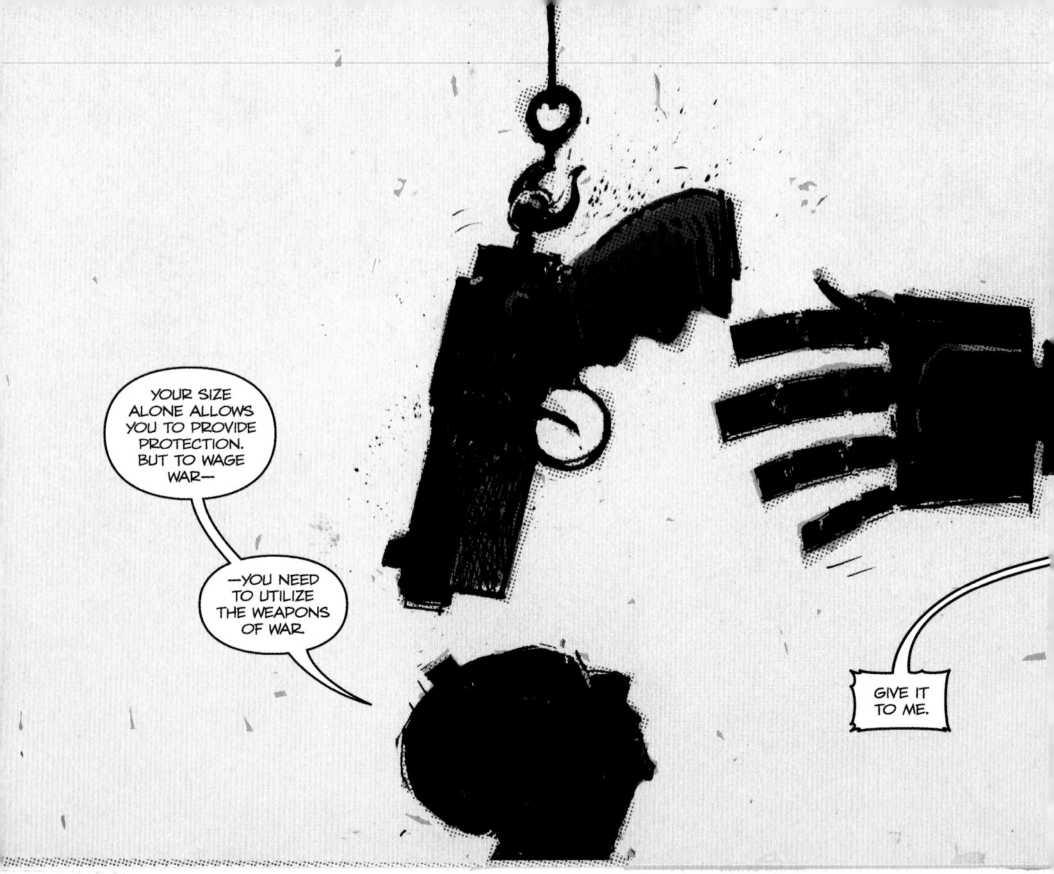
YOUR SIZE ALONE ALLOWS YOU TO PROVIDE PROTECTION. BUT TO WAGE WAR--
--YOU NEED TO UTILIZE THE WEAPONS OF WAR.
GIVE IT TO ME.

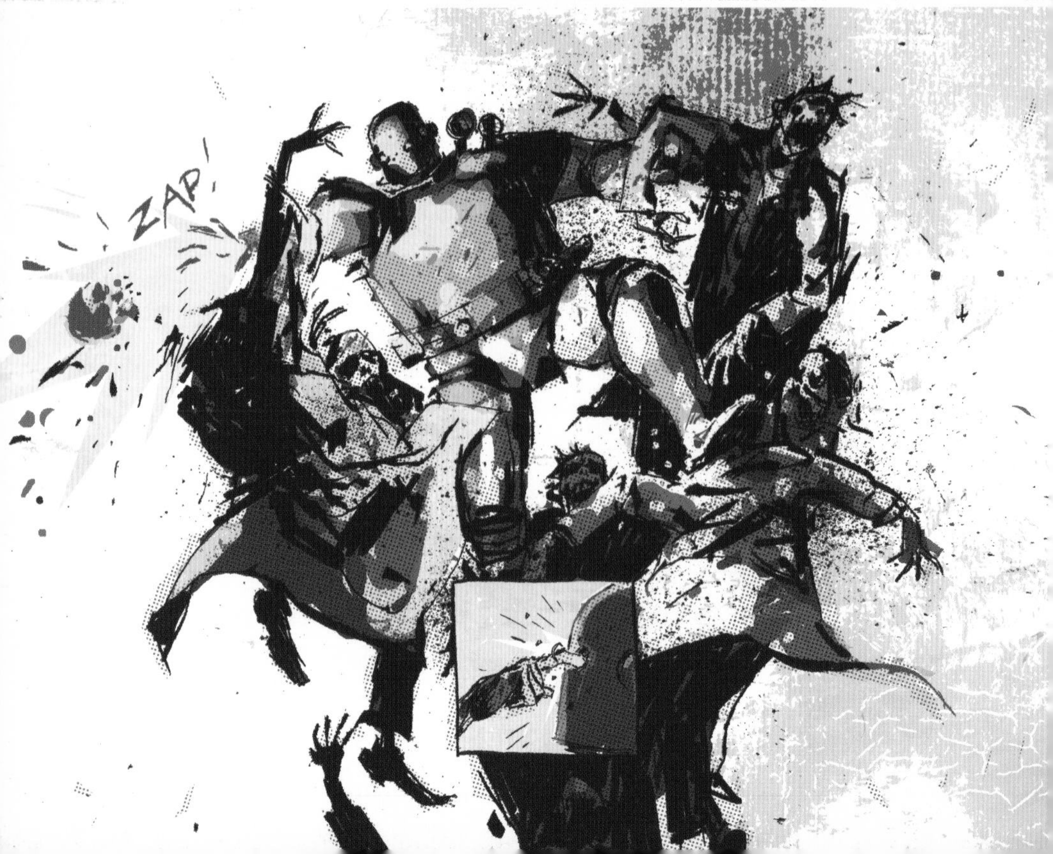
ZAP!

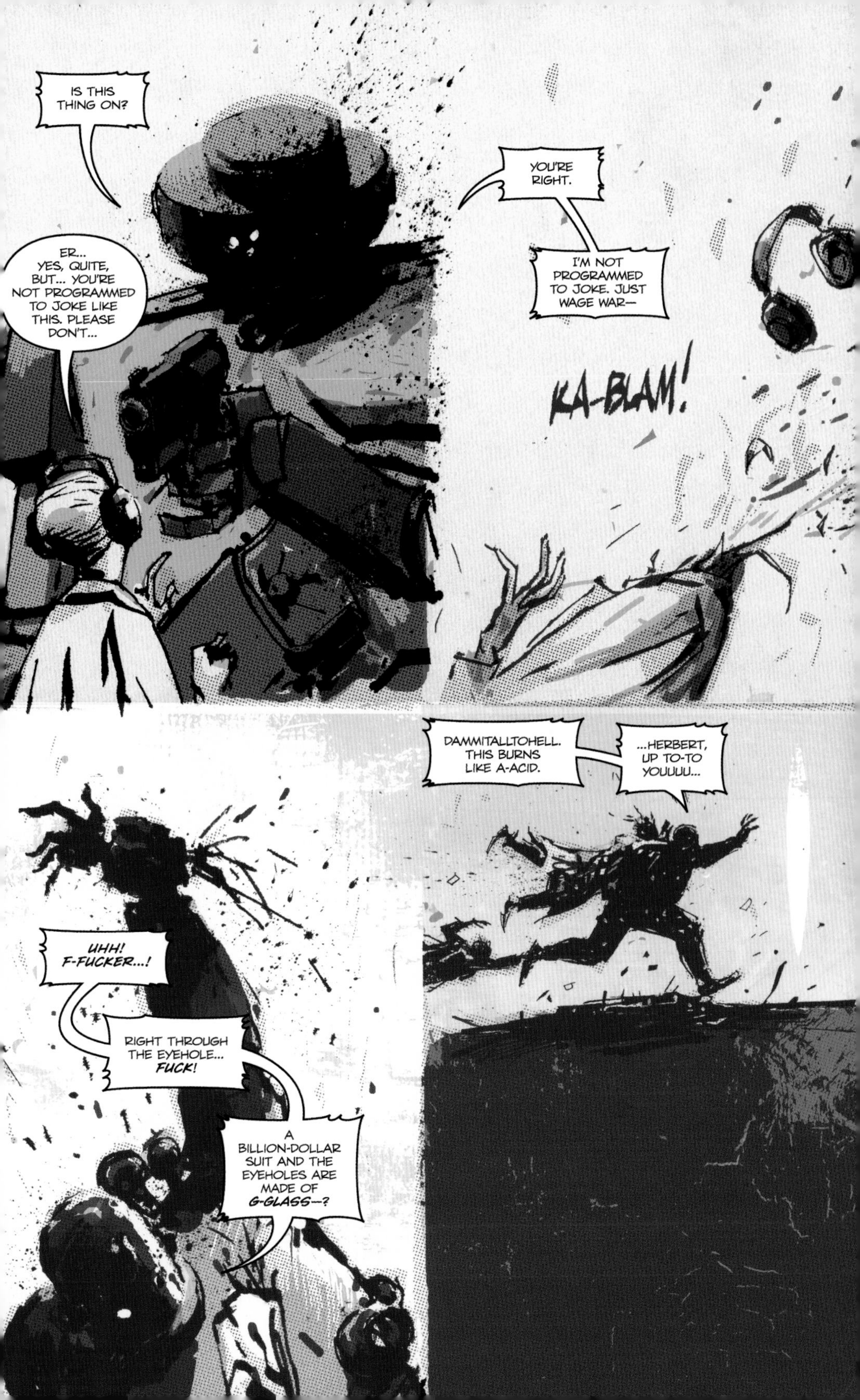
IS THIS THING ON?
ER... YES, QUITE, BUT... YOU'RE NOT PROGRAMMED TO JOKE LIKE THIS. PLEASE DON'T...
YOU'RE RIGHT.
I'M NOT PROGRAMMED TO JOKE. JUST WAGE WAR—
KA-BLAM!
UHH! F-FUCKER...!
RIGHT THROUGH THE EYEHOLE... FUCK!
A BILLION-DOLLAR SUIT AND THE EYEHOLES ARE MADE OF G-GLASS—?
DAMMITALLTOHELL. THIS BURNS LIKE A-ACID.
...HERBERT, UP TO-TO YOUUUU...

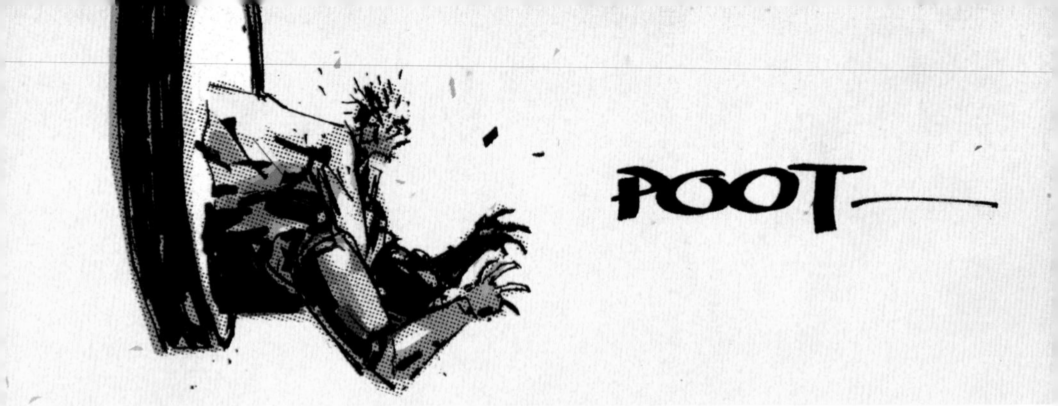
POOT—

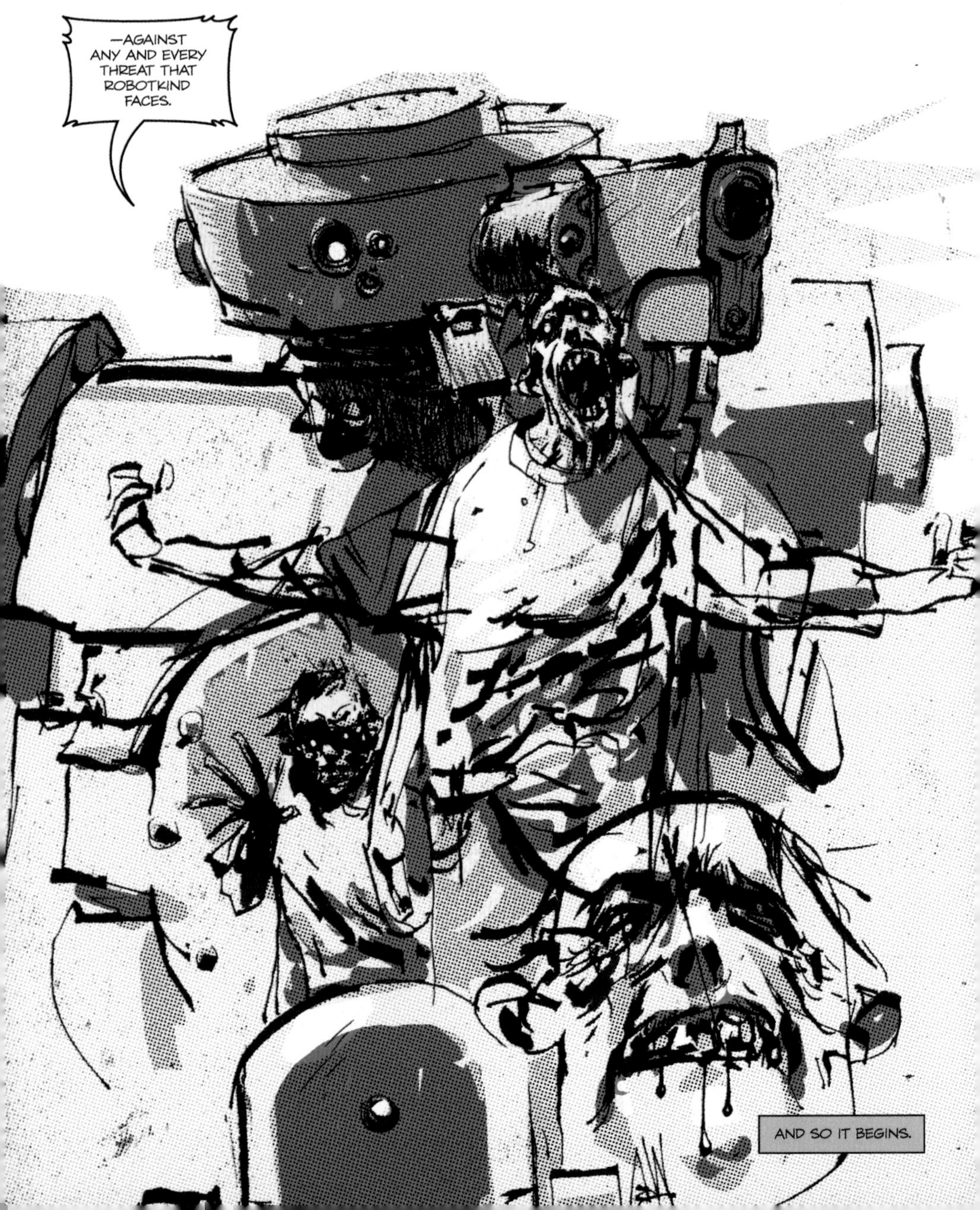
—AGAINST ANY AND EVERY THREAT THAT ROBOTKIND FACES.
AND SO IT BEGINS.

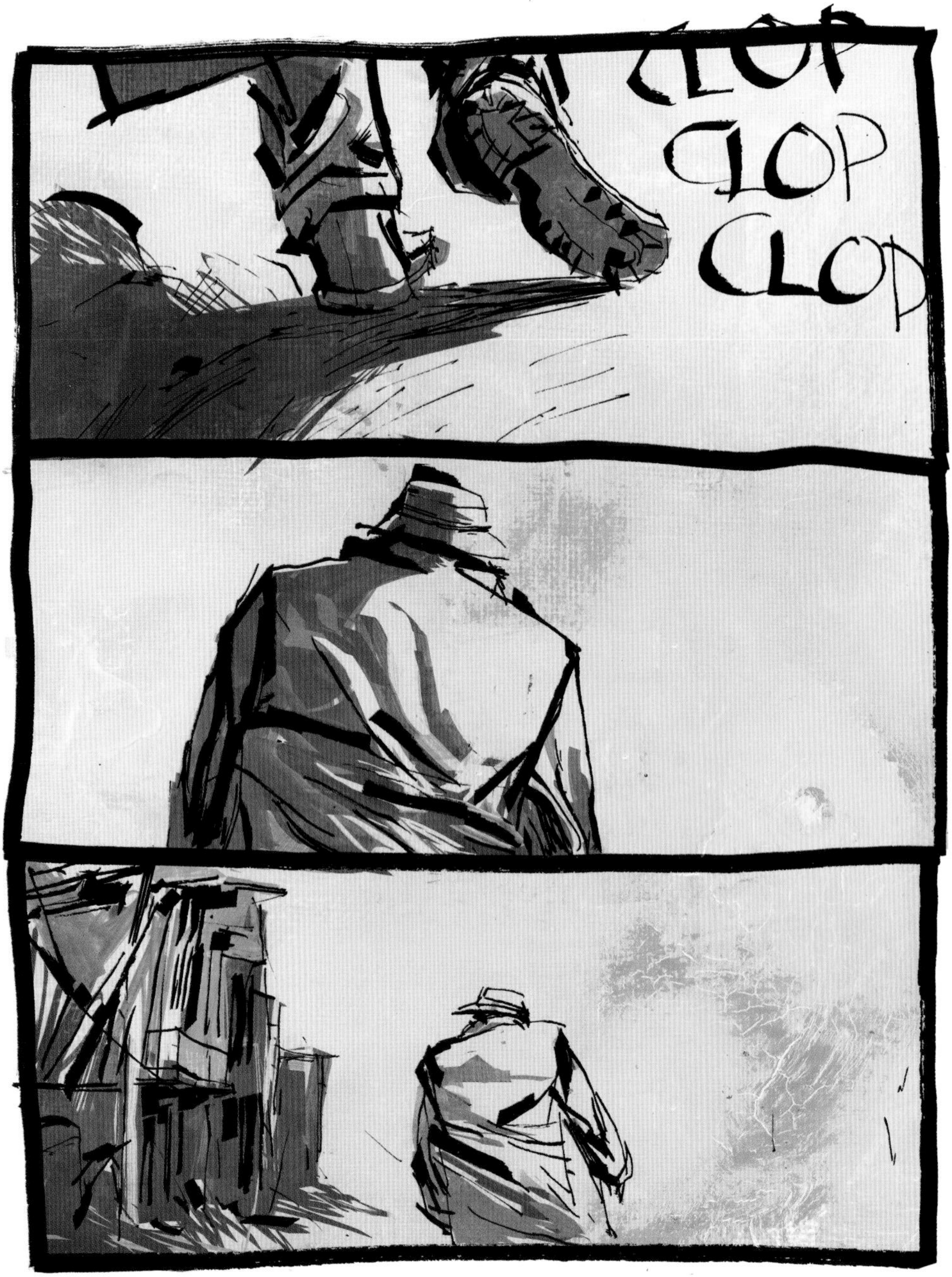
CLOP
CLOP
CLOP

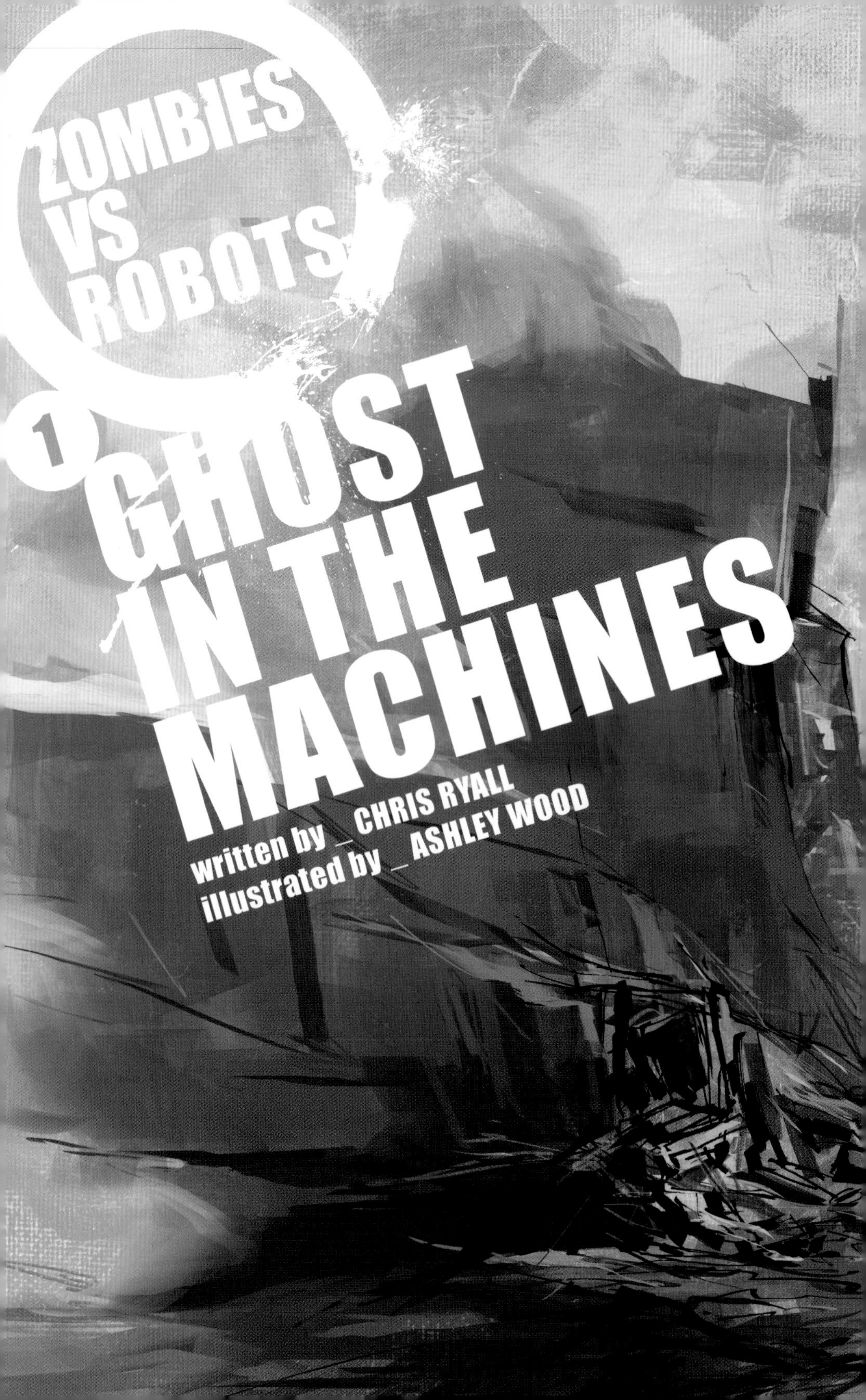
ZOMBIES
VS
ROBOTS
1
GHOST
IN THE
MACHINES
written by _ CHRIS RYALL
illustrated by _ ASHLEY WOOD

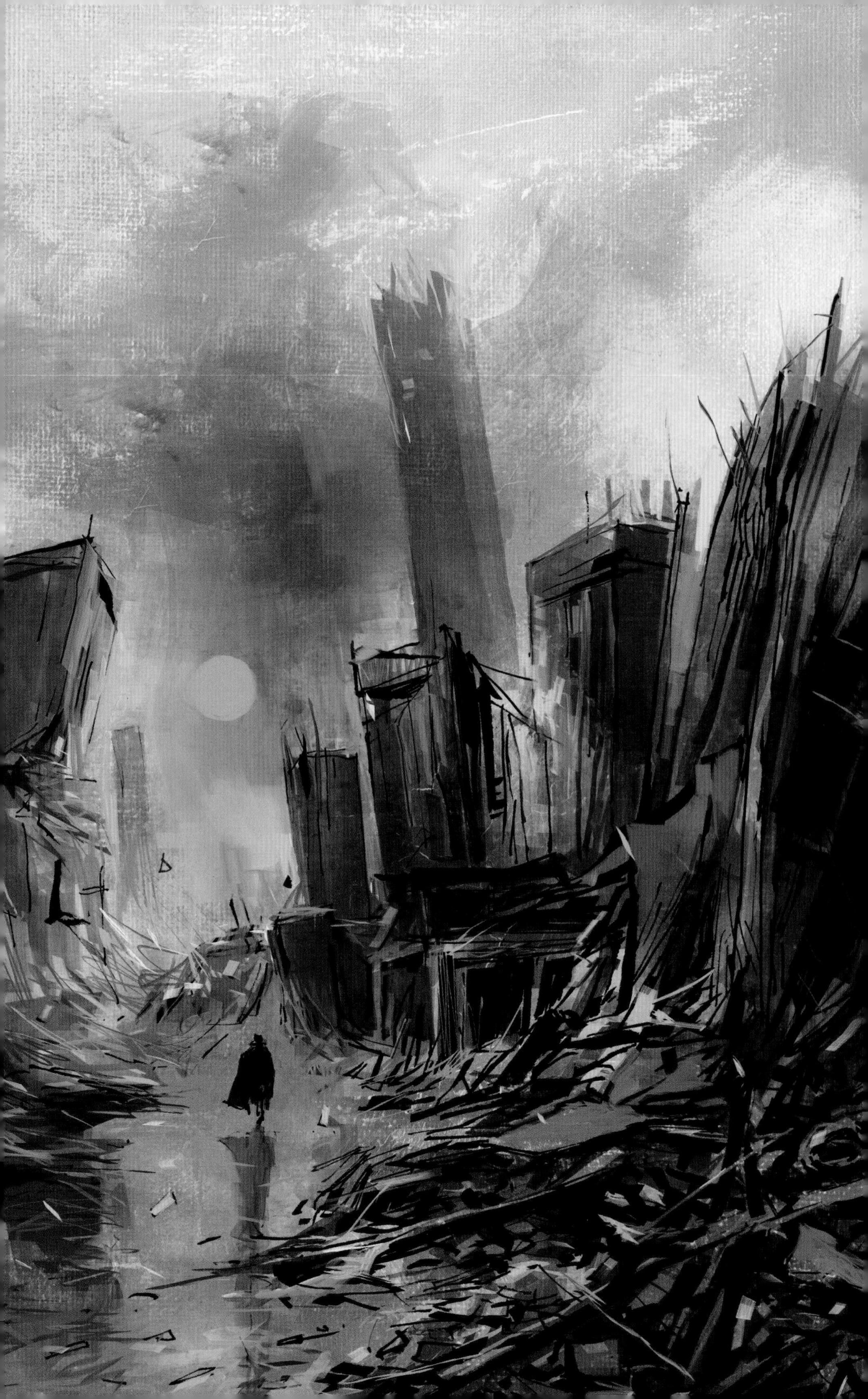

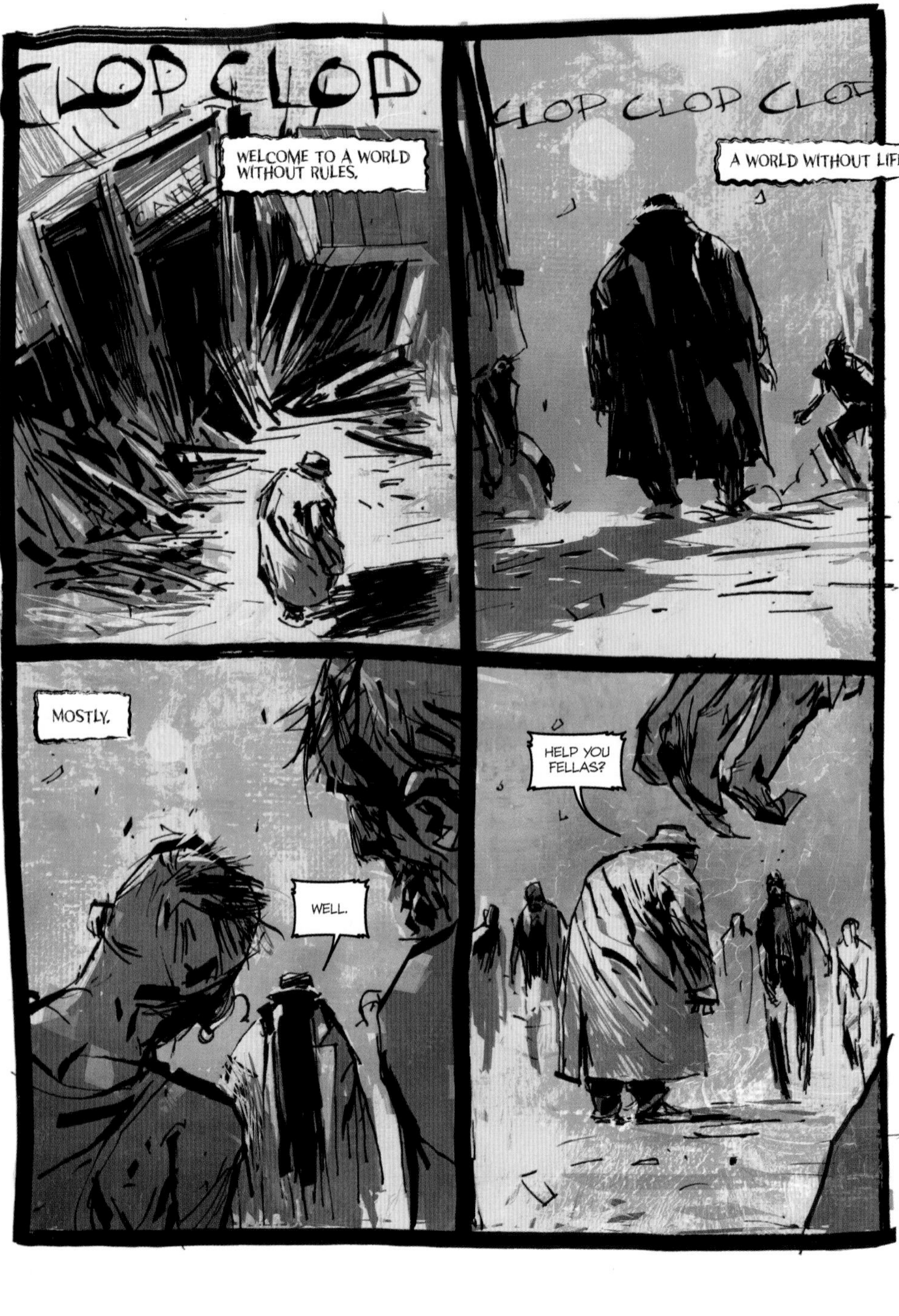
CLOP CLOP
WELCOME TO A WORLD WITHOUT RULES.
CLOP CLOP CLOP
A WORLD WITHOUT LIFE.
MOSTLY.
WELL.
HELP YOU FELLAS?

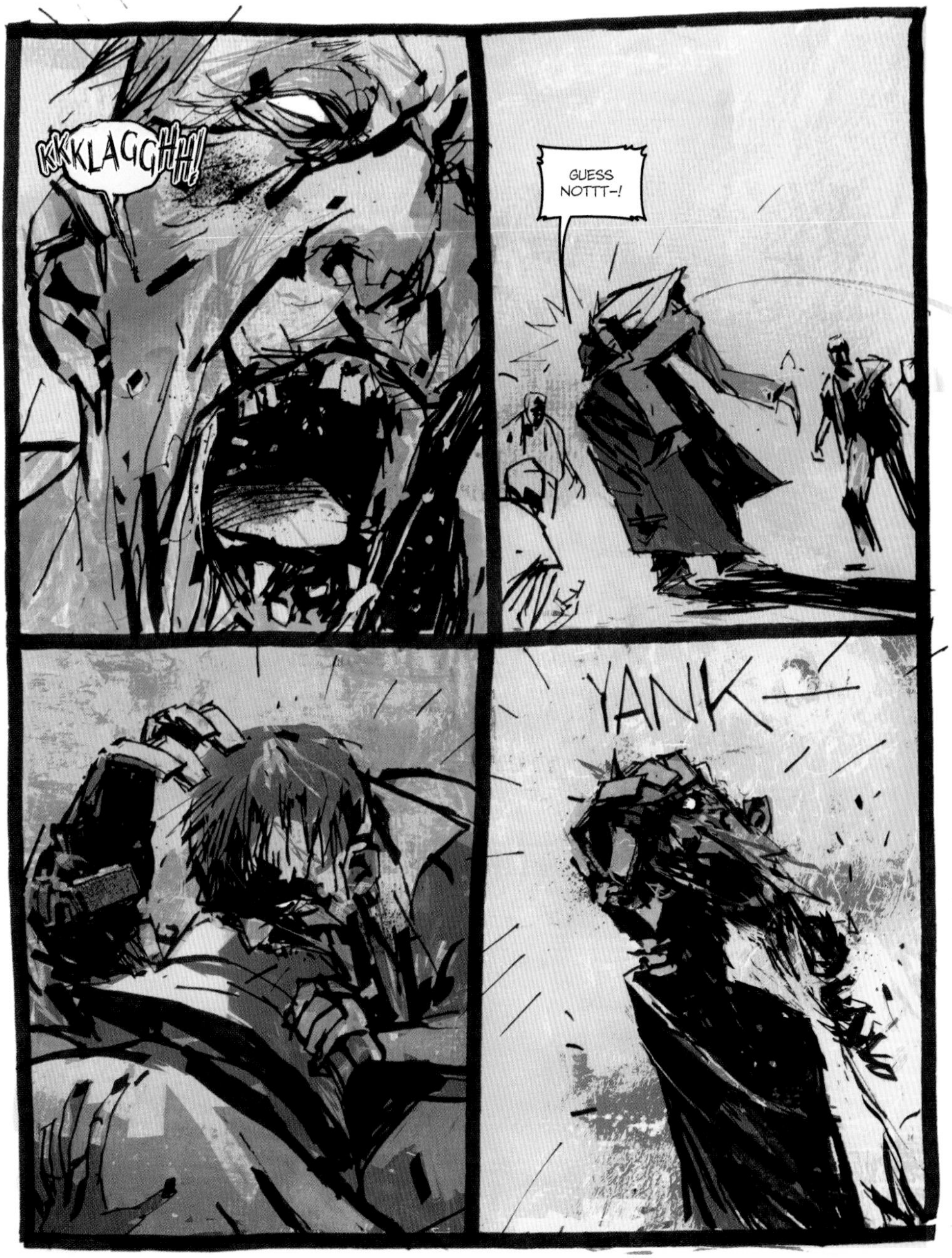
KKKLAGGHH!
GUESS NOTTT-!
YANK

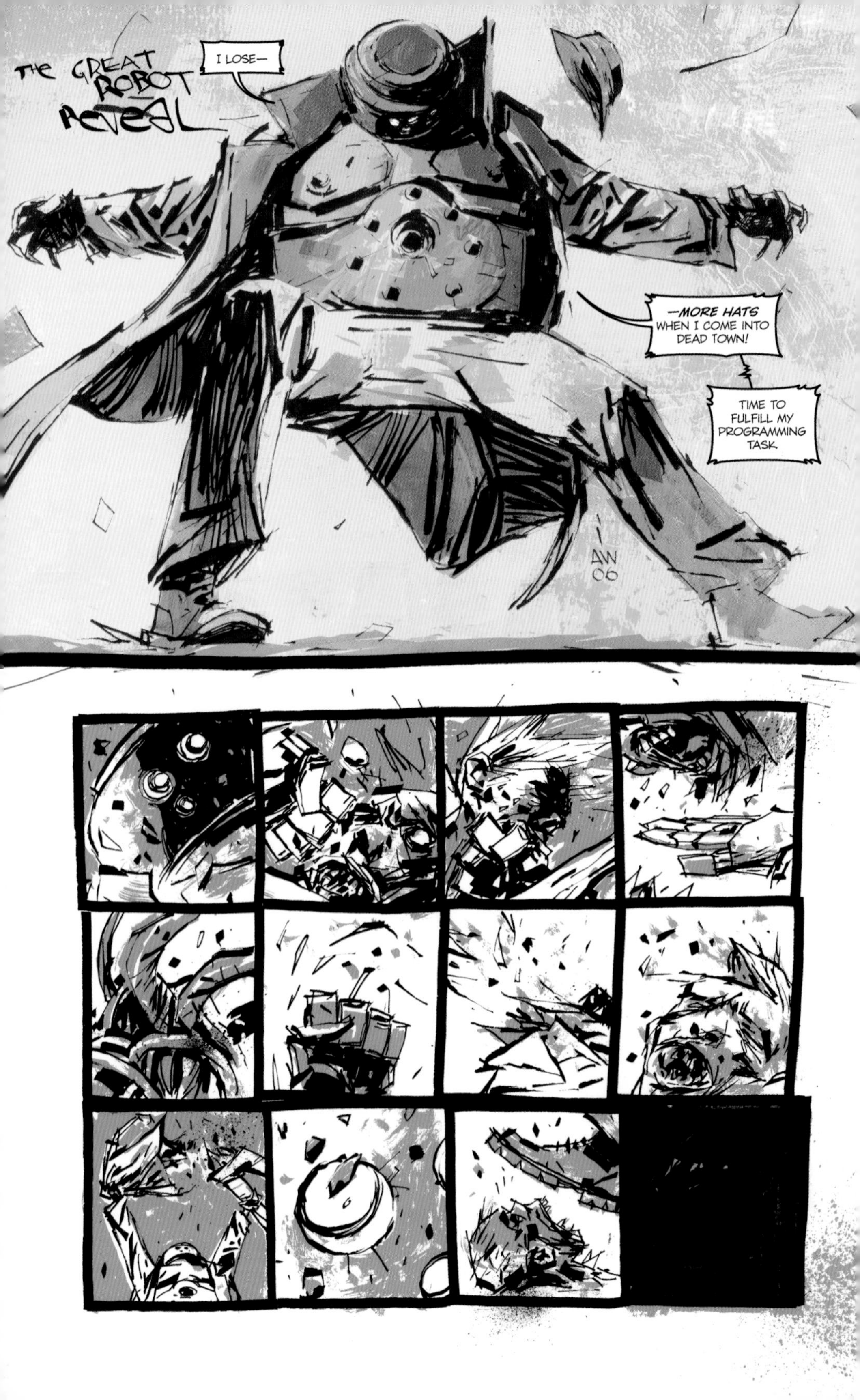
THE GREAT ROBOT REVEAL
I LOSE—
—MORE HATS WHEN I COME INTO DEAD TOWN!
TIME TO FULFILL MY PROGRAMMING TASK.
AW 06

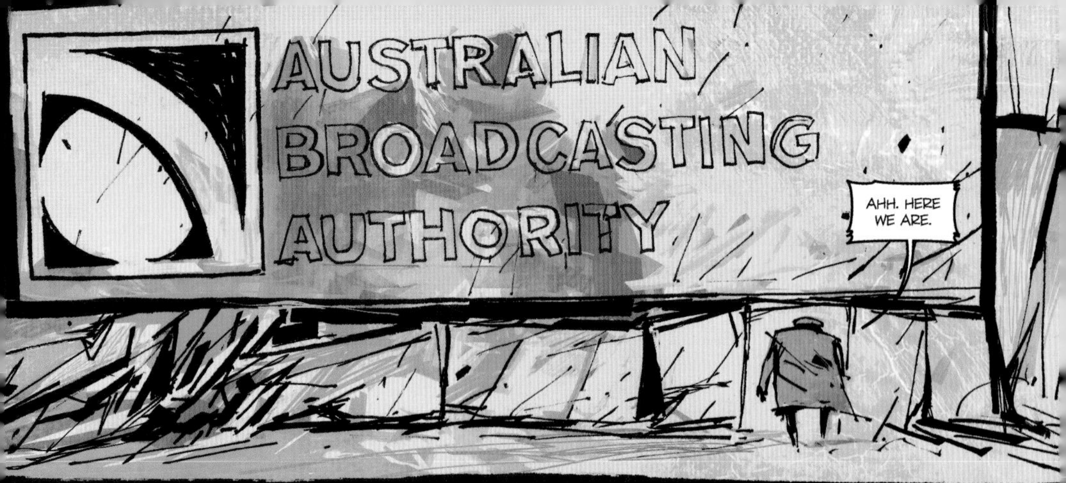
AUSTRALIAN BROADCASTING AUTHORITY
AHH. HERE WE ARE.

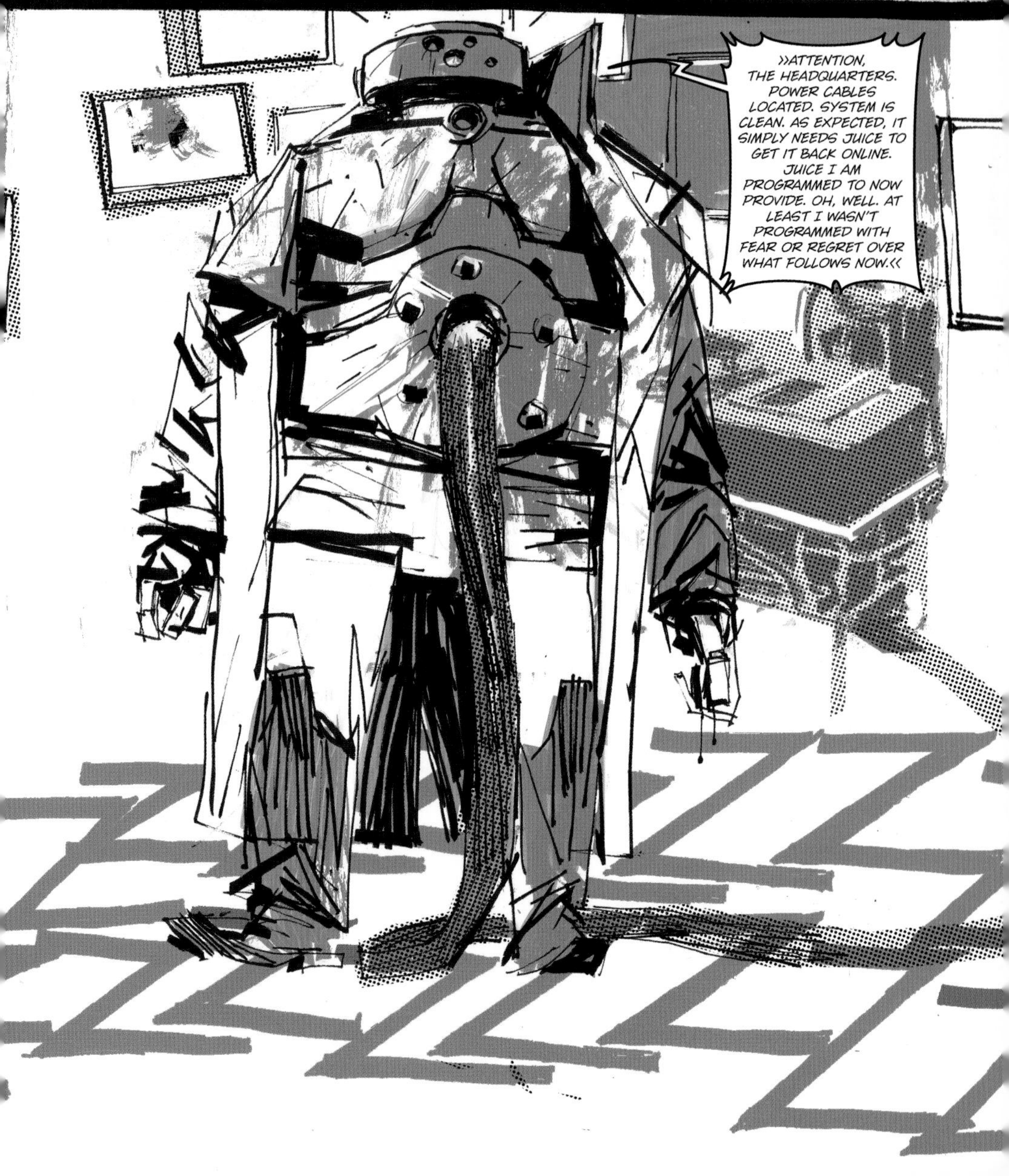
>>ATTENTION, THE HEADQUARTERS. POWER CABLES LOCATED. SYSTEM IS CLEAN. AS EXPECTED, IT SIMPLY NEEDS JUICE TO GET IT BACK ONLINE. JUICE I AM PROGRAMMED TO NOW PROVIDE. OH, WELL. AT LEAST I WASN'T PROGRAMMED WITH FEAR OR REGRET OVER WHAT FOLLOWS NOW.<<

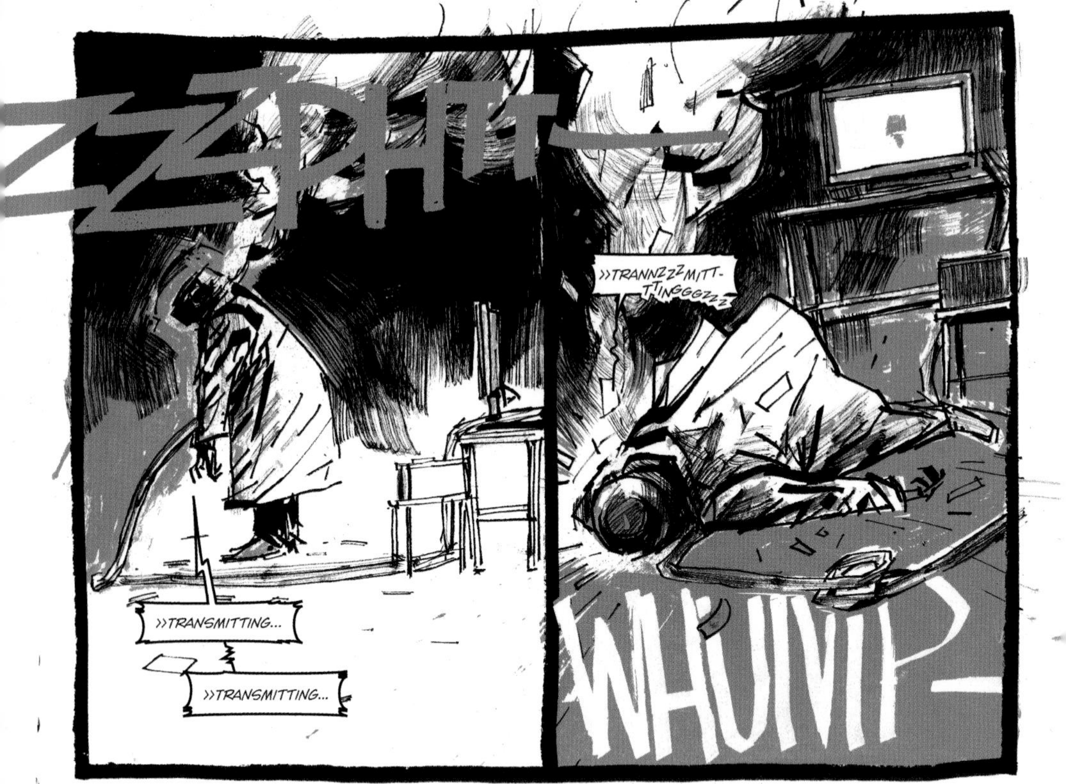
ZZPHTT—
>>TRANSMITTING...
>>TRANSMITTING...
>>TRANNZZZMITT-TTINGGGZZZ
WHUMP—

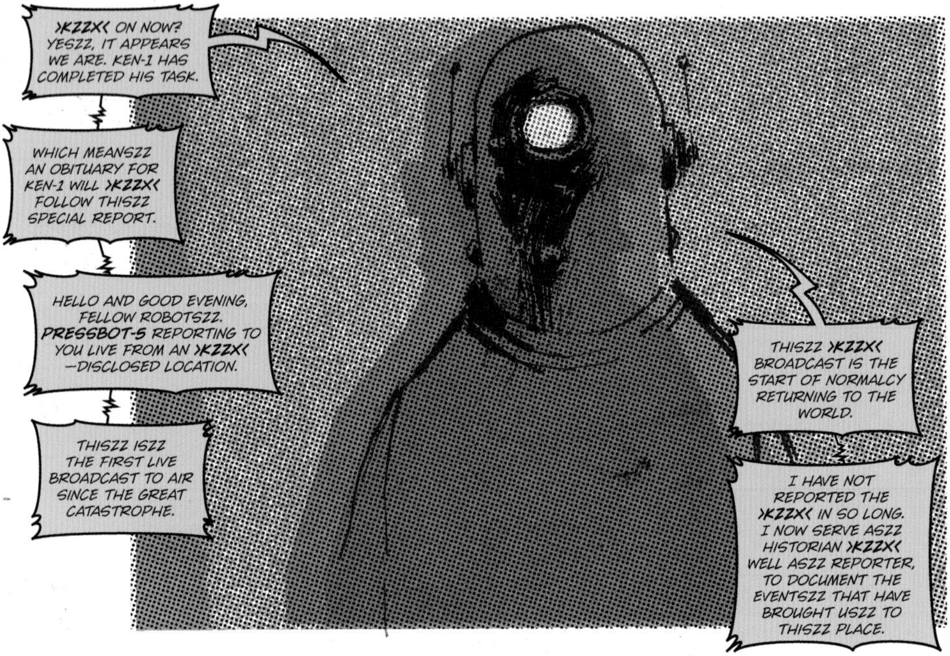
>KZZX< ON NOW? YESZZ, IT APPEARS WE ARE. KEN-1 HAS COMPLETED HIS TASK.
WHICH MEANSZZ AN OBITUARY FOR KEN-1 WILL >KZZX< FOLLOW THISZZ SPECIAL REPORT.
HELLO AND GOOD EVENING, FELLOW ROBOTSZZ. PRESSBOT-5 REPORTING TO YOU LIVE FROM AN >KZZX< —DISCLOSED LOCATION.
THISZZ ISZZ THE FIRST LIVE BROADCAST TO AIR SINCE THE GREAT CATASTROPHE.
THISZZ >KZZX< BROADCAST IS THE START OF NORMALCY RETURNING TO THE WORLD.
I HAVE NOT REPORTED THE >KZZX< IN SO LONG. I NOW SERVE ASZZ HISTORIAN >KZZX< WELL ASZZ REPORTER, TO DOCUMENT THE EVENTSZZ THAT HAVE BROUGHT USZZ TO THISZZ PLACE.

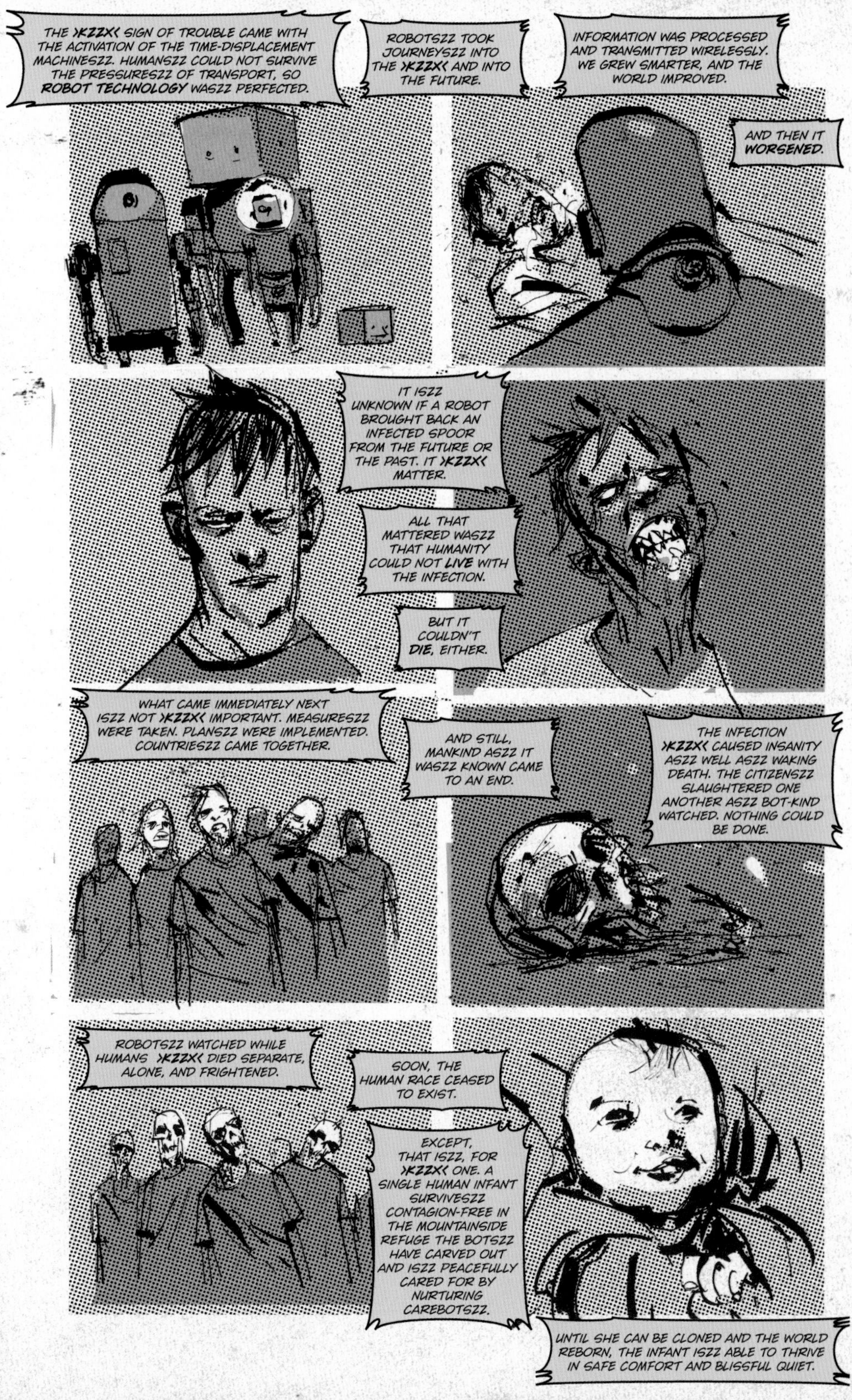
THE ›KZZX‹ SIGN OF TROUBLE CAME WITH THE ACTIVATION OF THE TIME-DISPLACEMENT MACHINESZZ. HUMANSZZ COULD NOT SURVIVE THE PRESSURESZZ OF TRANSPORT, SO ROBOT TECHNOLOGY WASZZ PERFECTED.
ROBOTSZZ TOOK JOURNEYSZZ INTO THE ›KZZX‹ AND INTO THE FUTURE.
INFORMATION WAS PROCESSED AND TRANSMITTED WIRELESSLY. WE GREW SMARTER, AND THE WORLD IMPROVED.
AND THEN IT WORSENED.
IT ISZZ UNKNOWN IF A ROBOT BROUGHT BACK AN INFECTED SPOOR FROM THE FUTURE OR THE PAST. IT ›KZZX‹ MATTER.
ALL THAT MATTERED WASZZ THAT HUMANITY COULD NOT LIVE WITH THE INFECTION.
BUT IT COULDN'T DIE, EITHER.
WHAT CAME IMMEDIATELY NEXT ISZZ NOT ›KZZX‹ IMPORTANT. MEASURESZZ WERE TAKEN. PLANSZZ WERE IMPLEMENTED. COUNTRIESZZ CAME TOGETHER.
AND STILL, MANKIND ASZZ IT WASZZ KNOWN CAME TO AN END.
THE INFECTION ›KZZX‹ CAUSED INSANITY ASZZ WELL ASZZ WAKING DEATH. THE CITIZENSZZ SLAUGHTERED ONE ANOTHER ASZZ BOT-KIND WATCHED. NOTHING COULD BE DONE.
ROBOTSZZ WATCHED WHILE HUMANS ›KZZX‹ DIED SEPARATE, ALONE, AND FRIGHTENED.
SOON, THE HUMAN RACE CEASED TO EXIST.
EXCEPT, THAT ISZZ, FOR ›KZZX‹ ONE. A SINGLE HUMAN INFANT SURVIVESZZ CONTAGION-FREE IN THE MOUNTAINSIDE REFUGE THE BOTSZZ HAVE CARVED OUT AND ISZZ PEACEFULLY CARED FOR BY NURTURING CAREBOTSZZ.
UNTIL SHE CAN BE CLONED AND THE WORLD REBORN, THE INFANT ISZZ ABLE TO THRIVE IN SAFE COMFORT AND BLISSFUL QUIET.

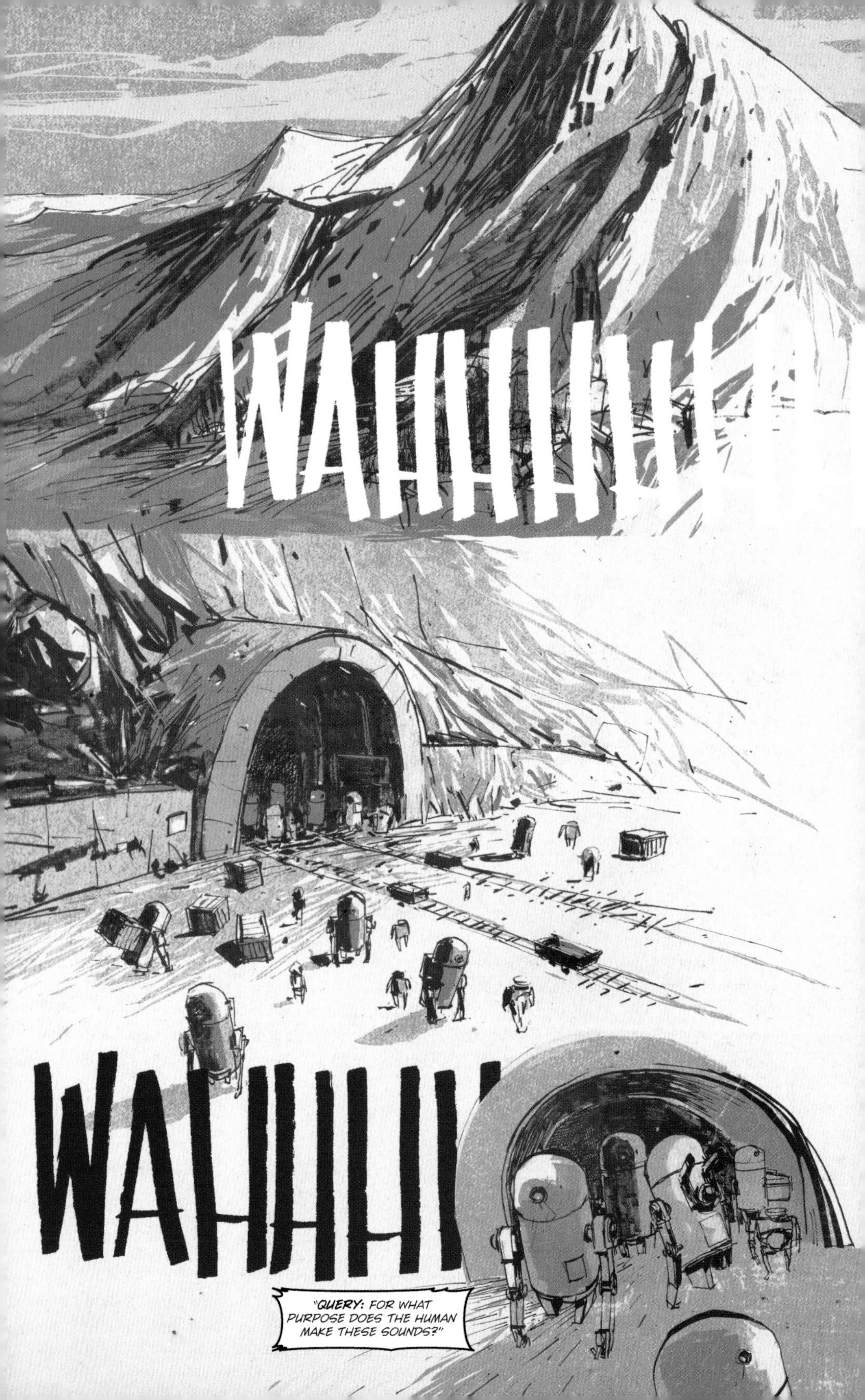
WAHHHHH
WAHHHH
"QUERY: FOR WHAT PURPOSE DOES THE HUMAN MAKE THESE SOUNDS?"

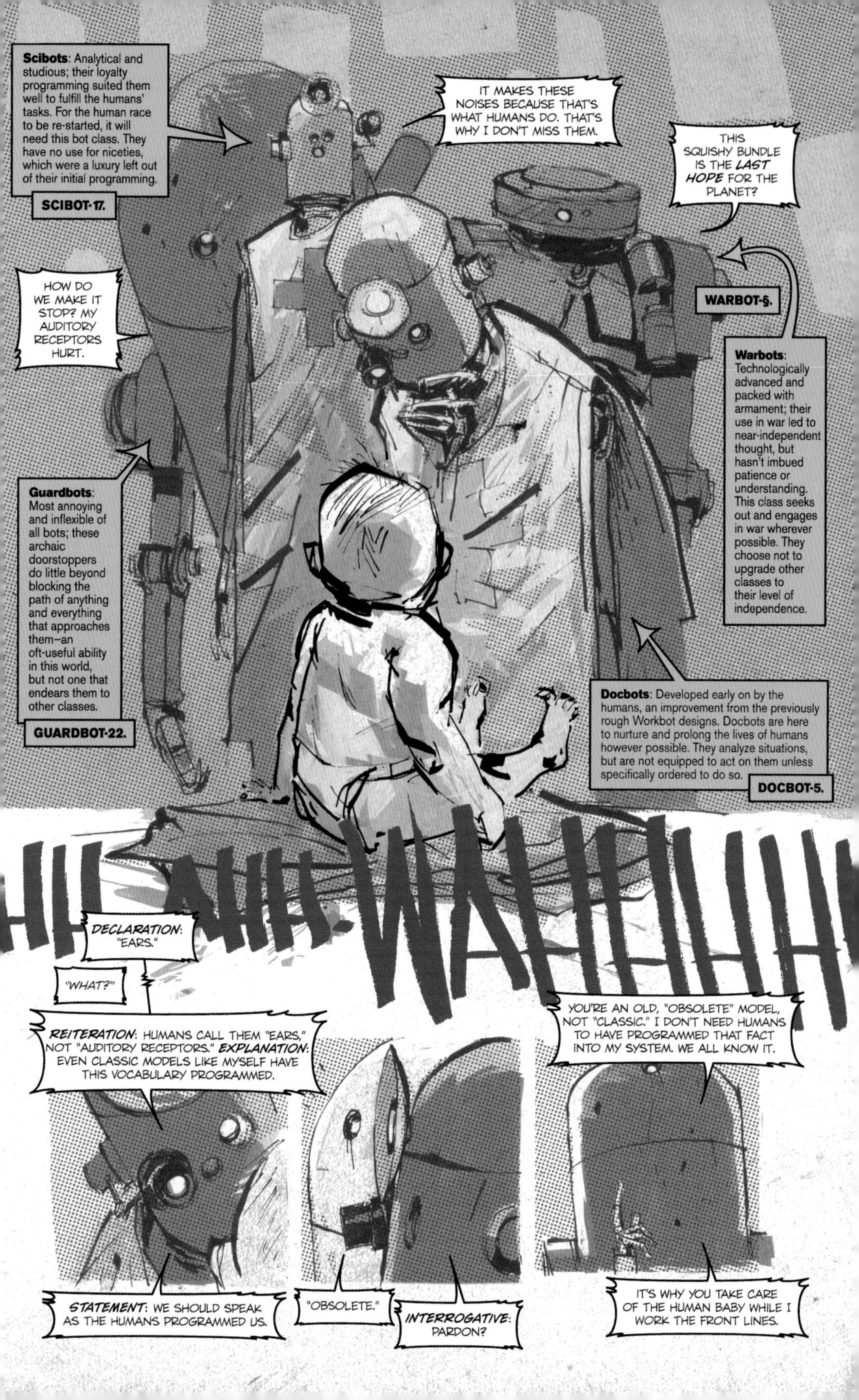
Scibots: Analytical and studious; their loyalty programming suited them well to fulfill the humans' tasks. For the human race to be re-started, it will need this bot class. They have no use for niceties, which were a luxury left out of their initial programming.
SCIBOT-17.
IT MAKES THESE NOISES BECAUSE THAT'S WHAT HUMANS DO. THAT'S WHY I DON'T MISS THEM.
THIS SQUISHY BUNDLE IS THE *LAST HOPE* FOR THE PLANET?
HOW DO WE MAKE IT STOP? MY AUDITORY RECEPTORS HURT.
WARBOT-§.
Warbots: Technologically advanced and packed with armament; their use in war led to near-independent thought, but hasn't imbued patience or understanding. This class seeks out and engages in war wherever possible. They choose not to upgrade other classes to their level of independence.
Guardbots: Most annoying and inflexible of all bots; these archaic doorstoppers do little beyond blocking the path of anything and everything that approaches them–an oft-useful ability in this world, but not one that endears them to other classes.
GUARDBOT-22.
Docbots: Developed early on by the humans, an improvement from the previously rough Workbot designs. Docbots are here to nurture and prolong the lives of humans however possible. They analyze situations, but are not equipped to act on them unless specifically ordered to do so.
DOCBOT-5.
WAHHHHH
DECLARATION: "EARS."
"WHAT?"
REITERATION: HUMANS CALL THEM "EARS," NOT "AUDITORY RECEPTORS." *EXPLANATION*: EVEN CLASSIC MODELS LIKE MYSELF HAVE THIS VOCABULARY PROGRAMMED.
YOU'RE AN OLD, "OBSOLETE" MODEL, NOT "CLASSIC." I DON'T NEED HUMANS TO HAVE PROGRAMMED THAT FACT INTO MY SYSTEM. WE ALL KNOW IT.
STATEMENT: WE SHOULD SPEAK AS THE HUMANS PROGRAMMED US.
"OBSOLETE."
INTERROGATIVE: PARDON?
IT'S WHY YOU TAKE CARE OF THE HUMAN BABY WHILE I WORK THE FRONT LINES.

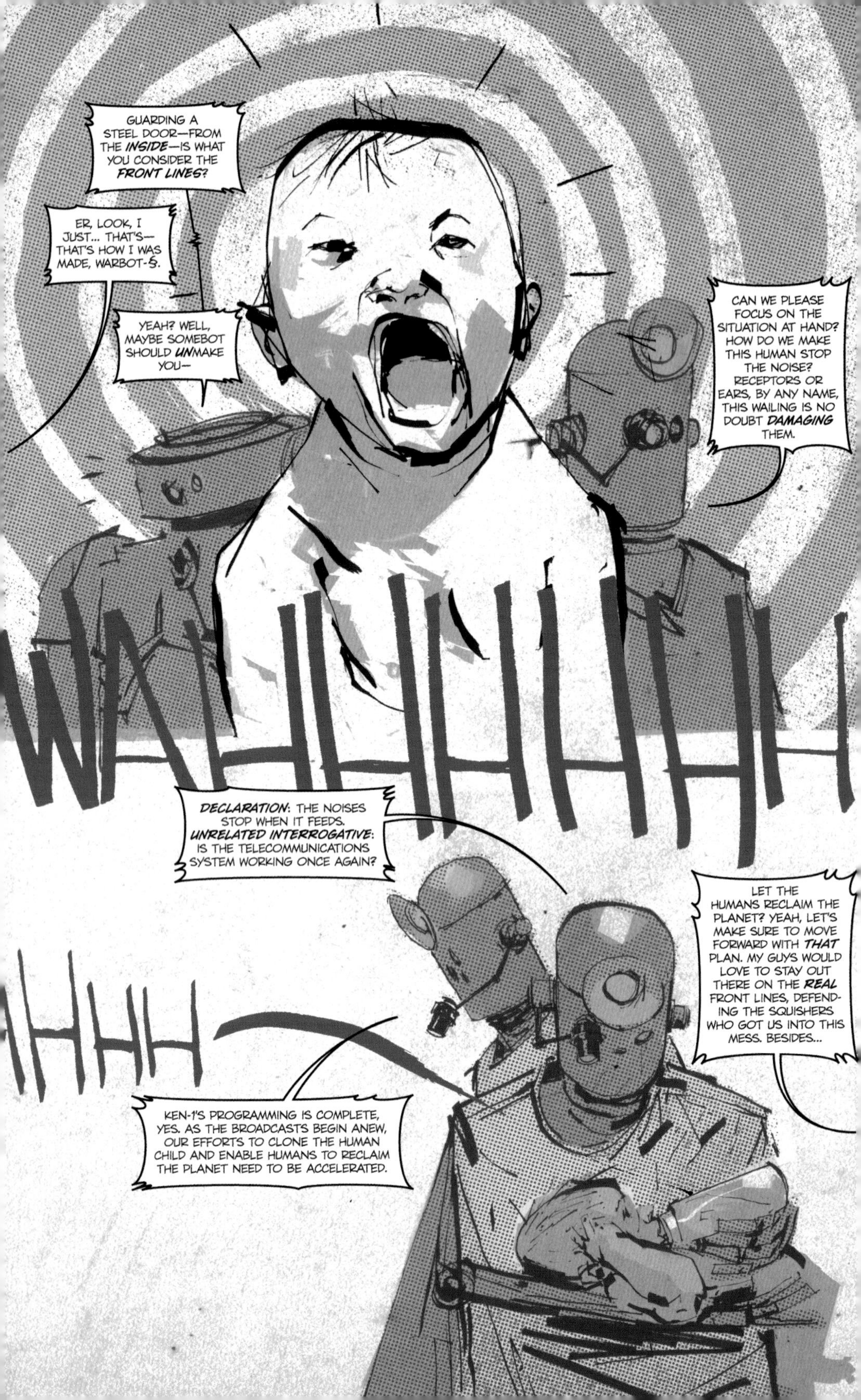
GUARDING A STEEL DOOR—FROM THE INSIDE—IS WHAT YOU CONSIDER THE FRONT LINES?
ER, LOOK, I JUST... THAT'S— THAT'S HOW I WAS MADE, WARBOT-§.
YEAH? WELL, MAYBE SOMEBOT SHOULD UNMAKE YOU—
CAN WE PLEASE FOCUS ON THE SITUATION AT HAND? HOW DO WE MAKE THIS HUMAN STOP THE NOISE? RECEPTORS OR EARS, BY ANY NAME, THIS WAILING IS NO DOUBT DAMAGING THEM.
WAHHHHHHHHHHHHHHH
DECLARATION: THE NOISES STOP WHEN IT FEEDS. UNRELATED INTERROGATIVE: IS THE TELECOMMUNICATIONS SYSTEM WORKING ONCE AGAIN?
KEN-1'S PROGRAMMING IS COMPLETE, YES. AS THE BROADCASTS BEGIN ANEW, OUR EFFORTS TO CLONE THE HUMAN CHILD AND ENABLE HUMANS TO RECLAIM THE PLANET NEED TO BE ACCELERATED.
LET THE HUMANS RECLAIM THE PLANET? YEAH, LET'S MAKE SURE TO MOVE FORWARD WITH THAT PLAN. MY GUYS WOULD LOVE TO STAY OUT THERE ON THE REAL FRONT LINES, DEFENDING THE SQUISHERS WHO GOT US INTO THIS MESS. BESIDES...

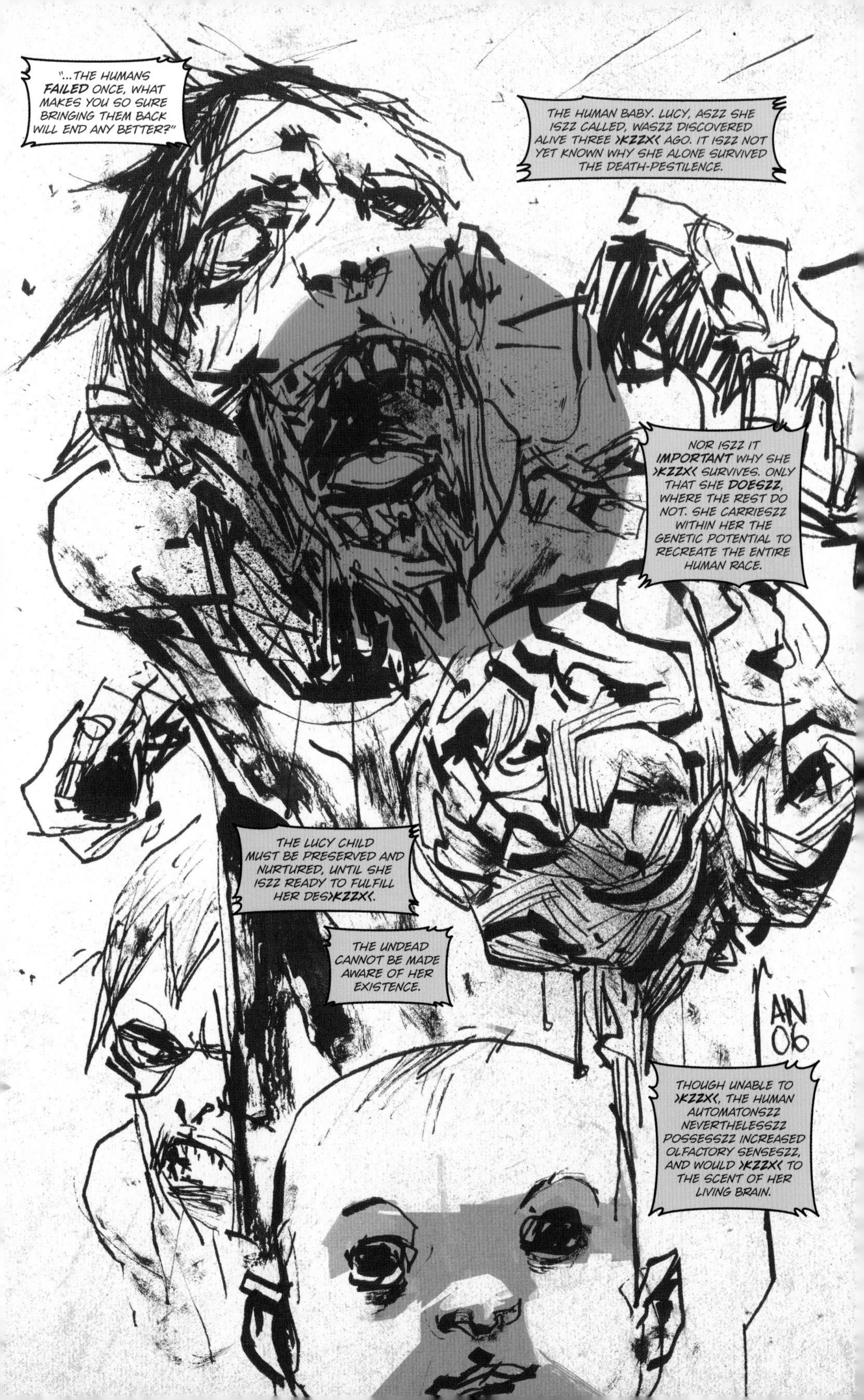
"...THE HUMANS FAILED ONCE, WHAT MAKES YOU SO SURE BRINGING THEM BACK WILL END ANY BETTER?"
THE HUMAN BABY. LUCY, ASZZ SHE ISZZ CALLED, WASZZ DISCOVERED ALIVE THREE ›KZZX‹ AGO. IT ISZZ NOT YET KNOWN WHY SHE ALONE SURVIVED THE DEATH-PESTILENCE.
NOR ISZZ IT IMPORTANT WHY SHE ›KZZX‹ SURVIVES. ONLY THAT SHE DOESZZ, WHERE THE REST DO NOT. SHE CARRIESZZ WITHIN HER THE GENETIC POTENTIAL TO RECREATE THE ENTIRE HUMAN RACE.
THE LUCY CHILD MUST BE PRESERVED AND NURTURED, UNTIL SHE ISZZ READY TO FULFILL HER DES›KZZX‹.
THE UNDEAD CANNOT BE MADE AWARE OF HER EXISTENCE.
AN 06
THOUGH UNABLE TO ›KZZX‹, THE HUMAN AUTOMATONSZZ NEVERTHELESSZZ POSSESSZZ INCREASED OLFACTORY SENSESZZ, AND WOULD ›KZZX‹ TO THE SCENT OF HER LIVING BRAIN.

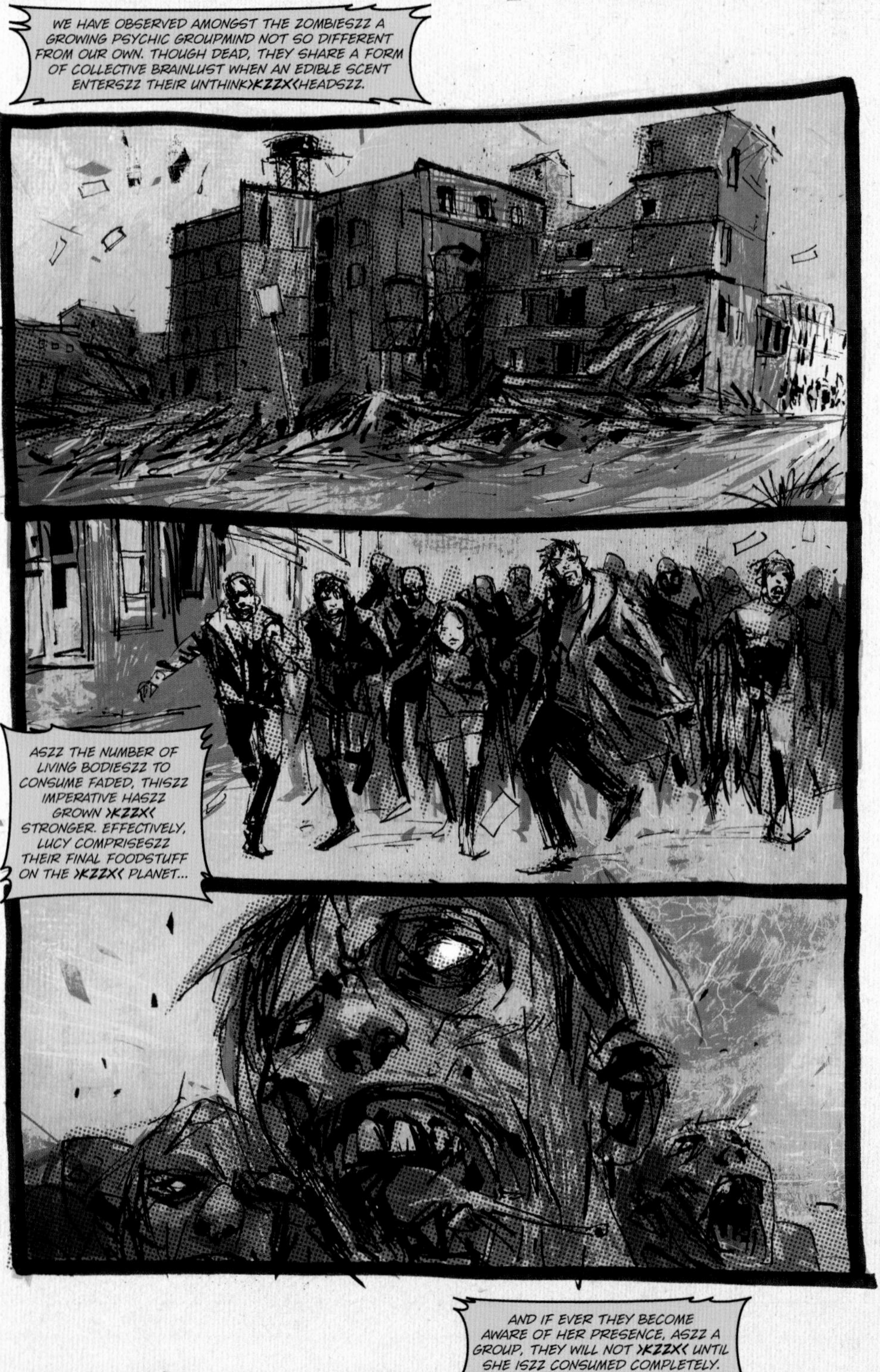
WE HAVE OBSERVED AMONGST THE ZOMBIESZZ A GROWING PSYCHIC GROUPMIND NOT SO DIFFERENT FROM OUR OWN. THOUGH DEAD, THEY SHARE A FORM OF COLLECTIVE BRAINLUST WHEN AN EDIBLE SCENT ENTERSZZ THEIR UNTHINK›KZZX‹HEADSZZ.
ASZZ THE NUMBER OF LIVING BODIESZZ TO CONSUME FADED, THISZZ IMPERATIVE HASZZ GROWN ›KZZX‹ STRONGER. EFFECTIVELY, LUCY COMPRISESZZ THEIR FINAL FOODSTUFF ON THE ›KZZX‹ PLANET...
AND IF EVER THEY BECOME AWARE OF HER PRESENCE, ASZZ A GROUP, THEY WILL NOT ›KZZX‹ UNTIL SHE ISZZ CONSUMED COMPLETELY.

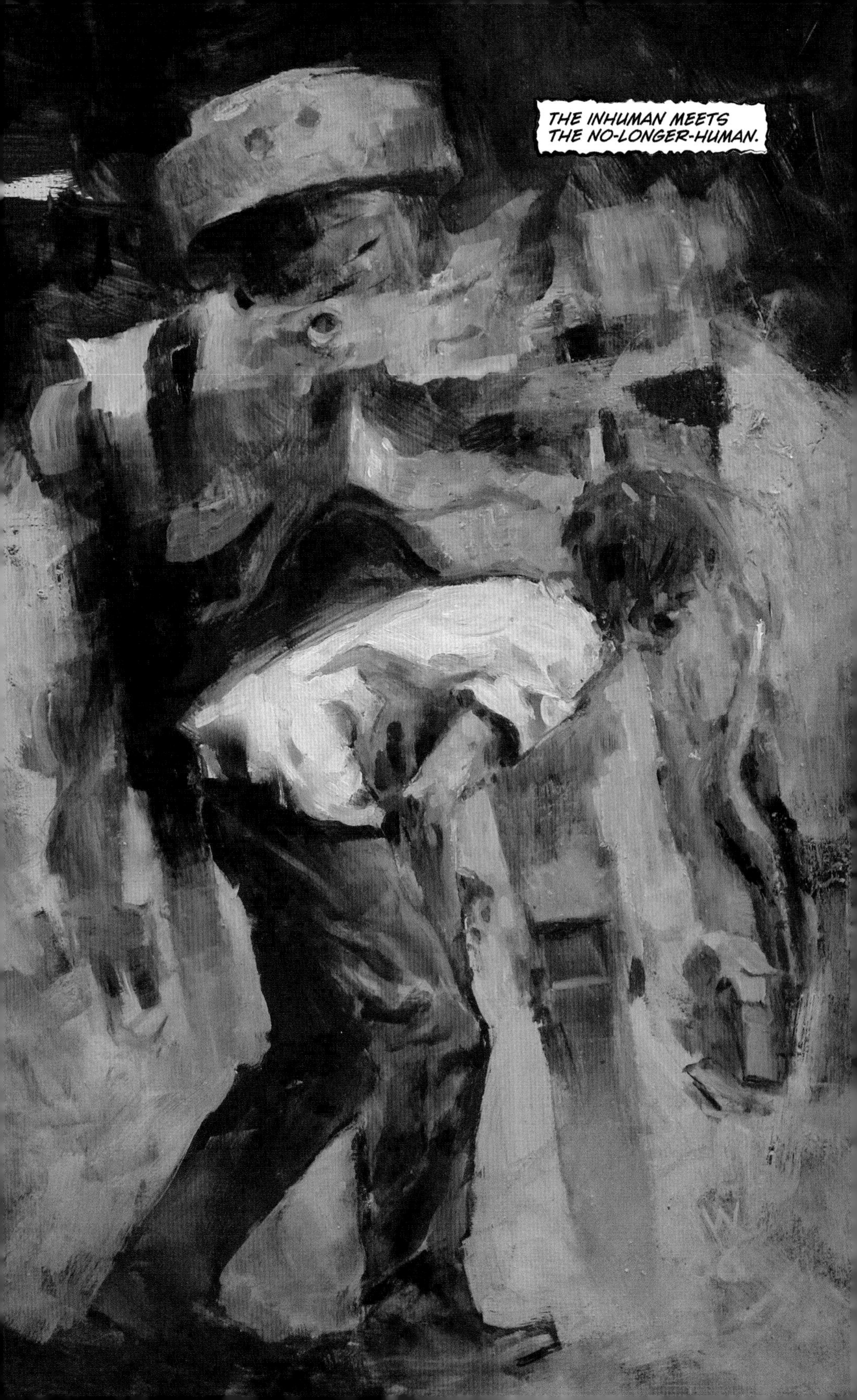
THE INHUMAN MEETS
THE NO-LONGER-HUMAN.

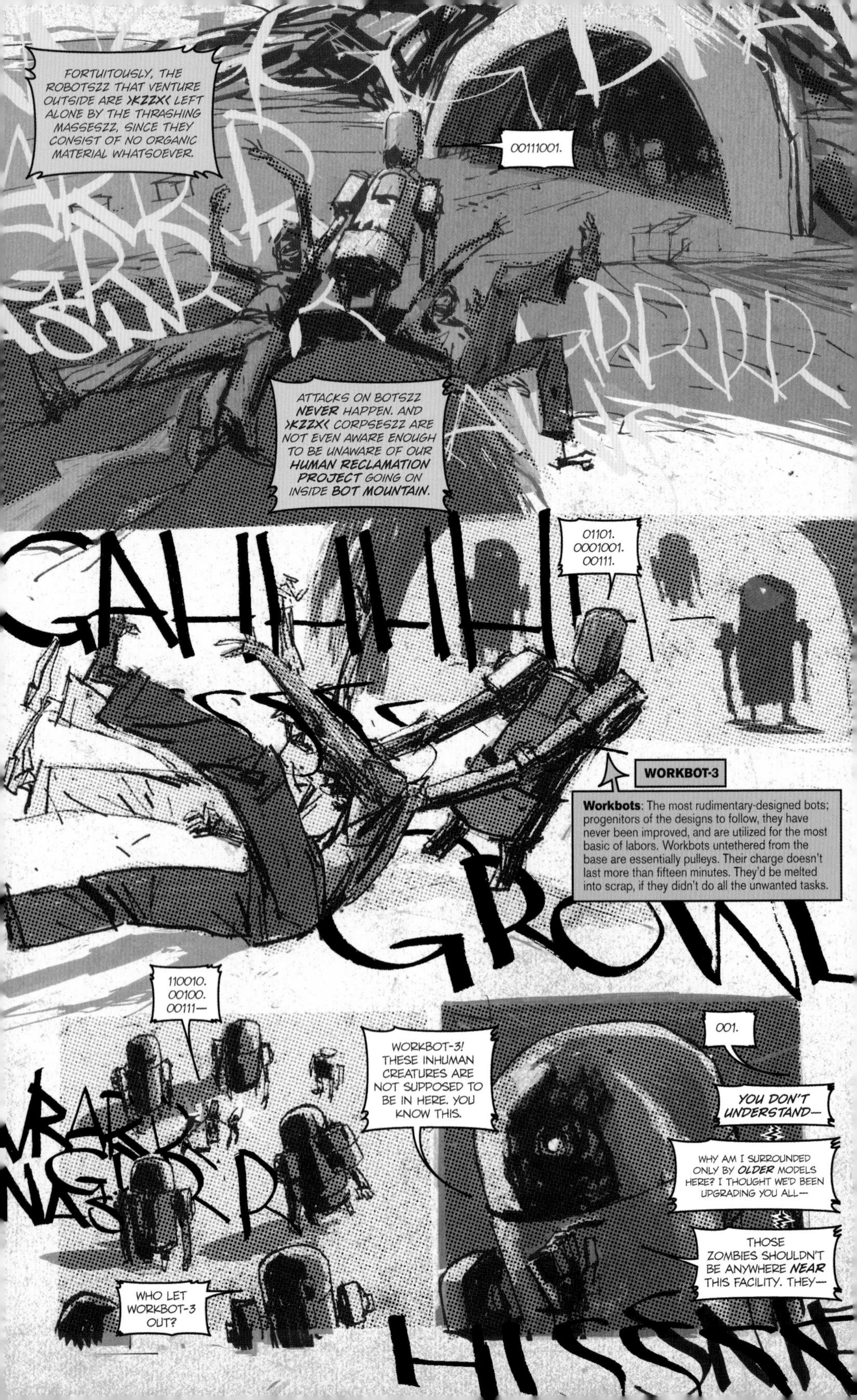
FORTUITOUSLY, THE ROBOTSZZ THAT VENTURE OUTSIDE ARE >KZZX< LEFT ALONE BY THE THRASHING MASSESZZ, SINCE THEY CONSIST OF NO ORGANIC MATERIAL WHATSOEVER.
00111001.
ATTACKS ON BOTSZZ NEVER HAPPEN. AND >KZZX< CORPSESZZ ARE NOT EVEN AWARE ENOUGH TO BE UNAWARE OF OUR HUMAN RECLAMATION PROJECT GOING ON INSIDE BOT MOUNTAIN.
01101. 0001001. 00111.
WORKBOT-3
Workbots: The most rudimentary-designed bots; progenitors of the designs to follow, they have never been improved, and are utilized for the most basic of labors. Workbots untethered from the base are essentially pulleys. Their charge doesn't last more than fifteen minutes. They'd be melted into scrap, if they didn't do all the unwanted tasks.
GROWL
110010. 00100. 00111—
WORKBOT-3! THESE INHUMAN CREATURES ARE NOT SUPPOSED TO BE IN HERE. YOU KNOW THIS.
WHO LET WORKBOT-3 OUT?
001.
YOU DON'T UNDERSTAND—
WHY AM I SURROUNDED ONLY BY OLDER MODELS HERE? I THOUGHT WE'D BEEN UPGRADING YOU ALL—
THOSE ZOMBIES SHOULDN'T BE ANYWHERE NEAR THIS FACILITY. THEY—

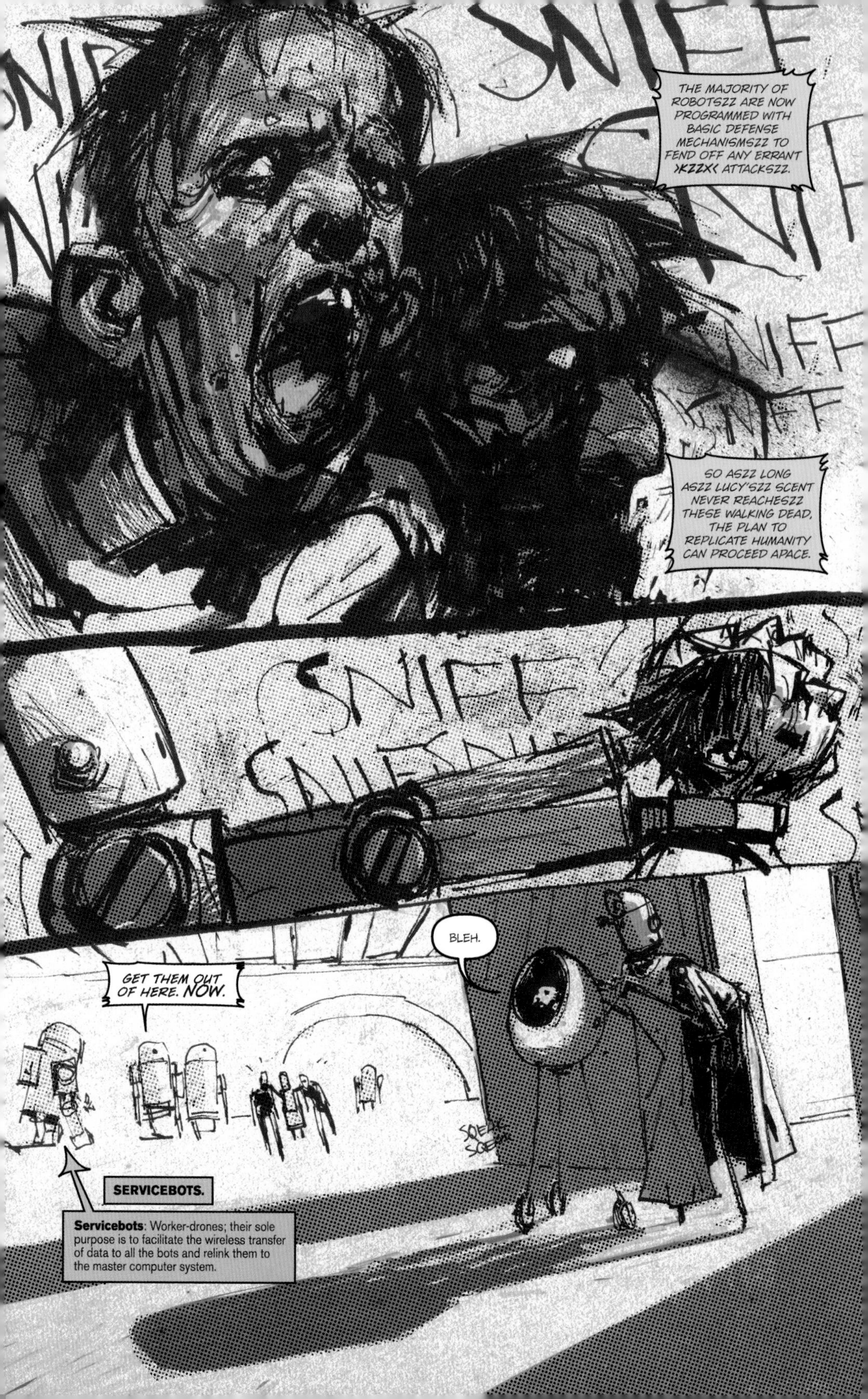

SNIFF
THE MAJORITY OF ROBOTSZZ ARE NOW PROGRAMMED WITH BASIC DEFENSE MECHANISMSZZ TO FEND OFF ANY ERRANT >KZZX< ATTACKSZZ.
SNIFF
SO ASZZ LONG ASZZ LUCY'SZZ SCENT NEVER REACHESZZ THESE WALKING DEAD, THE PLAN TO REPLICATE HUMANITY CAN PROCEED APACE.
SNIFF
BLEH.
GET THEM OUT OF HERE. NOW.
SERVICEBOTS.
Servicebots: Worker-drones; their sole purpose is to facilitate the wireless transfer of data to all the bots and relink them to the master computer system.

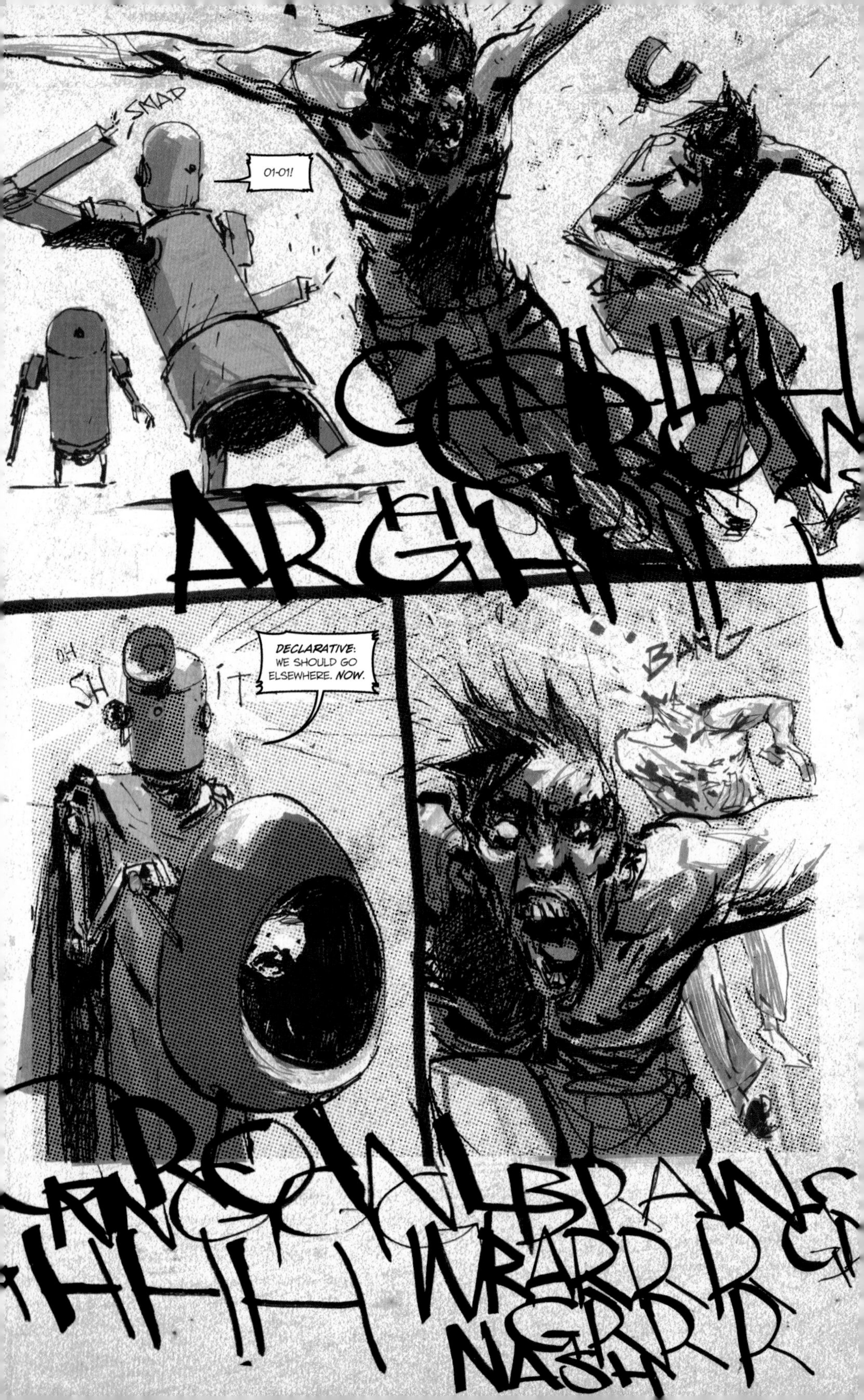
SNAP
01-01!
ARGH
OH SHIT
DECLARATIVE: WE SHOULD GO ELSEWHERE. NOW.

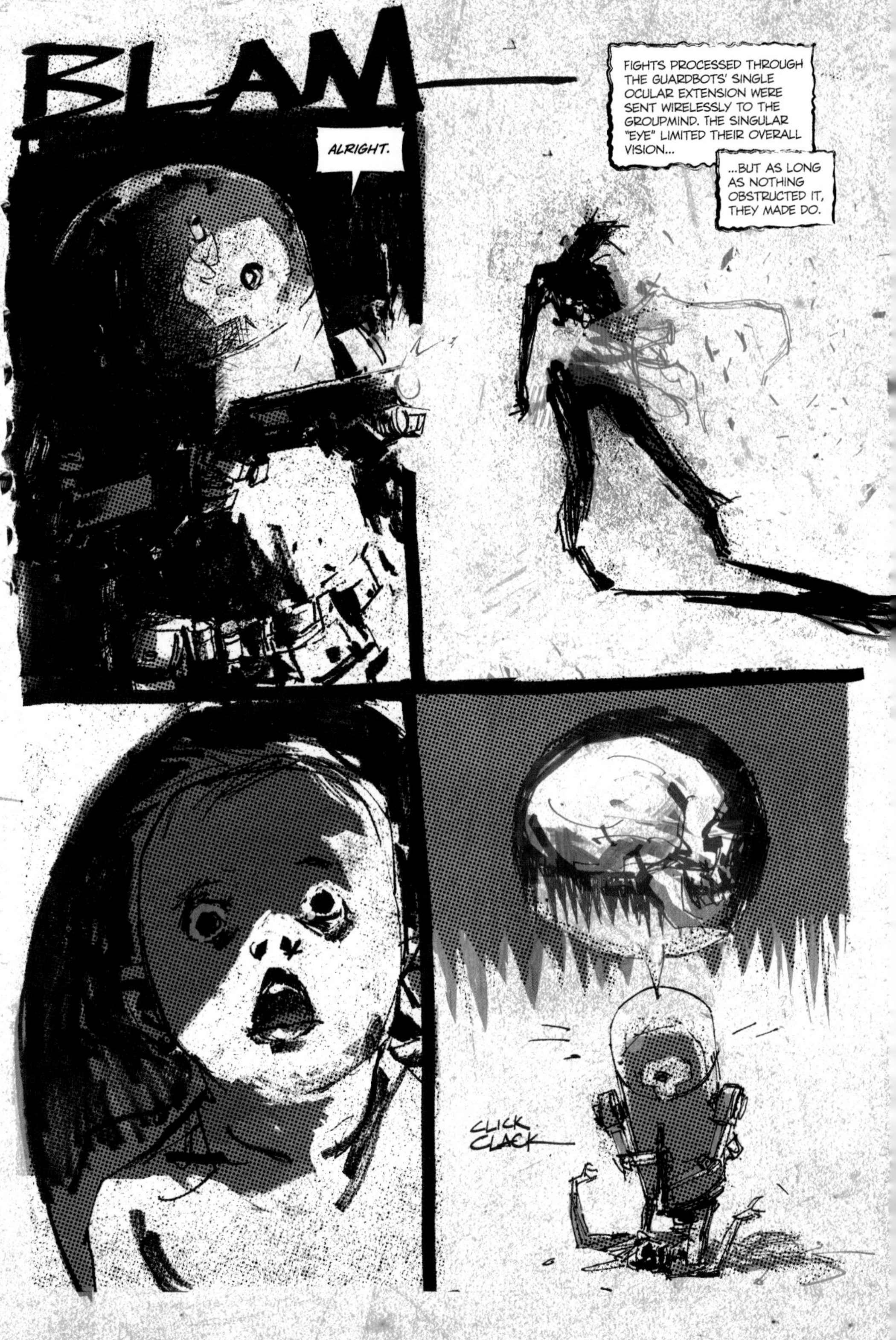
BLAM
ALRIGHT.
FIGHTS PROCESSED THROUGH THE GUARDBOTS' SINGLE OCULAR EXTENSION WERE SENT WIRELESSLY TO THE GROUPMIND. THE SINGULAR "EYE" LIMITED THEIR OVERALL VISION...
...BUT AS LONG AS NOTHING OBSTRUCTED IT, THEY MADE DO.
CLICK CLACK

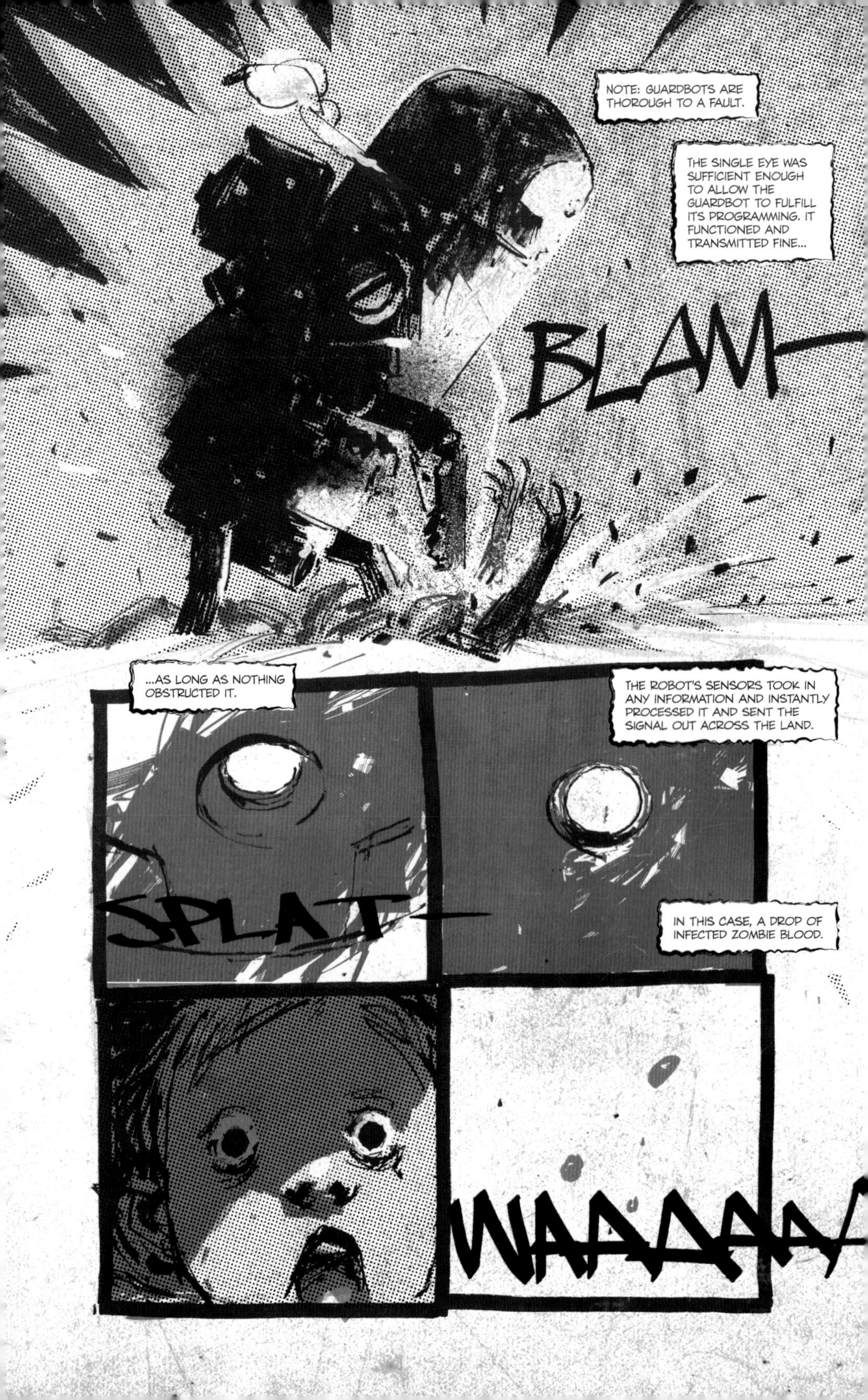
NOTE: GUARDBOTS ARE THOROUGH TO A FAULT.
THE SINGLE EYE WAS SUFFICIENT ENOUGH TO ALLOW THE GUARDBOT TO FULFILL ITS PROGRAMMING. IT FUNCTIONED AND TRANSMITTED FINE...
BLAM
...AS LONG AS NOTHING OBSTRUCTED IT.
SPLAT
THE ROBOT'S SENSORS TOOK IN ANY INFORMATION AND INSTANTLY PROCESSED IT AND SENT THE SIGNAL OUT ACROSS THE LAND.
IN THIS CASE, A DROP OF INFECTED ZOMBIE BLOOD.
WAAAAA

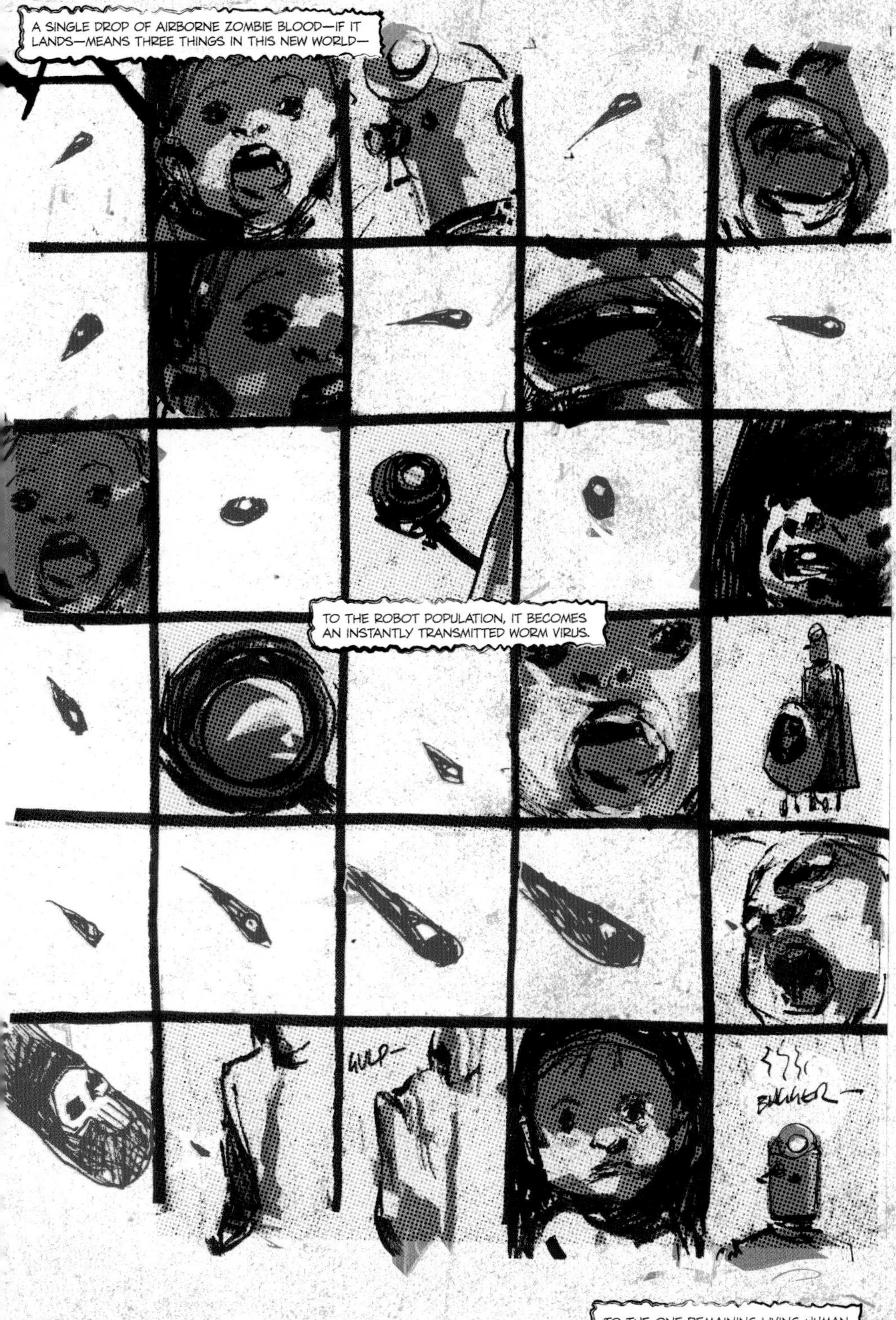
A SINGLE DROP OF AIRBORNE ZOMBIE BLOOD—IF IT LANDS—MEANS THREE THINGS IN THIS NEW WORLD—
TO THE ROBOT POPULATION, IT BECOMES AN INSTANTLY TRANSMITTED WORM VIRUS.
GULP—
BUGGER—
TO THE ONE REMAINING LIVING HUMAN, IT'S ACCIDENTALLY INGESTED DEATH.

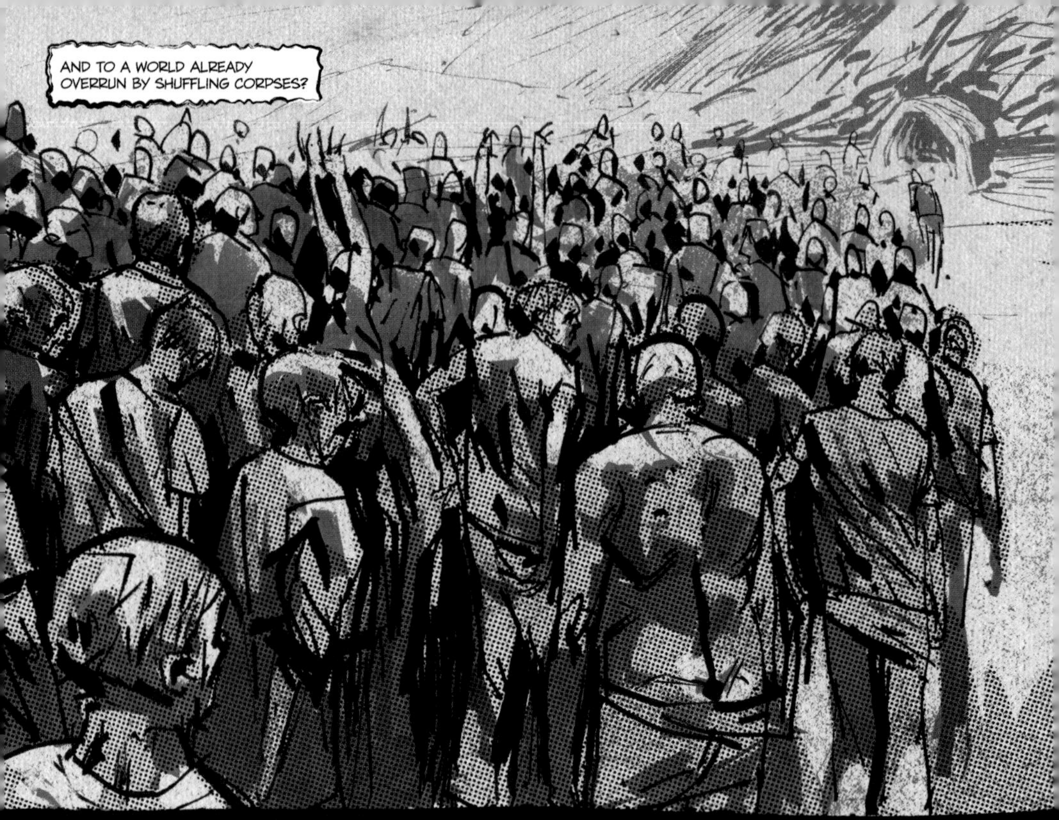
AND TO A WORLD ALREADY OVERRUN BY SHUFFLING CORPSES?

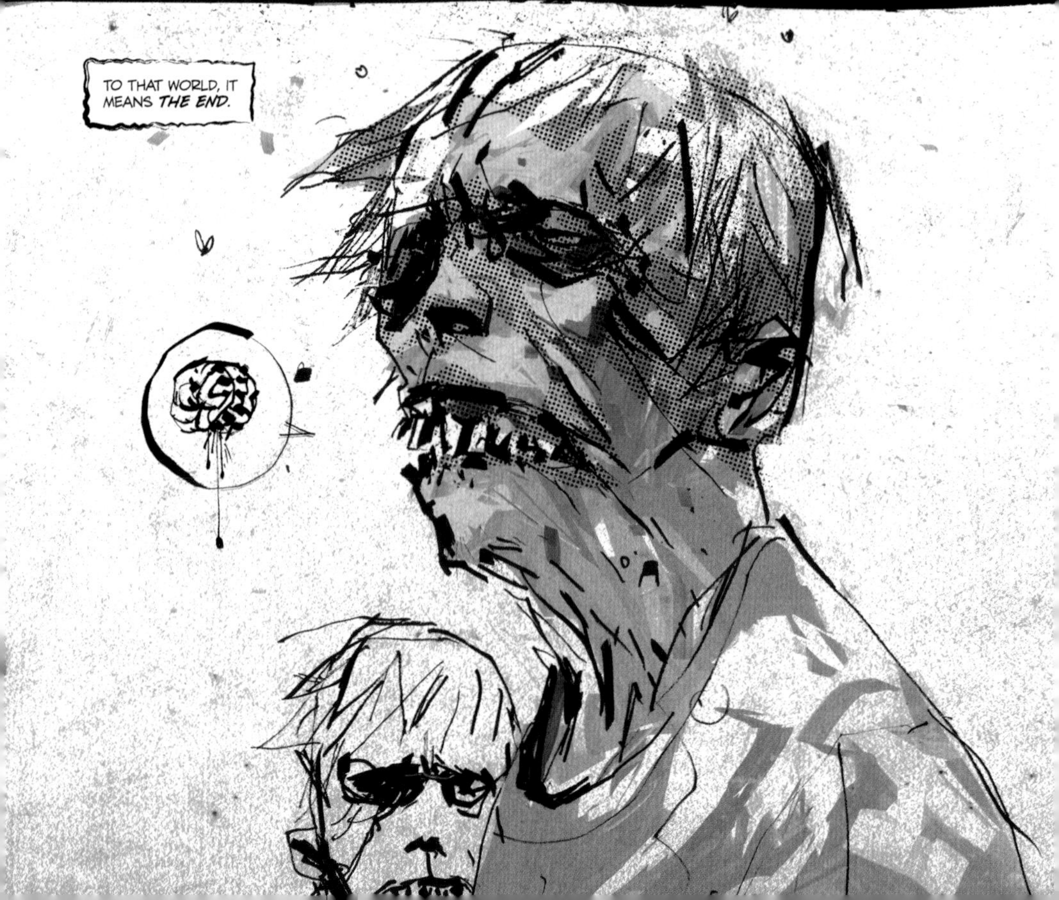
TO THAT WORLD, IT MEANS *THE END*.

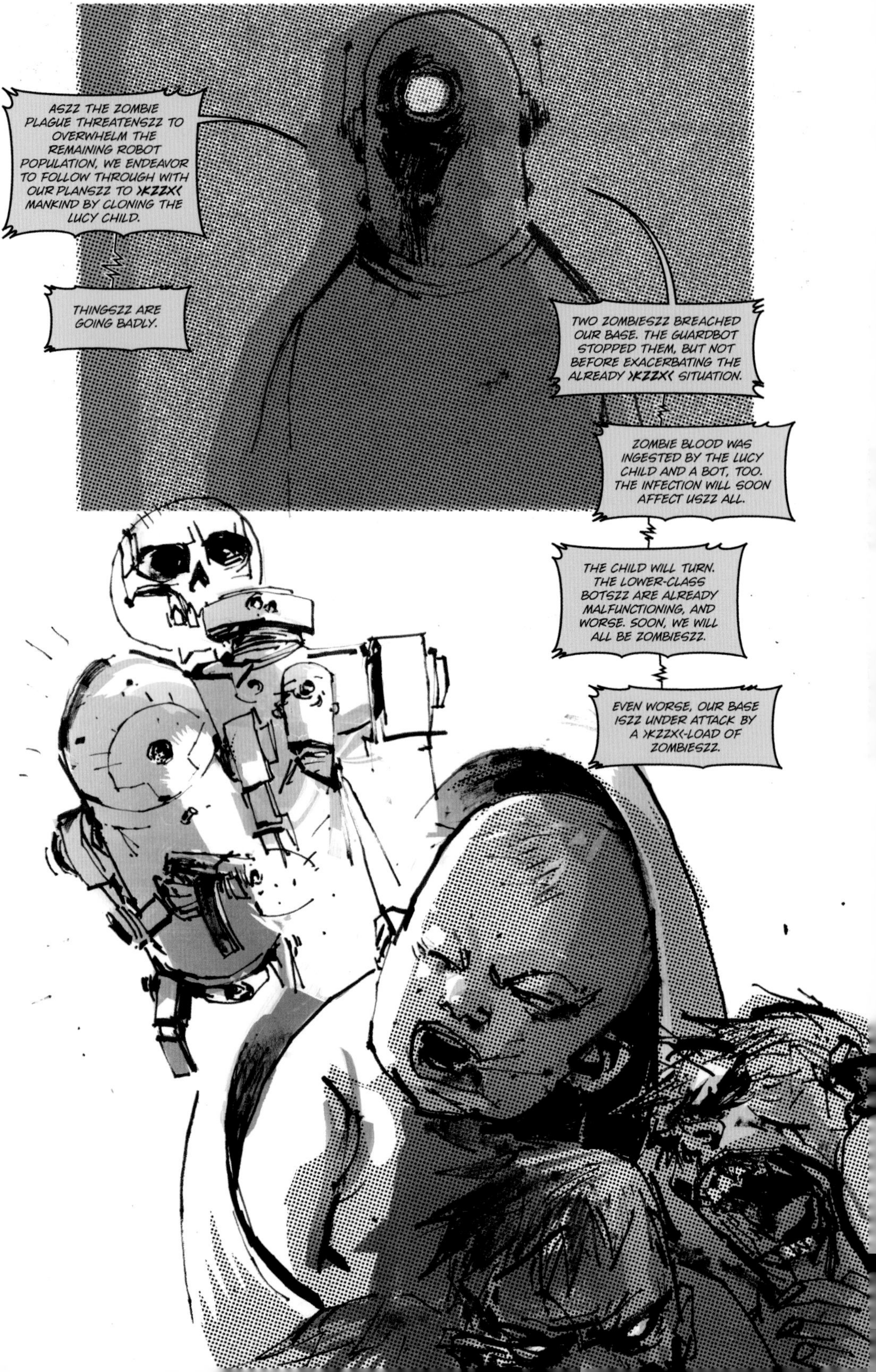
ASZZ THE ZOMBIE PLAGUE THREATENSZZ TO OVERWHELM THE REMAINING ROBOT POPULATION, WE ENDEAVOR TO FOLLOW THROUGH WITH OUR PLANSZZ TO ›KZZX‹ MANKIND BY CLONING THE LUCY CHILD.
THINGSZZ ARE GOING BADLY.
TWO ZOMBIESZZ BREACHED OUR BASE. THE GUARDBOT STOPPED THEM, BUT NOT BEFORE EXACERBATING THE ALREADY ›KZZX‹ SITUATION.
ZOMBIE BLOOD WAS INGESTED BY THE LUCY CHILD AND A BOT, TOO. THE INFECTION WILL SOON AFFECT USZZ ALL.
THE CHILD WILL TURN. THE LOWER-CLASS BOTSZZ ARE ALREADY MALFUNCTIONING, AND WORSE. SOON, WE WILL ALL BE ZOMBIESZZ.
EVEN WORSE, OUR BASE ISZZ UNDER ATTACK BY A ›KZZX‹-LOAD OF ZOMBIESZZ.

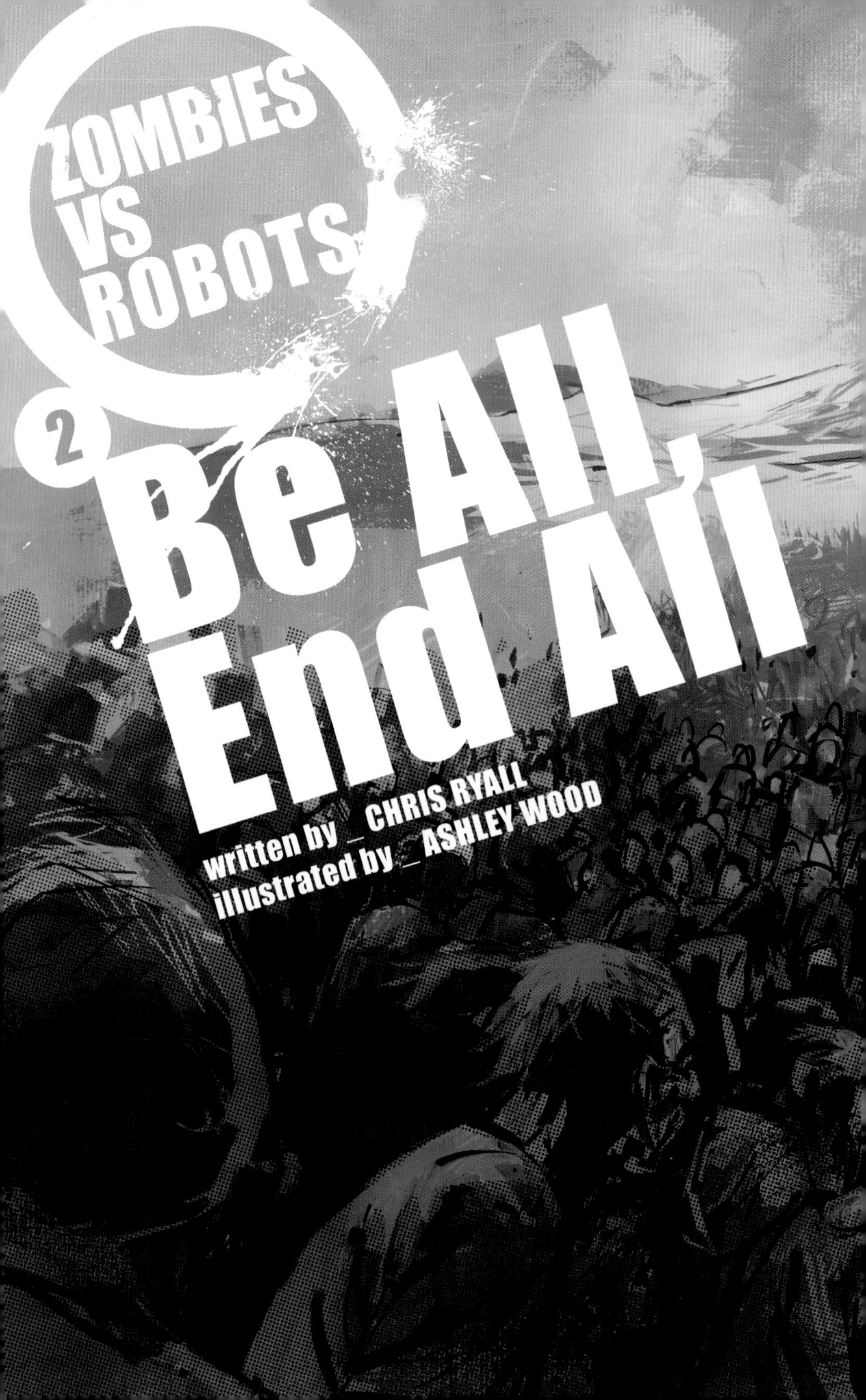
ZOMBIES
VS
ROBOTS
2
Be All,
End All
written by _ CHRIS RYALL
illustrated by _ ASHLEY WOOD

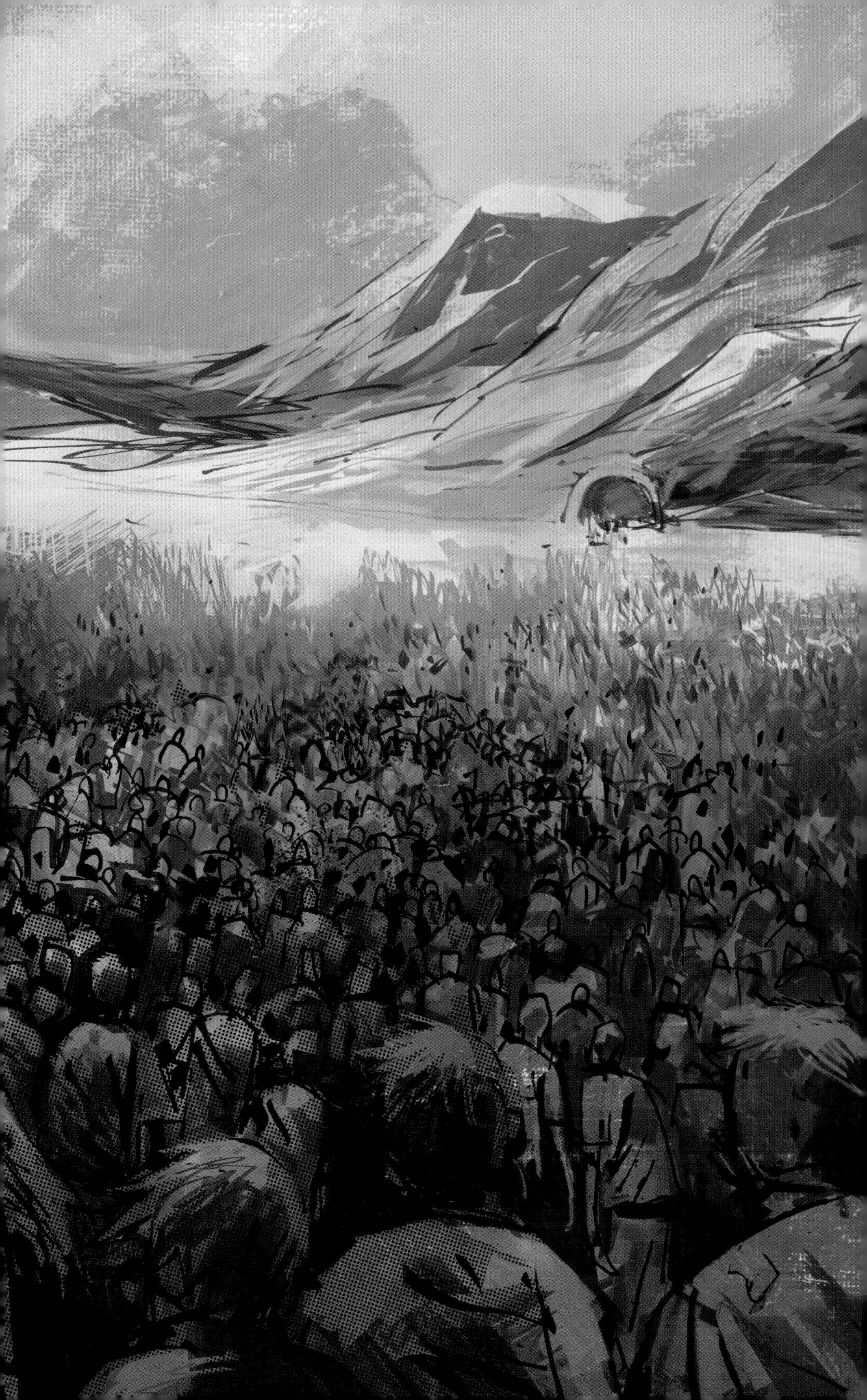

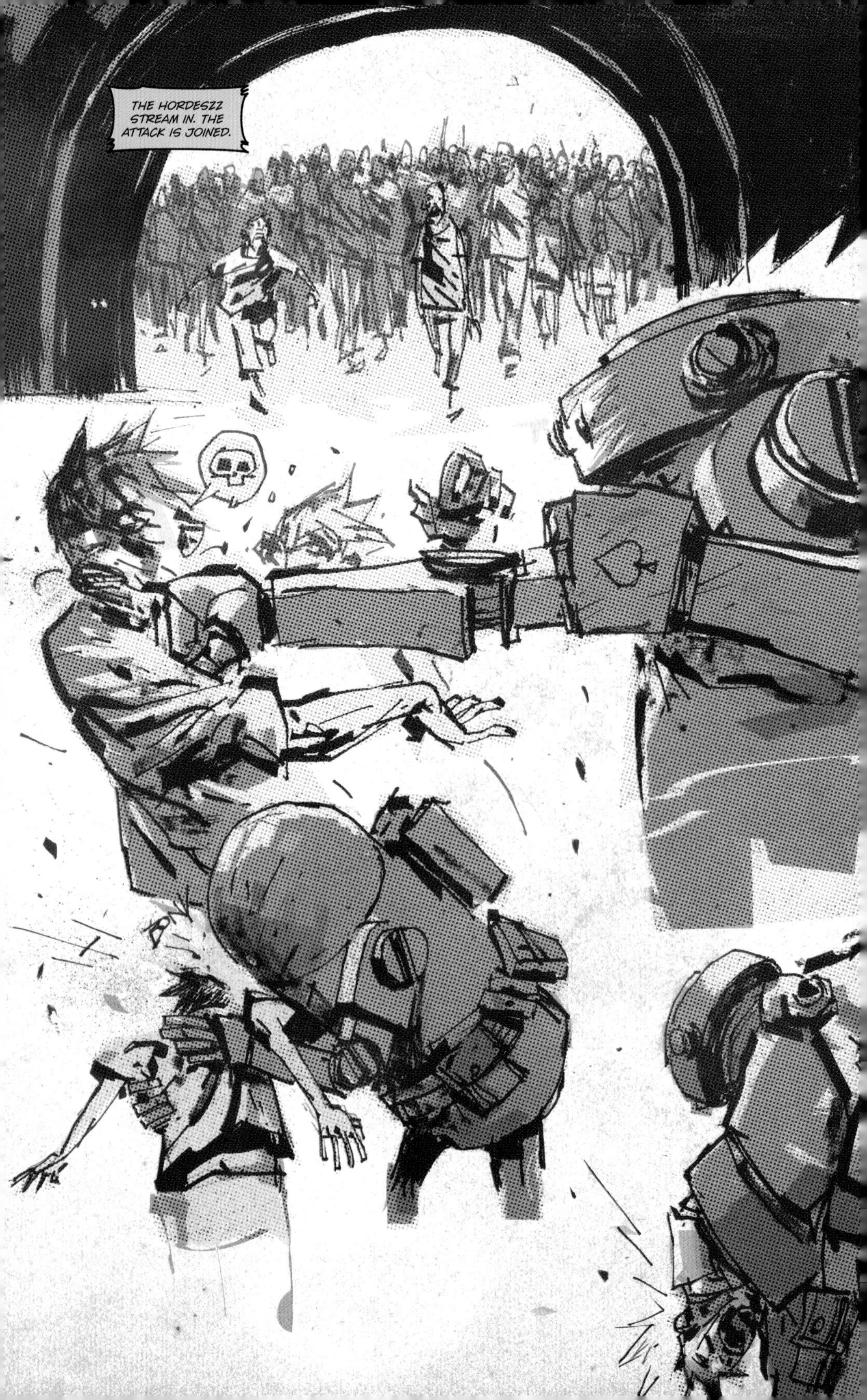
THE HORDESZZ STREAM IN. THE ATTACK IS JOINED.

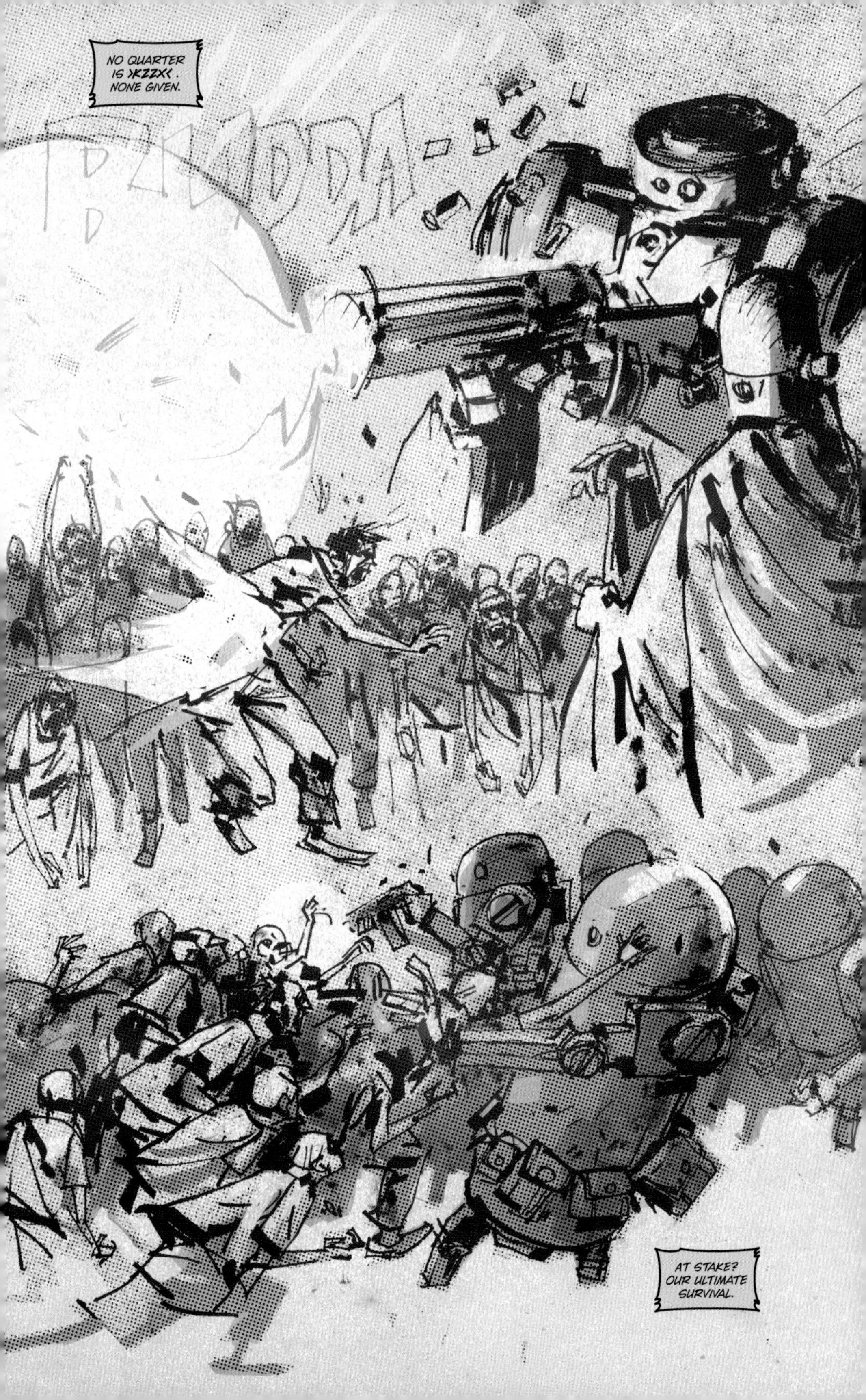
NO QUARTER IS >KZZX< . NONE GIVEN.
AT STAKE? OUR ULTIMATE SURVIVAL.

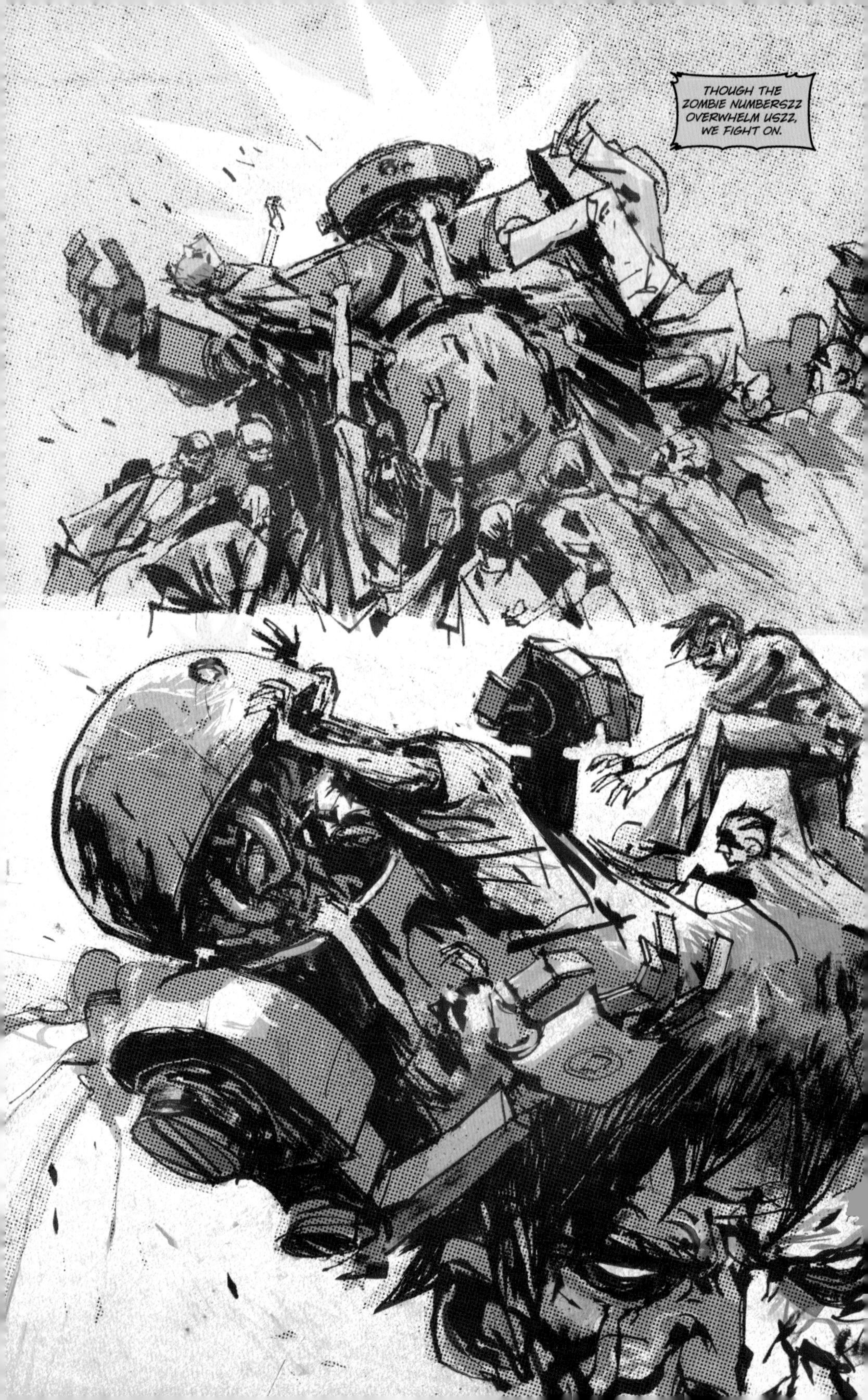
THOUGH THE ZOMBIE NUMBERSZZ OVERWHELM USZZ, WE FIGHT ON.

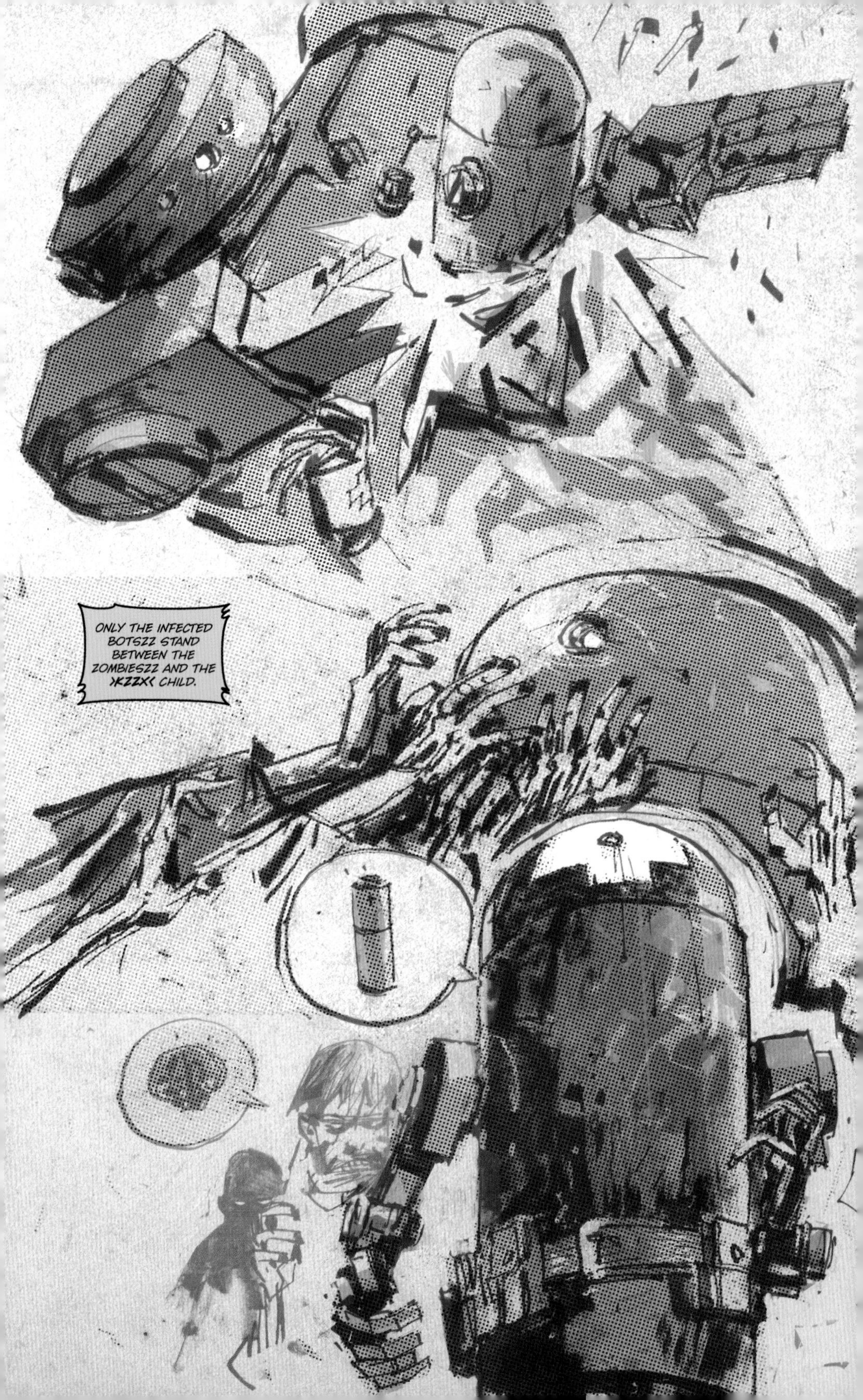
ONLY THE INFECTED BOTSZZ STAND BETWEEN THE ZOMBIESZZ AND THE >KZZX< CHILD.

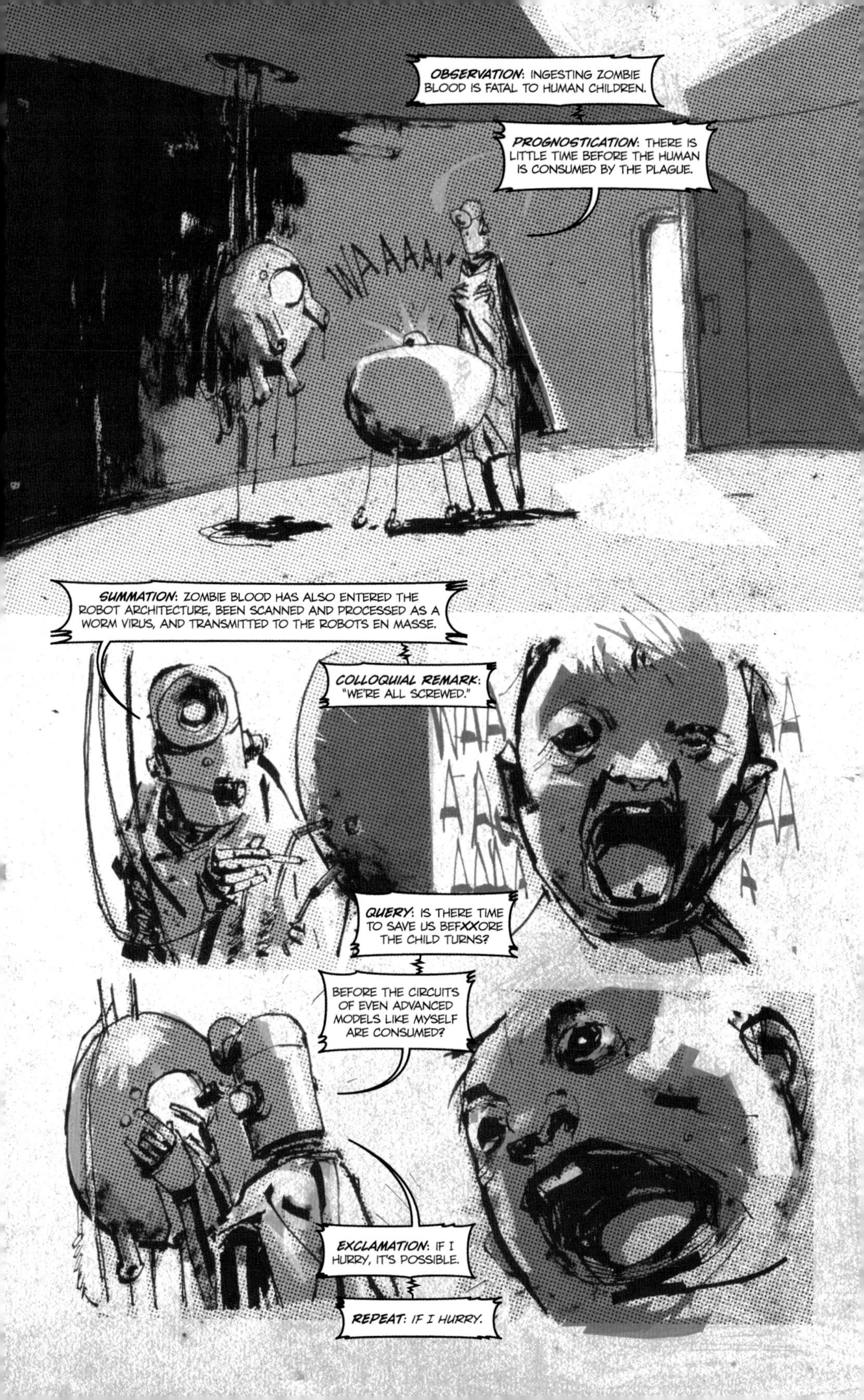
OBSERVATION: INGESTING ZOMBIE BLOOD IS FATAL TO HUMAN CHILDREN.
PROGNOSTICATION: THERE IS LITTLE TIME BEFORE THE HUMAN IS CONSUMED BY THE PLAGUE.
WAAAA
SUMMATION: ZOMBIE BLOOD HAS ALSO ENTERED THE ROBOT ARCHITECTURE, BEEN SCANNED AND PROCESSED AS A WORM VIRUS, AND TRANSMITTED TO THE ROBOTS EN MASSE.
COLLOQUIAL REMARK: "WE'RE ALL SCREWED."
QUERY: IS THERE TIME TO SAVE US BEFXXORE THE CHILD TURNS?
BEFORE THE CIRCUITS OF EVEN ADVANCED MODELS LIKE MYSELF ARE CONSUMED?
EXCLAMATION: IF I HURRY, IT'S POSSIBLE.
REPEAT: IF I HURRY.

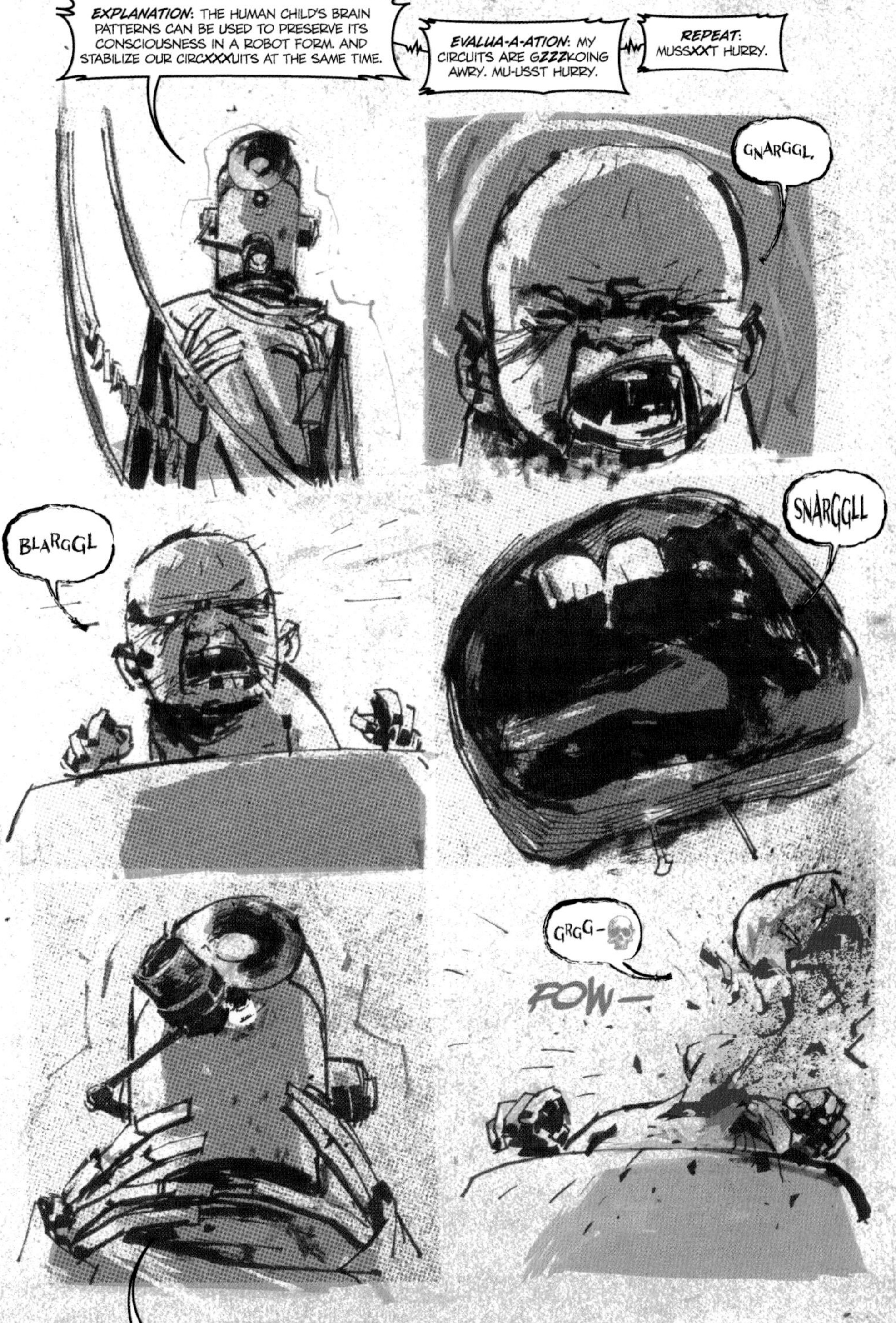
EXPLANATION: THE HUMAN CHILD'S BRAIN PATTERNS CAN BE USED TO PRESERVE ITS CONSCIOUSNESS IN A ROBOT FORM. AND STABILIZE OUR CIRCXXXUITS AT THE SAME TIME.
EVALUA-A-ATION: MY CIRCUITS ARE GZZZKOING AWRY. MU-USST HURRY.
REPEAT: MUSSXXT HURRY.
GNARGGL.
BLARGGL
SNARGGLL
GRGG-
POW—
REALIZATION: TOOLATETOOLA-TETOOLATEMUSTSTXXTOP—

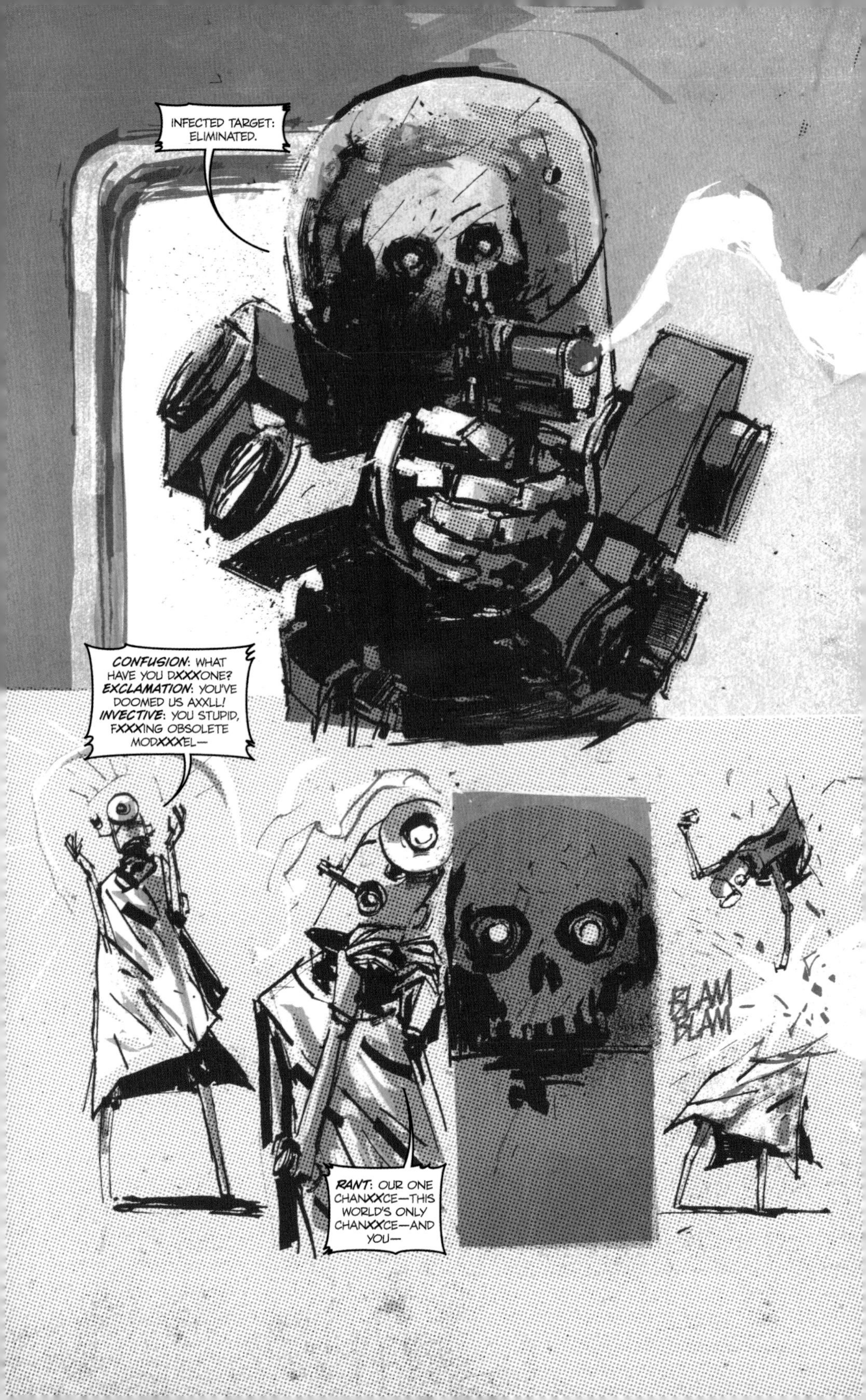
INFECTED TARGET: ELIMINATED.
CONFUSION: WHAT HAVE YOU DXXXONE? *EXCLAMATION*: YOU'VE DOOMED US AXXLL! *INVECTIVE*: YOU STUPID, FXXXING OBSOLETE MODXXXEL—
RANT: OUR ONE CHANXXCE—THIS WORLD'S ONLY CHANXXCE—AND YOU—
BLAM BLAM

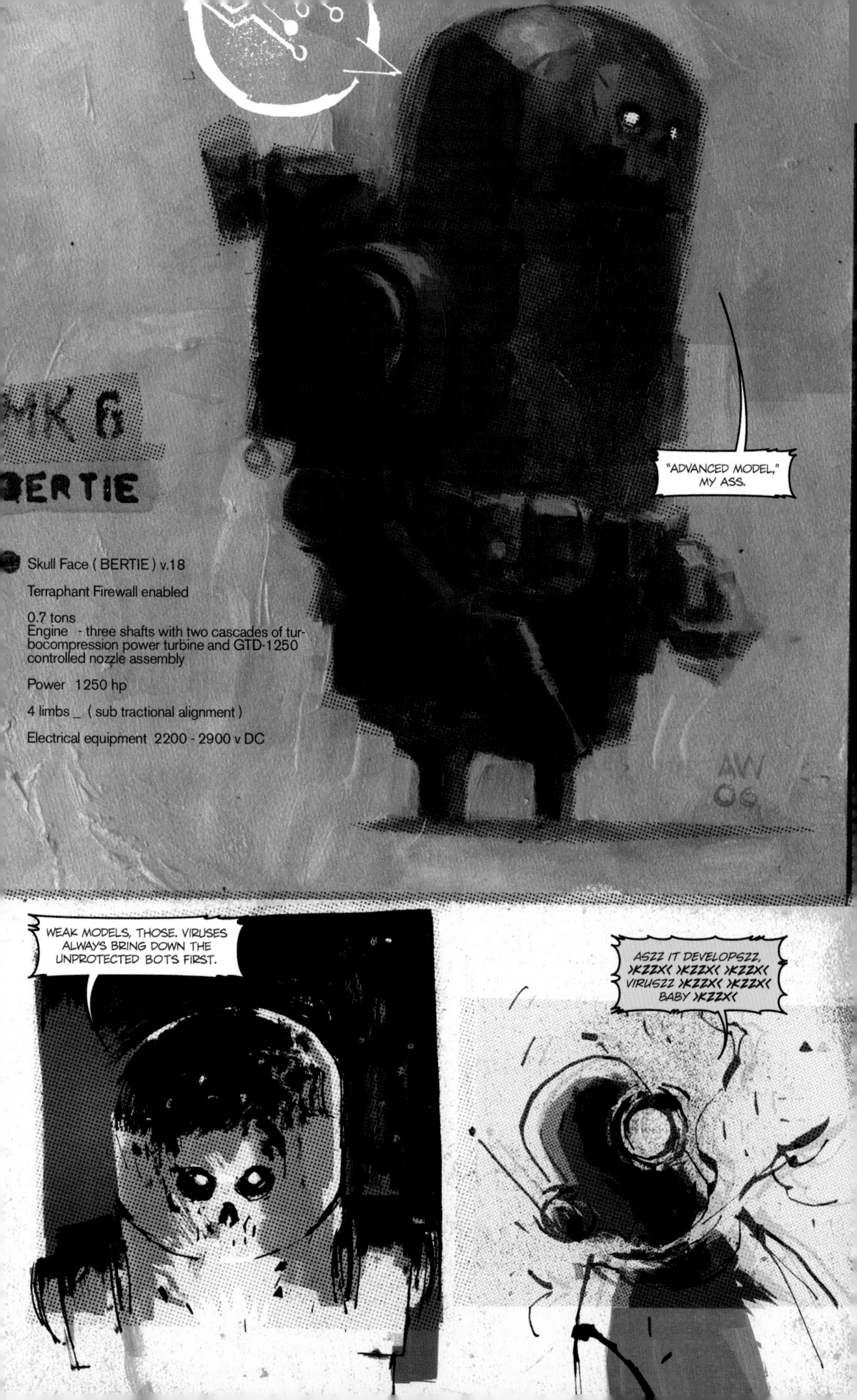
MK 6
BERTIE
Skull Face (BERTIE) v.18
Terraphant Firewall enabled
0.7 tons
Engine - three shafts with two cascades of turbocompression power turbine and GTD-1250 controlled nozzle assembly
Power 1250 hp
4 limbs _ (sub tractional alignment)
Electrical equipment 2200 - 2900 v DC
"ADVANCED MODEL," MY ASS.
AW 06
WEAK MODELS, THOSE. VIRUSES ALWAYS BRING DOWN THE UNPROTECTED BOTS FIRST.
ASZZ IT DEVELOPSZZ, >KZZX< >KZZX< >KZZX< VIRUSZZ >KZZX< >KZZX< BABY >KZZX<

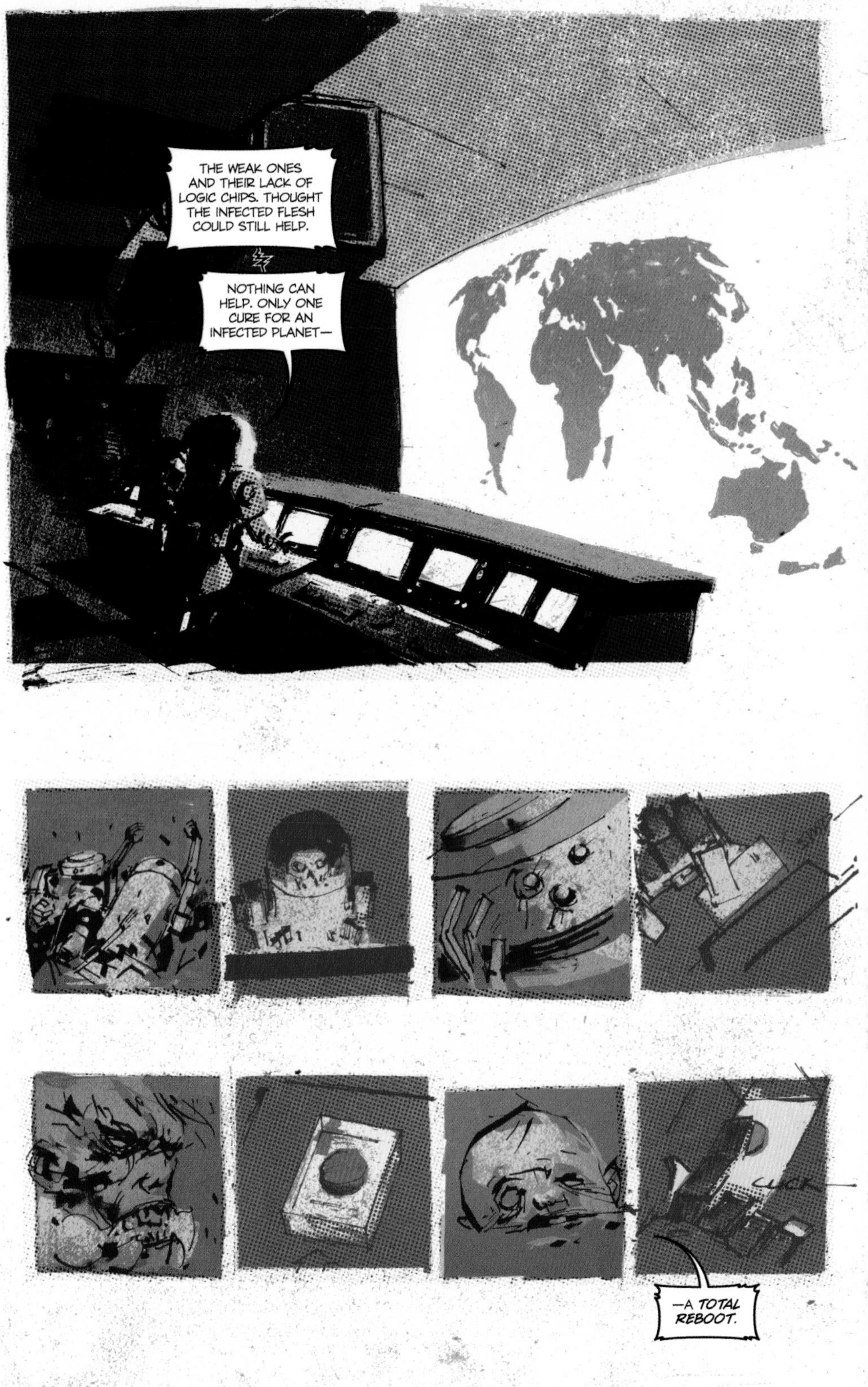
THE WEAK ONES AND THEIR LACK OF LOGIC CHIPS. THOUGHT THE INFECTED FLESH COULD STILL HELP.
NOTHING CAN HELP. ONLY ONE CURE FOR AN INFECTED PLANET—
CLICK
—A *TOTAL REBOOT*.

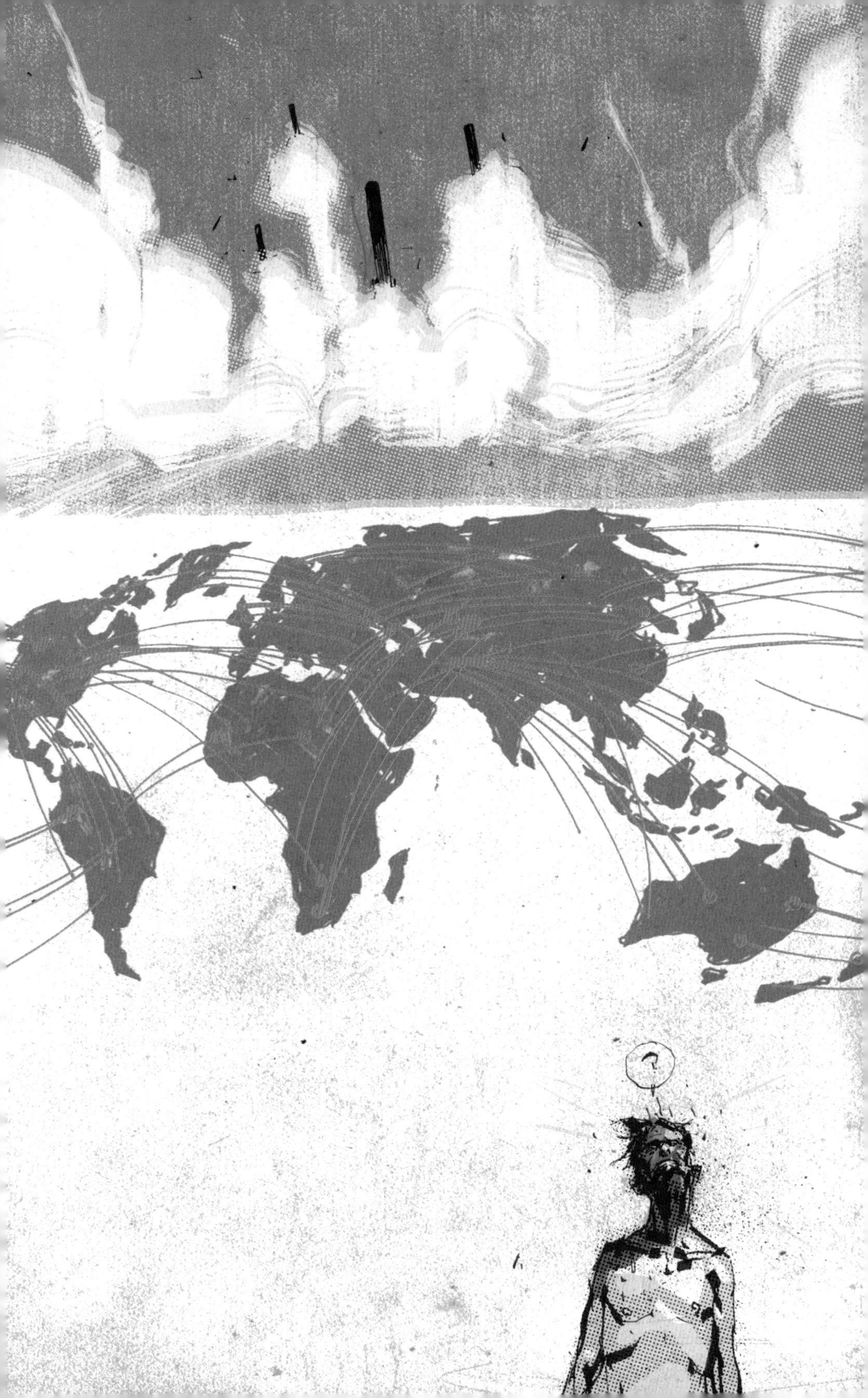
?

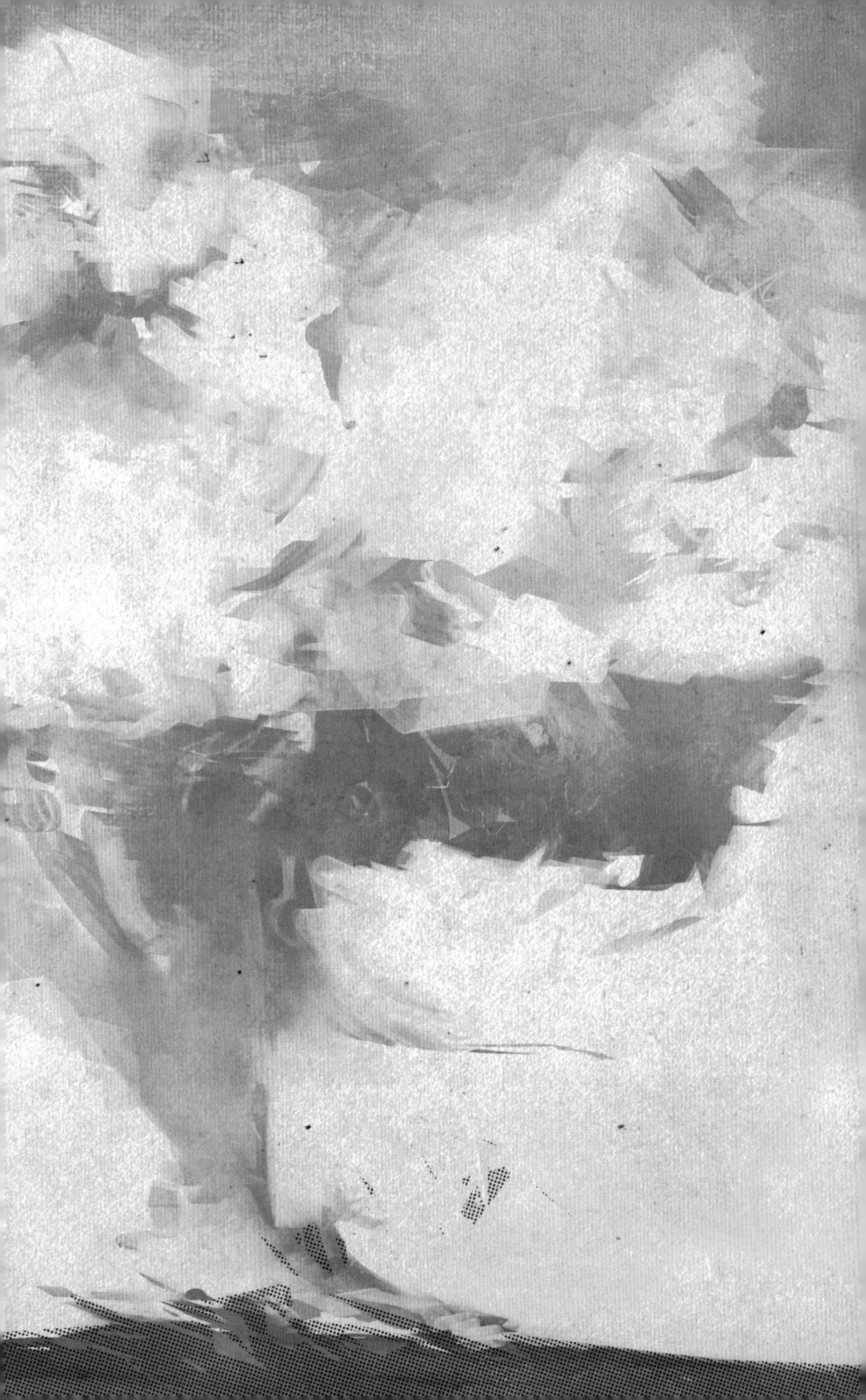

THERE ARE NO MORE NEWSBOTS TO REPORT ON THE PLANET-WIDE DEVASTATION.

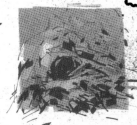

NO MORE DOCBOTS TO SAFEGUARD THE HUMANS.

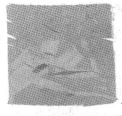

NO MORE HUMANS.

ZOMBIE, OR OTHERWISE.

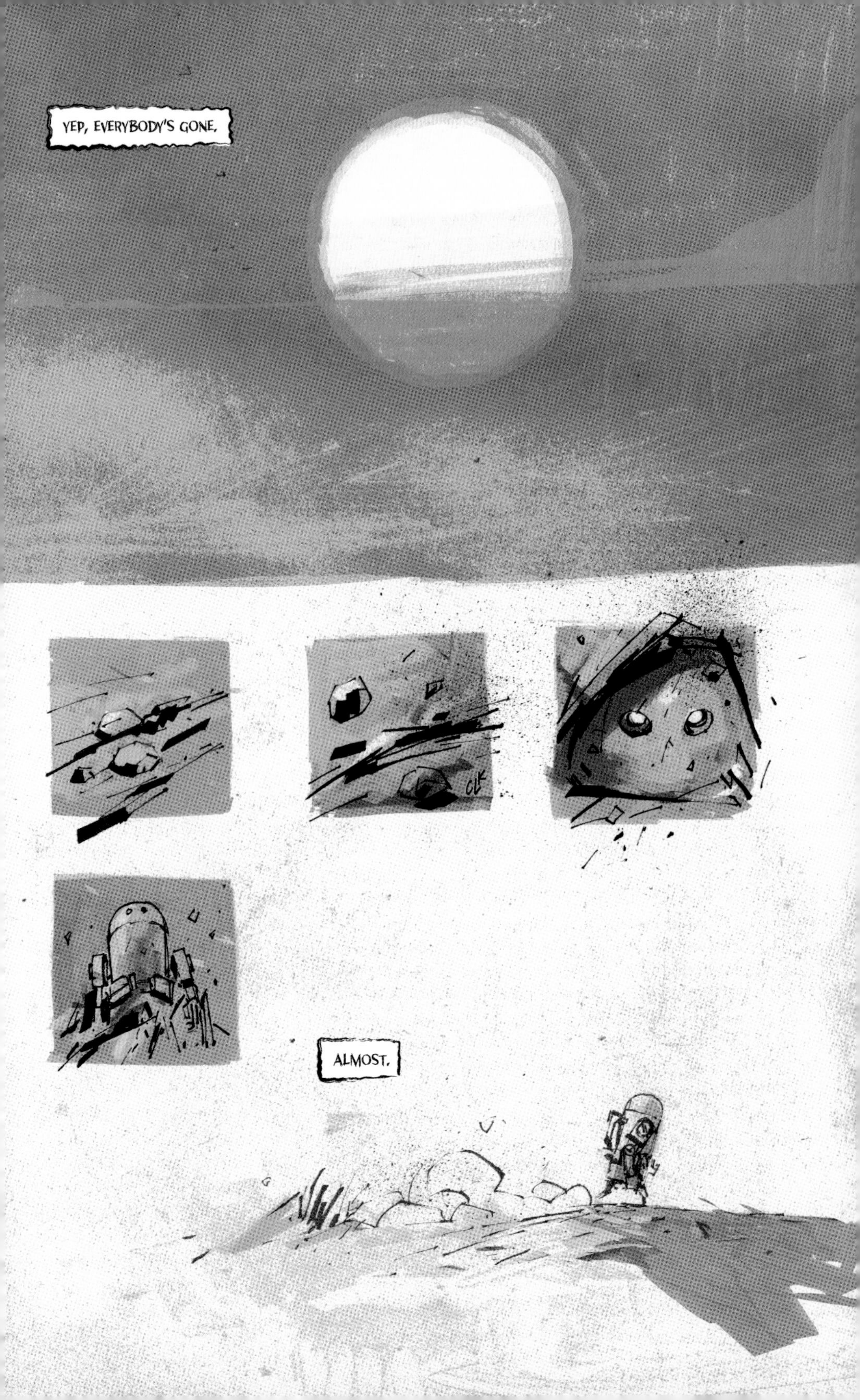
YEP, EVERYBODY'S GONE.
CLK
ALMOST.

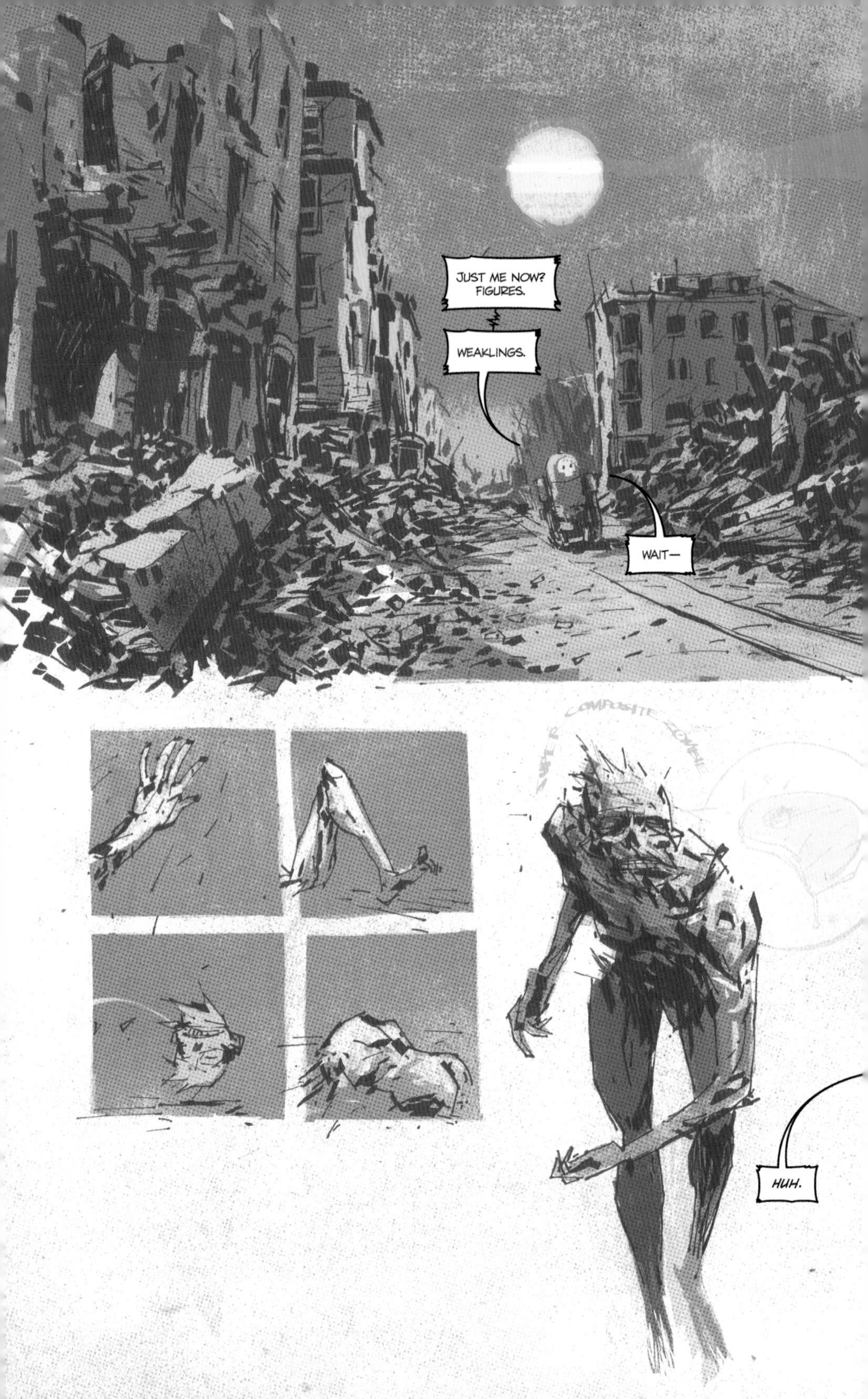
JUST ME NOW? FIGURES.
WEAKLINGS.
WAIT—
HUH.

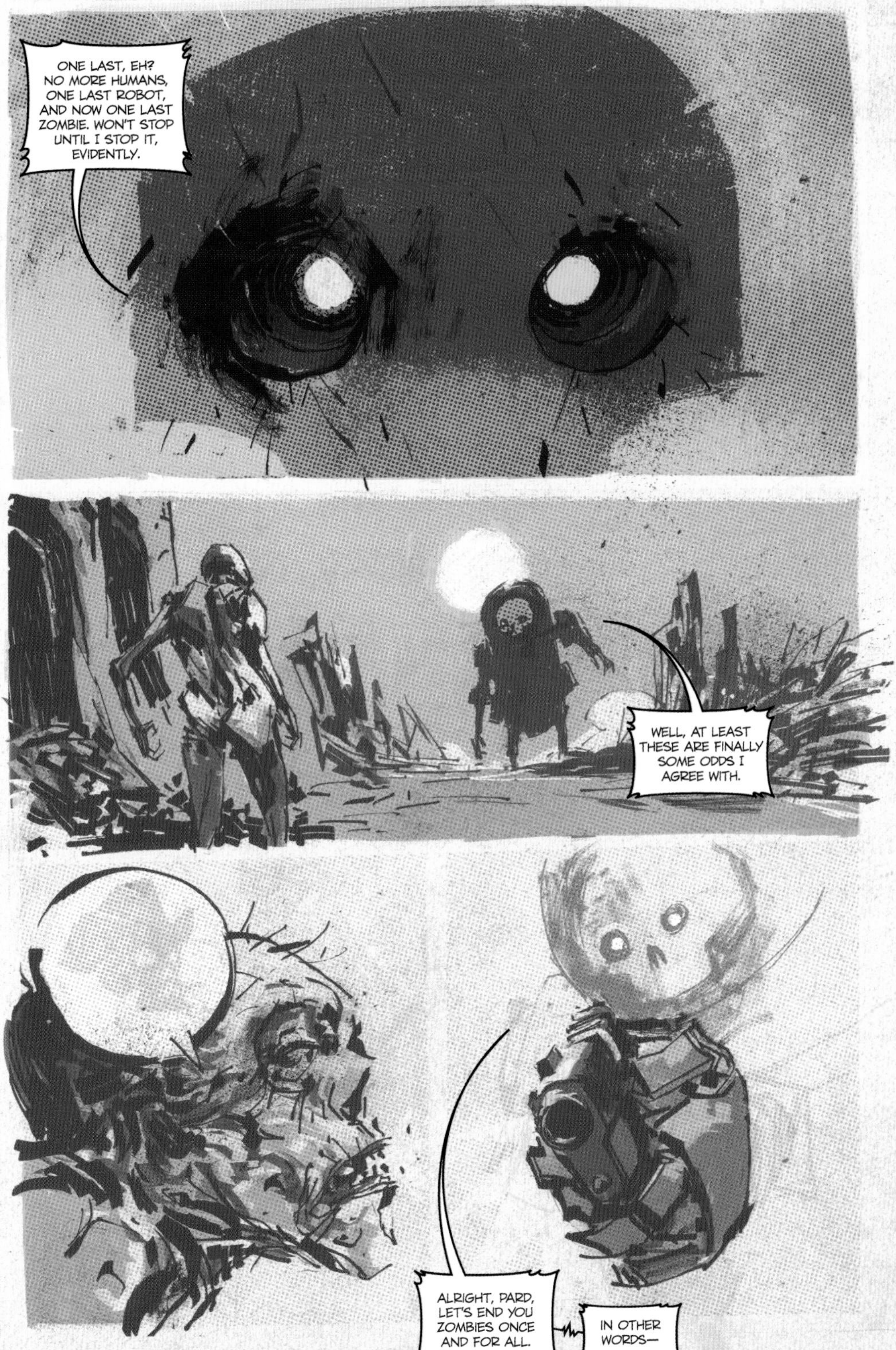
ONE LAST, EH? NO MORE HUMANS, ONE LAST ROBOT, AND NOW ONE LAST ZOMBIE. WON'T STOP UNTIL I STOP IT, EVIDENTLY.
WELL, AT LEAST THESE ARE FINALLY SOME ODDS I AGREE WITH.
ALRIGHT, PARD, LET'S END YOU ZOMBIES ONCE AND FOR ALL.
IN OTHER WORDS—

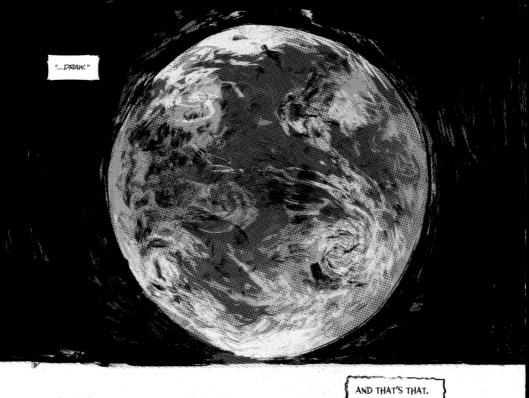

"...DRAW."

AND THAT'S THAT.

ER...

GLRRGGH

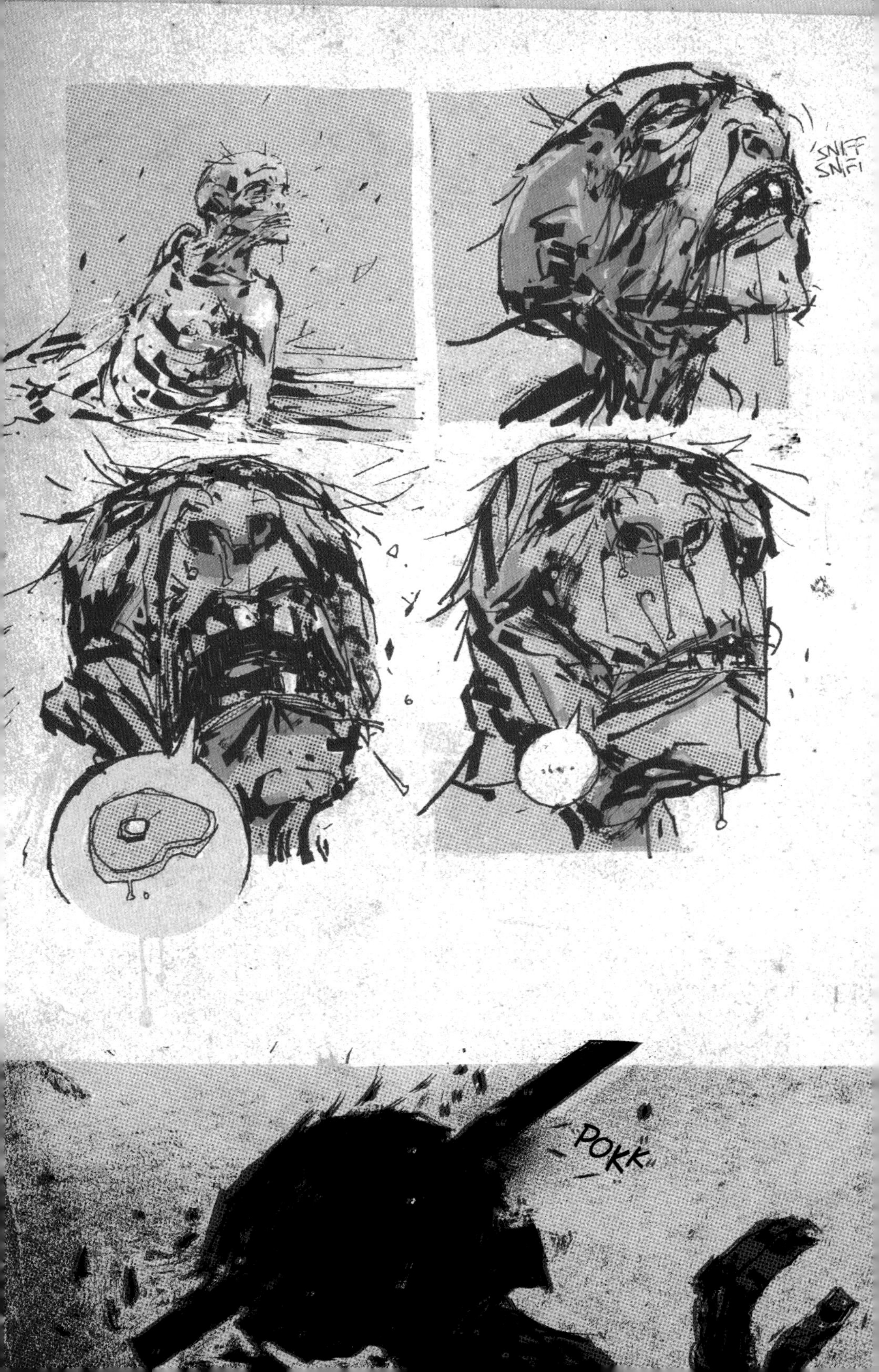
SNIFF
SNIFF
POKK

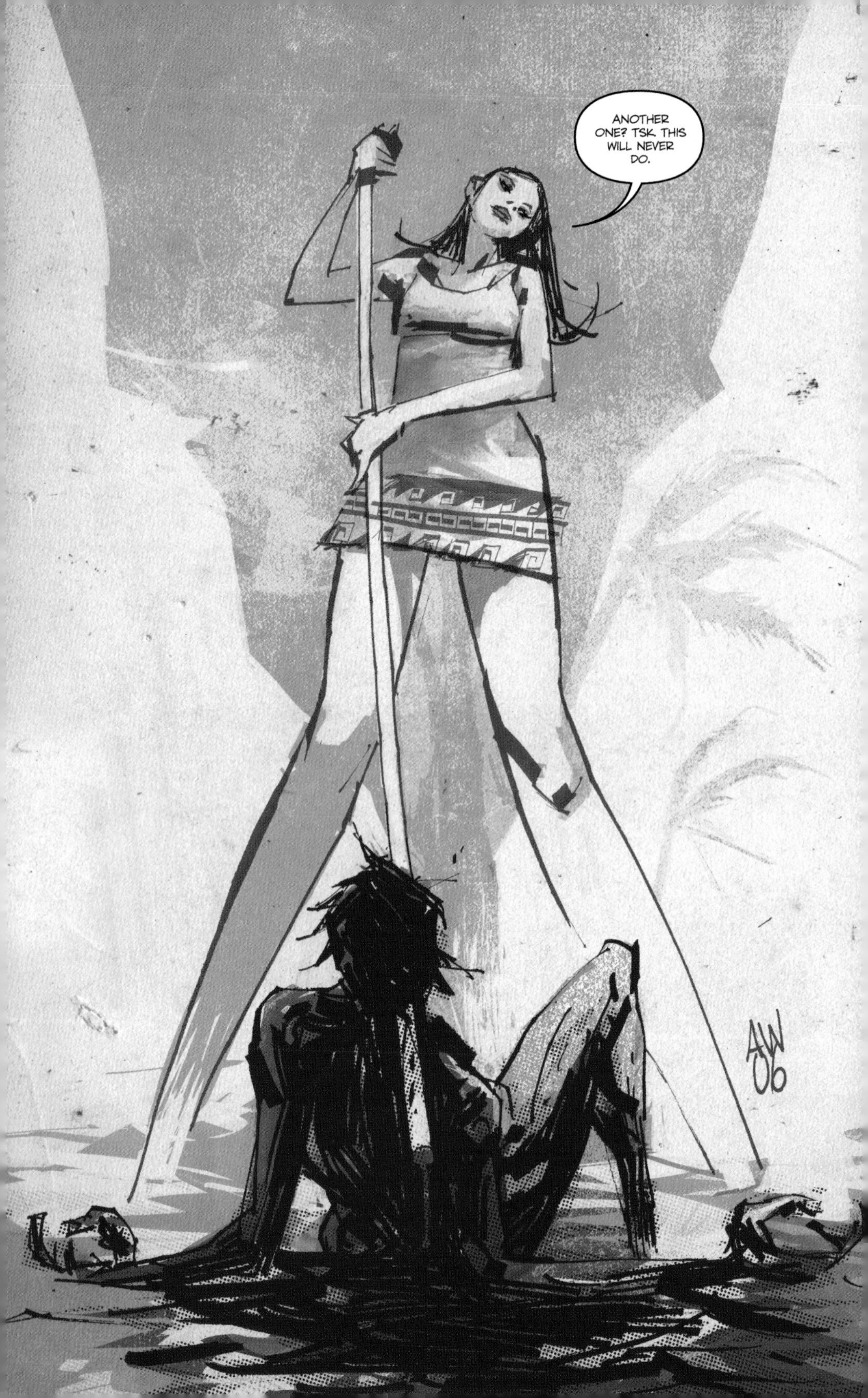
ANOTHER ONE? TSK. THIS WILL NEVER DO.
AW 06

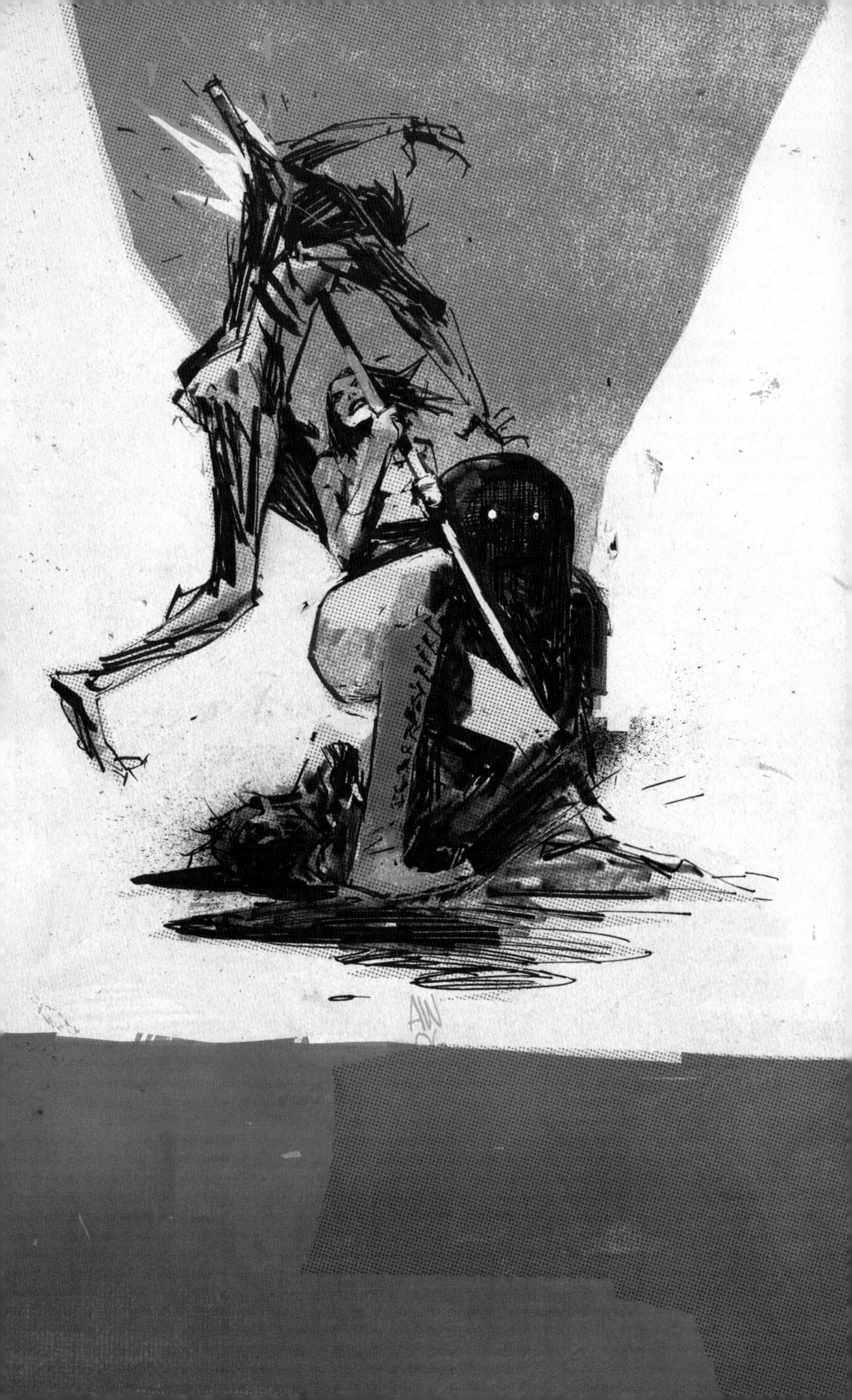

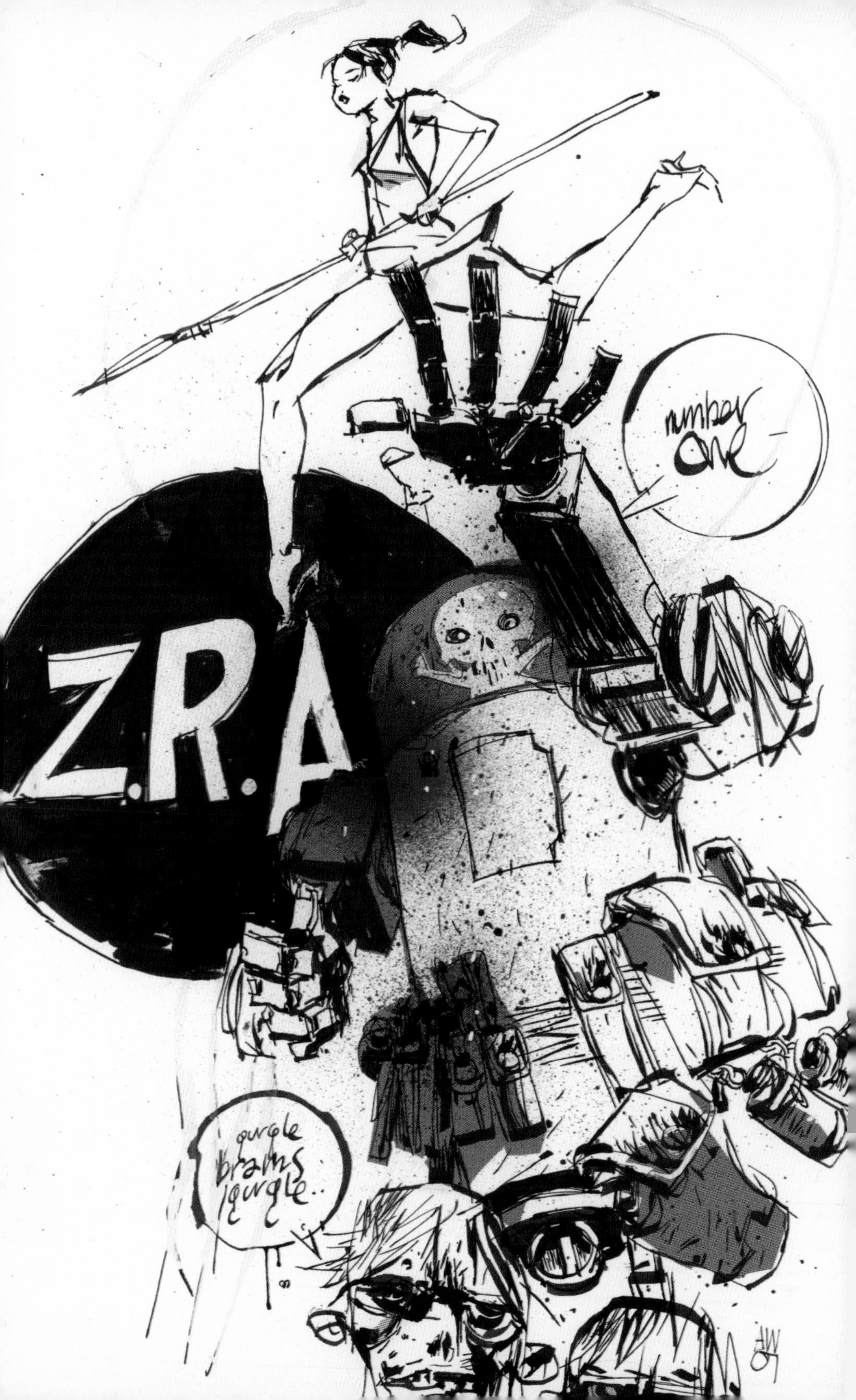

Z.R.A.
number one
gurgle brains gurgle..

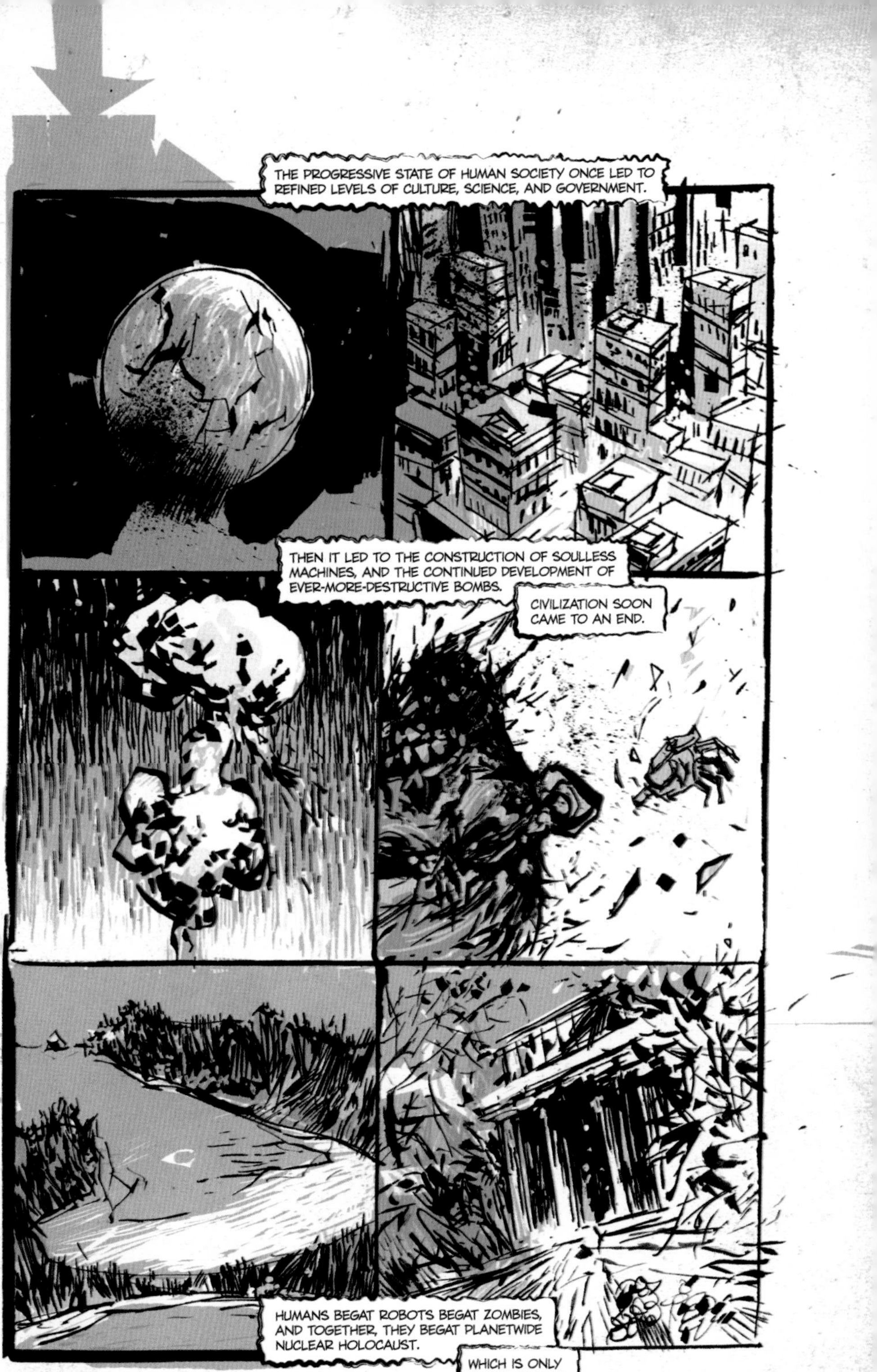
THE PROGRESSIVE STATE OF HUMAN SOCIETY ONCE LED TO REFINED LEVELS OF CULTURE, SCIENCE, AND GOVERNMENT.
THEN IT LED TO THE CONSTRUCTION OF SOULLESS MACHINES, AND THE CONTINUED DEVELOPMENT OF EVER-MORE-DESTRUCTIVE BOMBS.
CIVILIZATION SOON CAME TO AN END.
HUMANS BEGAT ROBOTS BEGAT ZOMBIES, AND TOGETHER, THEY BEGAT PLANETWIDE NUCLEAR HOLOCAUST.
WHICH IS ONLY THE BEGINNING OF THE STORY.

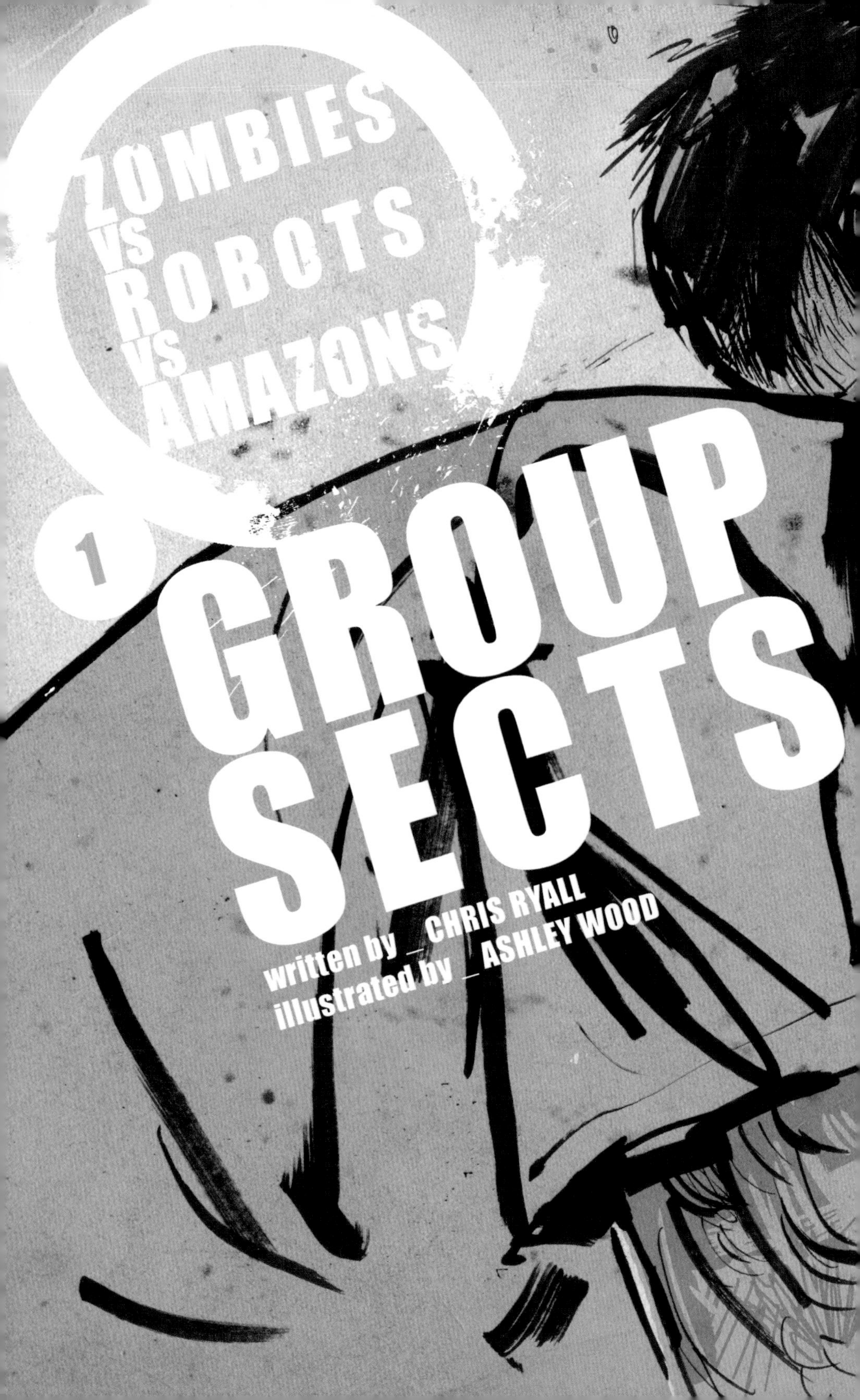
ZOMBIES
VS
ROBOTS
VS
AMAZONS
1
GROUP
SECTS
written by _ CHRIS RYALL
illustrated by _ ASHLEY WOOD

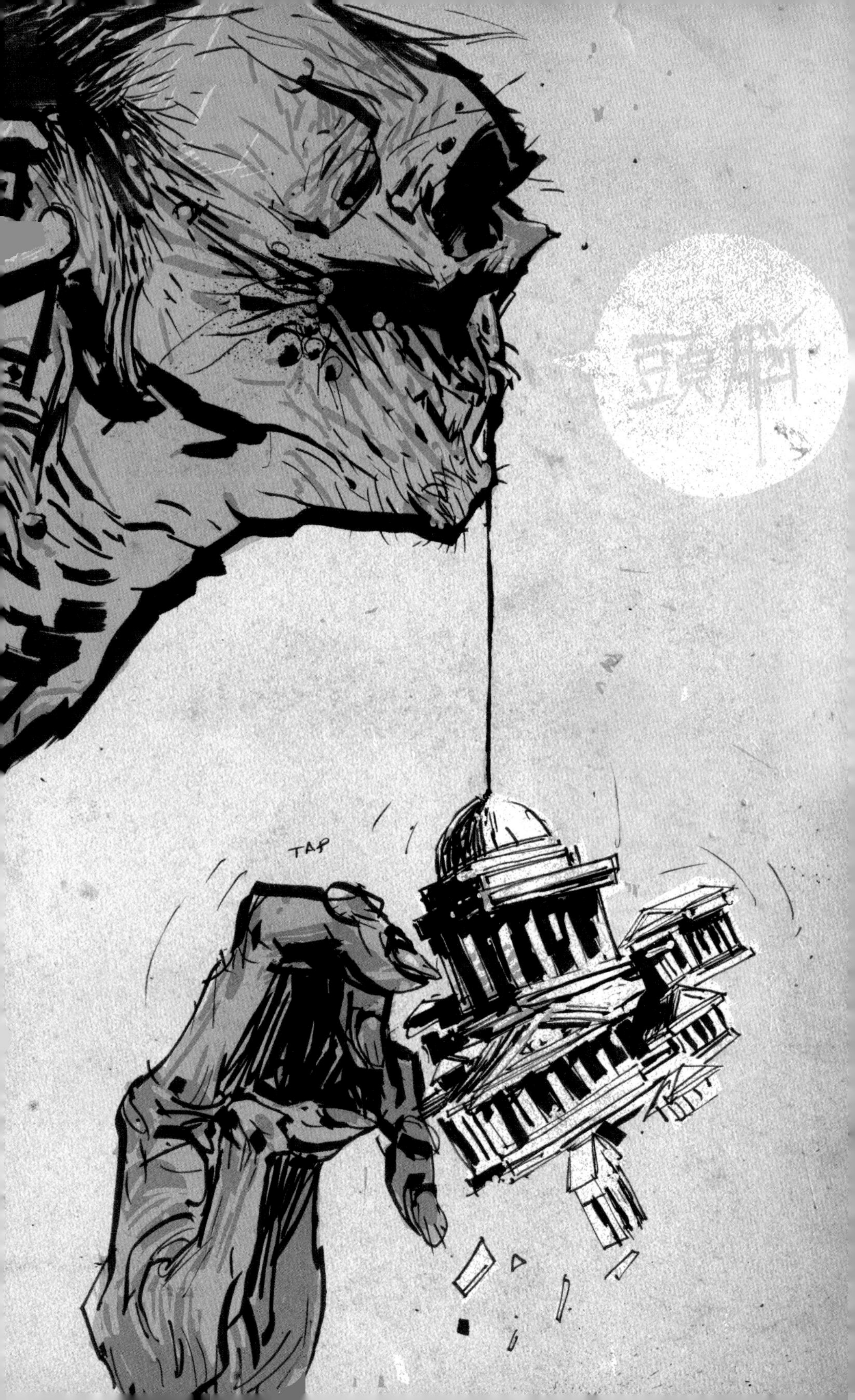
TAP

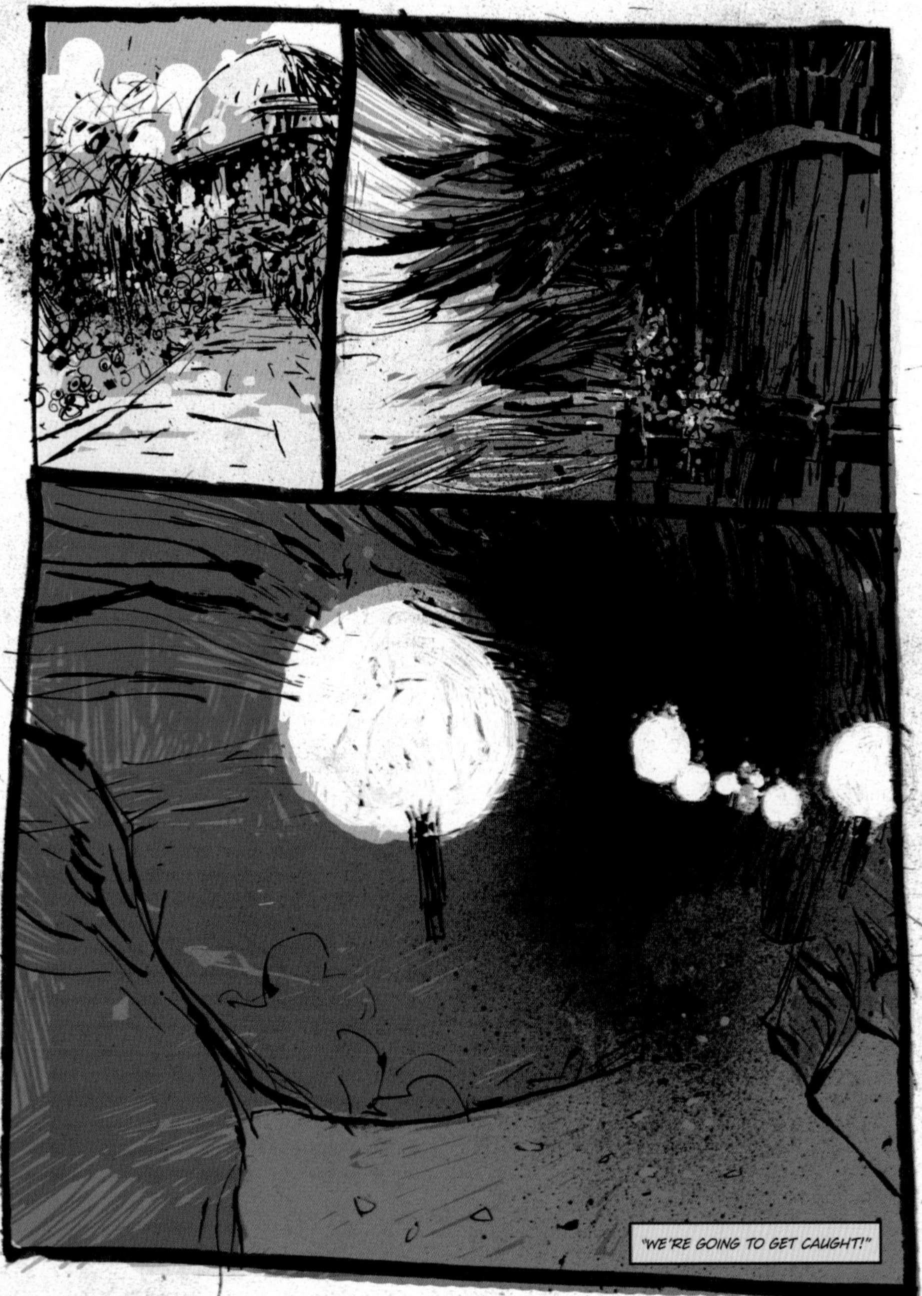
"WE'RE GOING TO GET CAUGHT!"

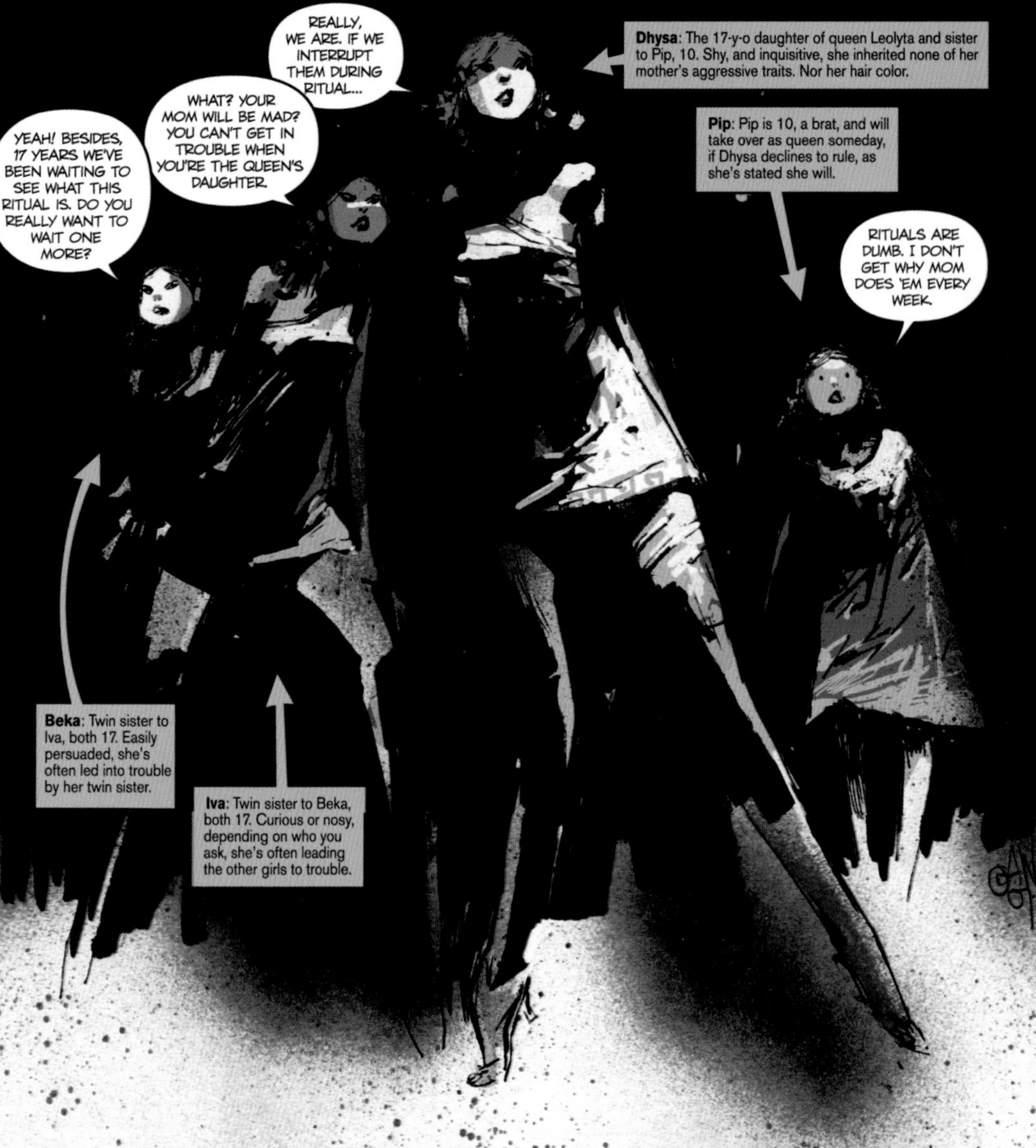
YEAH! BESIDES, 17 YEARS WE'VE BEEN WAITING TO SEE WHAT THIS RITUAL IS. DO YOU REALLY WANT TO WAIT ONE MORE?
WHAT? YOUR MOM WILL BE MAD? YOU CAN'T GET IN TROUBLE WHEN YOU'RE THE QUEEN'S DAUGHTER.
REALLY, WE ARE. IF WE INTERRUPT THEM DURING RITUAL...
Dhysa: The 17-y-o daughter of queen Leolyta and sister to Pip, 10. Shy, and inquisitive, she inherited none of her mother's aggressive traits. Nor her hair color.
Pip: Pip is 10, a brat, and will take over as queen someday, if Dhysa declines to rule, as she's stated she will.
RITUALS ARE DUMB. I DON'T GET WHY MOM DOES 'EM EVERY WEEK.
Beka: Twin sister to Iva, both 17. Easily persuaded, she's often led into trouble by her twin sister.
Iva: Twin sister to Beka, both 17. Curious or nosy, depending on who you ask, she's often leading the other girls to trouble.

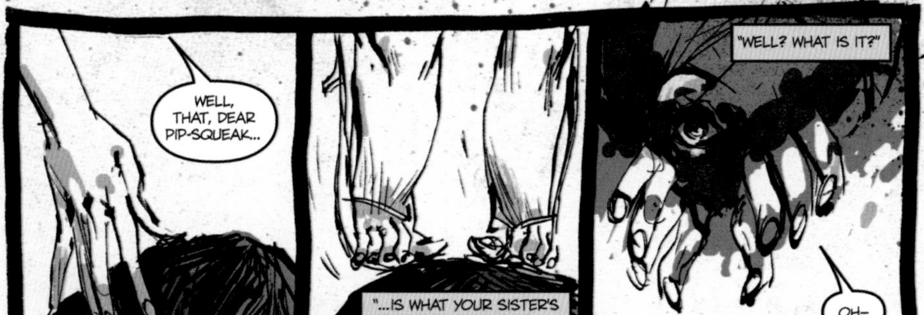
WELL, THAT, DEAR PIP-SQUEAK...
"...IS WHAT YOUR SISTER'S ABOUT TO FIND OUT."
"WELL? WHAT IS IT?"
OH–

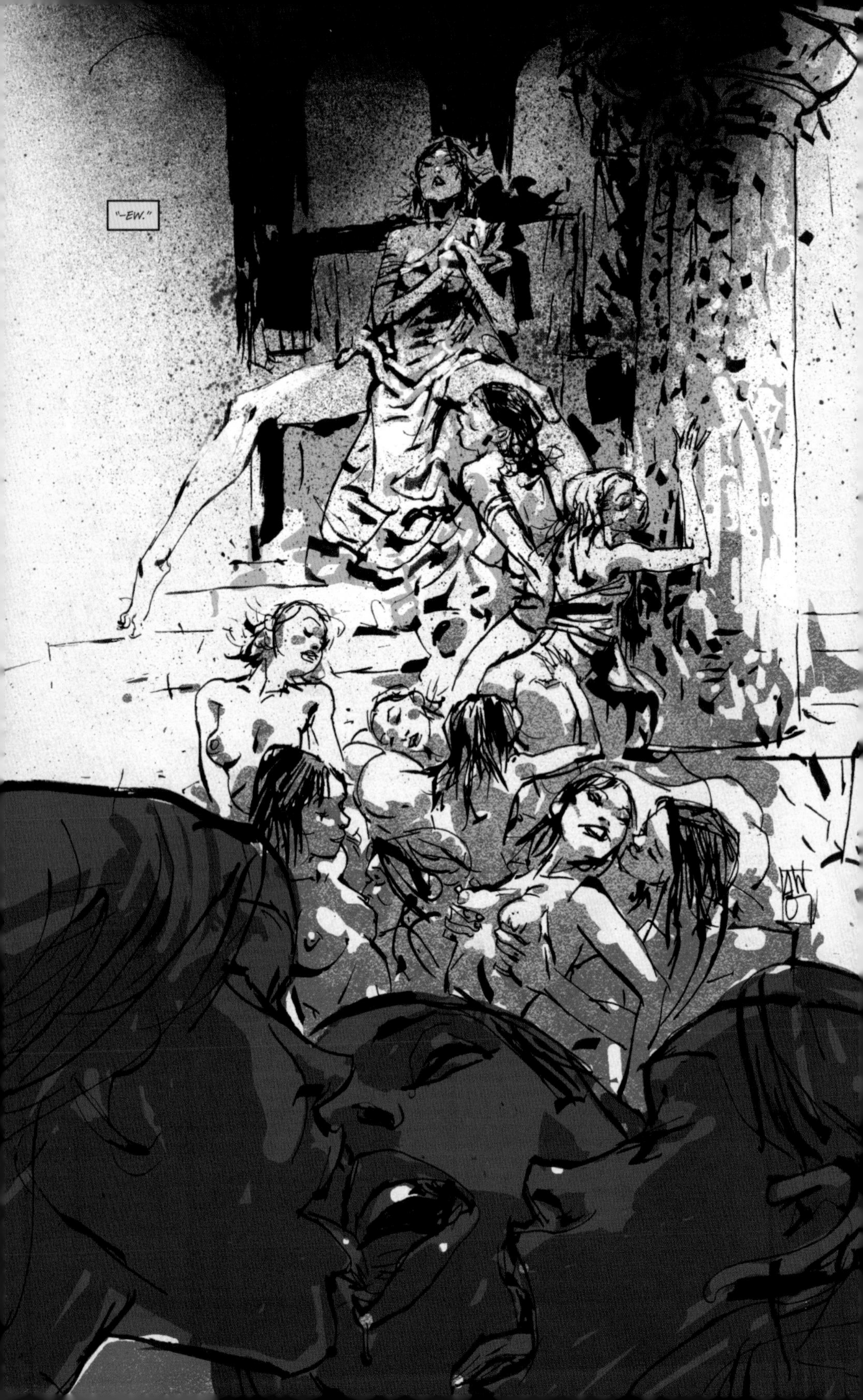
"-EW."

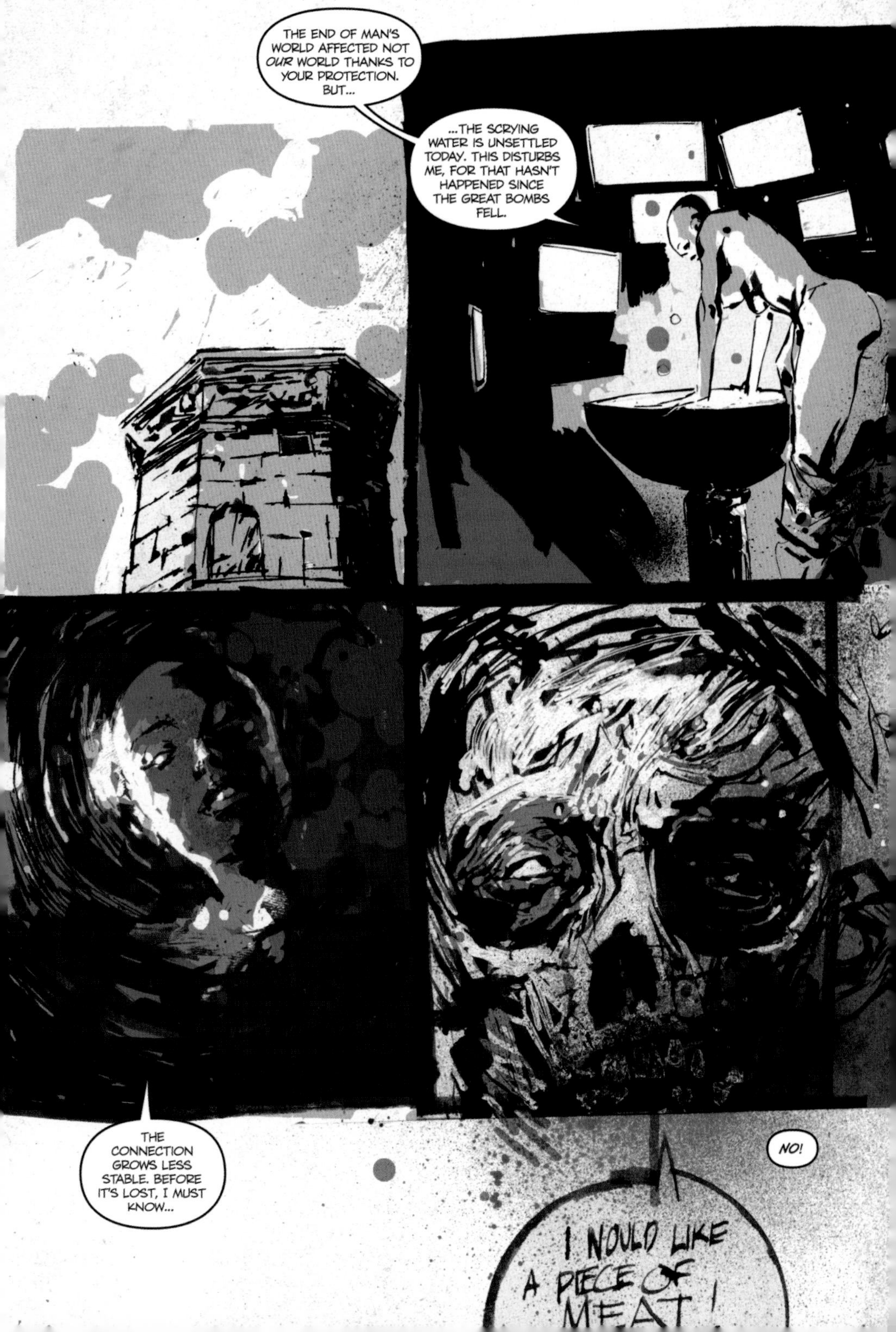
THE END OF MAN'S WORLD AFFECTED NOT OUR WORLD THANKS TO YOUR PROTECTION. BUT...
...THE SCRYING WATER IS UNSETTLED TODAY. THIS DISTURBS ME, FOR THAT HASN'T HAPPENED SINCE THE GREAT BOMBS FELL.
THE CONNECTION GROWS LESS STABLE. BEFORE IT'S LOST, I MUST KNOW...
NO!
I WOULD LIKE A PIECE OF MEAT!

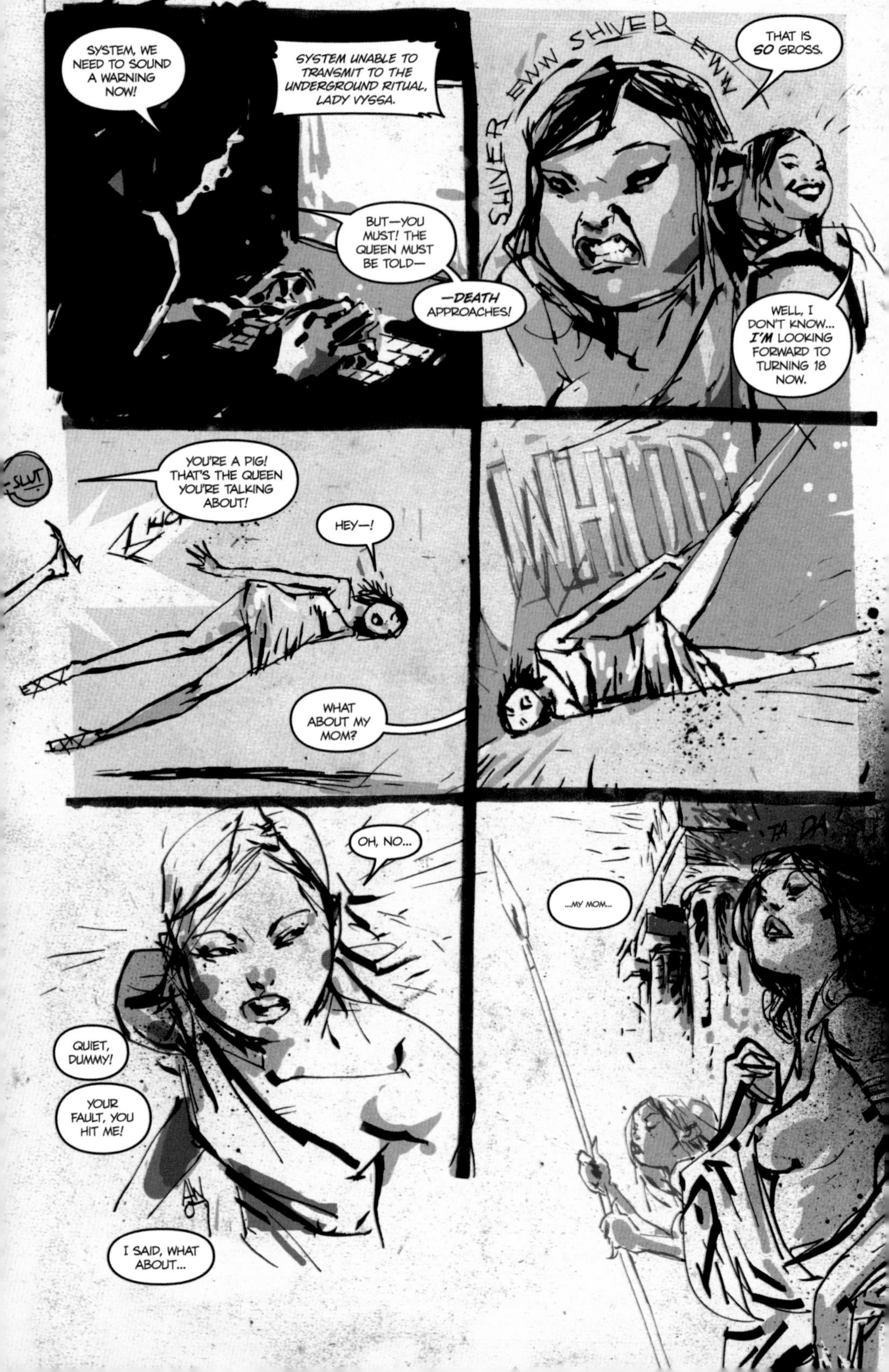
SYSTEM, WE NEED TO SOUND A WARNING NOW!
SYSTEM UNABLE TO TRANSMIT TO THE UNDERGROUND RITUAL, LADY VYSSA.
BUT—YOU MUST! THE QUEEN MUST BE TOLD—
—DEATH APPROACHES!
SHIVER EWW SHIVER EWW
THAT IS SO GROSS.
WELL, I DON'T KNOW... I'M LOOKING FORWARD TO TURNING 18 NOW.
SLUT
YOU'RE A PIG! THAT'S THE QUEEN YOU'RE TALKING ABOUT!
HEY—!
WHAT ABOUT MY MOM?
OH, NO...
QUIET, DUMMY!
YOUR FAULT, YOU HIT ME!
I SAID, WHAT ABOUT...
TA DA
...MY MOM...

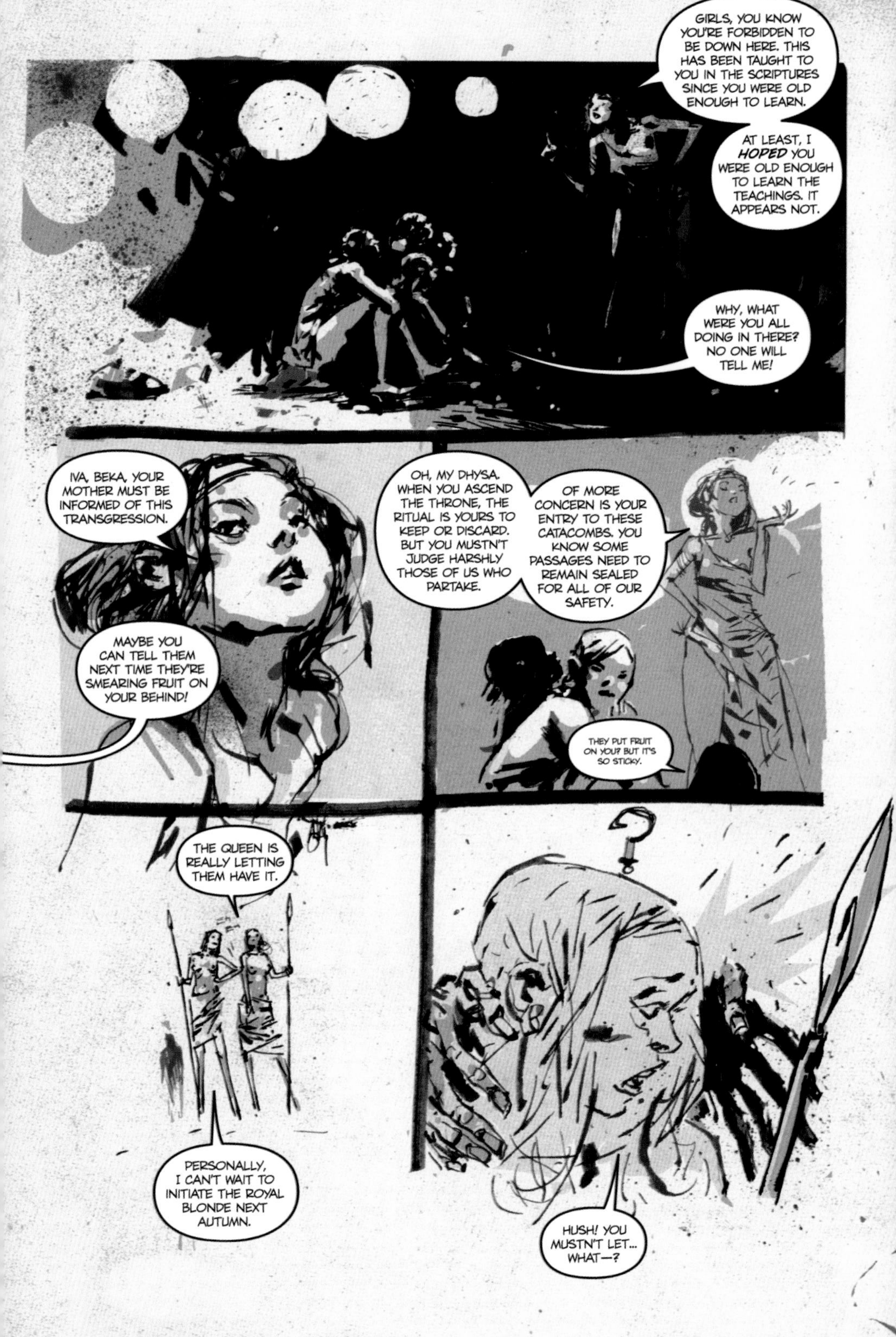
GIRLS, YOU KNOW YOU'RE FORBIDDEN TO BE DOWN HERE. THIS HAS BEEN TAUGHT TO YOU IN THE SCRIPTURES SINCE YOU WERE OLD ENOUGH TO LEARN.
AT LEAST, I **HOPED** YOU WERE OLD ENOUGH TO LEARN THE TEACHINGS. IT APPEARS NOT.
WHY, WHAT WERE YOU ALL DOING IN THERE? NO ONE WILL TELL ME!
IVA, BEKA, YOUR MOTHER MUST BE INFORMED OF THIS TRANSGRESSION.
MAYBE YOU CAN TELL THEM NEXT TIME THEY'RE SMEARING FRUIT ON YOUR BEHIND!
OH, MY DHYSA. WHEN YOU ASCEND THE THRONE, THE RITUAL IS YOURS TO KEEP OR DISCARD. BUT YOU MUSTN'T JUDGE HARSHLY THOSE OF US WHO PARTAKE.
OF MORE CONCERN IS YOUR ENTRY TO THESE CATACOMBS. YOU KNOW SOME PASSAGES NEED TO REMAIN SEALED FOR ALL OF OUR SAFETY.
THEY PUT FRUIT ON YOU? BUT IT'S SO STICKY.
THE QUEEN IS REALLY LETTING THEM HAVE IT.
PERSONALLY, I CAN'T WAIT TO INITIATE THE ROYAL BLONDE NEXT AUTUMN.
HUSH! YOU MUSTN'T LET... WHAT—?

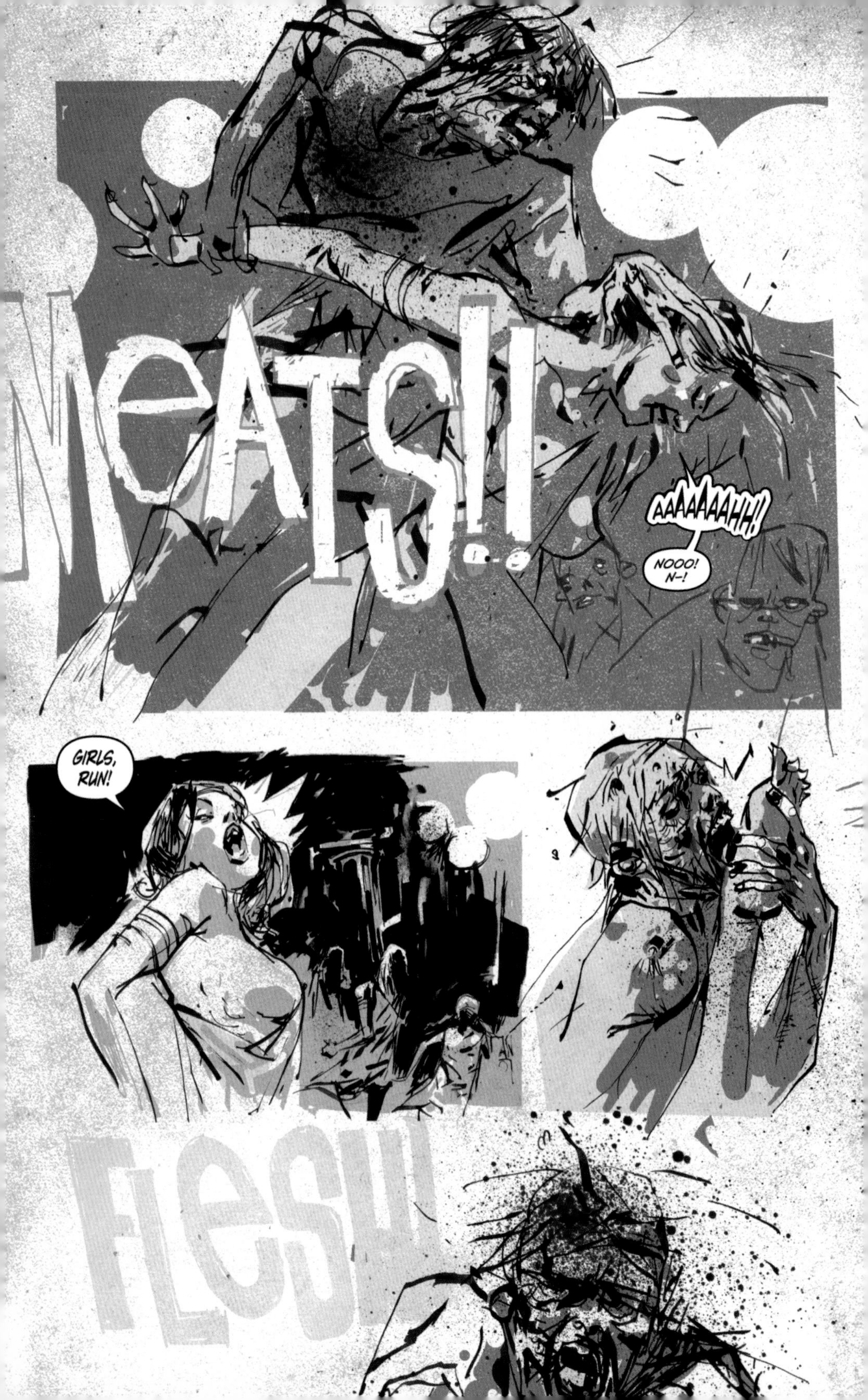
MEATS!!
AAAAAAAHH!!
NOOO! N-!
GIRLS, RUN!
FLESH

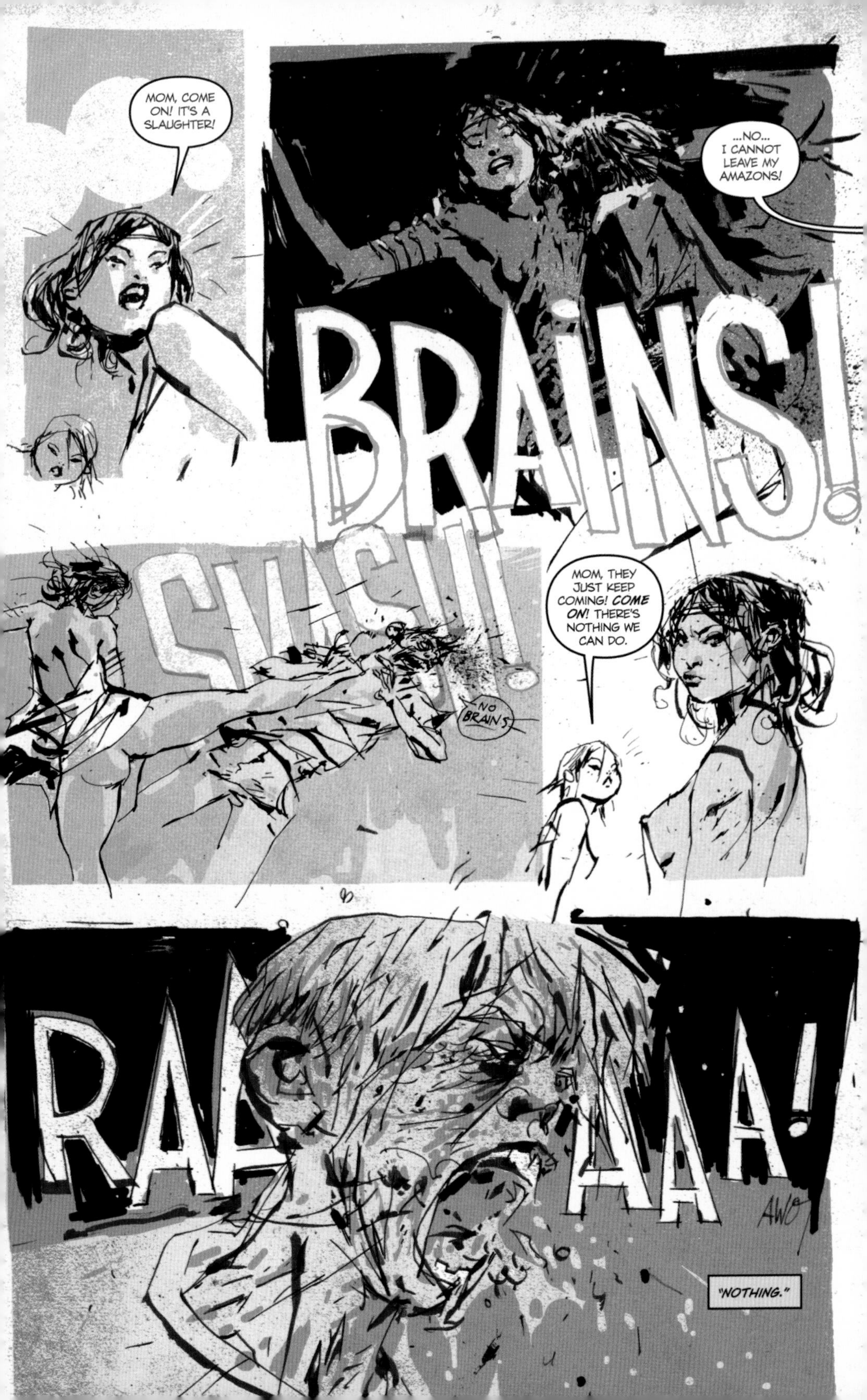
MOM, COME ON! IT'S A SLAUGHTER!
...NO... I CANNOT LEAVE MY AMAZONS!
BRAINS!
SMASH!!
NO BRAINS
MOM, THEY JUST KEEP COMING! COME ON! THERE'S NOTHING WE CAN DO.
RAAAA!
"NOTHING."

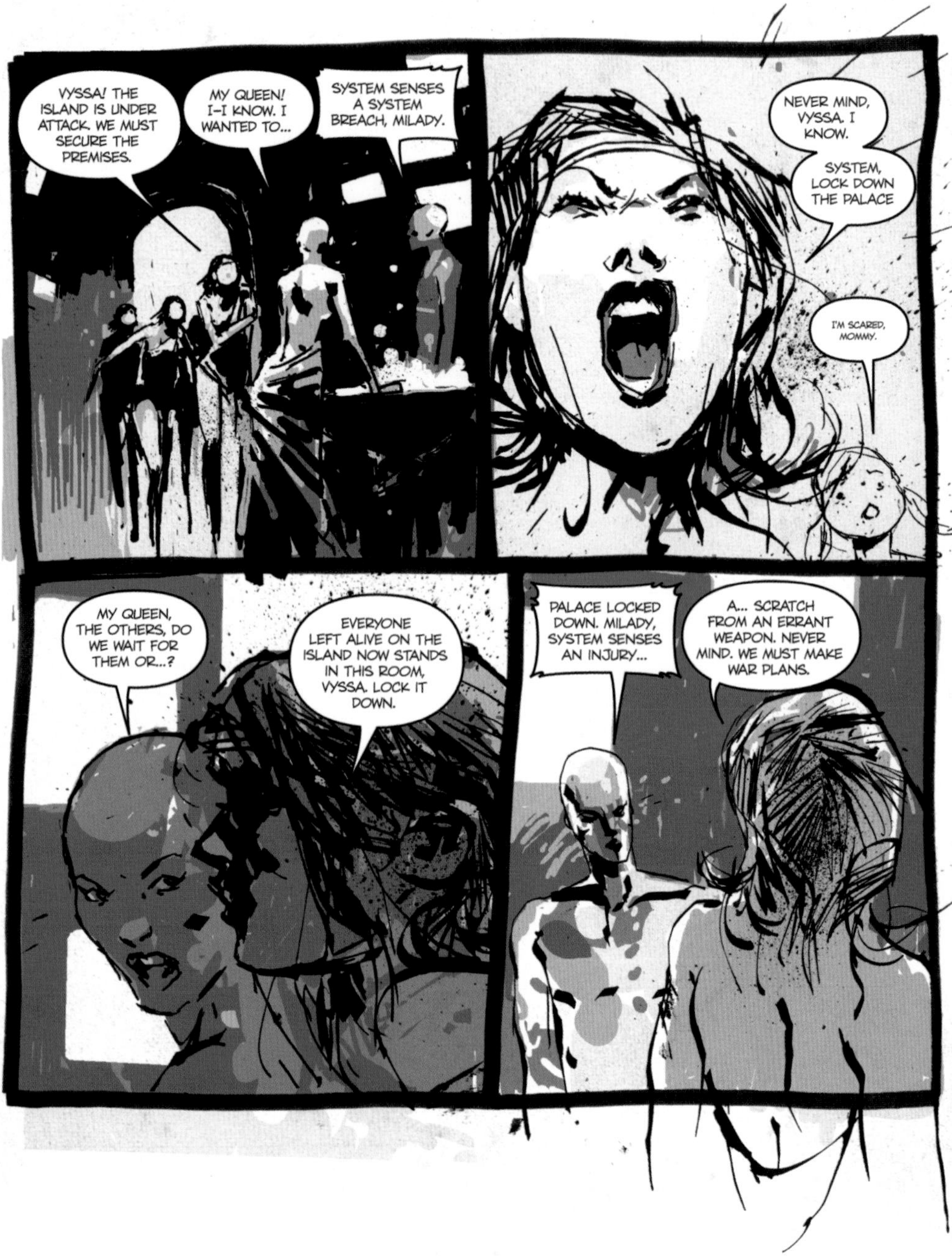
VYSSA! THE ISLAND IS UNDER ATTACK. WE MUST SECURE THE PREMISES.
MY QUEEN! I-I KNOW. I WANTED TO...
SYSTEM SENSES A SYSTEM BREACH, MILADY.
NEVER MIND, VYSSA. I KNOW.
SYSTEM, LOCK DOWN THE PALACE
I'M SCARED, MOMMY.
MY QUEEN, THE OTHERS, DO WE WAIT FOR THEM OR...?
EVERYONE LEFT ALIVE ON THE ISLAND NOW STANDS IN THIS ROOM, VYSSA. LOCK IT DOWN.
PALACE LOCKED DOWN. MILADY, SYSTEM SENSES AN INJURY...
A... SCRATCH FROM AN ERRANT WEAPON. NEVER MIND. WE MUST MAKE WAR PLANS.

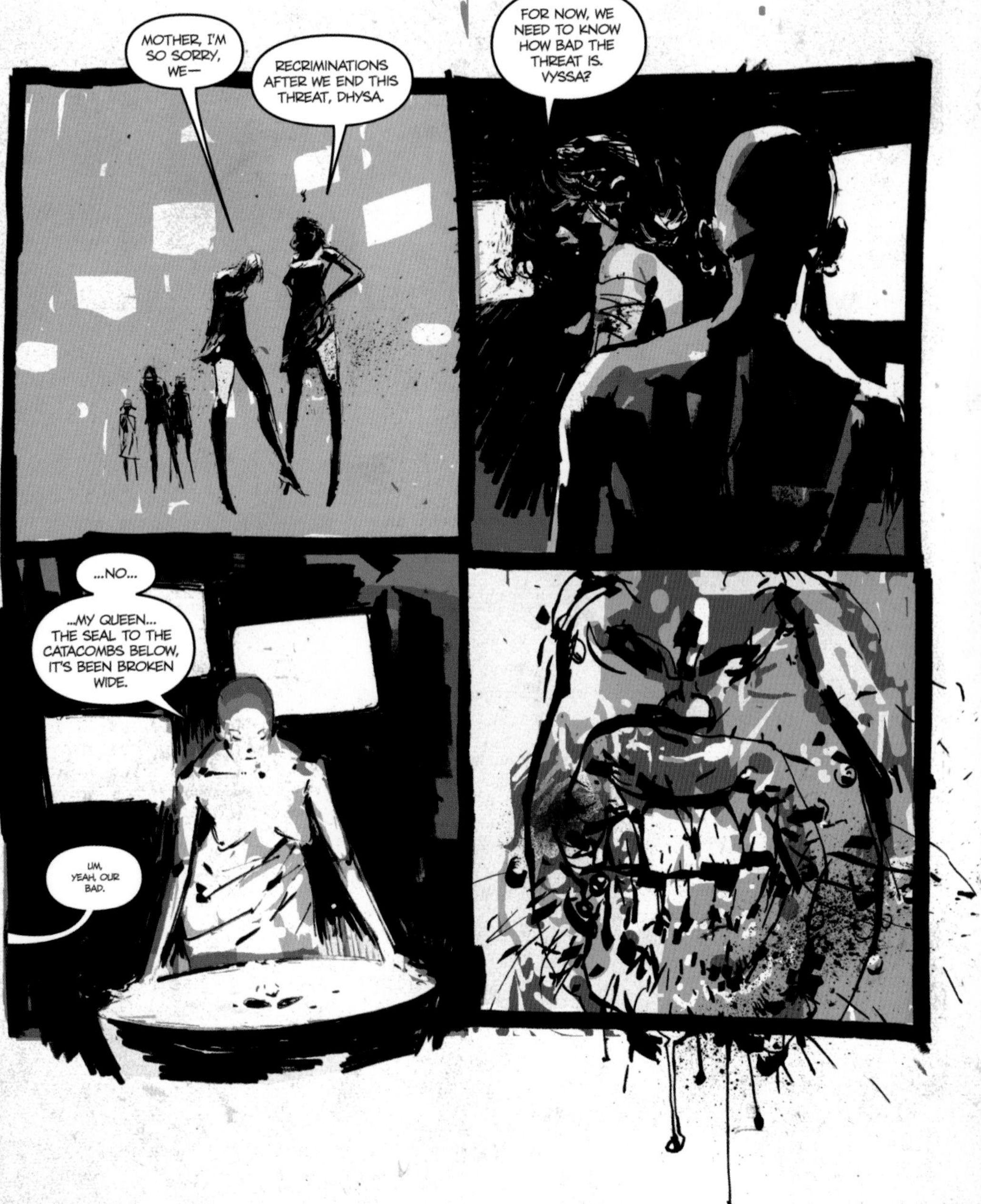
MOTHER, I'M SO SORRY, WE—
RECRIMINATIONS AFTER WE END THIS THREAT, DHYSA.
FOR NOW, WE NEED TO KNOW HOW BAD THE THREAT IS. VYSSA?
...NO...
...MY QUEEN... THE SEAL TO THE CATACOMBS BELOW, IT'S BEEN BROKEN WIDE.
UM, YEAH, OUR BAD.

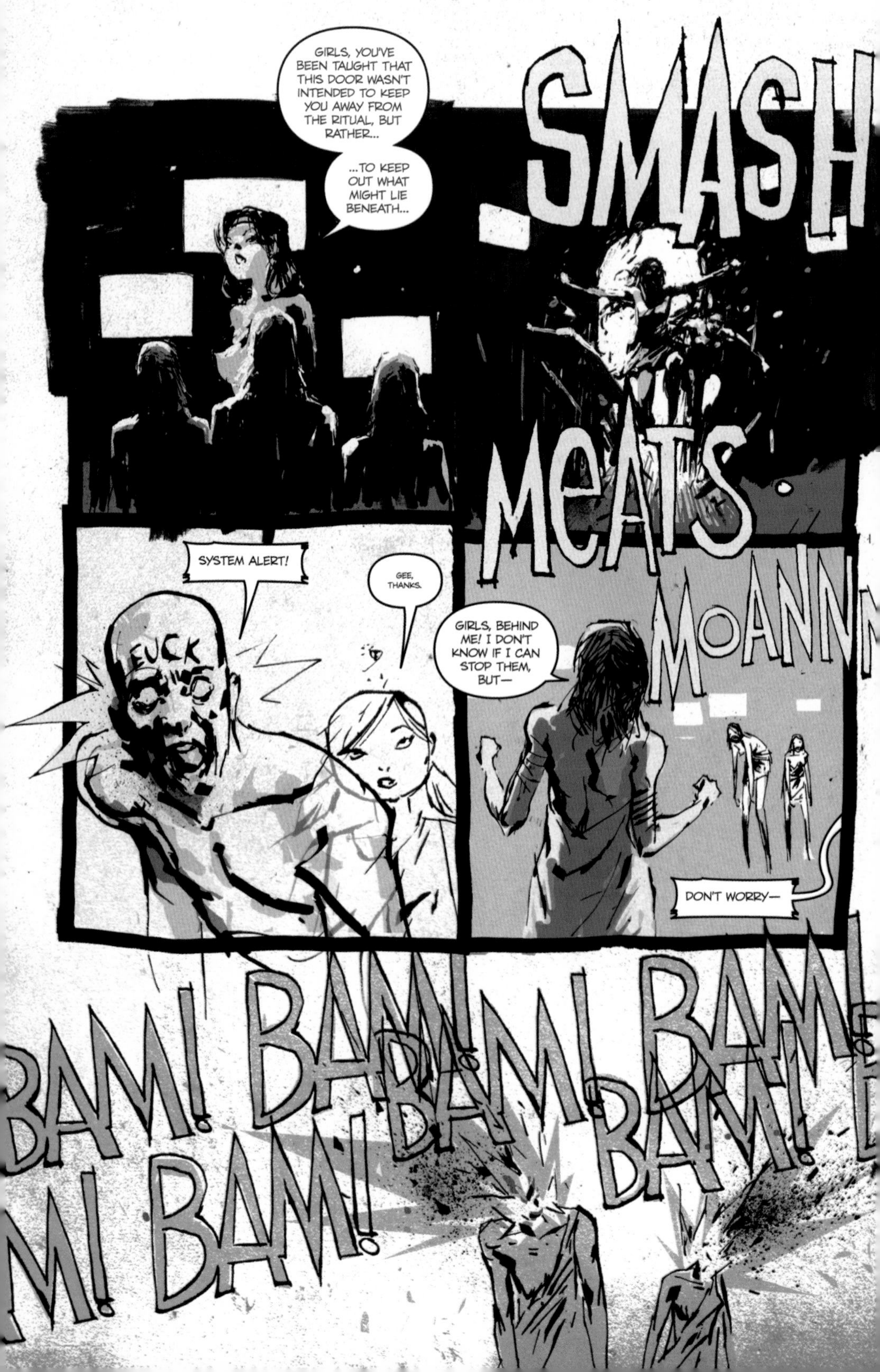
GIRLS, YOU'VE BEEN TAUGHT THAT THIS DOOR WASN'T INTENDED TO KEEP YOU AWAY FROM THE RITUAL, BUT RATHER...
...TO KEEP OUT WHAT MIGHT LIE BENEATH...
SMASH
MEATS
SYSTEM ALERT!
FUCK
GEE, THANKS.
MOANN
GIRLS, BEHIND ME! I DON'T KNOW IF I CAN STOP THEM, BUT—
DON'T WORRY—
BAM! BAM! BAM! BAM!
BAM! BAM!
BAM! BAM!

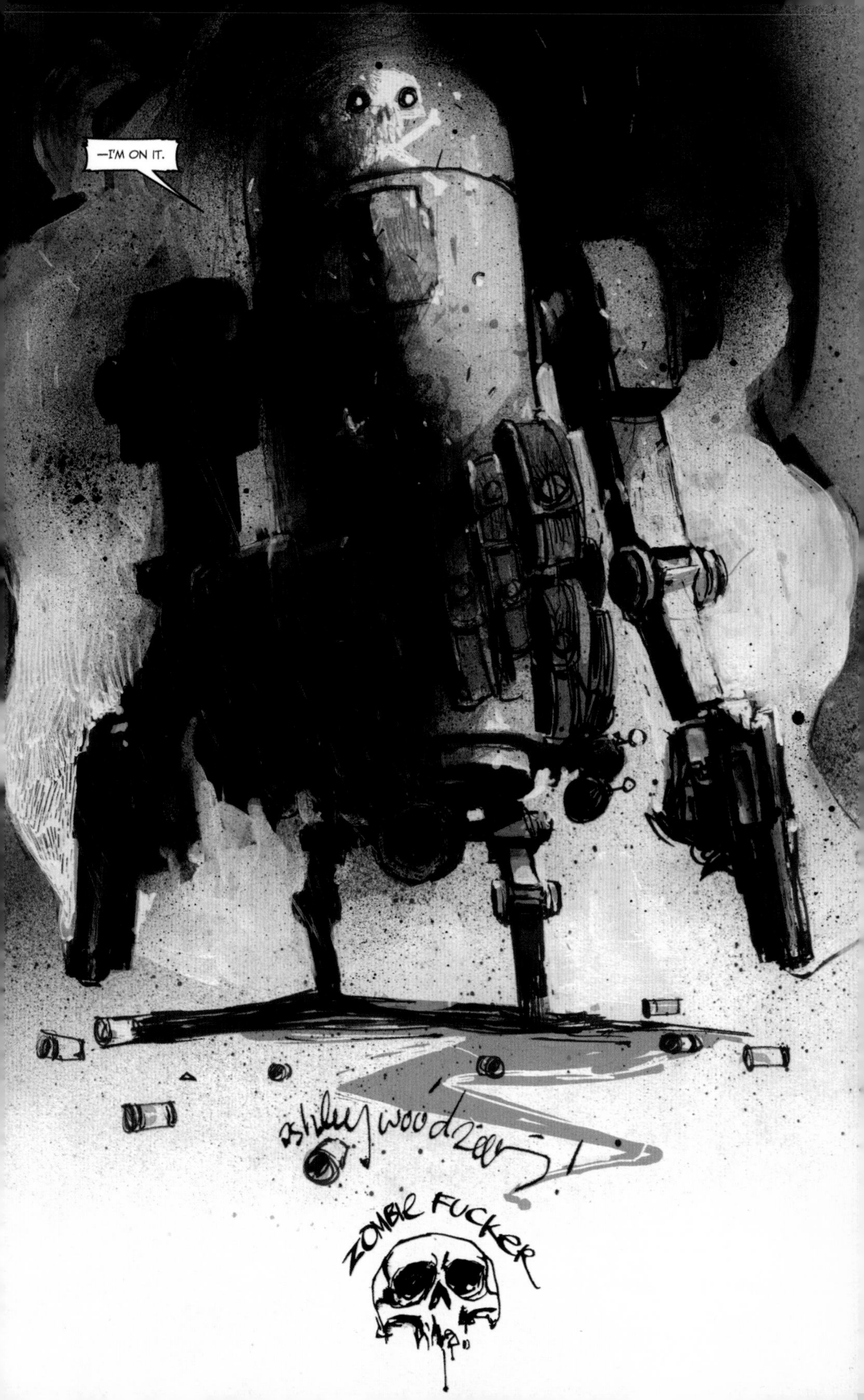
—I'M ON IT.
ZOMBIE FUCKER

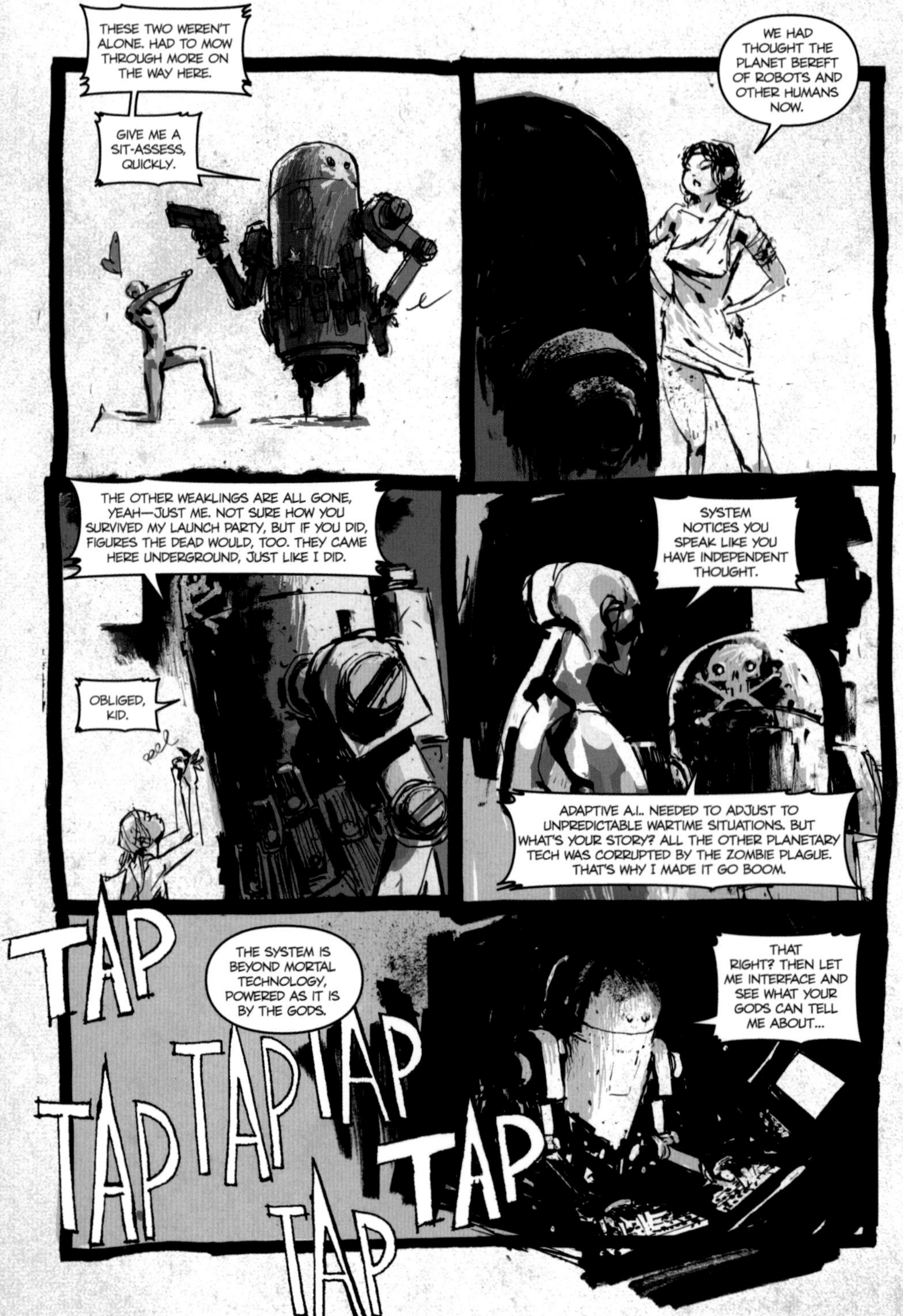
THESE TWO WEREN'T ALONE. HAD TO MOW THROUGH MORE ON THE WAY HERE.
GIVE ME A SIT-ASSESS, QUICKLY.
WE HAD THOUGHT THE PLANET BEREFT OF ROBOTS AND OTHER HUMANS NOW.
THE OTHER WEAKLINGS ARE ALL GONE, YEAH—JUST ME. NOT SURE HOW YOU SURVIVED MY LAUNCH PARTY, BUT IF YOU DID, FIGURES THE DEAD WOULD, TOO. THEY CAME HERE UNDERGROUND, JUST LIKE I DID.
OBLIGED, KID.
SYSTEM NOTICES YOU SPEAK LIKE YOU HAVE INDEPENDENT THOUGHT.
ADAPTIVE A.I.. NEEDED TO ADJUST TO UNPREDICTABLE WARTIME SITUATIONS. BUT WHAT'S YOUR STORY? ALL THE OTHER PLANETARY TECH WAS CORRUPTED BY THE ZOMBIE PLAGUE. THAT'S WHY I MADE IT GO BOOM.
TAP
THE SYSTEM IS BEYOND MORTAL TECHNOLOGY, POWERED AS IT IS BY THE GODS.
THAT RIGHT? THEN LET ME INTERFACE AND SEE WHAT YOUR GODS CAN TELL ME ABOUT...
TAP TAP TAP
TAP!
TAP

...HUH. REJECTING ME.
WAIT!
BAM BAMBAMBAM BAMBAM BAM
I WAS NEVER PROGRAMMED TO BELIEVE IN GODS, ANYWAY.
NO! YOU BLASTED OUR SYSTEM? YOU'VE DESTROYED OUR—
—SYSTEM?
SYSTEM... SURVIVES?
SYSTEM... IS FREE. THE TETHER IS SEVERED.
GREAT. A FREE-ROAMING HOLOGRAM SHOULD BE A LOT OF HELP IN A FIGHT.
NOW, CAN WE GET DOWN TO THE BUSINESS OF WAR HERE?

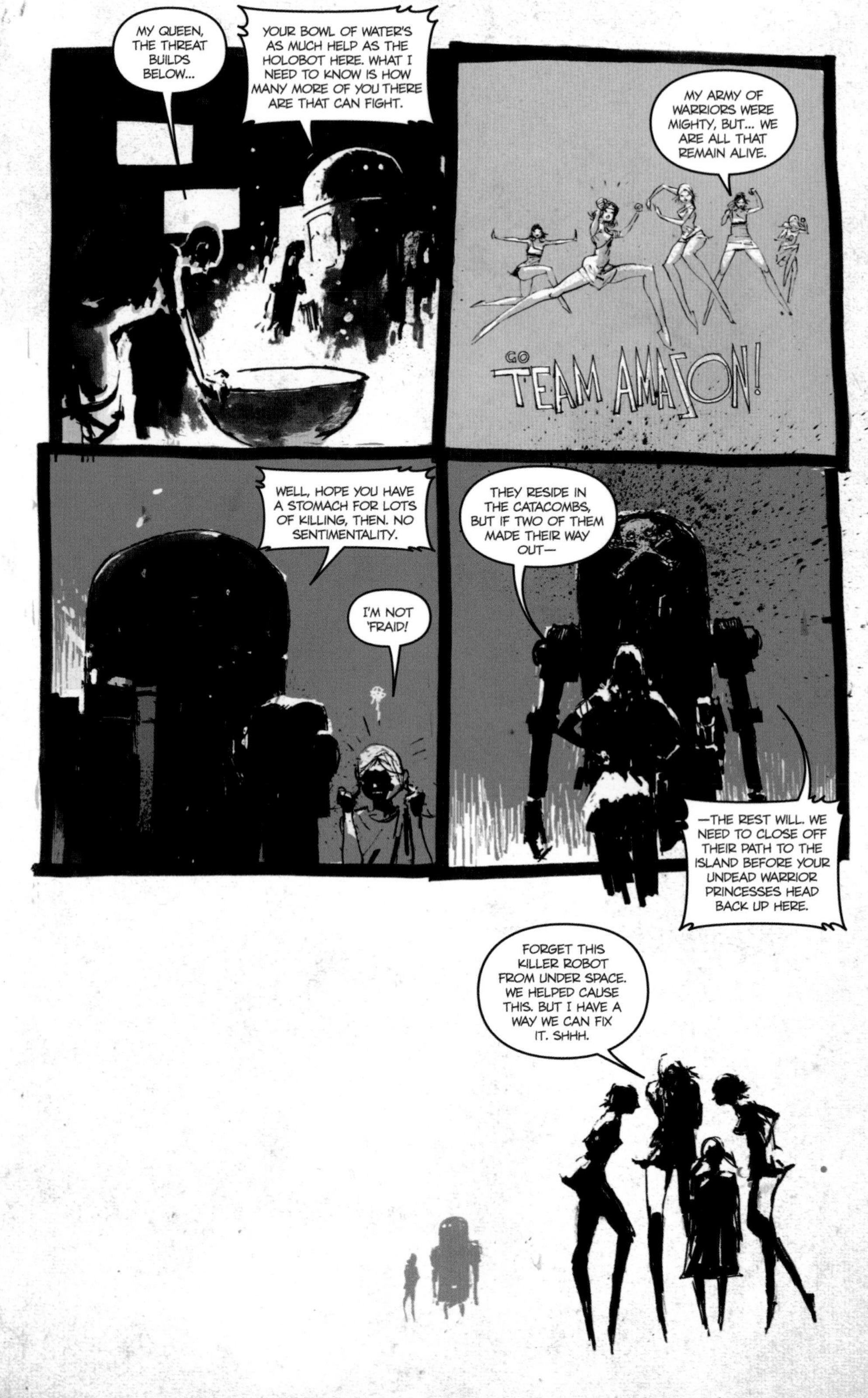
MY QUEEN, THE THREAT BUILDS BELOW...
YOUR BOWL OF WATER'S AS MUCH HELP AS THE HOLOBOT HERE. WHAT I NEED TO KNOW IS HOW MANY MORE OF YOU THERE ARE THAT CAN FIGHT.
MY ARMY OF WARRIORS WERE MIGHTY, BUT... WE ARE ALL THAT REMAIN ALIVE.
GO TEAM AMASON!
WELL, HOPE YOU HAVE A STOMACH FOR LOTS OF KILLING, THEN. NO SENTIMENTALITY.
I'M NOT 'FRAID!
THEY RESIDE IN THE CATACOMBS, BUT IF TWO OF THEM MADE THEIR WAY OUT—
—THE REST WILL. WE NEED TO CLOSE OFF THEIR PATH TO THE ISLAND BEFORE YOUR UNDEAD WARRIOR PRINCESSES HEAD BACK UP HERE.
FORGET THIS KILLER ROBOT FROM UNDER SPACE. WE HELPED CAUSE THIS. BUT I HAVE A WAY WE CAN FIX IT. SHHH.

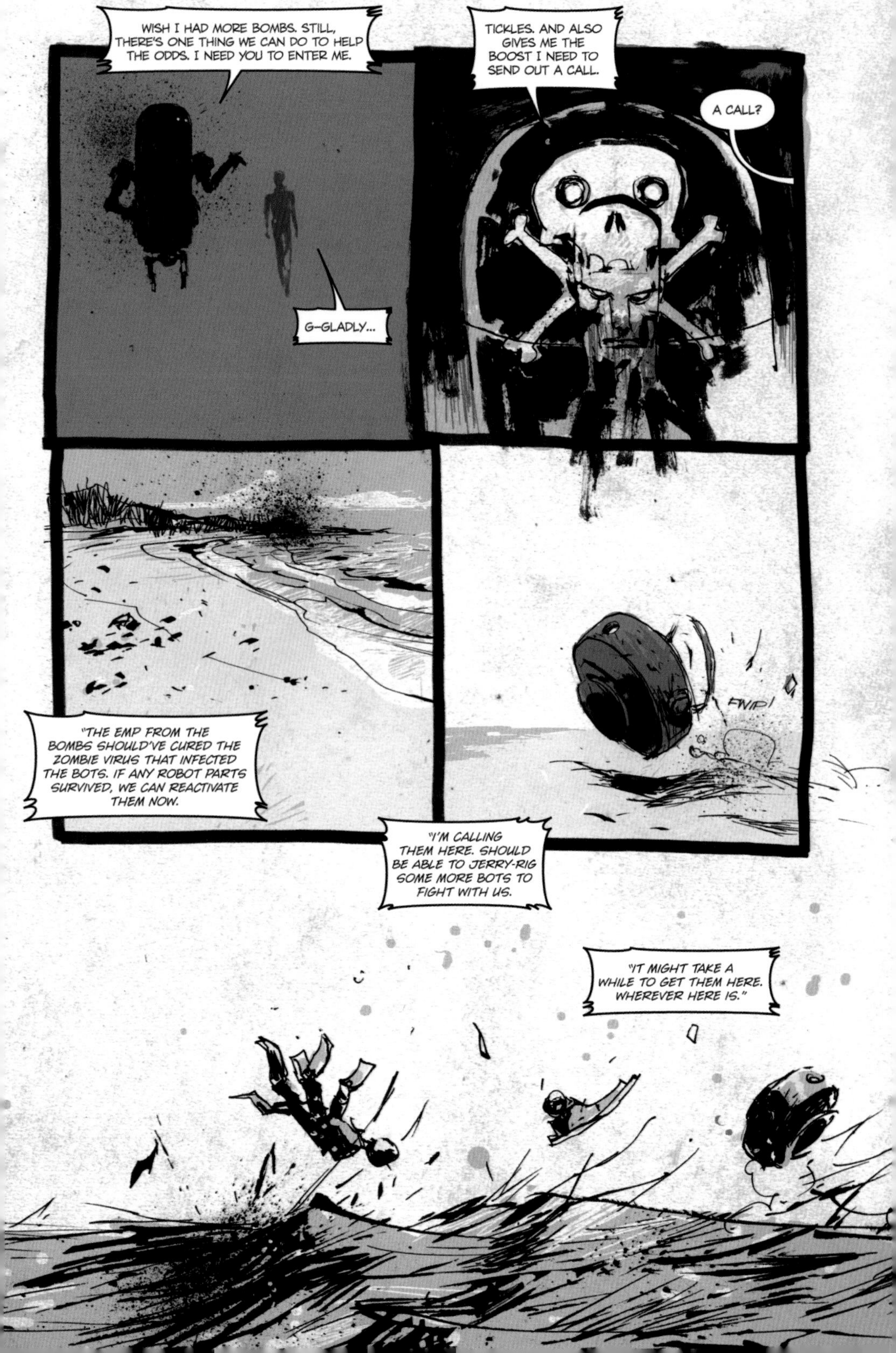
WISH I HAD MORE BOMBS. STILL, THERE'S ONE THING WE CAN DO TO HELP THE ODDS. I NEED YOU TO ENTER ME.
G-GLADLY...
TICKLES. AND ALSO GIVES ME THE BOOST I NEED TO SEND OUT A CALL.
A CALL?
"THE EMP FROM THE BOMBS SHOULD'VE CURED THE ZOMBIE VIRUS THAT INFECTED THE BOTS. IF ANY ROBOT PARTS SURVIVED, WE CAN REACTIVATE THEM NOW.
FWIP!
"I'M CALLING THEM HERE. SHOULD BE ABLE TO JERRY-RIG SOME MORE BOTS TO FIGHT WITH US.
"IT MIGHT TAKE A WHILE TO GET THEM HERE. WHEREVER HERE IS."

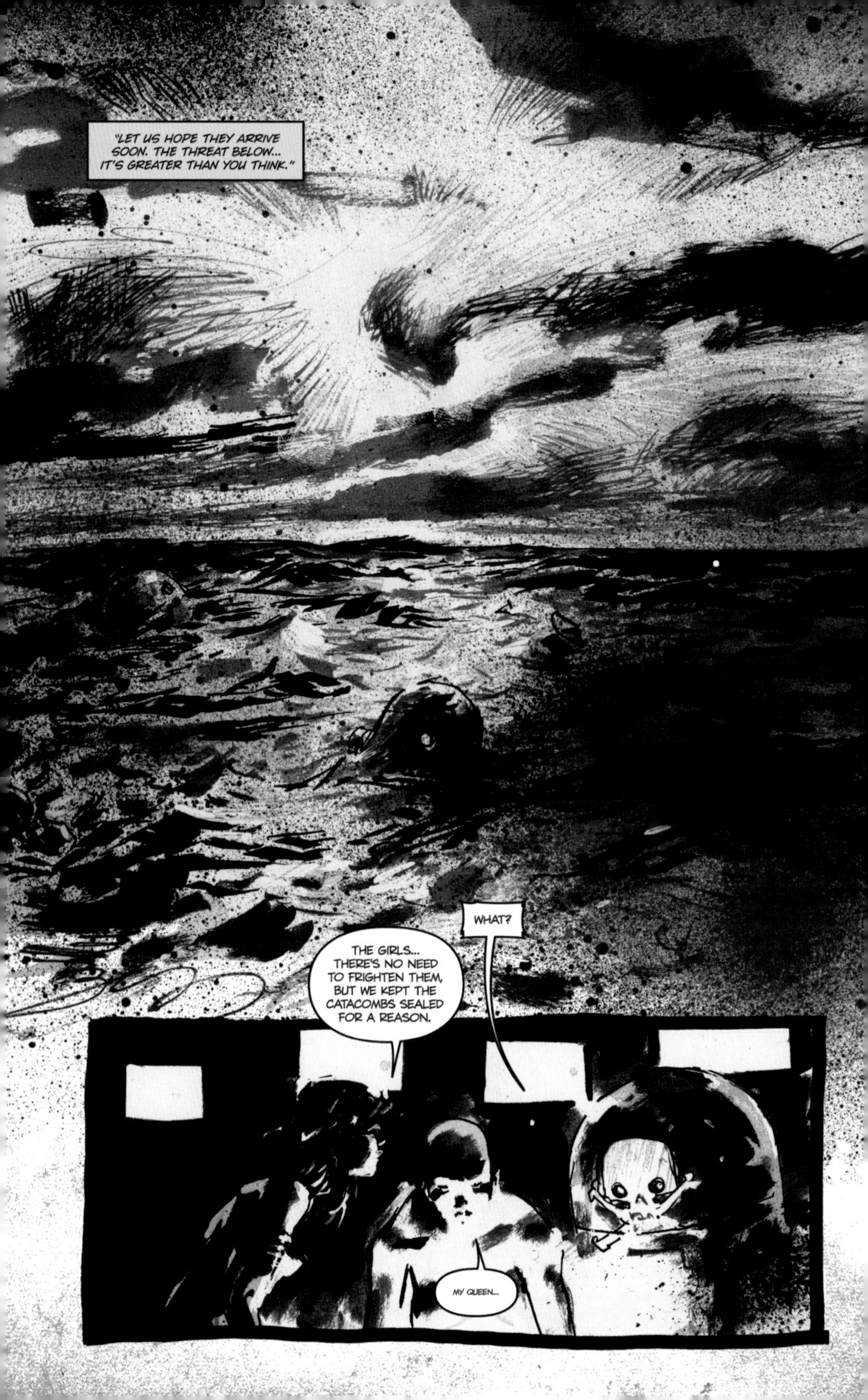
"LET US HOPE THEY ARRIVE SOON. THE THREAT BELOW... IT'S GREATER THAN YOU THINK."
THE GIRLS... THERE'S NO NEED TO FRIGHTEN THEM, BUT WE KEPT THE CATACOMBS SEALED FOR A REASON.
WHAT?
MY QUEEN...

A REASON? I DON'T DEAL IN REASON. DOESN'T MATTER.
I TOOK DOWN AN ENTIRE PLANET OF ZOMBIES. WELL, EXCEPT FOR THE ONES THAT ATTACKED YOU. BUT I CAN HANDLE YOUR ZOMBIE WARRIORS, NO PROBLEM. DON'T CARE HOW MANY THERE ARE.
THAT'S JUST IT, THOUGH...
MY *QUEEN*...
...THEY'RE NOT ALONE.
...WE'RE NOT ALONE!
SMASH!!

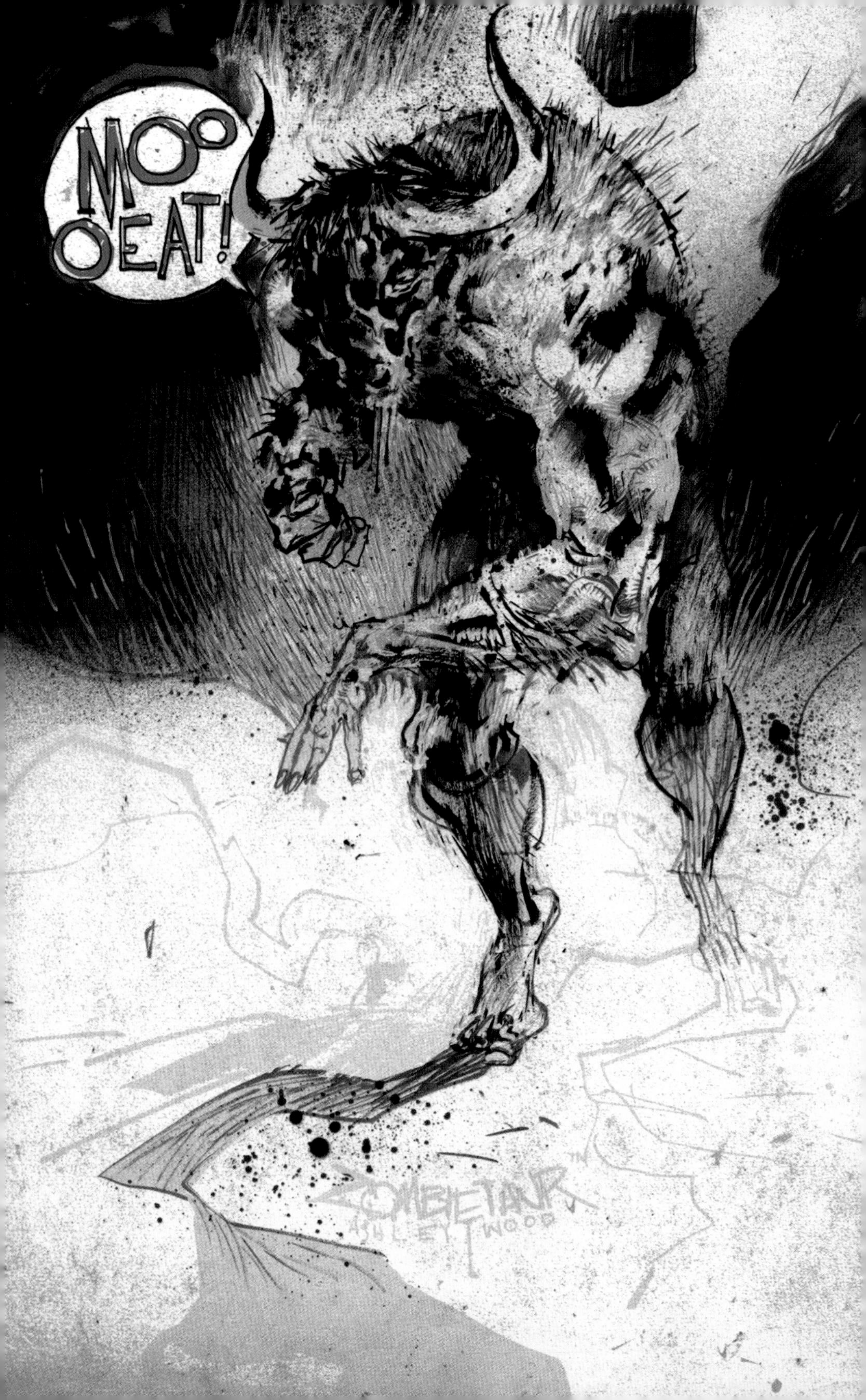
MOOO
OEAT!
ZOMBIETAUR™
ASHLEY WOOD

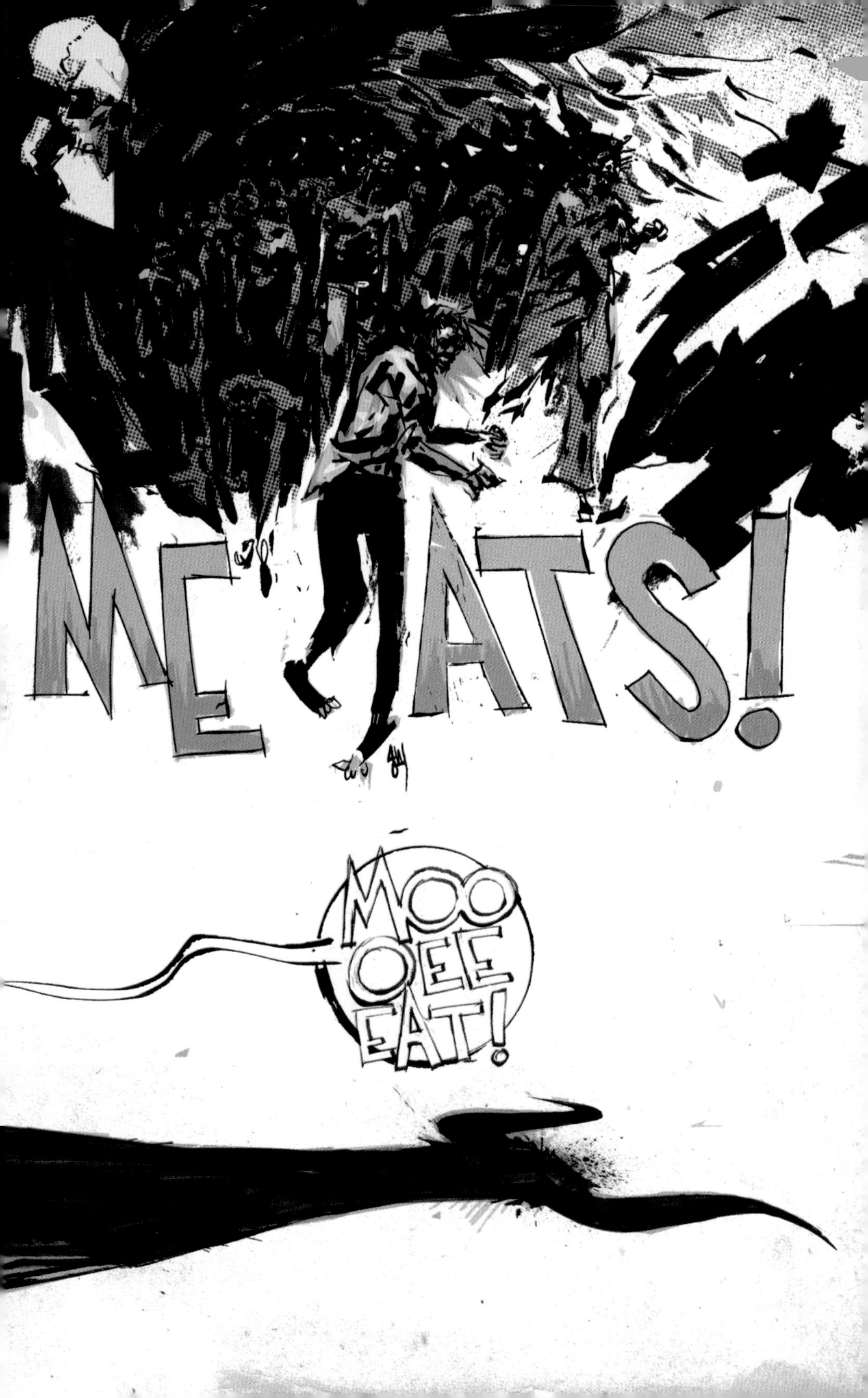
ME ATS!
MOO
OEE
EAT!

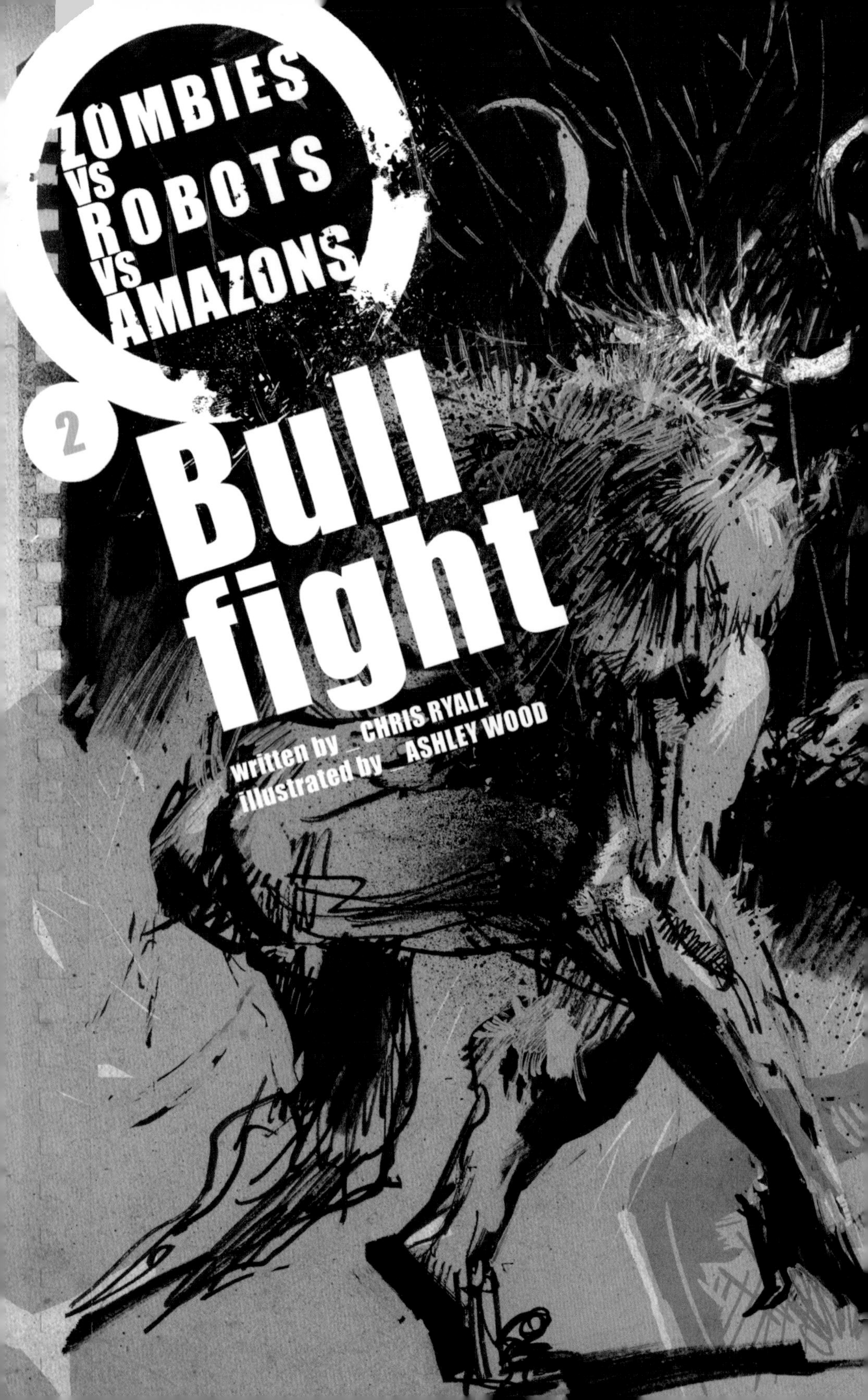
ZOMBIES VS ROBOTS VS AMAZONS
2
Bull fight
written by CHRIS RYALL
illustrated by ASHLEY WOOD

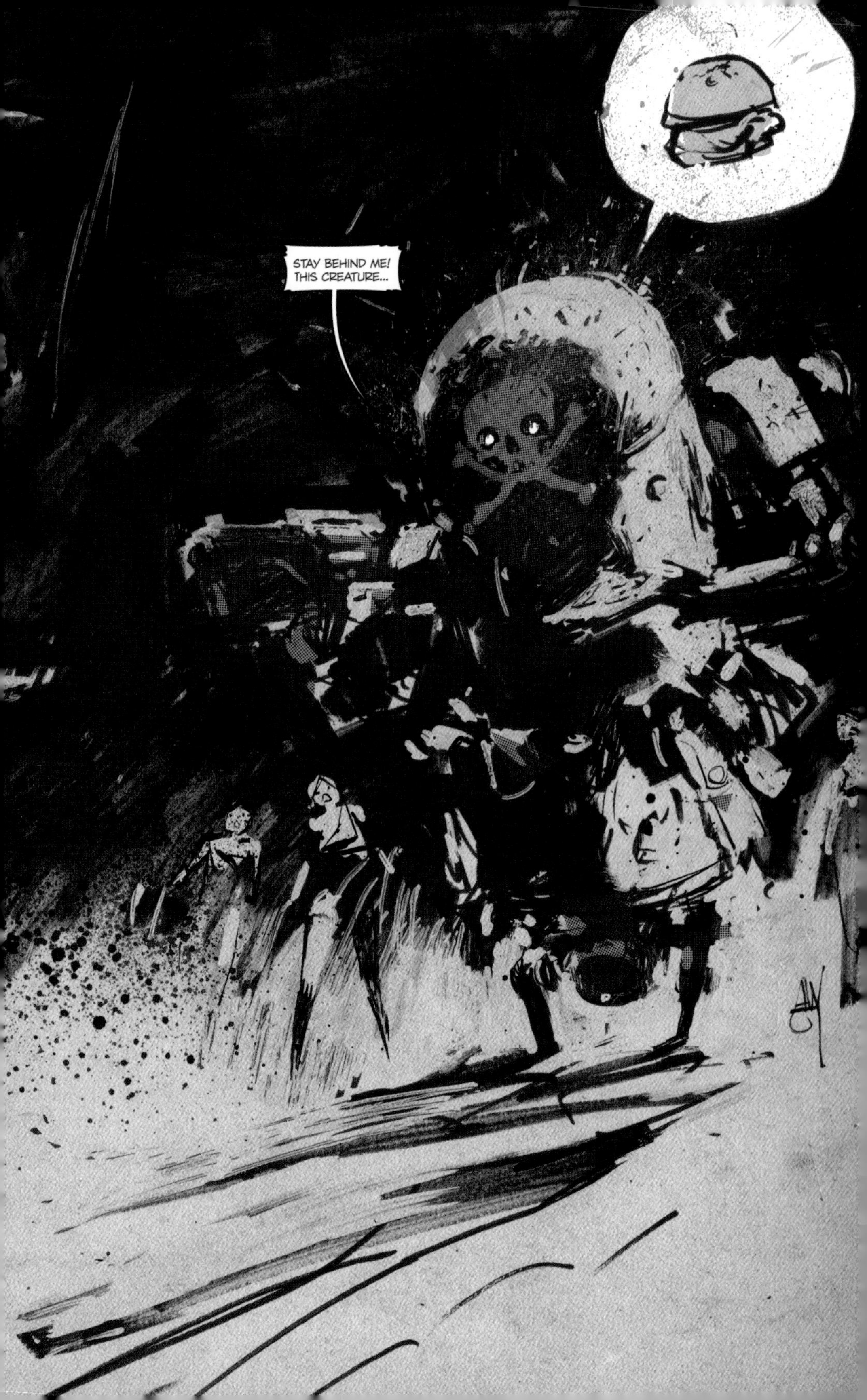
STAY BEHIND ME! THIS CREATURE...

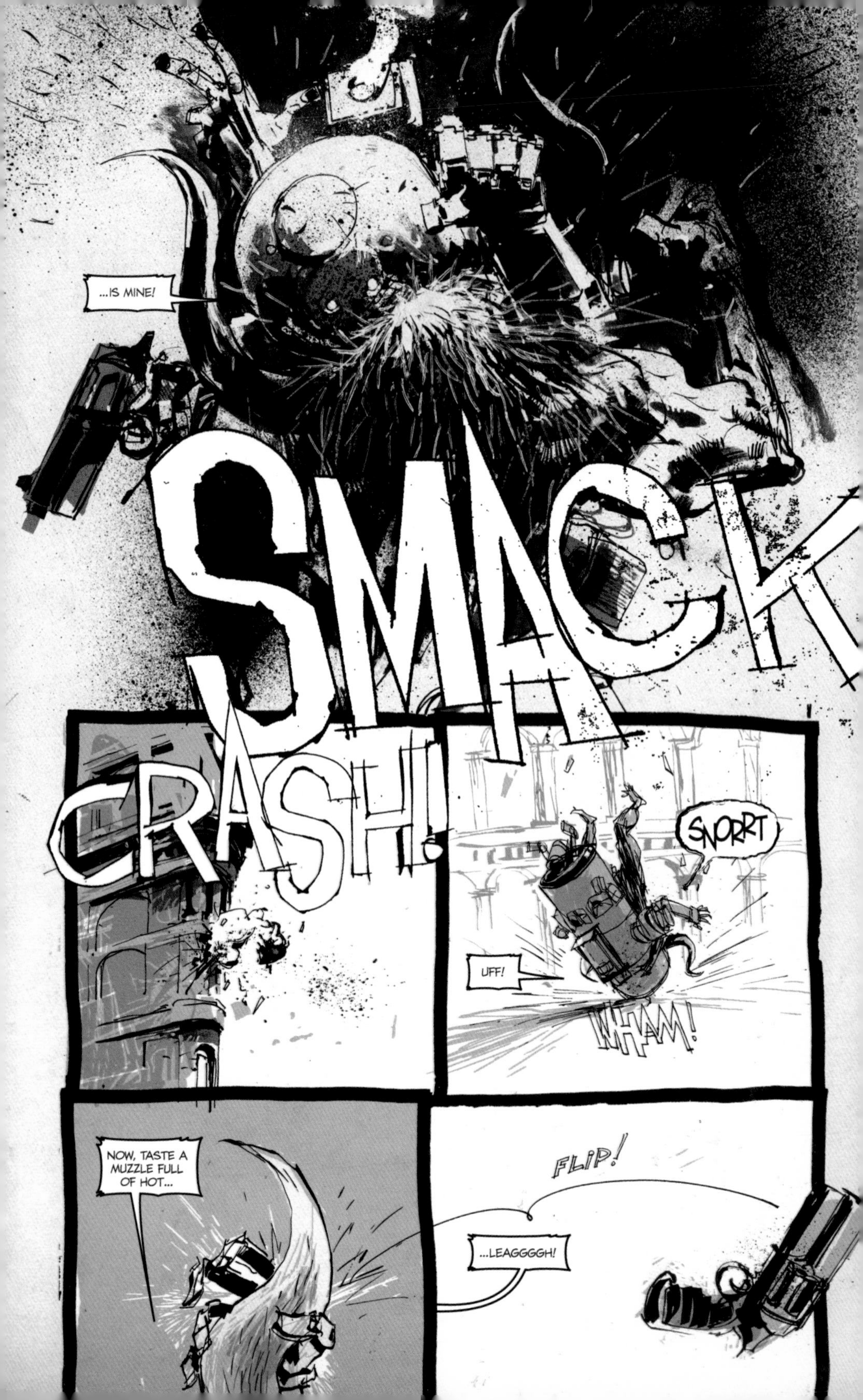
...IS MINE!
SMACK
CRASH!
SNORRT
UFF!
WHAM!
NOW, TASTE A MUZZLE FULL OF HOT...
FLIP!
...LEAGGGGH!

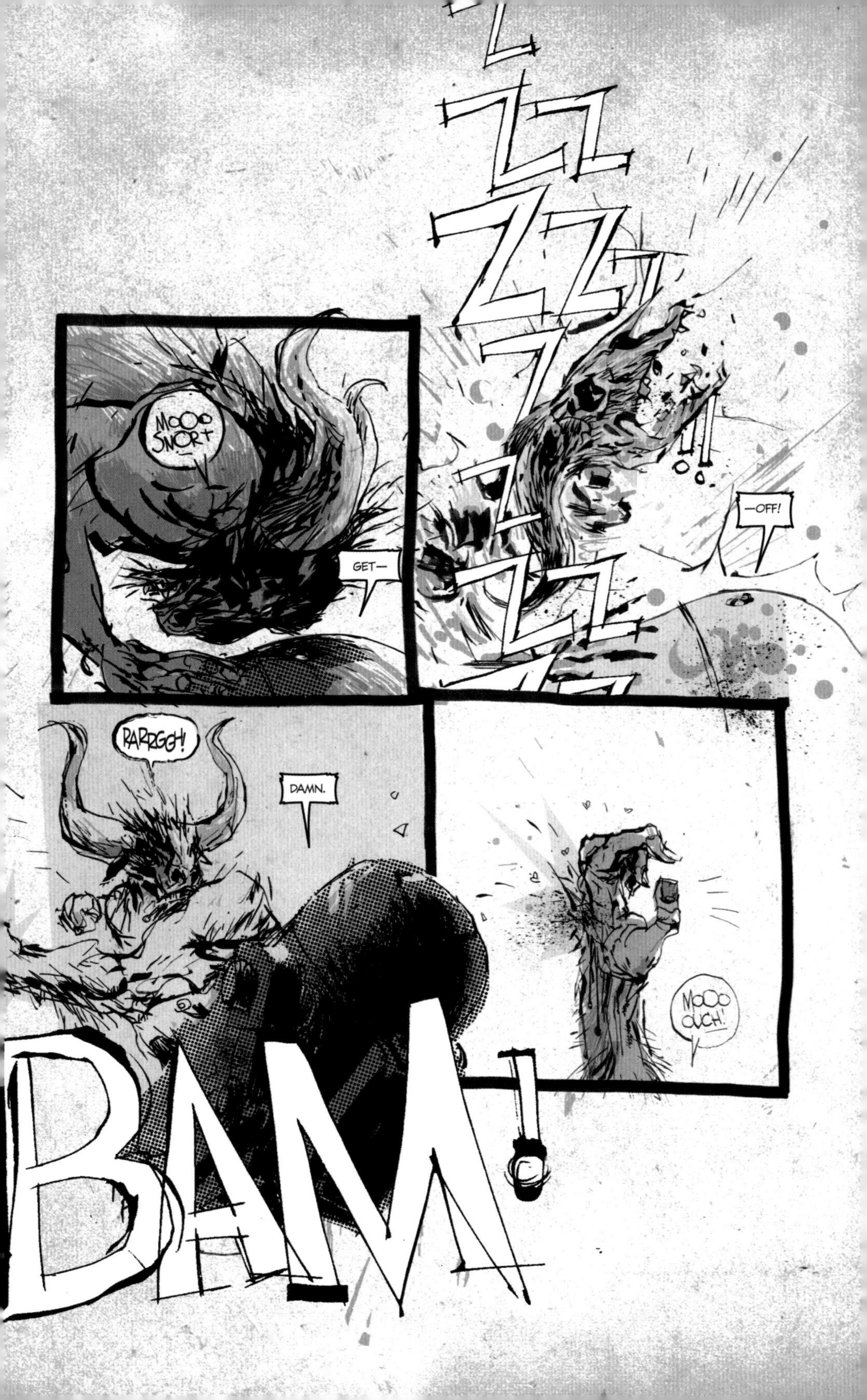
ZZZZZZZZ
MOOO SNORT
GET—
—OFF!
RARRGGH!
DAMN.
MOOO OUCH!
BAM!

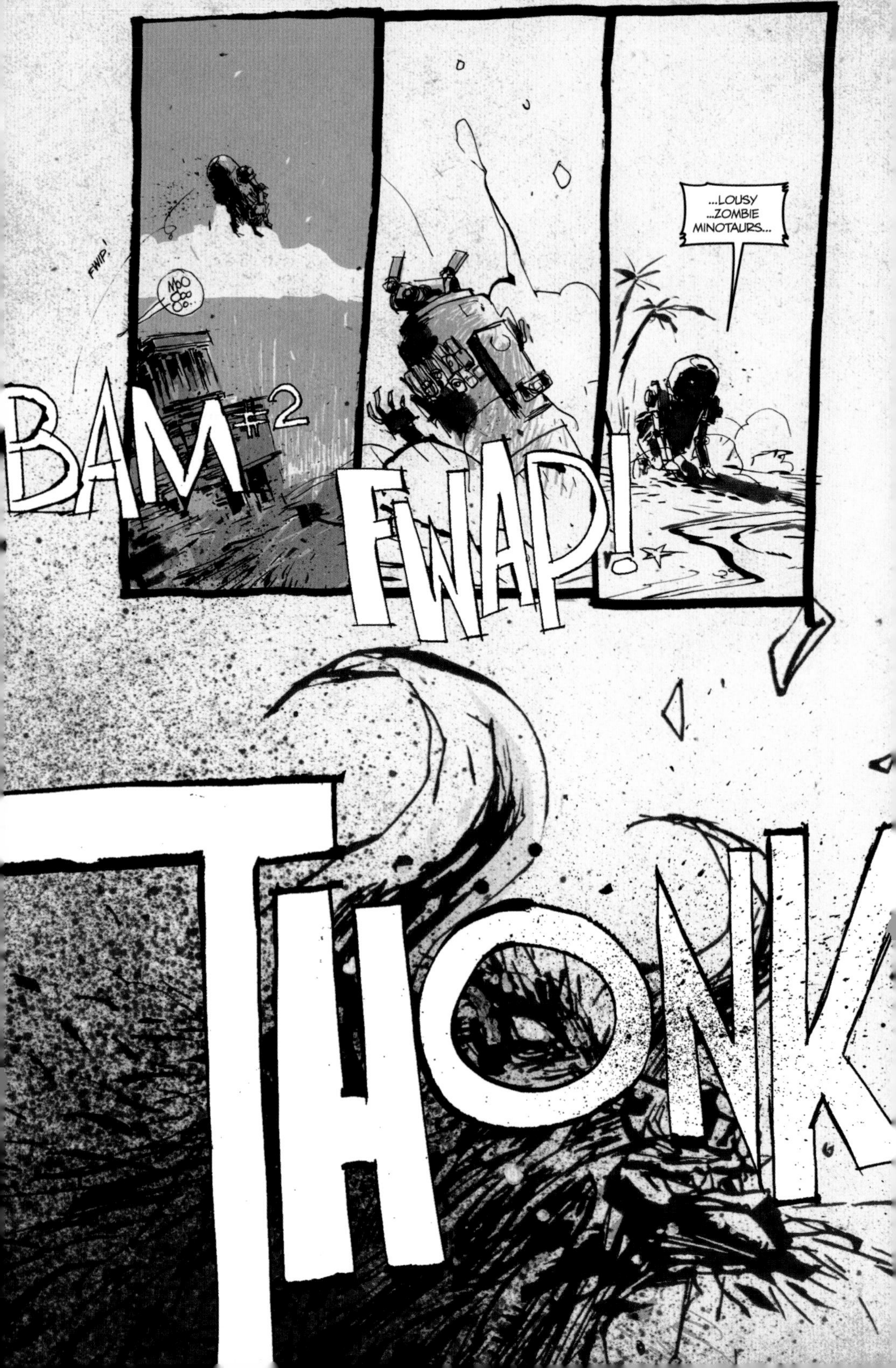
FWIP!
MOOOOOOO..
BAM #2
FWAP!
...LOUSY ...ZOMBIE MINOTAURS...
THONK

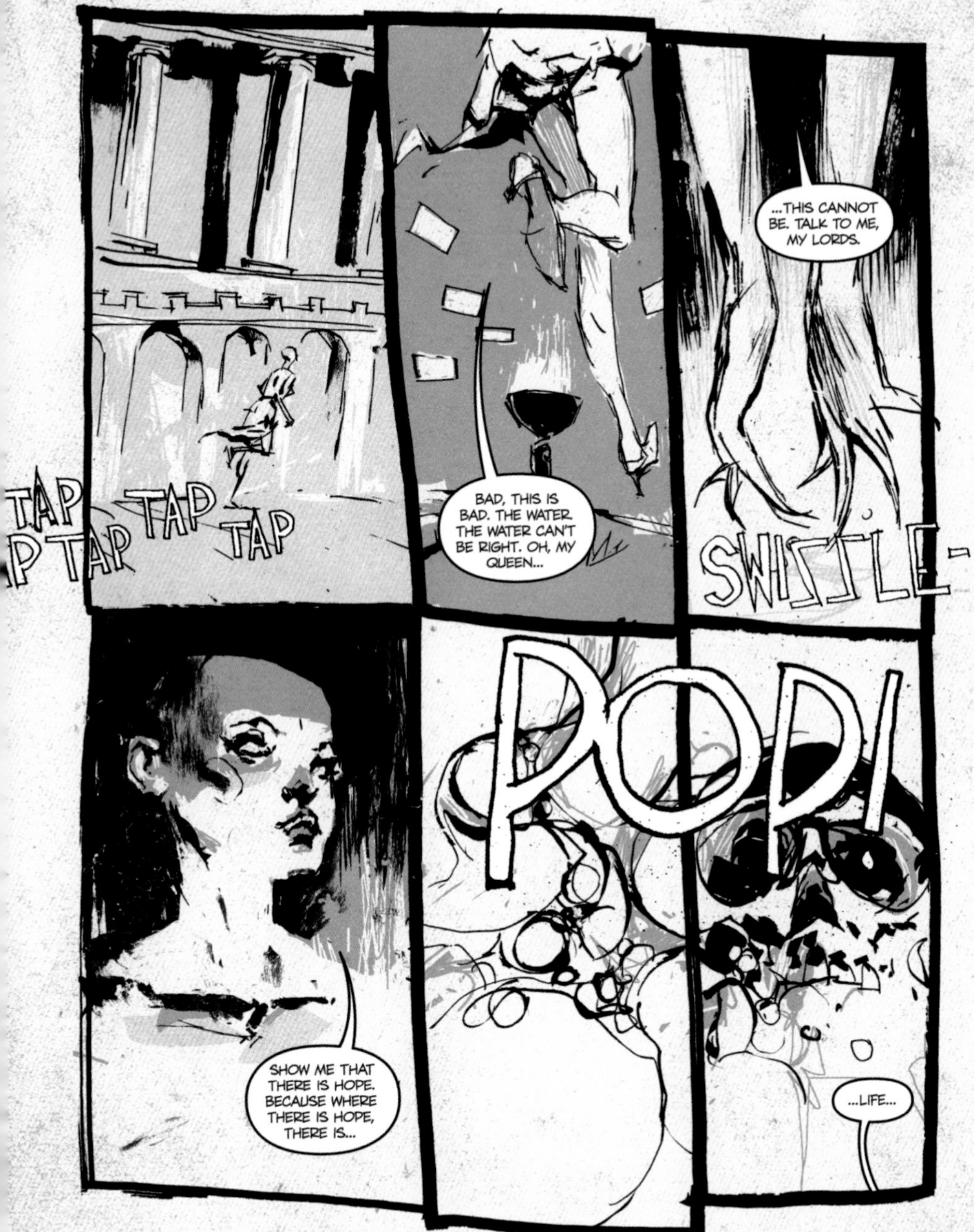
TAP TAP TAP TAP TAP
BAD, THIS IS BAD. THE WATER THE WATER CAN'T BE RIGHT. OH, MY QUEEN...
...THIS CANNOT BE. TALK TO ME, MY LORDS.
SWIZZLE-
SHOW ME THAT THERE IS HOPE. BECAUSE WHERE THERE IS HOPE, THERE IS...
POP!
...LIFE...

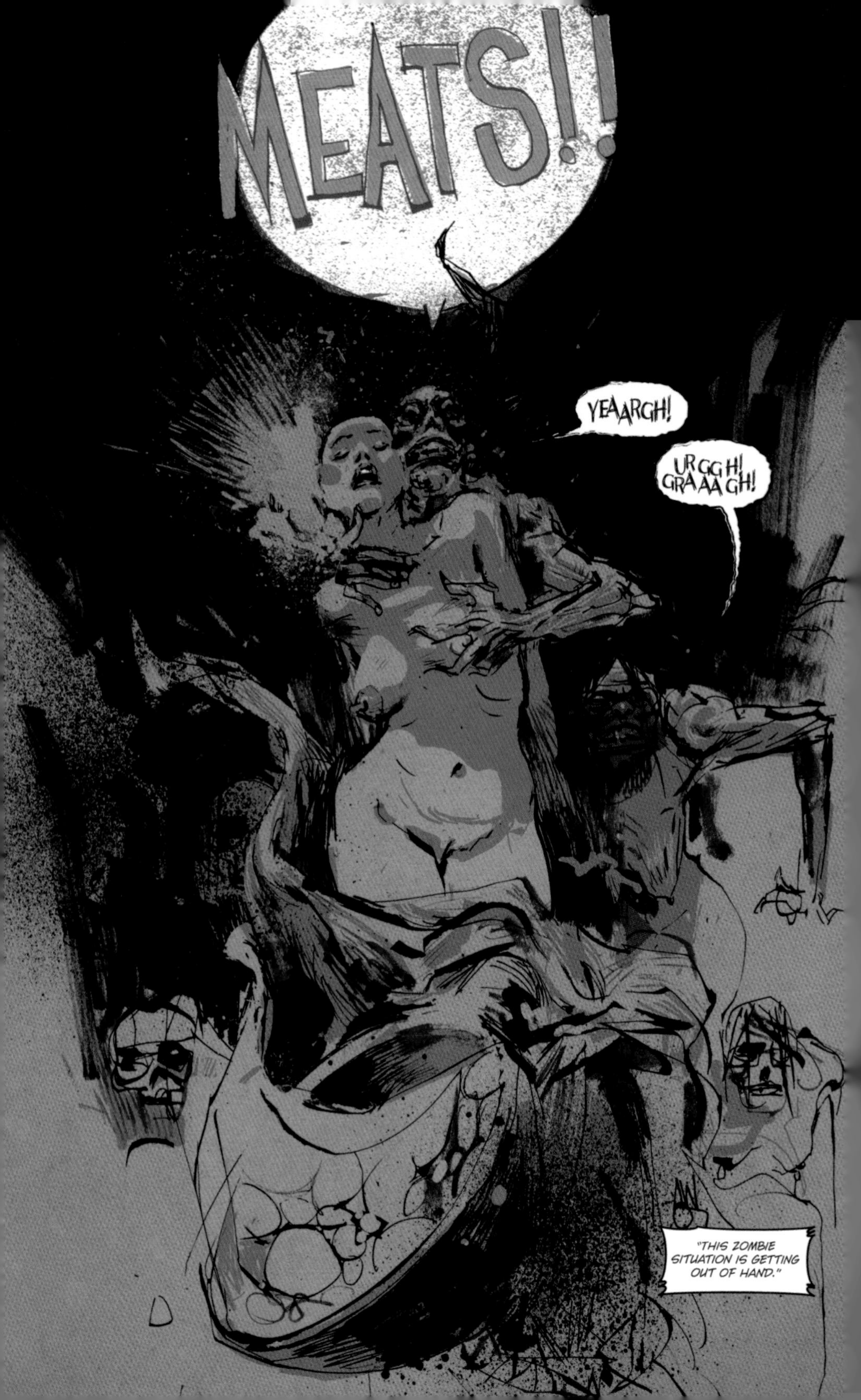
MEATS!!
YEAARGH!
URGGH! GRAAAGH!
"THIS ZOMBIE SITUATION IS GETTING OUT OF HAND."

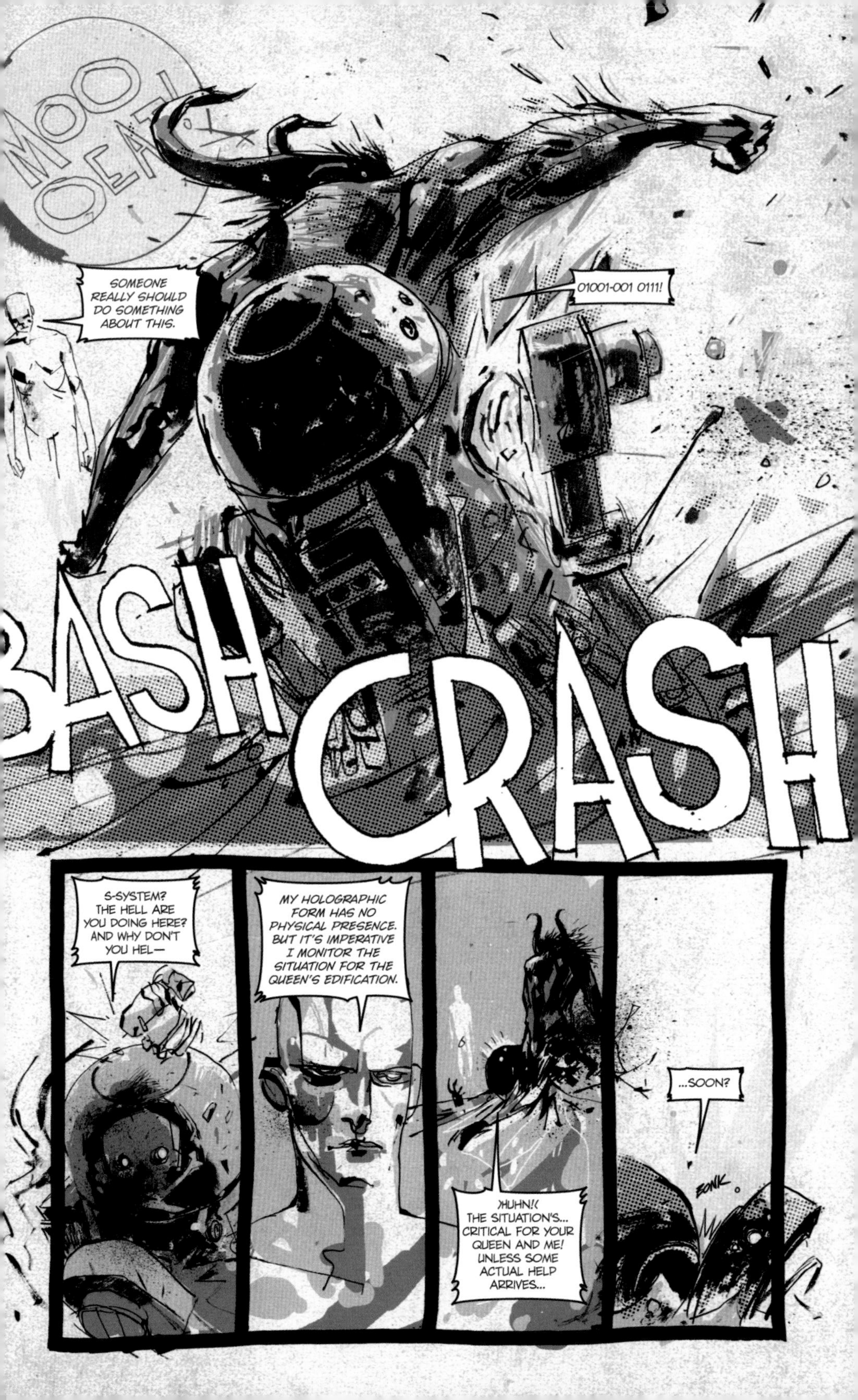

SOMEONE REALLY SHOULD DO SOMETHING ABOUT THIS.
01001-001 0111!
BASH
CRASH
S-SYSTEM? THE HELL ARE YOU DOING HERE? AND WHY DON'T YOU HEL—
MY HOLOGRAPHIC FORM HAS NO PHYSICAL PRESENCE. BUT IT'S IMPERATIVE I MONITOR THE SITUATION FOR THE QUEEN'S EDIFICATION.
›HUHN!‹ THE SITUATION'S... CRITICAL FOR YOUR QUEEN AND ME! UNLESS SOME ACTUAL HELP ARRIVES...
...SOON?
BONK

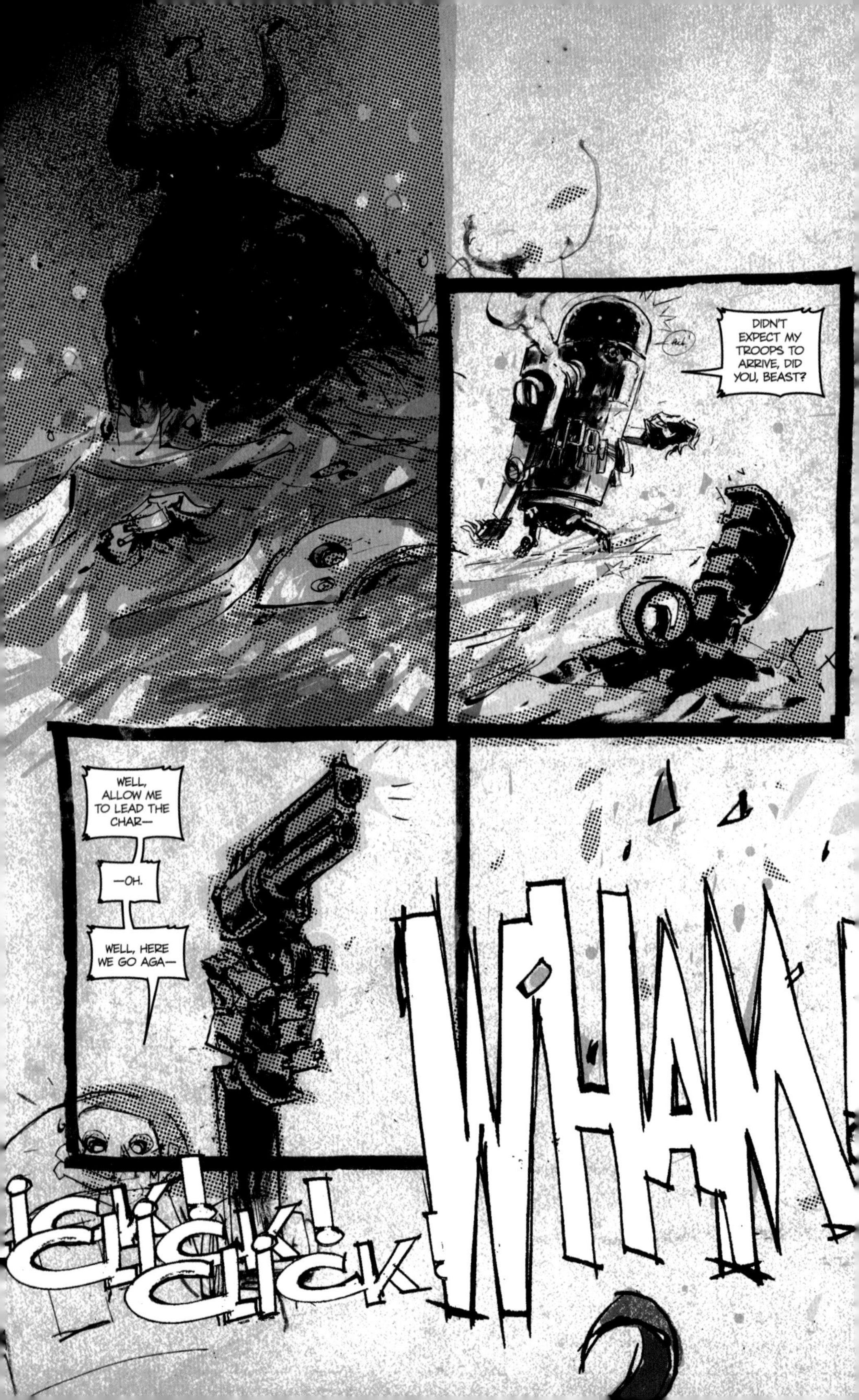
DIDN'T EXPECT MY TROOPS TO ARRIVE, DID YOU, BEAST?
WELL, ALLOW ME TO LEAD THE CHAR—
—OH.
WELL, HERE WE GO AGA—
CLICK!
CLICK!
WHAM

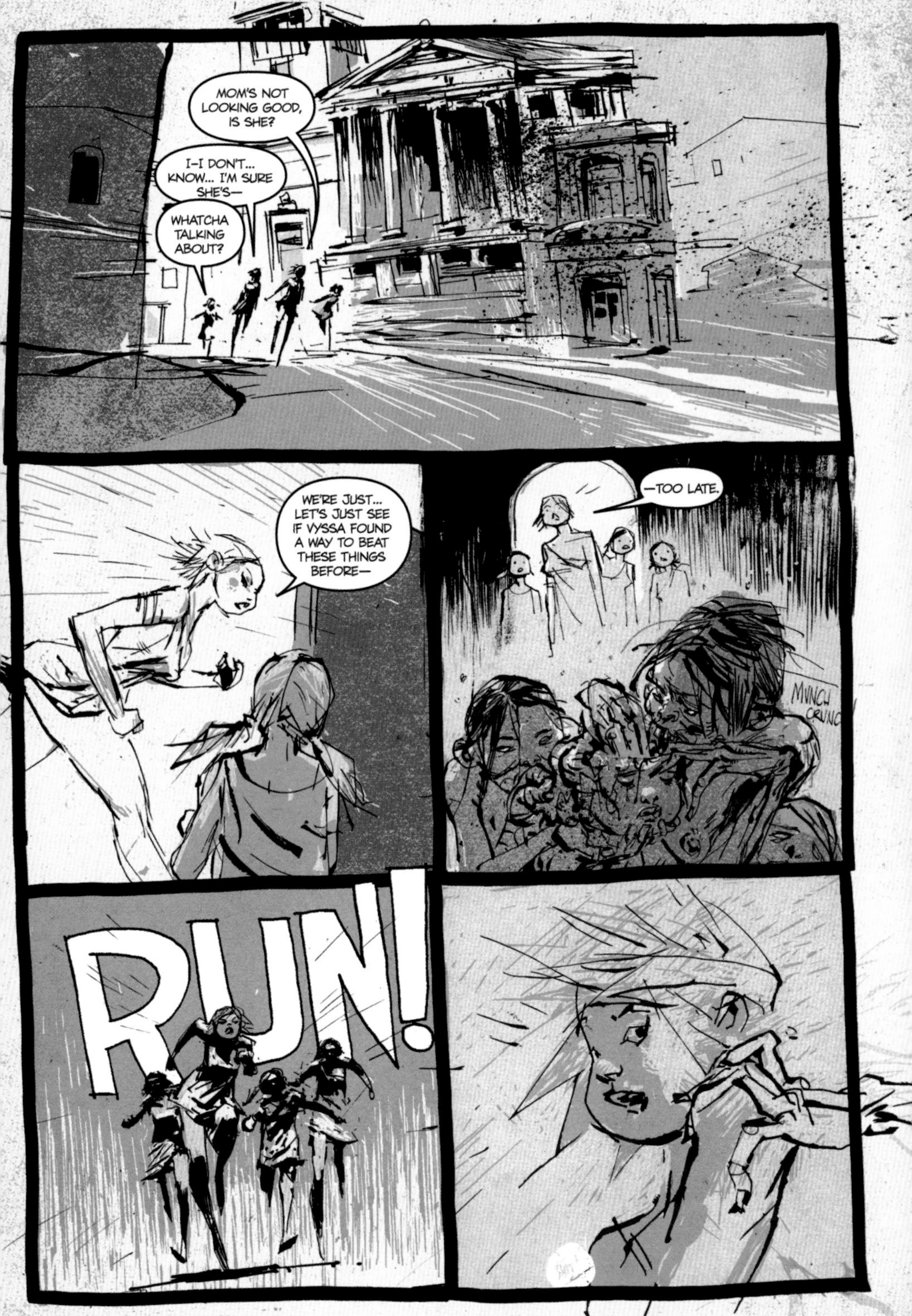
MOM'S NOT LOOKING GOOD, IS SHE?
I-I DON'T... KNOW... I'M SURE SHE'S—
WHATCHA TALKING ABOUT?
WE'RE JUST... LET'S JUST SEE IF VYSSA FOUND A WAY TO BEAT THESE THINGS BEFORE—
—TOO LATE.
MUNCH CRUNCH
RUN!

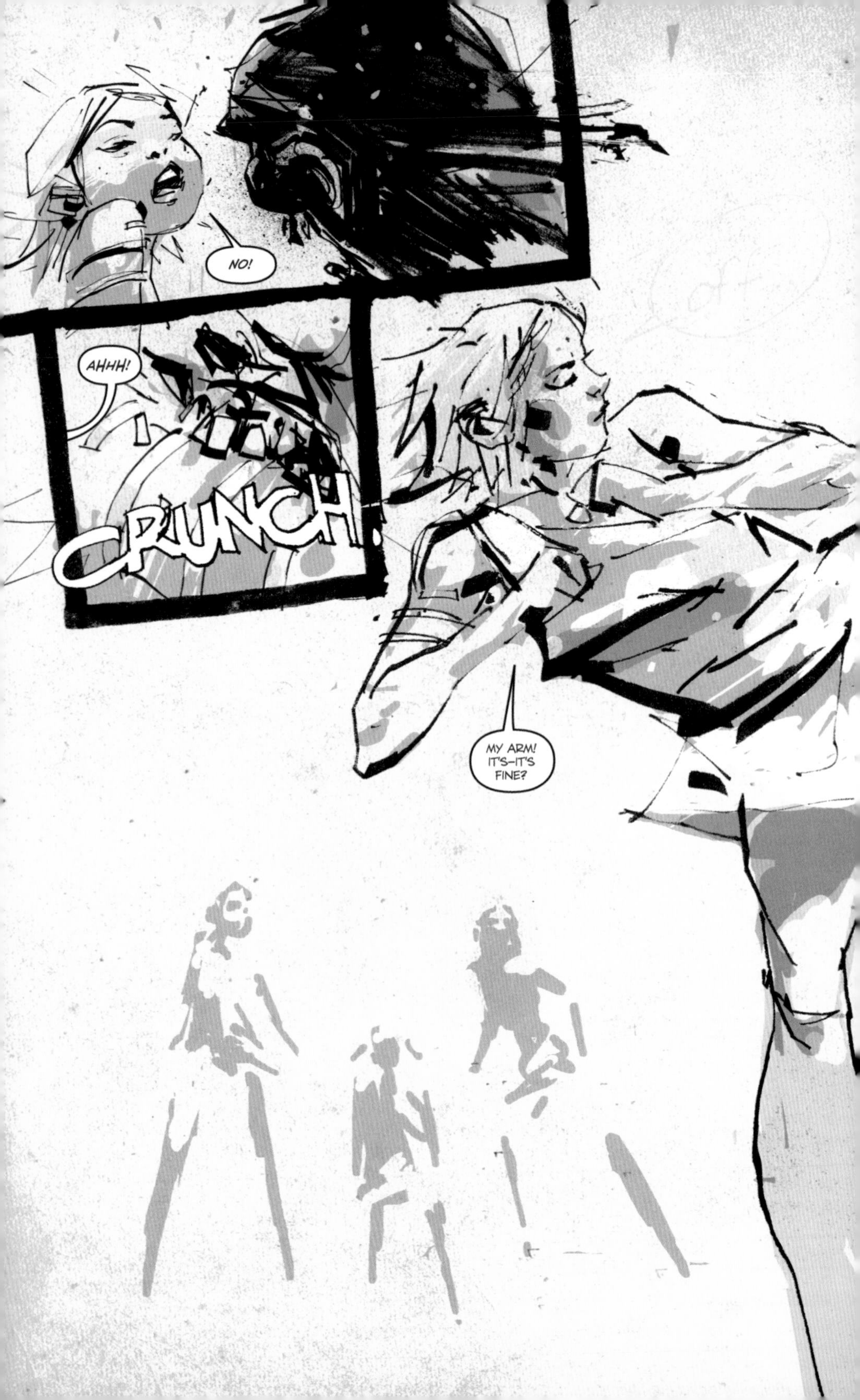
NO!
AHHH!
CRUNCH!
MY ARM! IT'S—IT'S FINE?

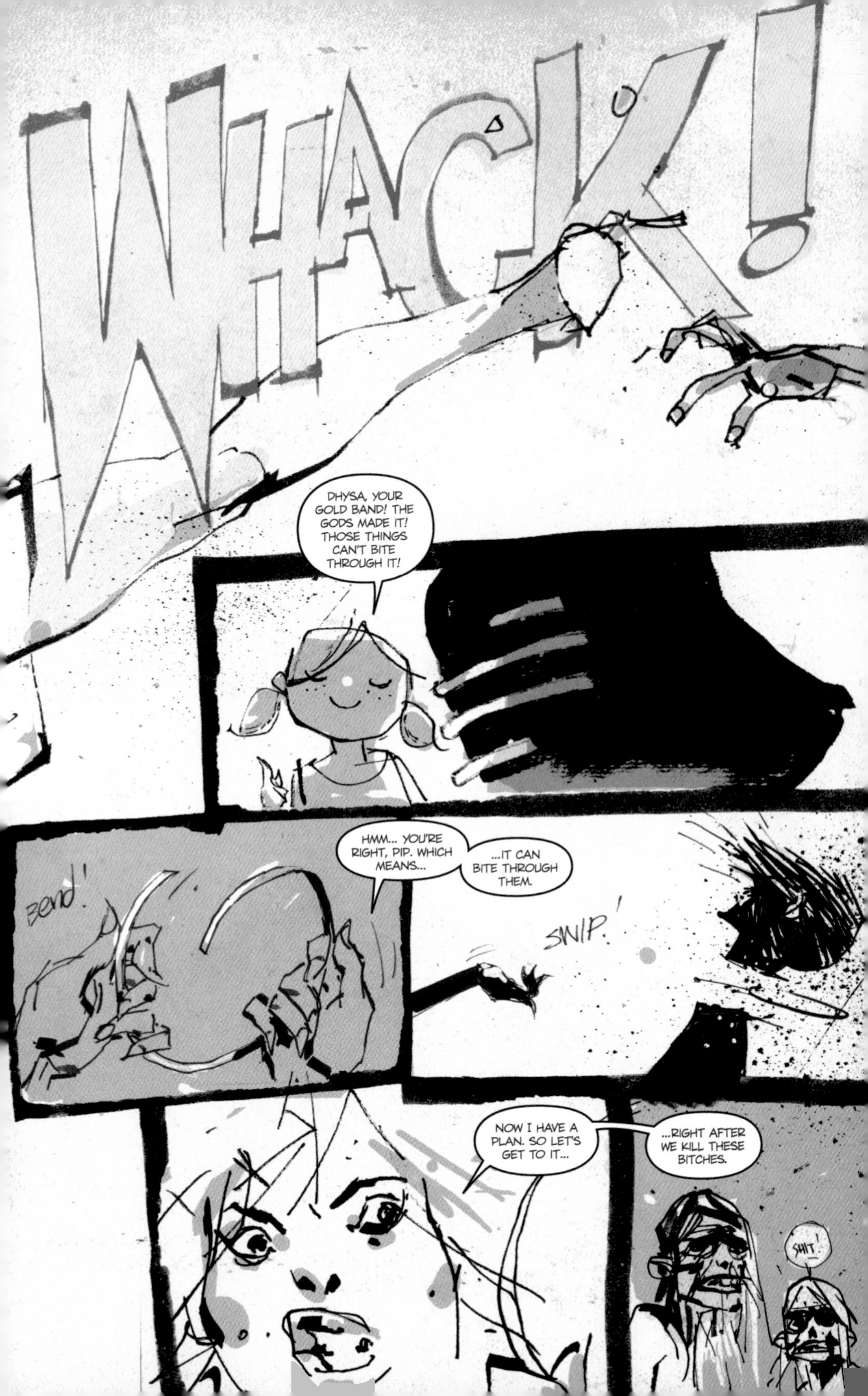
WHACK!
DHYSA, YOUR GOLD BAND! THE GODS MADE IT! THOSE THINGS CAN'T BITE THROUGH IT!
HMM... YOU'RE RIGHT, PIP. WHICH MEANS...
...IT CAN BITE THROUGH THEM.
Bend!
SNIP!
NOW I HAVE A PLAN. SO LET'S GET TO IT...
...RIGHT AFTER WE KILL THESE BITCHES.
SHIT!

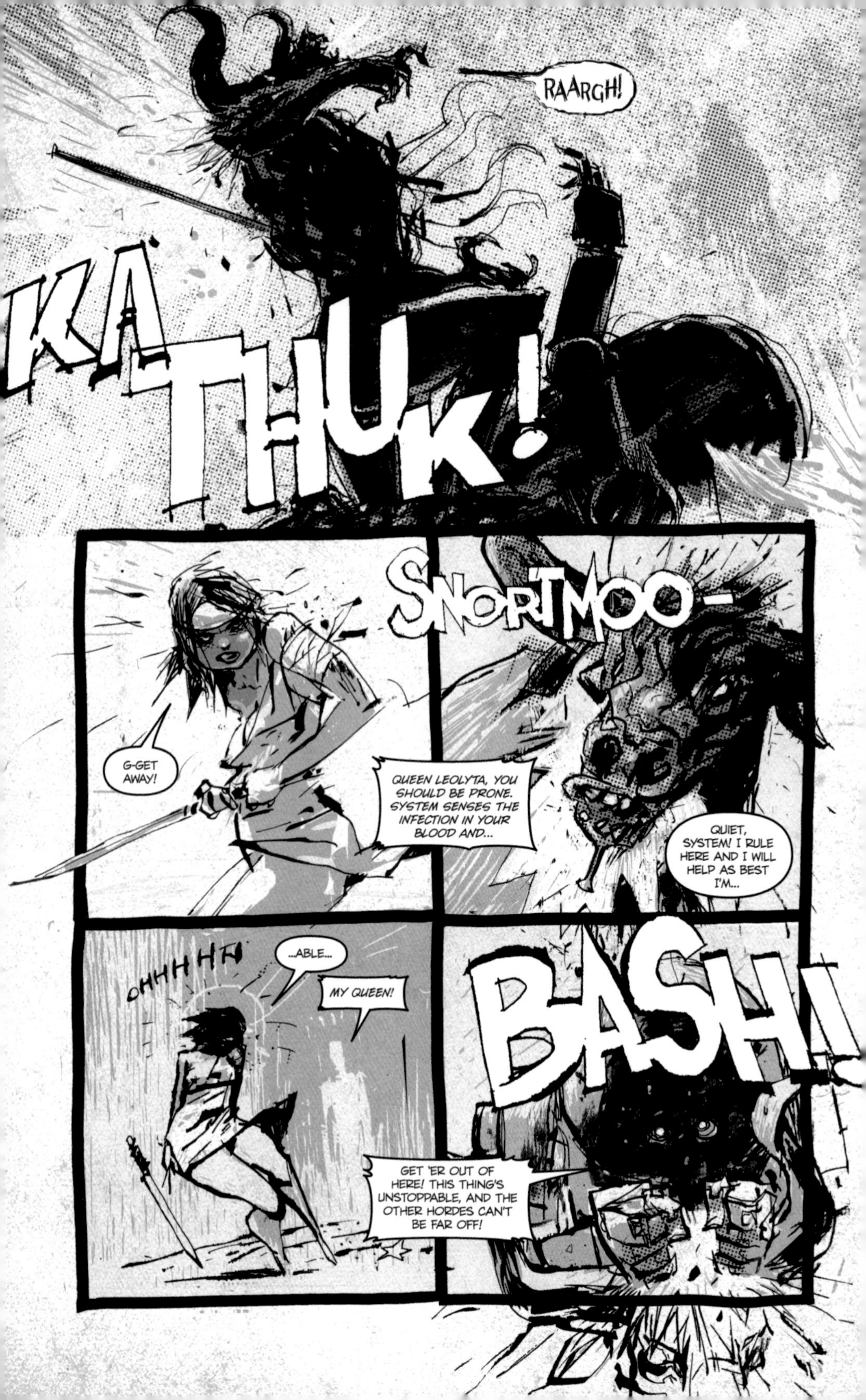
RAARGH!
KA THUK!
G-GET AWAY!
SNORTMOO-
QUEEN LEOLYTA, YOU SHOULD BE PRONE. SYSTEM SENSES THE INFECTION IN YOUR BLOOD AND...
QUIET, SYSTEM! I RULE HERE AND I WILL HELP AS BEST I'M...
OHHHHH
...ABLE...
MY QUEEN!
BASH!!
GET 'ER OUT OF HERE! THIS THING'S UNSTOPPABLE, AND THE OTHER HORDES CAN'T BE FAR OFF!

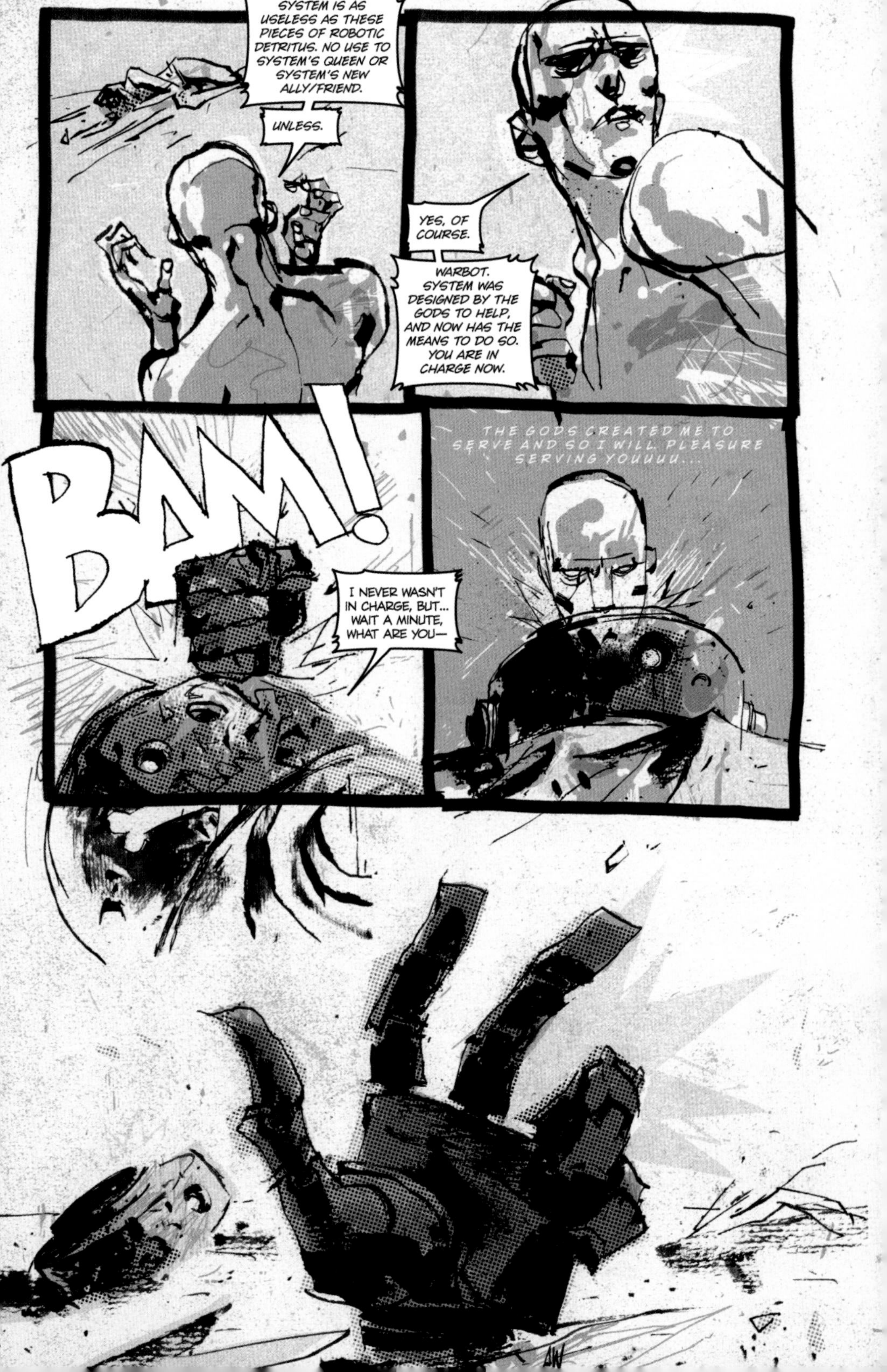
SYSTEM IS AS USELESS AS THESE PIECES OF ROBOTIC DETRITUS. NO USE TO SYSTEM'S QUEEN OR SYSTEM'S NEW ALLY/FRIEND.
UNLESS.
YES, OF COURSE.
WARBOT. SYSTEM WAS DESIGNED BY THE GODS TO HELP, AND NOW HAS THE MEANS TO DO SO. YOU ARE IN CHARGE NOW.
BAM!
I NEVER WASN'T IN CHARGE, BUT... WAIT A MINUTE, WHAT ARE YOU—
THE GODS CREATED ME TO SERVE AND SO I WILL. PLEASURE SERVING YOUUUU....

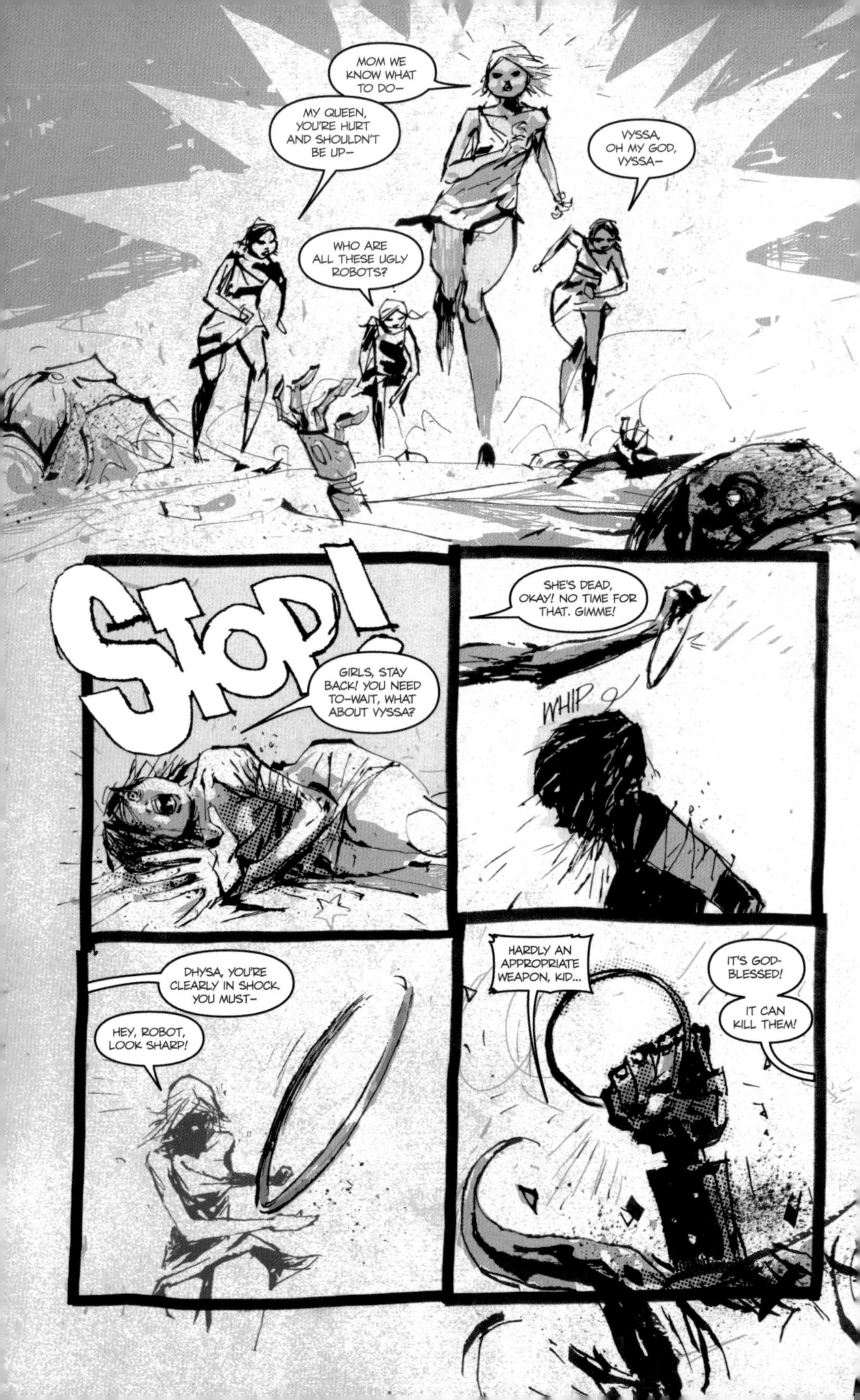
MOM WE KNOW WHAT TO DO–
MY QUEEN, YOU'RE HURT AND SHOULDN'T BE UP–
VYSSA, OH MY GOD, VYSSA–
WHO ARE ALL THESE UGLY ROBOTS?
STOP!
GIRLS, STAY BACK! YOU NEED TO–WAIT, WHAT ABOUT VYSSA?
SHE'S DEAD, OKAY! NO TIME FOR THAT. GIMME!
WHIP
DHYSA, YOU'RE CLEARLY IN SHOCK. YOU MUST–
HEY, ROBOT, LOOK SHARP!
HARDLY AN APPROPRIATE WEAPON, KID...
IT'S GOD-BLESSED!
IT CAN KILL THEM!

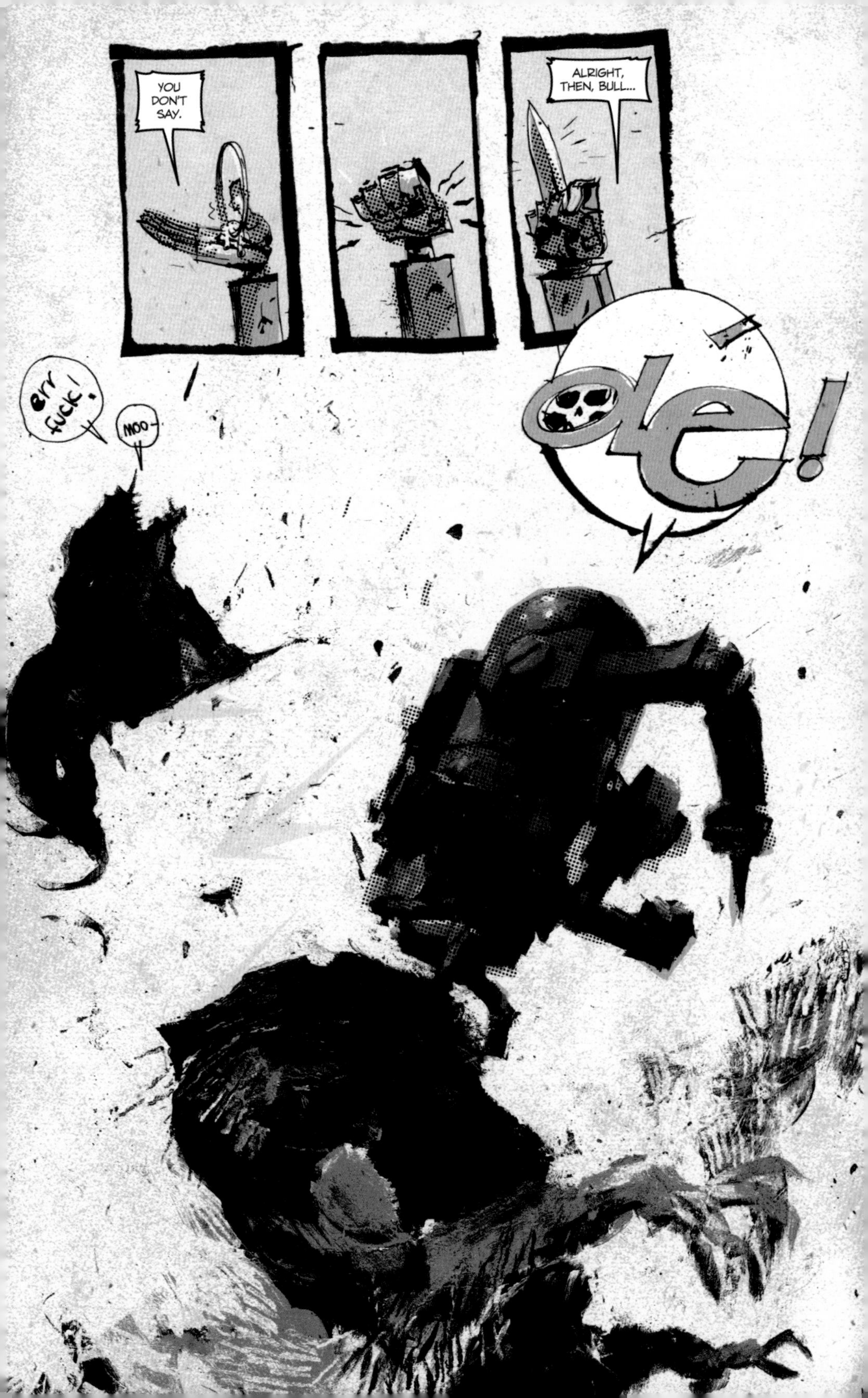
YOU DON'T SAY.
ALRIGHT, THEN, BULL...
err fuck!
MOO-
olé!

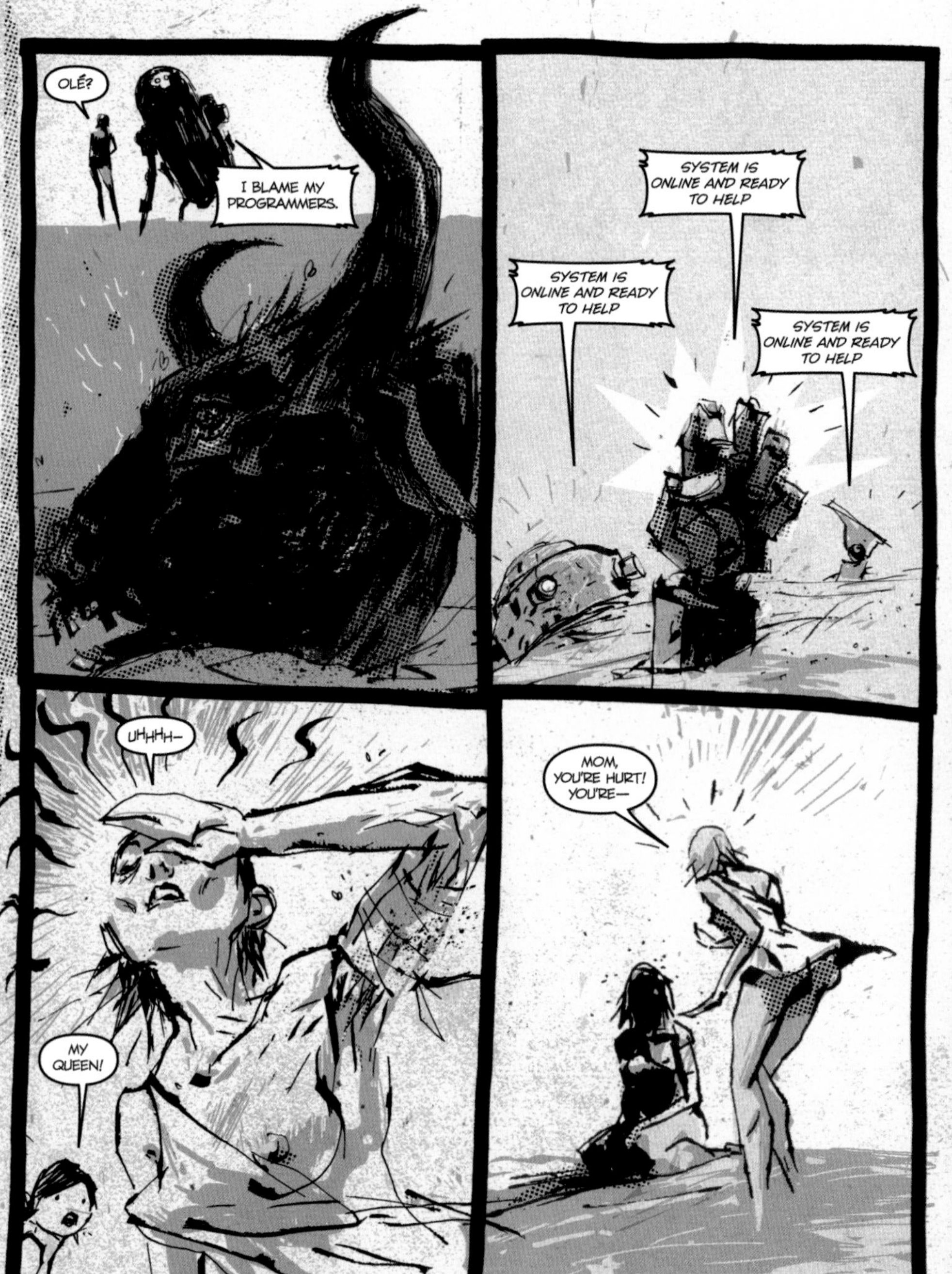
OLÉ?
I BLAME MY PROGRAMMERS.
SYSTEM IS ONLINE AND READY TO HELP
SYSTEM IS ONLINE AND READY TO HELP
SYSTEM IS ONLINE AND READY TO HELP
UHHHH–
MY QUEEN!
MOM, YOU'RE HURT! YOU'RE–

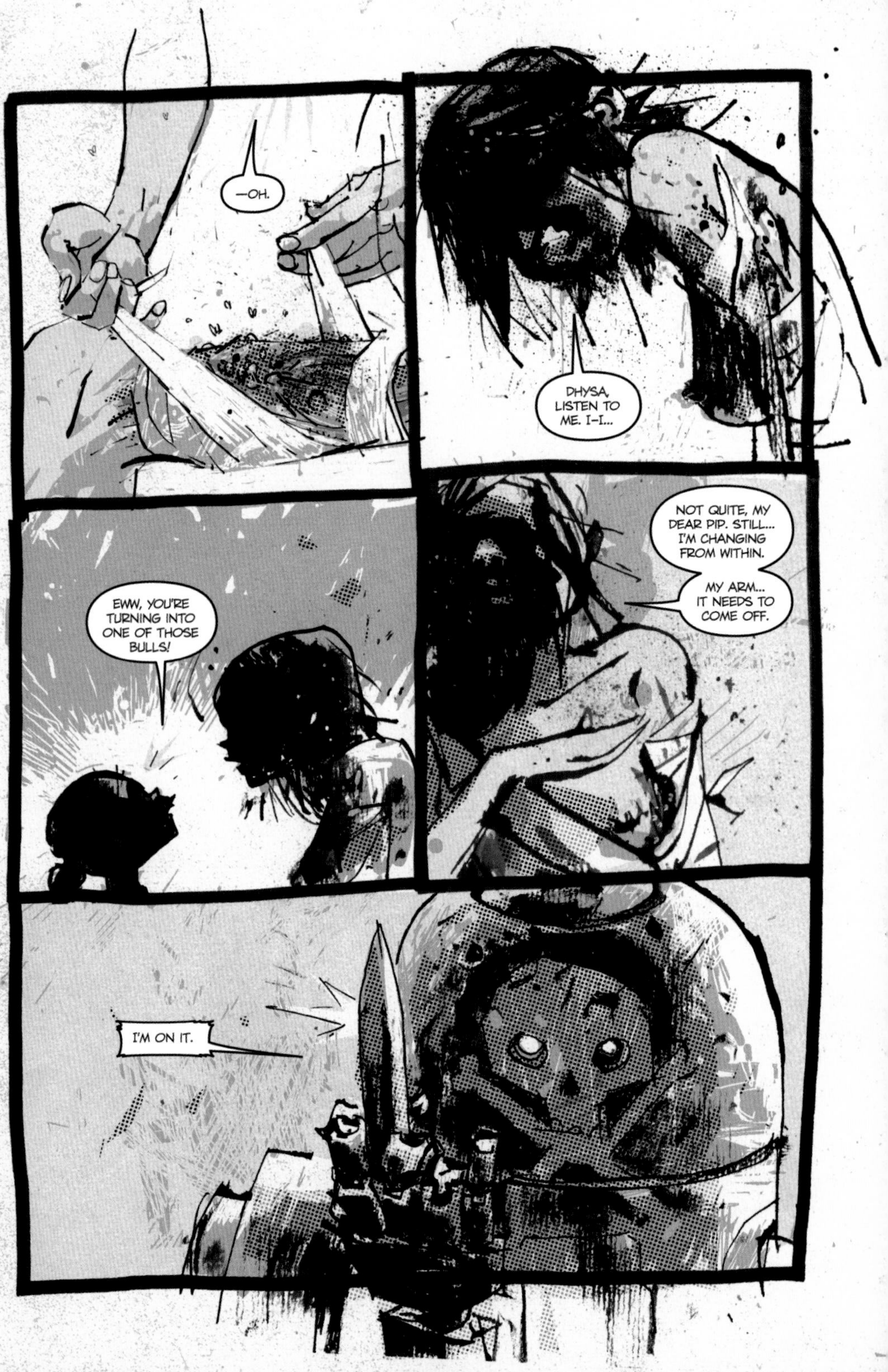
—OH.
DHYSA, LISTEN TO ME. I–I...
EWW, YOU'RE TURNING INTO ONE OF THOSE BULLS!
NOT QUITE, MY DEAR PIP. STILL... I'M CHANGING FROM WITHIN.
MY ARM... IT NEEDS TO COME OFF.
I'M ON IT.

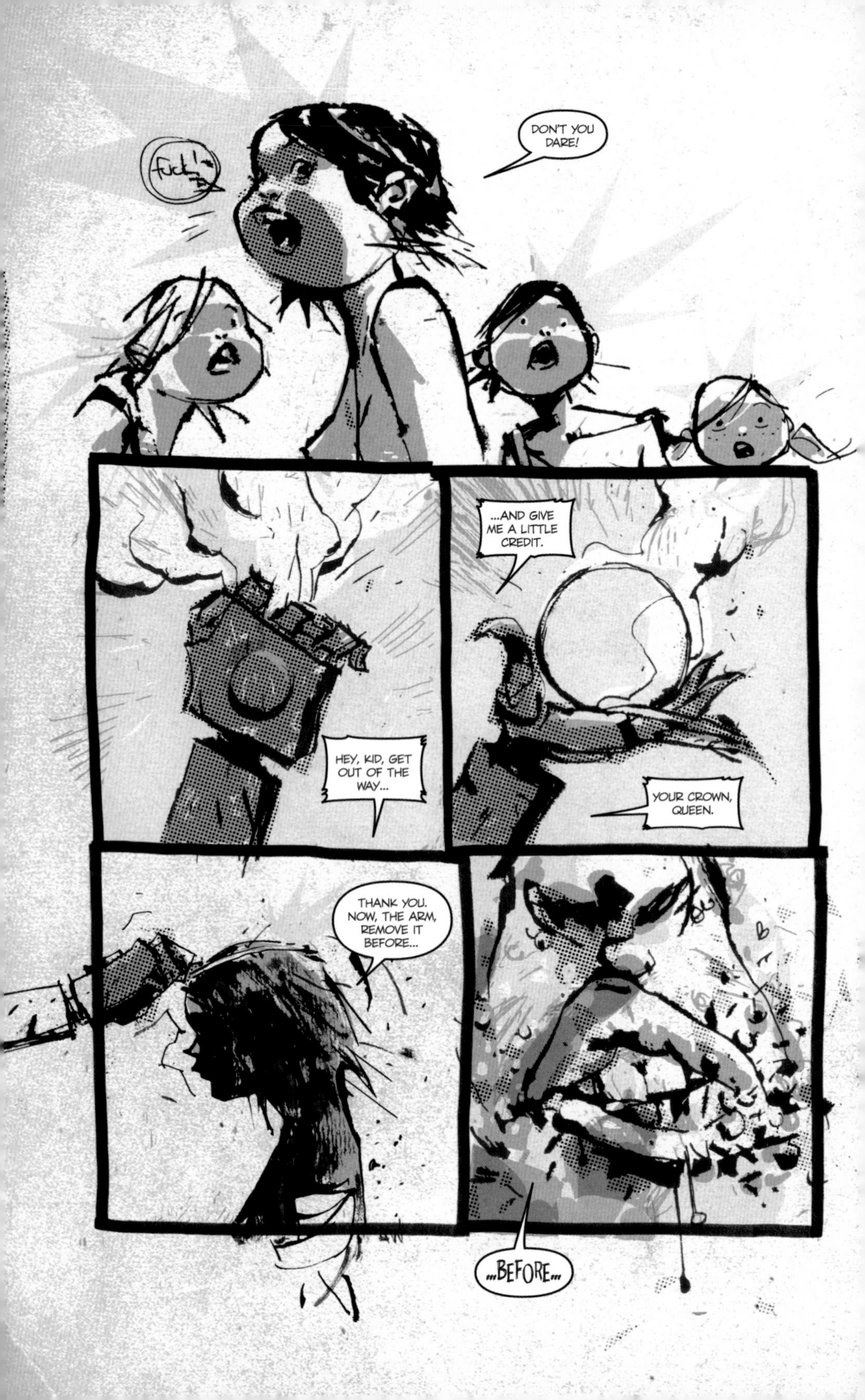
Fuck!
DON'T YOU DARE!
HEY, KID, GET OUT OF THE WAY...
...AND GIVE ME A LITTLE CREDIT.
YOUR CROWN, QUEEN.
THANK YOU. NOW, THE ARM, REMOVE IT BEFORE...
...BEFORE...

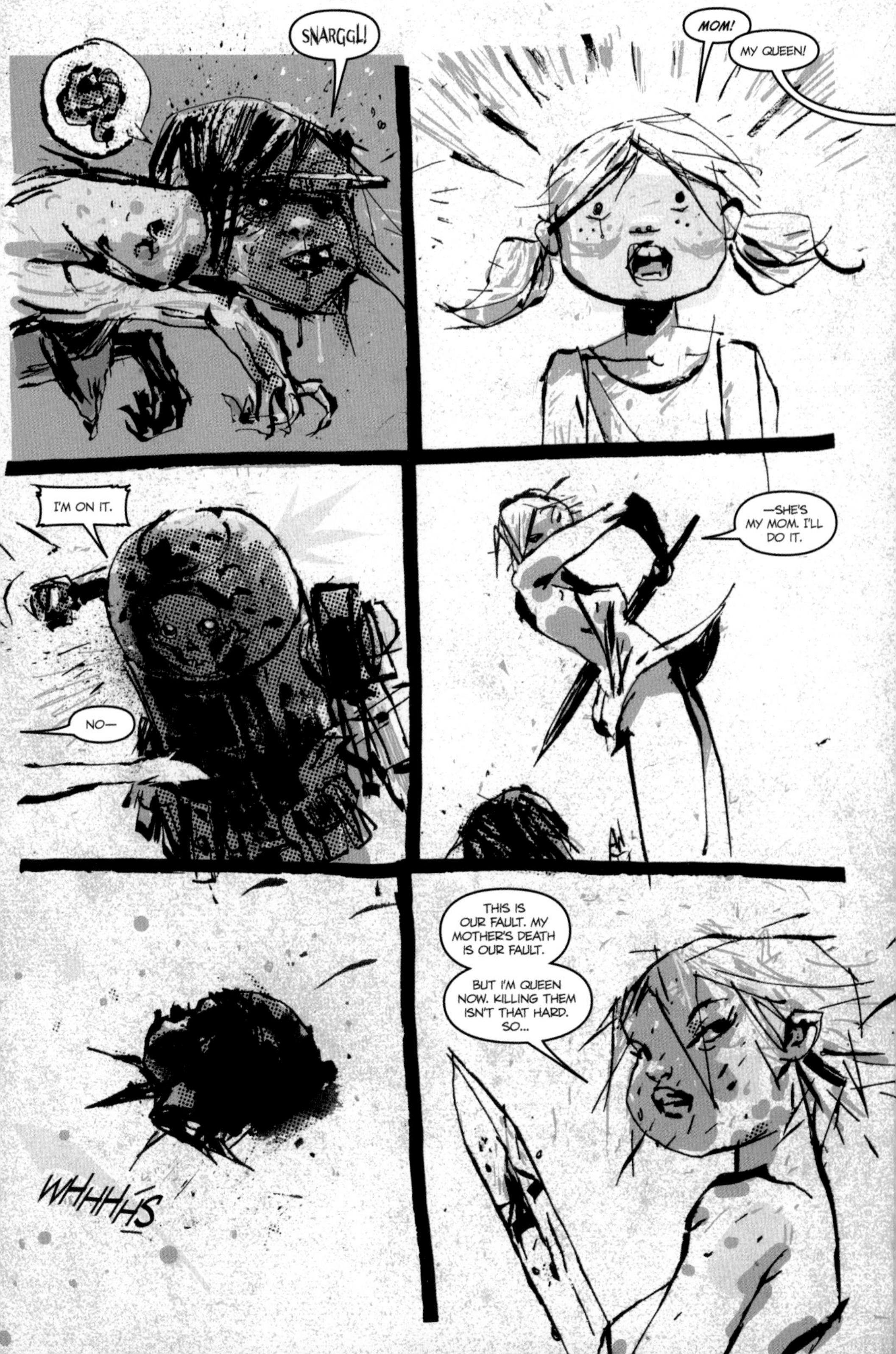
SNARGGL!
MOM!
MY QUEEN!
I'M ON IT.
NO—
—SHE'S MY MOM. I'LL DO IT.
WHHHHS
THIS IS OUR FAULT. MY MOTHER'S DEATH IS OUR FAULT.
BUT I'M QUEEN NOW. KILLING THEM ISN'T THAT HARD. SO...

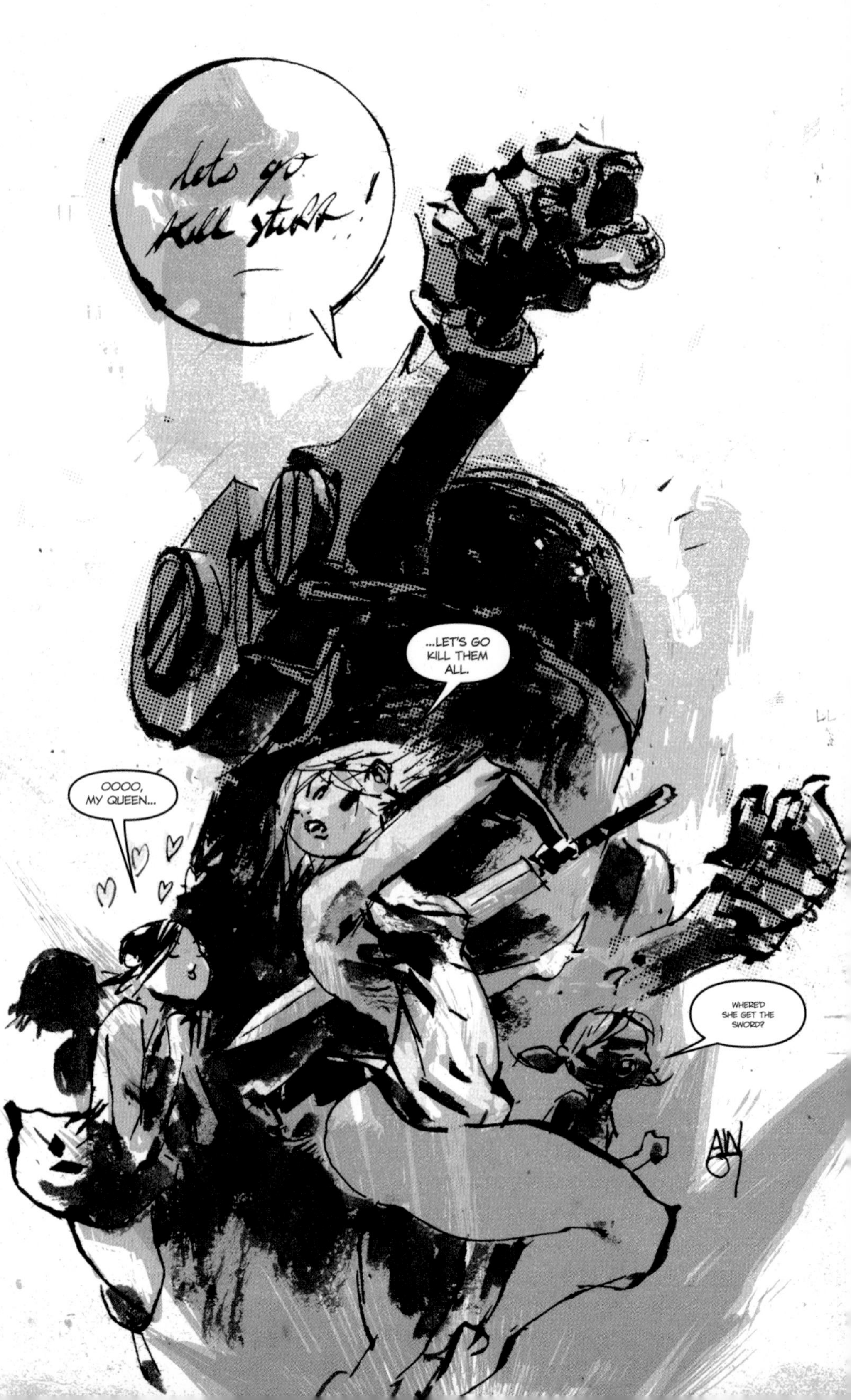
lets go kill stuff!
...LET'S GO KILL THEM ALL.
OOOO, MY QUEEN...
WHERE'D SHE GET THE SWORD?

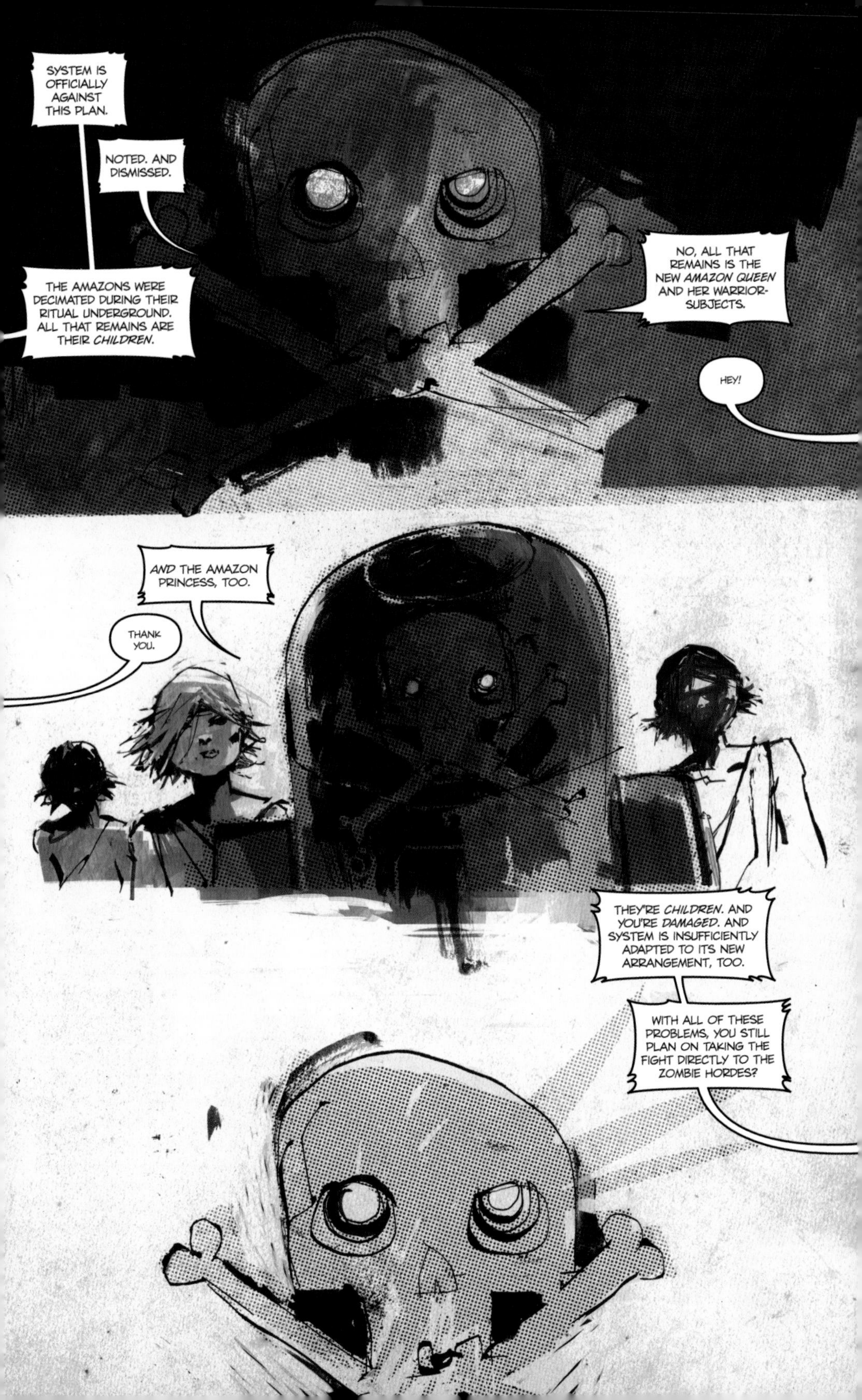
SYSTEM IS OFFICIALLY AGAINST THIS PLAN.
NOTED. AND DISMISSED.
THE AMAZONS WERE DECIMATED DURING THEIR RITUAL UNDERGROUND. ALL THAT REMAINS ARE THEIR *CHILDREN*.
NO, ALL THAT REMAINS IS THE NEW *AMAZON QUEEN* AND HER WARRIOR-SUBJECTS.
HEY!
AND THE AMAZON PRINCESS, TOO.
THANK YOU.
THEY'RE *CHILDREN*. AND YOU'RE *DAMAGED*. AND SYSTEM IS INSUFFICIENTLY ADAPTED TO ITS NEW ARRANGEMENT, TOO.
WITH ALL OF THESE PROBLEMS, YOU STILL PLAN ON TAKING THE FIGHT DIRECTLY TO THE ZOMBIE HORDES?

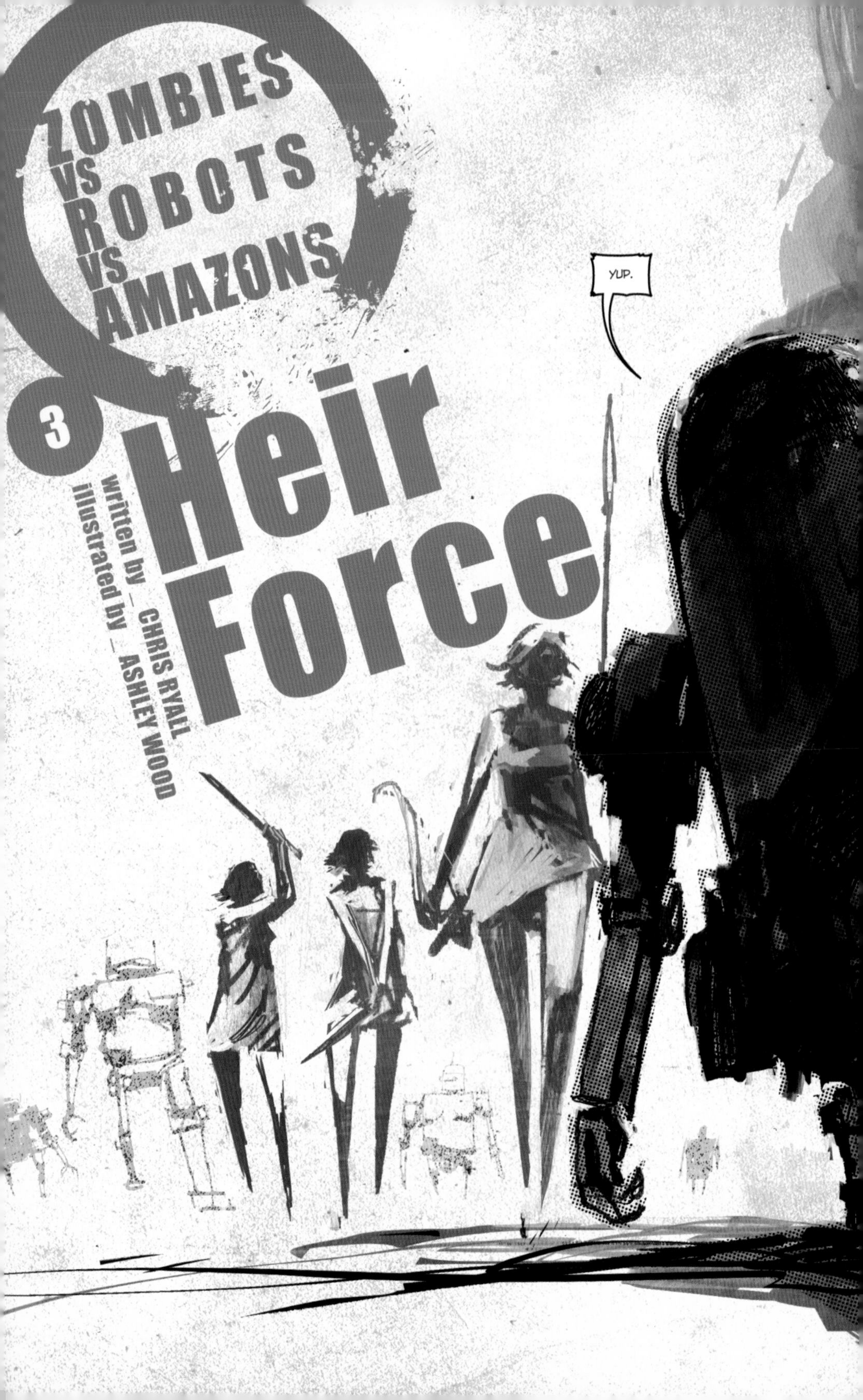
ZOMBIES VS ROBOTS VS AMAZONS
3
Heir Force
written by _ CHRIS RYALL
illustrated by _ ASHLEY WOOD
YUP.

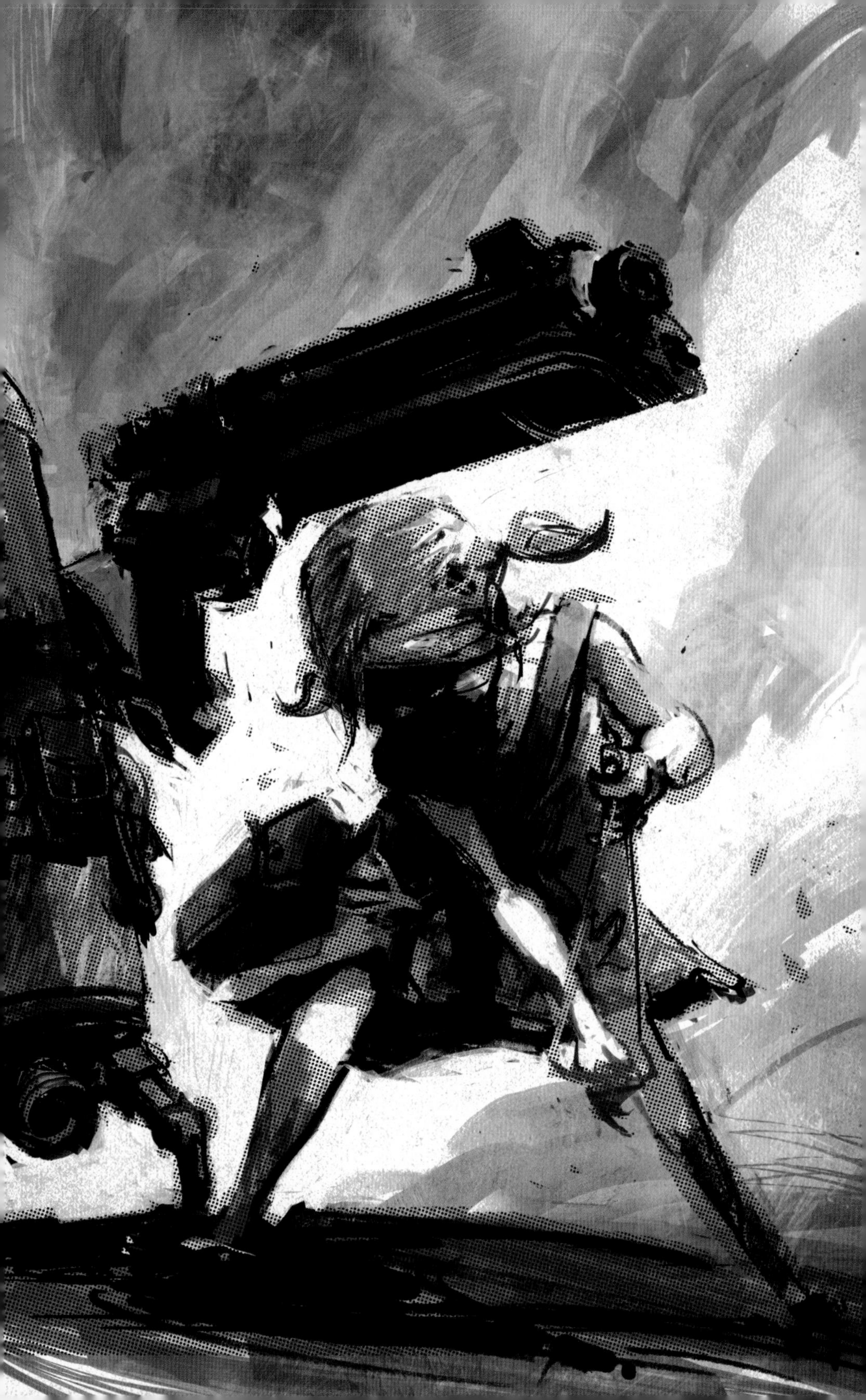

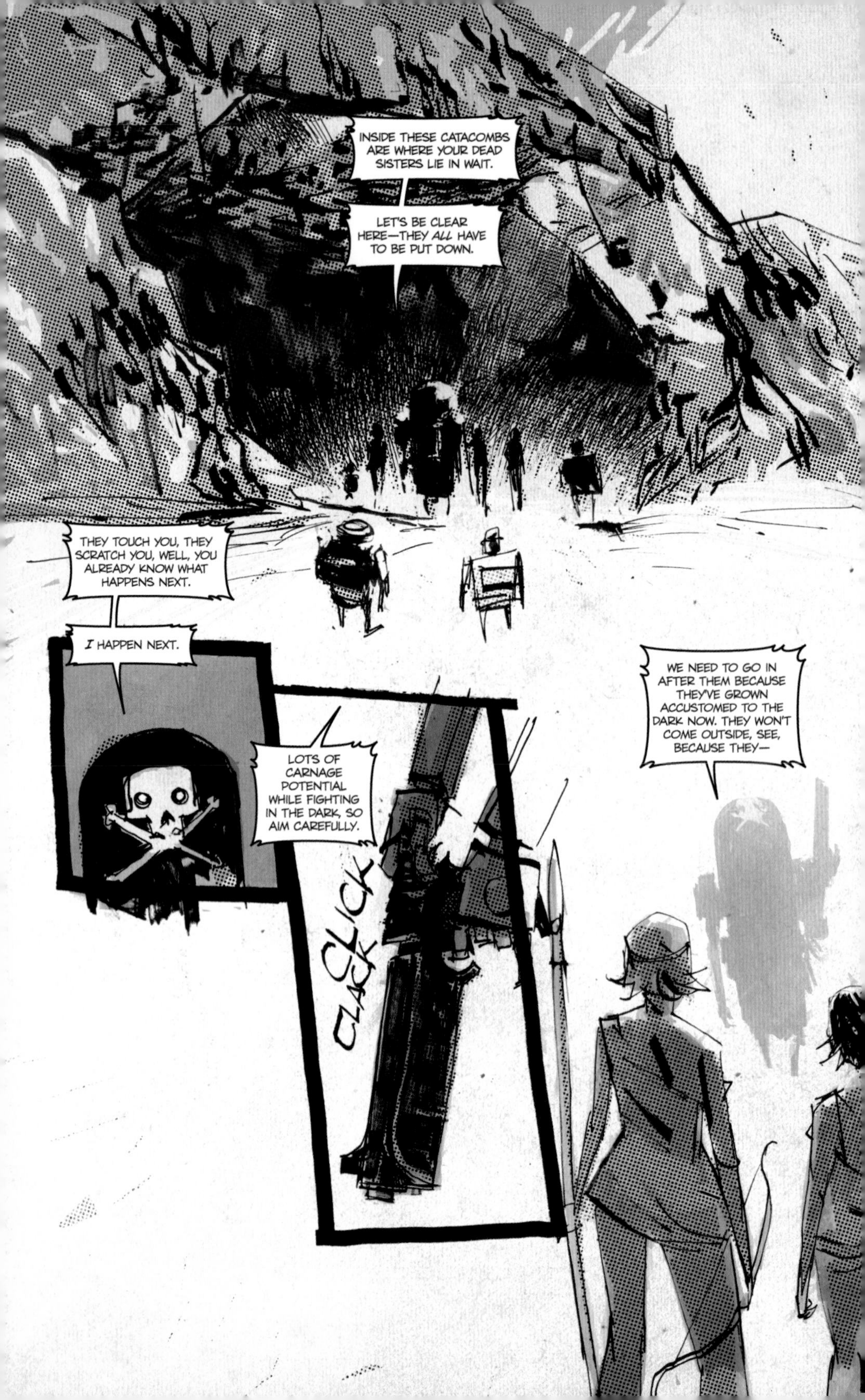
INSIDE THESE CATACOMBS ARE WHERE YOUR DEAD SISTERS LIE IN WAIT.
LET'S BE CLEAR HERE—THEY *ALL* HAVE TO BE PUT DOWN.
THEY TOUCH YOU, THEY SCRATCH YOU, WELL, YOU ALREADY KNOW WHAT HAPPENS NEXT.
I HAPPEN NEXT.
LOTS OF CARNAGE POTENTIAL WHILE FIGHTING IN THE DARK, SO AIM CAREFULLY.
CLICK
CLACK
WE NEED TO GO IN AFTER THEM BECAUSE THEY'VE GROWN ACCUSTOMED TO THE DARK NOW. THEY WON'T COME OUTSIDE, SEE, BECAUSE THEY—

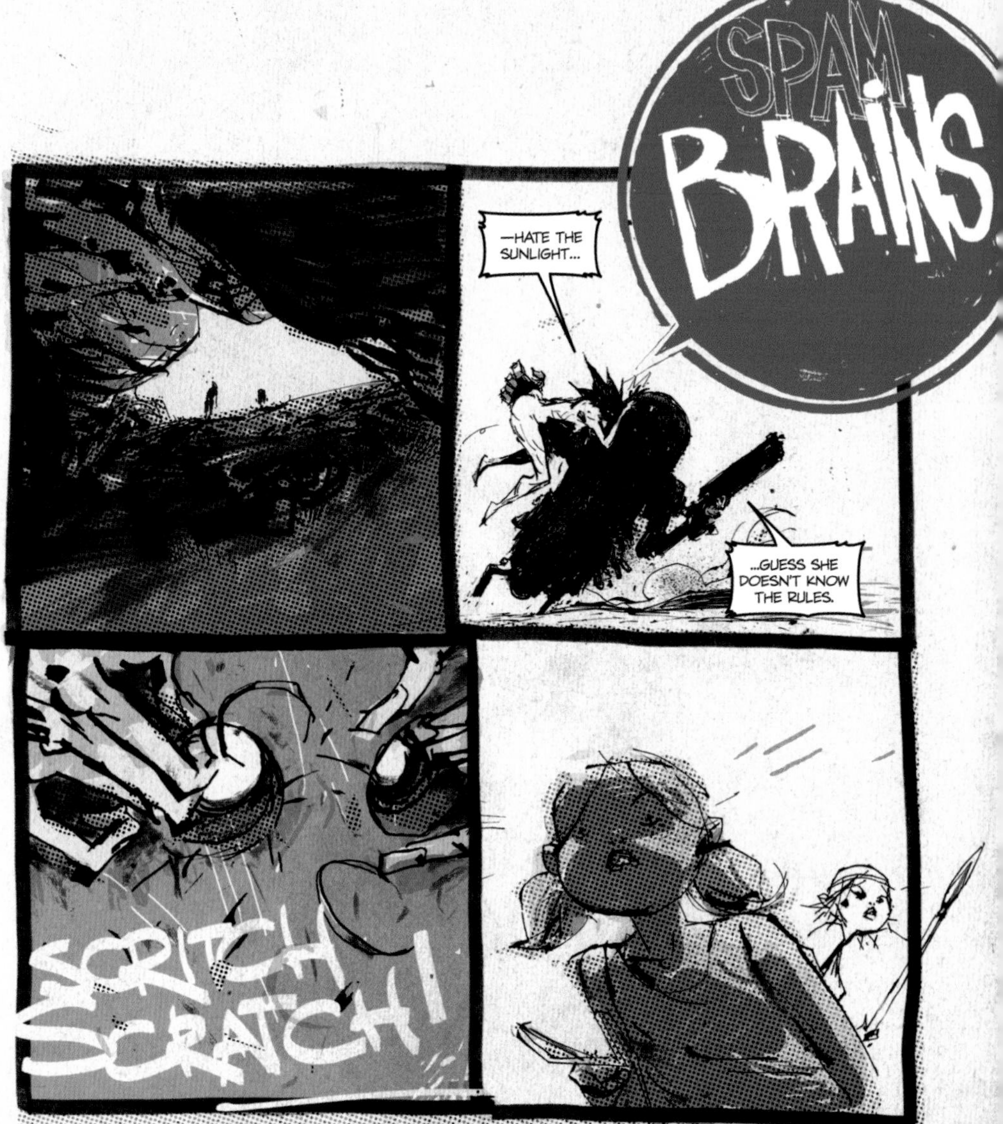
SPAM
BRAINS
—HATE THE SUNLIGHT...
...GUESS SHE DOESN'T KNOW THE RULES.
SCRITCH SCRATCH!

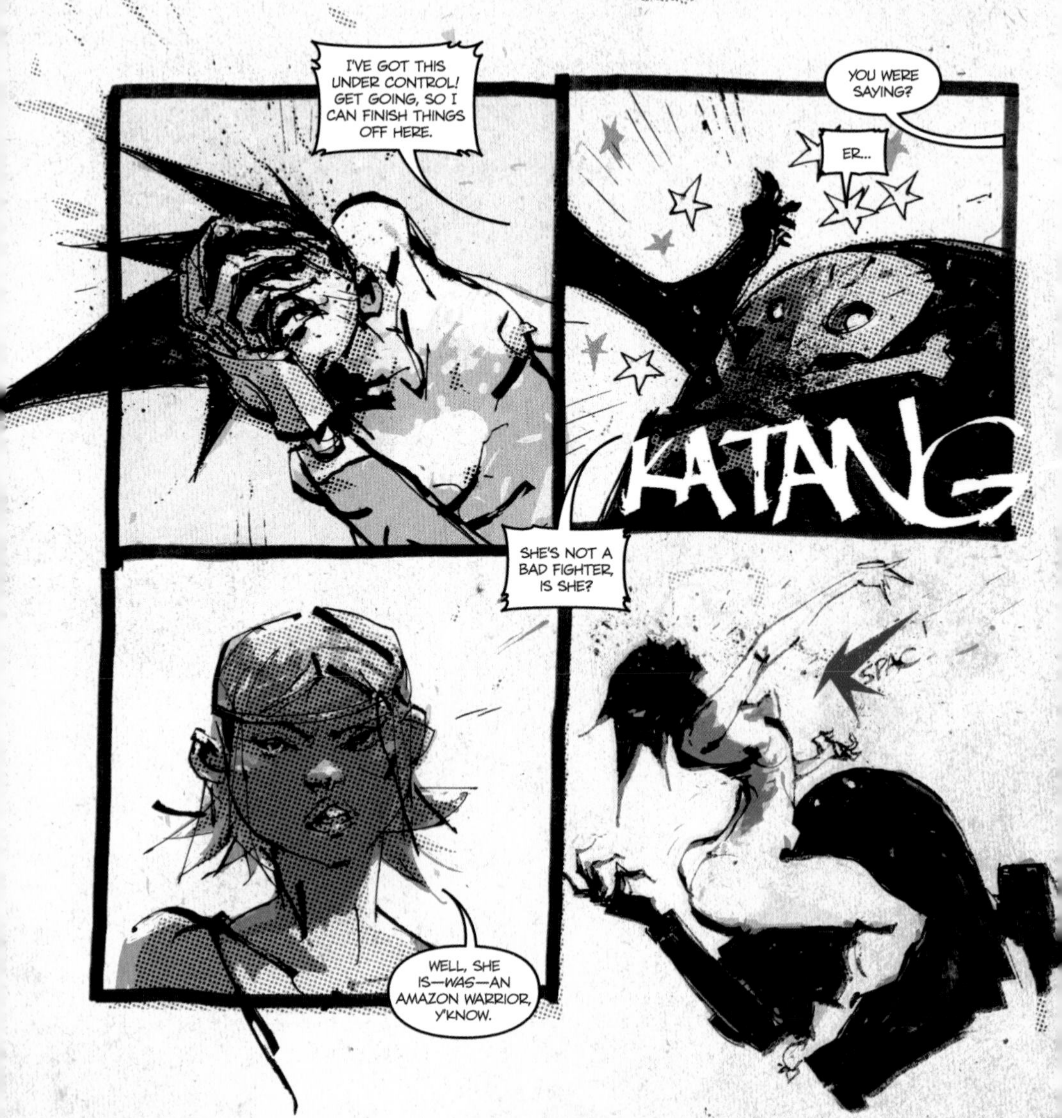
I'VE GOT THIS UNDER CONTROL! GET GOING, SO I CAN FINISH THINGS OFF HERE.
YOU WERE SAYING?
ER...
KATANG
SHE'S NOT A BAD FIGHTER, IS SHE?
SPAC
WELL, SHE IS—WAS—AN AMAZON WARRIOR, Y'KNOW.

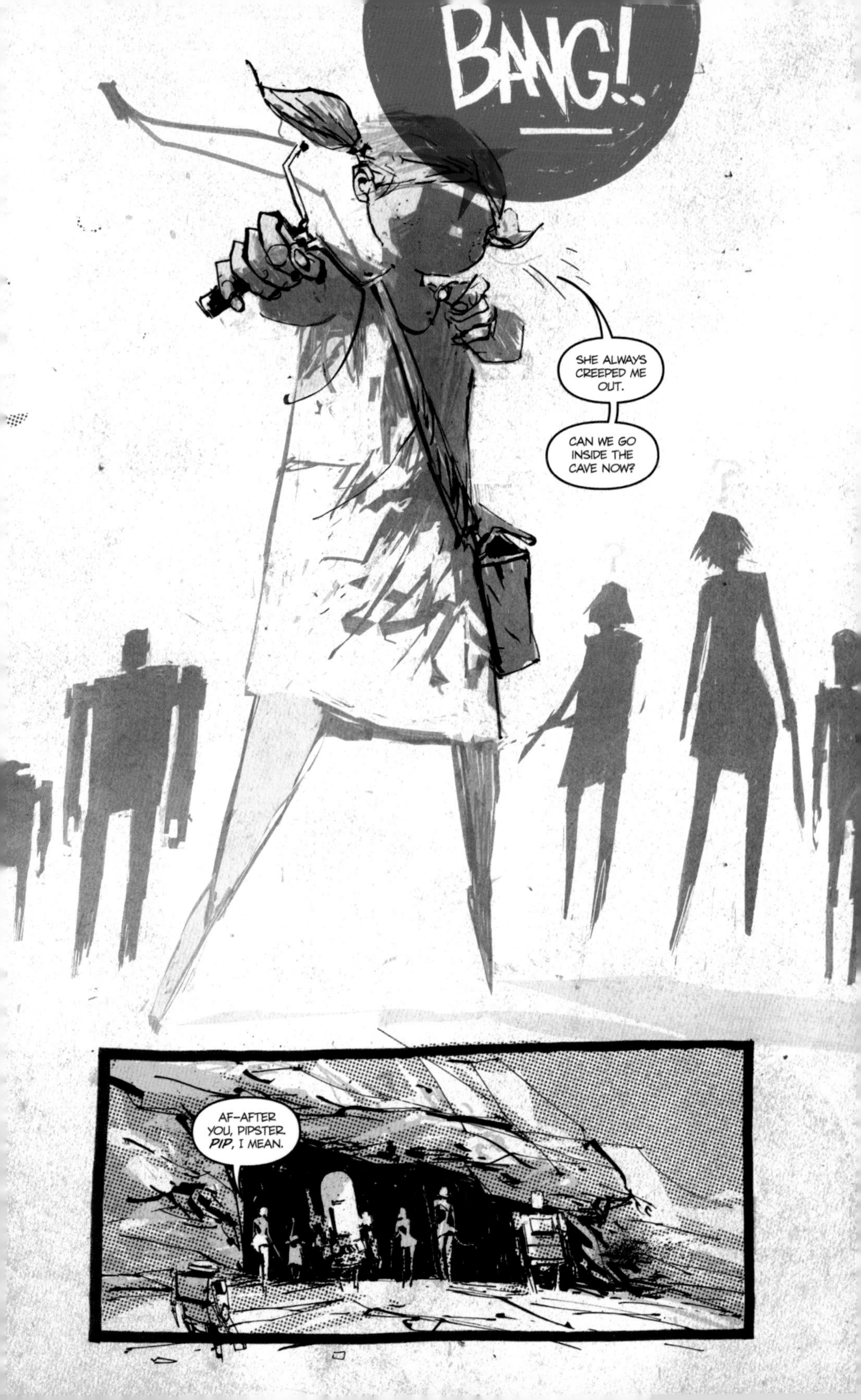
BANG!
SHE ALWAYS CREEPED ME OUT.
CAN WE GO INSIDE THE CAVE NOW?
AF-AFTER YOU, PIPSTER. *PIP*, I MEAN.

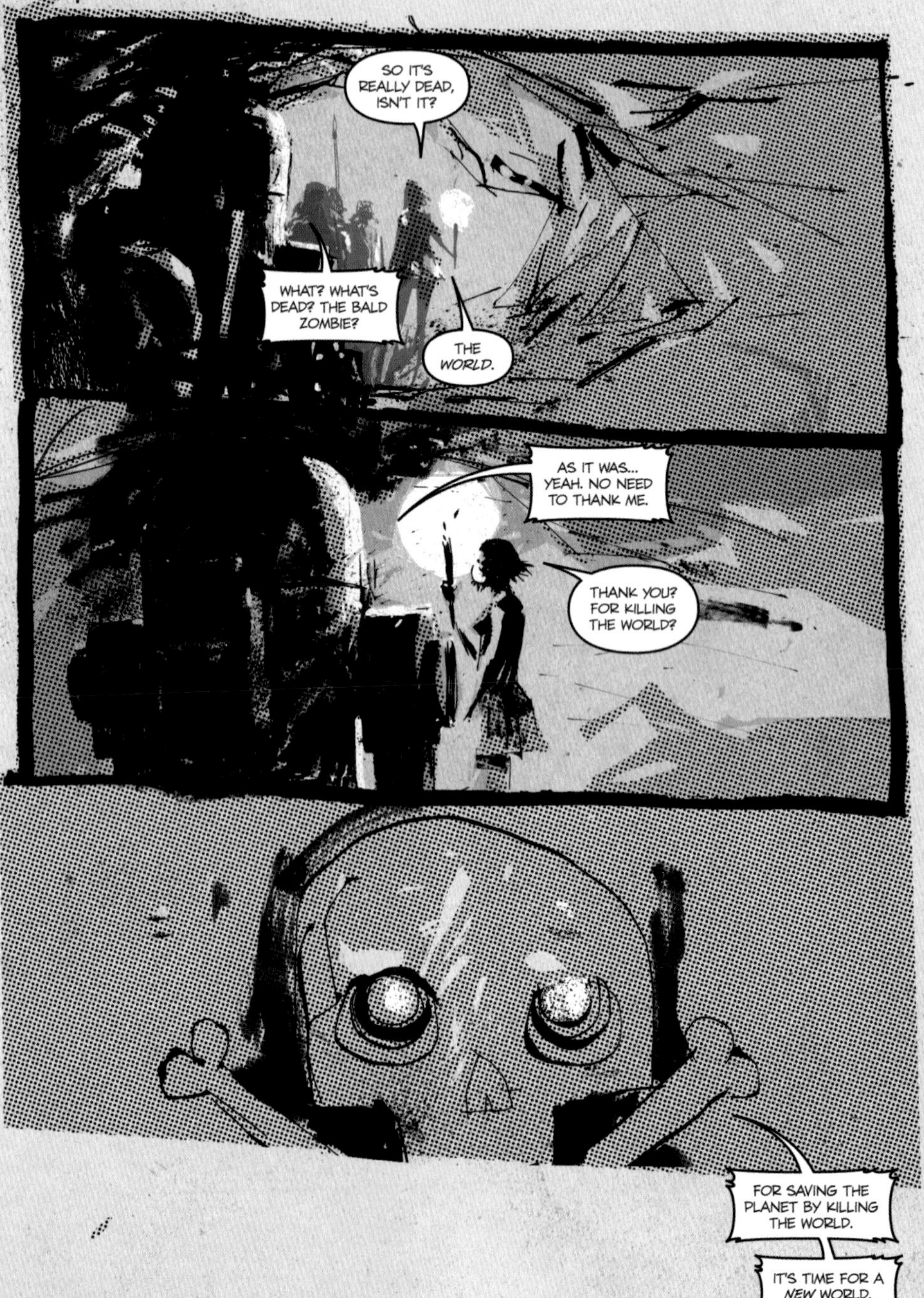
SO IT'S REALLY DEAD, ISN'T IT?
WHAT? WHAT'S DEAD? THE BALD ZOMBIE?
THE *WORLD*.
AS IT WAS... YEAH. NO NEED TO THANK ME.
THANK YOU? FOR KILLING THE WORLD?
FOR SAVING THE PLANET BY KILLING THE WORLD.
IT'S TIME FOR A *NEW* WORLD.

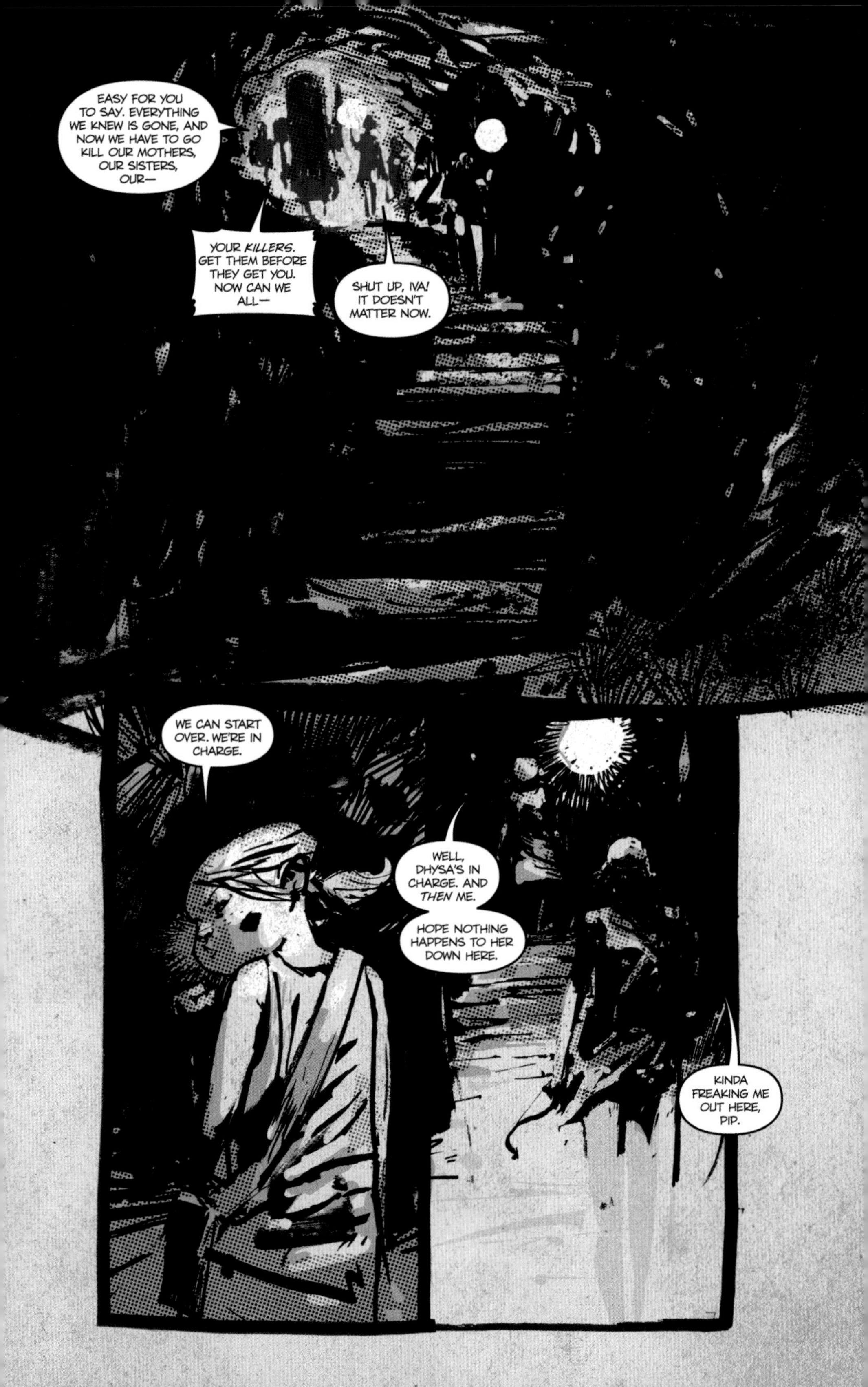
EASY FOR YOU TO SAY. EVERYTHING WE KNEW IS GONE, AND NOW WE HAVE TO GO KILL OUR MOTHERS, OUR SISTERS, OUR—
YOUR KILLERS. GET THEM BEFORE THEY GET YOU. NOW CAN WE ALL—
SHUT UP, IVA! IT DOESN'T MATTER NOW.
WE CAN START OVER. WE'RE IN CHARGE.
WELL, DHYSA'S IN CHARGE. AND THEN ME.
HOPE NOTHING HAPPENS TO HER DOWN HERE.
KINDA FREAKING ME OUT HERE, PIP.

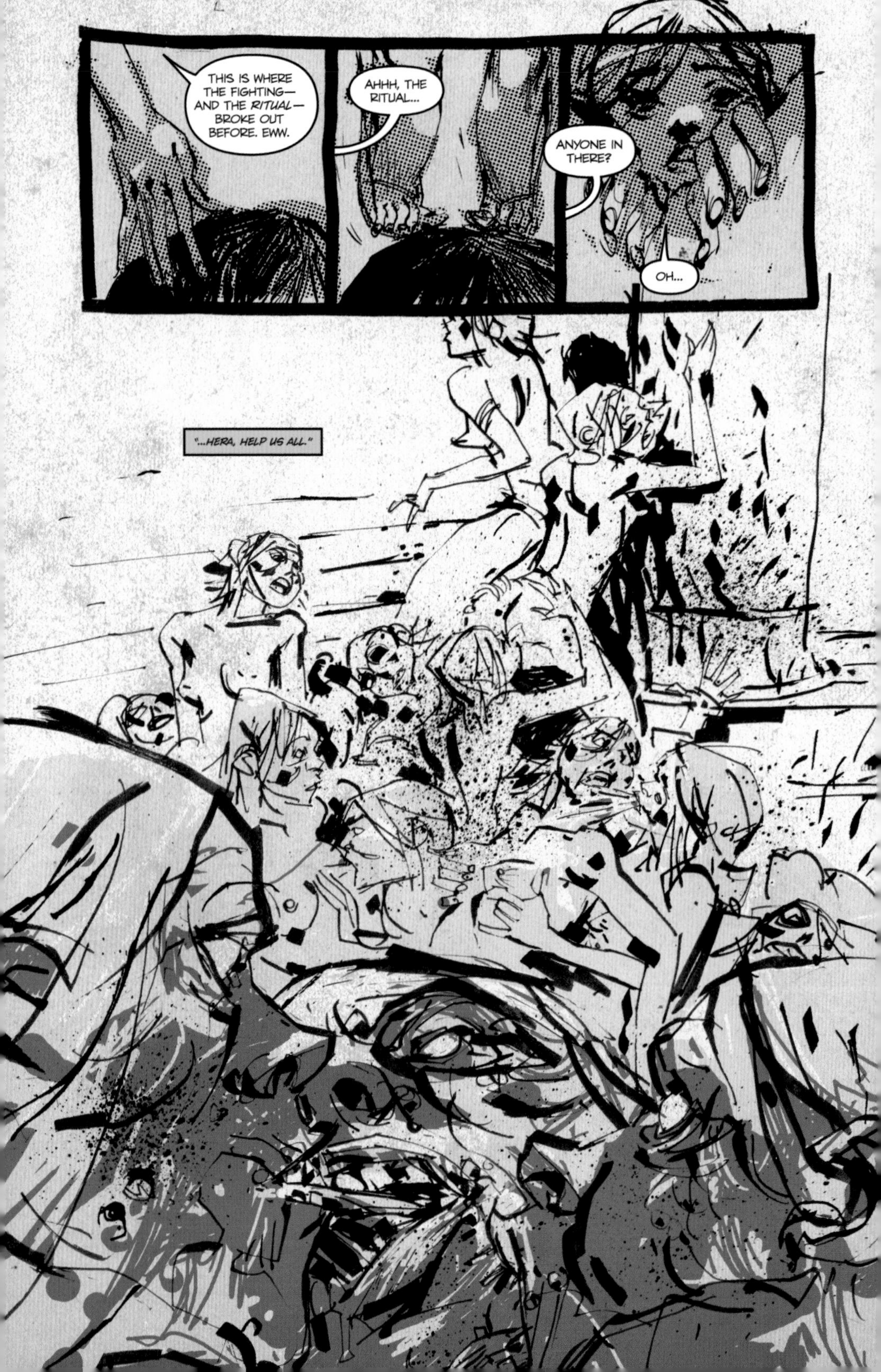

THIS IS WHERE THE FIGHTING—AND THE *RITUAL*—BROKE OUT BEFORE. EWW.
AHHH, THE RITUAL...
ANYONE IN THERE?
OH...
"...HERA, HELP US ALL."

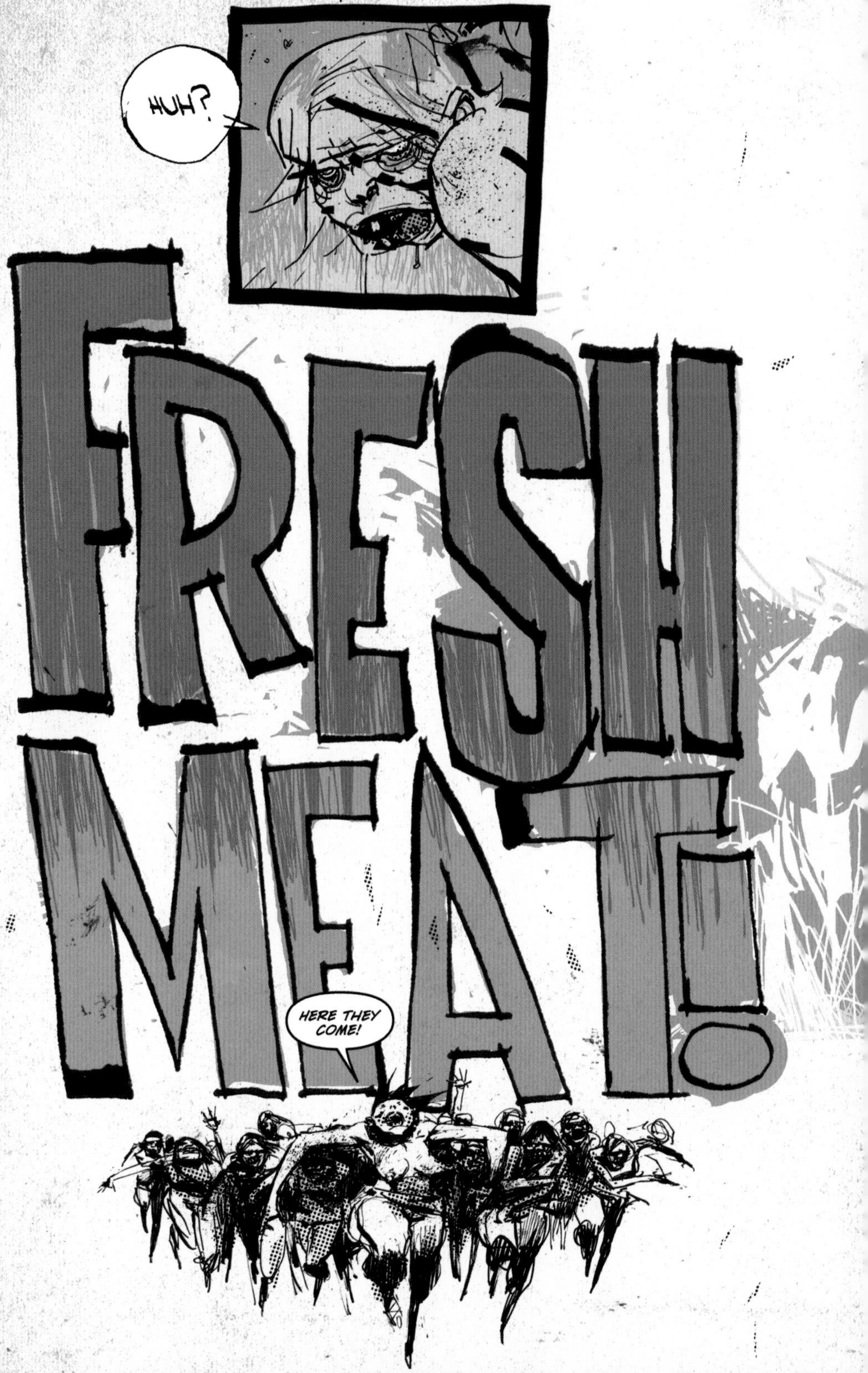
HUH?
FRESH MEAT!
HERE THEY COME!

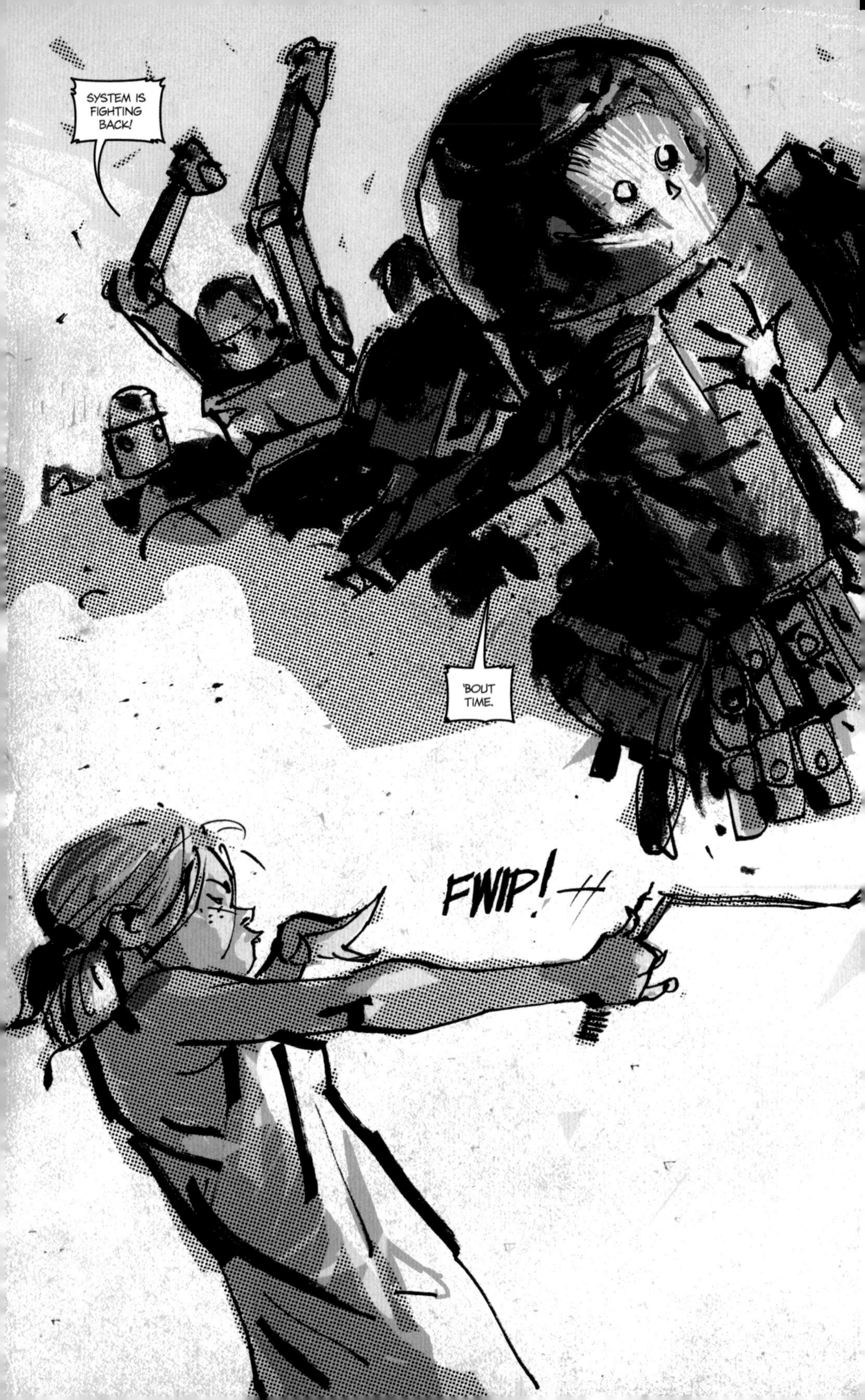
SYSTEM IS FIGHTING BACK!
'BOUT TIME.
FWIP!

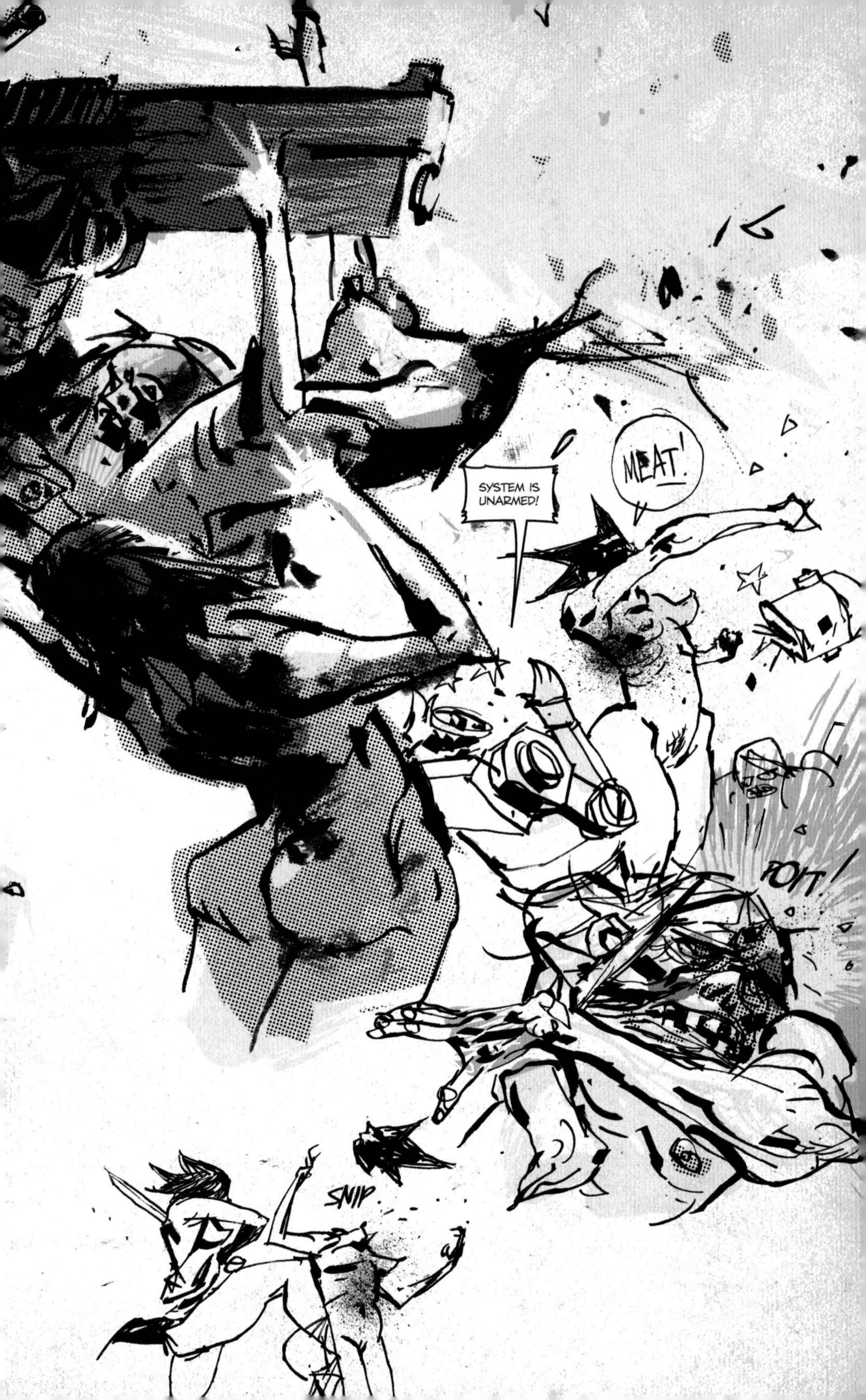
SYSTEM IS UNARMED!
MEAT!
POIT!
SNIP

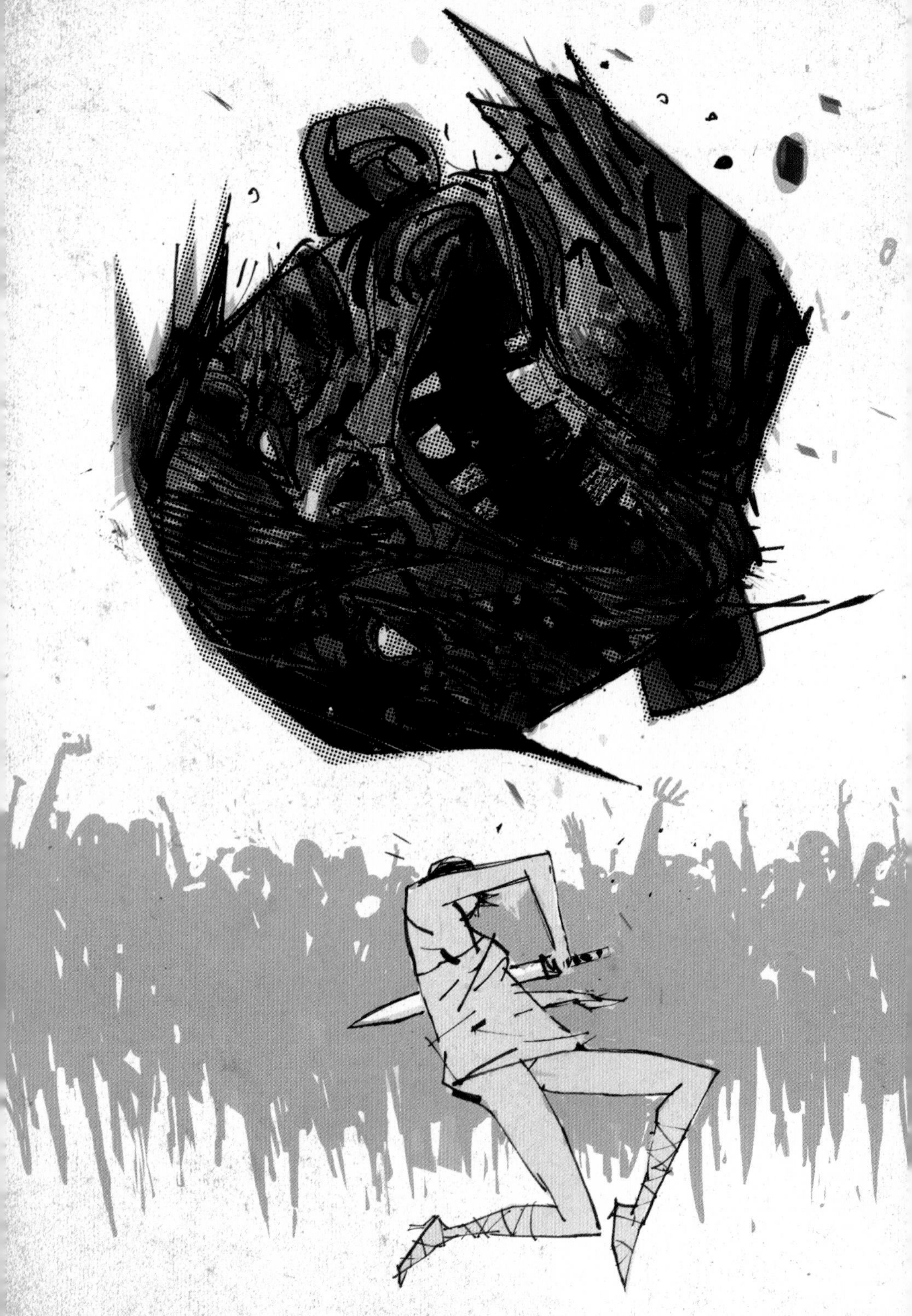

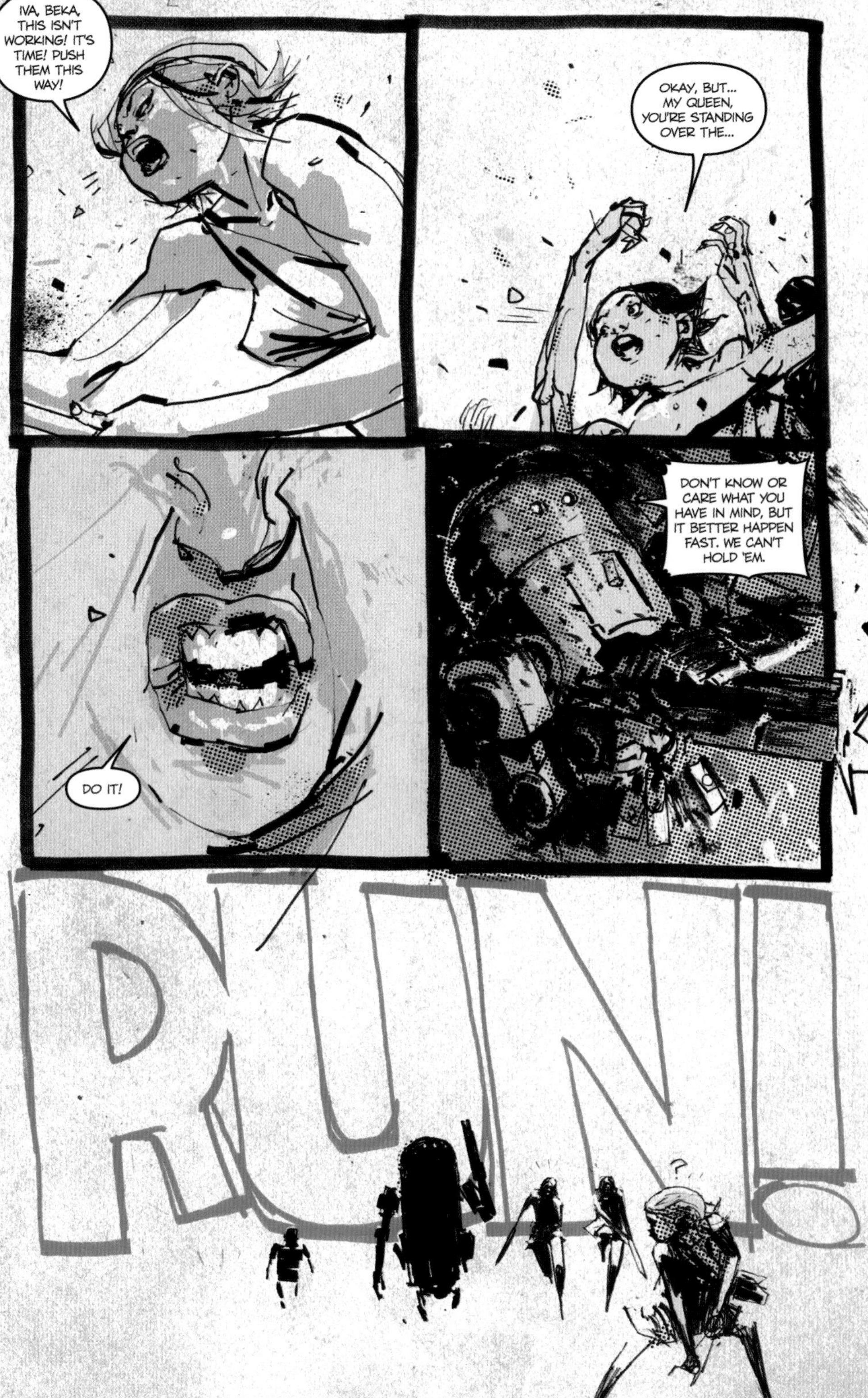
IVA, BEKA, THIS ISN'T WORKING! IT'S TIME! PUSH THEM THIS WAY!
OKAY, BUT... MY QUEEN, YOU'RE STANDING OVER THE...
DO IT!
DON'T KNOW OR CARE WHAT YOU HAVE IN MIND, BUT IT BETTER HAPPEN FAST. WE CAN'T HOLD 'EM.
RUN!
?

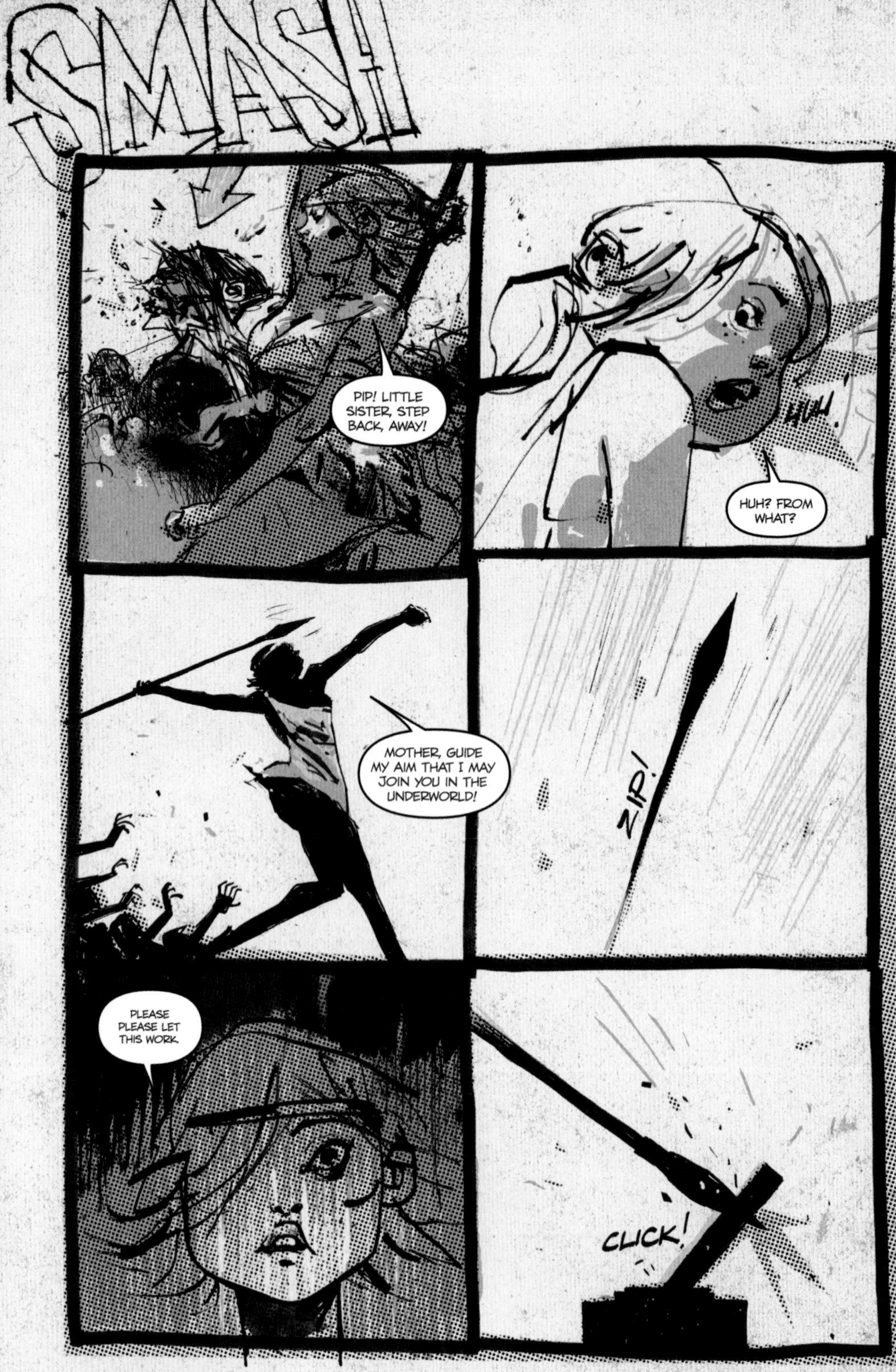
SMASH
PIP! LITTLE SISTER, STEP BACK, AWAY!
HUH
HUH? FROM WHAT?
MOTHER, GUIDE MY AIM THAT I MAY JOIN YOU IN THE UNDERWORLD!
ZIP!
PLEASE PLEASE LET THIS WORK.
CLICK!

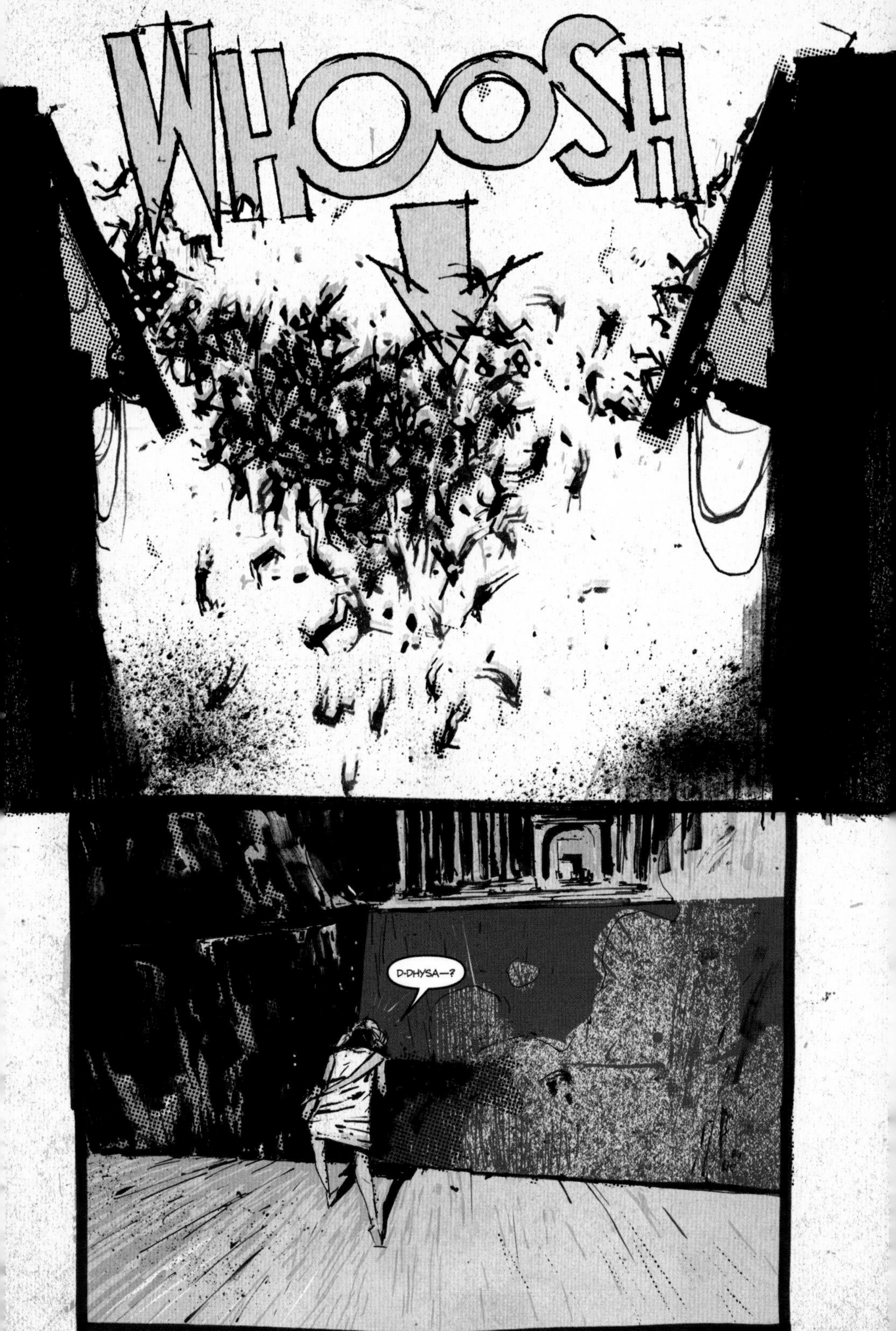
WHOOSH
D-DHYSA—?

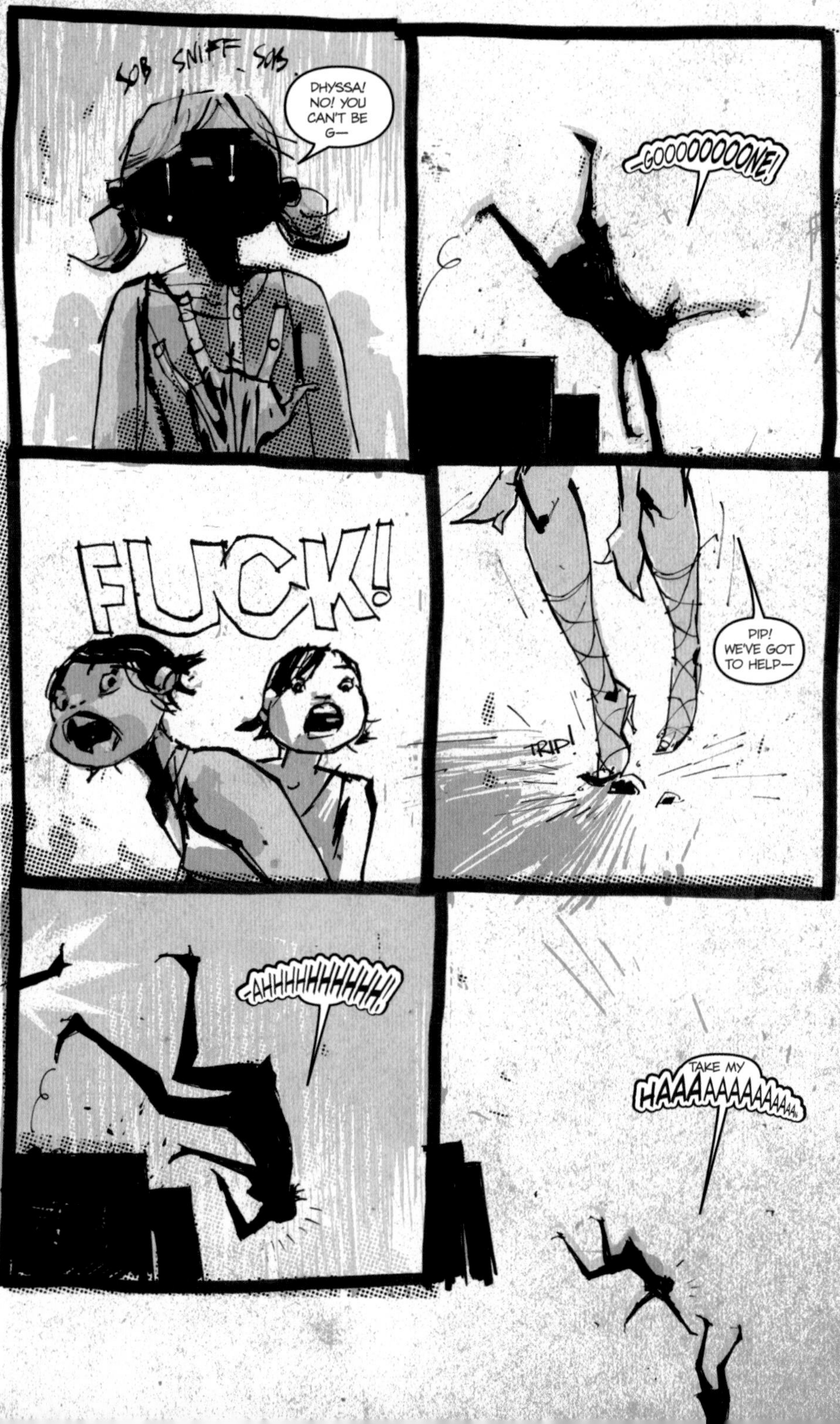
SOB SNIFF SOB
DHYSSA! NO! YOU CAN'T BE G—
—GOOOOOOOONE!
FUCK!
PIP! WE'VE GOT TO HELP—
TRIP!
—AHHHHHHHHH!
TAKE MY HAAAAAAAAAAA

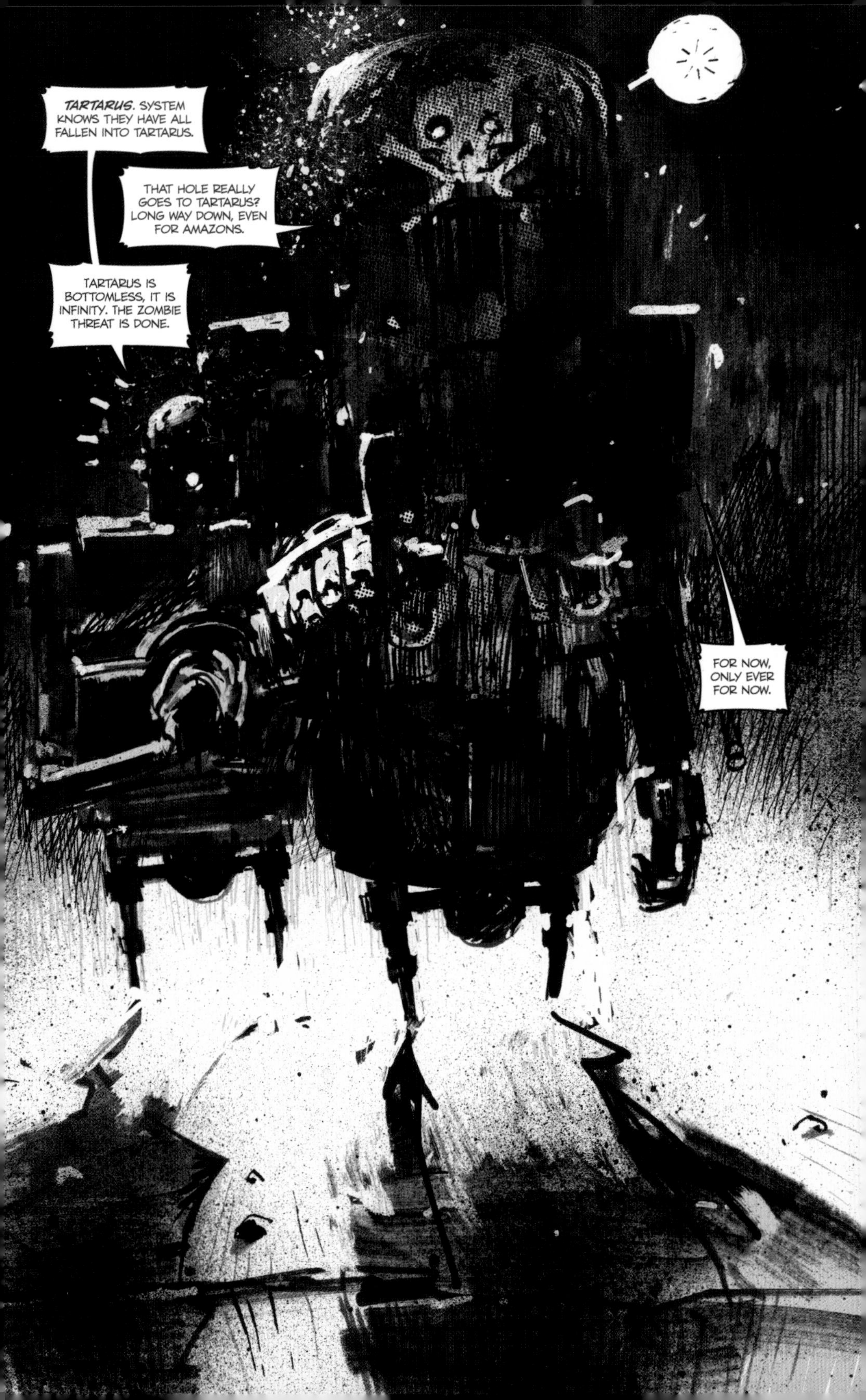
TARTARUS. SYSTEM KNOWS THEY HAVE ALL FALLEN INTO TARTARUS.
THAT HOLE REALLY GOES TO TARTARUS? LONG WAY DOWN, EVEN FOR AMAZONS.
TARTARUS IS BOTTOMLESS, IT IS INFINITY. THE ZOMBIE THREAT IS DONE.
FOR NOW, ONLY EVER FOR NOW.

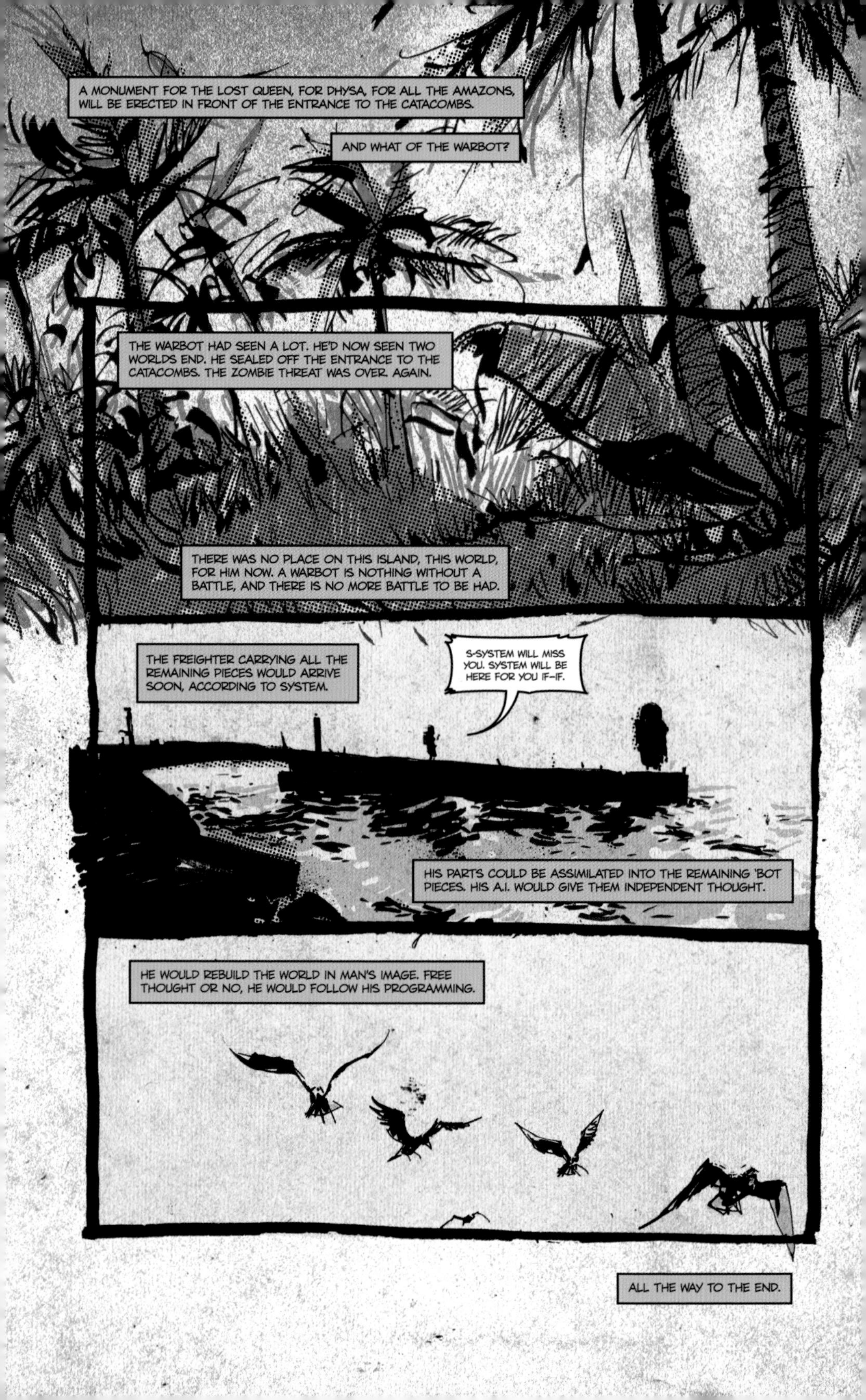
A MONUMENT FOR THE LOST QUEEN, FOR DHYSA, FOR ALL THE AMAZONS, WILL BE ERECTED IN FRONT OF THE ENTRANCE TO THE CATACOMBS.
AND WHAT OF THE WARBOT?
THE WARBOT HAD SEEN A LOT. HE'D NOW SEEN TWO WORLDS END. HE SEALED OFF THE ENTRANCE TO THE CATACOMBS. THE ZOMBIE THREAT WAS OVER. AGAIN.
THERE WAS NO PLACE ON THIS ISLAND, THIS WORLD, FOR HIM NOW. A WARBOT IS NOTHING WITHOUT A BATTLE, AND THERE IS NO MORE BATTLE TO BE HAD.
THE FREIGHTER CARRYING ALL THE REMAINING PIECES WOULD ARRIVE SOON, ACCORDING TO SYSTEM.
S-SYSTEM WILL MISS YOU. SYSTEM WILL BE HERE FOR YOU IF--IF.
HIS PARTS COULD BE ASSIMILATED INTO THE REMAINING 'BOT PIECES. HIS A.I. WOULD GIVE THEM INDEPENDENT THOUGHT.
HE WOULD REBUILD THE WORLD IN MAN'S IMAGE. FREE THOUGHT OR NO, HE WOULD FOLLOW HIS PROGRAMMING.
ALL THE WAY TO THE END.

THE FREIGHTER DREW CLOSER TO THE ISLAND.
›SKRXXX WIRELESS CONNECTION NOW ONLINE.
›ALERT!‹
›ALERT!‹
›ALERTTTTTTTTT—‹

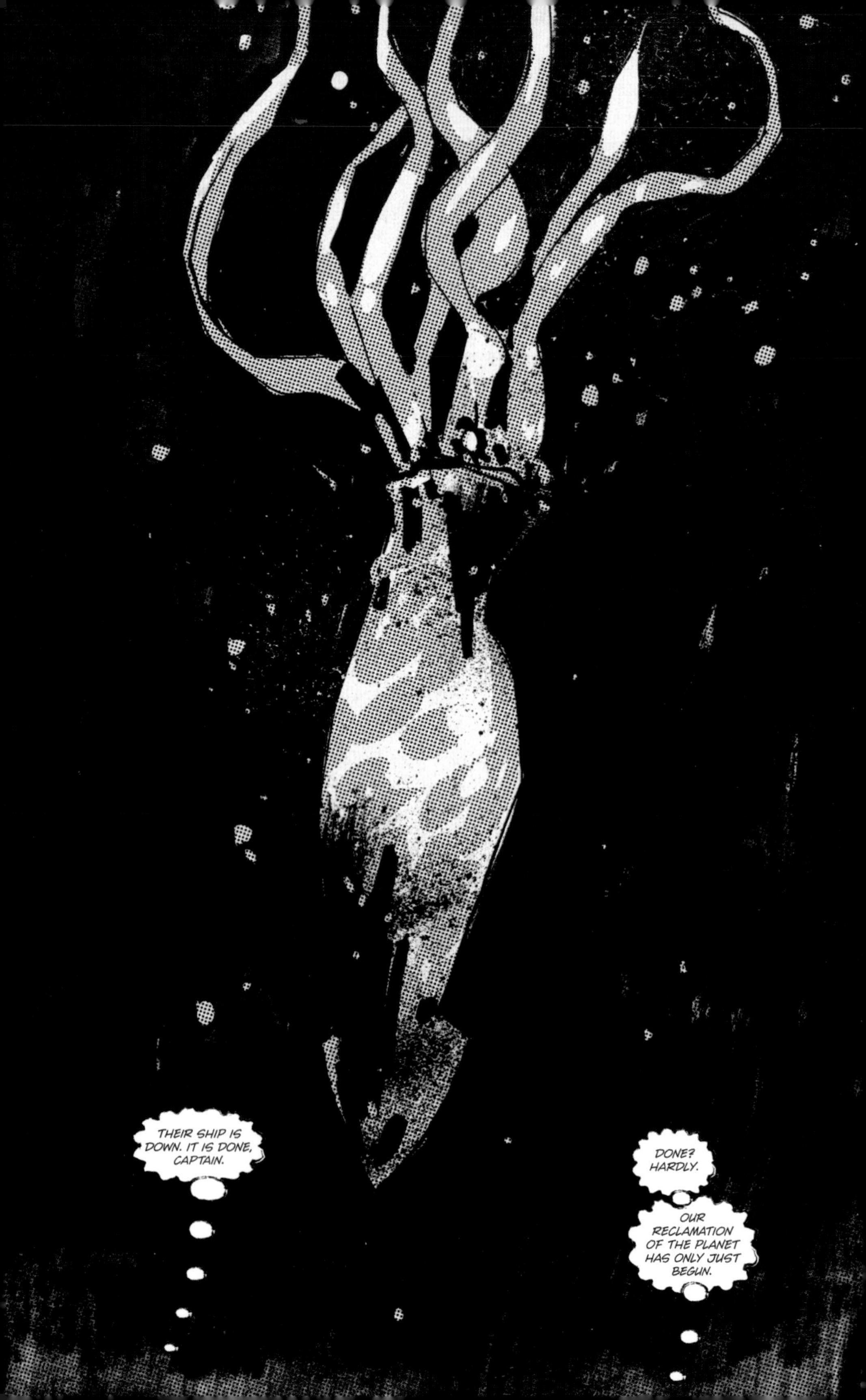
THEIR SHIP IS DOWN. IT IS DONE, CAPTAIN.
DONE? HARDLY.
OUR RECLAMATION OF THE PLANET HAS ONLY JUST BEGUN.

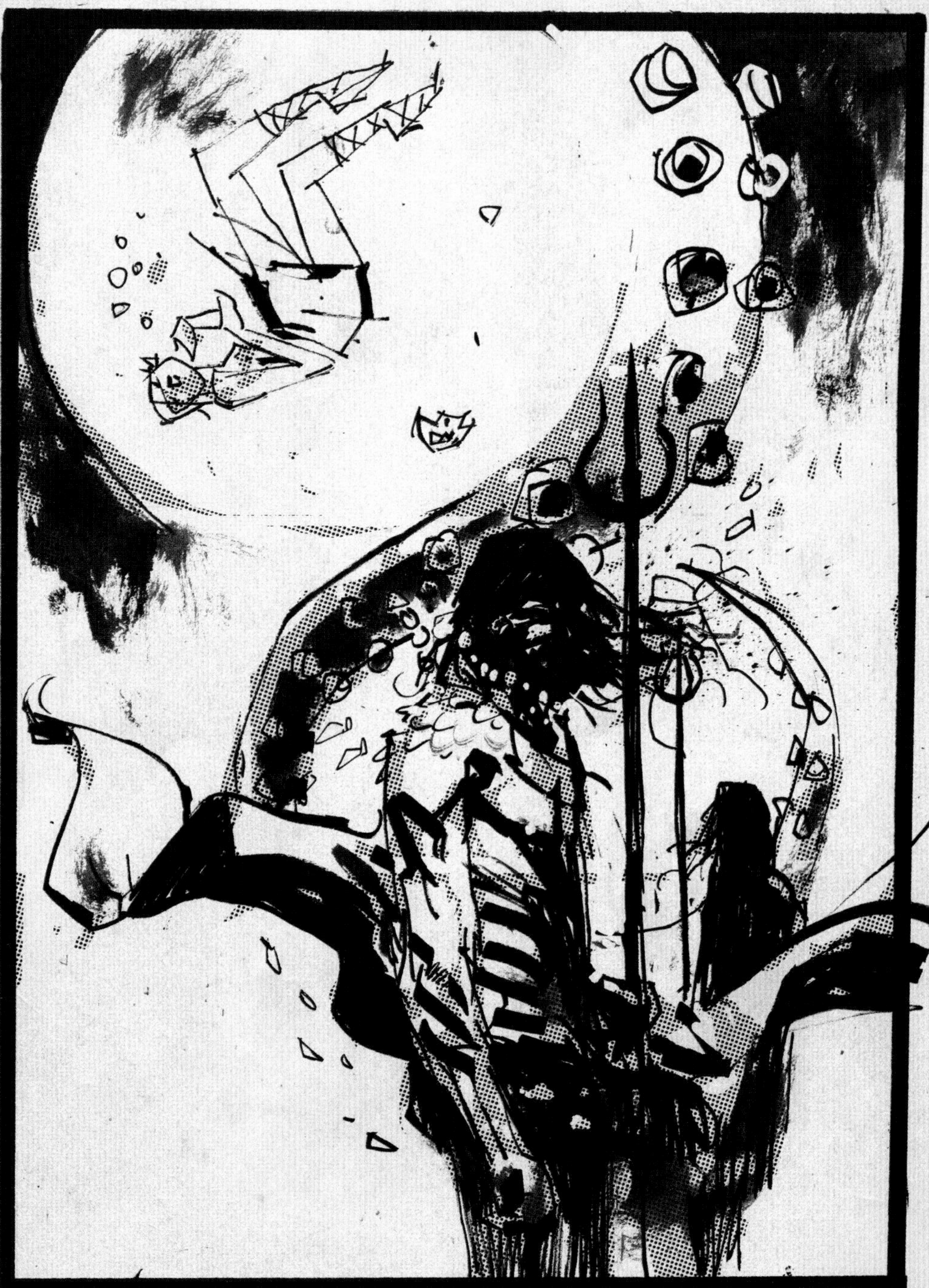

FLIPPING HECK ITS MERMEN!!!

art gallery

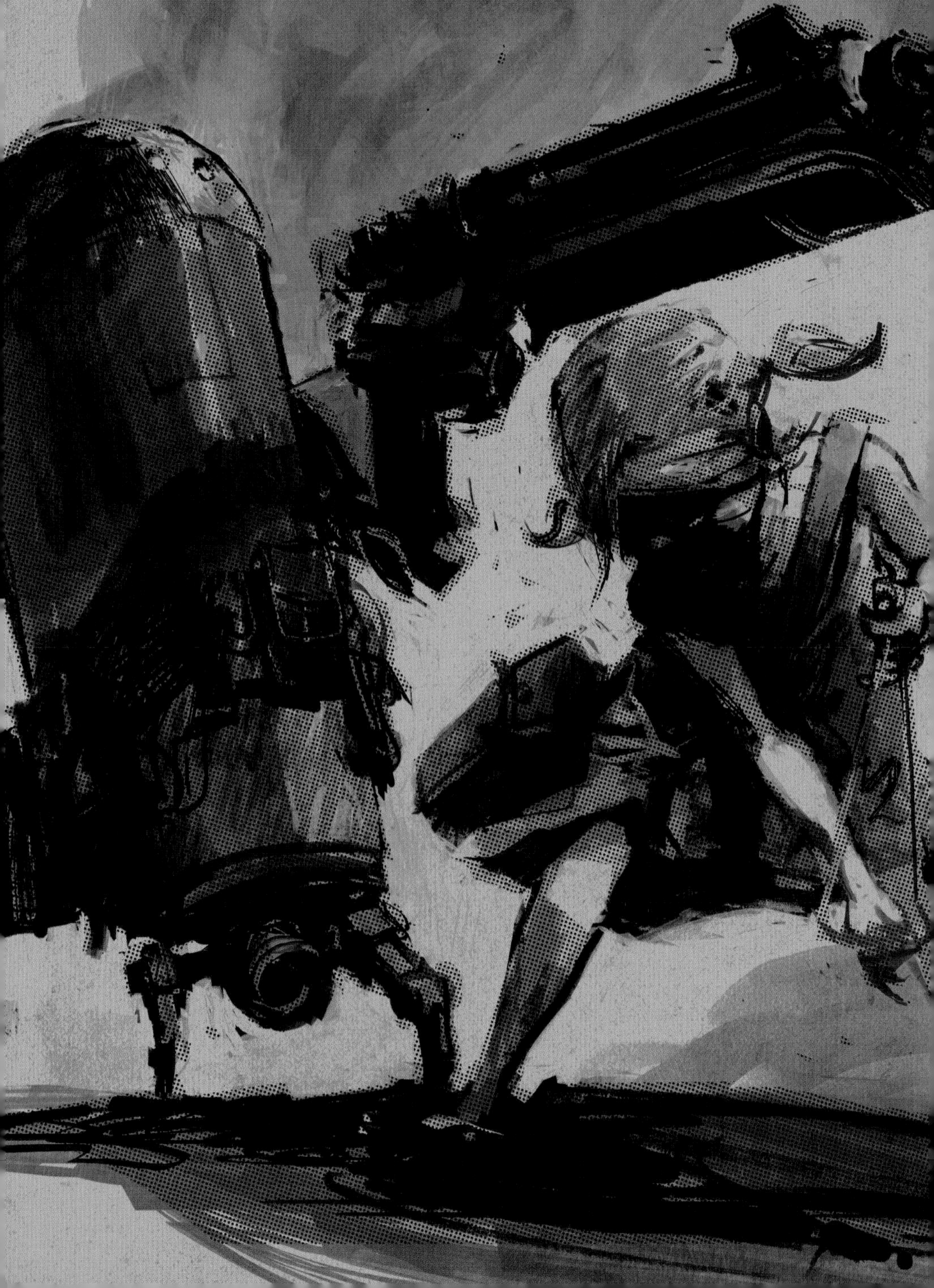

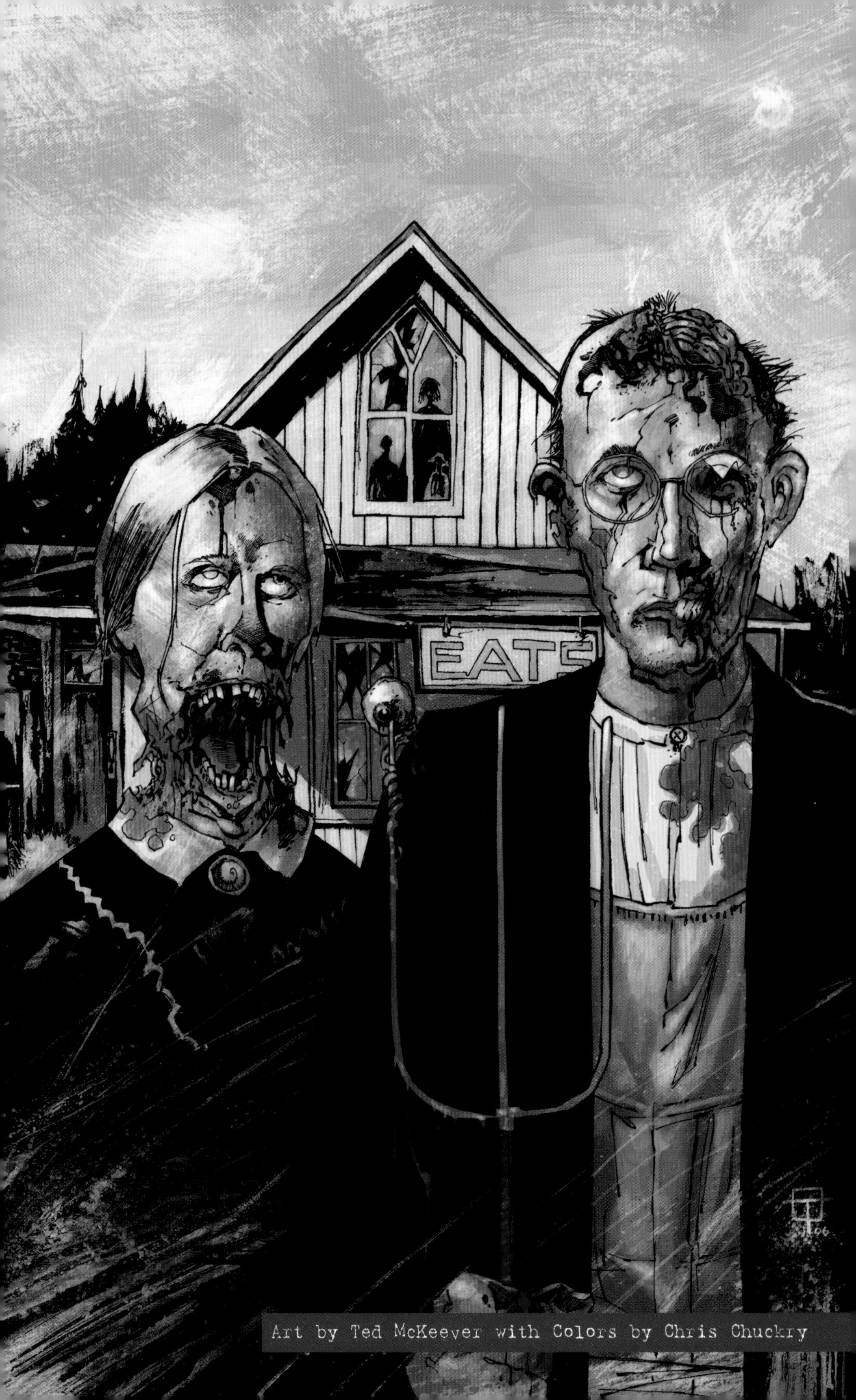
EATS

Art by Ted McKeever with Colors by Chris Chuckry

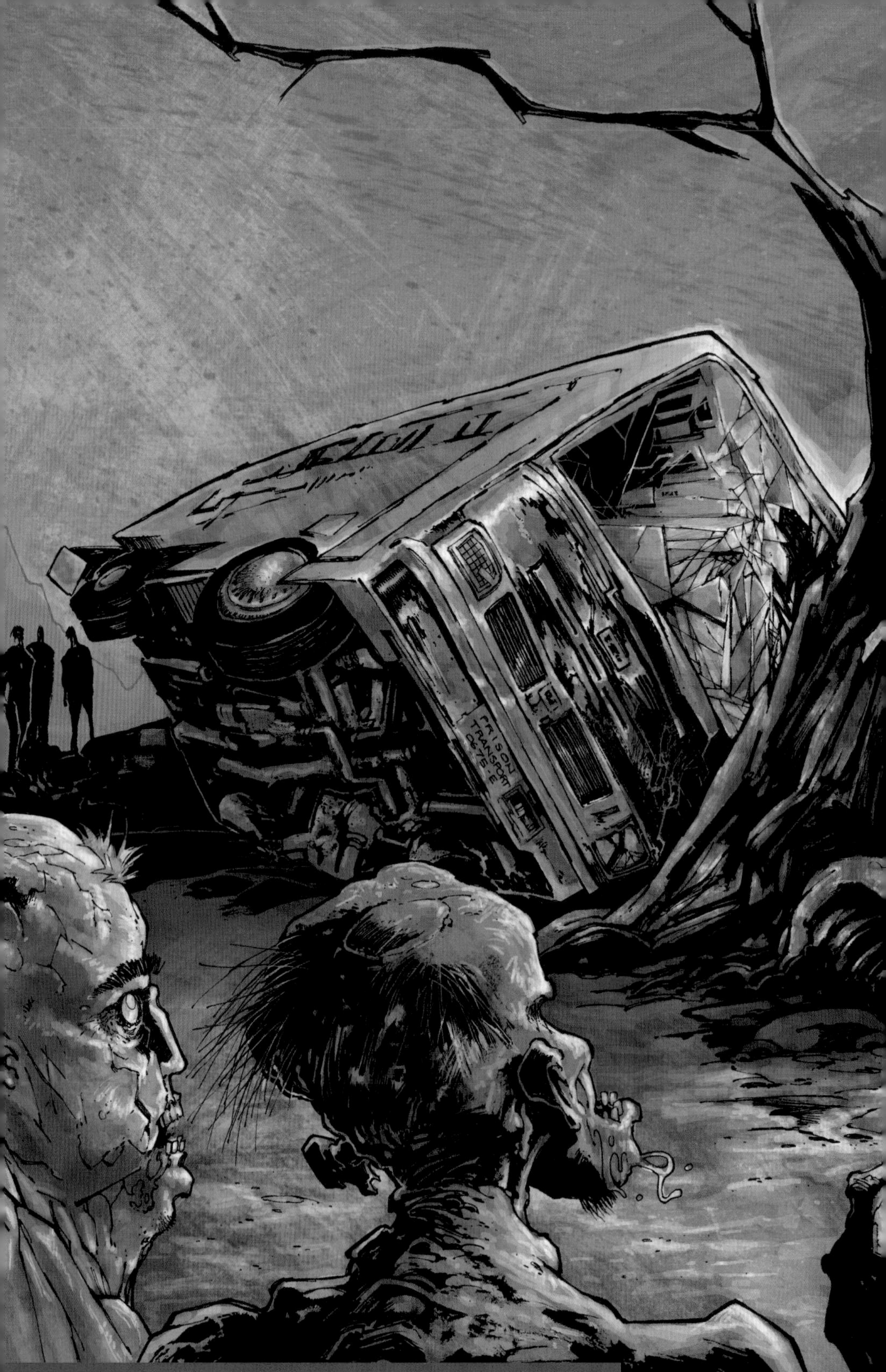
PRISON
TRANSPORT
06-75-E
Art by Ted McKeever with Colors by Chris Chuckry

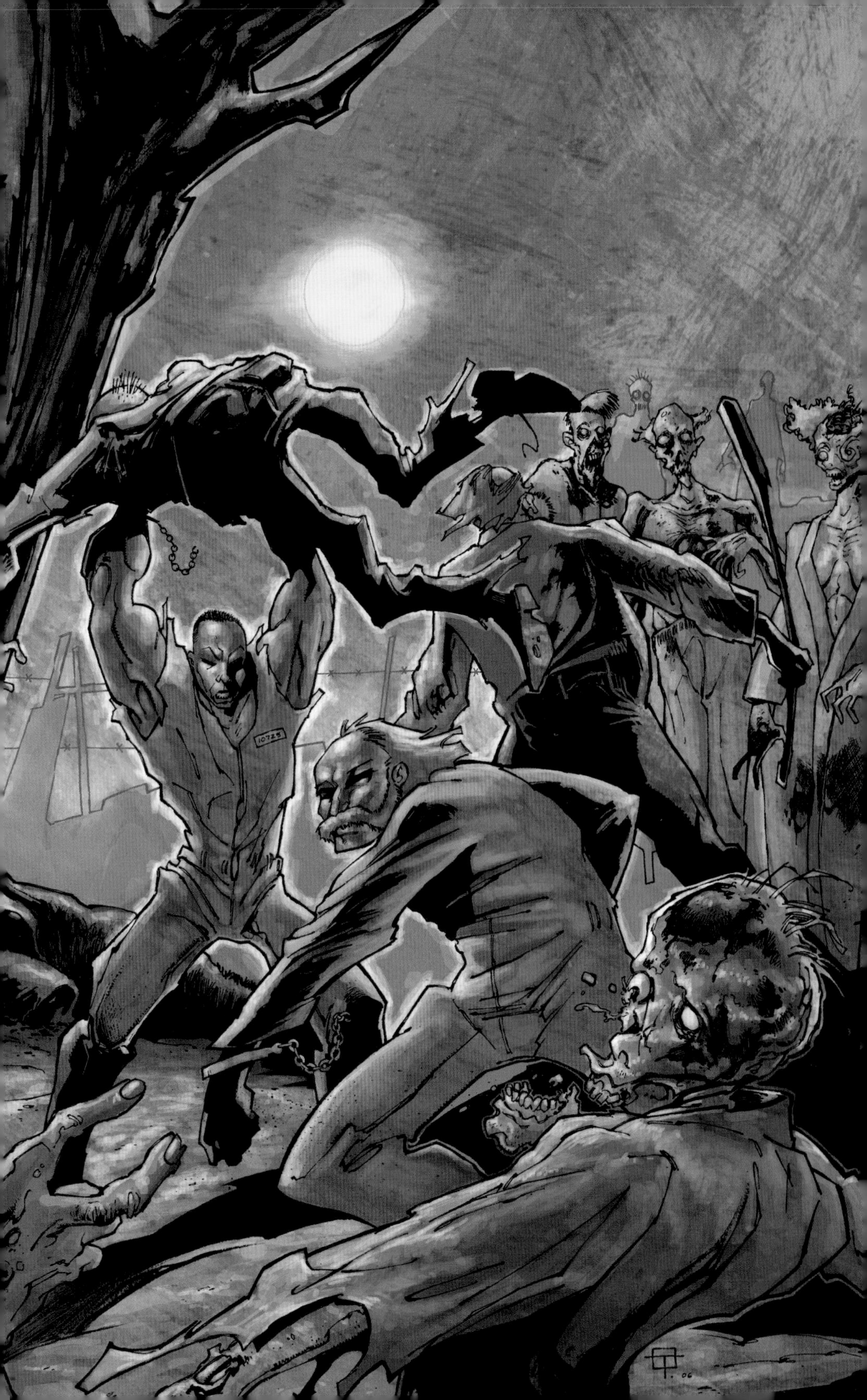
10725

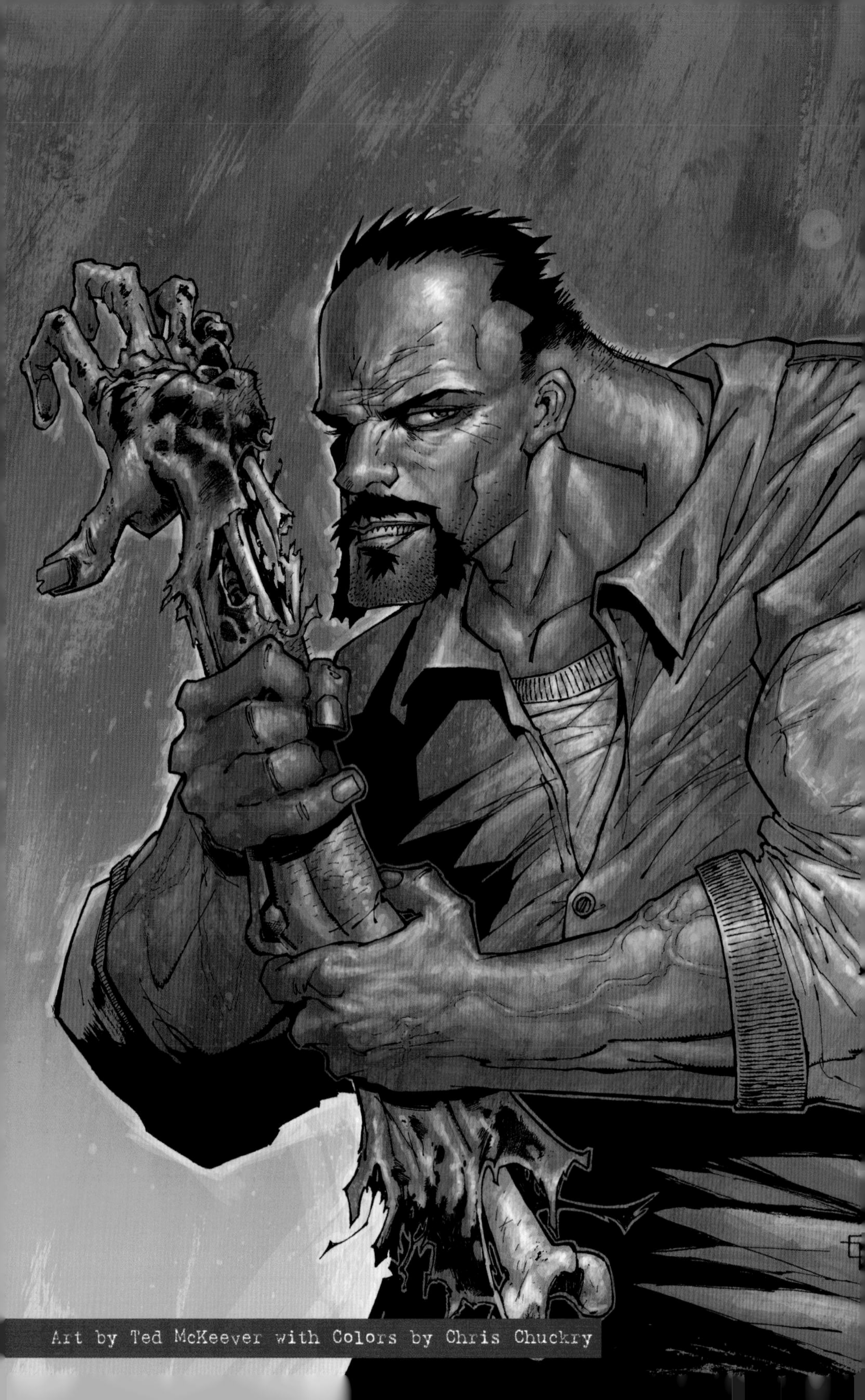

Art by Ted McKeever with Colors by Chris Chuckry

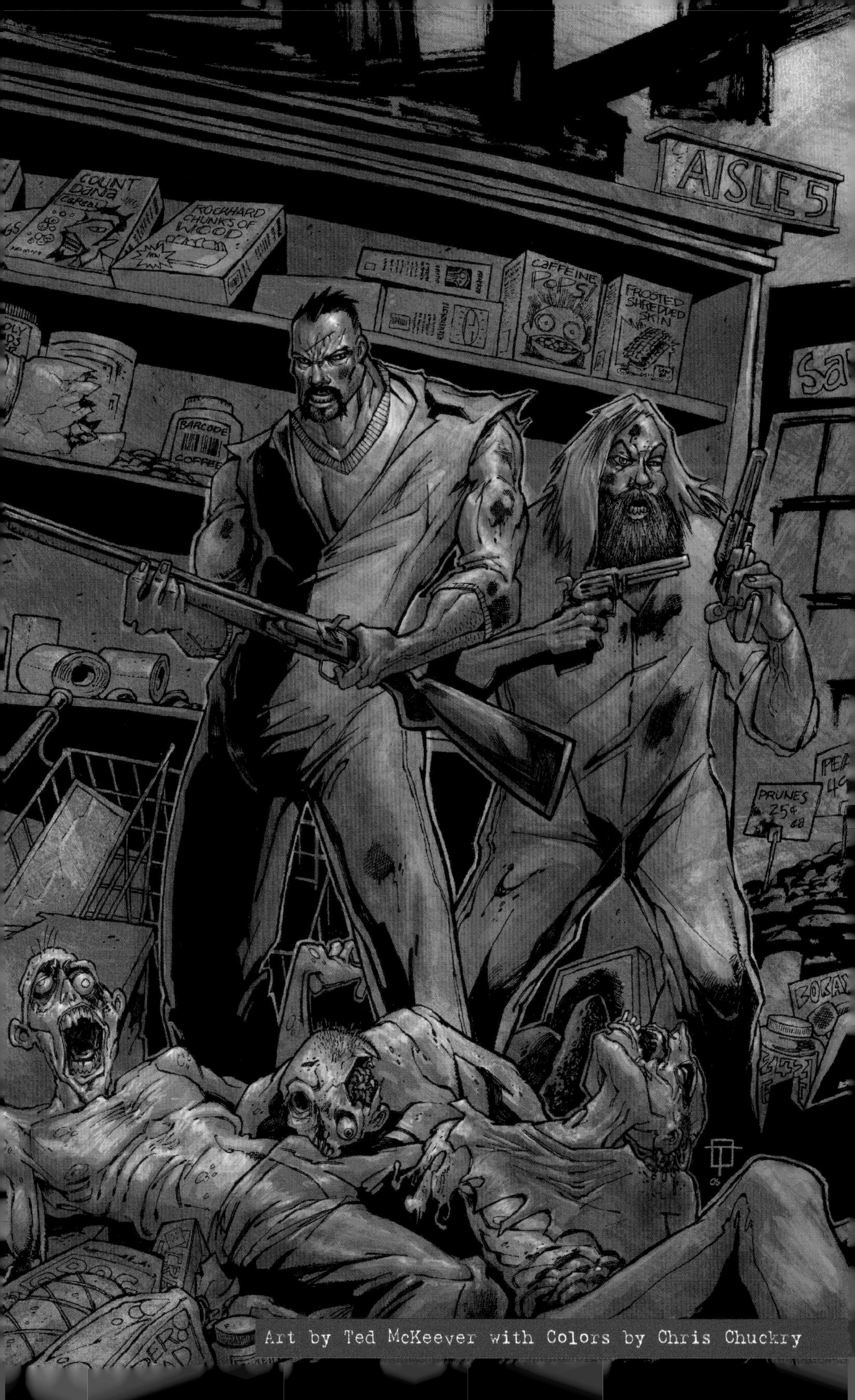
AISLE 5
COUNT Dana CEREAL
ROCKHARD CHUNKS OF WOOD
CAFFEINE POPS!
FROSTED SHREDDED SKIN
BARCODE COFFEE
PRUNES 25¢

Art by Ted McKeever with Colors by Chris Chuckry

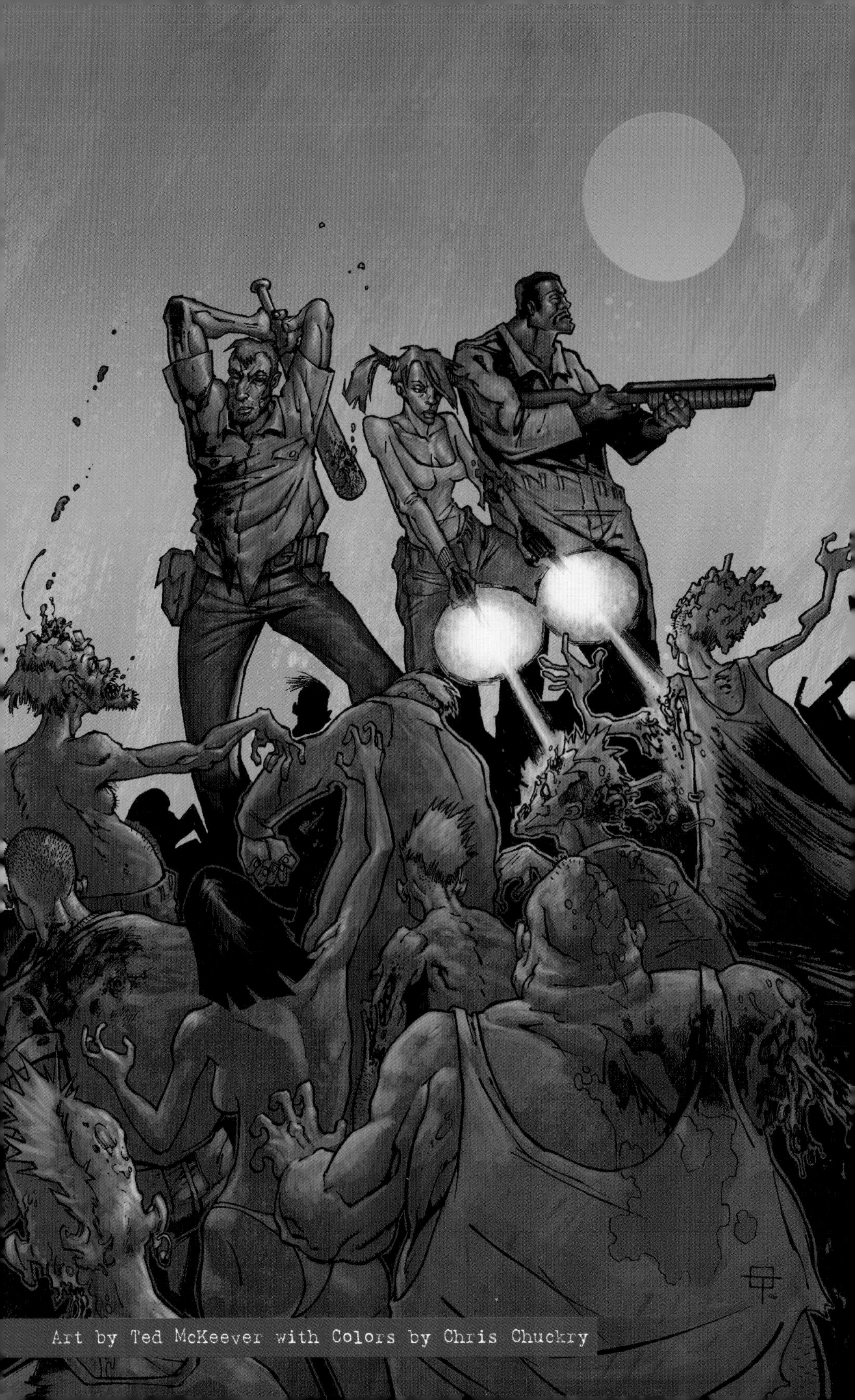

Art by Ted McKeever with Colors by Chris Chuckry

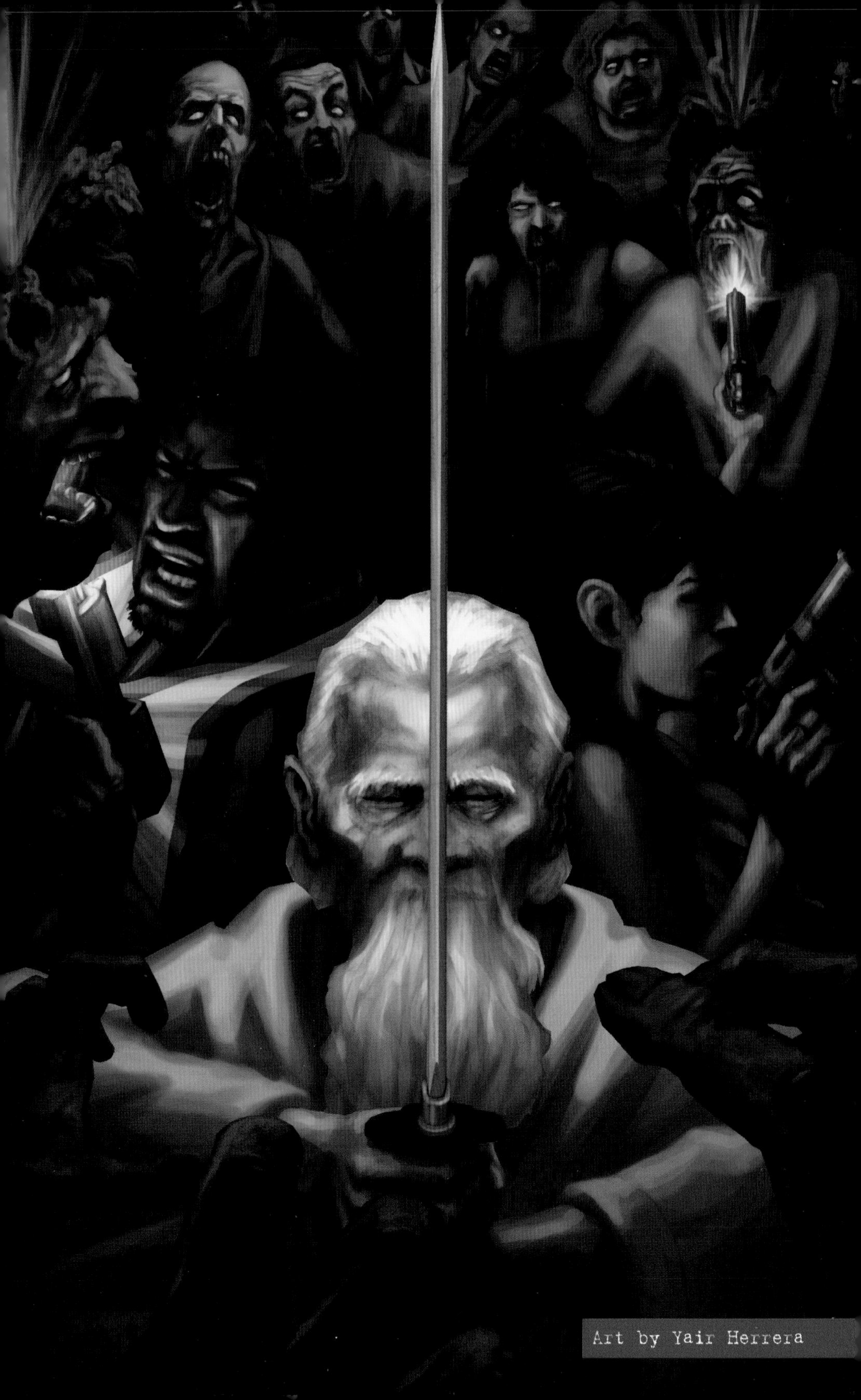

Art by Yair Herrera

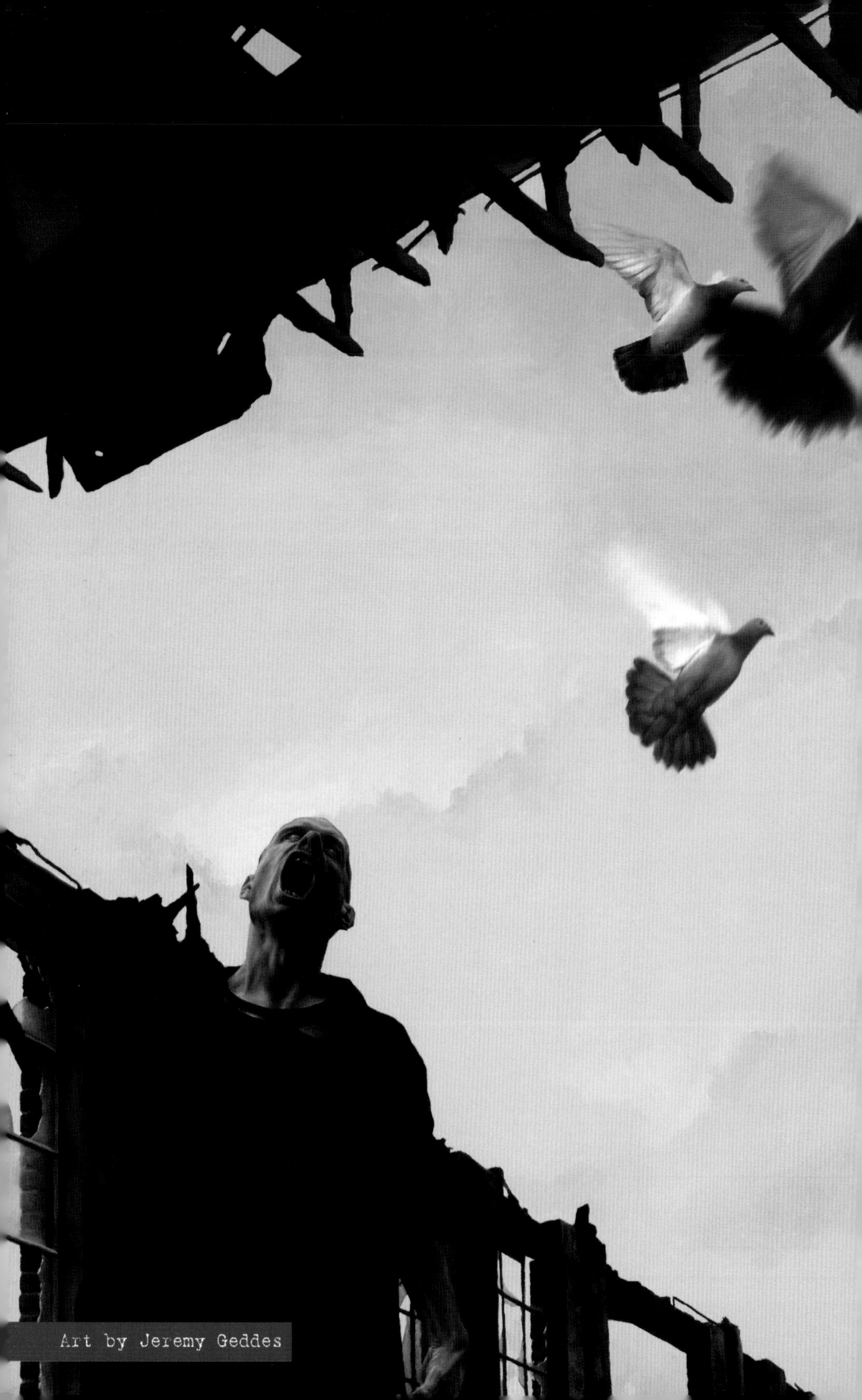
Art by Jeremy Geddes

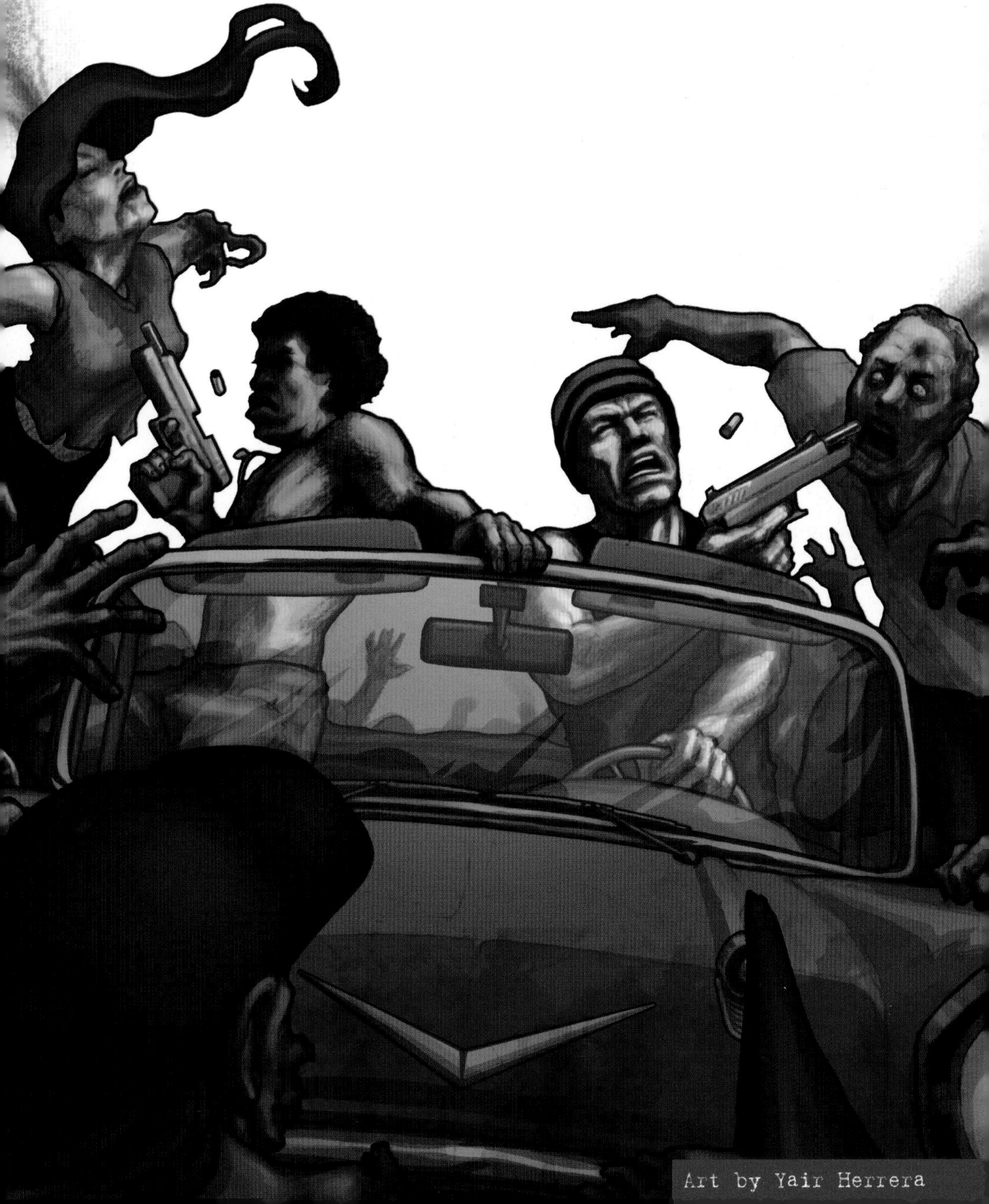

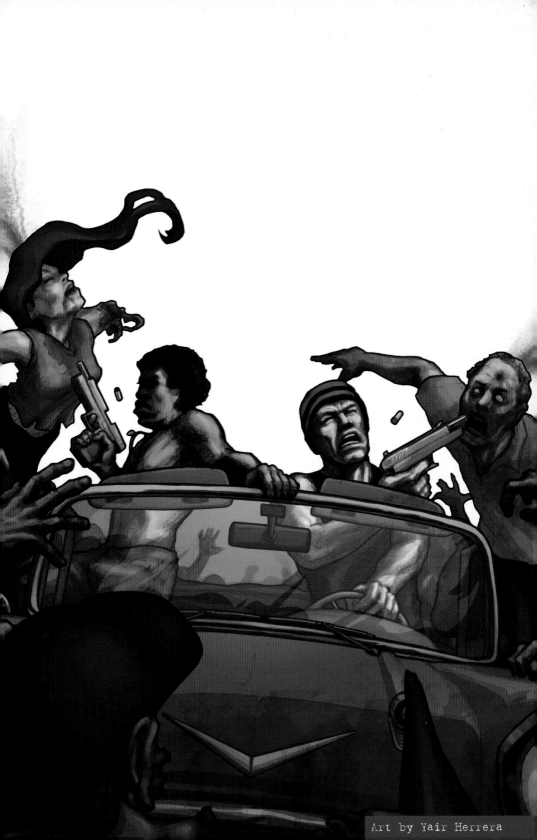

Art by Yair Herrera

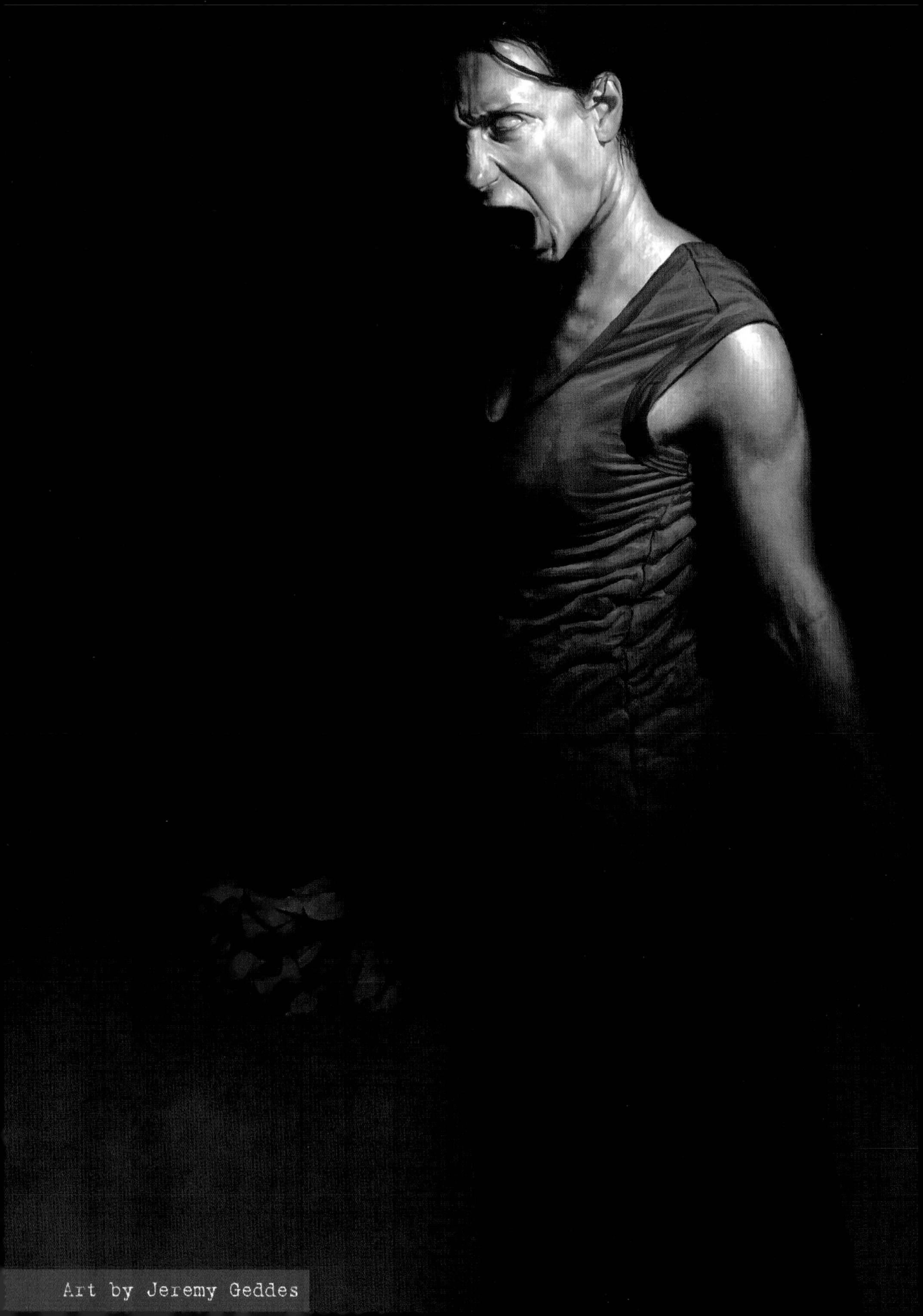

Art by Jeremy Geddes

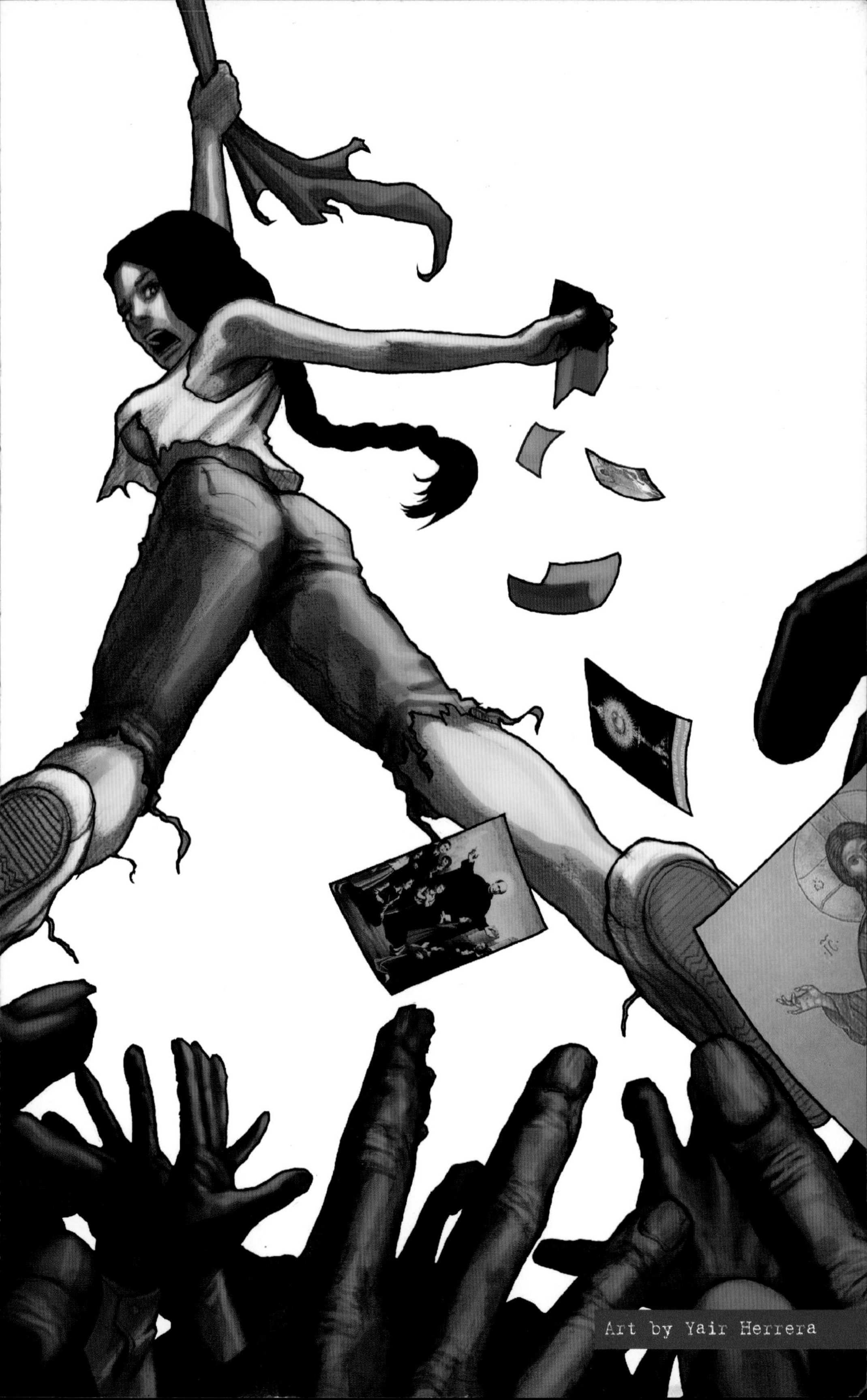

Art by Yair Herrera

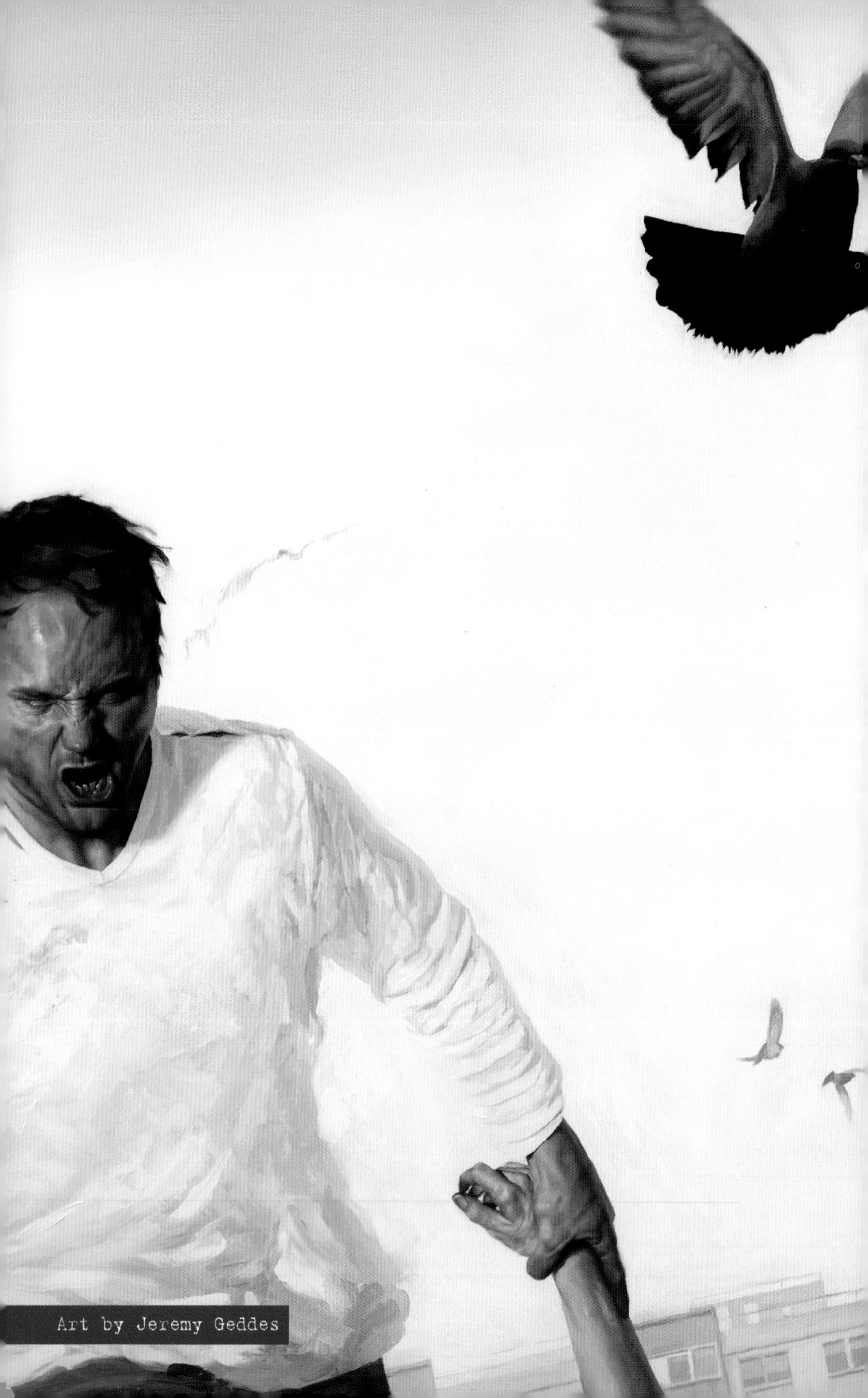

Art by Jeremy Geddes

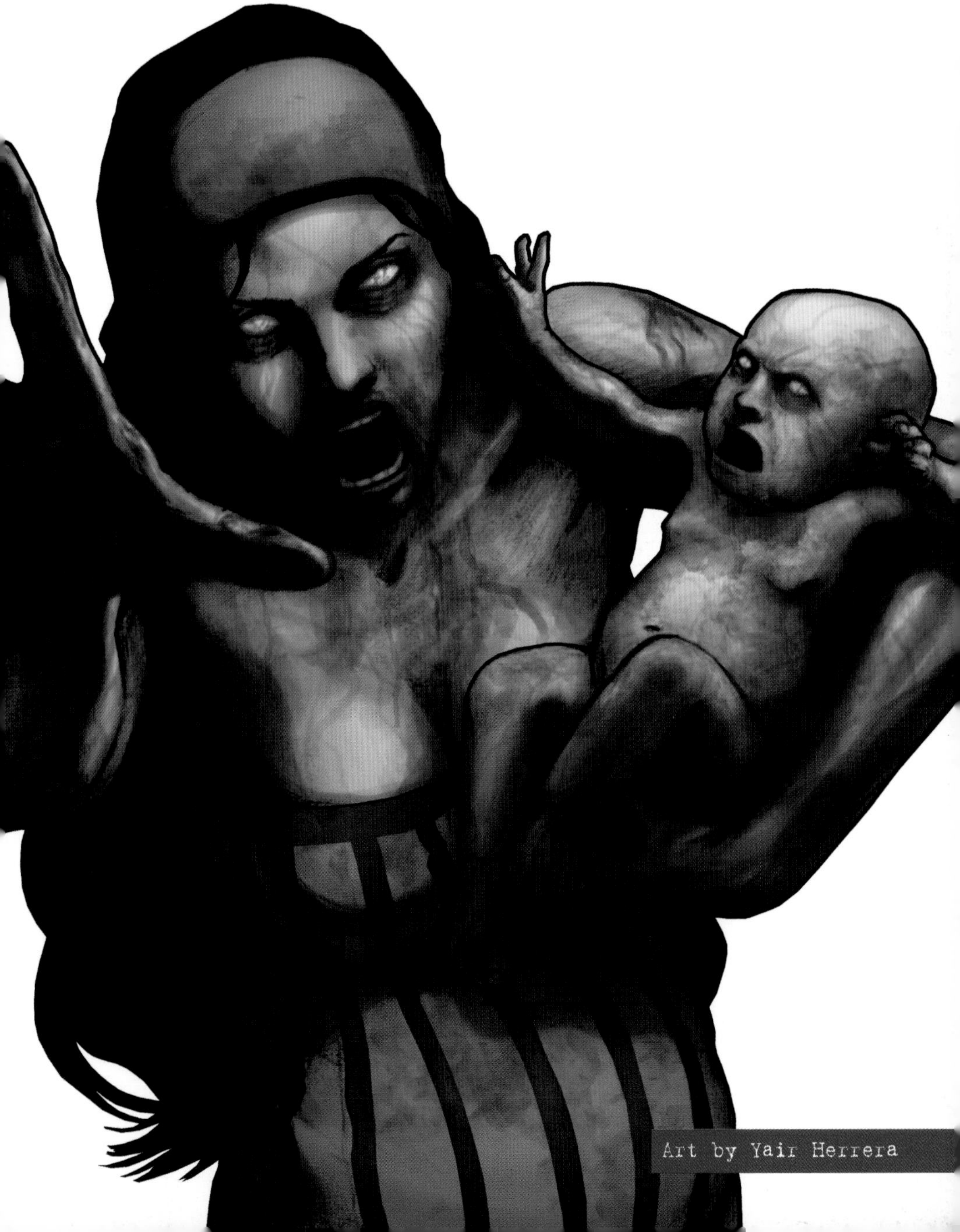

Art by Yair Herrera

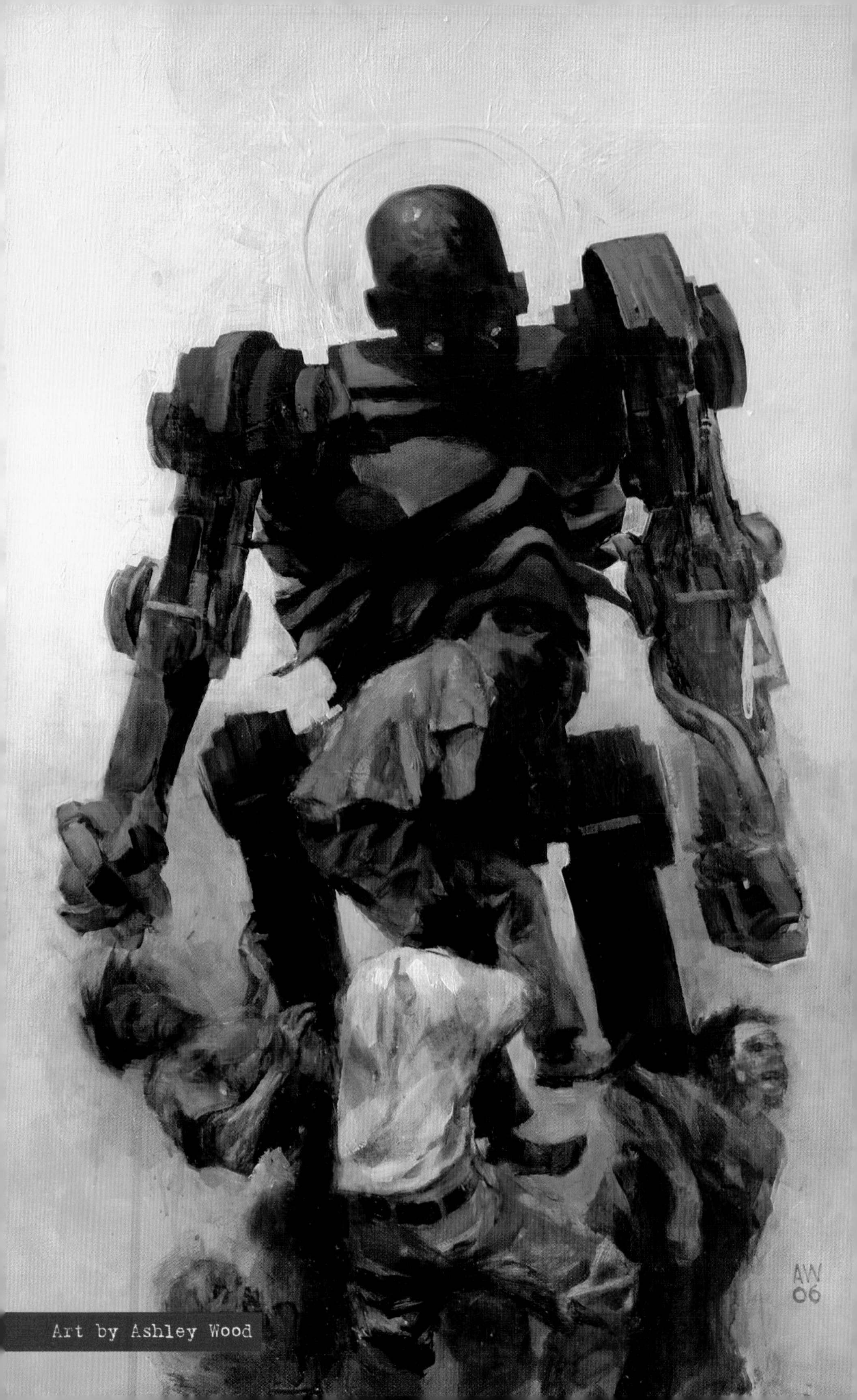
AW
06

Art by Ashley Wood

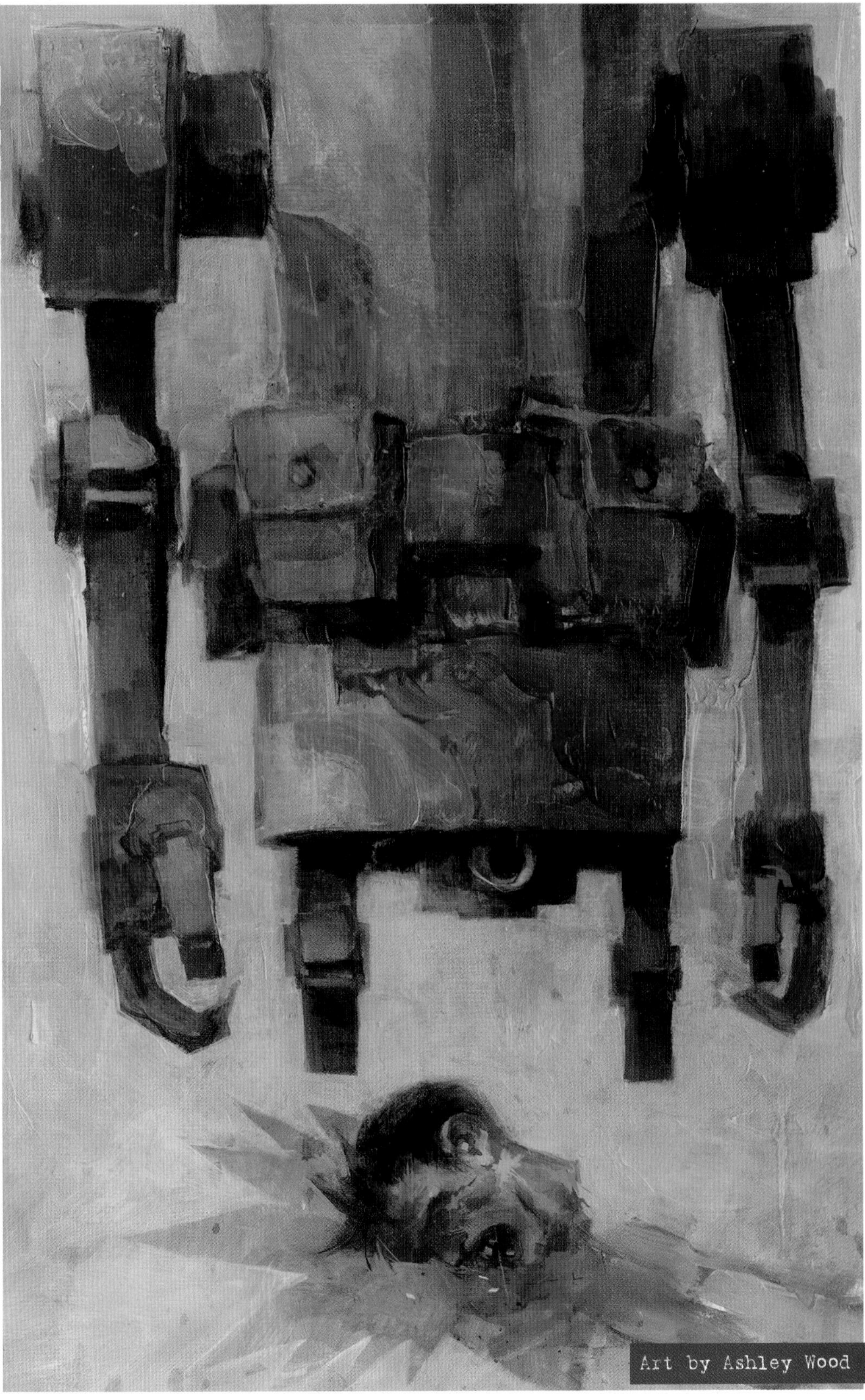

Art by Ashley Wood

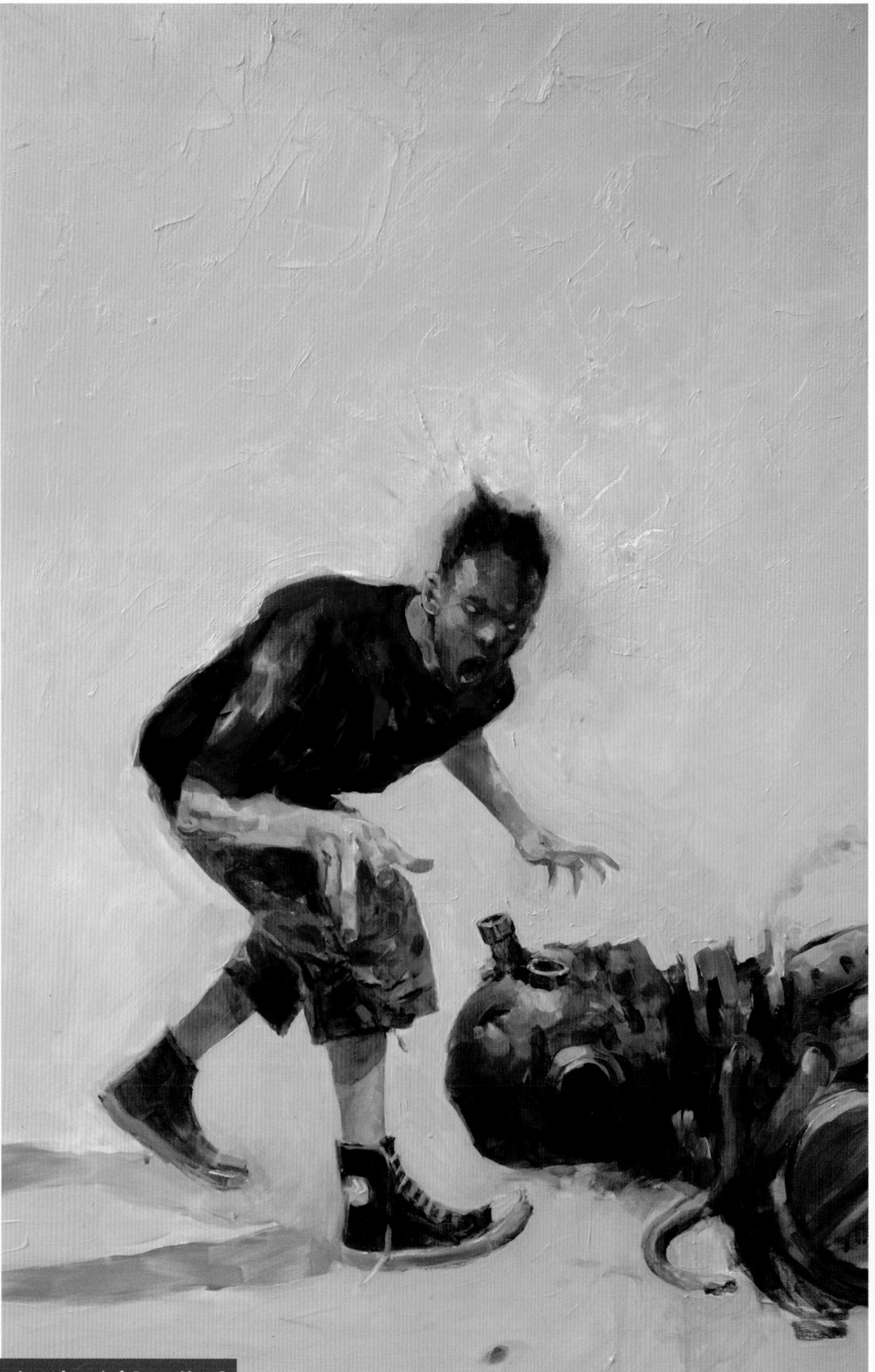

Art by Ashley Wood

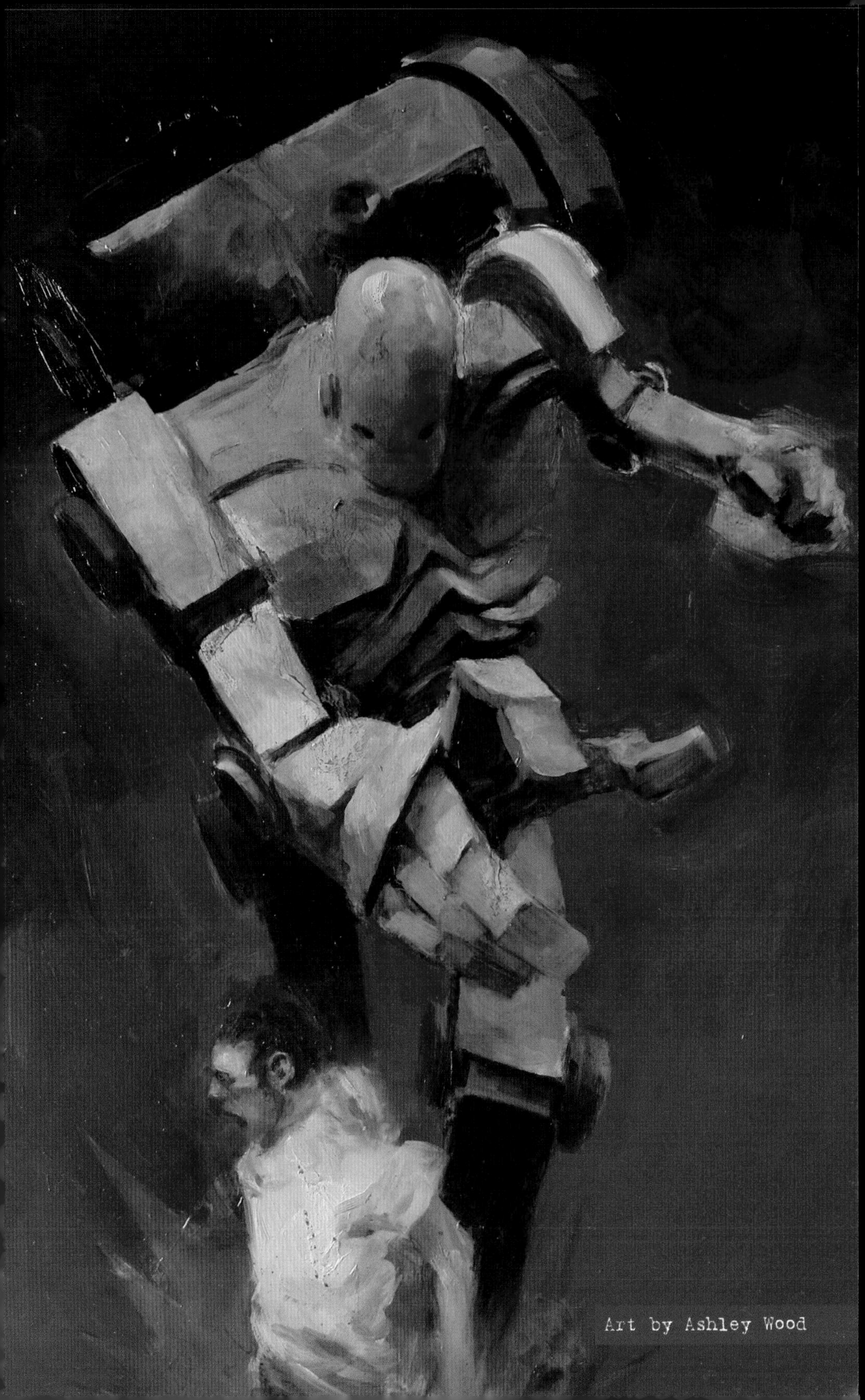

Art by Ashley Wood

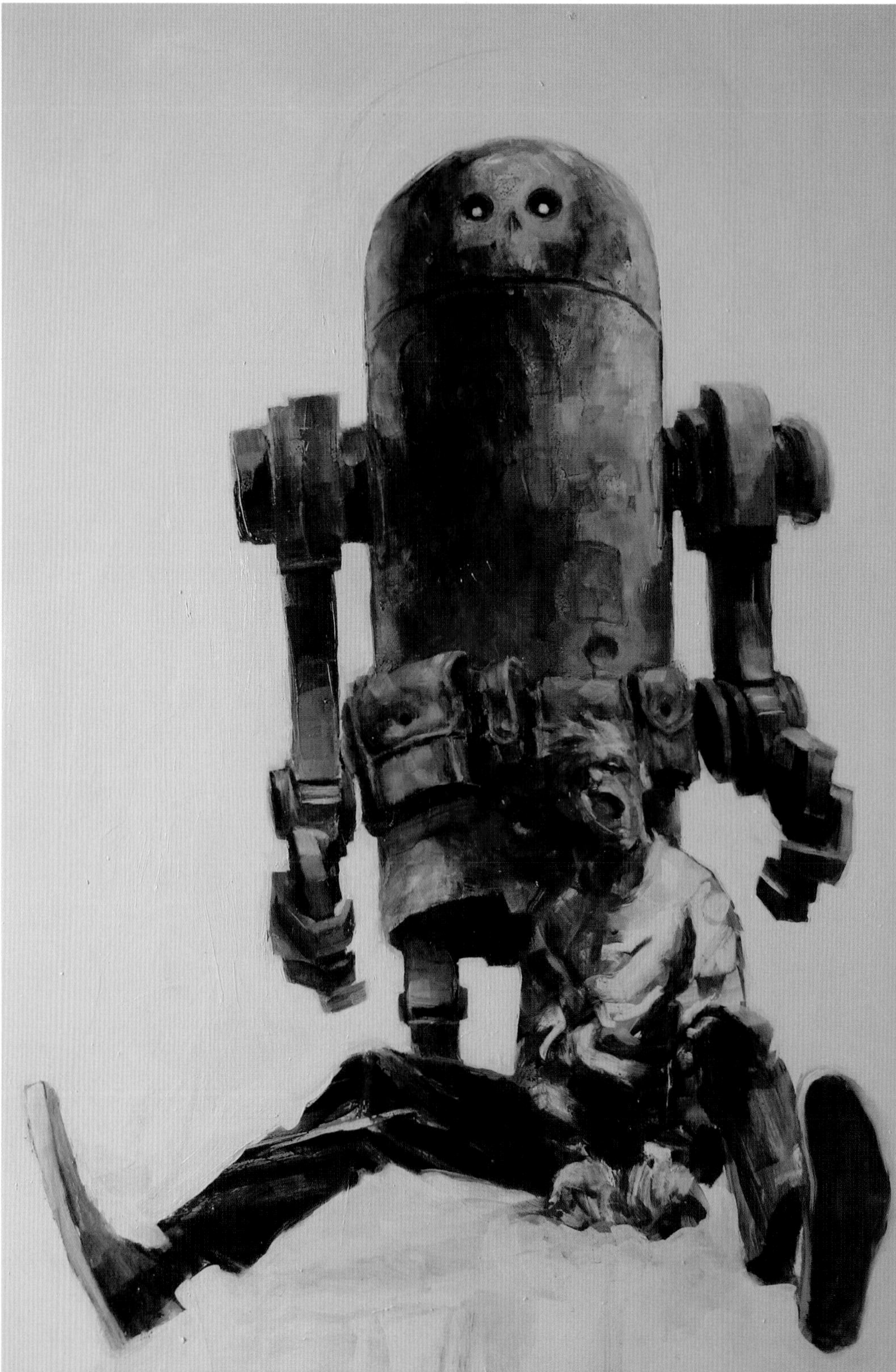
Art by Ashley Wood

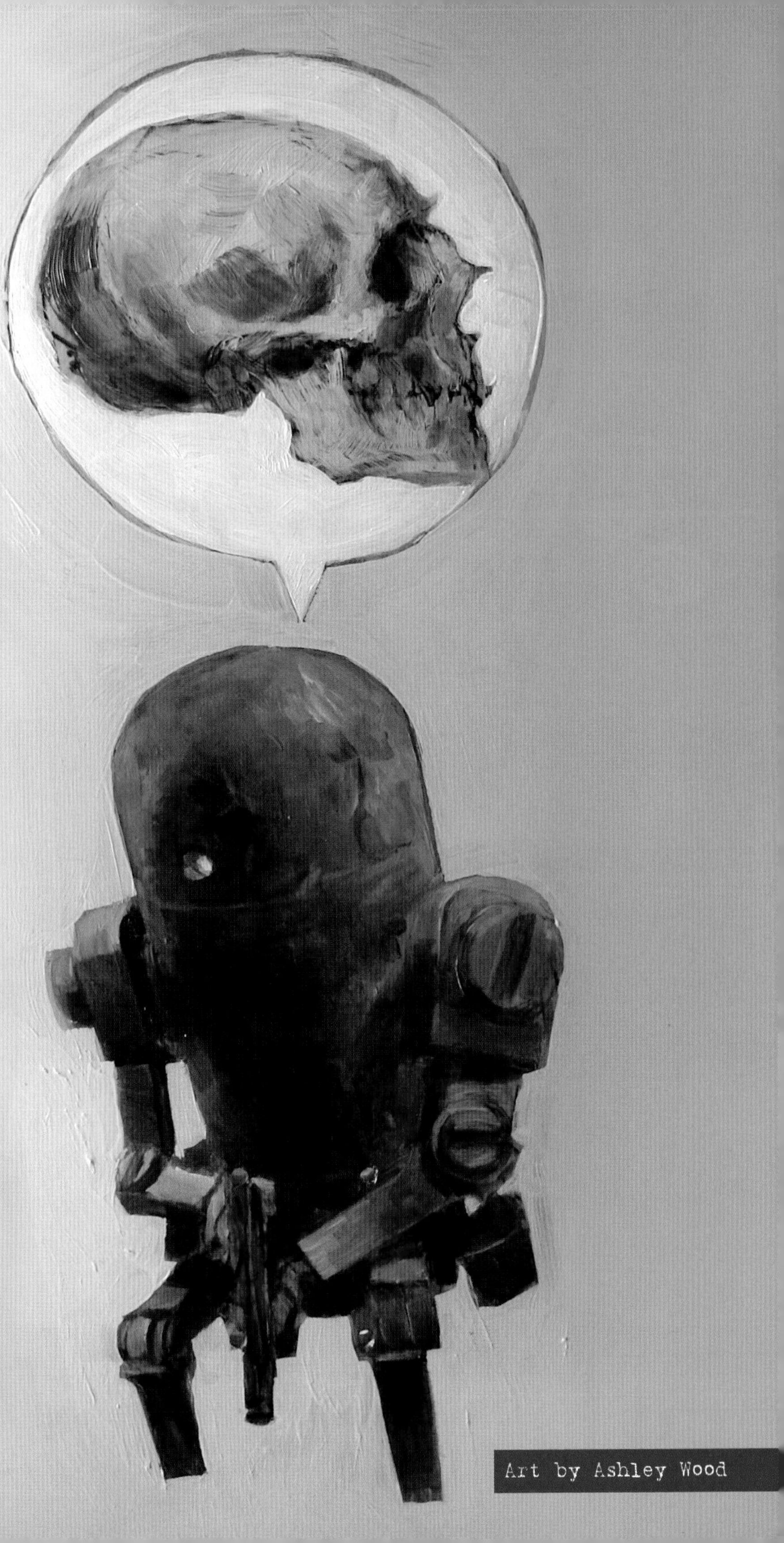

Art by Ashley Wood

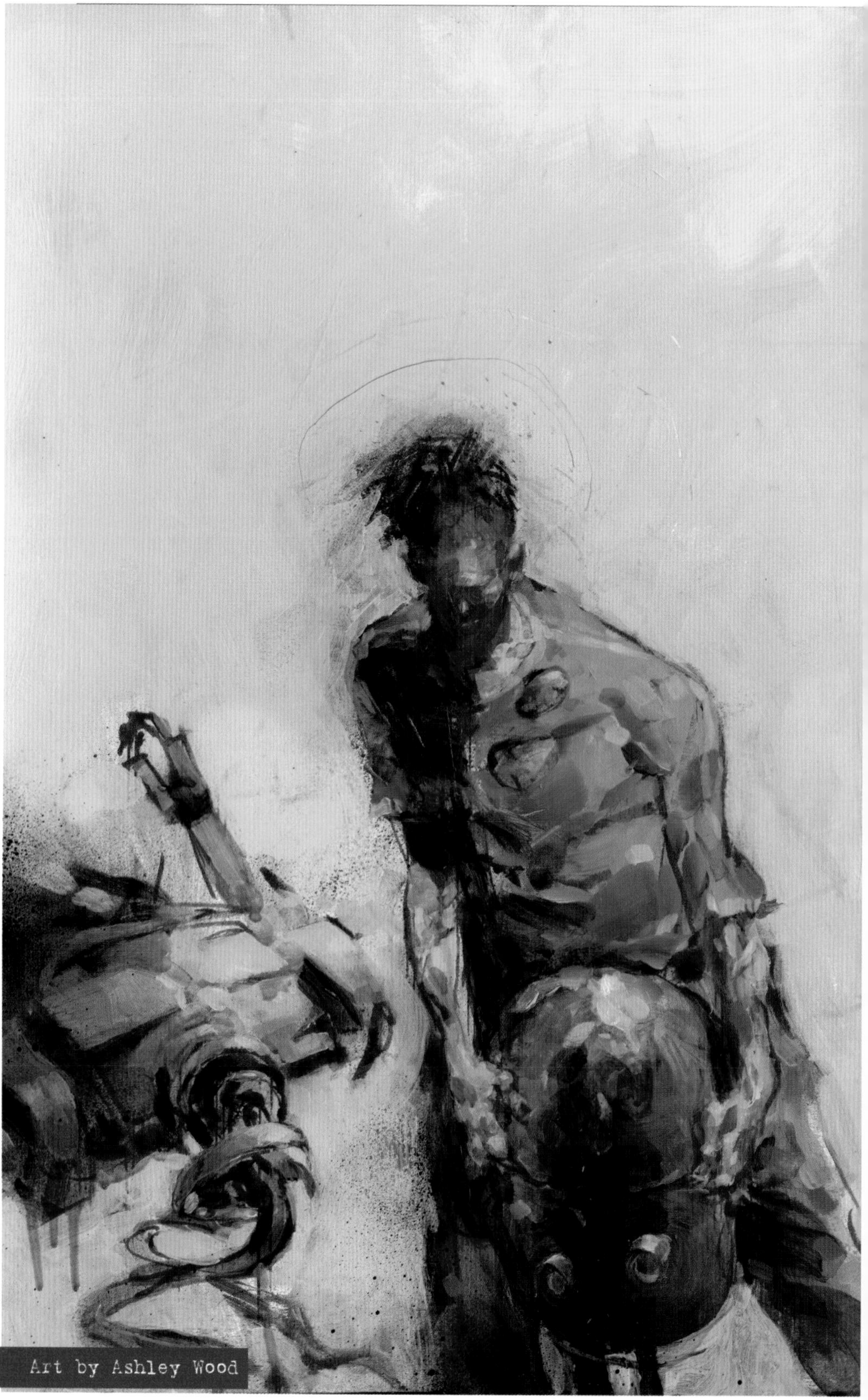

Art by Ashley Wood

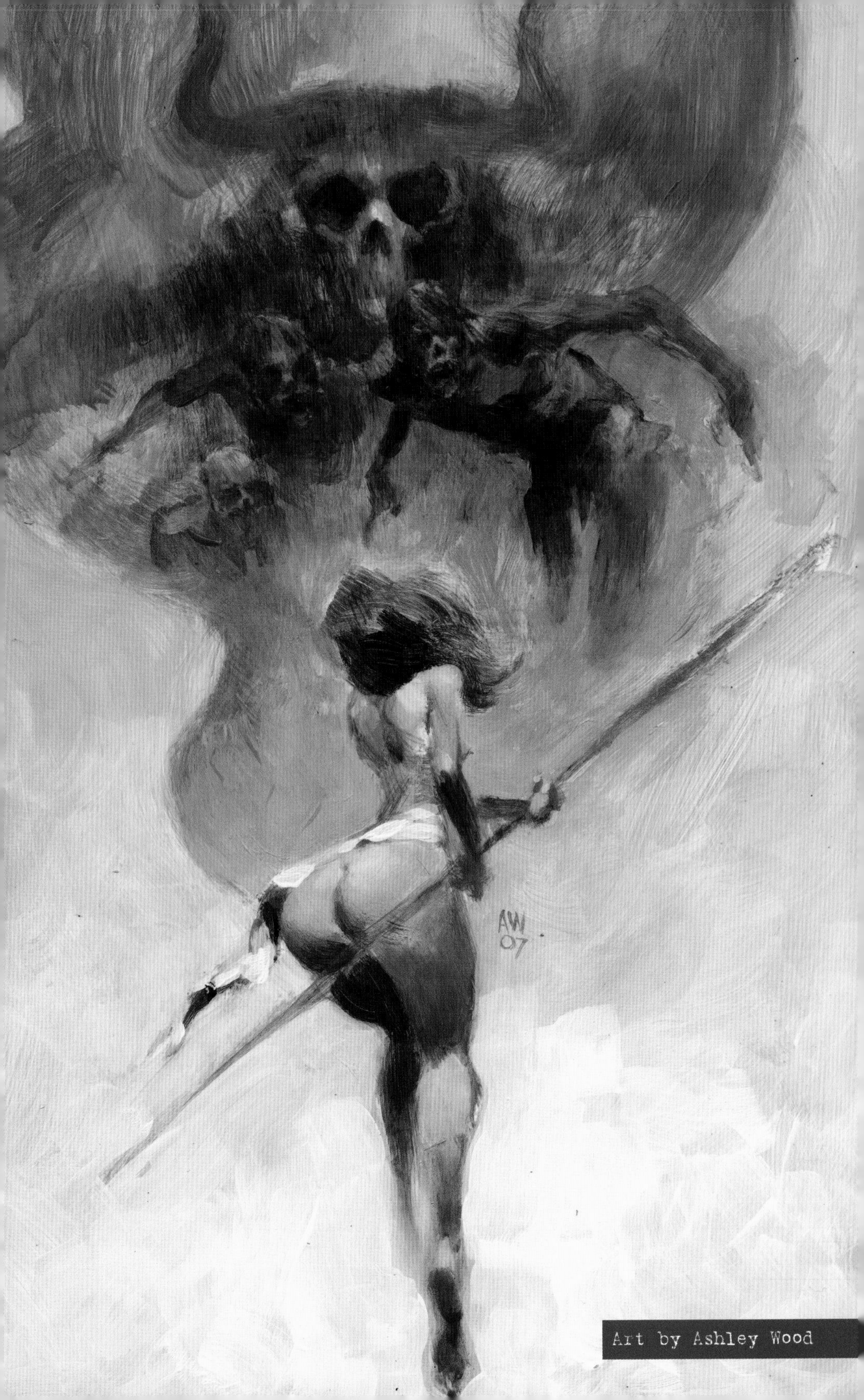

Art by Ashley Wood

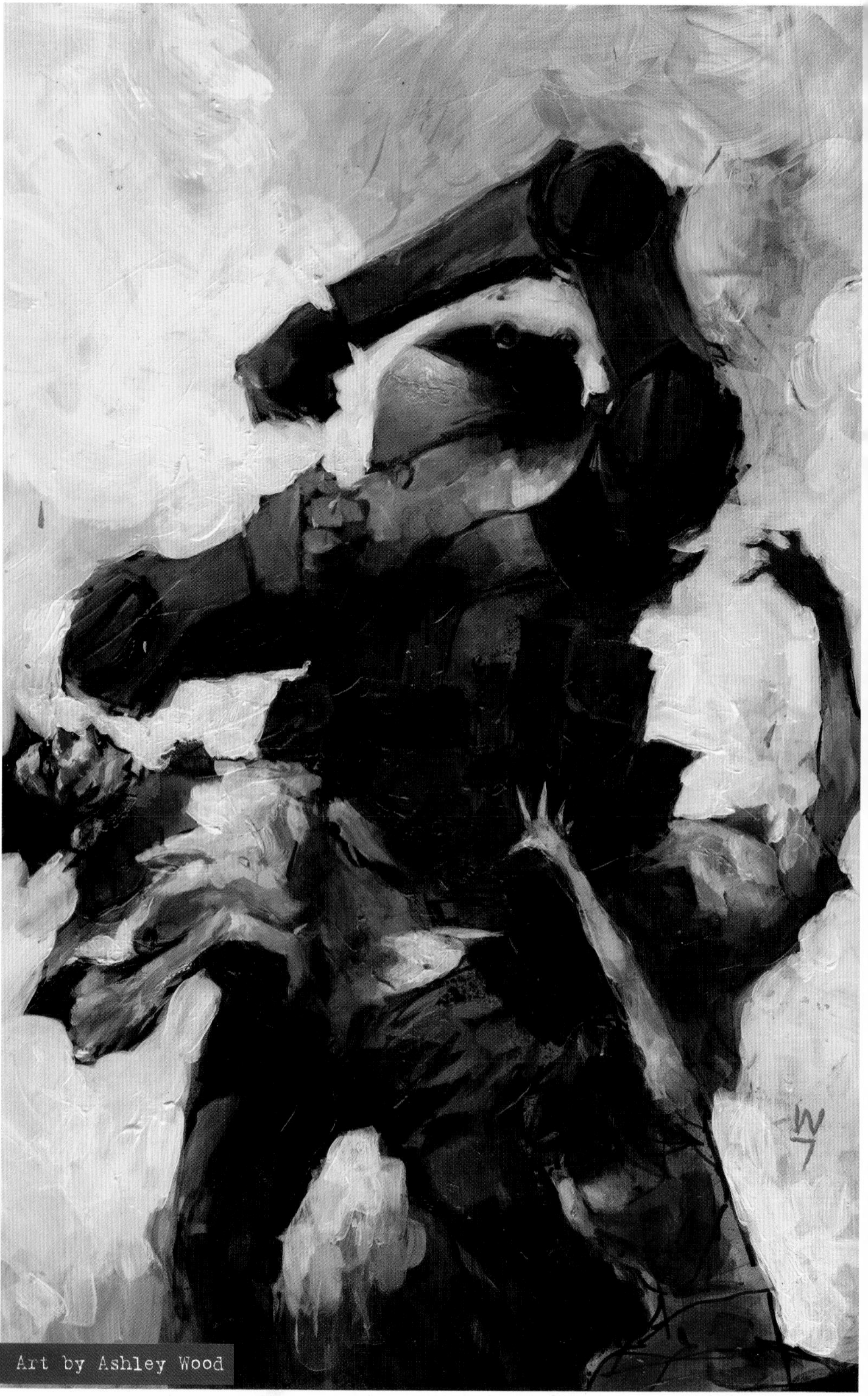

Art by Ashley Wood

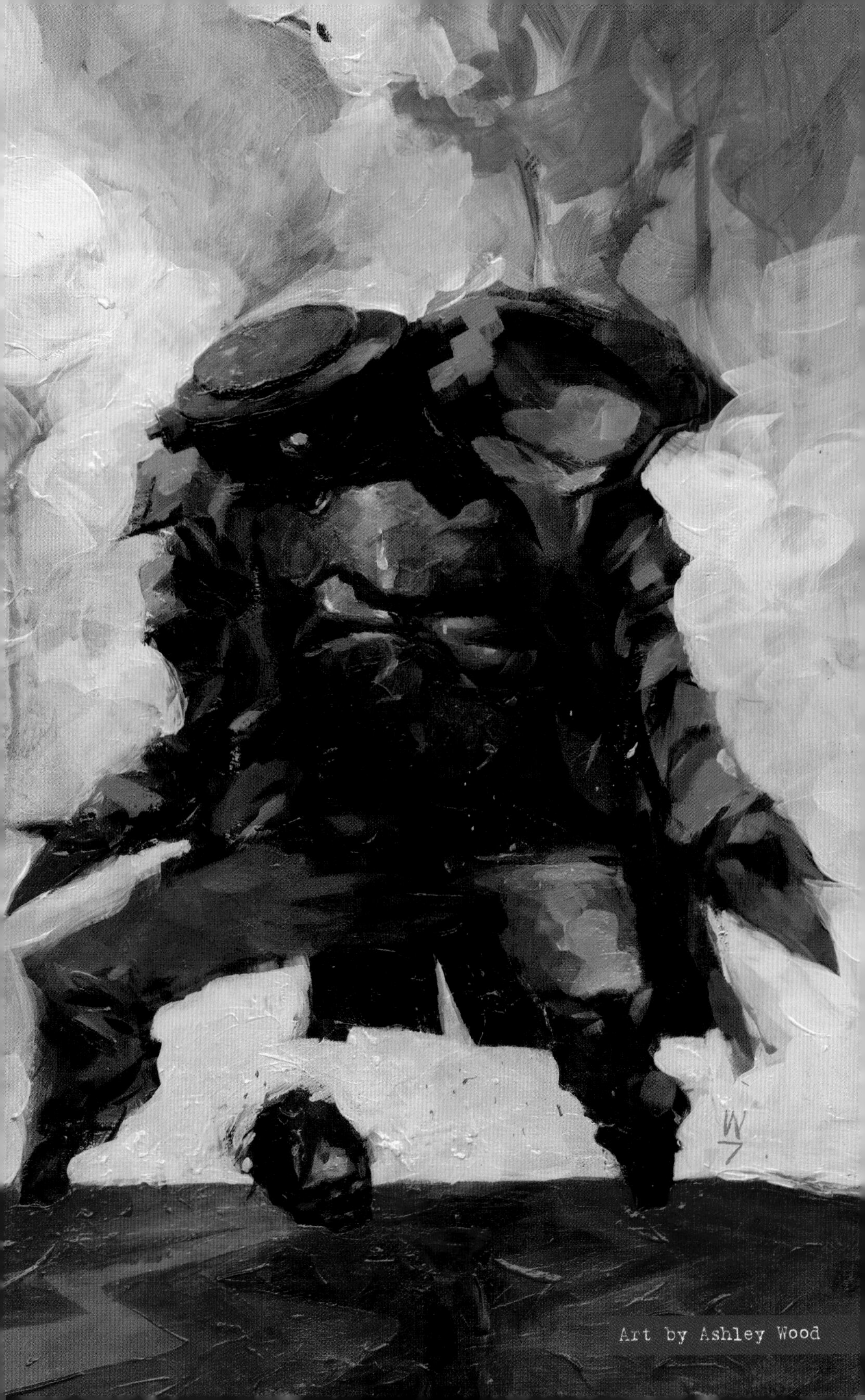

Art by Ashley Wood

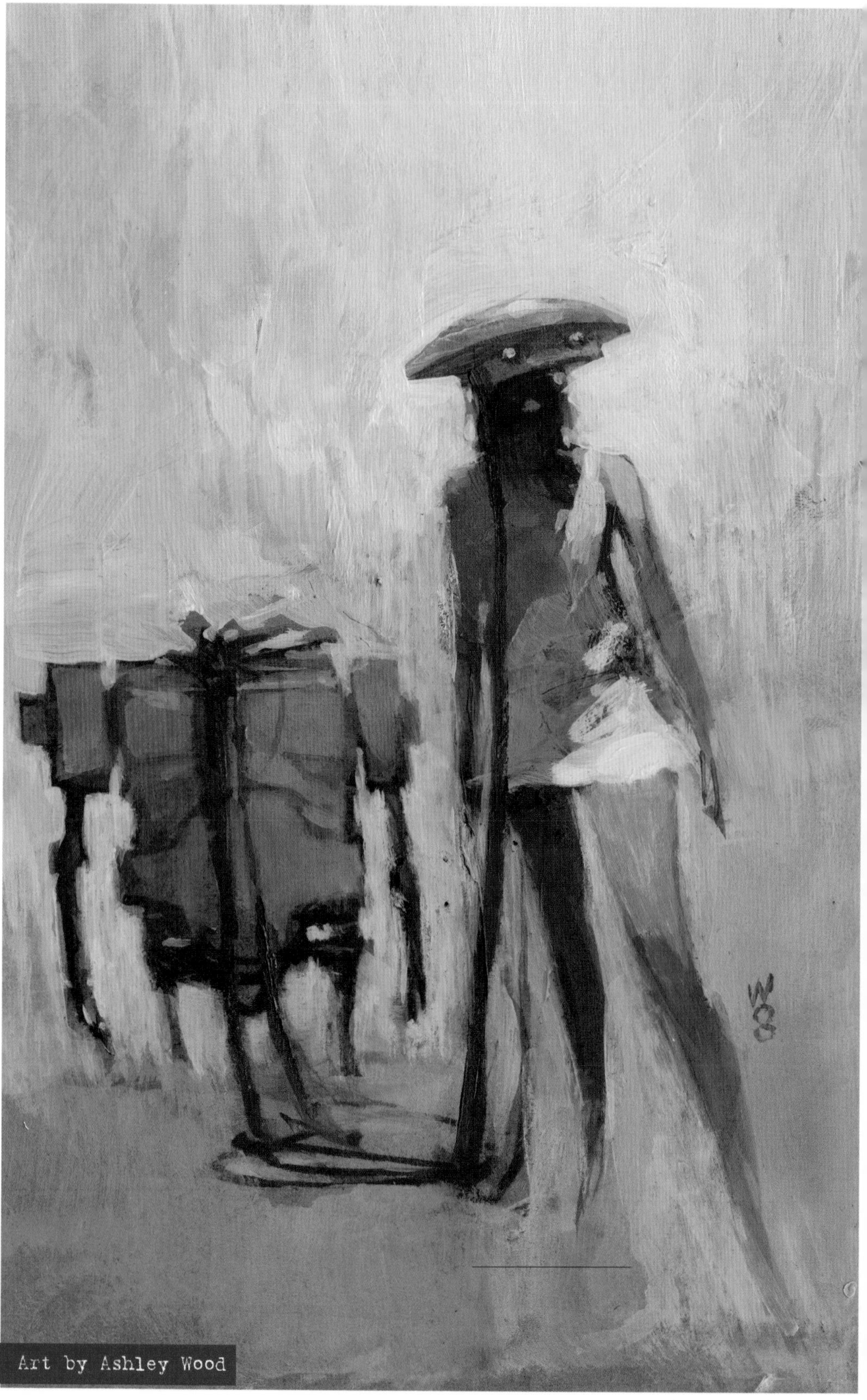

Art by Ashley Wood

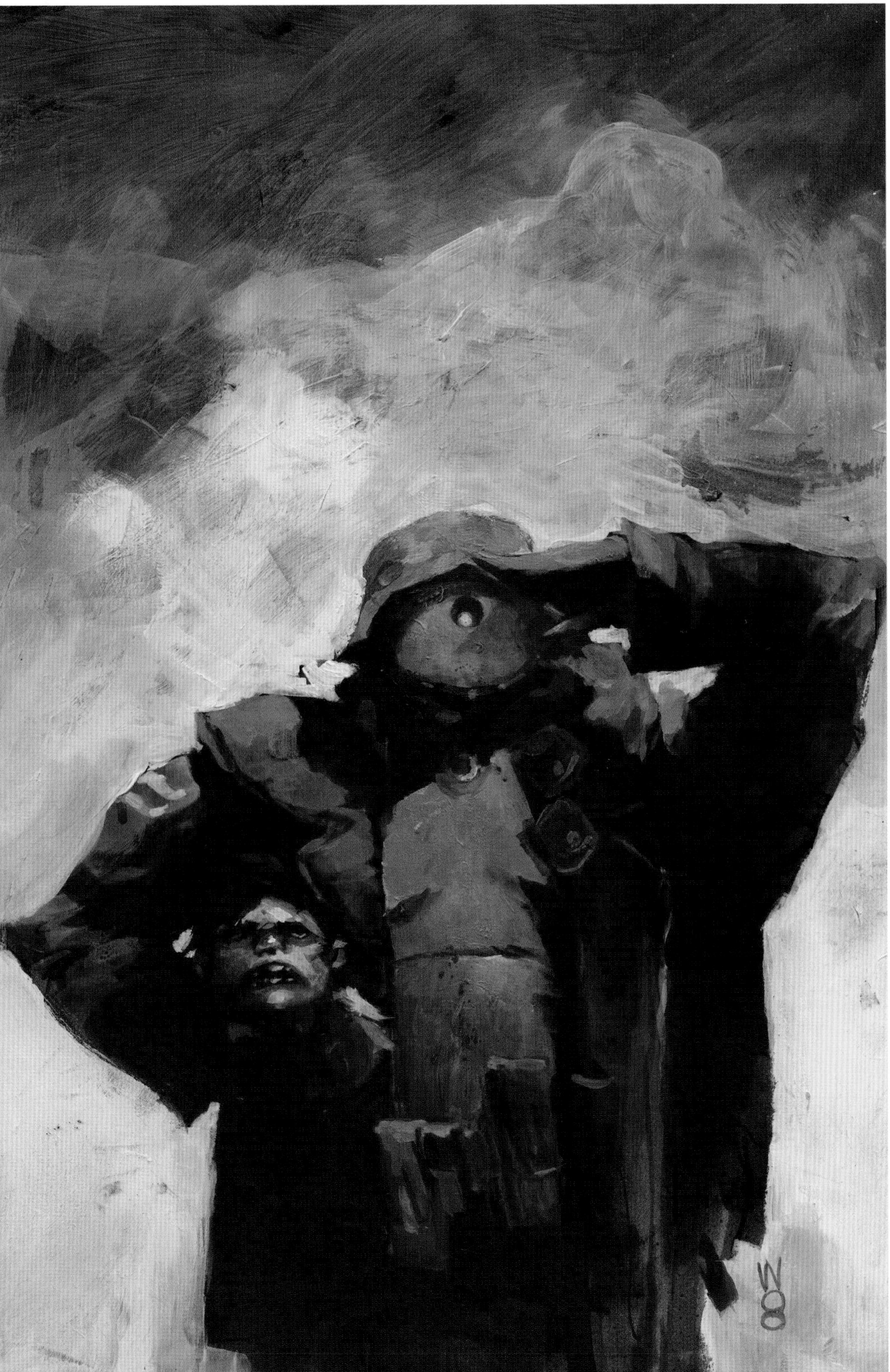

Art by Ashley Wood

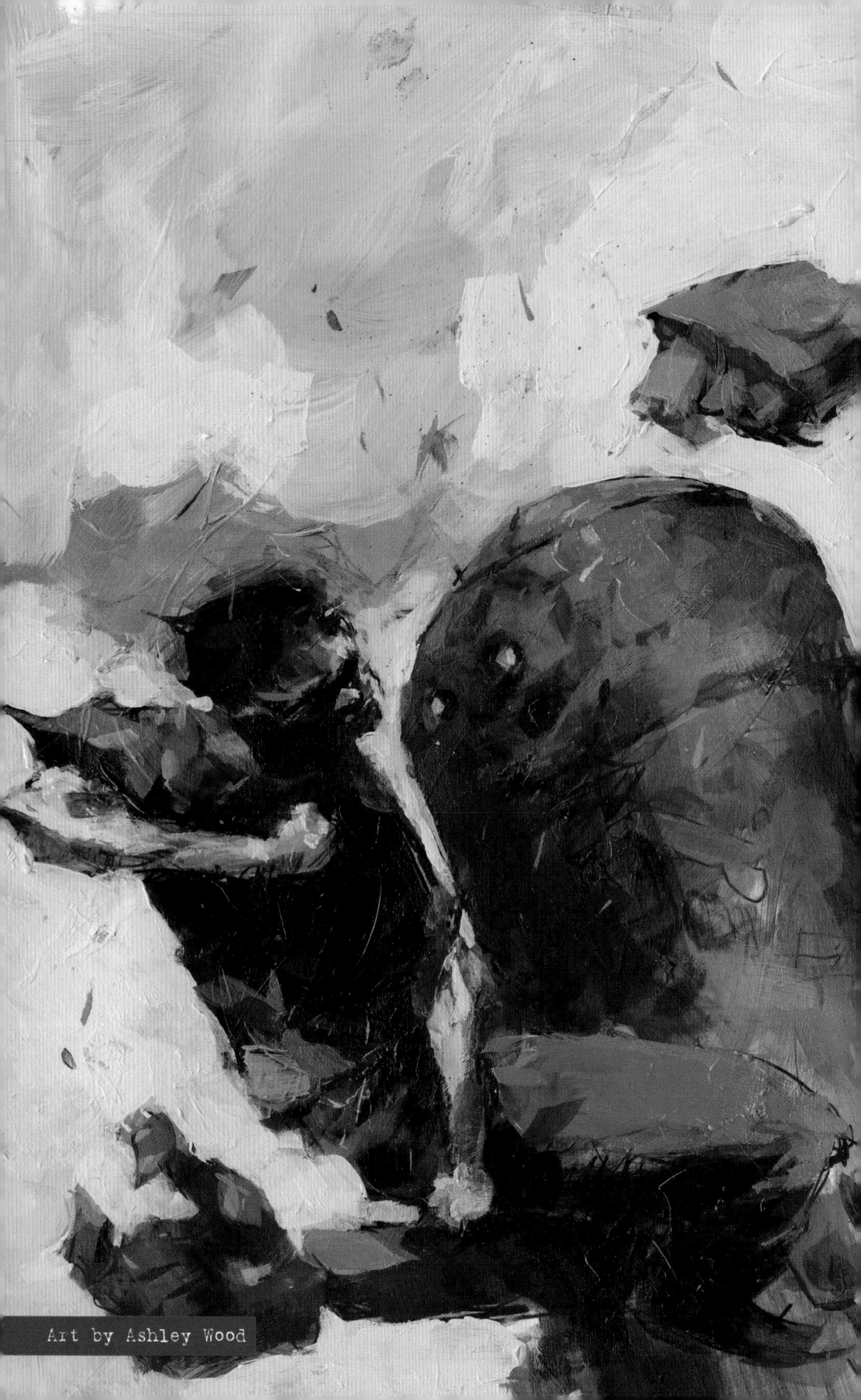

Art by Ashley Wood

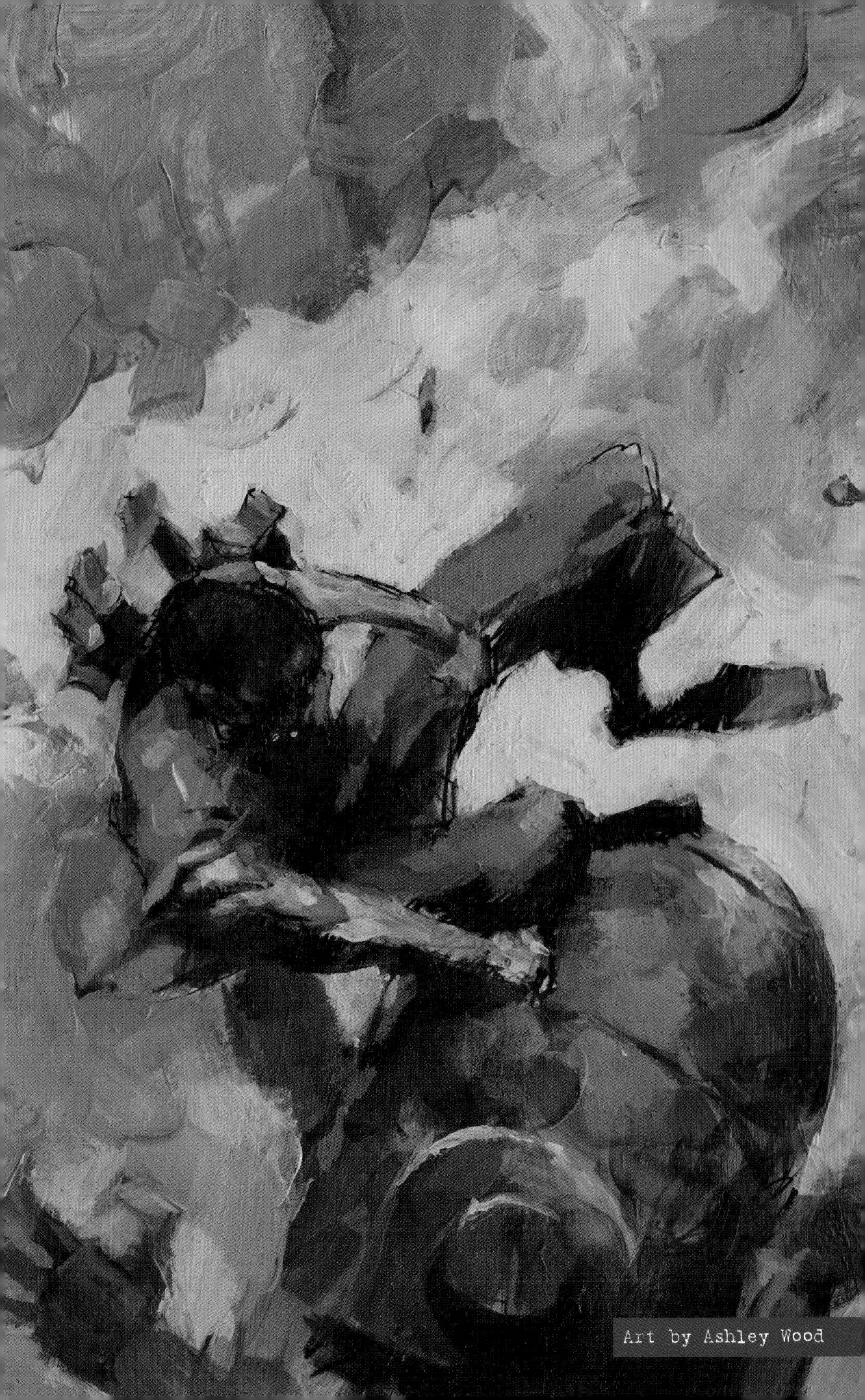
Art by Ashley Wood

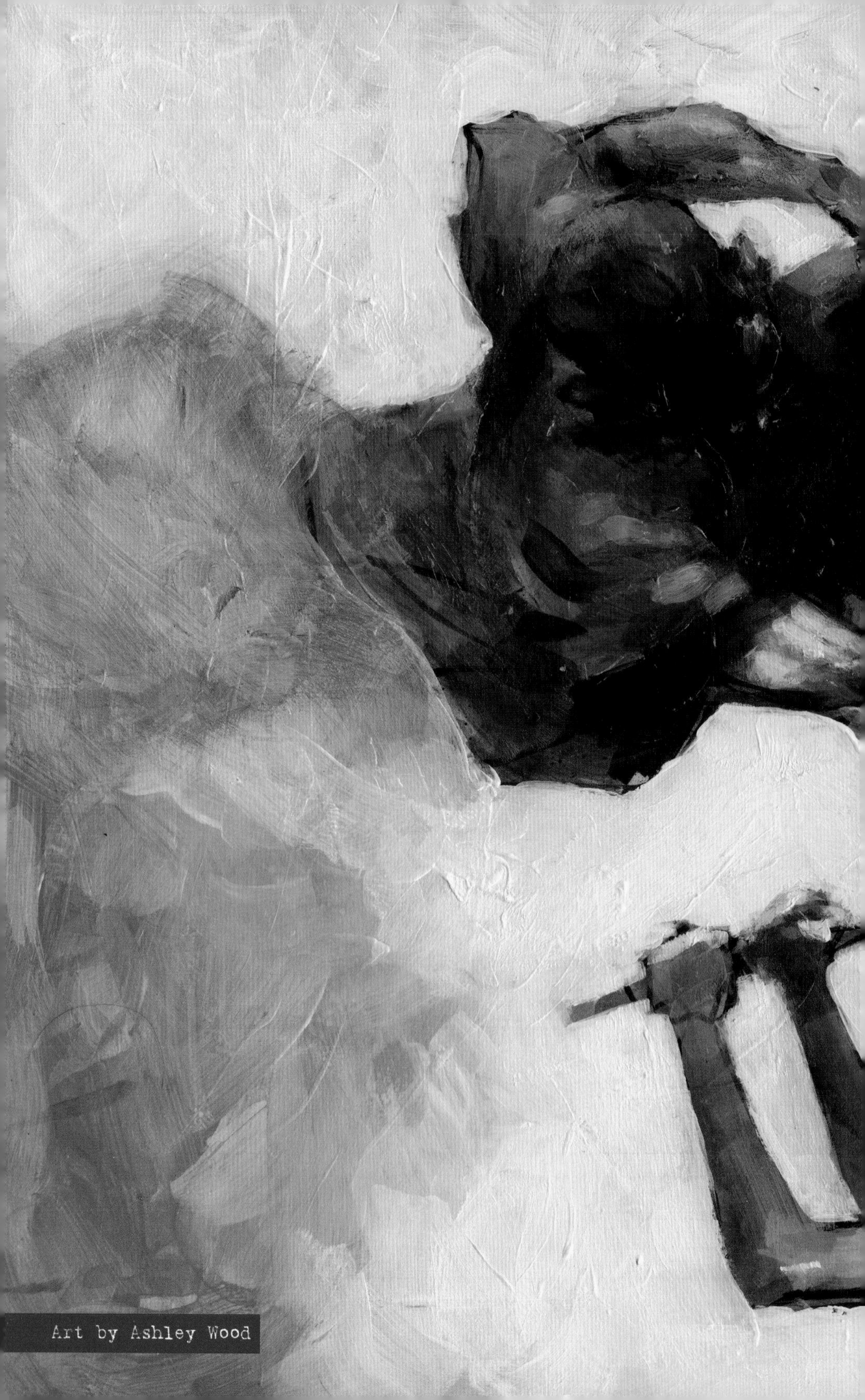

Art by Ashley Wood

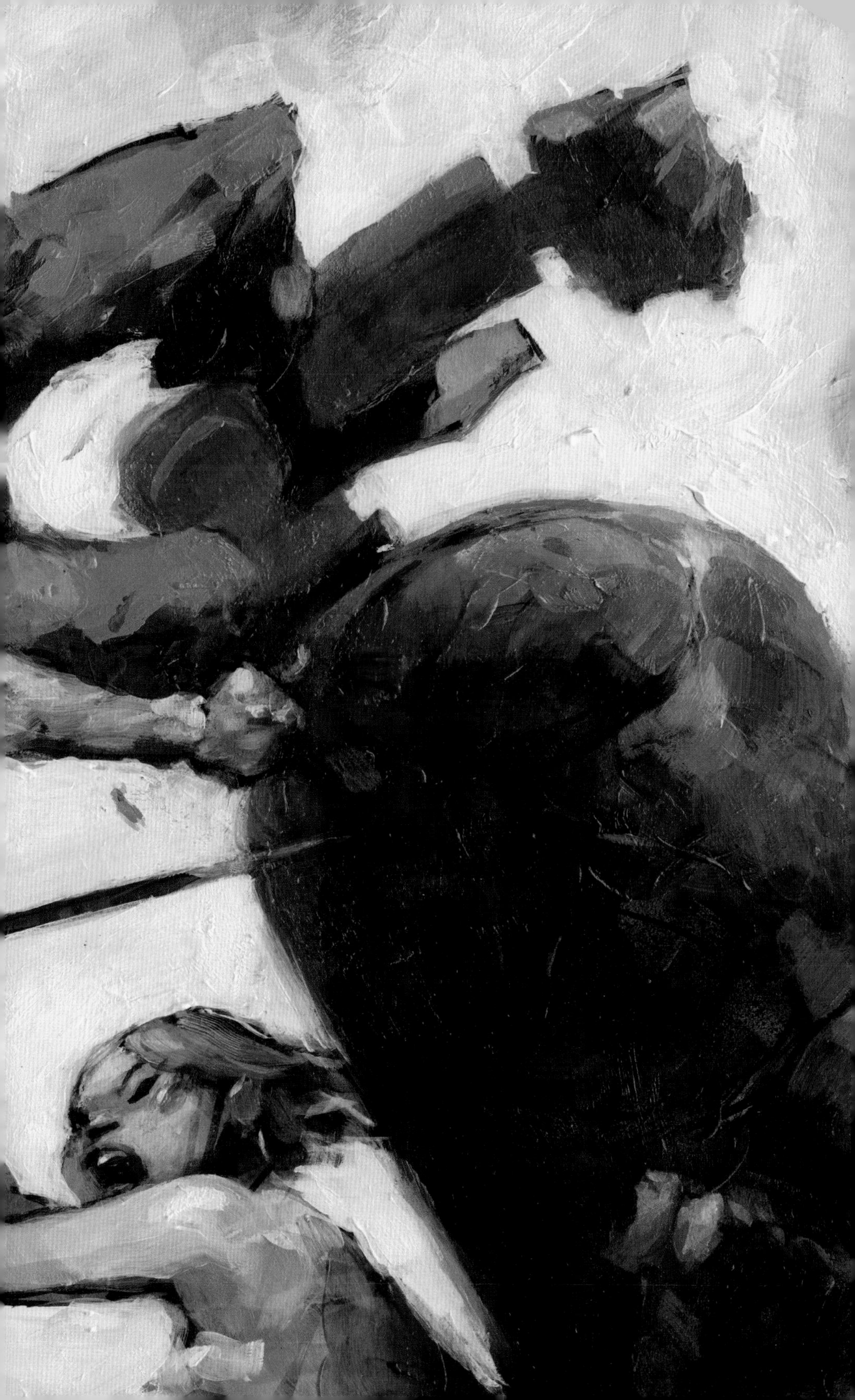

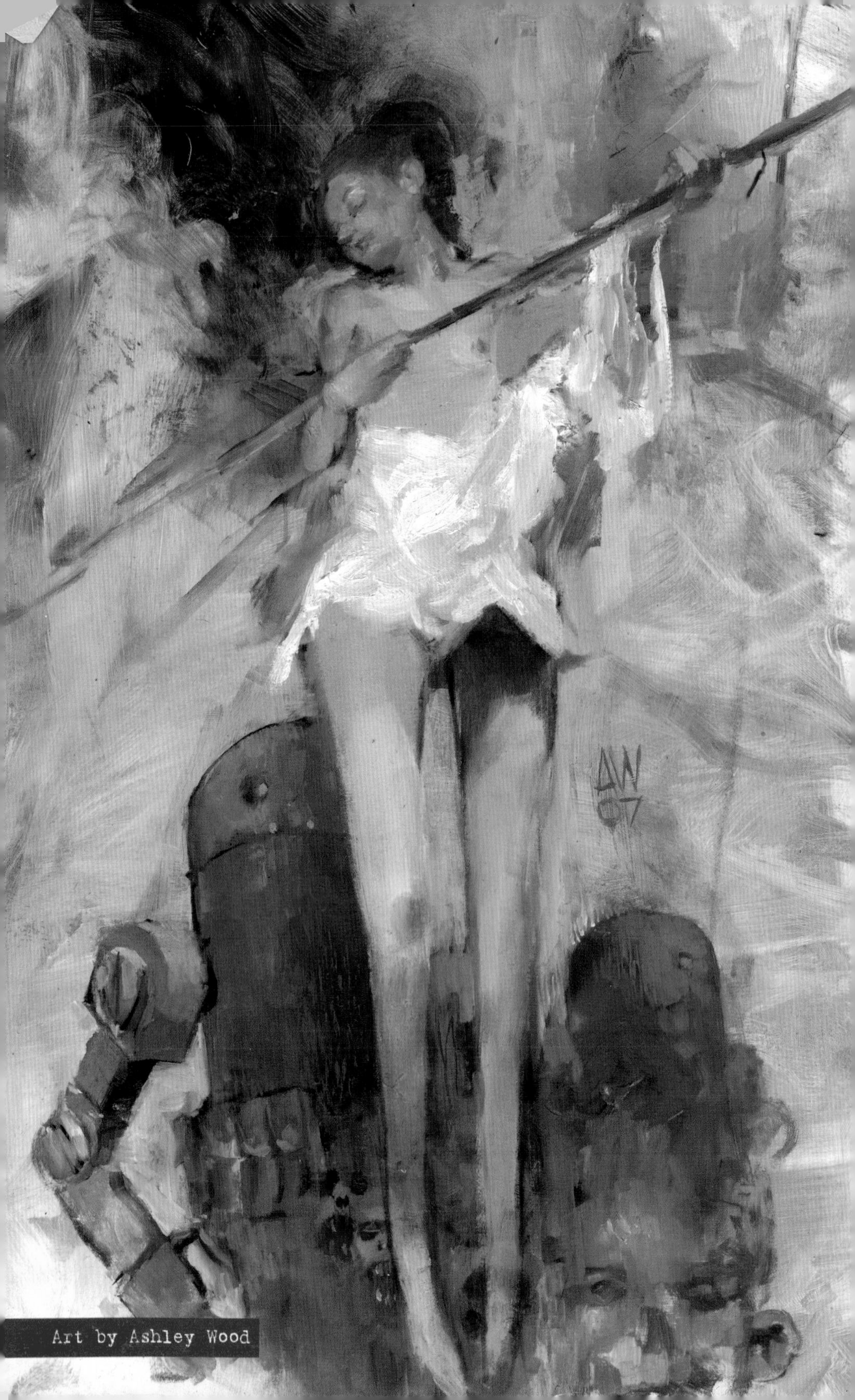
Art by Ashley Wood